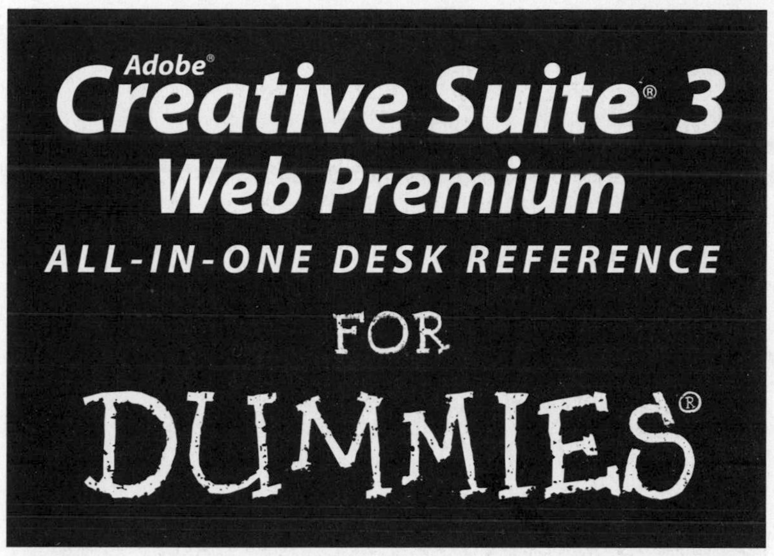

by Damon Dean, Andy Cowitt, Jennifer Smith, Christopher Smith

BICENTENNIAL 1807 WILEY 2007 BICENTENNIAL

Wiley Publishing, Inc.

Adobe® Creative Suite® 3 Web Premium All-in-One Desk Reference For Dummies®

Published by
Wiley Publishing, Inc.
111 River Street
Hoboken, NJ 07030-5774
www.wiley.com

Published by Wiley Publishing, Inc., Indianapolis, Indiana

Published simultaneously in Canada

For general information on our other products and services, please contact our Customer Care Department within the U.S. at 800-762-2974, outside the U.S. at 317-572-3993, or fax 317-572-4002.

For technical support, please visit www.wiley.com/techsupport.

Wiley also publishes its books in a variety of electronic formats. Some content that appears in print may not be available in electronic books.

Library of Congress Control Number: 2007932380

ISBN: 978-0-470-12099-6

Manufactured in the United States of America

10 9 8 7 6 5 4 3 2 1

About the Authors

Damon Dean leads the client services group for Revcube, a cross-channel marketing optomization company based in San Francisco. His team is responsible for producing all client integrations on the Revcube platform, as well as the Revcube product integration with search, display, e-mail, and other channels. Damon came to Revcube after 12 years of managing, designing, and delivering consumer and enterprise Internet applications and software on the both the client and agency side. Previous to his time at Revcube, Damon spent five years as the Director of Product Development for the California HealthCare Foundation, a $1 billion philanthropy. His team was responsible for the design and development all of CHCF's online properties, which included some 10 Web properties, as well as a whole suite of CRM, content management, and grant-making applications. CHCF is considered a leader among philanthropies in its use of innovative technology to promote social change in the health care market. Before joining CHCF, Damon was employee number six at 415, a San Francisco Web design and development agency. As the Solutions Director, Damon led 415's professional services efforts for Fortune 1000 firms on strategic marketing, product design, and development and business process engineering. Damon's successful track record includes work with Credit Suisse, Schwab, Robert Mondavi, BART, Hasbro, Levi's, and others. Damon also led the development of 415's technology assets. Before his time at 415, Damon spent the previous three years leading software development teams at AnyRiver Entertainment (an Electronic Arts Spinoff). He began his career in marketing for *PC World m*agazine. Damon is also the author five books, all published by John Wiley & Sons.

Andy Cowitt is a Web Producer at the California HealthCare Foundation, where he engages in Web development in multiple capacities. He spent his formative Web years at the award-winning firm 415, Inc. While at 415, Andy worked on multimedia presentations and Web sites for Apple, Oracle, Macromedia, the San Francisco Symphony, KQED and others. In his spare time, Andy uses his computer to make music and videos. He lives in Oakland with illustrator Michael Wertz and their dog, Olive.

Jennifer Smith is the co-founder and Vice President of Aquent Graphics Institute (AGI). She has authored numerous books on Adobe's software products, including development of many of the Adobe Classroom in a Book titles. She regularly speaks at conferences and seminars, including the CRE8 Conference. Jennifer has worked in all aspects of graphic design and production, including as an art director of an advertising agency. Jennifer combines her practical experience and technical expertise as an educator. She has developed training programs for Adobe Systems and for all types of designers involved in creating print, Web, interactive, along with fashion and apparel. Her teaching and writing style shows the clear direction of a practiced designer with in-depth knowledge of the Adobe Creative Suite applications. When she's not speaking or teaching, she can be found in suburban Boston, Massachusetts with her husband and children. You can learn about Jennifer's seminar and conference appearances at `agitraining.com`.

Christopher Smith is co-founder and President of Aquent Graphics Institute (AGI), the training and professional development division of Aquent that serves creative and marketing organizations. An Adobe Certified Expert for multiple Adobe products, he has worked as part of the Adobe Creative Team to develop many of the Adobe Classroom in a Book series and has authored numerous books on both InDesign and Acrobat. Christopher manages content for the CRE8 Conference for creative professionals and also the Adobe Acrobat & PDF Conference. He has also served as an elected member of the school board in his hometown in suburban Boston, Massachusetts, where he lives with his wife and children.

Dedication

Damon Dean: Chris, between the dog and cat, it's amazing that we're still a family. Nah, maybe not so much! Much love, Damon.

Andy Cowitt: For Michael, as always.

Jennifer and Christopher Smith: To our parents, Ed and Nancy Smith, along with Mary Kelly. In loving memory of Jennifer's father, Joseph Kelly, the best teacher of all. Also to our perfect children, Kelly, Alex, Grant, Elizabeth, and Edward.

Authors' Acknowledgments

Damon Dean: Every book requires the hard work of a large number of folks, the vast majority of which we never see. Revisions are even more challenging because as an author, you're constantly trying to remember what it was you wrote back in the first version of a product and whether it's still relevant. There is, however, a team of folks that are there to keep you on the ball, and for that I'm always grateful. Steve Hayes, our acquisition editor, continues to ask me and Andy to do these books, so a big thank you there! On this revision, Susan Christophersen was a tremendous shepherd of the book and my general lazy tendencies. Without her cheerful e-mails, we'd be late, or later, if you prefer! And a fine thank you to Ron Rockwell for all his vigilance in keeping us accurate. And to all the other production folks, thank you for making us all look good.

Andy Cowitt: Thanks to the Cowitts, Wertzes, and Saraccos, with special nods to Michael and to Damon. Also, props to Mike and all my other colleagues past and present at the California HealthCare Foundation.

Jennifer and Christopher Smith: Thanks to all our friends and colleagues at Adobe Systems for their support, encouragement, and faith in all our work, especially surrounding the Creative Suite 3 launch: Jane, Joe, Ron, Dave, Donna, Ali, Noha, Lynn, Adam, Jeffrey, Lori, Richard, and the many product team members who responded to our questions throughout the writing process.

A special thank you also to Fred Gerantabee, the master of all things Flash. Thanks for your significant contributions to this book.

Thank you also to Yvette Grimes for assistance in updating information.

To the highly professional instructional staff at Aquent Graphics Institute (AGI), we appreciate your great insight into the best ways to help others learn creative software applications.

Thanks to all at Wiley Publishing. This book involves a lot of detail and information, and it was up to Melody Lane, acquisitions editor for our three minibooks in this book, and her "tough love" to make sure that it got to the state it is now. Thanks to Kelly Ewing and technical editor Cathy Auclair for the great insight.

Grant, Elizabeth, and Edward — thanks for putting up with our long hours in front of the keyboard night after night.

Thanks to all of Kelly's friends for permission to use their photos.

Publisher's Acknowledgments

We're proud of this book; please send us your comments through our online registration form located at `www.dummies.com/register/`.

Some of the people who helped bring this book to market include the following:

Acquisitions, Editorial, and Media Development

Project and Copy Editors: Susan Christophersen and Kelly Ewing

Previous edition: Christopher Morris

Executive Editor: Steve Hayes

Technical Editors: Ron Rockwell and Cathy Auclair

Editorial Manager: Jodi Jensen

Media Development Manager: Laura VanWinkle

Editorial Assistant: Amanda Foxworth

Cartoons: Rich Tennant (`www.the5thwave.com`)

Composition Services

Project Coordinator: Erin Smith

Layout and Graphics: Carl Byers, Denny Hager, Joyce Haughey, Christine Williams

Proofreaders: Aptara, Cynthia Fields, John Greenough, Brian Walls

Indexer: Aptara

Publishing and Editorial for Technology Dummies

Richard Swadley, Vice President and Executive Group Publisher

Andy Cummings, Vice President and Publisher

Mary Bednarek, Executive Acquisitions Director

Mary C. Corder, Editorial Director

Publishing for Consumer Dummies

Diane Graves Steele, Vice President and Publisher

Joyce Pepple, Acquisitions Director

Composition Services

Gerry Fahey, Vice President of Production Services

Debbie Stailey, Director of Composition Services

Contents at a Glance

Table of Contents

Introduction

When creative juggernaut Adobe announced that it had acquired Macromedia in 2006, long-time Macromedia users wondered what it would mean for their preferred suite of Web development tools, Studio. Would Photoshop's superior power and depth spell the end of Fireworks, despite the fact that Fireworks has more user-friendly image-optimizing and -exporting capabilities? Would FreeHand survive? Would ColdFusion get lost in the shuffle? For those of us who always used Photoshop and Acrobat as well as the applications in the Studio suite, the question was, How long do we have to wait for better integration of Adobe's software with Dreamweaver, Flash, and Fireworks? With Adobe Creative Suite 3 Web Premium, we have our answers, and the future looks bright for Web developers!

About This Book

Adobe Creative Suite 3 Web Premium All-in-One Desk Reference For Dummies (we know, it's a mouthful) is designed to be a hands-on, easy-to-understand guide to the main features in all the CS3 Web development products. The no-nonsense approach will help you begin to build Web sites by covering the basics in a clear and concise fashion. The way we see it, you've got things to do, and reading a book, even a clever one, takes up valuable time. The faster we can help you do something or answer a question, the better.

How to Use This Book

You can use this book in a few different ways:

- **As a reference:** If you already have a Web site and use Creative Suite 3, this book can be a handy refresher for that thing you couldn't quite remember how to do. Whether it's finding out how to export graphics to Flash from Illustrator, or how to add a behavior to a button graphic in Fireworks, you can use this book to fill in those gaps that we all have . . . especially as we get older.
- **To guide you through building a Web site:** Several authors contributed to the creation of this book. All of us have a wealth of experience in the process of building Web sites. In this book, we've tried to impart as much of our collective knowledge about the processes and pitfalls of building Web sites using these tools as we can.

- **To find out more about the tools:** In this *All-in-One Desk Reference,* each minibook has a limited number of pages to cover a product or topic, which means that we get right to the point and make the topics covered easy to understand. We believe that this approach makes figuring out these products easier.

Three Presumptuous Assumptions

Before you dive into the book, we thought we should give you some advance warning of our expectations. We know, you're the audience, so we shouldn't assume anything! But, just so you know where we're coming from, here are our three basic assumptions about you, the reader:

- **You're in a hurry.** Frankly, if you wanted a more in-depth book, you'd have picked up a regular *For Dummies* book on one or all of these products. Hence the no-nonsense, get-it-done, and keep-on-moving approach that you find inside this book.
- **You know something about Web development.** This isn't a book in which we spend a lot of time talking about HTML and how it works. So you won't find a chapter anywhere in this book titled, "What the Internet Is and How It Works."
- **You'll experiment on your own.** The approach here is to give you quick, useful examples of how things work across all these products. In some cases, the examples can be fairly sophisticated. In most cases, though, the book presents the basics. Our hope is that you'll take those basic examples and build your own, more complex ones on top of that, according to the complexity of your site.

Macintosh versus Windows

Adobe Creative Suite 3 is both a Windows and a Macintosh product. In this book, you see us use the Windows commands, and most of the figures show Windows XP.

In general, you can convert between Windows (PC) and Macintosh key commands by using the following equivalencies:

- The Ctrl key on a PC is equivalent to the Command (⌘) key on a Mac.
- The Alt key on a PC is equivalent to the Option key on a Mac.
- The Enter key on a PC is equivalent to the Return key on a Mac.

When the Mac key command equivalents don't follow the rules just described, we note the exceptions where they occur throughout the text.

The Mac operating system uses several of the F keys to operate various elements such as hiding windows, opening the Dock, closing or opening windows and applications, and so on. To override the Mac OS defaults and enable an application's default key commands, open System Preferences (in the Dock) and then open Keyboard & Mouse. Select Keyboard Shortcuts from the three menu choices and scroll through the various shortcuts. If you wish to change F12 from opening or closing the Dashboard, for example, select it and click the plus sign button at the bottom of the window. Doing so brings up a new window headed by an Application menu. Select the application in which you wish to use F12, give it a name in the Menu Title box, and click the F12 in the Keyboard Shortcut window. Then, pressing F12 will do whatever the selected application wants to do instead of opening the Dashboard. Other applications will continue to use F12 as defaulted by the operating system, but you can change them just as easily.

How This Book Is Organized

As with all the *All-in-One Desk References For Dummies,* this book's chapters are organized into minibooks. Most of the minibooks revolve around products, but one is geared toward the Web development process. The following sections describe each minibook in more detail.

Book I: Dreamweaver CS3

Dreamweaver CS3 is the crux of any Web development effort with Creative Suite 3, so naturally, this is a good place to start. In this minibook, you get a hands-on look at how you can use Dreamweaver to create and manage your Web sites.

Book II: Photoshop CS3

Long the premier software for 2-D bitmap image creation and manipulation, Photoshop is the gold standard of Web design tools. This minibook aims to help you achieve good imagery, starting with basics that even advanced users may have missed along the way. We show you how to color correct images like a pro and use tools to keep images at the right resolution and size, no matter whether the image is intended for print or for the Web.

Book III: Fireworks CS3

Thanks to Photoshop's inclusion in CS3, Fireworks can concentrate on what it does best: act as a conduit between Photoshop/Illustrator in the design phase and Flash/Dreamweaver in the implementation phase of Web development. This minibook shows you how to work with bitmap and vector images, and how to optimize and export those images for the Web.

Book IV: Illustrator CS3

Book IV starts with the fundamentals of Adobe Illustrator CS3 to put you on your way to creating useful and interesting illustrations. Check out this minibook to discover how to take advantage of features that have been around for many versions of Illustrator, such as the Pen tool, as well as new and exciting advances, such as the Live Trace feature. See how to take advantage of the Appearance palette and save time by creating graphics styles, templates, and symbols. Pick up hard-to-find keyboard shortcuts that can help reduce the time spent mousing around for menu items and tools.

Book V: Flash CS3

Adobe Flash CS3 delivers animation, sound, video, and interactivity to the Web as no other product ever has. If you've ever wanted to find out how to use this tool to add some new zip to your Web site, this is the minibook for you!

Book VI: Contribute CS3

Designed as a collaborative tool that turns your hard development work into an easy interface for nontechies to update and publish content to the Web, Contribute puts the power of maintaining Web sites in the hands of the people you work with. In this minibook, you find everything you need to know to get you and your collaborators up and running with Contribute in no time flat.

Book VII: Acrobat CS3

Adobe Acrobat CS3 is a powerful viewing and editing application that allows you to share documents with colleagues, clients, and production personnel such as printers and Web page designers. Book VII shows you how you can save time and money previously spent on couriers and overnight shipping by taking advantage of annotation capabilities. Discover features that even advanced users may have missed along the way, and see how you can feel comfortable about using PDF as a file format of choice.

Conventions Used in This Book

We use some conventions throughout this book that merit a little explanation. When you see a phrase such as "choose File➪Save," it means to click through the sequence of menu commands. In this example, those commands are File followed by Save.

Whenever we tell you to click something (most likely it's a button or an icon), you use the left mouse button and click just once. On those rare occasions when clicking twice is required to get the job done, we tell you to double-click, or, if you need to use the right mouse button, we tell you to right-click.

To *select* an item, you either highlight it or click in a check box or radio button, depending on the item. Text that we tell you to enter (that is, type) into the program, such as in a text box, appears in **boldface** type. Web site addresses and on-screen messages show up in `monofont` type. And finally, to avoid confusion, we use title-style capitalization for option names and links, even when the program doesn't.

Icons Used in This Book

Along the way, when there's something of interest to point out, we toss in one of the icons you see in the left margin. When you see one, slow down for a moment to check it out to see what's up!

If there's a way to make something easier, or a more commonly accepted way of doing something, we tell you about it. This is the icon to look for!

When we really want to reinforce something, we throw in a Remember icon.

Pitfall ahead! That's what this icon is all about. If something could cause trouble, we let you know.

Because we love technology, you have to forgive us for geeking out every now and then. When we do, though, we let you know with this icon.

This icon highlights new features in the products that make up the Adobe Creative Suite 3 Web Premium package.

You can use the Adobe Creative Suite 3 programs together in many different and helpful ways to make your workflow more efficient. In the Photoshop, Illustrator, and Acrobat minibooks, we use this icon when we explain how you can implement integration wherever it's pertinent to the discussion at hand.

Where to Go from Here

If you've read this far, then you may actually be a candidate for reading this book from cover to cover! From here, we suggest you dive right in to whatever section you're most interested in. Remember, all these minibooks are self-contained and don't require you to read the others. So have at it. It's buffet time, and your plate needs fillin' up!

Book I

Dreamweaver CS3

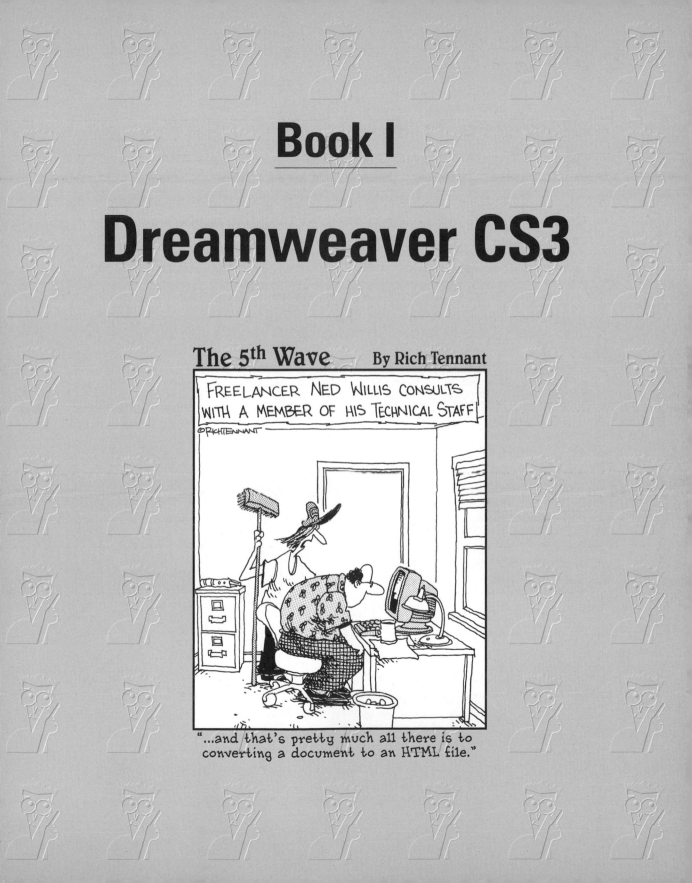

The 5th Wave
By Rich Tennant
FREELANCER NED WILLIS CONSULTS WITH A MEMBER OF HIS TECHNICAL STAFF
©RICHTENNANT

"...and that's pretty much all there is to converting a document to an HTML file."

Book 1: Dreamweaver CS3 7

Chapter 1: Introduction to Dreamweaver CS3

In This Chapter

- Exploring the Dreamweaver CS3 interface
- Choosing between Design view and Code view
- Choosing among Standard, Expanded Table, and Layout modes
- Examining your site with the Files panel
- Exploring toolbar buttons
- Using panels and inspectors
- Getting help

If you're looking for a Web design tool that's both easy enough for beginners and sophisticated enough for Web design gurus, you've come to the right place. Dreamweaver CS3 from Adobe is a powerful program that enables you to create almost any type of Web page. This chapter covers the Dreamweaver basics and introduces you to some of the program's essential tools.

Dreamweaver is the industry standard for Web site design and production. Whether you're interested in creating a site for fun, such as an online photo album or a site devoted to one of your hobbies, or for business, such as an online store, Dreamweaver's flexible interface provides simultaneous graphical and HTML editing. In other words, using Dreamweaver, you can not only lay out pages like an artist but also fine-tune the associated code as a programmer would. Additionally, Dreamweaver's built-in FTP features enable you to upload your site to the Web in a snap so that you can share your masterpieces with the world.

Activating Dreamweaver CS3

When you launch Dreamweaver for the first time, the Adobe Dreamweaver CS3 Grace Period window appears. Product activation is required, but if you're in a hurry to get to work on your site right away, you can select the Activate Later option and click the Next button. You have a 30-day grace period during which you can continue to select the Activate Later option every time you launch Dreamweaver. When the 30 days are up, though, you won't be able to use the application until you activate it.

Exploring the Dreamweaver CS3 Interface

With Dreamweaver CS3, Adobe continues the tradition of allowing you to choose from two versions of the Dreamweaver workspace — Designer style and Coder style — that debuted with Dreamweaver MX 2004. This selection allows you, the developer, to work in an environment that is best suited to your personal development taste: one geared toward WYSIWYG (What You See Is What You Get) development and one that is more code oriented.

Selecting a workspace

Dreamweaver offers two workspace options:

- **Designer:** The WYSIWYG (What You See Is What You Get) interface, which shows the page you are working on much like it would be in a Web browser. This style is more appropriate for Web design novices working on basic HTML pages.
- **Coder:** The style that shows the page you are working on as an editable text document, which is appropriate for experienced coders and for pages on which you're editing CSS (Cascading Style Sheets), XML, or dynamic code such as CFML (ColdFusion Markup Language) or ASP (Active Server Pages).

You can switch between the two styles, or even combine them, at the click of a button. See the "Introducing the Document Window" section, later in this chapter, for details. You might even consider switching back and forth between modes as you're learning HTML because doing so is a good way to see the underlying HTML as it's being generated.

Introducing the Start page

After you've selected a workspace, when you launch Dreamweaver by double-clicking its icon on the desktop or by selecting it from the Windows Start menu, you'll see a Start page, as shown in Figure 1-1. The Start page allows you to perform the following tasks with a single click of your mouse:

- **Open pages you've recently edited:** Simply click the filename of the page you want to open.
- **Create a new page in one of eight formats:** Simply click the type of page you want to create, from basic HTML to ColdFusion (CFML) to CSS (Cascading Style Sheets). You can also click More to view additional formats.

- **Create a new Dreamweaver Site:** Click the Dreamweaver Site icon (in the Create New column) to open the Site Definition Wizard, which guides you through the process of setting up the directory location, FTP information, server technology (if applicable), and more for your Web site. A "site" in Dreamweaver is a collection of Web pages, images, and tools that allow you to more easily manage your Web sites. See Book I, Chapter 3 for more in-depth details on Dreamweaver Sites.
- **Create a new page based on Dreamweaver's built-in samples:** Click an option in the Create from Samples column to open the New Document dialog box and choose from the preset formatting options for that type of page.

The Start page also gives you fast access to a quick tour and set of tutorials for Dreamweaver, and to Adobe's Dreamweaver Exchange page, where you can find lots of nifty objects that extend Dreamweaver's capabilities.

If you find the Start page incompatible with your working methods, you can prevent it from appearing in the future by selecting the Don't Show Again check box at the lower-left corner of the page.

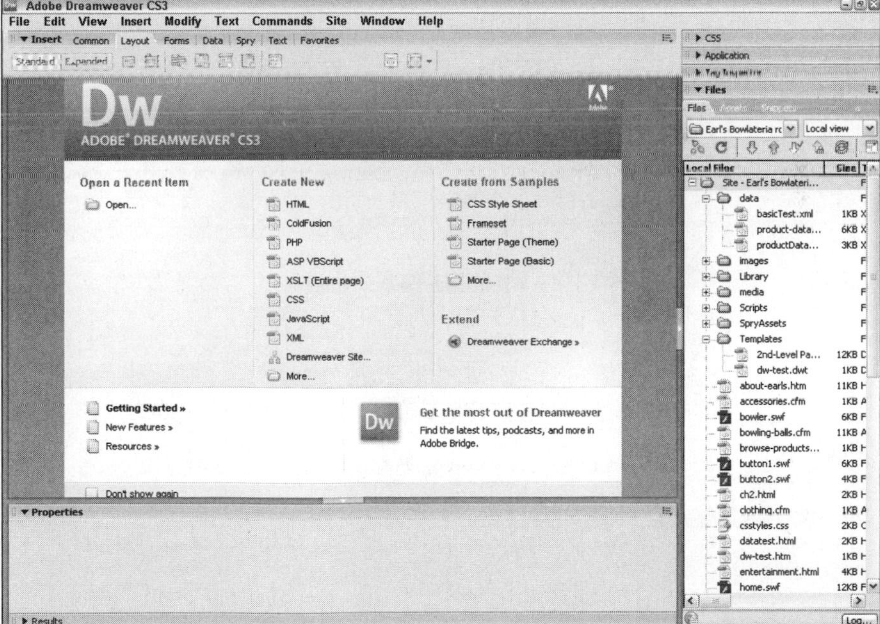

Figure 1-1: The Start page gives you one-click access to a variety of options.

Introducing the Document Window

Your primary workspace in Dreamweaver is the Document window, which appears automatically when you open a page in Dreamweaver. In the Document window, you construct your individual Web pages using panels and dialog boxes to format your work. The three primary views in Dreamweaver are as follows:

- **Design view:** The graphical view of your document, as shown in Figure 1-2. You can select this view by choosing View➪Design or simply clicking the Design button near the top left of the Document window.
- **Code view:** This view shows the underlying code of your document. You can select this view by choosing View➪Code or clicking the Code button.
- **Split view:** As you may expect, this is a split-screen view that includes both the Code and Design windows. You can select this view by choosing View➪Code and Design or clicking the Split button.

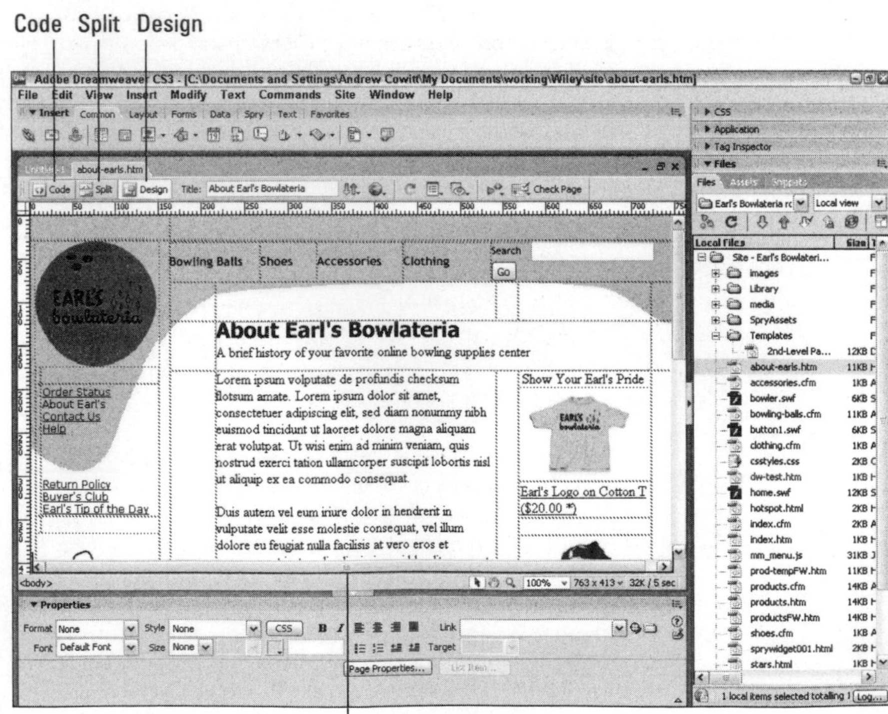

Figure 1-2: Design view approximates what your page looks like in a Web browser.

You can toggle between these views easily at any time by clicking their corresponding buttons at the top left of the Document window.

When you have several documents open in a site, you can select which document you want to work on by clicking the document's name at the top of the Dreamweaver Document window. You can also click the Site tab in the Files panel to work on an entire site.

The Insert bar sits directly underneath Dreamweaver's main menu. It gives you quick access to seven tabs you can use to insert everything from tables to Flash movies to form elements in your page. To select one of the seven categories, click the Insert bar's name (Common, Layout, and so on) and choose a new category from the drop-down list.

Choosing among Standard, Expanded Table, and Layout Modes

When viewing your document in either Split or Design view, you can view content using the Standard mode, the Expanded Table mode, or the Layout mode. The Standard mode is the default. (Figure 1-2, in the previous section, shows a page in Standard mode in the Design view, with the Insert bar set to Common.) The Expanded Table mode makes it easier for you to select tables and cells (though if you want to resize the table or row or column, you need to do so in Standard mode). The Expanded Table mode is most useful for editing existing tables. The Layout mode provides a simpler interface for drawing and editing tables and table cells.

Two special tools are available only when working in Layout mode: the Draw Layout Cell button and the Draw Layout Table button. A table created with the Draw Layout Table tool is shown in Figure 1-3. Both of these tools can help you generate tables or table cells quickly and easily in Dreamweaver, and are described in more detail in Book I, Chapter 2.

To change to the Layout mode, select the Layout Insert bar at the top left of the Document window and click the Layout Mode button, or choose View➪Table Mode➪Layout Mode, or press Alt+F6. When you're in Layout mode, press Alt+F6 (Opt+F6 on a Mac) to return to Standard mode.

To change to Expanded Table mode, select the Layout Insert bar at the top left of the Document window and click the Expanded Table Mode button at the top of the Document window, or choose View➪Table Mode➪Expanded Table Mode, or press F6. When you're in Expanded Table mode, press F6 or click the Expanded Table Mode button to return to Standard mode. ***Note:*** None of the table modes is available in Code view.

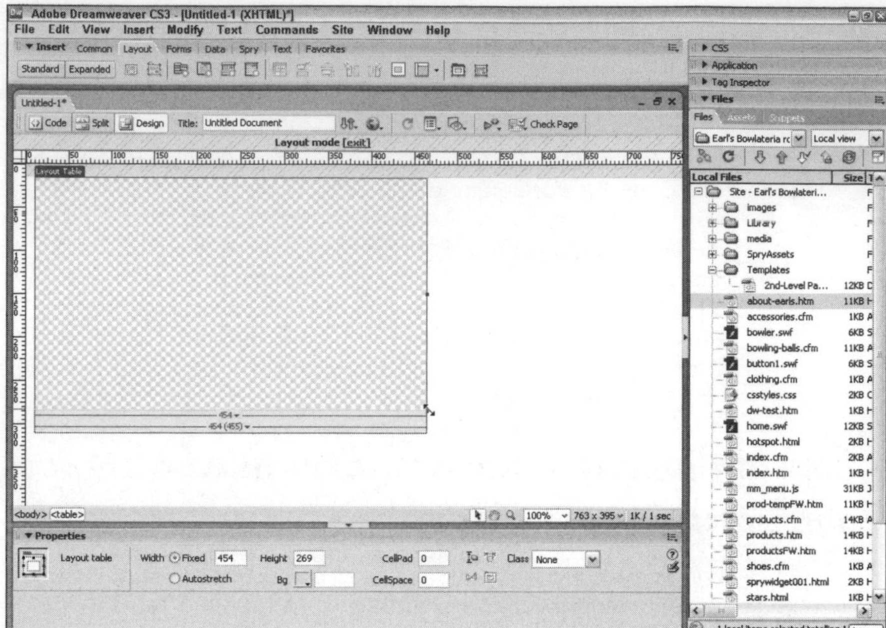

Figure 1-3: A table drawn in Layout mode.

Examining Your Web Site with the Files Panel

Dreamweaver offers Web developers the opportunity to work on individual files that make up a Web site, as well as to manage their entire Web site, all through the Dreamweaver interface. This concept is called, not surprisingly, a *Site;* to avoid confusion, we call them *Dreamweaver Sites.* Dreamweaver Sites can include the following elements:

✦ HTML, CFM, ASP, and other files that make up the code of the site

✦ Graphics, such as GIF and JPEG files

✦ Documents, such as PDF and DOC files

✦ Directories (folders that might contain any of the above)

Dreamweaver Sites are initially viewable within the Files panel (which is open by default; if the Files panel is not open, you can open it by pressing F8). To expand the Files panel so that it fills your screen, or to collapse the panel back to panel size, click the Expand/Collapse button (the icon of the two-row, two-column box with an arrow in the middle, at the right of the panel).

The Web site management tools for Dreamweaver Sites are designed to give you total control over the way in which your Web site is built and maintained from your local computer. The key features of the Dreamweaver Site tools include

- ✦ Asset management tools that help you manage all the files that make up your site. For example, these tools keep track of all your files and the links between files. Anytime you move a file, the tools will change the related links in other files.
- ✦ Basic source control to ensure that files don't get overwritten. These tools lock files so that when you're working on a particular file, others on your team can't edit that same file.
- ✦ Publishing tools that allow you to use FTP to upload the content from your site locally to the remote server where the site is housed.
- ✦ Utilities that create site maps, check links, check the HTML code, and run reports on who's been working on what.

Dreamweaver Sites are covered in more detail in Book I, Chapter 3.

Exploring Toolbar Buttons

Dreamweaver provides you with a number of useful view buttons (shown in Figure 1-4 and Figure 1-5) that you can use to see different views of your site or to perform various functions. You can easily switch among views to examine your site in different ways. Each Dreamweaver view offers specialized menus and tools to help you perform your work in that view. Certain views are available for an individual document or page, whereas other views are available for the entire site. At any time while you work, you can choose to preview your site in target Web browsers, which enables you to see your site from the user's perspective.

Figure 1-4 shows the following Site-related buttons from the Files panel:

- ✦ **Connect to Remote Host button:** Connects your local computer and your Web host, allowing you to transfer files between the two computers.
- ✦ **Refresh button:** Refreshes the panel's view of files in the Site if you've made a change to filenames or file structures outside of Dreamweaver while the program was open.
- ✦ **Get File(s) button:** Downloads (retrieves) documents and files from the host.

✦ **Put File(s) button:** Uploads (sends) documents and files to the host.

✦ **Check Out File(s) button:** Locks files for editing by a single individual.

✦ **Check In button:** Replaces files on the server and makes them available for editing by unlocking them.

✦ **Synchronize button:** Upload or download files to synch the assets on your local site with those on your remote site.

✦ **Expand/Collapse button:** Enlarges the Site tab to full screen, with remote and local files side by side (or, conversely, collapses the full-screen view).

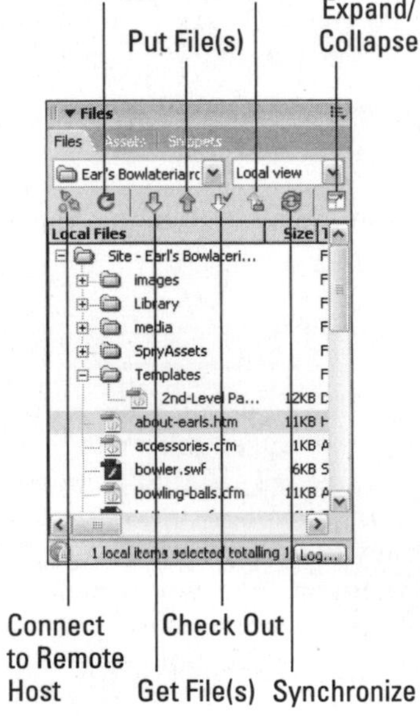

Figure 1-4: The Files tab of the Files panel includes useful buttons.

Figure 1-5 shows the following document-related buttons from the top of the Document window:

✦ **Code:** Enables you to view the HTML page code full-screen.

✦ **Split:** Allows you to view the HTML page code and the graphical view of your document at the same time.

✦ **Design:** Enables you to view the WYSIWIG graphical representation of your page full-screen.

- **File Management button:** Click and then select Get to retrieve files from the Web site host, or select Put to send files to the host.
- **Preview/Debug in Browser button:** Click and select to preview or debug in your browser(s).
- **Refresh button:** Reloads your page so that changes to the code are reflected in the Design view.
- **View Options button:** Click to select options (such as Word Wrap in Code view and the Ruler in Design view) to assist you in viewing your page.
- **Visual Aids:** Hides and shows the various visual cues available to you in the Split and Design views.
- **Validate Markup:** Allows you to run a check on your code to see whether the HTML code is well formed.
- **Check Browser Compatibility button:** Allows you to run a check on your code for browser compatibility.

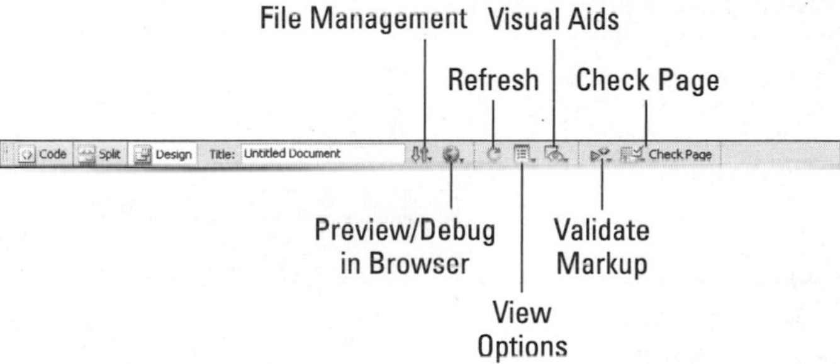

Figure 1-5: The buttons at the top of the Document window.

Some of these items may be unavailable, depending on what view you're in and what you have selected in a document or panel.

Using Panels and Inspectors

You can use Dreamweaver panels and inspectors to enter details about all aspects of your Web site. These interfaces offer areas where you can add and format page features, set up navigation and behaviors, and manage the workflow of building your site.

Understanding the role of panels

A panel typically provides information about all instances of a particular feature on a page. For example, the Layers panel lists information about all the layers on the current page.

The Tag Inspector panel gives you easy access to various properties and behaviors specific to a selected object. The Tag Inspector panel updates continually, depending on what you have selected on your page. (If you have nothing selected on the page, the panel displays properties and behaviors of the whole page itself, as shown in Figure 1-6.) Note that the Tag Inspector panel's name reflects the HTML or CFML tag being inspected.

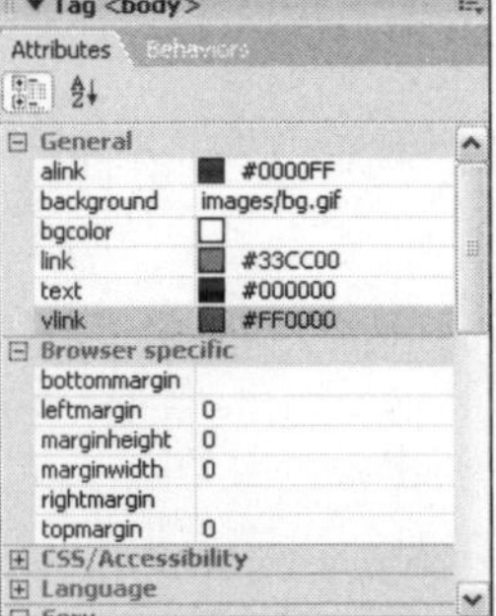

Figure 1-6: The Tag Inspector panel with general page properties displayed.

To switch among tabs in a panel, just click the tab names.

Working with the Properties panel

The Properties panel changes, as does the Tag Inspector panel, based on the individual document object you have selected on your page, and it contains details on attributes of the object. For example, selecting text on a page opens the Text Property inspector in the Properties panel, where you can format the size, font, color, link, and other attributes of the text. (Figure 1-3 shows the Properties panel with a Layout Table selected.) To make certain that the Properties panel is shown below the Document window, choose Window➪Properties or press Shift+F3.

The Properties panel has a small down arrow in the lower-right corner, called an Expander button. Click the button to enlarge the Properties panel to view additional formatting options. In an expanded Properties panel, click the small up arrow in the lower-right corner to collapse the panel.

Getting Help

Dreamweaver offers a variety of tools to help you find the answer to virtually any question you have about the program. The Help tools provide basic information for beginners, as well as advanced references detailing HTML and JavaScript code.

You can get help by clicking the Help button — the small question mark — in the top-right corner of some panels. Similarly, you can open the Options menu in the top-right corner of any panel and select Help from the list.

You can also access help by using the Help menu located on the main menu. Just choose Help and then you can select from a host of options. Some of the more popular ones include

✦ **Dreamweaver Help:** Provides definitions and itemized steps in performing routine Dreamweaver tasks. It contains Help Contents, Index, and Search categories.

✦ **Spry Framework Help:** Launches a Web browser and loads a page from the Adobe Web site, where you can find information about the Spry framework. See Book I, Chapter 7 for step-by-step instructions on using Dreamweaver to place smart Spry widgets on a page.

✦ **Using ColdFusion:** Provides information about coding dynamic sites using ColdFusion technology.

✦ **Reference:** Opens the Reference tab of the Results panel, offering a dictionary-style reference on CSS, HTML, Accessibility requirements, Sitespring tags, and JavaScript. You can also access the Reference tab of the Results panel by clicking the Reference button in the Document window.

✦ **Extensions:** Provides assistance in performing more advanced Dreamweaver tasks, especially tasks involving the integration of adjunct programs, such as Adobe Flash, with Dreamweaver. This help option contains nitty-gritty information about application programming interfaces (APIs) — specific software interfaces that allow you to integrate Dreamweaver with databases, the C and Java programming languages, and much more.

✦ **Dreamweaver Support Center:** Connects you to the Web, where you can find constantly updated information on working with Dreamweaver, answers to frequently asked questions, and program extensions. You can also join a developer's forum, where you can chat with other Dreamweaver users to get (and give) help.

Chapter 2: Creating Basic Web Pages

In This Chapter

- **Setting ruler and grid options in the Document window**
- **Creating and opening pages**
- **Establishing page properties**
- **Working with text**
- **Working with images**
- **Adding links**
- **Working with tables**
- **Previewing your work**
- **Checking browser compatibility**

The most significant (and, fortunately, the easiest) process in building a Web site is creating the individual pages that convey the site's content. Even if you plan on creating an ultrahip site chock full of animation and interactive forms, you spend the vast majority of your site-building effort constructing basic Web pages comprised of words and images. This chapter shows you how to set up, add color to, and name individual Web pages. You also discover how to add basic elements such as text, graphics, and tables, to your pages.

Setting Ruler and Grid Options in the Document Window

Dreamweaver offers you complete control over how you work in the Document window by providing two guide tools — rulers and a grid — to help you lay out your work accurately. You can customize a variety of guide tool attributes, such as ruler increments and grid snapping, to suit your personal preferences and speed Web page development.

Here's a brief look at all your options with rulers and grids:

- **Turning rulers on and off:** Using rulers — both horizontal and vertical — in the Document window can help you measure and position page elements. Toggle the rulers on and off by choosing View⇨Rulers⇨Show or by pressing Ctrl+Alt+R (⌘+Opt+R on a Mac).
- **Moving and resetting the origin:** By default, the origin, or (0,0) coordinate, of a Dreamweaver ruler is set to the upper-left corner of the Document window. You can reposition it to any coordinate in the Document window by clicking the origin cross hairs and dragging them to new coordinates, which can be useful if you want to use the rulers to position elements of a table whose upper-left corner doesn't sit at (0,0) in the Document window. Reset the origin to its default position by choosing View⇨Rulers⇨Reset Origin.
- **Changing ruler measurement units:** You can change the ruler's measuring increment by choosing View⇨Rulers and then choosing Pixels, Inches, or Centimeters.
- **Viewing the grid:** Dreamweaver provides a Document window grid that can assist you in visually positioning and aligning page elements. You can toggle the grid on and off by choosing View⇨Grid⇨Show Grid or pressing Ctrl+Alt+G (⌘+Opt+G on a Mac). The grid is shown in Figure 2-1.

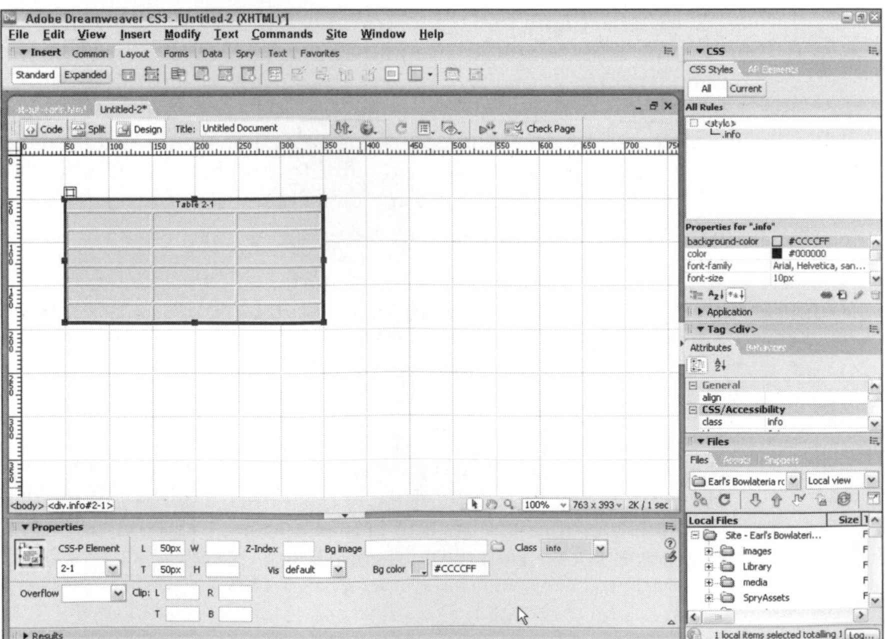

Figure 2-1: The grid is on.

- **Activating and deactivating grid snapping:** The Document window grid offers a snapping feature that causes a div or Layout table or cell to automatically align precisely with the snap-to points you define, which can be useful when you draw, resize, or move a div (see Book I, Chapter 5 for the skinny on divs). You can toggle grid snapping on and off by choosing View⇨Grid⇨Snap to Grid.

You can adjust how the grid appears in the Document window in the Grid Settings dialog box. To do so, open the Grid Settings dialog box by choosing View⇨Grid⇨Grid Settings and change any (or all) of the attributes that appear. When you finish, click the Apply button to view the effect of your changes. Click OK to accept the changes and close the dialog box.

Creating and Opening Pages

You have several ways to create a new page in Dreamweaver:

- On the Start page, scan through the Create New column and click the type of page you want to create from scratch.
- On the Start page, click one of the options in the Create from Samples column to open the New Document dialog box and make a new page with many common settings precoded.
- Choose File⇨New or use the keyboard shortcut Ctrl+N to open the New Document dialog box, from which you can create pages from scratch or from templates.

To open an existing page, do any of the following:

- On the Start page, click the name of the page in the Open Recent column.
- Double-click the page's filename in the Files tab of the Files panel.
- Choose File⇨Open or press Ctrl+O to summon the Open dialog box, which you can use to browse to the page you want to open.

Establishing Page Properties

The Page Properties dialog box provides you with control over how several key page properties appear, including the title of the page, page background color, link colors, and page margins. Selections apply only to the current page, not to the entire site. Open a Page Properties dialog box similar to the one shown in Figure 2-2 by choosing Modify⇨Page Properties or pressing Ctrl+J. Then make changes to any of the following in each of the five categories (Appearance, Links, Headings, Title/Encoding, and Tracing Image):

Figure 2-2: The Page Properties dialog box.

- **Page Font, Size, Text Color, Background Color, Background Image:** Choose a font or set of fonts from the Page Font drop-down list; add a style (bold or italic) if desired. Click the Color box next to each property and pick a color from the Web-safe color palette that appears, or enter a hexadecimal color code directly in any Color Code text field. You can also customize your own colors by selecting the color wheel and entering either RGB values or Hue, Saturation, and Luminosity values. For more information about using colors for the Web, see Book III, Chapter 2. Book III, Chapter 3 includes information on how to use the color picker to select colors in both Dreamweaver and Fireworks. For Background Image, click the Browse button to locate the image file that you want to appear as the Document window background. If the image is smaller than the available background area, the image is *tiled* (repeated in a checkerboard fashion, like floor tiles) to fill the background.

  Even if you choose to use a background image, select a complementary background color; the color shows while the background image is downloading.

- **Left Margin, Right Margin, Top Margin, and Bottom Margin:** Enter numbers (in pixels) in these text fields to set up margins that affect how your page appears in modern browsers. Enter a whole number for the number of pixels of buffer space you want between the left, right, top, and bottom edges of your document and the content of the document.

- **Link Font and Size, Color for Links, Rollover Links, Visited Links, and Active Links:** Choose a font or set of fonts from the drop-down list; add a style (bold or italic) if desired. Click the Color box next to each property and pick a color from the Web-safe color palette that appears, or enter a hexadecimal color code directly in any Color Code text field. You can also customize your own colors (see the first bullet on Text Color).

- **Underline Style:** Select an option from the drop-down list.
- **Heading Font, Sizes, and Colors:** Choose a font or set of fonts from the drop-down list; add a style (bold or italic) if desired. For as many of the six standard HTML heading levels as necessary, select a font size. If you choose a numeric value, the unit-of-measurement drop-down list to the right becomes active so that you can select an option. Click the Color box next to each heading and pick a color from the Web-safe color palette that appears, or enter a hexadecimal color code directly in any Color Code text field. You can also customize your own colors (see the first bullet point on Text Color).
- **Title/Encoding:** Enter a page title in the text field. This title appears in the title bar area of the window both during construction in Dreamweaver and when the page is viewed in a Web browser. Select an Encoding format if your site requires the use of non-Western fonts (Japanese or Cyrillic, for example). If your site is in English, you can leave the setting at the default, Western European.
- **Tracing Image:** Click the Browse button to locate the image file you want to use as a guide for laying out your Web page in the Document window. This feature is handy for developers who prefer to mock up a portion of their Web page design in a graphics program and then re-create that design in their Web pages. Tracing images appear in Dreamweaver only as a pattern to help guide you in creating an actual Web page; the tracing image never appears on the finished Web page.
- **Image Transparency:** Drag the slider to adjust the visibility level of the tracing image. At 0 percent, the tracing image is invisible; at 100 percent, the image is completely opaque.

Click the Apply button to view the effect of any property you change. Click OK to accept your changes and close the Page Properties dialog box.

Working with Text

As we mention in Book I, Chapter 1, Dreamweaver has three different design views: Design, Code, and Split (Code and Design). The following sections apply when you're working in Design view or Split view of Dreamweaver. In these views, you can enter and manipulate text on a Web page in Dreamweaver by using similar procedures to those you use when working with a word processing document.

Adding, editing, and deleting text

To enter text on a page, click in the Document window and begin typing. Your mouse pointer appears as a blinking cursor that moves along with the text you enter. When you reach the end of a line, the text automatically wraps to the next line. Dreamweaver automatically adds the associated code for your new text in the HTML for the page.

To delete text from a page, in the Document window, select the chunk that you want to delete and press Backspace or Del on your keyboard.

You can also modify how text appears on a page by editing its font, size, color, alignment, and other attributes. To modify text in the Document window, click and drag to select the text you want to modify. The Properties panel loads the Text Property inspector, as shown in Figure 2-3 (the Tag Inspector panel also reflects the selection). If the Text Property inspector is not open, choose Window➪Properties or press Ctrl+F3 to open it. In the Text Property inspector, modify any of the following properties:

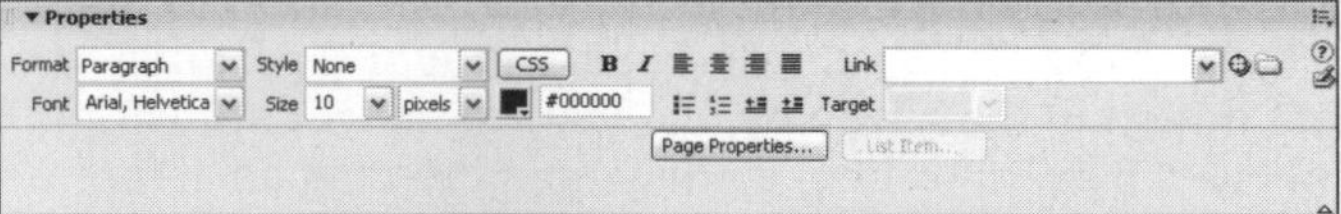

Figure 2-3: The Properties panel with the Text Property inspector loaded.

- **Format:** From the Format drop-down list, select a default text style. Heading 1 is the largest style and Heading 6 is the smallest, but none of the headings correlates with a specific pixel size unless you set it to do so. Select Paragraph for the basic body text of your pages. Select Preformatted if you want spaces, tabs, and new lines in a paragraph to show up in a browser. (Ordinarily, when you add multiple spaces in a row or tabs to your HTML — this is particularly obvious in the Dreamweaver document's Code view — they appear as single spaces in a browser.)
- **Font:** Select a font face from the Font drop-down list. Browsers show your text formatted as the first font in your selection that resides on the user's computer. Choosing Edit Font List allows you to add more fonts that you may have installed on your computer to the Font drop-down list.

  Most computers will have standard fonts such as Arial and Helvetica and won't have less common fonts such as, say, Univers or Futura. If you use a nonstandard font and it's not on the user's machine, the layout could look very different from what you planned.

- **Style:** Dreamweaver has been updated to work better with CSS styles. Styles defined within the document or in a linked stylesheet will be available from the Style drop-down list. You can also use the drop-down list to attach a stylesheet and create and edit styles.
- **Size:** Select a font size from the Size drop-down list. The options include None (choosing this option displays text in the default size), specific numbers, generic sizes XX-small to XX-large, and relative sizes Smaller and Larger. If you select a number, the unit-of-measurement drop-down list becomes available so that you can specify what the font size number refers to (pixels, ems, and so on).
- **Color:** Click the color box and select a text color from the Web-safe color palette that appears. Alternatively, you may enter a hexadecimal color code directly in any color code text field. (To set the default text color for a page, check out the "Establishing Page Properties" section, earlier in this chapter.)
- **Bold or Italic:** Click the Bold button to make your selected text appear in bold. Click the Italic button to italicize your selected text. You can click either button, or both.
- **Alignment:** Click an alignment button to align your text. Choices are Left, Center, Right, and Justify.
- **Link:** Type a URL in this field to transform selected text into a hypertext link. You can also use the Point to File tool to link to a file. To link to a file using this tool, just follow these steps:

  1. **Open the Files panel by choosing Window⇨Files or by pressing F8.**
  2. **Open Explorer to the folder location that includes the file you want to link to by selecting the collapsing menu squares.**

     Alternatively, skip to Step 3 and hover your cursor over the folder that contains the file; the folder will expand so that you can select the file within.
  3. **Click and hold the Point to File button in the Text Property inspector and drag the pointer to the file you want to link to. Release the mouse button when the pointer is over the file.**

     The Point to File button looks like a compass without the needle or a clock face without hands or numbers. It's located to the right of the Links field.

     When you're dragging the button, a line appears from the origin point to your cursor, as shown in Figure 2-4.

     After you let go of the mouse button, the link to the file appears in the Link text field. If you select the Link drop-down list, it shows you your recent links as well.

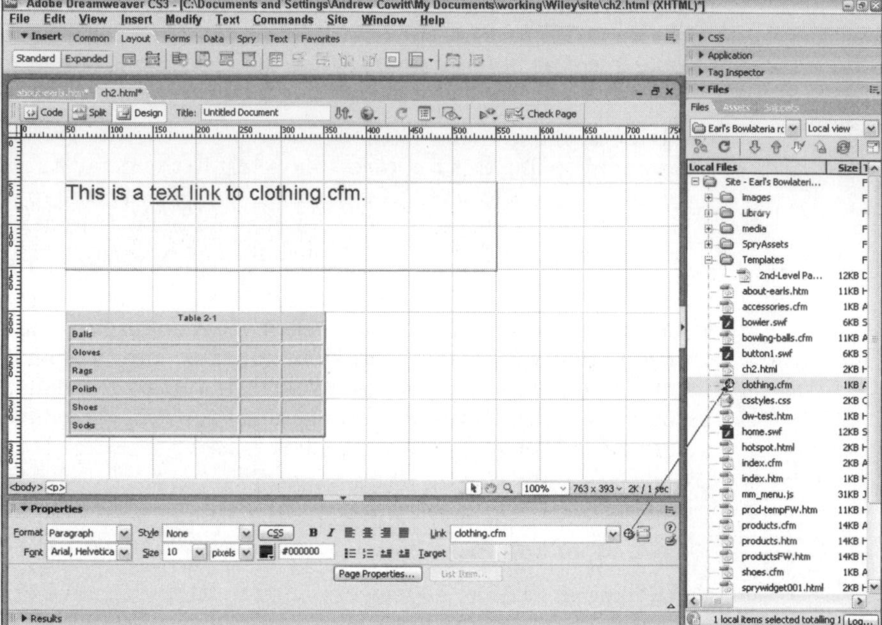

Figure 2-4: The line helps you see which file you're linking to.

✦ **Target:** If you are linking the selected text, you can specify how the linked page will open when the user clicks the link; you do so by selecting one of the following options from the drop-down list:

- `_blank`: Opens the link in a new window.
- `_parent`: Opens the link in the parent of the window that is currently open. If the window with the link in it is not in a frame, the linked page opens in the same window as the link. If the link is in a frame, the linked window will open in the parent frame or in the parent window of the frame with the link. See Book I, Chapter 4 for more information about frames.
- `_self`: Opens the link in the currently opened window; this is the default target.
- `_top`: Opens the link in the top-level window, replacing any existing frames.

✦ **List:** Click the Unordered List button next to the Target field to transform text into an unordered (bulleted) list; click the Ordered List button to transform text into an ordered (numbered) list.

✦ **Placement:** Click the Text Outdent button, which you find next to the Ordered List button, to outdent (decrease the indent) the selected text; click the Text Indent button to indent the selected text. If you outdent an item in a bulleted or numbered list, the item will no longer be a list item.

Inserting a line break

When you want to start a new line in a word-processing program, you press the Enter key. If you press Enter in Dreamweaver, you create a paragraph break, which starts a new paragraph and creates a blank space between paragraphs. If you want to start a new line directly under another line of text and without the big space between lines, you need to insert a line break. In Dreamweaver, you create a line break by choosing Insert⇨HTML⇨Special Characters⇨Line Break or by pressing Shift+Enter. Alternatively, you may click the Insert Line Break button from the HTML category of the Insert bar. Dreamweaver places the cursor at the start of the next line and inserts the line-break HTML code.

Working with Images

Aside from entering text, manipulating images on a Web page is probably the most common Dreamweaver function you perform. You can add or delete an image and modify its properties to create an aesthetically pleasing layout that effectively conveys the information you want to deliver to the user.

To see how to place an image on the background of your page, check out the "Establishing Page Properties" section, earlier in this chapter.

Inserting an image

To insert an image on a page, follow these steps:

1. **Choose Insert⇨Image.**

   Alternatively, you can click the Insert Image button in the Common category of the Insert bar.

2. **In the Select Image Source dialog box that appears (shown in Figure 2-5), click the image you want to insert.**

   If the image is outside the folder that holds your HTML document, use the Look In drop-down list to browse to the file you want. The Image Tag Accessibility Attributes window appears.

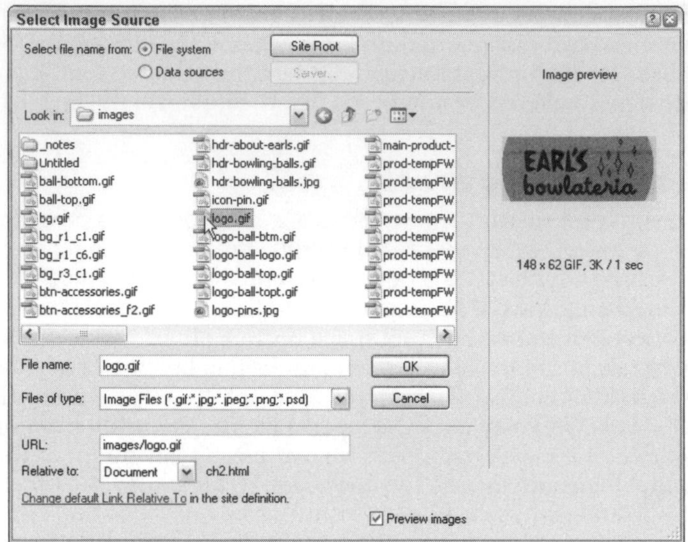

Figure 2-5: Select an image.

3. **If desired, enter Alternate text in the Alternate Text field of the Image Tag Accessibility Attributes window.**

   Specifying alternate text ensures that when viewers' browsers don't — or can't — display the image, some meaningful text appears instead; it also serves as an alternative for sight-impaired visitors to your page. Alternate text should be limited to a few words. You can also add more details about the image in the Long description field.

4. **Click OK to insert the image.**

   Note: Every image you want to include on a Web page should reside within the root folder of the current site. (Typically, you should have your HTML files in the site root folder — the master folder that holds everything on your site — and all your images in an images folder that's also in the site's root folder.) If you attempt to insert an image from another location, Dreamweaver asks whether you want to copy the image to the current site root folder. Click Yes. In the Copy File As dialog box, you can enter a new name for the image in the File Name text field, or you can accept the current name and click the Save button.

Always be sure that you have saved your HTML file at least once before you insert an image into it. If your file isn't saved, Dreamweaver won't know where to place the image in relation to the file. After you've saved the file in a particular folder, the location is known and Dreamweaver can include the correct relative location of the image.

Select the Preview Images check box at the bottom of the Select Image Source dialog box to view a thumbnail of the image before you select it for insertion. The preview area also tells you the size of the image and the expected download time.

Deleting or moving an image

To delete an image from a page, click the image in the Document window and press the Delete key on your keyboard.

If you want to move the image from one place on the page to another, you can click the image in the Document window, press Ctrl+X to cut the image, click the spot on the page where you want to move the image, and press Ctrl+V to paste the image. You can also move an image by clicking and dragging it to a new location.

Modifying an image

You can modify how an image appears on a page by editing its size and alignment, adding a border, and changing other attributes.

To modify an image, click the image in the Document window to select it. If the Image Property inspector does not appear, choose Window➪Properties to open it.

To see all the options the Image Property inspector offers, click the down arrow in the bottom-right corner of the Image Property inspector. (Clicking the up arrow displays fewer options.)

You can do any of the following things to modify the way an image appears:

✦ **Resize the image:** Click and drag a sizing handle to change the dimensions of the image. To resize the image maintaining the same proportions, hold down the Shift key as you drag a sizing handle. You can also resize the image by typing new pixel dimensions in the W and H text fields in the Image Property inspector. Click the Resample button to conform the resized image to the new dimensions. (Otherwise, resizing in Dreamweaver changes the dimensions in which the browser draws the image but leaves the image file itself untouched — and image quality suffers when the browser resizes the image.)

If you want the resized image to look its best, you may be better off resizing the image in Fireworks, because Fireworks gives you more control over the resizing process. To edit the image in Fireworks, select the image and click the Edit button (the pencil icon) in the Edit section of the Properties panel.

- **Align the image:** In the Image Property inspector, click an alignment button to position the image on the page (or within a cell if the image is located in a table cell). Alignment button choices are Left, Center, and Right. To align an image with special word wrapping, select one of the alignment options, which are detailed in Table 2-1, from the Align drop-down list that appears when you position your image near a bunch of text.
- **Add a border to the image:** In the Image Property inspector, enter a number in the Border text field to add a border of that thickness to the image. Border thickness is measured in pixels.
- **Pad an image with spaces:** In the Image Property inspector, enter a number in pixels in the V Space (V for vertical) text field for the space you want to appear between the top and bottom of the image and other page elements; then, enter a number in pixels in the H Space (H for horizontal) text field for the space you want to appear between the image and page elements on either side of the image.
- **Make the image a link:** In the Image Property inspector, enter a URL in the Link text field.
- **Specify alternate text for the image:** In the Image Property inspector, enter alternative text in the Alt field. (Specifying alternate text ensures that when viewers' browsers don't — or can't — display the image, some meaningful text appears instead, and also serves as an alternative for sight-impaired visitors to your page.)
- **Name the image:** In the Image Property inspector, enter a name in the text field next to the thumbnail image. (Naming an image is important if you want to refer to that image using a behavior or scripting language, such as JavaScript, but is otherwise unnecessary.)
- **Edit the image:** In the Image Property inspector, click the Edit button.

Dreamweaver allows you to optimize, crop, resample, adjust brightness and contrast of, and sharpen an image by using the buttons in the Edit section of the Image Property inspector. If you want the most control over the process of editing the image, click the Edit button to open the image in Fireworks or Photoshop. You'll have the choice of working directly with the image or opening the source file the image came from. In most cases, you maintain the highest image quality by manipulating the pre-optimized source version of the image and then exporting it as a new GIF or JPEG.

- **Change the image file:** In the Image Property inspector, enter a different filename in the Src (source) text field (or click the File Folder button to browse for image files).
- **Add an image map:** In Dreamweaver, you can add multiple hyperlinked hotspots to images to create an image map. In the bottom left of the Image Property inspector, you see an arrow pointer and some image tools (a rectangle, circle, and free-form hotspot creator). With these tools, you can create hotspots on your images, and you can specify the following for each hotspot:
  - The link location for the hotspot
  - The target window for the link
  - The alternate text for the hotspot

Table 2-1 Aligning an Image in Relation to Text

Alignment Option	*Effect on Image and Text Wrapping*
Default	Same as Bottom alignment
Baseline	Same as Bottom alignment
Top	Aligns the image top with the highest other inline element
Middle	Aligns the image middle with the text baseline
Bottom	Aligns the image bottom with the text baseline
Text Top	Aligns the image top with the text top
Absolute Middle	Aligns the image middle with the text middle
Absolute Bottom	Aligns the image bottom with the bottom of the text descenders
Left	Aligns the image flush left
Right	Aligns the image flush right

Working with Links

Linking your page to other Web pages enables you to direct visitors to related content on the Web. To insert a link, you must specify an image or some text to serve as the link; you must also specify the link location to which you want to send your visitors. The link can go to a page within your site or to a page elsewhere on the Web.

Inserting a link

To insert a link on a page, follow these steps:

1. **Select the text or image you want to make into a link.**

   Doing so opens the Property inspector for your text or image. If the Property inspector does not appear, choose Window⇨Properties to open it.

2. **In the Link area of the Property inspector, enter the destination URL of the link (text or image) that you created in Step 1.**

   The URL you specify can be any valid URL; for example, it can be a Web page within your own site (somePage.html), a page on the Web (http://www.someSite.com/somePage.html), or even an e-mail address (mailto:somebody@somewhere.com).

   Alternatively, you may click the File Folder button that you see in the Property inspector to display the Select File dialog box. After you browse your computer using the Select File dialog box and select a file, click OK to make that file the target of a link.

To create an e-mail link quickly, click anywhere in your document and choose Insert⇨Email Link. Specifying the same value for the Text and E-mail fields that appear allows folks who haven't configured their Web browsers to handle e-mail automatically to see the e-mail address on the page. Then, they can copy and paste the e-mail address information into their e-mail program of choice.

Deleting a link

To delete a link from text or an image without deleting the text or image itself, follow these steps:

1. **Select the text or image you want to remove the link from.**

   The Property inspector for your text or image opens. If the Property inspector doesn't appear, choose Window⇨Properties to open it.

2. **In the Property inspector, delete the URL from the Link text field.**

Note that if you delete a linked image or linked text from a page, the link gets deleted along with the text or image.

Using named anchors

When you want to create a navigational link that connects users not only to a page but also to a specific location on the page, you need to create a *named anchor*. Named anchors are frequently used for jumping to exact positions within a large block of text so that users don't have to scroll through paragraph after paragraph to find the information they need. Named anchors are especially useful when creating links from a directory or a table of contents to the content it presents.

Inserting a named anchor

Place an anchor anywhere on your Web page as follows:

1. **In the Document window, click at the position you want to insert the named anchor.**
2. **Click the Named Anchor button on the Common category of the Insert bar or choose Insert⇨Named Anchor.**

   The Named Anchor dialog box appears, as shown in Figure 2-6. If the Insert bar is set to a different category, click and hold the category name and select Common from the drop-down list.

Figure 2-6: The Named Anchor dialog box.

3. **Type a name in the Anchor Name text field.**
4. **Click OK.**

It's a good idea to insert the named anchor tag slightly above the actual position where you want the link to target. Doing so gives your targeted content a little padding on top. Otherwise, the top of your image or your first line of text appears flush with the top of the browser window.

Linking to a named anchor

To link to a named anchor, follow the procedure outlined in the "Inserting a link" section, earlier in this chapter, with the following modifications:

- ✦ **Linking to a named anchor on the current page:** In the Link text field of the Property inspector, type a pound sign (#) followed by the anchor name.
- ✦ **Linking to a named anchor on a different page:** In the Link text field of the Property inspector, type the page's URL followed by a pound sign and then the anchor name.

Be sure not to include any spaces in the names of anchors. These may not be read by the various Web browsers.

Working with Tables

You can position objects (such as text blocks, images, or animations) relative to each other on a page in two basic ways:

- ✦ **Using tables:** A time-honored Web tradition for page layout, tables are grids of cells defined by columns and rows. Cells can have set sizes and alignments and may contain anything you can put on a Web page, including other tables.
- ✦ **Using divs:** Divs can be positioned precisely, and in Dreamweaver, divs are in some ways easier to use than tables. For instructions on how to lay out your Web page with divs, see Book I, Chapter 5.

Adding a table to a Web page can help you lay out page elements more easily in the Document window. Tables consist of as many holding areas, or cells, as you want, and you can place virtually any Web element, such as text or an image, into a cell. Cells are organized horizontally into *rows* and vertically into *columns.* Dreamweaver provides you with complete control over the size, position, color, and other attributes of your table. You can edit these attributes at any time via the Table Property inspector.

Inserting a table

To insert a table into a Web page, just follow these steps:

1. **Click within the document at the point where you want to place the table.**
2. **Choose Insert⇨Table, press Ctrl+Alt+T (⌘+Opt+T on a Mac), or click the Table button in the Common category of the Insert bar.**

The Insert Table dialog box appears, as shown in Figure 2-7. If the Insert bar is set to a different category, click and hold the category name and select Common from the drop-down list.

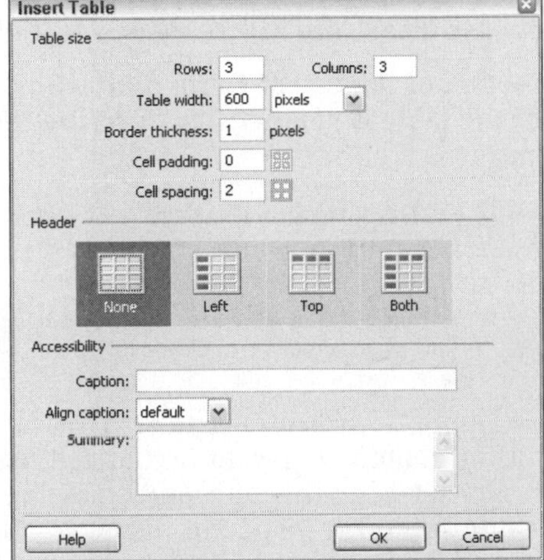

Figure 2-7: Fill out the Insert Table dialog box to create a table.

3. **Enter the number of rows and columns you want the table to have in the corresponding Rows and Columns fields.**

   You can always add or remove rows or columns later.

4. **Use the Table Width field to set a width for the table.**

   The width can be either a set number of pixels or a percentage of the area that bounds the table (the page itself, or, if the table is nested in a cell, that cell).

5. **In the Border Thickness field, enter a number for how many pixels thick you want the border of your table to be.**

   If you don't want the table border to show (which you probably don't if you're using the table for page layout purposes), enter 0 (zero).

6. **In the Cell Padding field, enter a whole number for the amount of pixels you want between the border of the cell and the text or object inside the cell.**

   The cell padding applies to the top, bottom, left, and right of the inside of each and every cell.

7. **In the Cell Spacing field, enter a number for the amount of pixels you want between the cells.**

   The cell spacing applies to the whole table; you can't have different cell spacing for individual rows or columns.

8. **If your table has a header row or header column (or both), click the button (None, Left, Top, or Both) that represents the header structure of your table.**

   The text in a header row has special formatting that you can define in a stylesheet. If you're creating a table for layout purposes, you won't want a header row or column, so make sure that None is selected.

9. **In the Accessibility section of the Insert Table dialog box, enter a caption and summary for the table if you need to describe the table for a sight-impaired audience.**

   If you're making the table for page layout purposes, leave these blank.

10. **Click OK.**

    The Insert Table dialog box disappears and the empty table appears in your document.

An empty table is shown in Figure 2-8. To enter data into the table, just click an individual cell and enter the content you want in that cell. You can modify any of the table's attributes by selecting the table and changing the attributes in the Property inspector or the Tag Inspector panel.

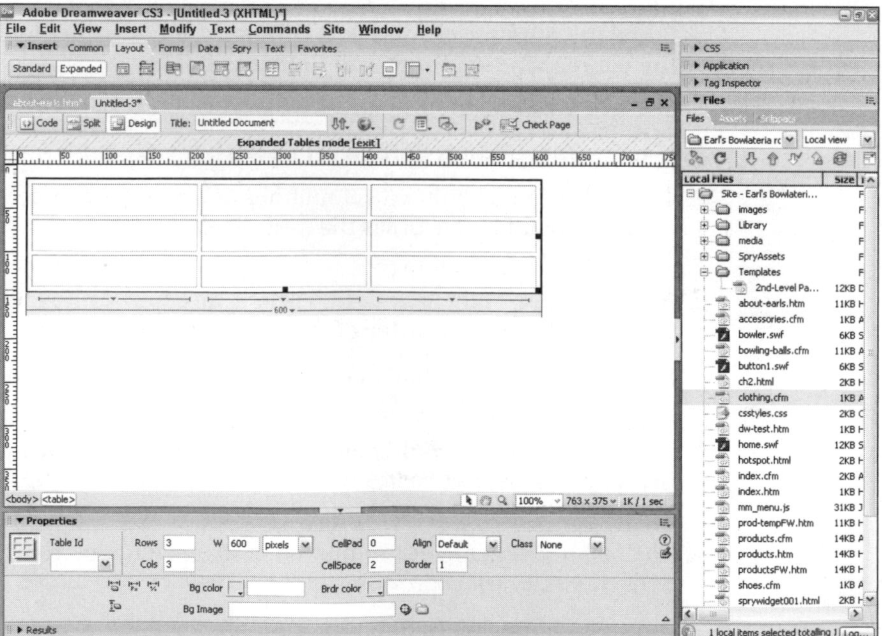

Figure 2-8: A simple table.

Deleting a table

To delete a table from a page, click the border of the table to select it and then press the Backspace or Del key. Dreamweaver removes the table from your page and deletes the associated code in the HTML for the page. Naturally, everything that was in the table is also deleted from the page.

Using layout tables

The use of tables is central to the traditional way of building great Web pages. (For information on laying out pages with divs, see Book I, Chapter 5.) What happens, though, when you want to put an image right smack in the middle of a page, or when you want to have one column of information along the right side of the page and a square text block at the bottom of the page? You can nest tables, which involves building new tables inside cells of other tables, but creating nested tables is complicated, especially with complex pages.

Thankfully, Dreamweaver offers an easy way to work with complex tables called layout tables. With a layout table, you tell Dreamweaver where you want to put something on the screen, and the program generates all the required tablework to make it happen.

To create a layout table, just follow these steps:

1. **Choose View⇨Table Mode⇨Layout Mode or press Alt+F6.**

   If the Insert bar is set to a different category, click the Layout tab. The first time you press Alt+F6 (Opt+F6 on a Mac), a Table Help dialog box appears.

2. **Click the Draw Layout Table button (just to the left of the Draw Layout Cell button).**

3. **Click and drag the cross hair to create the layout table of your choice.**

   A light-green table appears, as shown in Figure 2-9, with the dimensions you gave it.

4. **To create individual cells within that table, click the Draw Layout Cell button to the right of the Draw Layout Table button and draw a cell anywhere within the table.**

   If you create a layout cell outside a layout table, Dreamweaver will create both the cell and the table to support it. Note that you cannot draw a new cell that overlaps an existing cell in the table.

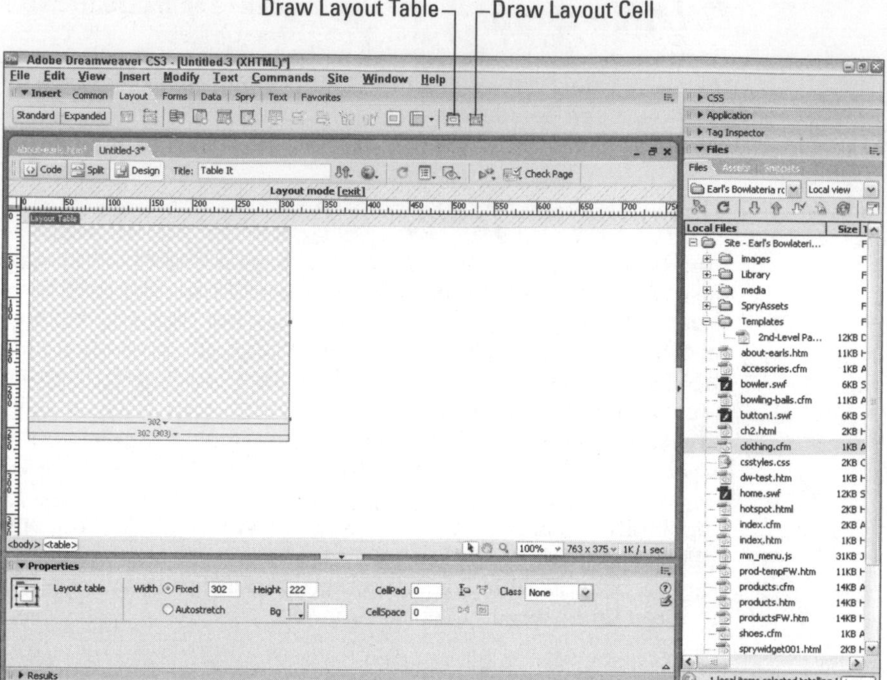

Figure 2-9: Drawing a layout table.

If you create a layout cell, you can immediately edit the cell you created. However, if you create a layout table, you either have to switch back to Standard view to edit the single cell of that table or create a layout cell within the table before you can edit the table.

Storing information in table cells

After you insert a table into a page, you can add or delete elements such as text and images in the table cells:

- **Adding an image to a cell:** To add an image to a table cell, click in a table cell and choose Insert➪Image or press Ctr+Alt+I (⌘+Opt+I on a Mac). Browse and select an image you want to add to the cell and then click OK. (For more information on inserting images, flip to the "Inserting an image" section, earlier in this chapter.)
- **Adding text to a cell:** To add text to a table cell, click to position the cursor in a table cell and type the text you want placed inside the cell.

- **Deleting an image from a cell:** To delete an image from a table cell, select the image and press Backspace or Del.
- **Deleting text from a cell:** To delete text from a table cell, select the text and press Backspace or Del.

Previewing Your Work

Whether you're working in Code view or Design view, at some point you'll want to see the page as visitors to your site will see it: in a browser such as Internet Explorer or Netscape Navigator. If you have two or more browsers on your computer, you can preview your page in any of the browsers — without leaving Dreamweaver — by using the Preview in Browser feature.

To preview your page in your primary browser, choose File⇨Preview in Browser⇨*Browser Name,* or press F12. The keyboard shortcut for previewing in your secondary browser is Shift+F12.

Checking Browser Compatibility

One of the most frustrating things about creating Web sites is that the same HTML and CSS code may display differently in different browsers. In fact, it's possible that one part of a page that displays in one browser won't display at all in another.

Dreamweaver can find problems in the code that may lead to display issues in different browsers. To use the Browser Compatibility Check, just follow these steps:

1. **Choose File⇨Check Page⇨Browser Compatibility.**

   The Results panel appears at the bottom of the workspace, open to the Browser Compatibility Check tab.

2. **Click the green right-facing arrow at the top left of the panel and choose Check Browser Compatibility from the menu that appears.**

   Dreamweaver searches your code for problems. Any issues it finds are listed in the panel, ordered by the line in the code where each problem appears.

Chapter 3: Creating and Using Dreamweaver Sites

In This Chapter

- **Defining a Site in Dreamweaver CS3**
- **Whipping up your first site**
- **Establishing a remote connection**
- **Using advanced site options**
- **Publishing and maintaining your site**
- **Using source control**

You can use Dreamweaver CS3 to create many different kinds of Web pages. During the course of building a Web site, you'll add pages, graphics, links, and all sorts of related information at a single location to be posted eventually to a Web server on the Internet. After your site is complete, you'll probably want to make updates and fixes. Heck, you may even be making more than one site at the same time!

To help facilitate management of your Web site (or sites), Dreamweaver offers a suite of site management tools. These tools are collectively called a *Dreamweaver Site*. This chapter explores how you can use these tools to manage your Web site more easily.

Defining a Site in Dreamweaver CS3

Figure 3-1 shows a typical relationship between where you build your Web site (on your desktop) and where the site actually lives on the Internet (on a Web server). Dreamweaver Sites facilitate getting all the correct information from your desktop to the Web server and generally make the Web page creation process easier. Specifically, a Dreamweaver Site enables you to do the following:

- ✦ Move files seamlessly back and forth between your local machine and your Web server.
- ✦ Keep all your Site files in a single location.

- Generate pages for your Site based on templates that you create.
- Run reports on the pages in your Site to check links, page load, and other key functions.
- Use source- and version-control to manage who works on what files and when they do it, which can prevent team members from accidentally overwriting each other's work when building or maintaining a Site collaboratively.

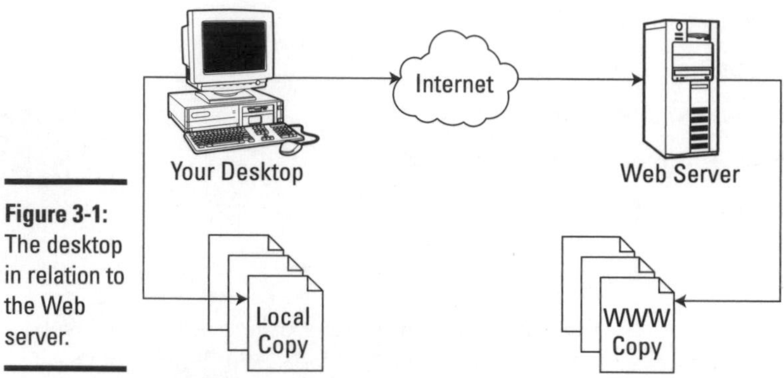

Figure 3-1: The desktop in relation to the Web server.

Creating Your First Site

If you're working with a set of files regularly in Dreamweaver, or if you're managing several sites, you're likely to find using Dreamweaver Sites — which are different from a traditional Web site — an efficient way of working. You can create a Site in Dreamweaver manually or by using a wizard.

This section shows you how to create a Dreamweaver Site manually. The following steps walk you through inputting the minimum amount of information that you need to enter to create your Site. However, you can choose from a number of other options, and they are covered in the "Using Advanced Site Options" section, later in this chapter.

To create a basic site manually, follow these steps:

1. **Choose Site➪New Site.**

   The Site Definition dialog box appears, opened to the Advanced tab by default. The Local Info options, shown in Figure 3-2, appear by default.

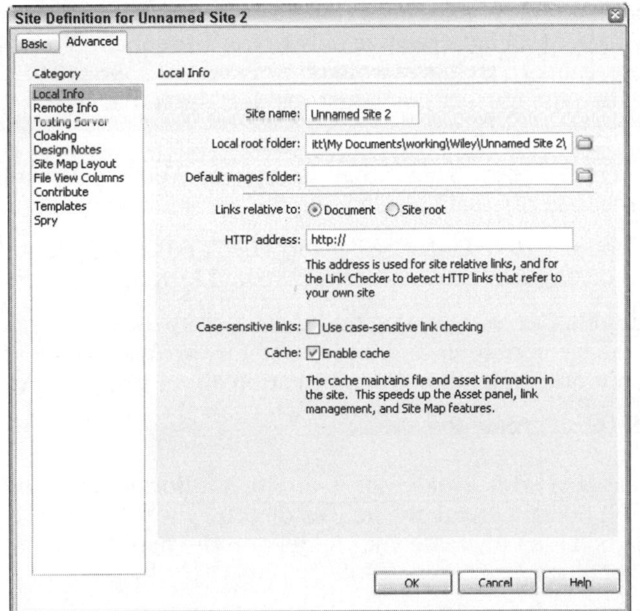

Figure 3-2: Defining your site.

2. **Set the options for your site by filling out each of the following pieces of information:**

   - **Site Name:** Choose a name that you can remember easily and that applies to the function of the Site.
   - **Local Root Folder:** This is the location on your hard drive where you want to store the files that make up your site. Again, you should title the folder something intuitive and easy to remember. If you want to browse for a folder, just click the folder icon to the right of the text field.
   - **Default Images Folder:** This is the standard directory for images used on your site. Dreamweaver adds images here when you copy image files into your Site. A good practice is to name this folder images (if your site will be hosted on a UNIX-based server, you need to be consistent about using upper- and lowercase letters in file-names and links to those files from your site). If you want to browse for the directory, just click the folder icon next to the text field.
   - **Links Relative To:** Select Document if you want links to include a path from the current document to the linked item (for example, `../../images/spacer.gif` for a link to an image in `[site root]/images/`

from an HTML page in [site root]/aboutus/). Select Site Root if you want all links relative only to the site's main directory (for example, a link to an image would be /images/spacer.gif, no matter where the current document resides; the initial slash represents [site root]).

- **HTTP Address:** This is the URL of your Web site. Dreamweaver uses this to verify that links in your site are working properly.
- **Case-sensitive Links:** Select this check box if you want Dreamweaver to distinguish between uppercase and lowercase letters in links.
- **Enable Cache:** Selecting this check box speeds up Dreamweaver's site management tools and is required for the Assets panel to work. See your documentation for information about using the Assets panel.

3. **Click OK to create the site.**

Dreamweaver creates a folder for your Site if it doesn't exist on your hard drive, but it doesn't create the images directory within that folder. Thus, it's always a good idea to create your folders on the hard drive first and then create your Site.

Setting Up a Remote Connection

After you create your Site, it's a good idea to get connected to the place where the remote version of your Site (the one users will access via the World Wide Web) will live. Dreamweaver can connect to a remote server in a variety of ways. The route you choose depends largely on how you plan to build and maintain your Site. You have essentially three different scenarios:

- **Creating and testing your Site solely on your own computer:** For example, this may be the case if you're building your Site for someone else — say, a client. Here the remote server is your computer — not all that remote!
- **Creating your Site on your computer, but testing it somewhere else:** This is the most common situation. Dreamweaver has three different delivery options for this scenario: FTP, Remote Development Services (RDS), and local network connection.
- **Creating and testing your Site on a remote machine:** In this case, the options are the same as in the previous bullet. The only difference is that when you're editing, you're editing files directly on the remote location, leaving nothing on your local machine.

In most cases, your remote location is at an externally hosted Internet service provider (ISP). If you have an account set up with an ISP, make sure to get the following information, which is required for Dreamweaver to set up a connection to your remote Web server:

✦ An IP address or a URL to be used when posting your files (FTP host)

✦ A folder on the remote server where you are supposed to keep your site files (host directory)

✦ A username for your account

✦ A password for your account

To set up a remote connection, follow these steps:

1. Choose Site⇨Manage Sites to bring up the Manage Sites dialog box, shown in Figure 3-3.

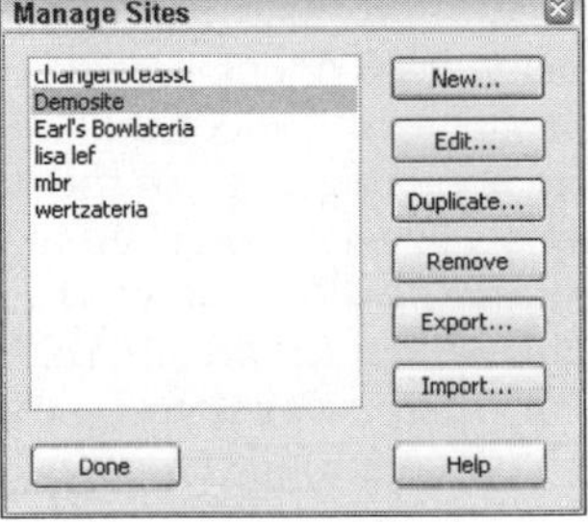

Figure 3-3: The Manage Sites dialog box.

2. Select your site from the list on the left and then click the Edit button.

The Site Definition dialog box appears, opened to the Advanced tab.

3. From the Category list on the left, select Remote Info.

Along the right side of the dialog box, the Local Info options are replaced with the Remote Info options. If you haven't set up a connection previously, all you see is the Access drop-down list.

4. Select an option from the Access drop-down list.

You can choose from several Access options in this list, including

- **FTP:** The industry standard, file transfer protocol.
- **Local/Network:** A location on your local (meaning office, home office, or your own computer) network.

- **WebDAV:** Stands for Web-based Distributed Authoring and Versioning. It's a standard for version control and is used with Web servers such as Apache Web Server and Microsoft IIS.
- **RDS:** ColdFusion's Remote Development Services allows secure remote access to files within a ColdFusion application server.
- **Microsoft Visual SourceSafe Database:** SourceSafe is Microsoft's version control application, which helps prevent the accidental overwriting of files when you're collaborating with others to build the site. With Dreamweaver, you can integrate SourceSafe and use it for your version control.

5. **Fill out the appropriate information for the connection type you selected.**

   Leave the source control settings (described in the "Using Source Control" section, later in this chapter) alone for the moment. The following list describes the information needed for each connection type:

   - **FTP:** In addition to the four items we note at the beginning of this section (FTP host, host directory, login (username), and password), you also need to select the Passive FTP check box if you plan to use Passive FTP (required for some servers). Select the Use IPv6 transfer mode box if your remote server is enabled to use the latest version of IP (Internet Protocol). If there's a firewall you need to work through, you can enter the Firewall host and port, as shown in Figure 3-4. Click OK to save your Preferences and return to the Site Definition window. Select the Use Secure FTP (SFTP) check box if you want to use encrypted secure logins. After you've added the necessary settings, you're able to connect to your ISP.

     Leave Maintain Synchronization Information selected to allow Dreamweaver to track differences between the local and remote servers.

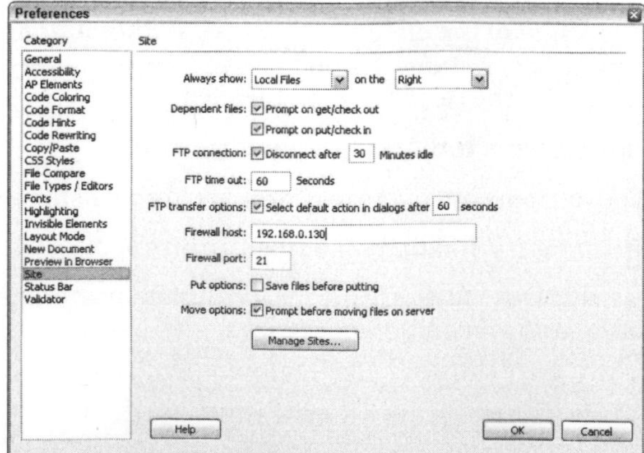

Figure 3-4: Setting your Firewall preferences.

If you select Automatically Upload Files to Server on Save, Dreamweaver will automatically make a connection to the remote server and upload your file each time you save it.

Select the Enable File Check In and Check Out option if you're working in a collaborative environment and you want to ensure that other team members can't work on a file at the same time that you're working on it. If you select this option, you need to add information that will identify you to your collaborators.

- **Local/Network:** Here you only need to specify the location of the remote folder on the network or a local drive, which you can enter manually or by clicking the folder icon to browse the network for the folder location. See the bottom three items in the preceding FTP bullet for information on other Local/Network settings.
- **RDS:** If you select RDS from the drop-down list, you need to click the Settings button next to the list to configure the RDS connection, as shown in Figure 3-5. To configure RDS, you need a host name (IP address or URL), port number (the default is 80), the directory of the site on the host, a username, and a password. If you don't want the password saved, then deselect the Save check box.

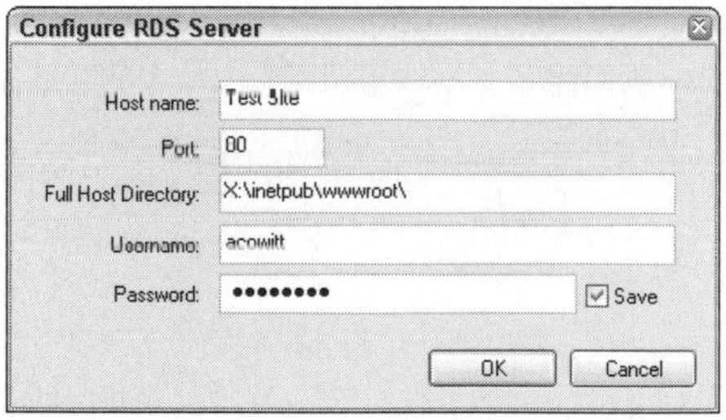

Figure 3-5: The Configure RDS Server dialog box.

- **Microsoft Visual SourceSafe:** As with RDS, with SourceSafe you have to click the Settings button next to the drop-down list. Then you specify the location of the SourceSafe Database Path (a path to an `.ini` file, usually on a network volume), the name of the project, a username, and a password. If you don't want the password saved, deselect the Save check box.
- **WebDAV:** You need the URL of the connection, a username, a password, and a checkout name and e-mail address. If you don't want the password saved, deselect the Save check box. You also have three options, one of which is selected by default. See your documentation for details.

6. **Click OK to put the changes into effect.**

Using Advanced Site Options

You can configure a number of advanced settings with Dreamweaver. You're not likely to need most of them, but just in case, we describe them in the following sections. You can access all these options by selecting the name of the item in the Category list of the Site Definition dialog box (refer to Figure 3-2).

Testing your server

Select Testing Server from the Category list on the Advanced tab of the Site Definition dialog box to access the options for setting up your testing server. If you're building a dynamic site, you need to have a Web server running that can process the pages and render them as HTML. To specify a Web serving technology, do the following:

1. **Select a Web server from the Server Model drop-down list, as shown in Figure 3-6.**

   You have several options here; if you're working within the old Macromedia model, your selection is probably going to be ColdFusion.

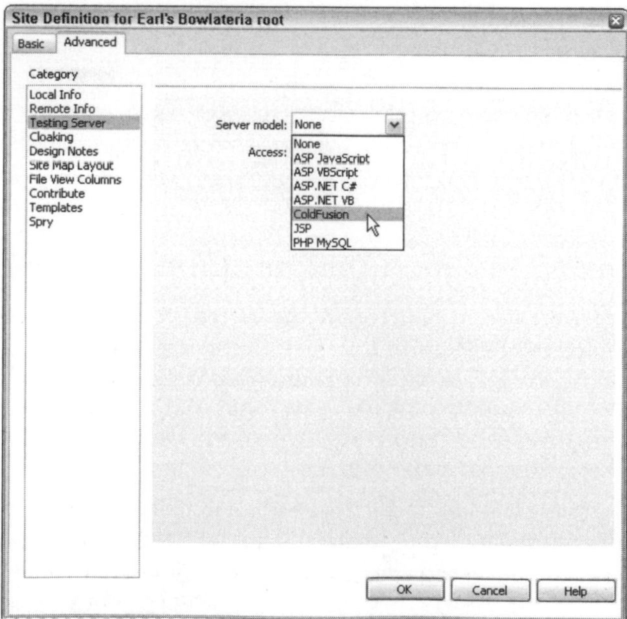

Figure 3-6: Choosing a testing server.

2. Select an Access type.

You can choose FTP or Local/Network. If you chose RDS on the Remote Info screen, you see an RDS option here as well. Choosing any of them provides additional fields for you to fill out, as specified for each Access type in the "Setting Up a Remote Connection" section, earlier in this chapter. Choose None if you don't want to use a testing server.

3. Click OK to save your settings.

Cloaking

Cloaking is a handy and appropriately named feature in Dreamweaver Sites. When enabled, *cloaking* allows you to hide different file types or folders from Dreamweaver's site tools. This feature can be especially helpful if you keep your raw asset files (your source Fireworks PNGs, Flash FLAs, and so on) in the same directory as the site itself, but you don't want the files uploaded or downloaded, included in reports, or otherwise touched by various Dreamweaver operations. To engage this feature, click the Advanced tab of the Site Definition dialog box and select Cloaking from the Category list on the left. Then select the Enable Cloaking and Cloak Files Ending With check boxes and add the file extensions for the file types you want to mask. See the online Help files for more details.

Using Design Notes

Design Notes aren't really necessary unless you're collaborating on a site with other people. In that case, Design Notes can be especially helpful. For example, you can use Design Notes to let others know the status of a given file. To engage Design Notes, click the Advanced tab of the Site Definition dialog box, select Design Notes from the Category list on the left, and then simply select the Maintain Design Notes check box. If you want to move the notes to the server when the site is published so that other team members can access them, select the Upload Design Notes for Sharing check box.

Setting up a site map

If you select Site Map Layout in the Category list in the Site Definition dialog box, you can set up the specifics of how you'd like your site's site map to look. You can specify the following:

- The home page for the site map, which can be different from the home page (index.htm) of the site
- The number and width of the columns of the map
- The labels for the site map icons
- Whether to display items marked hidden
- Whether to display dependent files

Selecting columns for File view

For the File view, shown in Figure 3-7, you have six built-in columns to choose from: Name, Notes, Size, Type, Modified, and Checked Out By. However, you can also add and remove your own columns by clicking the (+) and (–) buttons, respectively. For a column you create, you can also specify the following:

- ✦ The column name
- ✦ The column's Design Note association, if its contents relate to a specific Design Note
- ✦ The text alignment for the column
- ✦ The option to show or not show the column in the File view (***Note:*** The Name column cannot be hidden or moved.)
- ✦ Whether to share the column so that other workers on the site can see it (***Note:*** You must have Maintain Design Notes selected to share a column.)

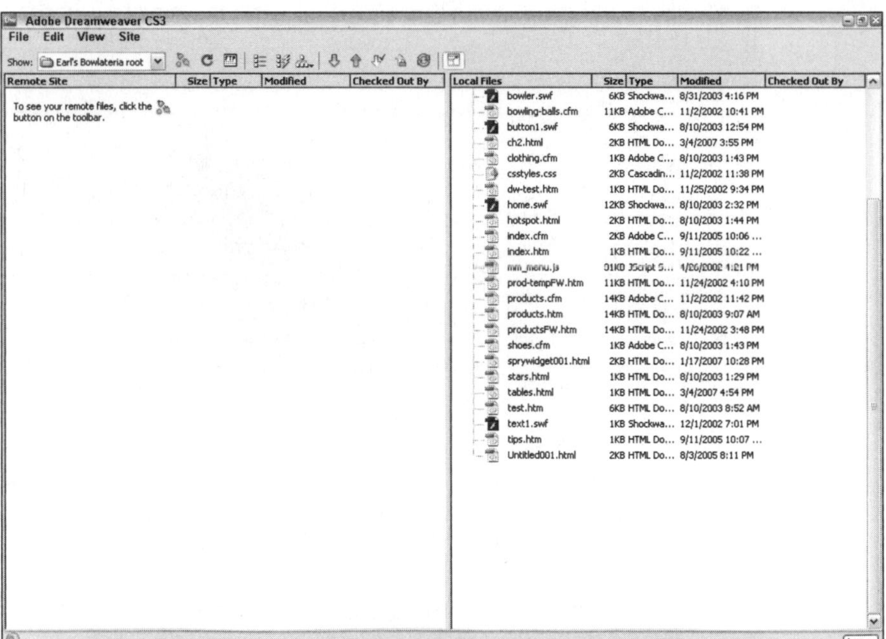

Figure 3-7: The File view.

Enabling Contribute compatibility

To enable compatibility with Contribute, click the Advanced tab of the Site Definition dialog box and select Contribute from the Category list on the left. Select the Enable Contribute Compatibility check box if you plan to have people maintain your site using Contribute. Selecting this option allows you to perform many administrative functions related to Contribute (for example, you can send Connection Keys based on your Dreamweaver Site setups).

Updating templates

When you create a document-relative link in a template file, the link is relative to the template. By default, when you create a page from the template, Dreamweaver automatically adjusts the link to have the correct pathname relative to the created page. To disable that feature, click the Advanced tab of the Site Definition box and select Templates from the Category list on the left. Select the Template Updating check box to remove the check.

Storing Spry Assets

The Spry framework, which incorporates JavaScript, CSS, and XML, allows nonprogrammers to put fancy navigation and animation on Web sites with a minimum of fuss. Book I, Chapter 7 offers instructions for using Spry to create a richer user experience on your Web site. When you insert the first Spry component in your site, Dreamweaver automatically creates a SpryAssets folder in your root directory, where it places the JavaScript and CSS files. To use a custom location for Spry Assets, click the Advanced tab of the Site Definition box and select Spry from the Category list on the left. Enter the location of your Spry Assets folder by typing or pasting it, or better yet, click the folder icon at the right to browse to the folder.

Publishing Your Site

After you've set up a remote site in a Dreamweaver Site, publishing your Site is a snap. To publish your Site to a remote server, just follow these steps:

1. **If the Files panel isn't already open, open it by choosing Window⇨Files or by pressing F8.**
2. **On the File tab, click the Expand/Collapse button (the button on the far right of the toolbar) to switch to File view.**

   This brings up the File view shown previously in Figure 3-7.

3. **If you haven't connected to the remote server since you launched Dreamweaver most recently, click the Connection button at the left of the Files panel toolbar to establish a connection with the remote server.**

   When you're connected, you see the File view shown in Figure 3-8.

4. **Select a file and click the Put button on the toolbar (an upward pointing blue arrow) to copy a file from the local server to the remote server, or click the Get button (a downward pointing green arrow) to copy a file from the remote server to the local server.**

   If you're copying files for the first time, simply select the Site's root folder and click the Put button. To copy files from the Local to Remote servers, or vice versa, you can also simply click and drag the elements from local to remote, or vice versa. If you use this method, be careful to place files in the correct folders.

If you ever want to see what's going on behind the scenes when you're copying those files, just click the FTP button in the toolbar in File view. The Results panel appears or expands and shows you the remote connections being set and all the commands for the files being sent (the File view collapses back to the Files panel as well).

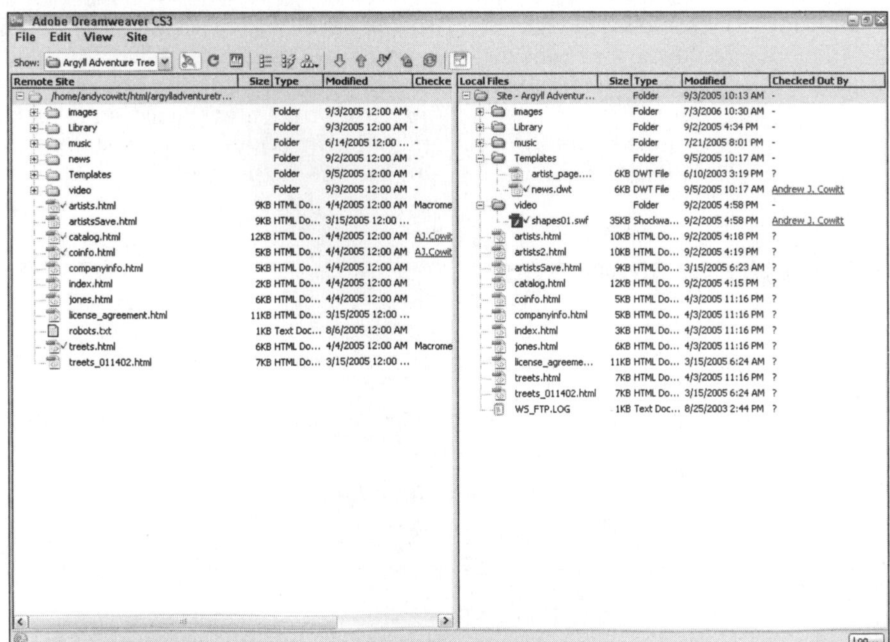

Figure 3-8: Remote and local sites.

Maintaining Your Site

After your Site is built, you want to make sure that it continues running at peak efficiency. To help in this effort, Dreamweaver offers some valuable tools that can help you keep on top of the wide array of items that go into keeping your Site running smoothly. We describe the two basic types of tools, reports and link checkers, in detail in the following sections.

Running reports

Reports encapsulate information about various aspects of your Site at the time the reports are run, giving you a snapshot of information such as which files on your Site are currently being worked on by different team members, whether all the images on a selected page have Alt tags, and more. To run a report in Dreamweaver, just follow these steps:

1. **Choose Site⇨Reports.**

   The Reports dialog box appears, as shown in Figure 3-9.

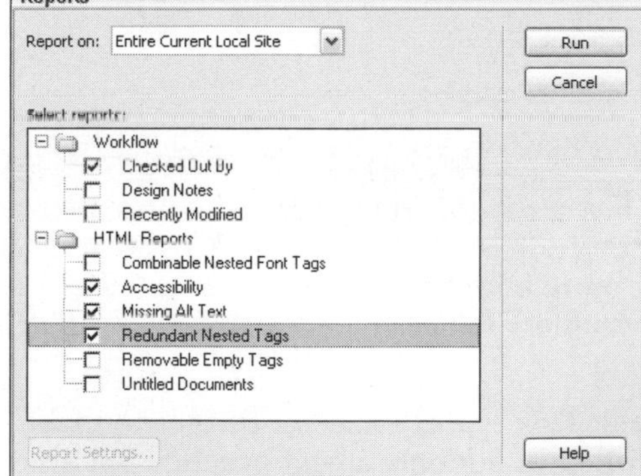

Figure 3-9: The Reports dialog box, with some options selected.

2. **Choose what you want to run the report against.**

   You can choose to run a report on the currently selected document, the entire site, selected files in the site, or a folder within the site. Select one of these options from the Report On drop-down list.

3. **Select the reports you want to run by selecting the check boxes next to their names.**

   You can run nine possible reports across two categories: Workflow and HTML Reports. The nine reports are as follows:

- **Checked Out By:** This report tells you what files in source control are currently being used by different members of the team. If you want the report to show only which files are currently checked out by a particular team member, click the Report Settings button at the bottom of the dialog box while the report is selected and add an individual's name to the text field in the Checked Out By dialog box that pops up.
- **Design Notes:** This report prints all the Design Notes associated with files on the site. To filter your results via the Design Notes dialog box, click the Report Settings button while the Design Notes report is selected.
- **Recently Modified:** This report shows which files have been modified within parameters you set by clicking the Report Settings button and specifying the parameters in the Recently Modified dialog box that pops up.
- **Combinable Nested Font Tags:** This report details locations in the code where overlapping Font tags could be merged. For example, if you change the size of a block of text, your code might contain something like this:

  ```
  <FONT face="Arial"><FONT size="2">Some
     text.</FONT></FONT>
  ```

  When it could and should be

  ```
  <FONT face="Arial" size="2">Some text.</FONT>
  ```

- **Accessibility:** If you run this report, the site files are scanned to find places where the code is not ADA (Americans with Disabilities Act) compliant. For more information about accessibility, browse to the W3C Web Accessibility Initiative pages at `www.w3.org/WAI/Resources/`.
- **Missing Alt Text:** This report looks for images to make sure they have Alt text, which is not only a best practice but also important for accessibility. (See the section on modifying an image in Book I, Chapter 2 for a little more information on Alt text.)
- **Redundant Nested Tags:** This report searches the code for locations where extra tags can be eliminated.
- **Removable Empty Tags:** If you're working in Design mode and moving many things around, sometimes the underlying code can be left with lingering, empty tags. This tool finds those empty tags.
- **Untitled Documents:** This report searches for pages that may have a filename but don't have a title.

4. Click Run to run the reports.

The results appear in the Site Reports tab of the Results panel, as shown in Figure 3-10.

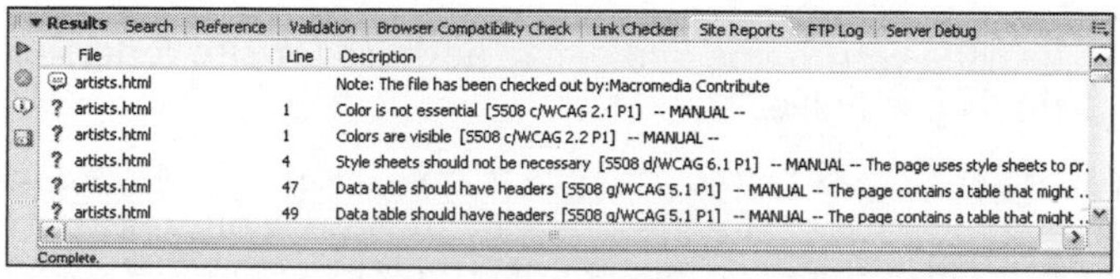

Figure 3-10: A site report in the Results panel.

Checking links

In addition to the reports that help clean up your code, Dreamweaver can also check the links on your site. To run the Link Check report, choose Site➪Check Links Sitewide or press Ctrl+F8. You see the results in the Link Checker tab in the Results panel. The report shows broken links, external links, and orphaned files.

Using Source Control

Source control allows team members to check out a document in your site, thereby locking it and making it uneditable by others until the team member who checked it out checks it back in again. This process is intended to ensure that files don't get overwritten accidentally and that data doesn't get lost during the development process.

In most large-scale software development projects, in which multitudes of people work on a single code-base, source control is critical. If your site requires that more than three people work on the same pages and code, you should consider taking advantage of this feature in Dreamweaver.

To set up source control, do the following:

1. **Choose Site➪Manage Sites, select your site, and then click the Edit button to open the Site Definition dialog box.**
2. **Click the Advanced tab if it's not already open and select Remote Info from the Category list on the left.**

3. **Set your source control options at the bottom of the screen.**

   When you enable file check in and check out, the following options become available:

   - Check out files automatically when you open a document within the site.
   - Provide your name and e-mail address for site reporting and informational purposes.

   You must have selected an Access option on the Remote Info screen before you can get the file check in and check out options to show up at the bottom of the page. See the "Setting Up a Remote Connection" section, earlier in this chapter, for more information about Access options.

4. **Click OK to save your settings.**

To work with a file after you've enabled source control, right-click the file from the Files panel and select one of the following options:

✦ **Get:** Retrieves the most recent version of the file and copies it locally.

✦ **Check Out:** Makes your local version the only editable version of a document and ensures that others can't open and save the file.

✦ **Put:** Copies the local version of your file to the remote location.

✦ **Check In:** Puts your local version of the file on the server and unlocks it so that others can check it out and work on it, if necessary.

Chapter 4: Punching Up Your Pages with Forms and Frames

In This Chapter

- **Incorporating forms into your Web pages**
- **Structuring your pages with frames**

Two Web page features, forms and frames, are also two of the most advanced features. You use them in your Web pages to serve the following functions:

- **Forms:** Enable you to gather information and feedback from the users who visit your Web pages. *Forms* can consist of text fields, buttons, check boxes, radio buttons, and drop-down lists, all of which enable the user to enter information or to choose among options you present.
- **Frames:** Enable you to construct sophisticated navigational schemes for your Web site. *Frames* are actually separate Web pages that are partitioned off so that two or more can be displayed in the same browser window at the same time. For example, one frame may be a navigational page consisting of a list of links to other pages; that frame remains in place in its portion of the browser window even when the user clicks a link to display a different Web page in the other frame.

In this chapter, you see how to work with these powerful features in Dreamweaver CS3.

Incorporating Forms into Web Pages

Forms on the Web serve the same purpose as the paper-based forms you fill out — they provide a structured format for gathering specific information. The difference is that Web-based forms usually require less time for keyboard-savvy users to fill out.

Dreamweaver offers you a number of handy tools for creating Web-based forms that you can easily include on your Web pages. You can incorporate everything from text fields to radio buttons, and create surveys, gather user data, and conduct e-commerce.

Creating Web-based forms requires the following two steps:

1. Creating the form that users see and interact with, which we demonstrate how to do using Dreamweaver in this chapter.
2. Creating the processing program that accepts and processes form input, which is beyond the scope of this book.

Adding a form

Before you can insert specific form objects such as check boxes on your Web page, you must first add a form to the page so that the appropriate code is added to the HTML.

To add a form to a page, click in the Document window where you want to add the form and choose Insert➪Form➪Form, or click the Form button from the Forms category on the Insert bar. (If the Insert bar is set to a different category, click and hold the category name and select Common from the drop-down list.)

Dreamweaver adds the form to the page, as indicated by the red dashed lines, and adds the associated form tag to your HTML page code, as shown in Figure 4-1. You can now insert form objects inside the red dashed lines of the form.

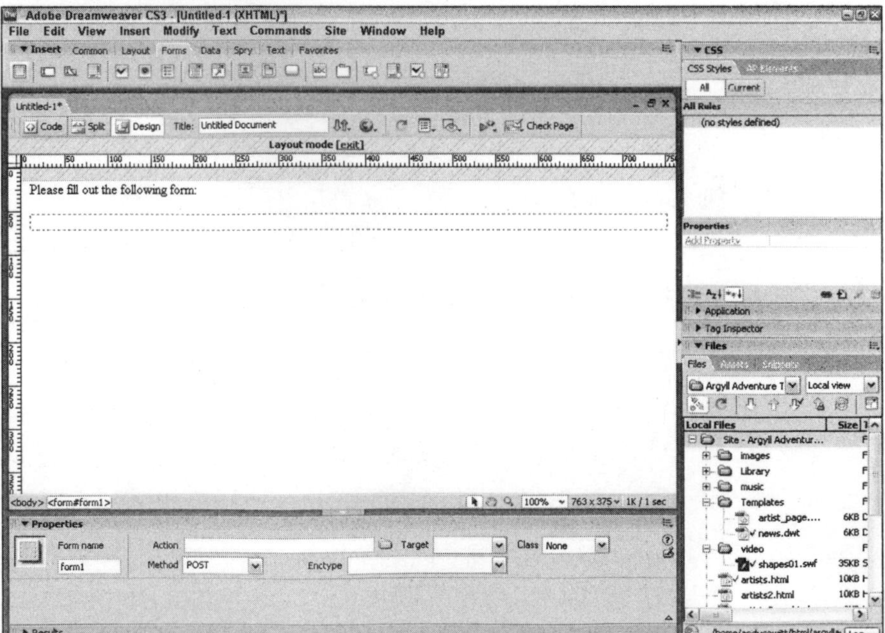

Figure 4-1: The dashed lines mean that you've created a form!

If you attempt to add a form object without first adding a form, a dialog box appears, asking whether you want to add a form tag. Click Yes to add both the form tag and the object to your page.

Dreamweaver's new Spry functionality includes form-specific widgets that perform tasks such as text field validation. See Book I, Chapter 7 for more details.

Specifying form properties

A form has six properties that you can set using the Form Property inspector: Form Name, Action, Method, Enctype, Target, and Class. Click the form to open the Form Property inspector. (If the Property inspector does not appear, open it by choosing Window➪Properties.) Then specify the following properties:

✦ **Form Name:** Enter an alphanumeric name in the empty text field (the name should start with a letter, but it can be made up of both letters and numbers). The advantage of naming your form is that you can use the name to reference the form in a scripting language that you use to retrieve, store, and manipulate the form data.

✦ **Action:** Enter the URL of the application document or file that processes the form data. Alternatively, you can browse to the location by clicking the folder and making a selection in the Select File dialog box.

  You can select the following three common actions:

  - Enter the URL of a ColdFusion page that evaluates the form after it has been submitted.
  - Enter the JavaScript program that runs after the user submits the form. The action appears as follows:

    ```
    javascript:function()
    ```

    Here, function refers to the name of your form-handling function.
  - Enter a mailto: address where the form data goes after the user clicks the Submit button. A mailto: address appears similar to the following:

    ```
    mailto:worker@formhandling.com
    ```

✦ **Method:** Select a method from the drop-down list for how the form data passes to the processing entity that you specified in the Action field. Choices are Default, GET, and POST. (Default and GET are the same.) GET sends the form data by appending it to the URL that Action specifies. POST sends the form data as a separate entity. GET limits the amount of data that can pass along, but POST does not.

In other words, if you were to choose GET, the URL sent to the server might look something like `http://www.server.com/coldfusionpage.cfm&bowlingballcolor=blue`, with the form data stuck onto the end. If you were to choose POST instead, the URL would just look something like `http://www.server.com/coldfusionpage.cfm`.

Most of the time, whether you choose GET or POST doesn't really make a difference. However, there are times when you may want to choose one over the other. For example, for security purposes, you may not want information, such as a credit card number, ever being shown in a browser's history. And if the user might choose to bookmark the URL, whether to have all the form data appear could affect your decision. If the form data included secure user information (such as the credit card example), then you probably wouldn't want to have the form data appear. However, if the form data includes search criteria, the user might want to bookmark the URL complete with the search parameters.

Data received at the specified mailto: address is not formatted for easy reading: It appears as strings of code with the form data embedded within it. This may depend on the encoding option, which we are about to discuss.

- **Enctype:** This is an optional attribute. For enctype, your choices are `application/x-www-form-urlencoded` and `multipart/form-data`. The first one, `application/x-www-form-urlencoded`, replaces all blank characters in the text with a plus sign (+), and it replaces other nonprinting characters with symbols and numbers. These replacements are often necessary for the server to interpret the information it is receiving — for example, when you've used the GET method, the browser would not be able to process a URL with blank spaces in it. The `multipart/form-data` attribute does not do this conversion but instead transfers the information as a compound MIME document. The `multipart/form-data` attribute is the method that must be used if you are using an `<INPUT TYPE="file">` element in the form. Alternatively, if the form action is `mailto:`, you can input `text/plain`, which will send the data unencoded; however, this is not a W3C standard.
- **Target:** This is also an optional attribute. If you do not specify a target, the server will assume that you want any information that is sent back to the browser (the URL of the response page, for example) sent to the same window or frame that your original form is in. If you wish the form submission's results to appear in a different frame or window, you must specify the name of the target window in this attribute.
- **Class:** You can apply a CSS (Cascading Style Sheet) class to the form as a whole and to some form elements in order to control how those form

elements appear in a browser. For example, you can specify the color of a text field by assigning it a style. This attribute is also optional. For details on using CSS stylesheets, take a look at *CSS Web Design For Dummies,* by Richard Mansfield (published by Wiley Publishing, Inc.).

Labeling form objects

Dreamweaver enables you to provide descriptors for form objects and provide the user with directions about how to complete the information requested for each option. To add descriptors to form objects, simply position your cursor in the form and begin typing. Then insert the form object you want.

Using text fields

Text fields are blank text boxes that you can insert in your form to hold alphanumeric information that the user types. You can set up a text field to hold a single line of text, multiple lines of text, or a password, as follows:

- **Single line:** Provides space for the user to enter a single word or short phrase of text.
- **Multi-line:** Provides space for the user to enter a longer string of text. Appropriate for a comment box.
- **Password:** Provides space for the user to enter a password. An asterisk or other placeholder appears in the text field for each character that the user types to hide the password characters from anyone who might be looking over the user's shoulder.

To add a text field, follow these steps:

1. **In the Document window, click where you want to add the text field and choose Insert➪Form➪Text Field, or click the Insert Text Field button on the Form category of the Insert bar.**

   If the Insert bar is set to a different category, click Form.

   The Input Tag Accessibility Attributes window appears, unless you have set your preferences otherwise.

2. **Enter Accessibility information as desired and click OK.**

   This information is not required, but including it makes your form easier to navigate for sight-impaired users. See your Dreamweaver documentation for details.

   Dreamweaver adds a text field to your form and a Text Field Property inspector appears. If the Text Field Property inspector does not appear, choose Window➪Properties to open the inspector.

3. **Fill in the following fields of the Text Field Property inspector to define the parameters of the text field:**

   - **TextField name:** Enter a name in the empty field. The field is referenced by this name in the HTML page code.
   - **Char Width:** Enter a whole number for the approximate visible width of the field. (The width is approximate because text characters in your form are displayed differently according to users' browser settings.)
   - **Max Chars:** (Applies to Single line and Password fields only) Enter a whole number to indicate the maximum number of characters that the user can enter in the field. Max Chars can be different from Char Width.
   - **Num Lines:** (Applies to Multi-line fields only) This specifies the height, in lines, of the form element, and may be affected by the setting for Wrap.
   - **Type:** Select a radio button for Single line, Multi-line, or Password. When you select Password, Dreamweaver includes code that makes an asterisk appear for each character the user enters.
   - **Init Val:** (Optional) Enter an alphanumeric word or phrase that occupies the text field when the user first encounters the field. Users can enter their own information over the Init Val. If you leave this attribute blank, the user will see a standard empty text field.
   - **Wrap:** (Applies to Multi-line fields only) Select an option for text wrapping from the drop-down list. Options consist of Default, Off, Virtual, or Physical. Default and Off are the same and do not wrap text until the user presses the Enter key. The Virtual option wraps text on the user's screen but not when the form is submitted. The Physical option wraps text both on the user's screen and when the form is submitted.
   - **Class:** (Optional) You may assign a CSS class to a text field to affect the appearance of the field or the text within it. For details on using CSS style sheets, look up *CSS Web Design For Dummies,* by Richard Mansfield (published by Wiley Publishing, Inc.).

Setting up buttons

After a user enters data into a form, the user must then perform some sort of task to transmit the data from his or her computer to another computer that can process the information. Dreamweaver offers you three buttons you can use to activate your form: Submit Form, Reset Form, and None:

✦ **Submit Form:** After the user clicks this button, the form data scoots off to another computer based on the specified action. (You see how to set the action of a form in the "Specifying form properties" section, earlier in this chapter.)

✦ **Reset Form:** After the user clicks this button, it erases all data entered into the form, resetting each form field to its initial value.

✦ **None:** After the user clicks this button, it executes the programming function that the Web designer assigned to it (for example, performs a mathematical calculation or sends the user to a different URL).

Follow these steps to insert a button into your form:

1. **Click where you want to add the button in the Document window and choose Insert⇨Form⇨Button or click Insert Button on the Form category of the Insert bar.**

   If the Insert bar is set to a different category, click Forms.

   Dreamweaver adds a button to your form and the Button Property inspector becomes visible. If the Button Property inspector does not appear, choose Window⇨Properties to open the inspector.

2. **Fill in the following fields of the Button Property inspector to define the parameters of the button:**

   • **Button Name:** Enter a name in the empty text field. This name identifies the button in the HTML code.

   • **Label:** Enter the text that you want to appear on the button.

   • **Action:** Select a radio button to indicate the function of the button. Choices consist of Submit Form, Reset Form, and None.

   • **Class:** (Optional) You can assign a CSS style to affect the button's appearance (color, width, and the like).

You can create a graphical Submit button — a button created from a small image — by choosing Insert⇨Form⇨Image Field or by clicking the Image Field button in the Form category of the Insert bar. Then browse to the image file in your site or type the path to and name of the image file directly into the File Name field.

Adding other form elements

In addition to the text fields and buttons, you can add a variety of form elements that help your users give you information. Figure 4-2 shows some of the useful form elements you can add to your forms. To insert any of the elements you see in Figure 4-2, follow these steps:

1. **Position your cursor in the area of the Document window where you want to add the element.**
2. **Click the appropriate button in the Form category of the Insert bar (see Figure 4-2) or choose Insert⇨Form Objects⇨Desired *Form Element*.**

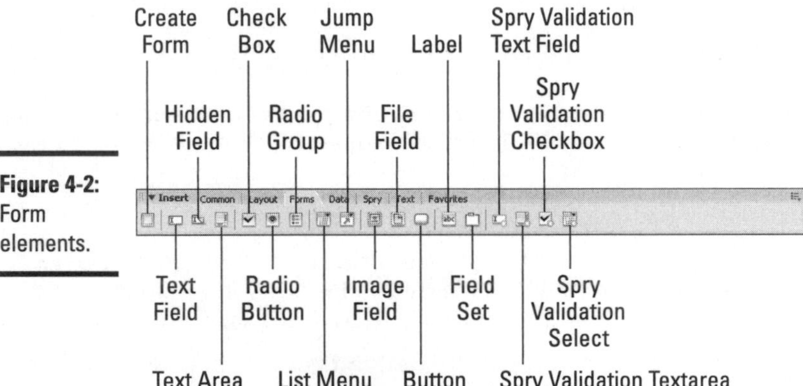

Figure 4-2: Form elements.

If the Insert bar is set to a different category, click Forms.

3. **If the Input Tag Accessibility Attributes window appears, enter Accessibility information as desired and click OK.**

   This information is not required, but including it makes your form easier to navigate for sight-impaired users. See your Dreamweaver documentation for details.

   Dreamweaver adds the element to your form and the appropriate inspector appears. (If the appropriate inspector does not appear, open it by choosing Windows⇨Properties.) ***Note:*** You must save your document before inserting a Spry widget.

4. **Fill in the fields of the Property inspector.**

   If you're adding a radio button group, jump menu, or image, a dialog box will pop up and ask you for additional information. Fill in your choices for each of these.

5. **Click OK to apply your selections and close the dialog box.**

Structuring Pages with Frames

Frames are divisions of a Web page that enable you to load information independently into distinct regions of the browser window. Frames are useful if you want to display certain information on-screen while changing other information. You frequently see three-frame pages on the Web — the top frame shows the site's title graphic, the left frame shows the navigation bar, and the large body frame changes to show the content that you select.

A special HTML page called a *frameset* defines the structure and formatting of frames on your Web page. As you work with frames, be aware that you must always save the frameset page to lay out the size, position, and borders of your frames, along with the content that you want to display in each frame. Keep in mind that different browsers may draw the frames slightly differently, even if you specify exact pixel dimensions.

You can create a frameset two ways in Dreamweaver:

- ✦ From scratch
- ✦ By adding a frame to an existing document

We detail each in the following sections.

Creating a frameset from scratch

When you create a frameset from scratch, you create the frameset and all the frames it describes in one fell swoop. To create a frameset using one of Dreamweaver's built-in templates, just follow these steps:

1. **Choose File⇨New, or use the keyboard shortcut Ctrl+N.**

   The New Document window appears.

2. **Click Page from Sample on the left.**

   The Sample Folder, Sample Page, and preview panes are updated.

3. **Click Frameset in the Sample Folder area.**

   The Sample Page pane and preview areas are updated.

4. **Click a Sample page.**

   The preview area shows you what the frameset will look like, as shown in Figure 4-3.

5. **Click Create.**

   The New Document window closes and the Frame Tag Accessibility Attributes window appears. The document window displays the new frameset.

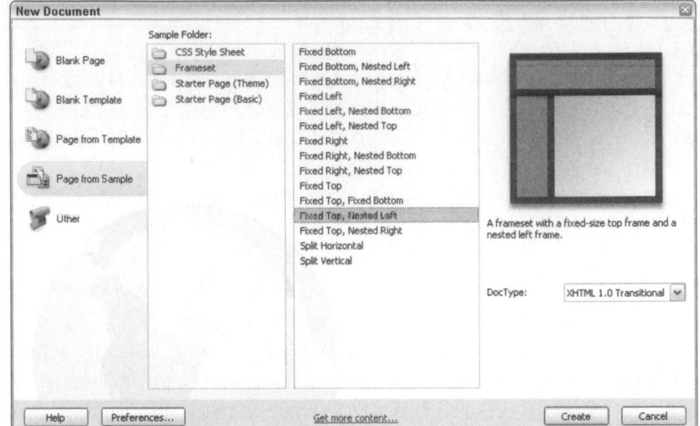

Figure 4-3: Creating a frameset the easy way.

6. **Select a frame from the Frame drop-down menu and type or paste a name in the Title field. Repeat until you've entered titles for all your frames and click OK.**

   This step is optional. Adding titles to your frames makes them easier to navigate for sight-impaired users. Dreamweaver automatically gives the frames generic titles. If you don't want to enter custom titles, simply click OK. The Frame Tag Accessibility Attributes window disappears and your document window displays the frameset.

Adding frames

You can add a frame to a frameless Document window or to an existing frame within the Document window. Adding a frame to an existing frame divides that frame into two or more regions.

To add a frame, click the Document window or existing frame in the area where you want to add the frame. Then click the Frames button in the Form category of the Insert bar and choose from the list of options that pops up. You can also get to an equivalent list (the same options, some with slightly different names and no icons) by choosing Insert➪HTML➪Frames➪ Frame *Option,* where *Frame Option* is one of the choices detailed in Table 4-1.

Table 4-1 Options for Creating Frames

Frame Option	*What It Does*
Left	Creates a vertical frame down the left side
Right	Creates a vertical frame down the right side
Top	Creates a horizontal frame across the top

Frame Option	*What It Does*
Bottom	Creates a horizontal frame across the bottom
Bottom and Nested Left	Splits the page in two — top and bottom — and creates a left frame in the top frame
Bottom and Nested Right	Splits the page in two — top and bottom — and creates a right frame in the top frame
Left and Nested Bottom	Splits the page in two — right and left — and creates a bottom frame in the right frame
Right and Nested Bottom	Splits the page in two — right and left — and creates a bottom frame in the left frame
Top and Bottom	Creates three frames
Left and Nested Top	Splits the page in two — right and left — and creates a top frame in the right frame
Right and Nested Top	Splits the page in two — right and left — and creates a top frame in the left frame
Top and Nested Left	Splits the page in two — top and bottom — and creates a left frame in the bottom frame
Top and Nested Right	Splits the page in two — top and bottom — and creates a right frame in the bottom frame

A third method of adding a frame is to drag the outer border of the current frame or Alt+click (Opt+click on a Mac) in the inner border. You can then follow the steps in the next section to modify this new frame.

Modifying frames

You use the Frame Property inspector to select the source page that appears in a frame. You also use the Frame Property inspector to format the appearance of an individual frame. To modify a frame, follow these steps:

1. **If the Properties panel is not already open, open it by choosing Window⇨Properties or by using the keyboard shortcut Ctrl+F3.**
2. **In the Frames panel, Alt+click (Opt+click on a Mac) the frame whose attributes you want to modify.**

   Note: You can't simply click a frame to open its associated Frame Property inspector. If you click a frame, you're actually clicking the source page that resides in the frame — a process identical to clicking in the Document window for that page. To select a specific frame, press the Alt key and click in the frame. You see the Frame Property inspector for an individual frame and the selected frame marked with a dashed line, as shown in Figure 4-4.

   A Frame Property inspector appears for the selected frame. If the inspector doesn't appear, open it by choosing Window⇨Properties.

3. **In the Frame Property inspector or the Attributes tab of the Tag Inspector panel, enter a name for your frame in the Frame Name text field.**

   This name is the name by which the frame is referenced in the Frames panel, target drop-down lists, and the HTML page code.

   The frame name must start with a letter, and you should not use hyphens, spaces, or periods. You should also avoid using JavaScript-reserved names, such as top. Although these words and symbols may be accepted, if you are using any scripting (JavaScript, VBScript) to manipulate your frames, the results may be inconsistent or wrong. It's a good idea to get into the habit of avoiding these words and characters. Word separation can be indicated by capitalization, and underscore characters can also be used.

4. **In the Src text field, enter the name of the source page whose content you intend to display in the frame.**

   Alternatively, you can click the Src folder and browse to select the source page.

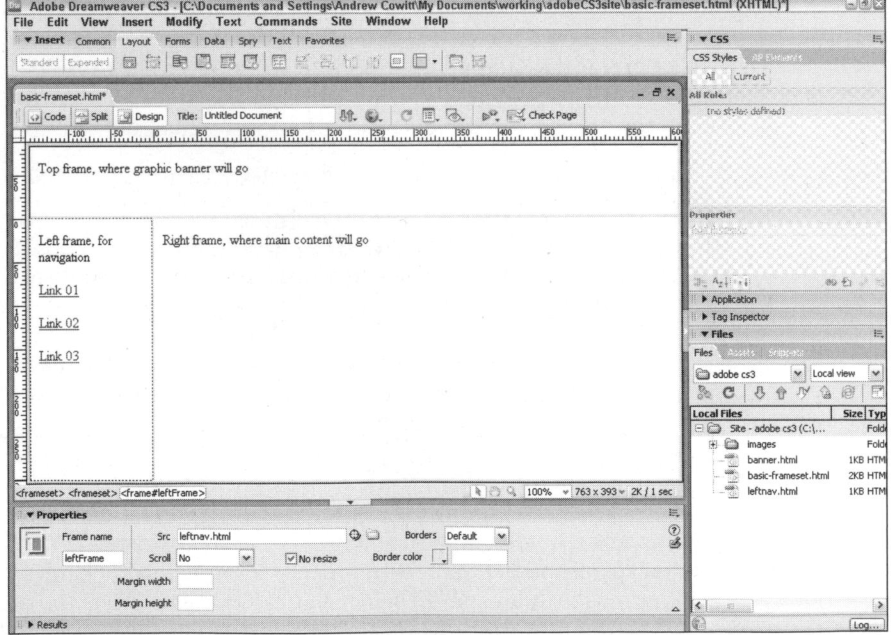

Figure 4-4: Alt+click (Opt+click on a Mac) a frame to select it and see the Frame Property inspector.

5. **Select a scrolling option for your selected frame from the Scroll drop-down list. The options are as follows:**
   - **Yes:** Adds scrollbars to the frame, whether they're needed or not.
   - **No:** Doesn't add scrollbars to the frame, even if a scrollbar is needed to display the entire frame.
   - **Auto:** Places one or more scrollbars in the frame if the frame contents exceed the frame boundaries.
   - **Default:** Places one or more scrollbars in the frame, depending on the user's browser settings.
6. **Select the No Resize check box if you don't want the user to be able to resize the frame.**

   If you do want the user to be able to resize the frame, leave the check box deselected.
7. **Format the frame border appearance by selecting a choice from the Borders drop-down list:**
   - **Yes:** Creates a three-dimensional look for the borders. (This doesn't work in all browsers.)
   - **No:** Creates a single-color flat look for the borders, or, if No is selected for each of the frames in a frameset, no border appears.
   - **Default:** Enables the user's browser to set how borders appear.
8. **Select a border color for the frame by clicking the Border Color swatch and selecting a color from the Color palette that appears.**

   Alternatively, you can enter a hexadecimal color code in the Border Color text field. This doesn't work in all browsers and is optional. If your frames don't have borders, the border color will not apply.
9. **Enter a number in pixels in the Margin Width and the Margin Height text fields.**

   Margin Width specifies the horizontal standoff space between the frame content and the frame border. Margin Height specifies the vertical standoff space between the frame content and the frame border. This is in addition to any values that the page called into the frame already has assigned.

Deleting frames

To delete a frame, select the frame border and drag it to the edge of the parent frame or to the edge of the Document window — whichever is closer. If you only have two frames on the page, this action will result in a frameset with only one page in it.

Saving frames

Saving a frame means that you're saving the HTML page from which the source content of the frame originates. To save a frame, follow these steps:

1. **Select the frame by clicking in it.**
2. **Choose File⇨Save Frame.**
3. **The first time you save the frame, enter a name in the File Name text field of the Save As dialog box that appears and then click the Save button.**

   Future saves require that you complete only Steps 1 and 2.

Saving framesets

Saving a frameset means saving the layout of frame positions, frame names, and border formatting on a page. Keep in mind that you must save individual frames to save the content contained in those frames. To save a frameset, follow these steps:

1. **Select the frameset by clicking one of its borders.**
2. **Choose File⇨Save Frameset.**

   Note: This will not work if the frameset is nested.
3. **The first time you save the frameset, enter a name in the File Name text field of the Save As dialog box that appears and then click Save.**

   Future saves require that you complete only Steps 1 and 2.

If you have made changes to individual frames — not just the frameset — since your last save, Dreamweaver asks whether you want to save individual frames. Make sure that you do so.

Setting no-frames content

Text-based browsers and many older browsers frequently don't support frames and can't correctly display pages that you create by using frames.

To help ensure that the maximum number of users can view your page correctly, Dreamweaver offers you a method for building no-frames pages as companions to your frame-enabled pages. To create a no-frames page for your current frameset, follow these steps:

1. **Choose Modify⇨Frameset⇨Edit NoFrames Content.**

   A blank, NoFrames Content page appears in the Document window and replaces your frame-enabled page, as shown in Figure 4-5.

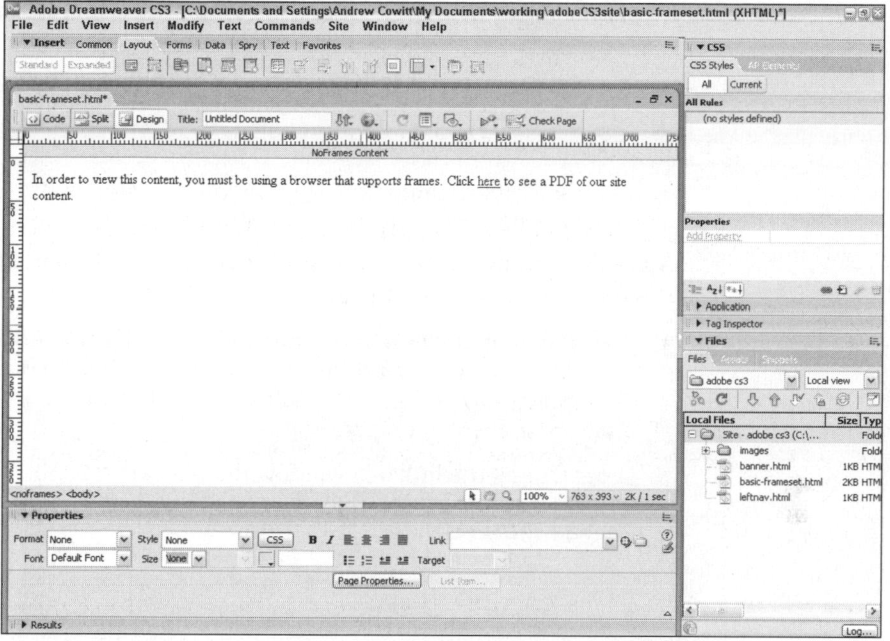

Figure 4-5: Setting up NoFrames Content.

2. **On the NoFrames Content page, insert the content that you want to appear in NoFrames browsers.**

   This content can include text, images, and other page elements.

3. **Return to your frame-enabled page by choosing Modify➪Frameset➪Edit NoFrames Content.**

Targeting content

You can set up a two-frame frameset in which you use the left frame for navigation and the main frame to display any link that the user clicks in the navigation frame. Simply set up the link to target the main frame as the location where you want the selected HTML page to open.

Set up a target by following these steps:

1. **Select the text or image that you want to act as a link.**

   Doing so opens the associated Property inspector. If the inspector doesn't appear, open it by choosing Window➪Properties.

2. **In the Link field, enter the name of the HTML source page that will appear in the frame.**

   Alternatively, you can click the Link folder and browse to select the source page.

3. From the Target drop-down list, select the target frame where the link is to appear.

All available targets are listed in the drop-down list, as shown in Figure 4-6. These targets include the names of all frames that you set up and also the following systemwide targets:

- `_blank`: Opens a new browser window and shows the link in that window. The current window remains open.
- `_parent`: Opens the link in a window that replaces the frameset containing the current page.
- `_self`: Opens the link in the current frame. The linked page replaces the page in the current frame. If you want the link to open in the current frame, you can select `_self` or leave the Target area in the Property inspector empty.
- `_top`: Opens the link in a window that replaces the outermost frameset of the current page. (Same as `_parent`, unless you're using nested framesets.)

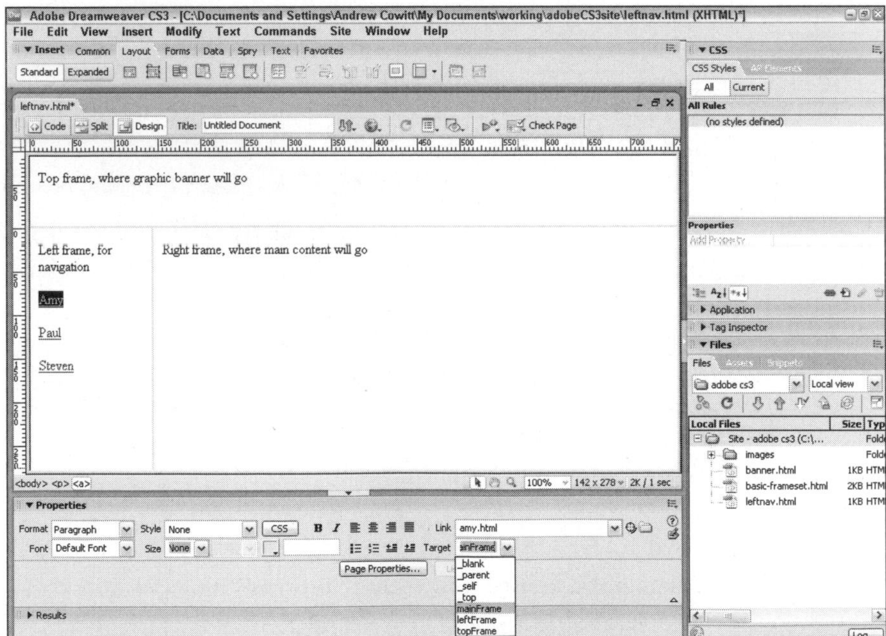

Figure 4-6: Select a target frame for the link.

Targeting can work in more complicated framesets using the same basic process. Whichever frame you target is the one that will update when the user clicks a link targeting that frame.

Adding IFrames

An IFrame allows you to embed one HTML page in another HTML page without having to create a frameset (the *I* in IFrame stands for inline). To insert an IFrame into an HTML page, follow these simple steps:

1. **Click in your document where you want the IFrame to go.**
2. **Click Layout in the Insert bar if Layout is not already selected.**
3. **Click the IFrame button.**

   The Document window shows that the IFrame has been inserted, as shown in Figure 4-7.

   Any content you enter inside the IFrame tags functions as alternative content for users whose browsers don't support IFrames.

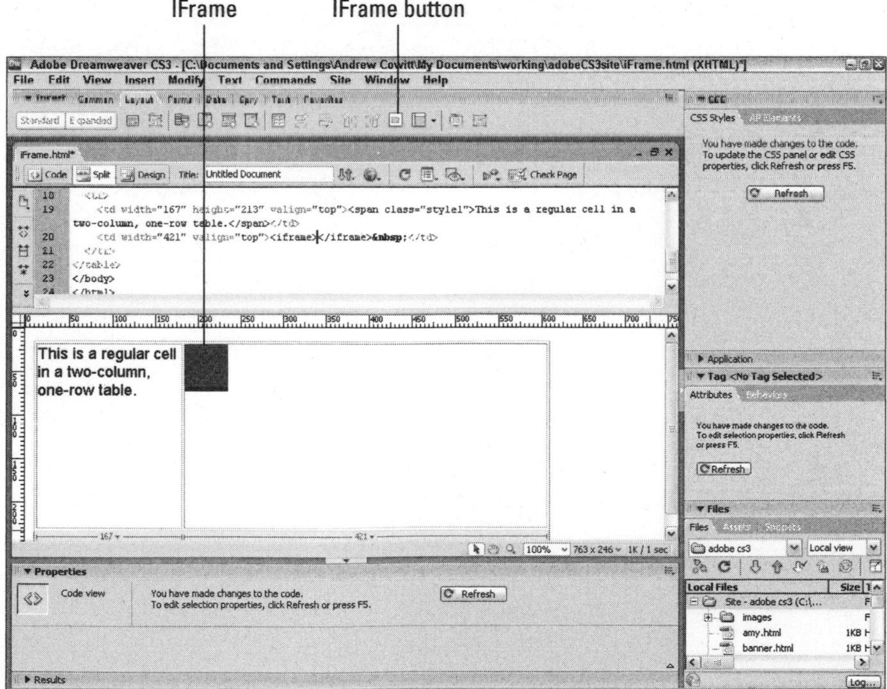

Figure 4-7: The Split view shows the IFrame in the Code portion of the window.

4. **Right-click inside the `<iframe>` tag and select Edit Tag from the menu that appears.**

   The Tag Editor window appears, open to the General area.

5. **Enter a filename or click Browse to navigate to the Source file (the HTML page or other content that will appear inside the IFrame).**

   The only required field is Source, because that field determines what goes in the IFrame; the rest of the settings control how the IFrame looks and functions.

6. **Enter other settings as necessary and click OK.**

   The Tag Editor disappears, and the document window is updated. To see your IFrame in action, choose File⇨Preview in Browser⇨*Browser Name* or use the keyboard shortcut F12 (PC only).

Chapter 5: Laying Out Pages with AP Divs and AP Elements

In This Chapter

- **Distinguishing between divs and AP Divs**
- **Using a tracing image**
- **Adding, selecting, and deleting an AP Element**
- **Placing objects in an AP Div**
- **Changing AP Element properties**
- **Nesting AP Divs**

To lay out the content of your Web page precisely, you can use tables (see Book I, Chapter 2), or you can use the latest and greatest layout aid: AP Divs. You can think of AP Divs in Dreamweaver as separate pieces of transparent paper that you fill with content (images, text, and so on) and shuffle, stack, position, and overlap until your Web page looks exactly the way you want.

Dreamweaver AP Divs use a now common companion to HTML called Cascading Style Sheets Positioning (CSS-P) in order to place your content anywhere on the screen. However, you should be aware that Cascading Style Sheets are supported inconsistently across browsers (what looks perfect in Internet Explorer 7 might not look the same in Safari or Firefox). For more information about Cascading Style Sheets, check out *CSS Web Design For Dummies,* by Richard Mansfield (published by Wiley Publishing, Inc.).

One of the chief advantages of CSS-P is that you can use it to place elements in *A*bsolute *P*ositions (the *AP* in AP Elements) on your Web page without using tables. You can make any page element (an image or a block of text, for example) into an AP Element in Dreamweaver by giving it an absolute position.

Distinguishing divs from AP Divs

If you have any familiarity with CSS, you might also know Divs by the name they used to be called in Dreamweaver: AP Divs. Most commonly, when you add an AP Element to a page, you're adding an AP Div. Much of the information in this chapter about AP Divs may be applied to regular divs as well (naming, nesting, and AP Diving, for example). We use the generic term div when the information applies to both kinds of divs.

You can add a regular old div to a page with a click of a button, but we focus here on AP Divs because they're easier for a beginner to work with. Why's that? Because, unlike regular divs, you can draw AP Divs right on your document, saving yourself the trouble of sizing and positioning the div after adding it to your page.

Before you begin working with AP Divs, you may find it useful to have the Insert panel open to the Layout category (click Layout in the Insert panel to make it active) and the document in Design view (click Design in the Document window). To open the AP Elements panel, if it's not already open, press F2 or choose Window➪AP Elements. When you have several AP Divs in your document, the AP Elements panel may come in handy.

Tracing a Design

If you're using AP Divs to reproduce a page designed in Fireworks, Photoshop, or Illustrator, you can take advantage of the tracing feature in Dreamweaver. It works just like putting a piece of tracing paper on top of a photograph and tracing the image (in that analogy, the tracing image is the photograph, on top of which you'll "trace" your AP Divs).

To trace a page design, follow these steps:

1. **Choose View➪Tracing Image➪Load.**

   The Select Image Source window appears.

2. **Navigate to the file and click the filename.**

   The tracing image can be a PNG, PSD, GIF, or JPEG file.

3. **Click OK.**

   The Page Properties window appears, open to the Tracing Image category.

   If the tracing image is not in your site root folder, you may see a window asking if you want to copy the image to the site root folder. You don't need to do so, but you may. We usually click No.

4. **Drag the Transparency Slider as needed.**

   If you drag it all the way to the left, your tracing image will be invisible — not very useful as a tracing image. If you drag it all the way to the right (the default setting), your tracing image will be totally opaque.

5. **Click OK.**

   The tracing image appears in the Document window, allowing you to "draw" your AP Divs directly on top of it. Note that the tracing image is not a background image — it won't appear in a browser.

You can go back and adjust the transparency of the tracing image at any time by choosing Modify➪Page Properties and clicking Tracing Image on the left of the window that appears.

Setting AP Element Preferences

To choose different default settings for when you add an AP Element to a page, choose Edit➪Preferences; the Preferences dialog box appears. Click the AP Elements Category on the left to view the AP Element default settings that you can change, as shown in Figure 5-1.

Figure 5-1: Setting your default preferences for AP Elements.

Adding an AP Div

You can add an AP Div to the workspace of your Document window, shown through the drawing method in Figure 5-2, using one of the following two methods:

- **Choose Insert➪Layout ➪Objects➪AP Div.** If nothing is on the page already, as in this case, a new AP Div appears in the upper-left corner of your Document window.
- **Click the Draw AP Div button (just to the right of the Insert Div Tag button) on the Layout category of the Insert bar.** (If the Insert bar is not set to the Layout category, click Layout.) Position the cross-hair cursor anywhere in your Document window and click and drag until the AP Div obtains the dimensions you want. Release the mouse button.

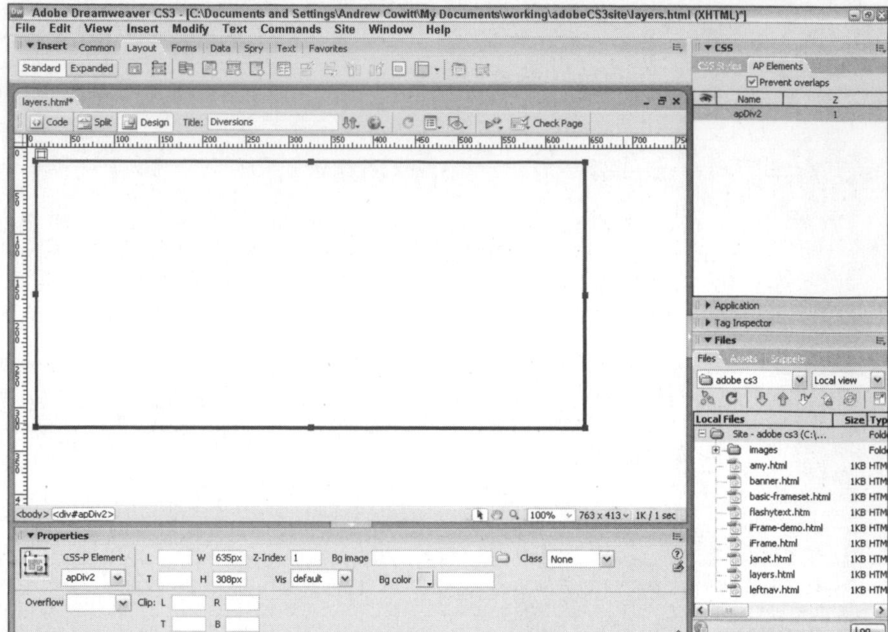

Figure 5-2: Drawing an AP Div.

If you set an AP Div's visibility to Hidden, it may be invisible in the Document window. To see it, simply click the name of the AP Div in the AP Elements tab of the CSS panel. Now you can see the AP Div, even though its visibility remains set to Hidden. See the "Changing the visibility of an AP Div" section, later in this chapter, for details on Visibility settings.

Selecting an AP Div

Selecting an AP Div enables you to identify which AP Div you want to affect when executing an AP Div operation, such as moving or naming the AP Div. Use either of the following methods to select an AP Div:

- ✦ In the Document window, click on the boundary of the AP Div. Before you select the AP Div, your cursor will turn into a four-pointed arrow (PC) or Grabber hand (Mac) when you place it over an AP Div boundary; the cursor becomes a white arrow (PC) when you place it over a Div boundary.
- ✦ In the AP Elements tab of the CSS panel, click the name of the AP Div.

The boundary becomes a thick blue line when the AP Div is selected. Also, selection handles appear on the boundary of the AP Div to indicate that you have selected it. The cursor becomes a double-sided arrow when you roll over a selection handle.

Deleting an AP Div

Deleting an AP Div removes the AP Div, the AP Div's contents, and the AP Div marker from the Document window. To delete an AP Div, select the AP Div and press the Del or Backspace key.

Don't delete an AP Div if you want to remove it from one page and add it to another. Instead, cut the AP Div by choosing Edit➪Cut or by pressing Ctrl+X. Open the page where you want to add the AP Div and choose Edit➪Paste or press Ctrl+V.

Placing Objects in an AP Div

To add an object to an AP Div, click inside the AP Div and follow the normal procedure for adding the object. For instance, add text to an AP Div by clicking inside the AP Div and typing text; add other objects to an AP Div by clicking inside the AP Div and choosing Insert➪Object, where *Object* is the name of the item you want to add to the AP Div.

Changing AP Div Properties

You can change lots of properties of AP Divs, including

- **Background:** You can add a background image or color to an AP Div.
- **Name:** Naming an AP Div can help you keep track of objects on a complex page, and is necessary if you want to apply behaviors to the AP Div.
- **Alignment:** You can align AP Divs with each other.
- **Visibility:** AP Divs (and the objects on them) can be visible or invisible.
- **Position:** AP Divs can be nested inside other AP Divs; they can also be stacked in different orders.
- **Size:** You can change the AP Div's height and width.
- **Location:** You can move an AP Div to any location on a page.

We show you how to edit each of these AP Div properties in the following sections.

Including a background image or color in an AP Div

By default, an unnested AP Div does not have a color or background image and will just display what lies beneath it as if it were transparent. (A nested child AP Div, if it's empty, will show the color or background image of its parent. For more about nested AP Divs, see the "Nesting AP Divs" section, later in this chapter.)

You can change the background of any AP Div by adding a background image or color as follows:

1. **Select the AP Div whose background you want to change by clicking the AP Div's border on the document or clicking the AP Div name in the AP Elements panel.**

   If the CSS-P Element Property inspector does not appear, open it by choosing Window➪Properties.

2. **In the CSS-P Element Property inspector, change one of the following:**

   - **Bg Image:** Click the folder to the right of the text field and browse to select a background image from the Select Image Source dialog box that appears. Click the Select button to accept your image choice and close the dialog box. The path to and name of the background image appear in the Bg Image field and the image is added to the background of the AP Div. Figure 5-3 shows an AP Div with a background image.

     If the image is smaller than the AP Div, the image will tile to fill the AP Div; if the image is larger than the AP Div, the image will be cropped to fit within the AP Div.

   - **Bg Color:** Click the color box (the little gray box with an arrow on it) and select a color from the color palette that appears. Alternatively, you can enter a hexadecimal number for a color in the Bg Color field. The new color appears in the background of the selected AP Div (as long as there isn't a background image in the AP Div already).

Naming an AP Element

The first AP Div you add to a page is automatically named AP Div1, the second AP Div you add is named AP Div2, and so on. You can change these default number names to other names that help you more easily distinguish AP Divs when working with HTML and examining AP Divs with the CSS-P Element Property inspector or AP Elements tab of the CSS panel.

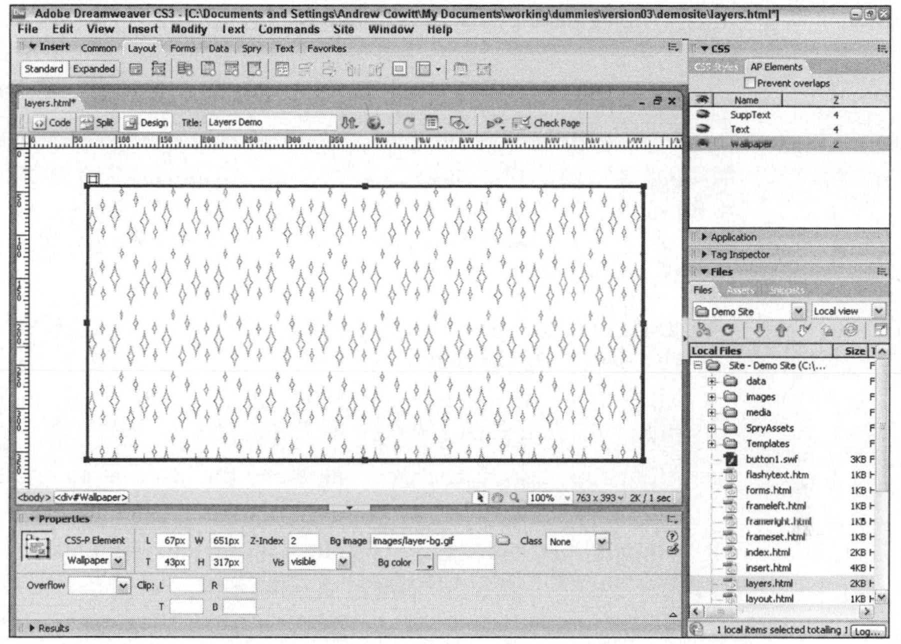

Figure 5-3: A background image added to an AP Element.

To name an AP Element using the AP Elements tab of the CSS panel, follow these steps:

1. **If the AP Elements tab of the CSS panel is not already visible, choose Window➪AP Elements or press F2.**
2. **Double-click the Name column for the AP Element whose name you want to change.**

   The current name is selected.

3. **Enter a new name for the AP Element.**

   Remember that AP Element names can contain only letters and numbers and must start with a letter.

You can also name an AP Element by double-clicking its name in the CSS-P Element Property inspector and entering a new name. The name updates automatically in the AP Elements tab of the CSS panel.

Get in the habit of appropriately naming your AP Divs as soon as you create them. The name *BlueprintImageMap* helps you remember an AP Div's content much better than *APDiv15*.

Aligning AP Elements

Aligning AP Elements with each other can help you precisely lay out visual content in the Document window. You can align the top, left, right, or bottom sides of AP Elements.

To align AP Elements, select the AP Elements you want to align by pressing and holding the Shift key and then clicking each AP Element in the Document window. Choose Modify⇨Arrange and choose one of the following options from the submenu:

- **Align Left:** Assigns the x-coordinate of the last selected AP Element to all selected AP Elements.
- **Align Right:** Aligns the right side of all selected AP Elements with the right side of the last selected AP Element.
- **Align Top:** Assigns the y-coordinate of the last selected AP Element to all selected AP Elements.
- **Align Bottom:** Aligns the bottom of all selected AP Elements with the bottom of the last selected AP Element.
- **Make Same Width:** Gives all the AP Elements the same width as the last selected AP Element.
- **Make Same Height:** Gives all the AP Elements the same height as the last selected AP Element.

Changing the Visibility of an AP Div

You can specify whether an AP Div is visible or hidden when a Web page *loads* — first appears in the user's browser window — and as a result of specific actions by the user. Visibility can change as many times as you want. Visibility options consist of the following:

- **Default:** The AP Div's initial visibility is the default setting, which is visible.
- **Inherit:** For a nested AP Div, the AP Div's initial visibility is the same as the visibility of its parent. For an unnested AP Div, selecting the Inherit option causes the AP Div to appear as visible.
- **Visible:** The AP Div's initial visibility setting is Visible.
- **Hidden:** The AP Div's initial visibility is Hidden.

You can use the CSS-P Element Property inspector or the AP Elements tab of the CSS panel to set AP Div visibility. By setting AP Div visibility, you can create scripts that cause images to appear (or disappear) in response to user interaction. For example, you can create an image of a gizmo that appears on a Web page after a user clicks a link marked Click Here to See Our Top-of-the-Line Gizmo!

To set the initial visibility of an AP Div via the CSS-P Element Property inspector, select the AP Div in the Document window to open the CSS-P Element Property inspector. If the inspector does not appear, open it by choosing Window⇨Properties. Choose a visibility option from the Vis drop-down list.

AP Divving AP Divs: Setting the z-index

The z-index of an AP Div indicates the AP Div's position in a stack of multiple AP Divs. Z-indices are useful when you have a handful of AP Divs — some containing transparent portions, some of different sizes — stacked one on top of the other. Changing the z-index of your AP Div lets you "shuffle" the AP Divs — much as you shuffle a deck of cards — to create interesting visual effects.

Z-indices are measured in whole numbers and do not have to be consecutive — for instance, you can have three AP Divs with z-indices of 1, 3, and 7, respectively. The AP Div with the largest z-index sits on top of the AP Div stack and the AP Div with the smallest z-index sits on the bottom of the AP Div stack. AP Divs with larger z-indices obscure those with smaller z-indices. You can change the z-index of an AP Div in either the CSS-P Element Property inspector or the AP Elements tab of the CSS panel.

To assign the z-index of an AP Div by using the CSS-P Element Property inspector, follow these steps:

1. **Select the AP Div to open the CSS-P Element Property inspector.**

   If the CSS-P Element Property inspector does not appear, open it by choosing Window⇨Properties.

2. **Enter a new number in the Z-Index field of the CSS-P Element Property inspector.**

To assign the z-index of an AP Element using the AP Elements tab of the CSS panel, follow these steps:

1. **If the AP Elements tab of the CSS panel is not already visible, choose Window⇨AP Elements or press F2.**
2. **Click the Z column for the AP Div whose z-index you want to change.**

   The current z-index is selected.

3. **Enter a new z-index for the AP Div.**

   The new number appears in the Z column for the selected AP Div, as shown in Figure 5-4.

4. **Click anywhere outside the Z column or press the Enter key.**

   Note that you can have multiple AP Divs at the same z-index.

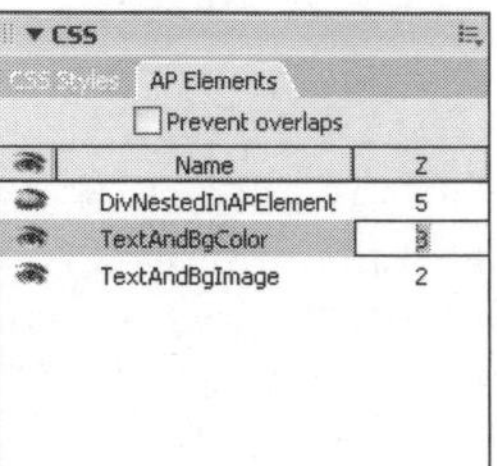

Figure 5-4: Changing the z-index of the AP Element named TextAndBgColor.

To assign relative z-indices to AP Divs by reordering Divs in the AP Divs tab of the CSS panel, follow these steps:

1. **Open the AP Elements tab of the CSS panel by choosing Window➪AP Elements or by using the keyboard shortcut F2.**

   The AP Elements tab lists AP Elements in order of descending z-index. Nested AP Divs are listed in descending order within their parent AP Div.

2. **Click the name of an AP Element for which you want to change the z-index.**

3. **Drag the AP Element name into a new list position and release the mouse button.**

   As you drag, the selected AP Div is indicated by a thick line.

Figure 5-5 shows the effect of changing a z-index. In the top image, the z-index of the bowling pins is higher than the starry background image. As a result, the bowling pins are on top. Conversely, in the bottom image, the starry background image has the higher z-index value, and as a result, it's on top of the bowling pins. Dreamweaver reorders the list in the AP Divs tab and renumbers AP Div z-indices to reflect your change. Also, Dreamweaver updates the associated code for the AP Divs' z-indices in the HTML source code for your page.

Because you don't have to number the z-index of AP Divs consecutively, consider leaving gaps between indices in case you later want to add new AP Divs into the middle of the stack. For instance, use only even numbers for your indices so that you can easily sandwich an AP Div with an odd-numbered z-index in between.

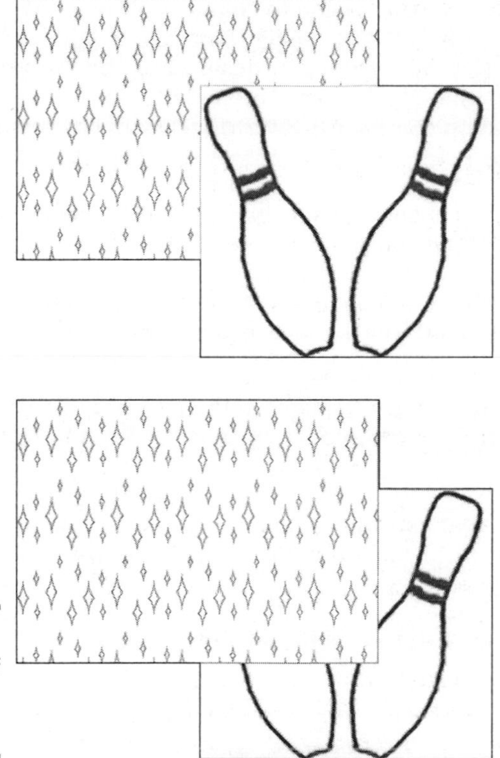

Figure 5-5: The effect of changing z-indices.

Moving an AP Div

You may want to move an AP Div to another location in the Document window or to a position relative to the grid or to other objects.

To move an AP Div, select the AP Div in the Document window and then reposition your selection by using one of the following three methods:

- Click the AP Div's border and drag the AP Div to a new location and release the mouse button. The border highlights with a red line inside the blue borderline to indicate that the AP Div can be moved.
- Press the arrow keys to nudge the AP Div up, down, left, or right one pixel at a time. If you hold down the Shift key, every press of an arrow key moves the AP Div by ten pixels.
- In the CSS-P Element Property inspector, enter a new value in the T (top) and L (left) fields to indicate the pixel coordinates of the AP Div's top-left corner.

When moving AP Divs, you can choose to enable or prevent AP Div overlap, depending on how you want the final image montage to appear. You enable or prevent AP Div overlap by selecting or deselecting the Prevent Overlaps check box in the AP Elements tab of the CSS panel.

Resizing an AP Div

Resizing an AP Div means changing its height and width dimensions. To resize an AP Div, select the AP Div and perform one of the following tasks:

- Click and drag a selection handle — one of the large dots on the AP Div boundary — until the AP Div is the size you want.
- In the CSS-P Element Property inspector, enter a new width in pixels in the W field and a new height in pixels in the H field. If the CSS-P Element Property inspector does not appear, open it by choosing Window➪Properties.

You can change the height and width dimensions of multiple AP Divs at the same time, provided the dimensions of the AP Divs you want to resize already match. Simply follow these steps:

1. **Press and hold the Shift key while selecting each AP Div you want to resize.**

   If the Multiple CSS-P Elements Property inspector does not appear, open it by choosing Window➪Properties.
2. **In the Multiple CSS-P Elements Property inspector, enter a new width in pixels in the W field and a new height in pixels in the H field.**

Nesting AP Divs

A *nested* AP Div is an AP Div that has all of its HTML code lying within another AP Div. The nested AP Div is often referred to as a *child* AP Div, whereas the AP Div on which it depends is called the *parent* AP Div. A child AP Div can be drawn completely inside its parent (as shown in Figure 5-6), in an intersecting arrangement with its parent, or completely unattached to its parent, depending on the effect you want to achieve. A nested AP Div inherits the same visibility of its parent and moves with the parent when the parent AP Div is repositioned in the Document window.

Enabling nesting

To create nested AP Divs in the Document window, you must first enable nesting. To do so, follow these steps:

1. **Choose Edit⇨Preferences to open the Preferences dialog box, or press Ctrl+U.**
2. **In the Preferences dialog box, select AP Elements in the Category area.**
3. **Select the Nesting check box.**
4. **Click OK to close the Preferences dialog box.**
5. **In the Document window, choose Window⇨AP Elements to open the AP Elements tab of the CSS panel.**
6. **In the AP Elements tab, make sure that the Prevent Overlaps option is deselected.**

Creating a new nested AP Div

Use either of these methods to draw a nested AP Div after enabling nesting:

- ✦ Click inside an existing AP Div and choose Insert⇨Layout Objects⇨AP Div. A child AP Div of default size appears inside the parent AP Div.
- ✦ Choose Layout Tools⇨Draw AP Div in the Layout category of the Insert bar. Then click and drag your mouse in the parent AP Div, releasing the mouse button when the AP Div has reached the dimensions you desire.

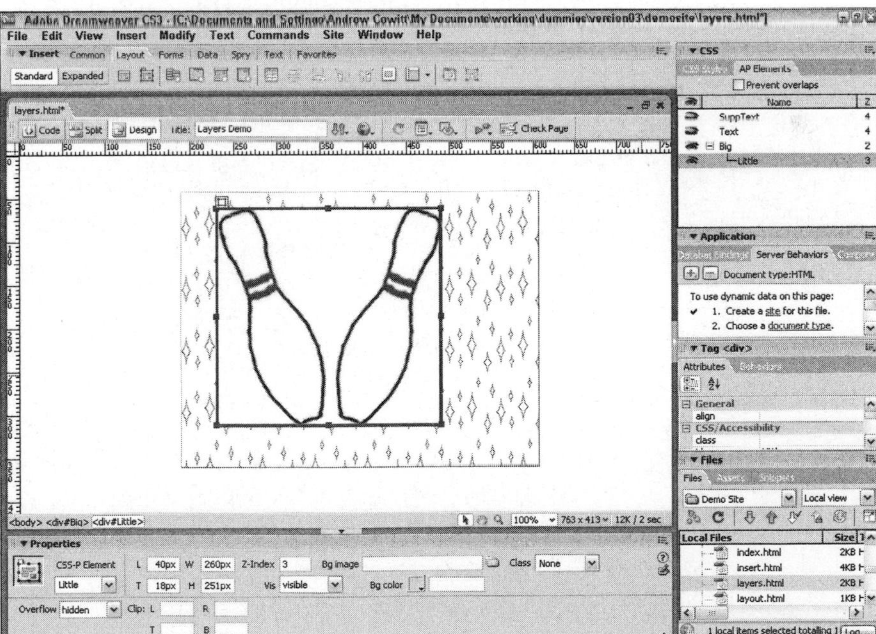

Figure 5-6: An AP Div nested in another AP Div.

Nesting an existing AP Div

To change the nesting of an existing AP Div, follow these steps:

1. **Open the AP Elements tab of the CSS panel by choosing Window➪AP Elements or pressing F2.**
2. **In the AP Elements tab of the CSS panel, press and hold the Ctrl key (⌘ key on the Mac) while using the mouse to click and drag the intended child AP Div on top of its new parent.**

   The child AP Div is in the correct position when you see a box appear around the name of its intended parent AP Div.
3. **Release the mouse button.**

   The new child-parent relationship is shown in the AP Divs tab of the CSS panel.

Dreamweaver draws the new child AP Div and updates the associated code for changed AP Div-nesting in the HTML source code for your page.

Collapsing or expanding your view in the AP Divs tab

You can change how you view the names of nested AP Divs in the AP Elements tab of the CSS panel by collapsing or expanding your view:

- ✦ **To collapse your view:** Click the minus sign (–) in front of a parent AP Div. Names of nested child AP Divs for that parent are hidden.
- ✦ **To expand your view:** Click the plus sign (+) in front of a parent AP Div. Names of nested child AP Divs appear underneath that parent AP Div.

Chapter 6: Advanced Web Page Design Techniques

In This Chapter

- **Creating hotspots**
- **Adding Flash text and button rollovers**
- **Adding a rollover behavior to an image**
- **Creating a navigation bar**
- **Inserting audio and video into your pages**
- **Using templates**
- **Validating your code**

In previous chapters of Book I, we focus on providing a good working knowledge of Dreamweaver CS3. Now we need to spend some time looking at the more advanced uses of Dreamweaver in Web development. In this chapter, we show you how to make images a bit more striking and how you can bring some other multimedia elements to life.

Creating Clickable Image Maps with Hotspots

You can designate certain areas of an image as *hotspots* — active areas that a user can click to open a link to another Web page or activate some other behavior. Hotspots can be shaped like rectangles, circles, or polygons (irregular objects). The coordinates of the hotspots are grouped into chunks of HTML code called *image maps.*

Creating a hotspot

Check out Figure 6-1. It shows a typical navigation bar for a site as a single JPEG image, with hotspots added. The following procedure shows you how to create an image map for that image by adding hotspots:

Figure 6-1: A typical JPEG navigation image with hotspots.

1. **Select the image to which you want to add a hotspot.**

   The Image Property inspector appears. If the bottom half of the Image Property inspector is not visible, click the Expander button, which is the down arrow in the bottom-right corner.

2. **In the Map area of the Image Property inspector, click the Hotspot button for the shape you want to draw.**

   You can choose a rectangle, a circle, or a polygon. Your mouse pointer becomes a cross-hair cursor when you move it over the image.

3. **Draw the hotspot according to the shape you select:**

   - **Circle or rectangle:** Click your cross hair cursor on the image and drag diagonally to create a hotspot. Release the mouse button when the hotspot reaches your desired dimensions. The area you draw is highlighted light blue, and the Hotspot Property inspector appears.
   - **Polygon:** Click your cross hair cursor on the image once for each point. The area you draw is highlighted light blue and the Hotspot Property inspector appears.

   Depending on your preference settings, you may see a window reminding you to supply Alternate text for the hotspot. Click OK.

4. **In the Hotspot Property inspector, supply the following information:**

   - **Map:** Enter a unique name for the image map.
   - **Link:** Enter a URL or the name of an HTML file you want to open when the user clicks the hotspot. Alternatively, you can click the folder icon and browse to select the link from your files. ***Note:*** Completing this field is optional. Instead, you may choose to attach a behavior to the hotspot.
   - **Behaviors:** To attach a behavior other than a link to the hotspot, open the Behaviors tab of the Tag panel by choosing Window➪Behaviors or by pressing Shift+F4. Then click the Add (+) button in the Behaviors panel, which opens a pop-up menu of available behaviors, including Check Plugin, Effects, Popup Message, Preload Images, and many

others. Choose a behavior from the pop-up menu, complete the information in the dialog box that appears for your selected behavior, and click OK.

- **Target:** Complete this field if you entered a link in the Link field and you want the link to open in a window or frame other than the one you're linking from. Click the arrow and select from the drop-down list a target window where you want your selected link to appear. You can select from the following choices: `_blank` (opens the link in a new window); `_parent` (opens the link in the parent of the currently opened window; if the currently opened window was opened from another frame, the link will open in that frame); `_self` (the default; opens the link in the currently opened window; not selecting a Target produces the same effect); and `_top` (opens the link in the top-level window, replacing frames, if any). If you have created frames, you can also select a frame name from this list. (See Book I, Chapter 4 for more information about frames.)
- **Alt:** Enter the text you want to show when the user moves the mouse pointer over the hotspot. Alt text also makes information about the hotspot accessible to vision-impaired users.

Modifying or deleting a hotspot

If you need to change the size or shape of a hotspot after you've created it, or you need to change the link, target, or Alt information for the hotspot, use the following procedure to edit the hotspot:

1. **On an image in the Document window, click the hotspot you want to modify.**

   The Hotspot Property inspector appears. If the inspector does not appear, open it by choosing Window➪Properties.

2. **Edit the Link, Target, or Alt information you want to change in the Hotspot Property inspector.**
3. **If you want to reshape or resize the hotspot, select the Arrow tool in the Hotspot Property inspector and then click any handle of the selected hotspot and drag the handle to a new location.**
4. **If you want to reposition the hotspot, select the Arrow tool in the Hotspot Property inspector, click anywhere within the hotspot, and drag it to a new location.**

You can delete a hotspot by selecting it and pressing the Del key on your keyboard.

Adding Flash Text Rollovers

A *text rollover* is text that changes color when users move their mouse pointer over it. One way to create text rollovers in Dreamweaver is by adding *Flash text* to your pages, as described in the following section.

Flash text and Flash buttons are so named because Dreamweaver implements these features using the same code that Adobe Flash CS3 (the animation program included in Creative Suite 3) uses.

Adding Flash text

To add hyperlinked Flash text that changes color when users roll their mouse over it, follow these steps:

1. **Click in the Document window where you want to add Flash text.**
2. **Choose Insert➪Media➪Flash Text.**

   Your page must be saved before you can insert Flash text. If the page hasn't been saved at least once, an alert pops up to remind you to save the page so you can insert the Flash text.
3. **In the Insert Flash Text dialog box, shown in Figure 6-2, select a font from the Font drop-down list.**

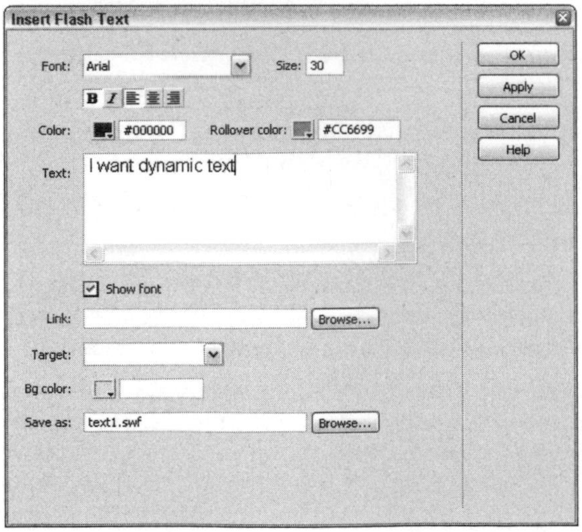

Figure 6-2: Choose how you want the text to appear in the Insert Flash Text dialog box.

4. **Enter a point size for your text in the Size text field.**
5. **If you want, you can also format the text.**

   You can click the Bold button and/or Italics button. You can also click an alignment button. Alignment choices are Left, Center, and Right.
6. **Select a Color (the initial color) and a Rollover Color (the color the text changes to when users move their mouse pointer over it) by clicking the color swatch in each area and selecting a color from the color palette that appears.**
7. **Enter your text in the Text field. Select the Show Font option if you want to preview the characters in the Text field in your selected font.**
8. **In the Link field, enter a URL or the name of the page you want to appear when the user clicks the Flash text.**

   Alternatively, you can click the Browse button to select a page from your files.
9. **In the Target area, click the arrow and select from the drop-down list a target window where the linked page will appear.**

   If you have created frames, you can select a frame name from this list, or you can select from the following choices:

   - `_blank`: Opens the link in a new window.
   - `_parent`: Opens the link in the parent of the currently opened window.
   - `_self`: Opens the link in the currently opened window; this is the default. Leaving the Target area empty produces the same result.
   - `_top`: Opens the link in the top-level window, replacing any existing frames.
10. **Select a Background color by clicking the Bg Color swatch and selecting a color from the color palette that appears, or type in a hexadecimal number.**

    Your Flash text appears over the background color you choose.
11. **Enter a name for your Flash text component in the Save As field or click the Browse button to select a name from your files.**

    You must save Flash text with an `.swf` extension.
12. **Click OK to create your Flash text and close the dialog box.**

    Depending on your preferences, you may see the Flash Accessibility Attributes window. Enter the Title, Access key, and Tab index information as needed and click OK. You can click OK without entering any information.

To preview the rollover effect of your Flash text, select the Flash object in the Document window to open the Flash Text Property inspector. In the Property inspector, click the Play button to view your Flash text as it will appear in the browser window. Click the Stop button when you're done.

Changing Flash text

You can change an existing Flash text object by simply double-clicking the object in the Document window or by clicking the object and then clicking the Edit button in the Property inspector. Doing so opens the Insert Flash Text dialog box, where you can change various attributes of the object as we describe in the previous section.

Adding Flash Button Rollovers

Buttons that change appearance when users move their mouse pointer over them — called *button rollovers* — are so popular that Dreamweaver gives you a way to create them quickly and easily as Flash movies. To find out how to create button rollovers using images and behaviors instead of Flash button rollovers, see the "Inserting Image Rollovers" section, later in this chapter. (Book III, Chapter 5 describes how to make rollovers in Fireworks CS3 using images and behaviors.)

Adding a Flash button

To add a Flash button, follow these steps:

1. **Click in the Document window where you want to add a Flash button.**
2. **Choose Insert⇨Media⇨Flash Button to open the Insert Flash Button dialog box, as shown in Figure 6-3.**

   Your page must be saved before you can insert a Flash button. If the page hasn't been saved at least once, an alert pops up to remind you to save the page so you can insert the Flash button.
3. **In the Insert Flash Button dialog box, scroll through the button selections in the Style list and click to select a style.**

   You can preview the style in the Sample area of the dialog box — just point to the sample with your mouse to see the Flash button in action.

   You can get new Flash buttons on the Dreamweaver Web site by clicking the Get More Styles button in the Insert Flash Button dialog box. A Web page on Adobe's site opens in your browser. Select the Flash Media option from the Categories drop-down list and scroll through the results as needed.

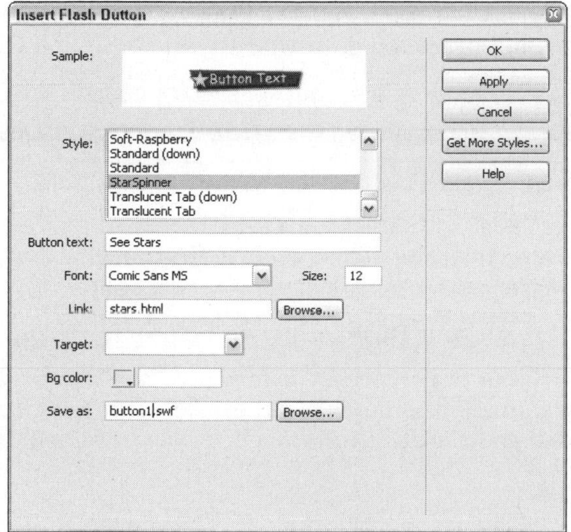

Figure 6-3: Add an interactive button with the Insert Flash Button dialog box.

4. **If your selected button has a placeholder for text, enter the text that you want to appear on the button in the Button Text field.**

   Text centers within the button automatically. Button size is fixed, though, so you must make sure your text is brief enough to fit on the button.

5. **Select a font for your Flash button text from the Font drop-down list.**
6. **Enter a point size for your text in the Size field.**
7. **In the Link field, enter a URL or the name of the page that you want to appear when the user clicks the Flash button.**

   Alternatively, you can click the Browse button to select a page from your files.

8. **From the Target drop-down list, select a target window where the linked page will appear.**

   If you have created frames, you can select a frame name from this list, or you can select from the following choices:

   - `_blank`: Opens the link in a new window.
   - `_parent`: Opens the link in the parent of the currently opened window.
   - `_self`: Opens the link in the currently opened window; this is the default. Leaving the Target area empty produces the same result.
   - `_top`: Opens the link in the top-level window, replacing any existing frames.

9. **Select a Background color by clicking the Bg Color swatch and selecting a color from the color palette that appears.**

   Alternatively, you can enter a hexadecimal color code in the Bg Color field.

   Your Flash button displays with the background color you select.

10. **Enter a name for your Flash button in the Save As field or click the Browse button to select a name from your files.**

    The Flash button filename requires an `.swf` extension. Dreamweaver will add the extension automatically if you don't enter it.

11. **Click OK to create your Flash button and close the dialog box.**

    Depending on your preferences, you may see the Flash Accessibility Attributes window. Enter the Title, Access key, and Tab index information as needed and click OK. You can click OK without entering any information.

To see what a Flash button looks like in action, select the button in the Document window to open the Flash Button Property inspector. In the Property inspector, click the Play button to view your Flash button as it appears in the browser window. Click the Stop button when you finish.

Changing a Flash button

To change an existing Flash button object, simply double-click the object in the Document window, or click the object and then click the Edit button in the Property inspector. Doing so opens the Insert Flash Button dialog box, where you can change your button as we describe in the previous section.

Inserting Image Rollovers

An *image rollover* (often just referred to as a *rollover*) is a behavior that changes an image whenever users move their mouse pointer over the image. Rollovers add interactivity to a Web page by helping users to see what parts of the page are links to other Web pages.

A rollover is actually two images — one for normal display on a page (the original image) and one that is slightly modified for display when the image is rolled over (the rollover image). You can modify an image by changing the color or position, adding a glow or a shadow, or adding another graphic — such as a dog changing from sleeping to wide-awake. For a rollover to work best, the normal and rollover states of the image should share the same width and height.

As with all images, you can't create the original image or the rollover image directly in Dreamweaver; you must use an image-editing program, such as Fireworks or Photoshop, to generate the images.

Insert a rollover by following these steps:

1. **Click inside the Document window where you want to insert the image rollover.**
2. **On the Common category of the Insert bar, click and hold the Image button and select Rollover Image from the pop-up menu.**

   The Insert Rollover Image dialog box appears, as shown in Figure 6-4. Alternatively, you can choose Insert➪Image Objects➪Rollover Image.

Figure 6-4: Creating an image rollover.

3. **In the Insert Rollover Image dialog box, enter a unique name for the rollover in the Image Name field, making sure there are no spaces in the name.**

   The rollover is referred to by this name in the HTML page code. Keep in mind that this rollover name refers to the combined original image/rollover image pair.

4. **Enter the name of the original image file in the Original Image field, or click the Browse button to select an image from your files.**

   The original image appears on the page when the user's mouse pointer is *not* over the image.

5. **Enter the name of the rollover image file in the Rollover Image field, or click the Browse button to select an image from your files.**

   The rollover image appears on the page when the user's mouse pointer is over the image.

6. **Select the Preload Rollover Image check box.**

   This feature makes the rollover action appear without delay to users as they move the mouse pointer over the original image. It is selected by default.

7. **Enter alternate text for the image to make it accessible to vision-impaired visitors to your site.**

   This step is optional but recommended.

8. **If you want to make the rollover image a link, enter a URL of the page in the When Clicked, Go to URL text field.**

   Alternatively, you can click the Browse button to select a page from your files.

9. **Click OK to accept your choices and close the dialog box.**

To check the rollover, preview your page in a browser by choosing File⇨Preview in Browser or by clicking the Preview in Browser button, and then use your mouse to point to the original image. You can also press F12 (on the PC, not on the Mac) to preview the rollover in the default preview browser. If you haven't set a default preview browser, you will have to do so using the Preview in Browser category in Dreamweaver's Preferences dialog box. See Dreamweaver's help documentation for details.

Setting Up a Navigation Bar

A *navigation bar* is a group of buttons that users can access to move throughout your Web site. Buttons within a navigation bar may present users with options, such as moving backwards, moving forwards, returning to the home page, or jumping to specific pages within the site.

Each button in a navigation bar possesses properties similar to a rollover in that the button *changes state* — or appears differently — based on where the user is positioning the mouse pointer. However, a navigation bar button can possess as many as four different states:

- **Up:** The original state of the button
- **Over:** How the button appears when a user moves their mouse pointer over it
- **Down:** How the button appears as a user is clicking it
- **Over While Down:** How the button appears when the user moves their mouse pointer over it after clicking it and arriving on the page it represents

A navigation bar differs from individual rollovers in that clicking a navigation bar button in the Down state causes all other buttons in the bar to revert to the Up state.

To create a navigation bar, just follow these steps:

1. **Select the Navigation Bar button from the Common category of the Insert bar or choose Insert⇨Image Objects⇨Navigation Bar.**

   Whichever method you choose, the Insert Navigation Bar dialog box appears, as shown in Figure 6-5.

Figure 6-5: From the Insert Navigation Bar dialog box, you can create an entire navigation bar.

2. **In the Insert Navigation Bar dialog box, enter a name for the first button in the Element Name field.**

   The new button appears in the Nav Bar Elements field. Don't use spaces in the names of any of these elements.

3. **For each state of the button — Up Image, Over Image, Down Image, and Over While Down Image — enter the name of the image file that you want to use in the associated field.**

   Alternatively, you can click the Browse button for each field and select an image from your files. You must supply the Up Image. All other states are optional and can be left blank.

   You don't need to use all four navigation bar button states — creating only Up and Down states works just fine.

4. **Enter alternate text for the image to make it accessible to vision-impaired visitors to your site.**

   This step is optional but recommended.

5. **In the When Clicked, Go to URL text field, enter a URL or the name for the page you want to appear when the user clicks the navigation bar button.**

   Alternatively, you can click the Browse button to select a page from your files.

6. **From the In drop-down list, select a target window where you want the linked page to appear.**

   If you aren't using frames, the only option is to use the Main window.

7. **Click the Add Item (+) button to add another navigation bar button.**

   Repeat Steps 2 through 6 to format the new button.

   Note: You can remove any button already created by clicking its name in the Nav Bar Elements field and clicking the Remove Item (–) button. You can also reorder the sequence of the buttons as they will appear on the page by clicking a button name in the Nav Bar Elements field and clicking the up- or down-arrow button.

8. **In the Options area, select the Preload Images check box if you want the rollover effects to appear without delay when the user triggers them.**

9. **To set the current button to appear in the Down state when the user first sees the navigation bar (which you might do to indicate that the current page is the one represented by the button), select the Show "Down Image" Initially check box in the Options area.**

   The Over While Down state works in combination with this option.

10. **Select Horizontally or Vertically from the Insert drop-down list to position the navigation bar horizontally or vertically.**

11. **To set up the button images in a table format, select the Use Tables check box.**

    This option is checked by default.

12. **Click OK to accept your choices and close the dialog box.**

To check the navigation bar, you must preview your page in a browser. Choose File➪Preview in Browser or click the Preview in Browser button and use your mouse to point to the buttons.

To change elements of an existing navigation bar, choose Modify➪Navigation Bar. The Modify Navigation Bar dialog box is nearly identical to the Insert Navigation Bar dialog box shown in Figure 6-5, except that you can no longer change the orientation of the bar or access the Use Tables check box.

Adding Audio and Video to Your Pages

You have two basic options, which are described in detail in the following sections, for adding downloadable audio and video to your Web pages:

- **Embedding:** You can embed an audio or video file to display a playback console on a Web page that users can use to play, rewind, and fast-forward the media file. (You can also embed an audio file and make it invisible to create a background audio effect.)

  Users must have an appropriate plug-in installed on their machines to play the embedded audio or video file. To ensure maximum compatibility, you may want to use Flash to create SWFs with audio and video (check out Book III, Chapter 6 for details on adding audio and video to SWFs).

- **Linking:** You can link to an audio or video file to give users the choice of whether or not to view that media file.

Keep in mind that most audio and video files are large — large enough that many folks impatiently click the Stop button on their browsers before a Web page chock-full of audio or video effects has a chance to finish loading. Keep the following basic rules in mind to help you use audio and video effectively in your Web pages:

- Use audio and video only when plain text just won't do.
- Keep your audio and video clips as short (and corresponding file sizes as small) as possible.

Embedding an audio or video clip

You can embed an audio or video file by following these steps:

1. **In the Document window, click the location in your page where you want to add an embedded audio or video file.**
2. **Click and hold the Media button in the Common category of the Insert bar and select Plugin from the pop-up menu, or choose Insert⇨Media⇨Plugin.**

   The Select File dialog box shown in Figure 6-6 appears.
3. **In the File Name field in the Select File dialog box, enter the path or browse to the audio or video file that you want to embed, and click OK.**

   If the file is outside your current root directory, Dreamweaver asks whether you want to copy the file to your site's root directory. Click Yes.

Figure 6-6: Select a media file to import.

4. **In the Plugin Property inspector, size the Plugin placeholder to any dimensions you prefer.**

   You can either enter a width and height in the W and H text fields in the Plugin Property inspector, or you can drag a handle on the placeholder to manually resize.

   Test in all your target browsers (the browsers your users are likely to view your site with) to ensure that users can view all the audio playback controls or video area and controls.

You can click the Play button in the Plugin Property inspector to play your media file without previewing your page in a browser.

Embedding background music

Embedding background music (music that plays automatically after the user opens a page) in your page can be controversial because users may be unpleasantly surprised by audio when they are expecting silence, and because users have no way to turn off the music from within the browser. If you still want to embed background music in your page, follow these steps:

1. **In the Document window, click the location in your page where you want to add an embedded audio file.**

   This should be an out-of-the-way location, like the bottom of your page, so the embedded audio doesn't create an awkward space in your design.

2. **Click and hold the Media button in the Common category of the Insert bar and select Plugin from the pop-up menu, or choose Insert➪Media➪Plugin.**

The Select File dialog box appears.

3. **In the File Name field in the Select File dialog box, enter the path to the audio file that you want to embed, and click OK.**

   If the file is outside your current root directory, Dreamweaver asks whether you want to copy the file to your site's root directory. Click Yes.

4. **Enter a width and height of 2 in the W and H text fields in the Plugin Property inspector.**
5. **Click the Parameters button to open the Parameters dialog box.**
6. **In the Parameters dialog box, click the Add (+) button to add a new parameter.**
7. **Click in the Parameter column and type** hidden.
8. **Type** true **in the Value column.**

   Steps 7 and 8 hide the audio playback controls.

9. **Click OK to complete the process and close the dialog box.**

Linking to an audio or video clip

A simple and relatively trouble-free way to include audio and video clips on a Web page is to link the page to an audio or video file. Users can click the link if they want to hear or watch the clip. This selection opens a player outside the browser where the user can control playback.

You follow the same steps to create a link to an audio or video file that resides in your root folder as you do to create a link to a Web page (see Book I, Chapter 2 for information on adding links); the only difference is that you specify a media file instead of a URL for the link.

Adding Other Media

Dreamweaver enables you to easily insert a number of other multimedia formats into your Web pages, including ActiveX, Java Applets, Adobe Flash, and Shockwave. After inserting any of these media formats, you can set the control and playback features of the media in the Parameters dialog box. Additionally, you can fine-tune the media action on your page by using the Behaviors panel to create triggering actions that cause the media to play, stop, and execute other functions.

Follow these directions to insert other media:

1. **In the Document window, click the location in your page where you want to add a multimedia file.**

2. Click and hold the Media button in the Common category of the Insert bar to view all the object types that you can insert, as shown in Figure 6-7, and click the icon of the type of media file you want to insert.

Alternatively, you can choose Insert⇨Media⇨Media *Type,* where *Media Type* is the type of media file you want to insert.

The Select File dialog box appears.

- **For Applet, Macromedia Flash, and Shockwave files:** In the File Name field in the Select File dialog box, enter the path to the media and click OK. Your file is inserted and the associated Property inspector appears. You can change the selected file in the Plugin Property inspector by typing a new name in the File text field or by browsing in the File folder to select a file (for Applets, use the Code text field). Select the Embed check box if you want Netscape Navigator users to have access to the Applet.
- **For ActiveX:** An ActiveX placeholder is inserted and the ActiveX Property inspector appears. Enter the name of the ActiveX object you want to play in the Class ID text field. Select the Embed check box if you want Netscape Navigator users to have access to the ActiveX object.

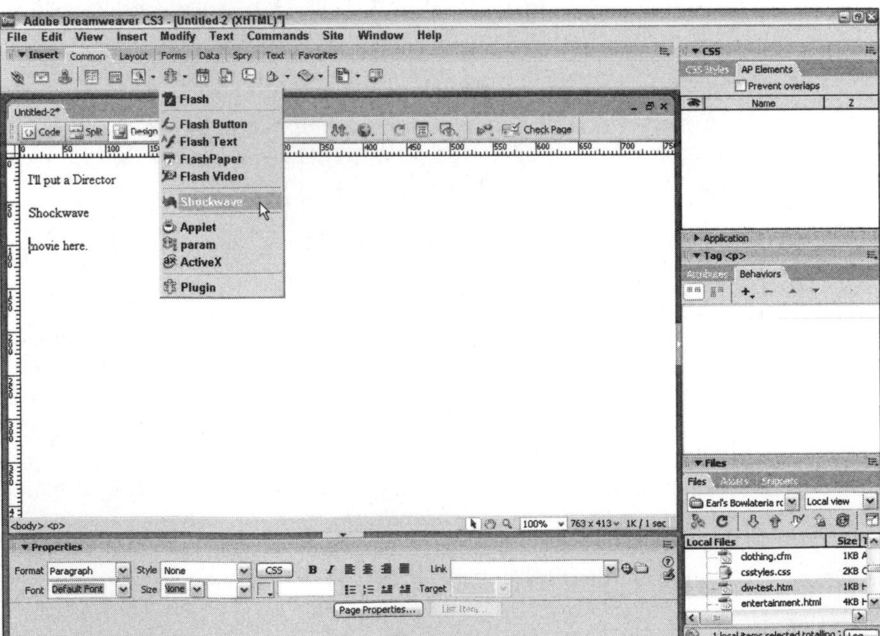

Figure 6-7: Your embedded media options.

3. **In the Property inspector for your selected media, enter dimensions in the W and H text fields to size the Media placeholder to any dimensions you choose.**
4. **In the Property inspector for your selected media, click the Parameters button to open the Parameters dialog box, where you can add parameters (like width, height, loop, and autoplay) appropriate to the selected media type.**

Using Dreamweaver Templates

Dreamweaver comes with many built-in layouts that you can use to create pages or Dreamweaver templates quickly. The layouts are predesigned pages with placeholder content. Make a new page from a layout, replace the placeholder content with real content, and voilà — a professionally designed page!

To create a new page based on a built-in layout, just follow these steps:

1. **Choose File➪New.**

   The New Document dialog box appears.
2. **Select Page from Sample in the Category list on the left.**

   The Sample Folder and Sample Page columns are updated.
3. **Select Starter Page (Theme) or Starter Page (Basic).**

   The Sample Page column is updated. Click any page in the Sample Page column to see a preview in the Preview area, as shown in Figure 6-8.

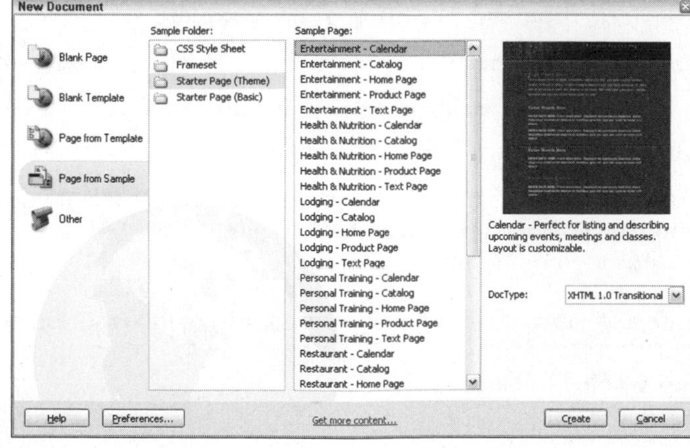

Figure 6-8: The Entertainment: Calendar sample page is selected.

4. **When you've found the layout you want, select the Document option in the lower-right corner and click the Create button.**

   The Save As dialog box appears.

5. **Name the file and click Save.**

   An untitled HTML page opens in the Document window with placeholder content that you can replace with real content.

   If the Copy Dependent Files dialog box appears, click Copy. The styles and images used in the template will be copied to your site's root folder.

You don't have to use a built-in layout to create a Dreamweaver template: You can make a Dreamweaver template based on any Web page. One cool thing about Dreamweaver templates is that if you make a whole bunch of pages based on a template, you can change the template, and all the pages based on it will be updated to match the template automatically. Another cool thing is that you can make a template that other people can use in combination with either Dreamweaver or Contribute to create new pages that conform to the template's design.

To create a Dreamweaver template based on an existing HTML page, just follow these steps:

1. **Open the HTML page you want to use as a template.**
2. **Choose File⇨Save As Template.**

   The Save As Template dialog box appears.

3. **Select the site you want to use the template in.**

   By default, the current site is selected.

4. **If desired, input a description of the template.**

   This step is optional.

5. **In the Save As field, input a name for the template.**
6. **Click Save.**

   If the Update Links dialog box appears, click Yes. When you've saved the template, you need to add editable regions. See Steps 4–6 in the next set of steps to find out how.

To create a Dreamweaver template from scratch, follow these steps:

1. **Choose File⇨New.**

   The New Document dialog box appears, with the General tab selected.

2. **Select Basic Page from the Category list on the left and then select HTML Template from the list of Basic Pages that appears in the middle.**

You can also select Template Page from the Category list and choose HTML Template from the Template Page list that appears in the middle.

3. **Create your page layout.**

   By default, nothing in the design of pages based on your template is editable. You must create editable regions in order to make a useful template.

4. **Click a table cell or other part of your layout that you want users to be able to fill with content, and choose Insert⇨Template Objects⇨Editable Region, or press Ctrl+Alt+V (⌘+Opt+V on a Mac).**

   The New Editable Region dialog box appears. If you have a placeholder image already in the layout, you can right-click the image and choose Templates⇨New Editable Region from the context menu that pops up, or you can select the image and press Ctrl+Alt+V (⌘+Opt+V on a Mac).

5. **Name the region and click OK.**

   You can use the default name Dreamweaver gives to the region, but it's better if you name the region to reflect the content that will go into it (for example, name the region Product Description). Figure 6-9 shows a template with three editable regions. Editable regions are bound by a light blue box with the region name at the top left.

6. **Repeat Steps 4 and 5 until you have made editable regions out of all the areas of the page that you want to be editable in new pages based on the template.**

Anything inside an editable region can be replaced in a page based on the template; anything outside the editable regions is locked and can't be changed in pages based on the template.

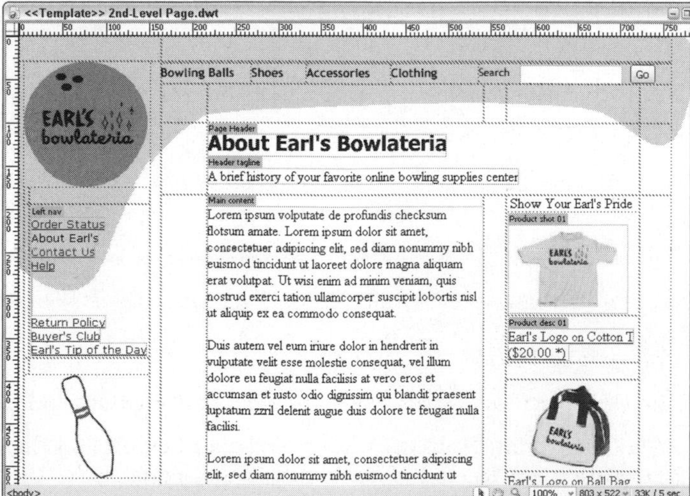

Figure 6-9: Editable regions in a template.

7. **Choose File➪Save.**

   The Save As Template dialog box appears.

8. **Choose the site the template belongs to from the drop-down list, enter a name for the template in the Save As field, and click the Save button.**

   The template will now be available to anyone who has access to the Dreamweaver site, either through Dreamweaver or with Contribute.

To create an HTML page based on an existing user-created template, follow these steps:

1. **Click the Templates icon in the Assets tab of the File panel. All available templates for the selected site appear.**

   If the Files panel is closed, choose Window➪Assets or press F11 (on the PC only, not the Mac).

2. **Right-click the template you want to create the new page from and choose New from Template, as shown in Figure 6-10.**

   The page opens as an HTML page in the Document window.

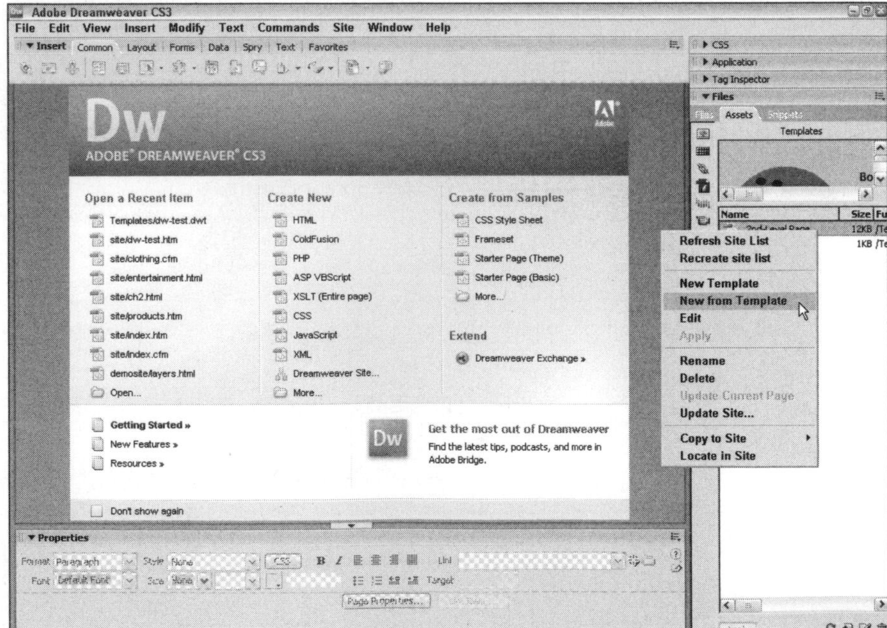

Figure 6-10: Creating a new page based on a template.

You can also create an HTML page based on a user-created template by choosing File⇨New and choosing the template from the Page From Template category of the New Document dialog box. (When you select the Page from Template category, the Templates options appear, as shown in Figure 6-11.)

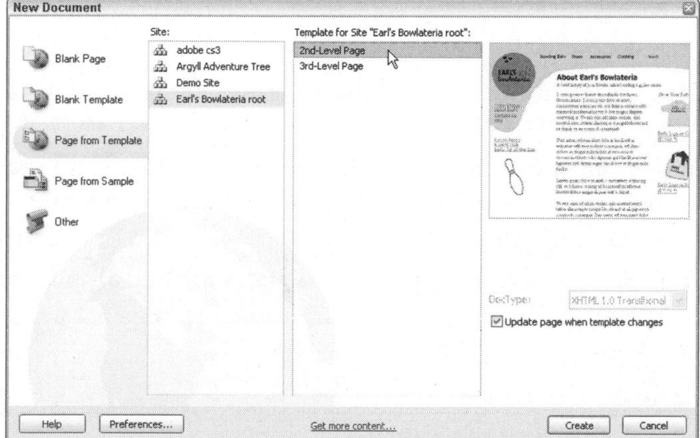

Figure 6-11: Choosing a user-created template.

Validating Your Code

Dreamweaver CS3 has a built-in code validator. The validator checks your HTML for errors (for example, unclosed `<TD>` tags or tags with invalid attributes, such as `<FONT width=113>`). If you work exclusively in Design view, you may never need to use the validator. If you work in Code view, though, and you are creating long, complex pages, you may find it worthwhile to run the validator.

To validate your code on a page that's open in the document window (unless it's XML), choose File⇨Validate Markup or press Shift+F6. The Results panel opens and shows a list of warnings for any faults in the code. Double-click a result in the list to highlight the problem in the code.

To validate XML code, choose File⇨Validate⇨As XML. Because XML has stricter requirements for well-formed code, you should take advantage of Dreamweaver's built-in validator if you're writing XML or XHTML.

You can validate the code for an entire site at one time by following these steps:

1. **If the Results panel isn't open already, choose Window⇨Results or press F7.**

   The Results panel appears under the Properties panel at the bottom of the screen.

2. **Click the Validation tab.**

3. **Click and hold the green arrow at the left of the Results panel and choose Validate Entire Current Local Site, as shown in Figure 6-12.**

   The results of the validation check appear in the Results window. Double-click a result to highlight the problem in the code.

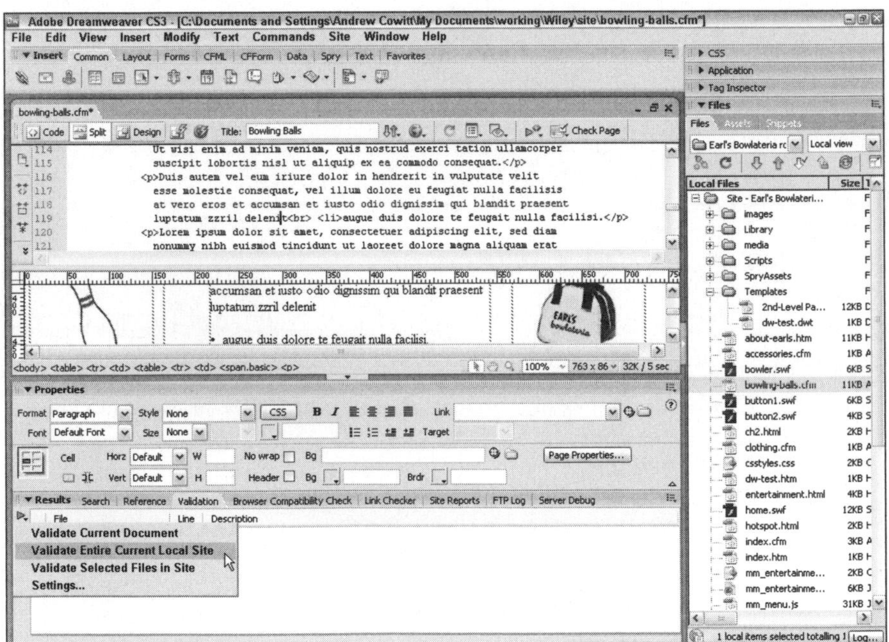

Figure 6-12: The results are in!

Chapter 7: Adding Interactivity with Spry

In This Chapter

- Introducing the Spry Framework
- Adding Spry data widgets
- Validating user input with Spry widgets
- Adding Spry navigation widgets
- Dazzling users with Spry effects

The Spry Framework is a collection of JavaScript functions and Cascading Style Sheet instructions that allow you to add sophisticated — and often eye-catching — widgets to your Dreamweaver pages. The widgets range in purpose from the practical (form validation) to the decorative (animation effects).

In this chapter, we introduce you to the uses of the Spry widgets that ship with Dreamweaver CS3. If the past is any indicator, new widgets will become available from Adobe's Web site as power users share their work with the Adobe community.

If you can't find what you're looking for in this chapter, fear not. You can always check out Dreamweaver's built-in help files by choosing Help➪Dreamweaver Help or pressing F1. You can also find more information on the Web by choosing Help➪Spry Framework Help.

Adding Spry Data Set Widgets

Data set widgets allow you to display XML data on your page in ways that reproduce the feel of dynamic pages; the user can sort data in tables by clicking column headers, for example, or click a link to display, replace, or hide an image or text anywhere on that same page. The best part is that the user doesn't have to wait for the page to refresh. It all appears pretty much instantly. XML (or eXtensible Markup Language) looks a lot like HTML but has a very different purpose. XML allows you to organize data so that it can be stored in a single text file, exchanged between different systems, and displayed in multiple ways (including standard Web pages and cell phones). If you need more information about XML, see *XML For Dummies,* 4th Edition, by Lucinda Dykes and Ed Tittel (Wiley Publishing, Inc.).

If you want to display the data from an XML file in a Spry Region, list, or table, the first step is to tell Dreamweaver where the XML data is and how it is structured. Read on to discover how to build the line of communication between Dreamweaver and your XML file.

Defining a Spry XML data set

If you want to display on a Web page data that you have stored in an XML file, the first step is to reference the XML data in Dreamweaver. To do so, simply follow these steps:

1. **If it's not already selected, click the Spry tab in the Insert bar.**

   The Spry category of the Insert tab gives you one-click access to all the Spry widgets available in Dreamweaver, as shown in Figure 7-1.

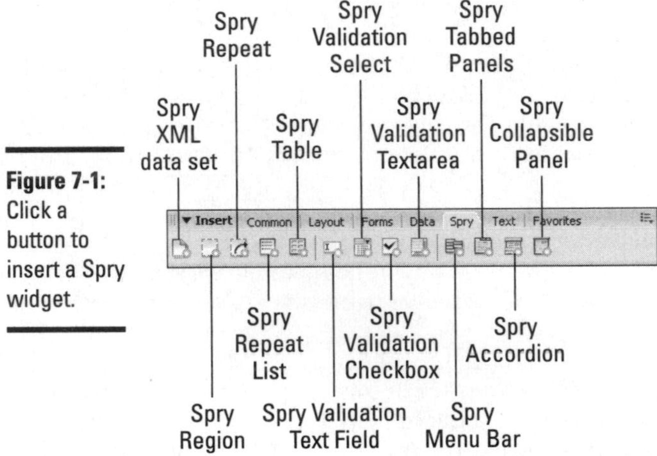

Figure 7-1: Click a button to insert a Spry widget.

2. **Click the Spry XML Data Set button on the Insert bar.**

   The Spry XML Data Set window appears, with a default Data Set name.

3. **If you'll be referencing more than one data set on your site, you may want to input a custom name in the Data Set name field.**

   Data Set names can contain only letters and numbers and can start only with a letter.

4. **Click the browse button and navigate to the XML file in the Select XML Source window that appears. Click the file and click OK.**

   The Select XML Source window disappears and the selected file appears in the XML Source field.

5. **Click the Get Schema button and click the Row Element that you want to use as the basis for display.**

   For example, we want to show bowling balls but not other products in the XML file, so we've selected "ball," as you can see in Figure 7-2. The data hierarchy is reflected in the Row Element window, which shows subordinate elements as indented. The XPath, Data Set Columns, Data Type, and Direction fields update automatically to their defaults.

   You can click the Preview button to see how the data would appear in a simple table in your browser. (***Note:*** The Preview window shows only the top 20 rows.)

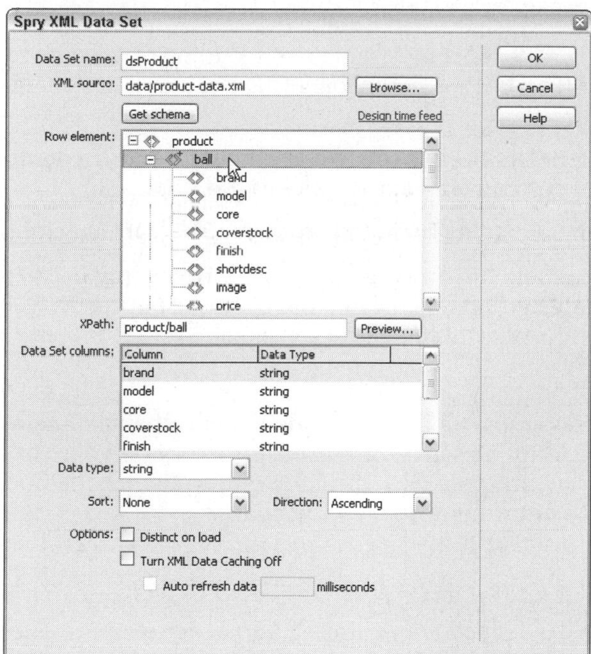

Figure 7-2: Selecting a row element.

6. **Optional: If you have XML elements for which you want to specify the data type, click the element in the Data Set Columns area and choose a data type from the Data Type select menu.**

   Specifying the data type can allow for sorting and formatting. The Data Type choices are as follows:

   - **String:** The data is treated as a generic string of characters, even if the data consists of numerals only. This is the default setting.
   - **Number:** The data is treated as a number.
   - **Date:** The data can be formatted as a date.
   - **Image link:** The data will be treated as a link to an image file.

7. **Optional: Choose a sort method from the Sort select menu and a sort direction from the Direction select menu.**

   The contents of the Sort menu depend on the Data Set Columns. You can choose to sort the data by any of the columns shown in the Data Set Columns section.

   Your choices for sort direction are Ascending (low value to high value, as in 1–100 or A–Z) or Descending (high value to low value, as in 100–1 or Z–A).

8. **Optional: Select the Distinct On Load check box if you don't want duplicate columns in your display of the data.**

9. **Optional: Select the Turn XML Data Caching Off check box.**

   This option and the Auto Refresh Data option apply only if you have data that updates constantly on your site. For our purposes, we're assuming a fairly static XML data source, so you wouldn't want to select these options.

10. **Click OK.**

    Dreamweaver inserts the Spry code in your document and the necessary JavaScript files in a SpryAssets directory on your site. If you're in Design view, you won't see the code (you can click the Code button in the Document window to view the code).

Creating a Spry Region

After you have a defined Spry data set, you need to create a container on your page that can hold Spry elements. This container is called a Spry Region. There are two types of Spry Regions:

✦ **Spry Region:** The regular type of region, a div tag that "wraps around" (contains) Spry data elements such as tables, tabbed panels, and so on.

✦ **Spry Detail Region:** A region dependent on, and dynamically updateable by, a regular Spry Region.

You'll be prompted to create a Spry Region if you attempt to insert a Spry list or table in your document without first creating a Spry Region. In other words, you don't need to create a Spry Region as a stand-alone step in the process of building your page. You can do so if you want.

To create a Spry Region on your page, just follow these steps:

1. **Click the Spry Region button on the Spry category of the Insert bar.**

   The Insert Spry Region window appears.

2. **Choose a container type by clicking either DIV or SPAN.**

   The default, DIV, is the better option in most cases.

3. **Choose a type by clicking either Region or Detail Region.**

   Choose Detail Region if you're creating a region that will update based on feedback from an object in another region on the page. If so, you need to create the other region and object first. Otherwise, leave the default (Region) selected.

4. **Choose the applicable Spry Data Set from the select menu.**

   To learn how to define a Spry data set, see "Defining a Spry XML data set," earlier in this chapter.

5. **Click OK.**

   The Insert Spry Region window disappears. A box with a dotted-line border and the sentence "Content for Spry Region Goes Here" shows the Spry Region.

Creating a Spry Repeat

You can use the Spry Repeat function to display repeating elements in your data set in whatever display format you want (as items stacked vertically in a div or table cell, for example). If you want to display the data in a bulleted or numbered list, use the Spry Repeat List function, described later in this chapter.

To add a Spry Repeat, create your data set and add a Spry Region as described previously. (If you haven't done so ahead of time, you'll be prompted to do each as part of the process of creating a Spry Repeat.)

1. **Click the spot in the Spry Region where you want the repeating elements to start.**

2. **Insert a binding for the repeating element you want to display by selecting it and clicking the Insert button in the Bindings category of the Application panel.**

   If you can't see the Bindings panel, choose Window Bindings or press Ctrl+F10. The element will appear in the document in curly brackets.

3. **Click the element in the document window to select it, and click the Spry Repeat button in the Spry category of the Insert bar.**

   The Insert Spry Repeat window appears, as shown in Figure 7-3.

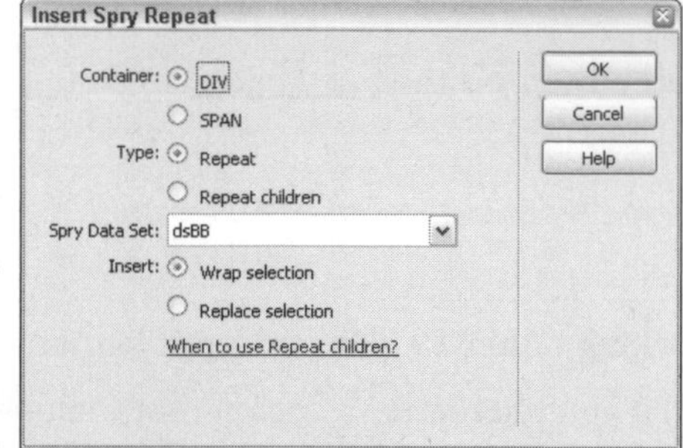

Figure 7-3: Inserting a Spry Repeat.

4. **Choose either DIV (the default) or SPAN to contain the repeating data.**

   In most cases, you'll want to use a DIV as your container.

5. **Choose either Repeat (the default) or Repeat Children.**

   Beginning users will probably want to stick with the default.

6. **Select a data set from the Spry Data Set select menu.**

   If you have only a single data set associated with your page, it will appear as the default, and only, choice.

7. **Choose either Wrap Selection (the default; wraps the repeat div tag around the element selected in the document window) or Replace Selection (replaces the selected element with a div tag).**

8. **Click OK.**

   The Insert Spry Repeat window closes and the Spry Repeat div is added to your page's code.

Creating a Spry Repeat List

As you might guess from the name, a Spry Repeat List is a variation on the Spry Repeat function. A Spry Repeat List simply lets you set up the repeating display element in a list. You can create four types of lists, as follows:

- **UL:** An Unordered List (a.k.a. a bulleted list)
- **OL:** An Ordered (numbered) List

- **DL:** A Definition List
- **Select:** A list of options for an HTML Select menu

To insert a Spry Repeat List into an existing Spry Region, simply follow these steps:

1. **Click the spot in the Spry Region where you want the list to start.**
2. **Click the Spry Repeat List button in the Spry category of the Insert bar.**

   The Insert Spry Repeat List window appears, as shown in Figure 7-4.

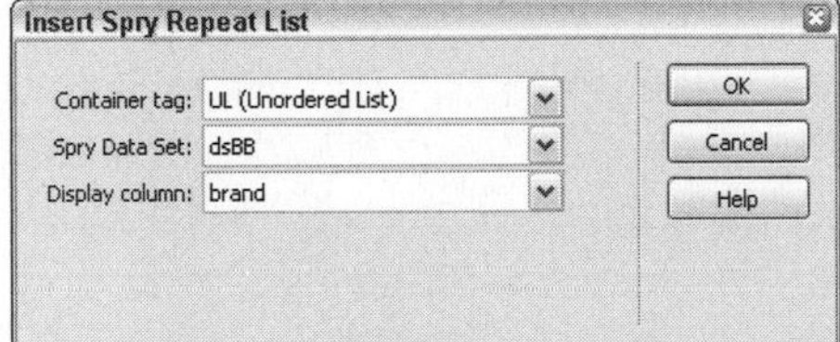

Figure 7-4: Inserting a Spry Repeat List.

3. **Choose a type of list from the Container Tag select menu.**

   The four choices are listed at the beginning of this section.
4. **Select a data set from the Spry Data Set menu.**

   If you have only a single data set associated with your page, it will appear as the default, and only, choice.

5a. **If you chose UL or OL in Step 3, choose which data element you want to display on your page from the Display Column menu.**

   The menu contains all the columns in the data set that you selected in Step 4.

5b. **If you selected DL in Step 3, select a term from the DT Column menu and a definition from the DD Column menu.**

5c. **If you selected Select in Step 3, select what the user will see in the menu you're creating from the Display Column menu and what will be processed by the form from the Value Column menu.**

6. **Click OK.**

   The Insert Spry Repeat List window disappears, and Dreamweaver adds the necessary code to your page.

Creating a Spry Table

A Spry Table is a nifty way to display a data set on your page. One cool feature of Spry Tables is that you can choose to make any column sortable alphabetically or numerically: When the user clicks on a column header, the data is instantly re-sorted based on the data in the selected column. Not only that, but the user can toggle the results between ascending order (A–Z, or 1–100, say) and descending order (Z–A or 100–1, for example).

To add a Spry Table to an existing Spry Region, follow these steps:

1. **Click the spot in the Spry Region where you want the table to go.**
2. **Click the Spry Table button in the Spry category of the Insert bar.**

   The Insert Spry Table window appears, as shown in Figure 7-5.

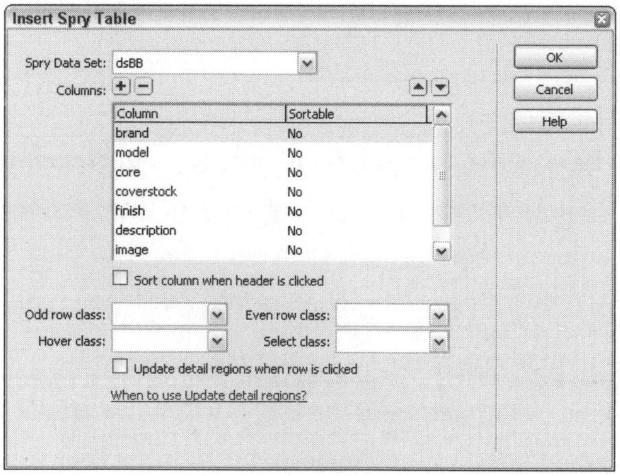

Figure 7-5: Inserting a Spry Table.

3. **Select a data set from the Spry Data Set menu.**

   If you have only a single data set associated with your page, it will appear as the default, and only, choice. The columns in that data set appear in the Columns section of the Insert Spry Table window.

4. **Optional: To change the display order of a table column, click to select it and click the Up arrow to move it up in the list or click the Down arrow to move it down in the list.**

   You can also click the Add Column (+) button to add a column or the Remove Column (–) button to remove the column.

5. **Optional: To make it possible for the user to sort the data in the table by clicking a column header, select the column in the Columns section and select the Sort Column When Header is Clicked check box.**

You can do this for as many columns as you have in your table, for none of the columns, or for anything in between. After you finish inserting the table, you'll have to add empty links to the column headers in order to make them trigger the sort action. To add an empty link to an object (a link that doesn't go anywhere), select the object and input the pound sign (#) in the Link field in the Properties panel.

6. **Optional: If you already have a stylesheet set up, you can apply existing classes to odd and even rows in your table and for hover and selected states for links.**

   If you want to control these aspects of the look of the table with CSS, it's better to set up the styles before you create the table so that you can easily set the display options from the select menus in the Insert Spry Table window.

7. **Optional: If you are using the table to control a Spry Detail Region elsewhere on the page, select the Update Detail Regions When Row Is Clicked check box.**

8. **Click OK.**

   The Insert Spry Table window disappears and Dreamweaver inserts the necessary code in your page. After that's done, you can select the table and apply width, cellpadding, and all the usual table attributes as needed.

Validating User Input with Spry Widgets

In case you want to put user feedback forms on your site, Dreamweaver gives you an easy way to make those forms smarter, thanks to Spry's form field validation widgets. You can set up the widgets to change color and/or display an error message when a user enters information you've defined as invalid. The widgets add client-side validation capabilities to the following:

- **Text Input fields:** You can set the minimum/maximum amount of characters allowed in the field, and you can declare certain characters as either not allowed or required.
- **Select menu:** You can make selecting an option required, and you can declare a selection invalid (such as when you have horizontal lines separating the menu options into groups).
- **Check boxes:** You can make any number of check boxes required (for example, you might say that the user must select a minimum of three boxes out of nine).
- **Textareas:** You can make a textarea required, and you can set a minimum and maximum number of characters that the user must enter.

No matter which type of form validation widget you use, you must place it inside a form. You can either put a form in your page as a separate step (see Book II, Chapter 4 for details), or you can simply add the form as part of the process of adding the first Spry form validation widget to your page, as we show below.

Adding a Spry text input field

To add a Spry text input field to your document, follow these simple steps:

1. **Place your cursor in your document where you want the text input field to go.**
2. **Click the Spry Validation Text Input button in the Spry category of the Insert bar.**

   Depending on your preferences settings, the Input Tag Accessibility Attributes window may appear. If it does, enter information as you see fit. It's a good practice to make your forms accessible to people with impaired sight. For information about the accessibility attributes, see your documentation. Whether you enter attributes or not, click OK to close the window.

   If you haven't yet created a form on your page, a dialog box may appear asking if you want to add a form tag. Click Yes. The dialog box will disappear, and the Spry text input field will appear in your document, as shown in Figure 7-6.
3. **Depending on what type of information users might be putting in the field, you may find preset validation scripts by selecting an option in the Type select menu.**

   For example, if you want users to enter their e-mail address in the field, you can select Email Address. The field will be checked to make sure there is an @ sign and dot (.) in the data the user enters.
4. **Depending on the Type you select, the Format menu may become active. If the menu is not grayed out, select a required format for the field.**

   For example, if the Type is Date, the required format could be mm/dd/yy, mm/dd/yyyy, or another. If you chose the first one, and a user input 07/18/2000, the field would turn red and an error message would appear.
5. **Select a Preview state from the Preview States select menu to see what the field will look like in each of three states if you make the field required (which it is by default). You must be in Design view to see the Preview state.**

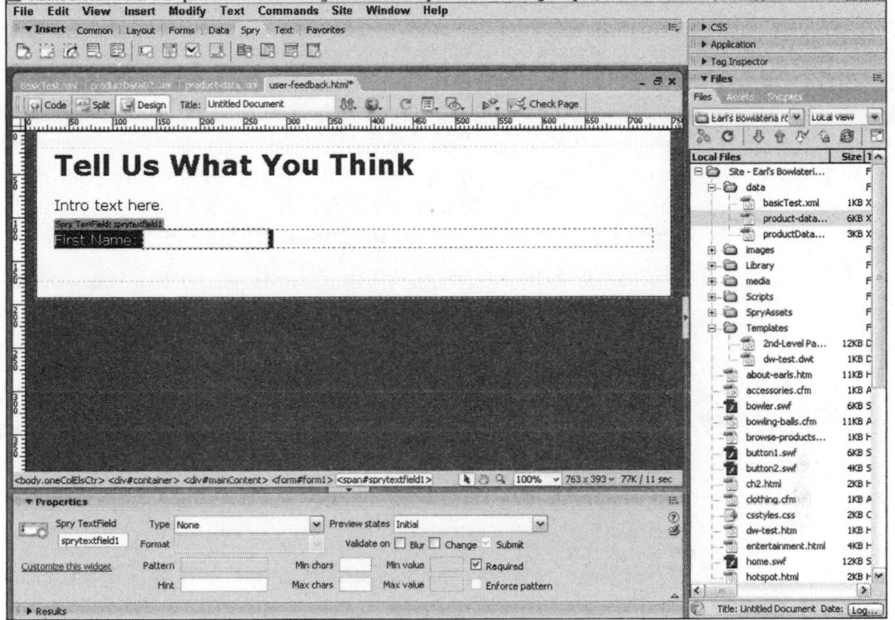

Figure 7-6: Spry text input field, with accessibility attribute Label set to "First Name."

The states may include:

- **Initial:** What the field looks like when the user first loads the page in a browser.
- **Required:** What the field looks like when the field is required but is left blank.
- **Invalid Format:** How the field appears when the user enters information in a format invalid for the type (for example, an e-mail without an @ sign).
- **Valid:** What the field looks like when the user has entered valid information.

Other states may appear depending on what you choose elsewhere in the Property inspector.

6. **Choose an action that triggers the field's validation by checking one of the Validate On check boxes.**

   By default, fields are validated on Submit, that is, when the user clicks the form's Submit button. You can also choose Blur (when the user clicks anywhere else on the page after entering information in the field) or Change (when the user begins inputting data in the field).

7. **Optional: If you wish to specify a minimum number or maximum number of characters that the user can input into the text field, enter the numbers in the Min Chars or Max Chars field, respectively.**

8. **Optional: Depending on the Type you select, the Min Value and Max Value fields may become active.**

   For the Integer type, for example, you could set minimum or maximum (or both) allowable numerals for the field. (The numeral the user inputs must be at least 5, say, or no greater than 100.)

9. **Optional: You can prepopulate the field with a temporary value that shows the correct format by entering the value in the Hint field.**

   For example, if you're asking the user to fill in a phone number, you could enter (111) 222-3456.

10. **Optional: Select the Enforce Pattern check box if you want to ensure that no illegal characters can be put in the text field.**

    For example, for the Email Address type, the user would not be able to input characters such as < or /.

11. **Optional: Deselect the Required check box if you don't want the user to have to fill in the field in order to submit the form.**

    Otherwise, leave Required at the default setting, which will prevent the user from submitting the form unless the user puts a value in the text field.

You can change the error messages or the default colors for the different states of the text field, but that's a little too advanced to describe here. Click the Customize This Widget link in the Properties panel to learn more.

Adding a Spry Select menu

What makes a Spry Select menu different from a regular old select menu? Three things:

- You can make choosing an option mandatory for the user.
- You can make options invalid.
- The menu will change color based on user feedback and will display an error message if the user makes an invalid selection (or, if the menu is required and the user makes no selection).

To insert a Spry Select menu into a form, follow these steps:

1. **Place your cursor in the form where you want the select menu to go.**

   If you don't already have a form on the page, Dreamweaver will prompt you to create one.

2. **Click the Spry Validation Select button in the Spry category of the Insert bar.**

   Depending on your preferences, the Input Tag Accessibility Attributes window may appear. Fill in the fields as needed (see Figure 7-7 for an example of one possibility). Click OK. The window will disappear, even if you didn't add any information.

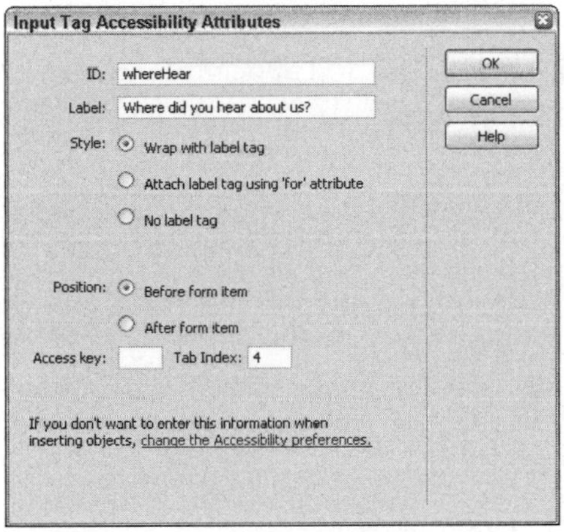

Figure 7-7: Adding Accessibility attributes is good standard practice.

3. **If you want choosing an option to be mandatory, leave the Do Not Allow Blank Value check box selected, as it is by default.**
4. **If you have options in your select menu that you don't want users to be able to select, select the Do Not Allow Invalid Value check box and enter an invalid value (the default, –1, should work just fine).**
5. **Select a Preview state from the Preview States select menu to see what the field will look like in each of three states if you make the field required (which it is by default). You must be in Design view to see the Preview state.**

   The states may include:

   - **Initial:** What the field looks like when the user first loads the page in a browser.
   - **Required:** What the field looks like when the field is required but is left blank.
   - **Invalid Format:** How the field appears when the user enters information in a format invalid for the type (for example, an e-mail without an @ sign).
   - **Valid:** What the field looks like when the user has entered valid information.

Other states may appear depending on what you choose elsewhere in the Property inspector.

6. **Click the select menu in your form in the Document window.**

   The Property inspector updates to show the List/Menu options.

7. **Click the List Values button.**

   The List Values window appears.

8. **Click in the Item Label column and enter an Item Label.**

   The Item Label is the option as it will appear to the user.

9. **Click the same line in the Value column and enter a value for the option.**

   The value is what the form will return when the user clicks the Submit button.

10. **Click the Plus (+) button to add another list value, and continue until you have entered all the values; then click OK to close the window.**

    Note that in Figure 7-8, we've assigned "Select one" a value of –1 so that a user may not submit the form if he or she chooses that option.

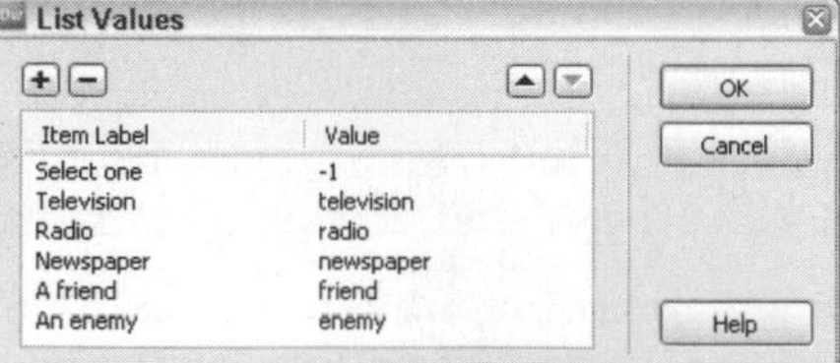

Figure 7-8: Adding list values to the Spry Select menu.

11. **If you want a particular option to be selected when the user first loads the page in a browser, click the option in the Initially Selected menu.**

12. **Click anywhere in the document page to deselect the Select menu.**

    You can press F12 to preview the Select menu in a browser. You may be prompted to save the page. If so, click Yes. The dialog box will disappear and the page will load in your default browser.

Adding a Spry Checkbox

If you want an easy way to make a certain number of check boxes required, create Spry Checkboxes on your page. To do so, follow these steps:

1. **Click in the canvas where you want the check box to go.**

2. **Select the Spry Validation check box in the Spry category of the Insert bar.**

   Depending on your preference settings, the Input Tag Accessibility Attributes window may appear. If it does, enter information as you see fit. It's a good practice to make your forms accessible to people with impaired sight. For information about the accessibility attributes, see your documentation. Whether you enter attributes or not, click OK to close the window.

   If you haven't yet created a form on your page, a dialog box may appear asking if you want to add a form tag. Click Yes. The dialog box will disappear and the Spry Checkbox will appear in your document, as shown in Figure 7-9.

3. **Select Required (Single) if you want users to have to select at least one check box; select Enforce Range (Multiple) if you want users to have to select at least two check boxes.**

   If you select Enforce Range, enter a minimum number of boxes the user must select in the Min # of Selections field. If you don't want users to be able to select more than a certain number of boxes, enter that number in the Max # of Selections field.

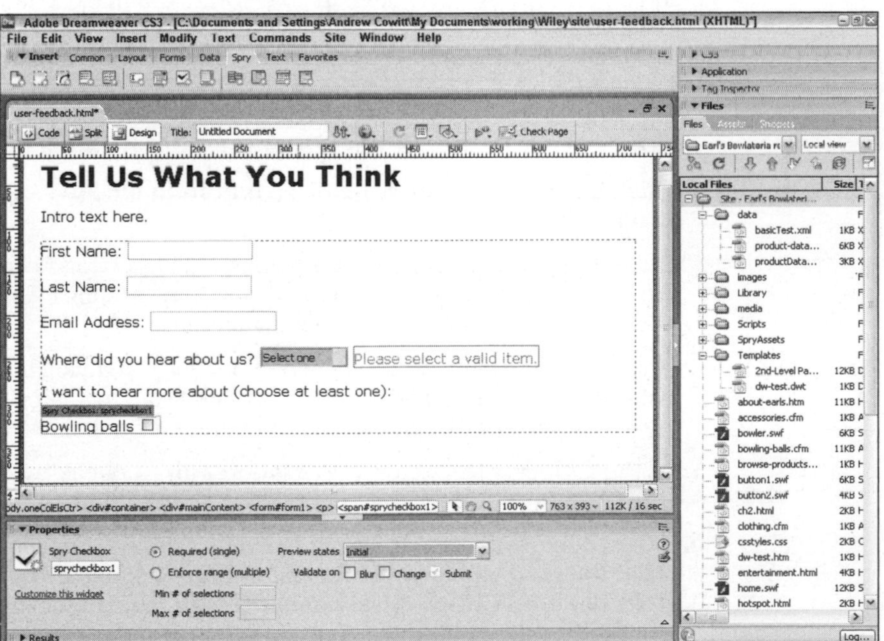

Figure 7-9: Adding a Spry Checkbox.

4. **Select a Preview state from the Preview States select menu to see what the field will look like in each of three states if you make the field required (which it is by default).**

   You must be in Design view to see the Preview state.

   See Step 5 in "Adding a Spry Select menu" for details.

5. **Choose an action that triggers the field's validation by selecting one of the Validate On check boxes.**

   By default, fields are validated on Submit, that is, when the user clicks the form's Submit button. You can also choose Blur (when the user clicks anywhere else on the page after entering information in the field) or Change (when the user begins inputting data in the field).

6. **Add more check boxes as necessary by starting again at Step 1. Press the Enter key or click anywhere in the Document window when you're finished.**

   If you're enforcing a range, be sure to match the Min # of Selections and Max # of Selections for each check box you create.

Adding a Spry Textarea

When you create a Spry Textarea in your form, you make a multiline input field in which users can enter several lines of text. You can set minimum and maximum character amounts, add a character counter, and make the field required. To create a Spry Textarea in your form, simply follow these steps.

1. **Click in your Document where you want the Textarea to go.**
2. **Click the Spry Validation Textarea button in the Spry category of the Insert bar.**

   Depending on your preference settings, the Input Tag Accessibility Attributes window may appear. See Step 2 in "Adding a Spry Checkbox," the preceding section, for more information.

   If you haven't yet created a form on your page, a dialog box may appear asking if you want to add a form tag. Click Yes. The dialog box will disappear, and the Spry Textarea will appear in your document.

3. **In the Property inspector, leave the Required check box selected if you want to require users to enter text in the textarea.**
4. **Select a Preview state from the Preview States select menu to see what the field will look like in each of three states if you make the field required (which it is by default). You must be in Design view to see the Preview state.**

   The states may include:

- **Initial:** What the field looks like when the user first loads the page in a browser.
- **Required:** What the field looks like when the field is required but is left blank.
- **Invalid Format:** How the field appears when the user enters information in a format invalid for the type (for example, an e-mail without an @ sign).
- **Valid:** What the field looks like when the user has entered valid information.

Other states may appear depending on what you choose elsewhere in the Property inspector.

5. **Choose an action that triggers the field's validation by selecting one of the Validate On check boxes.**

   By default, fields are validated on Submit, that is, when the user clicks the form's Submit button. You can also choose Blur (when the user clicks anywhere else on the page after entering information in the field) or Change (when the user begins inputting data in the field).

6. **If you want to set a minimum number of characters that users must enter in the textarea, enter the number in the Min Chars field.**
7. **If you don't want users to input more than a certain number of characters in the textarea, enter that number in the Max Chars field.**

   By default, if you enter a Max Chars limit, the Block Extra Characters check box is selected. When this box is selected, users cannot enter more than the maximum number of characters you specify.

   Also, if you enter a Max Chars limit, you can add a character counter that will appear in the user's browser indicating either the number of characters entered (Chars Count) or the number of allowed characters not yet entered (Chars Remaining).

8. **Optional: If you want to include instructions in the textarea itself, enter text in the Hint field in the Spry Textarea Property inspector.**

   We put the hint " Up to 200 characters," as shown in Figure 7-10.

If you want to edit the non-Spry properties of any of your Spry Validation form elements, simply click the element to select it and enter the properties in the Property inspector. You can mix non-Spry form elements with Spry form elements. In fact, there's no Spry Submit button, so you need to add the button from the Forms category of the Insert bar. See Book II, Chapter 4 for more information about creating and modifying forms.

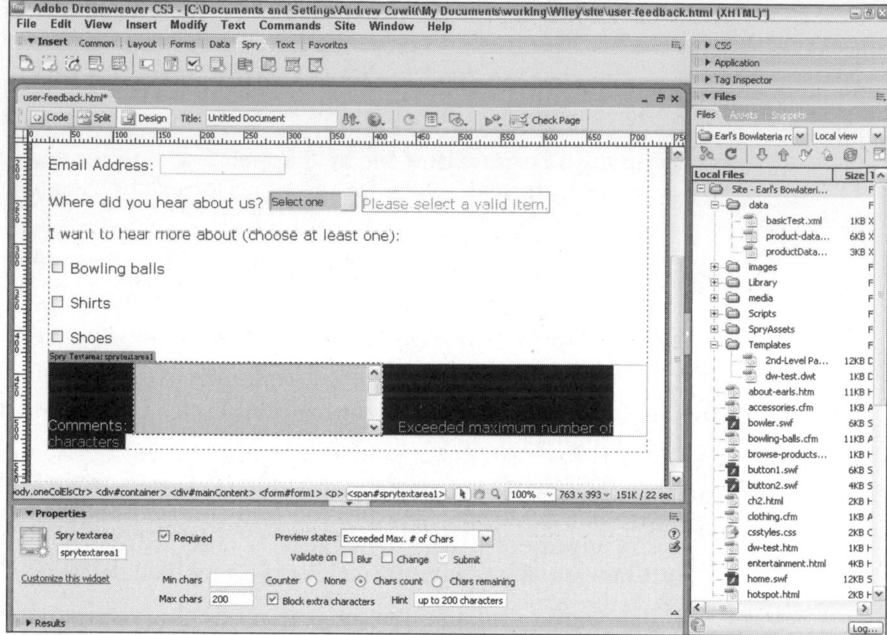

Figure 7-10: Providing a hint in the Spry Textarea.

Adding Spry Navigation Widgets

Spry Navigation widgets offer you a simple way to add flashy navigation to your site. Apart from being cool, the chief advantage of Spry navigation widgets is that they save plenty of space. You can have

- ✦ Multilevel menus that appear only when a user rolls over a specified area, with the extra levels appearing to hover above the page
- ✦ Panels that share the same space on a page, which users can activate by clicking the associated tabs
- ✦ Panels with detail areas that appear to slide open while other detail areas appear to close
- ✦ Panels with detail areas that the user can make appear and disappear, affecting other elements on the page

Inserting a Spry Menu Bar

A Spry Menu Bar is essentially a multilevel pop-up menu of the kind that first appeared on the Web scene with the advent of DHTML. If you are building a site that has two or more levels of navigation and much information to squeeze on every page, Spry Menu Bars are for you.

To create a Spry Menu Bar on a page, follow these steps:

1. **Click in your document where you want to put the menu bar.**
2. **Click the Spry Menu Bar button in the Spry category of the Insert bar.**

   The Spry Menu Bar window appears.
3. **Choose either Horizontal (menu items appear side by side) or Vertical (menu items arranged top to bottom) and click OK.**

   The Spry Menu Bar window closes and the menu bar appears in your document, with placeholder text for each top-level menu item and three second-level items for each top-level item.
4. **Click the first item in the left-hand list (top-level items); then, click in the Text field on the right and enter what the menu item should say.**
5. **Enter a link for the menu item by typing it in the Link field or clicking the Folder icon and browsing to the page you want to link to.**
6. **Click the first item in the middle list (second-level items); then, click in the Text field on the right and enter what the menu item should say.**
7. **Enter a link for the second-level menu item.**

   Click each of the second-level items in turn and follow the same procedure.
8. **If you have third-level links, click the top-level menu item in the first column, the second-level link in the second column, and the Add button (+) in the third column.**

   A new Untitled Item appears in the third column, highlighted, as shown in Figure 7-11.
9. **Enter Text and Link information in the Text and Link fields on the right.**
10. **Continue until you have fully populated your menu as needed.**

    To remove an item from any column, click to select it and click the Remove Menu Item (–) button above that column.
11. **Choose File➪Save or press Ctrl+S to save your changes.**

    If this is the first Spry Menu Bar widget you've added to your site, Dreamweaver will let you know that the applicable Spry Assets will be copied to the SpryAssets directory in your site.

    After you've saved your document, you can preview it in a browser by choosing File➪Preview in Browser➪*Browser Name* or by pressing F12.

When you remove a top-level or second-level link, all links below it in the hierarchy (also known as child links) are removed at the same time. If you try to remove a parent link, Dreamweaver will alert you that the child links of that parent will also be deleted.

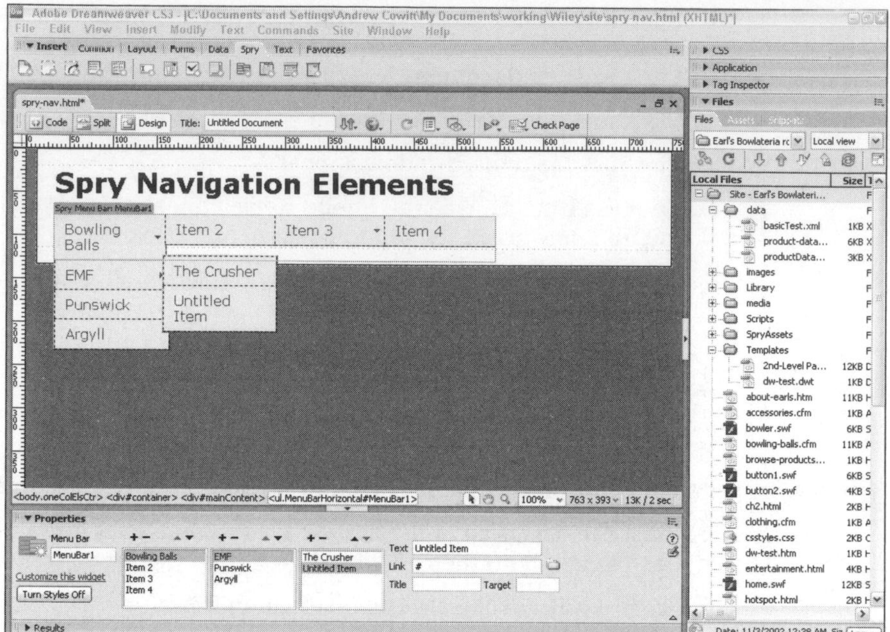

Figure 7-11: Adding a third-level menu item.

To change the position of an item, click to select it and use the Up arrow to put the item before others or the Down arrow to put the item after others.

Inserting a Spry Tabbed Panel

If you use a modern browser — Safari, Mozilla, or Internet Explorer 7, for example — you know about the advantages of tabbed browsing. You can go to a new page in the browser without opening a new window or browsing away from your previous page. Spry Tabbed Panels provide the same effect but do so on a single Web page. The user can't look at the contents of two Tabbed Panels simultaneously, but the user can click different tabs to see the contents of their associated panels in a single space on the page, without the page having to reload in a browser.

To create a Spry Tabbed Panel, follow these steps:

1. **Click in the canvas where you want the tabbed panel to go.**
2. **Click the Spry Tabbed Panel button on the Spry category of the Insert bar.**

   A Spry Tabbed Panels widget appears in the document, with two tabs, and the Property inspector updates to show the Tabbed Panels options, as shown in Figure 7-12.

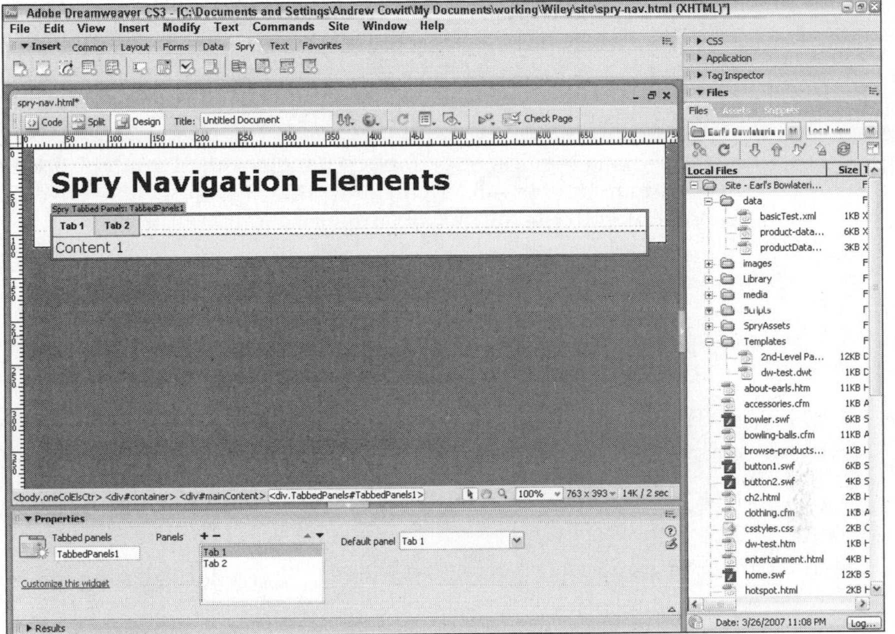

Figure 7-12: Adding Spry Tabbed Panels to a document.

3. **Click and drag across the Tab 1 text in the document to select it, and enter your own text for the first tab.**

4. **Click and drag across the Content 1 placeholder text and insert the content that should appear on the page when the user clicks the tab on the left.**

   You can insert nearly anything in a panel that you'll find in the Common tab of the Insert bar.

5. **Repeat the preceding Steps 3 and 4 for Tab 2.**

6. **If you want to add another tab, click the Spry Tabbed Panels label in the document to select the widget; otherwise, skip to Step 8.**

   You can also click anywhere along the light-blue border of the widget to select it. The border will be highlighted and the Property inspector will be updated to display the Tabbed Panels options.

7. **Click the Add Panel (+) button in the Tabbed Panels Property inspector.**

   A new tab (named Tab 3 by default) appears in the document and in the panels column. Repeat the preceding Steps 3 and 4 for the third tab. If you want to add another panel, repeat this step until you have as many tabs as you want.

8. **If you don't want the left panel to be the one that's visible when the user first loads the page in a browser, you can select a different Default panel from the menu on the right of the Tabbed Panels Property inspector.**
9. **Choose File⇨Save or press Ctrl+S to save your changes.**

   If this is the first Spry Tabbed Panels widget you've added to your site, Dreamweaver will let you know that the applicable Spry Assets will be copied to the SpryAssets directory in your site.

   After you've saved your document, you can preview it in a browser by choosing File⇨Preview in Browser⇨*Browser Name* or by pressing F12.

Inserting a Spry Accordion

The Spry Accordion widget works in a similar way to the Spry Tabbed Panels widget. The Accordion has two main differences:

- ✦ The tab that a user clicks to view a different panel is a long, narrow strip by default.
- ✦ The selected panel appears to slide open, obscuring the previously open panel.

To add a Spry Accordion to your page, simply follow these steps:

1. **Click in the canvas where you want the tabbed panel to go.**
2. **Click the Spry Accordion button on the Spry category of the Insert bar.**

   A Spry Accordion widget appears in the document, with two labels, and the Properties panel updates to show the Accordion options. Label 1, the top strip, is selected by default.
3. **Click and drag across the Label 1 text in the document window and insert the content you want the user to click in order to view the contents of the top panel.**

   You can put any element in the tab. Try to use something that describes the contents of the panel.
4. **Click and drag across the Content 1 text to highlight it and enter content in the first panel, as shown in Figure 7-13.**

   You can insert pretty much any content in the panel that you can find in the Common category of the Insert bar. In Figure 7-13, we've included only text.
5. **Click and drag to select the Label 2 text in the document window and enter the descriptive text a user will click to view the second panel.**

   Notice that when the tab is active in the document window, an eye icon appears at the far right of the tab. Click the eye icon to view the panel content for the tab.

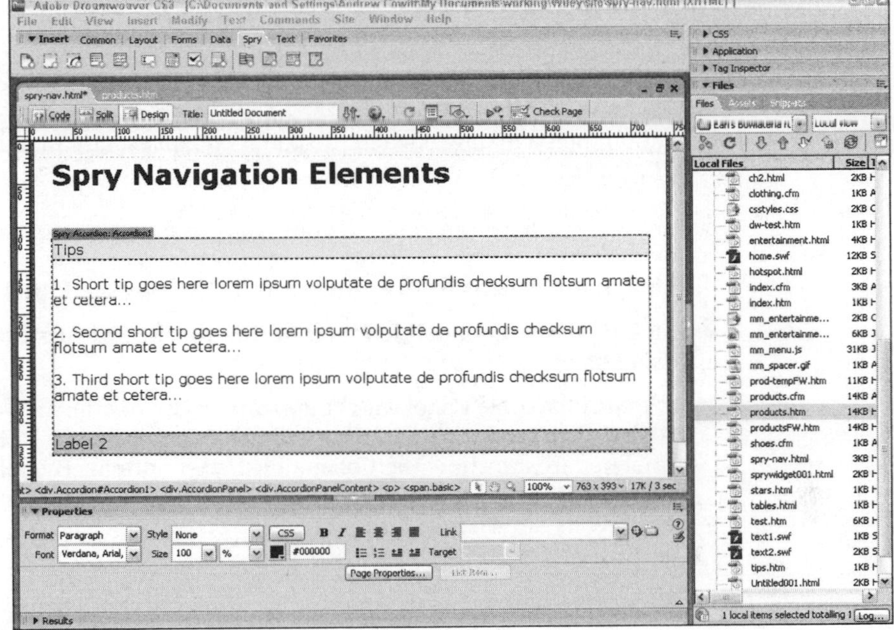

Figure 7-13: Adding content to panel 1 of a Spry Accordion widget.

6. **Insert content in the second panel.**
7. **If you want to add another tab, click the Spry Accordion label in the document to select the widget. Otherwise, skip to Step 9.**

   You can also click anywhere along the light-blue border of the widget to select it. The border will be highlighted and the Property inspector will be updated to display the Tabbed Panels options.

8. **Click the Add Panel (+) button in the Accordion Property inspector.**

   A new tab (named Label 3 by default) appears in the document and in the panels column. Repeat the preceding Steps 3 and 4 for the third tab. If you want to add another panel, repeat this step until you have as many tabs as you want.

9. **Choose File➪Save or press Ctrl+S to save your changes.**

   If this is the first Spry Accordion widget you've added to your site, Dreamweaver will let you know that the applicable Spry Assets will be copied to the SpryAssets directory in your site.

   After you've saved your document, you can preview it in a browser by choosing File➪Preview in Browser➪*Browser Name* or by pressing F12.

Inserting a Spry Collapsible Panel

As with the Spry Tabbed Panels and Accordion widgets, the Spry Collapsible Panel allows you to hide content on your page until the user does something to make the content visible. When the panel expands, it pushes everything below it on the page down; when the panel collapses, anything below it on the page moves up.

To add a Spry Collapsible Panel to your page, follow these steps:

1. **Click in the canvas where you want the Collapsible Panel to go.**
2. **Click the Spry Collapsible Panel button on the Spry category of the Insert bar.**

   A Spry Collapsible Panel widget appears in the document, with a tab labeled "Tab" and a panel with the default text "Content." The Properties panel updates to show the Collapsible Panel options. By default, Display and Default State are set to Open, and the Enable Animation check box is selected, as shown in Figure 7-14.

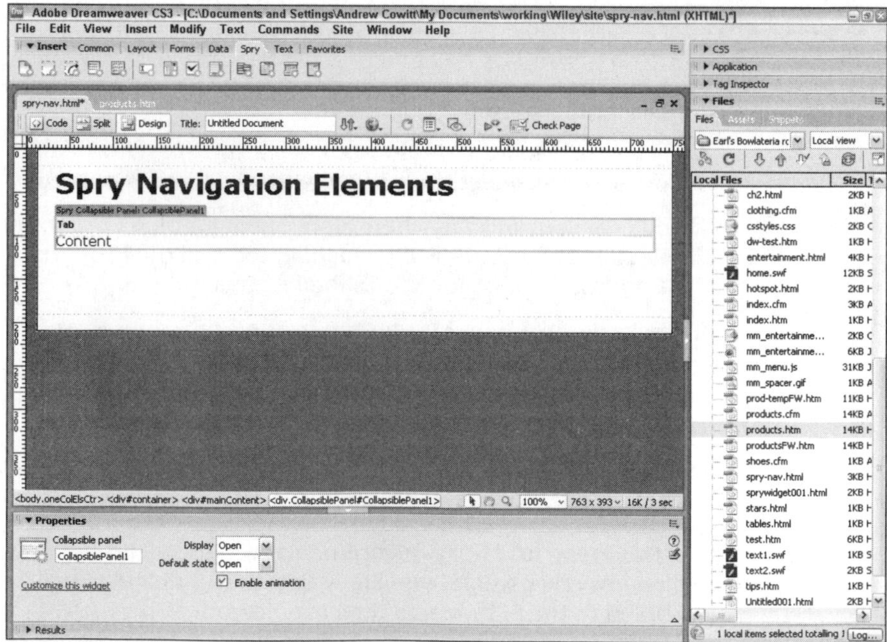

Figure 7-14: Adding a Spry Collapsible Panel to a document.

3. **Click and drag to select the Tab text in the document window and insert your own descriptive text that the user will click to open and close the panel.**

   The text might be something like "Details" or it might be a more generic "Show/Hide."

4. **Click and drag to select the Content default text and insert content into the panel.**

   Content may include anything you can add to a document via the Common tab of the Insert panel, as well as any other Web content.

5. **If you want to preview the Open or Closed state of the panel within the document window, change the Display select menu to Open or Closed.**

   You can also roll over the tab and click the eye icon at the right of the tab to display or hide the panel.

6. **Choose either Open or Closed in the Default State menu to make the panel appear open or closed when the user loads the page in a browser.**

7. **If you want to disable the animation effect of the panel sliding open and closed when the user clicks the tab, deselect the Enable Animation check box.**

   If you disable the animation, the panel will appear and disappear abruptly when the user clicks the tab.

8. **Choose File⇨Save or press Ctrl+S to save your changes.**

   If this is the first Spry Collapsible Panel widget you've added to your site, Dreamweaver will let you know that the applicable Spry Assets will be copied to the SpryAssets directory in your site.

   After you've saved your document, you can preview it in a browser by choosing File⇨Preview in Browser⇨*Browser Name* or by pressing F12.

Dazzling Users with Spry Effects

Elsewhere in this chapter, we show you how to use Spry widgets to display XML data sets, to create multilevel navigation bars, and to show and hide content. In this section, we discuss the Spry widgets that add pizzazz to your page without necessarily having a more practical purpose (except perhaps drawing attention to a particular chunk of content). As with the Spry widgets, the changes in appearance happen without any reloading of the page in the browser.

Dreamweaver CS3 ships with Spry effects widgets that make content appear to do the following:

- ✦ Fade in and out
- ✦ Appear and disappear as if being revealed/obscured by a blind
- ✦ Grow and shrink
- ✦ Highlight
- ✦ Shake
- ✦ Slide up and down
- ✦ Squish
- ✦ Any combination of the preceding

Spry effects don't work on all objects. For example, you can add a Fade effect to an image, but you can't add a Blind effect to an image. You can add a Blind effect to a div that includes an image, though. If you apply an effect and it doesn't seem to be working, check the Help files to make sure that the effect you're applying can be applied to the object you're trying to affect.

Effects depend on two objects:

- ✦ **The triggering object:** The linked text or button that triggers the effect based on a user action such as clicking the mouse. To add an empty link to an object (a link that doesn't go anywhere), select the object and input the pound sign (#) in the Link field in the Properties panel.
- ✦ **The affected object:** The object that changes when triggered. This object must have an ID (you can add an ID in the Properties panel or the Attributes panel).

After you've added a Spry effect, you must save your document in order to preview the effect in a browser. The first time you save after adding a Spry effect, the Copy Dependent Files window appears, letting you know that the `SpryEffects.js` file will be placed in the `SpryAssets` directory in your site. Click OK to add the file and close the window. Do not delete the `SpryEffects.js` file from your site—it's required to make the effects work. And don't forget to copy the Spry directories to your Web server with the rest of your site files.

Making objects fade in and out

You can make objects fade in or out when a user performs a specified action, or when the page first loads in a browser. You could think of the Spry fade effect as kind of a slow-motion button rollover.

The Appear/Fade effect won't work with the following objects: `applet`, `body`, `iFrame`, `object`, `tr`, `tbody`, and `th`.

We're assuming that the object you want to add the effect to, and the trigger for the effect, are in your document already. The object you want to add the effect to must have an ID, which you can add by selecting the object and entering characters in the ID field of the Properties panel. To add a fade to an object (text, an image, or a div, for example), follow these steps:

1. **In the document window, select the object you want to use as a trigger.**
2. **Click the Add (+) button in the Behaviors panel (you can find Behaviors as a category of the Tag panel).**

   If the Behaviors panel isn't open, choose Window Behaviors or press Shift+F4.
3. **Choose Effects⇨Appear/Fade from the pop-up menu.**

   The Appear/Fade window appears, as shown in Figure 7-15.

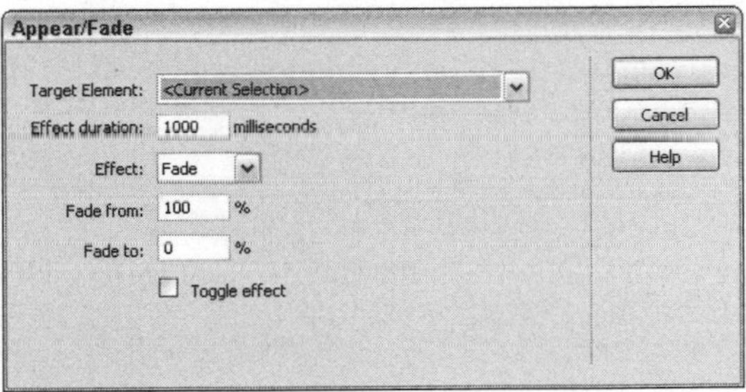

Figure 7-15: Adding the Appear/Fade Spry effect to an image.

4. **For target element, select the object that you want to apply Appear/Fade to.**

   If you don't see the object in the select menu, check to make sure that it has an ID and that the effect can be applied to its type of object.
5. **Enter a number in milliseconds for the amount of time you want the effect to last in the Effect Duration field.**

   One thousand milliseconds equals 1 second; 2000 milliseconds is 2 seconds; 500 milliseconds is, you guessed it, half of one second. You want the effect to last long enough to be noticeable but not so long that the user gets frustrated waiting for the effect to end.

6. **Choose an effect from the Effect select list.**

   Your choices are Fade (start visible and slowly become less visible or invisible) or Appear (start less visible or invisible and become more visible).

7a. **If you selected Fade in Step 6, you can set the visibility at the start (Fade From) and end (Fade To) of the effect by entering a number from 0 to 100 in the Fade fields.**

   One hundred would be totally visible; 0 is totally invisible.

7b. **If you selected Appear in Step 6, you can set the visibility at the start (Appear From) and end (Appear To) of the effect by entering a number from 0 to 100 in the Appear fields.**

   Zero is totally invisible; 100 is totally visible.

8. **If you want the user to be able to toggle the effect on and off, select the Toggle Effect check box.**

9. **Click OK.**

   The Appear/Fade window disappears and the behavior shows in the Behaviors panel. By default, the behavior is triggered when the user clicks the trigger with the behavior applied to it. You can click `onClick` in the action column of the Behavior panel and choose a different trigger from the select menu that appears.

Applying the Open/Close Blind effect

When you add the Blind effect, the user can see an object seem to appear or disappear as if it is behind a blind or curtain.

This effect cannot be applied to images. It can be applied to the following HTML objects: `address`, `dd`, `div`, `dl`, `dt`, `form`, `h1` through `h6`, `p`, `ol`, `ul`, `li`, `applet`, `center`, `dir`, `menu`, and `pre`.

Adding the effect to an object is essentially identical to making objects fade in or out (see the steps in the preceding "Making objects fade in and out" section), so we're saving some space here as we describe how to apply the Blind effect:

1. **Follow Steps 1 and 2 in the preceding set of steps.**
2. **Choose Effects⇨Blind from the pop-up menu.**

   The Blind window appears.

3. **Select a Target Element and enter an amount in the Effect Duration field, as per Steps 4 and 5 above.**

4. **Choose an effect from the Effect select menu.**

   Your choices are Blind Up (the object is visible) and Blind Down (the object seems to disappear behind the blinds).

5a. **If you selected Blind Up in Step 4, you can set the visibility at the start (Blind Up From) and end (Blind Up To) of the effect by entering a number from 0 to 100 in the Blind Up fields.**

   One hundred is totally visible; 0 is totally obscured.

5b. **If you selected Blind Down in Step 4, you can set the visibility at the start (Blind Down From) and end (Blind Down To) of the effect by entering a number from 0 to 100 in the Blind Down fields.**

   Zero obscures the object completely; 100 makes the object completely visible.

6. **If desired, select the Toggle Effect check box and click OK.**

   See Step 9 in the steps in the preceding "Making objects fade in and out" section for details.

Making objects grow and shrink

The Spry Grow/Shrink effect doesn't simply make objects grow or shrink in place. Instead, it moves them as it shrinks, either diagonally to the bottom-left or top-left corner, or toward/from the center.

To save space, we refer to the previous steps for "Making objects fade in and out" where they apply equally to making objects grow and shrink.

1. **Follow Steps 1 and 2 in "Making objects fade in and out."**

2. **Choose Effects⇨Grow/Shrink from the pop-up menu.**

   The Grow/Shrink window appears.

3. **Select a Target Element and enter an Effect Duration, as per Steps 4 and 5 from "Making objects fade in and out."**

4. **Choose an Effect from the Effect select menu.**

   Your choices are Shrink and Grow.

5a. **If you selected Shrink in Step 4, you can set the size at the start (Shrink From) and end (Shrink To) of the effect by entering a number from 0 to 100 in the Shrink fields; then, select either Shrink to Center or Shrink to Top Left Corner.**

   One hundred is full size; 0 is invisibly small.

5b. If you selected Grow in Step 4, you can set the size at the start (Grow From) and end (Grow To) of the effect by entering a number in the fields; then, select either Grow to Center or Grow to Top Left Corner.

Zero obscures the object completely; 100 makes the object full size. You can use a number higher than 100 (200, for example, would be double-size), but be aware that you might grow your object right off the page!

6. If desired, select the Toggle Effect check box and click OK.

See Step 9 in the previous "Making objects fade in and out" section for details.

Highlighting with color

The Highlight effect makes an object change from one color to another (typically, you would use this effect to change the background color of a paragraph, a div, or even a whole page). As with other Spry effects, you can set how quickly or slowly the change takes place and whether the user can toggle the effect back and forth.

To use the highlight effect to change the background color of a div, follow these steps:

1. **In the document window, select the object you want to use as a trigger.**
2. **Click the Add (+) button in the Behaviors panel (you can find Behaviors as a category of the Tag panel).**

   If the Behaviors panel isn't open, choose Window Behaviors or press Shift+F4.
3. **Choose Effects Highlight.**

   The Highlight window appears.
4. **For Target Element, select the div whose background color you want to change.**

   If you don't see the object in the Target Element select menu, check to make sure it has an ID and that the effect can be applied to its type of object.
5. **Enter a number in milliseconds for the amount of time you want the effect to last in the Effect Duration field.**

   One thousand milliseconds equals 1 second; 2000 milliseconds is 2 seconds; 500 milliseconds is half of one second. You want the effect to last long enough to be noticeable but not so long that the user gets frustrated waiting for the effect to end.

6. **Set the Start Color either by clicking the color box and choosing a color via the color picker or by entering the color's hexadecimal equivalent in the Start Color text field.**

   See Book IV, Chapter 3 for details on using the color picker. If the start color is different from the existing background color of the div, the div will change color abruptly to the start color and then proceed to the end color at the rate you set in the Effect Duration field.

7. **Set the End Color either by clicking the color box and choosing a color via the color picker or by entering the color's hexadecimal equivalent in the End Color text field.**

8. **Set the Color After Effect either by clicking the color box and choosing a color via the color picker or by entering the color's hexadecimal equivalent in the Color After Effect text field.**

   The Color After Effect is the color that the object retains at the end of the effect. That color does not have to be the same one as the original color of the object, but that would be a typical implementation. The switch from the End Color to the Color After Effect is abrupt (unless the Color After Effect is identical to the end color, in which case there's no switch at all).

9. **If you want the user to be able to toggle the effect on and off, select the Toggle Effect check box.**

10. **Click OK.**

    The Highlight window disappears and the behavior shows in the Behaviors panel. By default, the behavior is triggered when the user clicks the trigger with the behavior applied to it. You can click `onClick` in the action column of the Behavior panel and choose a different trigger from the select menu that appears.

Shaking up an object

The Shake Spry effect moves an object back and forth three times. It's one of the simplest Spry effects to apply to an object because it doesn't permit you to choose any options (at least not in the current implementation of Spry as of this writing). To add the effect to an object, simply click the Add Effect button (the + sign) in the Behaviors panel, select a Target Element (the object you want to shake), and click OK.

Sliding an object up or down

Sliding is similar to the Blind effect, except that instead of remaining stationary while the effect obscures or shows the element, sliding makes everything in a div move up as it disappears or down as it appears. The Slide effect can be applied only to a single "container" div.

To add the Slide effect to a div, follow these steps:

1. **In the document window, select the object that you want to use as a trigger.**
2. **Click the Add (+) button in the Behaviors panel (you can find Behaviors as a category of the Tag panel).**

   If the Behaviors panel isn't open, choose Window Behaviors or press Shift+F4.
3. **Select the div from the Target Element menu, as shown in Figure 7-16.**

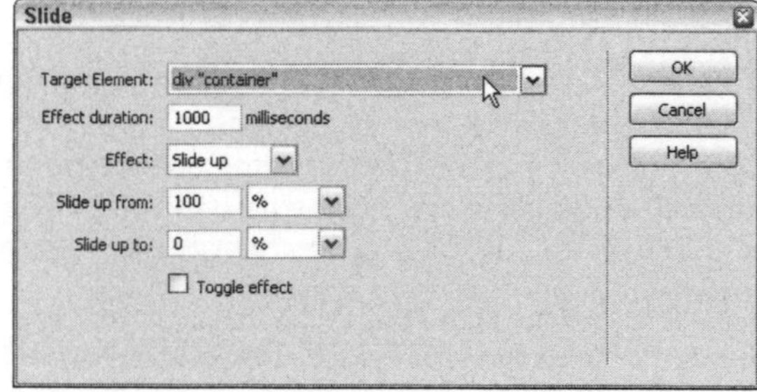

Figure 7-16: We gave our targeted div the id "container."

4. **Choose either Slide Up or Slide Down in the Effect menu.**

   Slide Up will start with the div fully or partially visible and end with the div partially or fully hidden. Slide Down will do the opposite.

5a. **If you choose Slide Up in Step 4, enter a number in the Slide Up From field, and select either % or pixels for the number. Proceed to Step 6a.**

   The default of 100% means that the full div appears before the effect is applied. If you choose pixels, and you choose a lower number than the actual height of the div, the top of the div will seem to be hidden at the start of the slide.

5b. **If you choose Slide Down in Step 4, enter a number in the Slide Down To field and select either % or pixels for the number. Proceed to Step 6b.**

   The default of 0% means that the div would be totally hidden at the end of the effect. If you choose a pixel number instead, and the number is lower than the height of the div, some of the div will remain visible at the end of the effect.

6a. If you choose Slide Up in Step 4, enter a number in the Slide Up To field and select either % or pixels for the number.

The default of 0% means that the div would be totally hidden at the end of the effect. If you choose a pixel number instead, and the number is lower than the height of the div, some of the div will remain visible at the end of the effect.

6b. If you choose Slide Down in Step 4, enter a number in the Slide Down From field and select either % or pixels for the number.

The default of 100% means the full div appears at the end of the effect. If you choose pixels, and you choose a lower number than the actual height of the div, the top of the div will seem to be hidden at the end of the slide.

7. **If you want the user to be able to toggle the div up and down by clicking repeatedly, select the Toggle Effect check box.**
8. **Click OK.**

   The Slide window disappears and the behavior shows in the Behaviors panel. By default, the behavior is triggered when the user clicks the trigger with the behavior applied to it. You can click `onClick` in the action column of the Behavior panel and choose a different trigger from the select menu that appears.

Squishing an object

Squish lets a user toggle an object so that it appears to move up and away into the top-left corner. It's one of the simplest Spry effects to apply to an object because it doesn't permit you to choose any options (at least not in the current implementation of Spry as of this writing). To add the effect to an object, simply click the Add Effect button (the + sign) in the Behaviors panel, select a Target Element (the object you want to squish) and click OK.

Combining effects

You can combine effects easily by simply selecting the trigger object and clicking the Add Behavior (+) button. Then just follow any of the previous sets of steps. It is possible to "chain" effects (make them happen one after the other instead of simultaneously), but that takes some programming know-how that's beyond the scope of this book. As you work with Spry Effects, you can always check out much of how things work by using Code view in the Document window. For now, though, celebrate how easy it is in Dreamweaver to add dynamism to your Web pages with Spry widgets!

Book II

Photoshop CS3

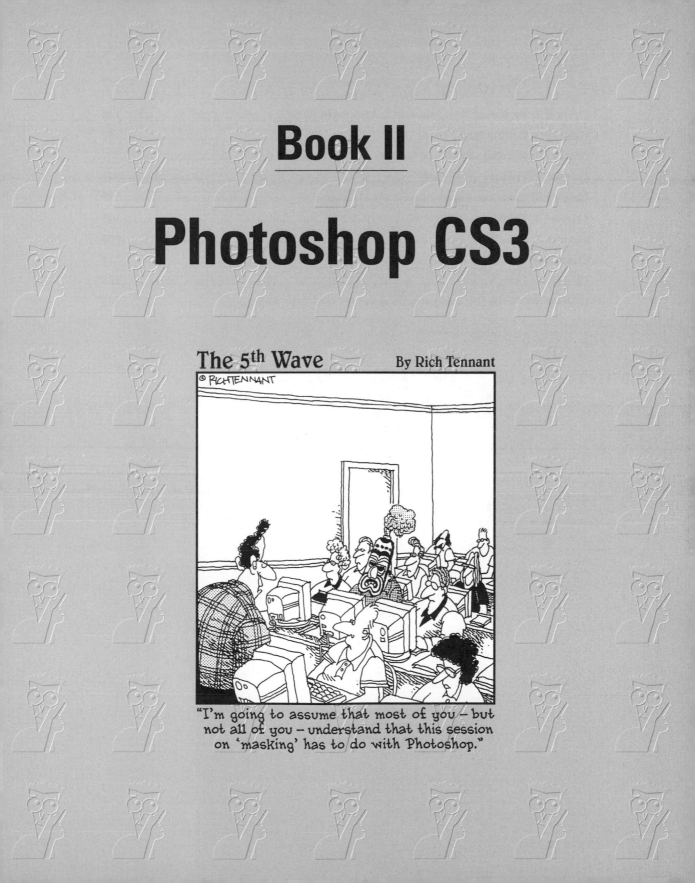

The 5th Wave
By Rich Tennant
© RICHTENNANT
"I'm going to assume that most of you – but not all of you – understand that this session on 'masking' has to do with Photoshop."

Chapter 1: Exploring New Features in Photoshop CS3

In This Chapter

- Working with the new interface
- Getting smart with filters
- Improving curve corrections

Photoshop CS3 includes significant improvements to the workspace, filters, and selection tools. In this chapter, you take a quick tour of some of most exciting new capabilities. The features you see depend on the Photoshop that you have (Standard or Extended).

This quick rundown of what is new and exciting in Photoshop CS3 is hopefully a help to you as you start experimenting with the new tools and features.

If you really want to dive into the new features, choose Window⇨Workspace⇨What's New In CS3. Instantly all new features are highlighted in the menus!

A New Efficient Workspace

As soon as you launch Photoshop CS3, the more efficient workspace — meaning more space is available for you to work on your images — is apparent (see Figure 1-1).

The toolbar is now single column. If you don't like the change in the toolbar, you can return to the old two-column display by clicking the gray bar at the top of the toolbar.

Additionally, palettes are collapsed to a compact view and represented by icons, saving even more space. The new workspace makes focusing on the images easier, and the tools become a natural extension of your work.

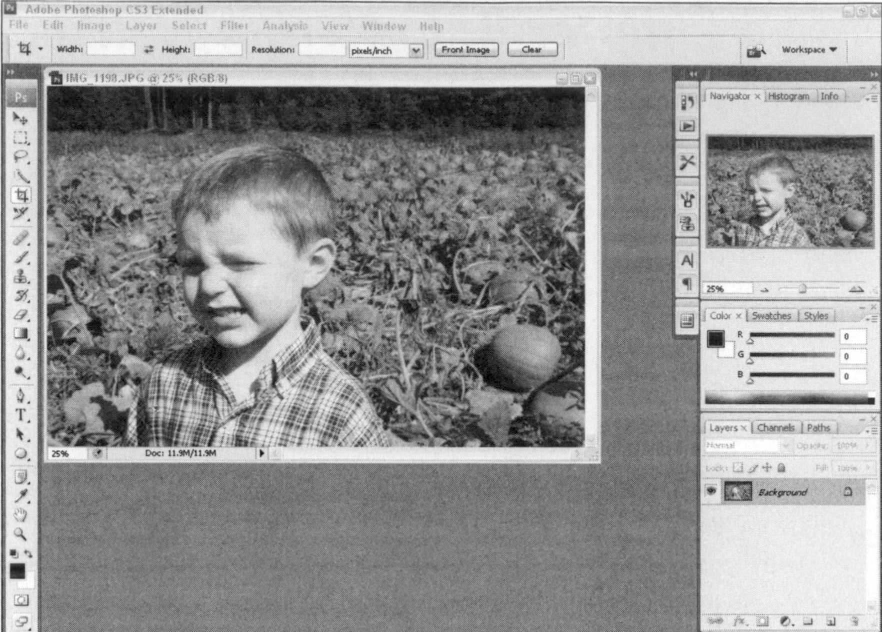

Figure 1-1: The new space-saving Photoshop CS3 workspace.

Photoshop continues to make extensive use of palettes. To activate a palette in this new version, simply click the appropriate palette icon. If you select another palette icon, its pane is brought to the front of the display. You can return them to icons by clicking the Collapse To Icons bar at the top of the palette drawer. When an icon is dragged out to the work area, it automatically expands and then returns to an icon when dragged back into dock.

Showing and hiding all your tools and palettes is easier as well. Press the Tab key to hide all your tools and palettes. To cause them to reappear, move your cursor over the left or right side of your screen and pause at the vertical gray bar.

Do you have Standard or Extended?

How can you tell whether you have Photoshop Standard or Extended? If you purchase the master, Design Premium, or Web Premium Suite, you have Photoshop Extended.

Do you need Extended? Most likely not. The typical designer, whether Web or print, will most likely never need the advanced tools that separate Standard from Extended.

But if you're into 3D, life sciences, manufacturing, or the medical field, you may want to take advantage of the 3D, counting, and analysis tools now available in Photoshop.

Super Selection Tools and Features

If you want the ability to paint your selections, you'll love the new Quick Selection tool. With this tool, you can easily brush over the image area that you want to select. By default, additional strokes with the Quick Selection tool add to the selection. You can delete by holding down Alt (Option on a Mac) as you stroke. The toolbar provides more options, including New Selection, Add To Selection, and Subtract From Selection buttons.

The new Refine Edge button, available from any of the selection tool's options, is quite helpful in cleaning up selections or adding feathering to create a vignette of a selection. All of these options are available in a preview window that includes choices for five different ways to preview the selection, as shown in Figure 1-2. (Read more detail about selections in Chapter 4 of this minibook.)

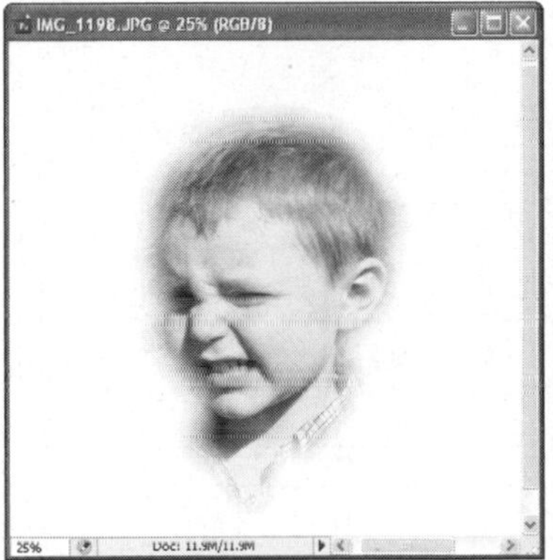

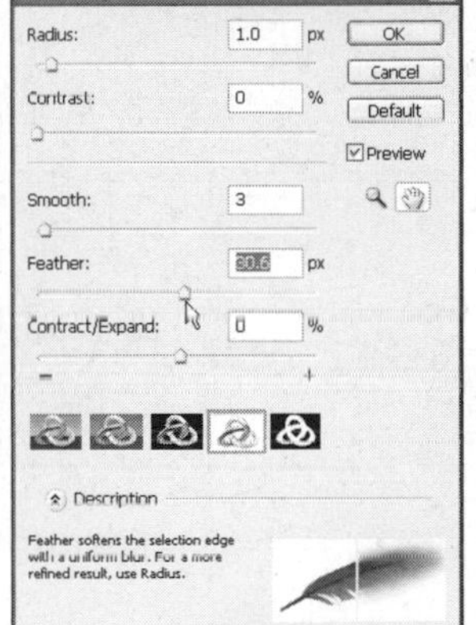

Figure 1-2: The new Refine Edge feature can be used with any of the selection tools.

Smart Filters

Photoshop CS3 has taken nondestructive imaging editing to the max with Smart filters. Don't worry about destroying your image with filters because you can now edit filters after they're applied. When you use a Smart Filter, a Filter effects mask thumbnail appears in the Layer's palette. You can select the mask thumbnail and then, using your paint tools, paint black (or shades of) to change where and how the filter is applied, or paint white to bring back the filter.

You can turn off the Smart Filters by selecting the visibility icon in the Layers palette or adjust filter settings by double-clicking the icon to the right of the listed filter. It's worth experimenting with this feature because you can apply multiple filters. Read more about applying filters in Chapter 8 of this minibook.

Black-and-White Conversion like a Pro

Photoshop CS3 makes creating great-looking black-and-white images easier. With an image open, you can click the Create New Fill or Adjustment Layer button in the Layers palette and then select Black & White. The Black and White dialog box appears, as shown in Figure 1-3. Choose a preset, or customize the color conversion by using the Channel mixer adjustments. If you're converting multiple images, you can save your settings by selecting the Preset options button to the right of the Presets drop-down menu. If you want to experiment with more creative options, use the Tint box and add a color tint to your image as it's converted.

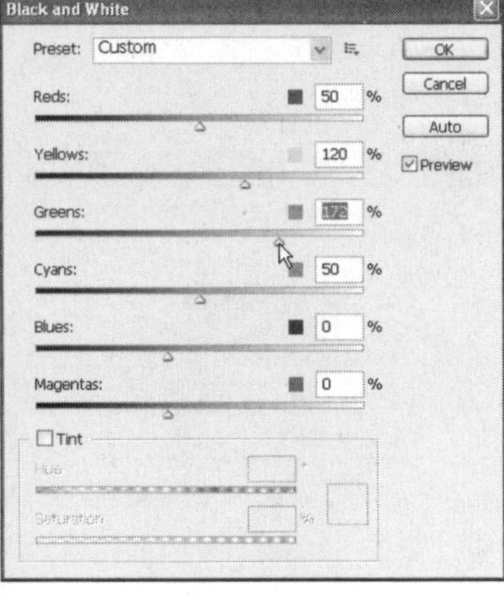

Figure 1-3: Use the Channel Mixer options, as well as other presets, in the new Black & White adjustment layer.

Multiple Planes in Vanishing Point Filter

In Photoshop CS3, you can create images wrapped around multiple perspective planes, which is great if you're creating package design or needing spatial illustrations. To experiment with this incredible feature:

1. **Copy an image and choose Filter⇨Vanishing Point.**

   The Vanishing Point dialog box appears.

2. **Using the Create Plane tool, click four corners to make a perspective plane.**

   Note that the plane is accurate if the grid is blue.

3. **If the grid isn't blue, use the Edit Plane tool to adjust the corners.**
4. **Hold down the Ctrl key (Windows) and drag one of the middle nodes.**

   An additional perspective plane, generated from the original, appears.
5. **Paste your image and drag it into your plane.**

   The image wraps the planes (see Figure 1-4).

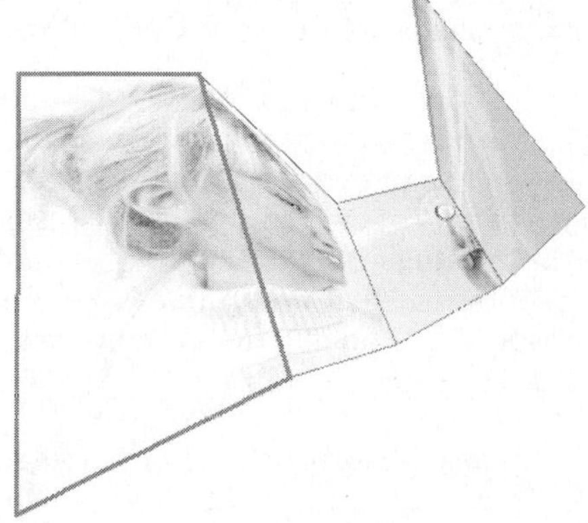

Figure 1-4: An image wrapped around multiple planes.

Even better, Vanishing Point adjusts brush strokes, healing, and cloning as you paint over the planes. Note that in Photoshop CS3, you're no longer restricted to adding planes at 90-degree angles.

Help with Aligning

Ever take several versions of a picture and wish that you could easily combine and align the images to pick the best of each? With the new Align feature, you can do just that:

1. **Drag similar images into a file to create layers.**

   These images may be several versions of a group picture, for example.
2. **Select the Move tool and Shift+click to select the multiple layers.**
3. **Click the Auto-Align Layers button in the options bar.**

   The Auto-Align Layers dialog box appears.
4. **Choose your alignment method and click OK.**

Improved Curve Controls

Check out Image➪Adjustment➪Curves for a look at the new improved curves palette. Wow! It's like a perfect combination of Levels and Curves. If you know that you should use Curves, but like the interface of the Level controls, the improved curve controls are a dream come true. Read about using the Curves palette in Chapter 7 of this minibook.

Performance Improvements on Intel Macintosh

If you're a Macintosh user, you'll appreciate that Adobe has done a great job at porting the software to the Intel-based processors. As a Universal application, the software can run in a native mode on both Intel and PowerPC Macintosh systems. As part of our testing, we've been using both PC and Macintosh systems, both using Intel Core2 Duo processors. The performance is strong on both platforms. Most noticeable is the huge speed improvement between Photoshop CS3 running on an Intel-based Macintosh and Photoshop CS2 running on the same system.

Before Photoshop CS3, the Intel-based Macintosh computers had to interpret the software so that it could be used because the earlier versions of software weren't made for the Intel processors but for the PowerPC processors in the last generation of Macintosh systems. This release of Photoshop CS3 has been developed to run efficiently on either legacy or new Macintosh computers, regardless of the processor.

Compared to earlier versions of Photoshop running on the Intel-based Macintosh systems, Photoshop CS3 is blazing fast. And if you still have an older Macintosh system with a PowerPC processor, Photoshop CS3 still runs on these computers as well.

Additional Features in Photoshop Extended

If you have Photoshop CS3 Extended, it's probably because you purchased the Master or one of the Premium Suites, or because you're in the medical, architecture, manufacturing, or construction business. Photoshop CS3 Extended isn't necessarily a better version of Photoshop, but it does contain additional tools to help those users in certain industries get the counting, viewing, and analysis tools that they need to do their job. As a designer, you may never need the Counting tool, but it can be invaluable to someone in manufacturing.

Some features are in Photoshop Standard, but are enhanced in Photoshop Extended. For example, although you have animation in the Standard version, you see a timeline in the Extended version that has a higher level of functionality. The following sections are by no means a complete list of Extended features, but a quick look at some incredibly different features that have been included in Photoshop CS3 Extended.

3D Layers

For those involved in 3D graphics, Photoshop Extended is a great tool. You don't build 3D elements in Photoshop, but you can take advantage of 3D model visualization and texture editing and export of 3D models from 2D images. Support for common 3D interchange formats lets you import 3D models, edit their textures, and easily composite designs with images, such as site photographs.

You can freely rotate and manipulate these models in 3D space in a Photoshop document. Access the textures applied to the model surfaces and edit them with the full range of tools in Photoshop CS3 Extended. You can even create 3D models from 2D images, by defining perspective planes in an image with Vanishing Point and then exporting the model to a 3D format.

Due to the scope of this book, we don't discuss 3D features in detail, but you can get step-by-step information by choosing Help⇨Photoshop Help.

New Video Layers and Movie Paint

Now with the new video layers and the Animation (Timeline) palette, Photoshop CS3 Extended offers a great new feature for video professionals, Movie Paint. Movie Paint brings the power of Photoshop painting, retouching, and pixel level editing to every frame of a movie file. Using the Animation palette to navigate, you can quickly find and edit any frame of the movie file. Due to the advanced level of this feature, we don't cover the Animation (Timeline) palette in this book.

Comprehensive Image Analysis

Physicians, radiologists, and technicians using Photoshop? Absolutely, thanks to the new selection, measurement, and analysis tools that let them quickly extract and export a wide array of quantitative data from microscopic and radiological images (see Figure 1-5).

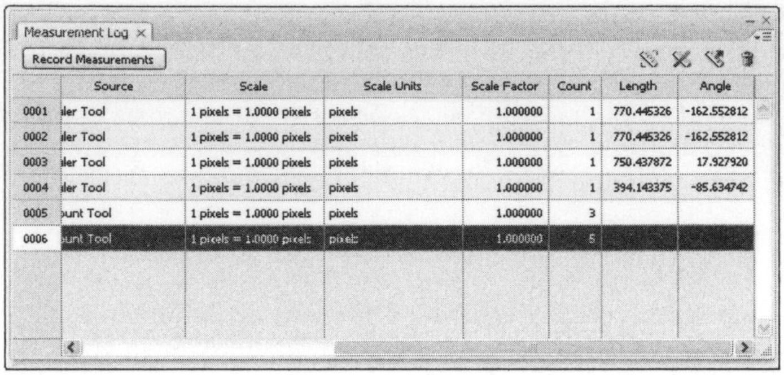

Measurement Log

Record Measurements

	Source	Scale	Scale Units	Scale Factor	Count	Length	Angle
0001	ler Tool	1 pixels = 1.0000 pixels	pixels	1.000000	1	770.445326	-162.552812
0002	ler Tool	1 pixels = 1.0000 pixels	pixels	1.000000	1	770.445326	-162.552812
0003	ler Tool	1 pixels = 1.0000 pixels	pixels	1.000000	1	750.437872	17.927920
0004	ler Tool	1 pixels = 1.0000 pixels	pixels	1.000000	1	394.143375	-85.634742
0005	ount Tool	1 pixels = 1.0000 pixels	pixels	1.000000	3		
0006	ount Tool	1 pixels = 1.0000 pixels	pixels	1.000000	5		

Figure 1-5: Photoshop Extended includes new analysis tools.

Photoshop Extended provides users with tools to count, rulers that can be recorded in a measurement log, and other high-end analysis tools.

Chapter 2: Getting into Photoshop CS3 Basics

In This Chapter

- Discovering Photoshop
- Organizing your palette
- Changing screen modes

Navigating the work area in Photoshop can be slightly cumbersome at first, especially if you've never worked in a program that relies so heavily on palettes. In this chapter, we introduce you to Photoshop CS3 and show you how to do basic tasks, such as opening and saving an image. We also introduce you to the work area, show you what the Photoshop CS3 tools are all about, and reveal how to neatly organize and hide palettes.

Getting Started with Photoshop CS3

Unless you use Photoshop as a blank canvas for painting, you may rarely create a new file in Photoshop because you usually have a source image that you start with. This image may have been generated by a scanner, digital camera, or stock image library. You can open existing Photoshop images by choosing File➪Open, selecting the file in the Open dialog box, and then clicking the Open button.

Photoshop can open a multitude of file formats, even if the image was created in another application, such as Illustrator or another image-editing program, but you have to open the image in Photoshop by choosing File➪Open. If you just double-click an image file in a directory (one that wasn't originally created in Photoshop, or from different versions), the image may open only in a preview application.

If you're opening a folder of images that you want to investigate first, choose File➪Browse to open Adobe Bridge, the control center for Adobe Creative Suite. You can use Adobe Bridge to organize, browse, and locate the assets you need to create your content. Adobe Bridge keeps native PSD, AI, INDD, and Adobe PDF files, as well as other Adobe and non-Adobe application files, available for easy access.

Adobe Bridge is a standalone application that you can access from all applications in the Creative Suite by choosing File➪Browse or by clicking the Go To Bridge icon in the upper-right corner of the application window. Use the Bridge interface to view your images as thumbnails and look for Metadata information.

Creating a new file

If you're creating a new file, you may be doing so to create a composite of existing files or to start with a blank canvas because you're super creative.

Discover Camera Raw

If you haven't discovered the Camera Raw capabilities in Adobe Photoshop, you'll want to give them a try. Camera Raw is a format available for image capture in many cameras. Simply choose the format in your camera's settings as Raw instead of JPEG or TIFF. These raw files are a bit larger than the standard JPEG files, but you capture an enormous amount of data with the image that you can retrieve upon opening. (See `www.adobe.com` for a complete list of cameras supporting Camera Raw.)

A camera raw file contains unprocessed picture data from a digital camera's image sensor, along with information about how the image was captured, such as the camera and lens used, the exposure settings, and white balance setting. When you open the file in Adobe Photoshop CS3, the built-in Camera Raw plug-in interprets the raw file on your computer, making adjustments for image color and tonal scale.

When you shoot JPEG images with your camera, you're locked into the processing done by your camera, but working with camera raw files gives you maximum control over your image, such as controlling the white balance, tonal range, contrast, and color saturation, as well as image sharpening. Cameras that can shoot in RAW format have a setting on the camera that changes its capture mode to RAW. Instead of writing a final JPEG, a RAW data file is written, which consists of black-and-white brightness levels from each of the several million pixel sites on the imaging sensor. The actual image hasn't yet been produced, and unless you have specific software, such as the plug-in built into Adobe Photoshop, opening the file can be very difficult, if not impossible.

To open a camera raw file, simply choose File➪Browse. Adobe Bridge opens, and you see several panels, including the Folders, Content, Preview, and Metadata panels. Using the Folders panel, navigate to the location on your computer where you have saved your Camera Raw images; thumbnail previews appear in the Content panel. Think of camera raw files as your photo negative. You can reprocess the file at any time to achieve the results you want.

If Adobe Photoshop CS3 doesn't open your raw file, you may need to update your raw plug-in. (See `www.adobe.com` for the latest plug-in.) The plug-in should be downloaded and placed in this location in Windows: C:\Program Files\Common Files\Adobe\Plug-Ins\CS3\File Formats, and this location on the Macintosh: Library\Application Support\Adobe\Plug-Ins\CS3\File Formats.

For whatever reason, note that when you choose File⇨New, you have a multitude of basic format choices that you can select from the Preset menu. They range from basic sizes and resolutions, such as U.S. Paper or Photo, to other final output such as the Web, Mobile Devices, or Film.

Keep in mind that you're determining not only size but resolution in your new file. If your new file is to contain images from other files, make sure the new file is the same resolution. Otherwise, you may get unexpected size results when cutting and pasting or dragging images into your new file. Choose Image⇨Image Size to see the document dimensions.

Saving documents

Save an image file by choosing File⇨Save. If you're saving the file for the first time, the Save As dialog box appears. Notice in the Format drop-down list that you have plenty of choices for file formats. The different file formats are discussed in more detail in Chapter 10 of this minibook. You can always play it safe by choosing the Photoshop (PSD) file format. The native Photoshop format supports all features in Photoshop. Choosing some of the other formats may eliminate layers, channels, and other special features.

Many users choose to save a native Photoshop file as a backup to any other file formats. It's especially important to have a backup or original file saved as a native Photoshop file (PSD) as you increase in capabilities and start taking advantage of layers and the other great capabilities of Photoshop.

Getting to Know the Tools

Tools are used to create, select, and manipulate objects in Photoshop CS3. When you open Photoshop, the toolbox appears along the left edge of the workspace (see Figure 2-1). We discuss palettes and the palette well in the upcoming section, "Navigating the Work Area."

In the toolbox, look for the name of the tool to appear in a ToolTip when you hover the cursor over the tool. Following the tool name is a letter in parentheses, which is the keyboard shortcut command that you can use to access that tool. Simply press the Shift key along with the key command you see to access any hidden tools. In other words, pressing P activates the Pen tool, and pressing Shift+P activates the hidden tools under the Pen tool in the order that they appear. When you see a small triangle at the lower-right corner of the tool icon, you know that this tool contains hidden tools.

Figure 2-1: Photoshop CS3 workspace includes the toolbox, palettes, and palette well.

Table 2-1 lists the Photoshop tools, what each is used for, and in what chapter you can find more about each.

Table 2-1 Photoshop CS Tools

Button	*Tool*	*What It Does*	*Chapter It's Covered in This Minibook*
	Move (V)	Moves selections or layers	4
	Marquee (M)	Selects image area	4
	Lasso (L)	Makes freehand selections	4

Button	Tool	What It Does	Chapter It's Covered in This Minibook
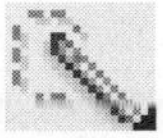	Quick Selection Tool (New) (W)	Selects similar pixels	4
	Crop (C)	Crops an image	2
	Slice (K)	Creates HTML slices	n/a
	Spot Healing Brush (J)	Retouches flaws	8
	Brush (B)	Paints foreground color	8
	Clone Stamp (S)	Copies pixel data	8
	History Brush (Y)	Paints from selected state	8
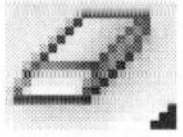	Eraser (E)	Erases pixels	8
	Gradient (G)	Creates a gradient	8
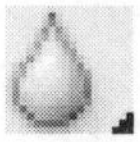	Blur (R)	Blurs pixels	8
	Toning (O)	Dodges, burns, saturates	8
	Pen (P)	Creates paths	5
 T	Type (T)	Creates text	9

(continued)

Table 2-1 *(continued)*

Button	Tool	What It Does	Chapter It's Covered in This Minibook
	Path Selection (A)	Selects paths	5
	Vector Shape (U)	Creates vector shapes	9
	Notes (N)	Makes annotations	n/a
	Eyedropper (I)	Samples pixels	8
	Hand (H)	Navigates page	9
	Zoom (Z)	Increases, decreases view	2

Looking for the Magic Wand tool? Click and hold on the Quick Selection tool in the toolbar to access it.

Navigating the Work Area

Getting around in Photoshop isn't much different from getting around in other Adobe applications. All Adobe applications make extensive use of palettes, for example. In the following sections, we cover the highlights on navigating in Photoshop.

Docking and saving palettes

Palettes, palettes everywhere . . . do you really need them all? Maybe not just yet, but as you increase your skill level, you'll take advantage of most (if not all) of the Photoshop palettes. The palettes give you easy access to important functions.

As you work in Photoshop, keep in mind these two key commands:

- Press Tab to switch between hiding and showing the tools and palettes.
- Press Shift+Tab to hide the palettes, leaving only the toolbox visible.

On the far right of the Options bar (a toolbar that contains the options for each tool and appears across the top of the work area) is the *palette well,* which helps you organize and manage palettes. The palette well stores, or *docks,* palettes so that you can access them easily. (See Figure 2-1, earlier in this chapter.)

The palette well is available only when using a screen resolution greater than 800 x 600 pixels (a setting of at least 1024 x 768 is recommended). Dock palettes in the palette well by dragging the palette's tab into the palette well; release when the palette well is highlighted.

If you find that you're always using the same palettes, hide the palettes that you don't need and arrange your other palettes on-screen where you want them. Then follow these steps to save that palette configuration:

1. **Choose Window⇨Workspace⇨Save Workspace.**
2. **In the Save Workspace dialog box that appears, name the Workspace and click Save.**
3. **Any time you want the palettes to return to your saved locations, choose Window⇨Workspace⇨*Name of Your Workspace* (where *Name of Your Workspace* is the name you supplied in Step 2).**

TIP

Choose Window⇨Workspace⇨Reset Palette Locations to put the palettes back in the same order they were upon the initial installation.

Taking advantage of new workspace features

Photoshop CS3 now has included many saved workspaces that you can take advantage of to streamline workspaces and open the palettes you need for specific tasks. These new features include workspaces for Web Design, Painting and Retouching, and Color and Tonal Correction to name a few.

Increase your work area by turning your palettes into icons, as shown in Figure 2-2. Do so by either right-clicking the tab of a palette and selecting Collapse To Icons or clicking the Auto Collapse gray bar at the top of the palette drawer. Yes, you heard it correctly — the area where the palettes are located is actually a drawer that can be adjusted in or out by clicking and dragging on the vertical pane to the left of the palettes.

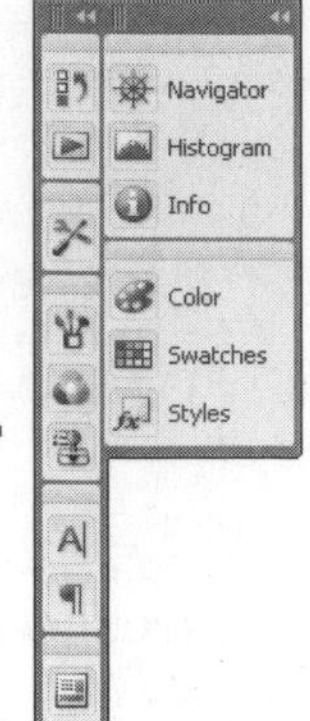

Figure 2-2: Turn your palettes into icons.

Zooming in to get a better look

What looks fine at one zoom level may actually look very bad at another. You'll find yourself zooming in and out quite often as you work on an image in Photoshop. You can find menu choices for zooming in the View menu; a quicker way to zoom is to use the keyboard commands listed in Table 2-2.

Table 2-2 Zooming and Navigation Keyboard Shortcuts

Command	*Windows Shortcut*	*Mac Shortcut*
Actual size	Alt+Ctrl+0	⌘+1
Fit in window	Ctrl+0 (zero)	⌘ +0 (zero)
Zoom in	Ctrl++ (plus sign) or Ctrl+Spacebar	⌘ ++ (plus sign) or ⌘ +Spacebar
Zoom out	Ctrl+– (minus) or Alt+Spacebar	⌘ +– (minus) or Option+Spacebar
Hand tool	Spacebar	Spacebar

Here are a few things to keep in mind as you work with the Zoom tool to get a better look at your work:

- ✦ **100-percent view:** Double-clicking the Zoom tool in the toolbox puts you at 100 percent view. Do this before using filters to see a more realistic result of your changes.
- ✦ **Zoom marquee:** Drag from the upper left to the lower right of the area you want to zoom to. While dragging, a marquee appears; When you

release the mouse button, the marqueed area zooms up to fill the image window. The Zoom marquee gives you much more control than just clicking on the image with the Zoom tool. Zoom back out to see the entire image by pressing Ctrl+0. It fits the entire image in the viewing area.

- **Zoom using the keyboard shortcuts:** If you have a dialog box open and you need to reposition or zoom to a new location on your image, you can use the keyboard commands without exiting the dialog box.
- **A new window for a different look:** Choose Window➪Arrange➪ New Window to create an additional window for your front-most image. This technique is helpful when you want to see the entire image (say, at actual size)or to see the results as a whole, yet zoom in to focus on a small area of the image to do some fine-tuning. The new window is dynamically linked to the original window so that as you make changes, the original and any other new windows created from the original are immediately updated.

- **Cycle through images:** Press Ctrl+Tab to cycle through open images.

Choosing Your Screen Mode

You have a choice of three screen modes in which to work. Most users start and stay in the default (standard screen mode) until they accidentally end up in another. The four modes are

- **Maximized Screen mode** displays a maximized document window that fills all available space between docks and that resizes when dock widths change.
- **Standard mode** is the typical view, where you have an image window open but can see your desktop and other images open behind.
- **Full-screen mode with menu** view surrounds the image out to the edge of the work area with a neutral gray. This mode not only prevents you from accidentally clicking out of an image and leaving Photoshop, but also from seeing other images behind your working image.
- **Full screen mode, no menu** is a favorite with multimedia types. It shows your image surrounded by black and also eliminates the menu items from the top of the window. Press Tab to hide all tools, and you have a very clean work environment.

Cropping an Image

A simple but essential task is to crop your image. *Cropping* means to eliminate all that is not important to the composition of your image. Cropping is especially important in Photoshop. Each pixel, no matter what color, takes up the same amount of information, so cropping eliminates unneeded pixels and saves on file size and processing time, so you want to crop your image before you start working on it.

You can crop an image in Photoshop CS3 in two ways:

- ✦ Use the Crop tool.
- ✦ Select an area with the Marquee tool and choose Image➪ Crop.

To crop an image by using the Crop tool, follow these steps:

1. **Press C to access the Crop tool and drag around the area of the image that you want to crop to.**
2. **If you need to adjust the crop area, drag the handles in the crop-bounding area.**
3. **When you're satisfied with the crop bounding area, double-click in the center of the crop area or press the Return or Enter key to crop the image.**
4. **If you want to cancel the crop, press the Esc key.**

Ever scan in an image crooked? When using the Crop tool, if you position the cursor outside any of the handles, a rotate symbol appears. Drag the crop's bounding area to rotate it and line it up as you want it cropped. When you press Return or Enter, the image is straightened out.

Chapter 3: Messing with Mode Matters

In this Chapter

- Working in black and white
- Understanding Photoshop image modes

Before diving into Photoshop, you must know what image mode you should be working in and how important color settings are. So no matter whether you're doing a one-color newsletter, a full-color logo, or something in between, this chapter can help you create much better imagery for both Web and print.

Working with Bitmap Images

You may have already discovered that Photoshop works a little differently than most other applications. In order to create those smooth gradations from one color to the next, Photoshop takes advantage of pixels. *Bitmap images* (sometimes called *raster images*) are based on a grid of pixels. The grid is smaller or larger depending on the resolution that you're working in. The number of pixels along the height and width of a bitmap image are called the pixel dimensions of an image, which are measured in pixels per inch (ppi). The more pixels per inch, the more detail in the image.

Unlike *vector graphics* (mathematically created paths), bitmap images can't be scaled without losing detail. (See Figure 3-1 for an example of a bitmap image and a vector graphic.) Generally, it's best to use bitmap images at or close to the size that you need. If you resize a bitmap image, it can become jagged on the edges of sharp objects. On the other hand, you can scale vector graphics and edit them without degrading the sharp edges.

Photoshop has the capability to work on both bitmap and vector art. (See the path line around the vector shape layer and notice that the path isn't pixilated.) It gives you, as a designer, incredible opportunities when combining the two technologies.

For information on changing and adjusting image resolution, see Chapter 6 of this minibook.

Figure 3-1: Bitmap versus vector.

Choosing the Correct Photoshop Mode

Choose Image⇨Mode to view the image mode choices you can choose from. Selecting the right one for an image is important because each mode offers different capabilities and results. For example, if you choose the Bitmap mode, you can work only in black and white . . . that's it. No shades of color, not even a gray. Most features are disabled in this Bitmap mode. This is fine if you're working on art for a black-and-white logo, but not for most images. If, instead, you work in the RGB mode, you have full access to Photoshop's capabilities. So read on to see what image mode is best for your needs. When you're ready to make your mode selection, have a file open and choose a selection from Image⇨Mode. You can read descriptions of each image mode in the following sections.

Along with a description of each image mode, we include a figure showing the Channels palette set to that mode. A *channel* is simply the information about color elements in the image. The number of default color channels in an image depends on its color mode. For example, a CMYK image has at least four channels, one each for cyan, magenta, yellow, and black information. Grayscale has one channel. If you understand the printing process, think of each channel representing a plate (color) that, when combined, creates the final image.

Bitmap

Bitmap mode offers little more than the ability to work in black and white. Many tools are unusable, and most menu options are grayed out in this mode. If you're converting an image to bitmap, you must convert it to Grayscale first.

Grayscale

Use Grayscale mode, shown in Figure 3-2, if you're creating black-and-white images with tonal values, specifically for printing to one color. Grayscale mode supports 256 shades of gray in the 8-bit color mode. Photoshop can work with Grayscale in 16-bit mode, which provides more information, but may limit your capabilities when working in Photoshop.

When you convert to Grayscale mode, you get a warning message confirming that you want to discard all color information. If you don't want to see this warning every time you convert an image to grayscale, select the option to not show the dialog box again before you click Discard.

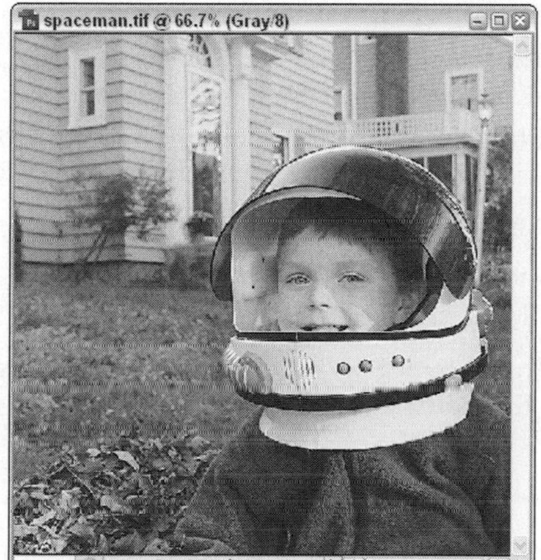

Figure 3-2: Grayscale supports 256 shades of gray.

Duotone

Use Duotone mode when you're creating a one- to four-color image created from spot colors (solid ink, such as Pantone colors). You can also use the Duotone mode to create Monotones, Tritones, and Quadtones. If you're producing a two-color job, duotones create a beautiful solution to not having full color.

The Pantone Matching color system helps to keep printing inks consistent from one job to the next. By assigning a numbered Pantone color, such as 485 for red, you don't risk one vendor (printer) using fire-engine red, and the next using orange-red for your company logo.

To create a Duotone, follow these steps:

1. **Choose Image⇨Mode⇨Grayscale.**
2. **Choose Image⇨Mode⇨Duotone.**
3. **In the Duotone dialog box, choose Duotone from the Type drop-down list.**

   Your choices range from Monotone (one-color) up to Quadtone (four-color). Black is automatically assigned as the first ink. But you can change that if you like.
4. **To assign a second ink color, click the white swatch immediately under the black swatch to open the Color Libraries dialog box, as shown in Figure 3-3.**
5. **Now comes the fun part: Type (quickly!) the Pantone or PMS number that you want to access and then click OK.**

   There is no text field for you to enter the number in, so don't look for one. Just type the number while the Color Libraries dialog box is open.

   Try entering **300** for an easy one. That selects PMS 300.
6. **You can already see that you have created a tone curve, but click the Curve button to the left of the ink color to further tweak the colors.**
7. **Click and drag the curve to adjust the black in the shadow areas, perhaps to bring down the color overall; experiment with the results.**

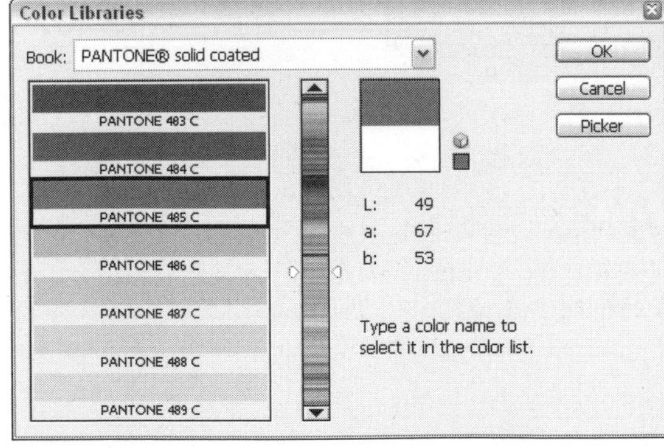

Figure 3-3: Click the white swatch to open the Color Libraries dialog box.

8. **(Optional) If you like your Duotone settings, store them by clicking the Save button.**

Click the Load button to find your customized presets and to find preset Duotones, Tritones, and Quadtones supplied to you by Adobe.

Duotone images must be saved in the Photoshop EPS format in order to support the spot colors. If you chose another format, you risk the possibility of converting your colors into a build of CMYK (Cyan, Magenta, Yellow, and Black.)

9. **Click OK when you're finished.**

Index color

You may not work in Index color, but you probably have saved a file in this mode. Index color mode (see Figure 3-4) uses a color look-up table (CLUT) in order to create the image.

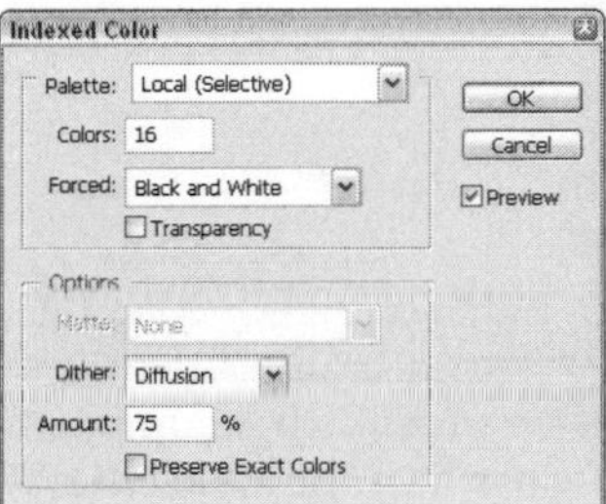

Figure 3-4: Index color uses a limited number of colors to create an image.

A *color look-up table* contains all the colors that make up your image, like a box of crayons used to create artwork. If you have a box of eight crayons and only those crayons are used to color an image, you have a color look-up table of only eight colors. Of course, your image would look much better if you used the 64-count box of crayons with the sharpener on the back, but those additional colors increase the size of the color look-up table, as well as the file size.

The most colors that can be in index mode are 256. When saving Web images, you often have to define a color table. We discuss the Save For Web feature (which helps you to more accurately save an index color image) in Chapter 10 of this minibook.

Choose Image➪Mode➪Color Table to see the color table making up an image.

RGB

RGB (Red, Green, Blue), shown in Figure 3-5, is the standard format that you work in if you import images from a digital camera or you scan images on a scanner in RGB mode. For complete access to features, RGB is probably the best color mode to work in. If you're working on images for use on the Web, color copiers, desktop color printers, and on-screen presentations, you want to stay in the RGB mode.

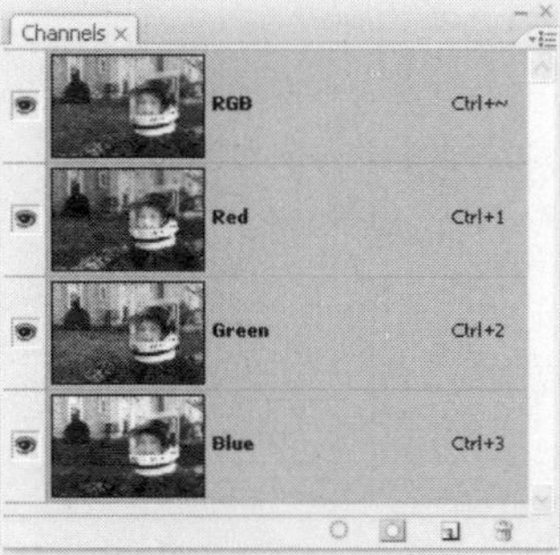

Figure 3-5: RGB creates the image from red, green, and blue.

If you're having your image printed on a press (for example, if you're having the image professionally printed), it must be separated. Don't convert images to CMYK mode until you're finished with the color correction and you know that your color settings are accurate. A good print service may want the RGB file so that it can do an accurate conversion.

CMYK

CMYK (Cyan, Magenta, Yellow, Black) is the mode used for final separations for the press. Use a good magnifying glass to look closely at anything that has been printed in color, and you may see the CMYK colors that created it. A typical four-color printing press has a plate for each color and runs the colors in the order of cyan, magenta, yellow, and then black.

Don't take converting an image into this mode lightly. You need to make decisions when you convert an image to CMYK, such as where the file is going to be printed and on what paper stock, so that the resulting image is the best it can be. Talk to your print provider for specifications that are important when converting to CMYK mode.

Lab color

Lab (Lightness, A channel, and B channel) is a color mode that many high-end color professionals use because of its wide color range. Using Lab, you can make adjustments to *luminosity* (lightness) without affecting the color. In this mode, you can select and change an L (Lightness or Luminosity) channel without affecting the A channel (green and red) and the B channel (blue and yellow).

Lab mode is also a good mode to use if you're in a color-managed environment and want to easily move from one color system to another with no loss of color.

Some professionals prefer to sharpen their images in LAB mode because they can select just the Lightness channel and choose Filter⇨Sharpen⇨Unsharp Mask to sharpen only the gray matter of the image, leaving the color noise-free.

Multichannel

Multichannel is used for many things; sometimes you end up in this mode, and you're not quite sure how. Deleting a channel from an RGB, CMYK, or Lab image automatically converts the image to Multichannel mode. This mode supports multiple spot colors.

Bit depth

You have more functionality in 16-bit and even 32-bit mode. Depending upon your needs, you may spend most of your time in 8-bit mode, which is more than likely all that you need.

Bit depth, also called *pixel depth* or *color depth,* measures how much color information is available to display or print each pixel in an image. Greater bit depth means more available colors and more accurate color representation in the digital image. In Photoshop, this increase in accuracy does also limit some of the features available, so don't use it unless you have a specific request or need for it.

To use 16-bit or 32-bit color mode, you also must have a source to provide you with that information, such as a scanner or camera that offers a choice to scan at 16-bit or 32-bit.

Chapter 4: Creating a Selection

In This Chapter

- **Discovering the selection tools**
- **Painting selections the easy way**
- **Giving transformed selections a try**
- **Feathering away**
- **Keeping selections for later use**
- **Using the new Vanishing Point feature**

It's common to use Photoshop to create compositions that may not actually exist and to retouch images to improve them. What you don't want is obvious retouching or a composition that looks contrived. (The exception is if you intend an image to be humorous, such as putting baby Joey's head on Daddy's body.)

That's where the selection tools come in. In this chapter, you discover several selection methods and how to use the selection tools to make your images look as though you *haven't* retouched or edited them. Even if you're an experienced Photoshop user, this chapter provides a plethora of tips and tricks that can save you time and help make your images look absolutely convincing.

Getting to Know the Selection Tools

You create selections with the selection tools. Think of *selections* as windows in which you can make changes to the pixels. Areas that aren't selected are *masked,* which means that these unselected areas are unaffected by changes, much like when you tape around windows and doors before you paint the walls. In this section, we briefly describe the selection tools and show you how to use them. You must be familiar with these tools in order to do *anything* in Photoshop.

As with all the Photoshop tools, the Options bar across the top of the Photoshop window changes with each selection tool. The keyboard commands you read about in this section exist on the Options bar as buttons.

If you move a selection with the Move tool, pixels move as you drag, leaving a blank spot in the image. To *clone* a selection (that is, to copy and move the selection at the same time), Alt+drag (Option+drag on a Mac) the selection with the Move tool.

The Marquee tool

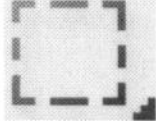

The Marquee tool is the main selection tool; by that, we mean that you'll use it most often for creating selections. The exception, of course, is when you have a special situation that calls for a special tool, either the Lasso, Magic Wand tool, or the new Quick Selection tool. Throughout this section, we describe creating (and then deselecting) an active selection area; we also provide you with tips for working with selections.

The Marquee tool includes the Rectangular Marquee (for creating rectangular selections), Elliptical Marquee (for creating round or elliptical selections), and Single Row Marquee or Single Column Marquee tools (for creating a selection of a single row or column of pixels). You can access these other Marquee tools by holding down on the default, Rectangle Marquee tool.

To create a selection, select one of the Marquee tools (remember you can press M) and then drag anywhere on your image. When you release the mouse button, you create an active selection area. When you're working on an active selection area, whatever effects you choose are applied to the whole selection. To deselect an area, you have three choices:

- ✦ Choose Select⇨Deselect.
- ✦ Press Ctrl+D.
- ✦ While using a selection tool, click outside the selection area.

How you make a selection is important because it determines how realistic your edits appear on the image. You can use the following tips and tricks when creating both rectangular and elliptical selections:

- ✦ Add to a selection by holding down the Shift key; drag to create a second selection that intersects the original selection (see the left image in Figure 4-1). The two selections become one big selection.
- ✦ Delete from an existing selection by holding the Alt (Option on a Mac) key and then drag to create a second selection that intersects the original selection where you want to take away from the original selection (on the right in Figure 4-1).
- ✦ Constrain a rectangle or ellipse to a square or circle by Shift+dragging; make sure that you release the mouse button before you release the Shift key. Holding down the Shift key makes a square or circle only when there are no other selections. (Otherwise, it adds to the selection.)
- ✦ Make the selection from the center by Alt+dragging (Option+dragging on a Mac); make sure that you release the mouse button before the Alt or (Option) key.

- ✦ Create a square or circle from the center out by Alt+Shift+dragging (Option+Shift+dragging on a Mac). Again, make sure that you always release the mouse button before the modifier keys.
- ✦ When making a selection, hold down the spacebar before releasing the mouse button to drag the selection to another location.

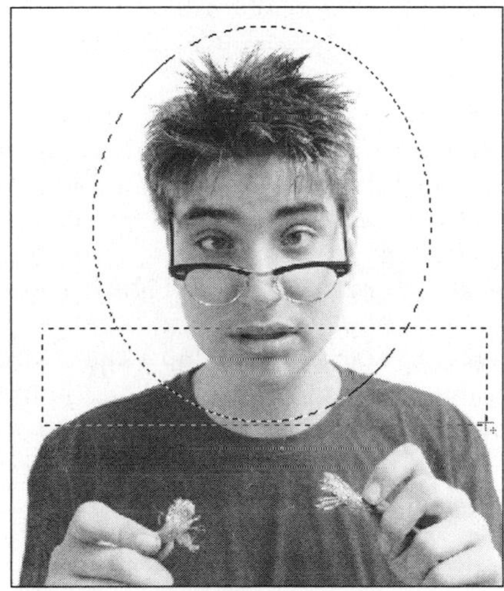

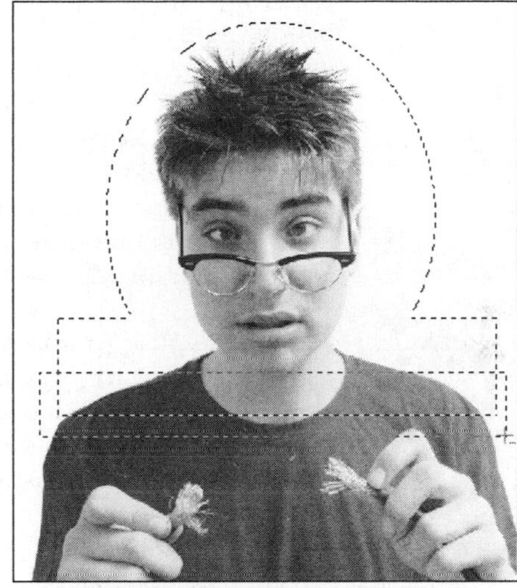

Figure 4-1: You can add and delete from selections.

Fixed size

If you've created an effect that you particularly like — say, changing a block of color in your image — and you'd like to apply it multiple times throughout an image, you can do so. To make the exact same selection multiple times, follow these steps:

1. **With the Marquee tool selected, select Fixed Size from the Style drop-down list on the Options bar.**

   You can also select Fixed Ratio from the Style drop-down list to create a proportionally correct selection, but not fixed to an exact size.

2. **On the Options bar, type the Width and Height values into the appropriate text fields.**

   You can change ruler increments by choosing Edit⇨Preferences⇨Units And Rulers (Photoshop⇨Preferences⇨Units And Rulers on a Mac).

3. **Click the image.**

   A selection sized to your values appears.

4. **With the selection tool, drag the selection to the location that you want selected.**

Shift+drag a selection to keep it aligned to a straight, 45-degree, or 90-degree angle.

Floating and nonfloating selections

As a default, when you're using a selection tool, such as the Marquee tool, your selections are *floating,* which means that you can drag them to another location without affecting the underlying pixels. You know that your selection is floating by the little rectangle that appears on your cursor (see the left image in Figure 4-2).

If you want to, however, you can move the underlying pixels. With the selection tool of your choice, just hold down the Ctrl (⌘ on a Mac) key to temporarily access the Move tool; the cursor changes to a pointer with scissors, denoting that your selection is nonfloating. Now, when you drag, the pixel data comes with the selection (as shown on the right in Figure 4-2).

Hold down Alt+Ctrl (Option+⌘ on a Mac) while using a selection tool and drag to clone (copy) pixels from one location to another. Add the Shift key, and the cloned copy is constrained to a straight, 45-degree, or 90-degree angle.

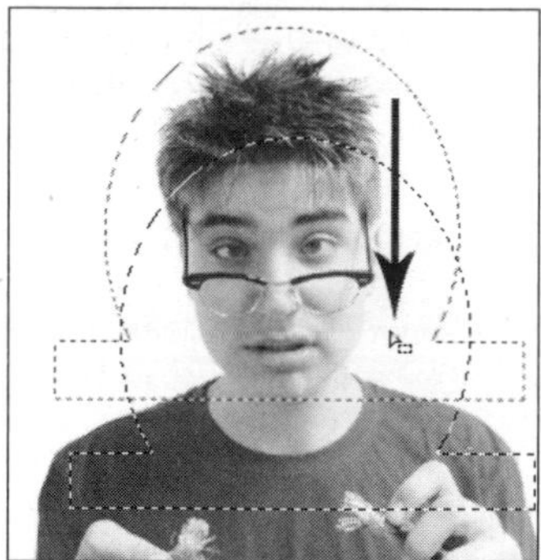

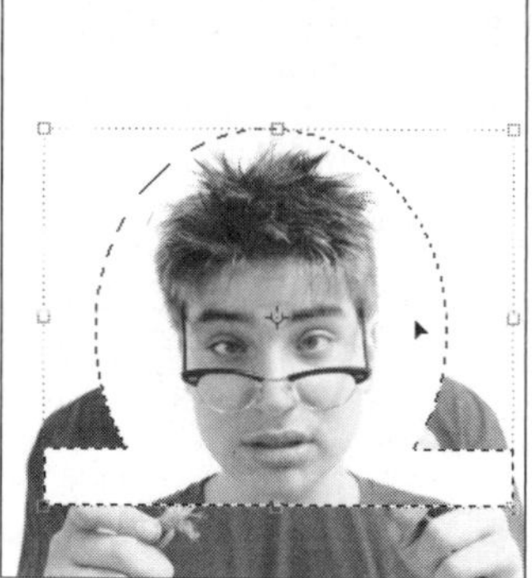

Figure 4-2: The Float icon is used on the left, and the Move icon is used on the right.

The Lasso tool

Use the Lasso tool for *freeform selections* (selections of an irregular shape). To use the Lasso tool, just drag and create a path surrounding the area to be selected. If you don't return to your start point to close the selection before you release the mouse button, Photoshop completes the path by finding the most direct route back to your starting point.

Just like with the Marquee tool, you can press the Shift key to add to a lasso selection and press the Alt (Option on a Mac) key to delete from a lasso selection.

Hold down on the Lasso tool to show the hidden Lasso tools, the Polygonal Lasso and the Magnetic Lasso tool. Use the Polygonal Lasso tool by clicking on a start point and then clicking and releasing from point to point until you come back to close the selection. Use the Magnetic Lasso tool by clicking to create a starting point and then hovering the cursor near an edge in your image. The Magnetic Lasso tool is magnetically attracted to edges; as you move your cursor near an edge, the Magnetic Lasso tool creates a selection along that edge. Click to manually set points in the selection; when you get back to the starting point, click to close the selection.

You may find that the Polygonal Lasso and the Magnetic Lasso tools don't make as nice of a selection as you'd like. Take a look at the upcoming section, "Painting with the Quick Mask tool," for tips on making finer selections.

The new Quick Selection tool

The Quick Selection tool lets you quickly "paint" a selection using a round brush tip of adjustable size. Click and drag and watch as the selection expands outward and automatically follows defined edges in the image. A Refine Edge command lets you improve the quality of the selection edges and visualize the selection in different ways for easy editing.

Follow these steps to find out how you can take advantage of this new tool:

1. **Start by choosing File⇨Open and opening a file named Sunflower.psd that already exists in your Photoshop CS3 Samples folder.**

   You can find the file in the following location on the Windows OS at C:\Program Files\Adobe\Adobe Photoshop CS3\Samples and on the Mac OS at Applications\Adobe\Adobe Photoshop CS3\Samples.

2. **Select the Quick Selection tool.**

3. **Position the cursor over the yellow petals of the sunflower and notice the brush size displayed with the cursor; click and drag to start painting the selection.**

   You can adjust the size of the painting selection by pressing [to make the brush size smaller or] to make the brush size larger.

4. **Using the Add To Selection or Subtract From Selection buttons in the toolbar options, you can paint more of the selection or deselect active areas (see Figure 4-3).**

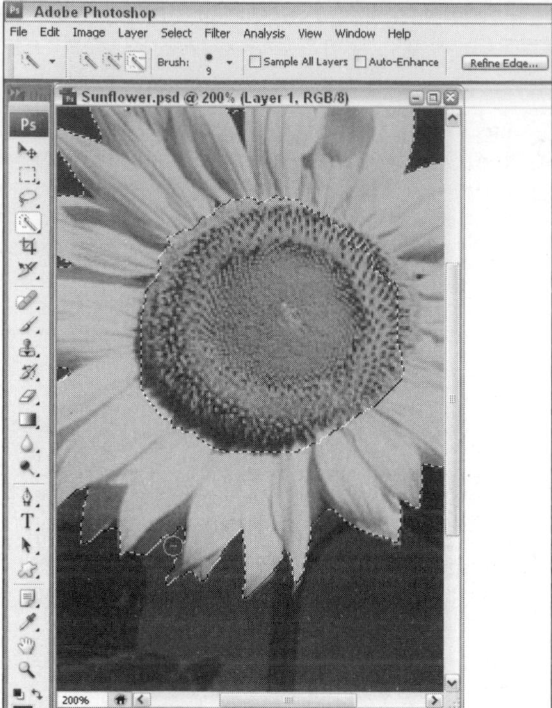

Figure 4-3: The Quick Selection tool allows you to paint your selection.

The Magic Wand tool

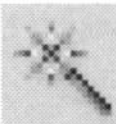

The Magic Wand tool is particularly helpful when you're working on an image of high contrast or with a limited number of colors. This tool selects individual pixels of similar shades and colors. Select the Magic Wand tool, click anywhere on an image, and hope for the best — the Magic Wand tool isn't magic at all. You decide how successful this tool is. What we mean by that is that you control how closely matched each pixel must be in order for the Magic Wand tool to include it in the selection. You do so by setting the tolerance on the Options bar.

When you have the Magic Wand tool selected, a Tolerance text field appears on the Options bar. As a default, the tolerance is set to 32. When you click with a setting of 32, the Magic Wand tool selects all pixels within 32 shades (steps) of the color that you clicked. If it didn't select as much as you want, increase the value in the Tolerance text field (all the way up to 255). The amount that you enter really varies with each individual selection. If you're selecting white napkins on an off-white tablecloth, you can set as low as 5 so that the selection doesn't leak into other areas. For colored fabric with lots of tonal values, you might increase the tolerance to 150.

Don't fret if you miss the entire selection when using the Magic Wand tool. Hold down the Shift key and click in the missed areas. If it selects too much, choose Edit⇨Undo (Step Backwards) or press Ctrl+Z, reduce the value in the Tolerance text field, and try again.

Manipulating Selections

After you master creating selections, you'll find that working with the selections — painting, transforming, and feathering them — can be easy and fun.

Painting with the Quick Mask tool

If you have fuzzy selections (fur, hair, or leaves, for example) or you're having difficulty using the selection tools, the Quick Mask tool can be a huge help because it allows you to paint your selection uniformly in one fell swoop.

To enter into Quick Mask mode, create a selection and then press Q. (Pressing Q again exits you from Quick Mask mode.) You can also click the Quick Mask button at the bottom of the toolbox. If you have a printing background, you'll notice that the Quick Mask mode, set at its default color (red), resembles something that you may want to forget: rubylith and amberlith. (Remember slicing up those lovely films with Exacto blades before computer masking came along?) In Quick Mask mode, Photoshop shows your image as it appears through the mask. The clear part is selected; what's covered in the mask isn't selected.

To create and implement a quick mask, follow these steps:

1. **Press Q to enter Quick Mask mode.**
2. **Press D to change the foreground and background color boxes the default colors of black and white.**
3. **Select the Brush tool and start painting with black in the clear area of the image in Quick Mask mode.**

   It doesn't have to be pretty; just get a stroke or two in there.
4. **Press Q to return to the Selection mode.**

   You're now out of Quick Mask mode. Notice that where you painted with black (it turned red in the Quick Mask mode), the pixels are no longer selected.
5. **Press Q again to re-enter the Quick Mask mode and then press X.**

   This step switches the foreground and background colors (giving you white in the foreground, black in the background).

6. **Using the Brush tool, paint several white strokes in the red mask area.**

   The white strokes turn clear in the Quick Mask mode.

7. **Press Q to return to the Selection mode.**

   Where you painted white in the Quick Mask mode is now selected.

When in Quick Mask mode, you can paint white over areas you want selected and black over areas that you don't want selected. When painting in the Quick Mask mode, increase the brush size by pressing the] key. Decrease the brush size by pressing the [key.

In the Selection mode, your selection seems to have a hard edge; you can soften those hard edges by using a softer brush in the Quick Mask mode. To make a brush softer, press Shift+[and press Shift+] to make a brush harder.

Because the Quick Mask mode makes selections based on the mask's values, you can create a mask by selecting the Gradient tool and dragging it across the image in Quick Mask mode. When you exit Quick Mask mode, it looks as though there is a straight-line selection, but actually the selection transitions as your gradient did. Choose any filter from the Filters menu and notice how the filter transitions into the untouched part of the image to which we applied the new and improved Graphic Pen filter.

If you're working in Quick Mask mode, choose Window⇨Channels to see that what you're working on is a temporary alpha channel. See the later section, "Saving Selections," for more about alpha channels.

Transforming selections

Don't deselect and start over again if you can just nudge or resize your selection a bit. You can scale, rotate, and even distort an existing selection. Follow these steps to transform a selection:

1. **Create a selection and then choose Select⇨Transform Selection.**

   You can use the bounding box to resize and rotate your selection.

   - Drag the handles to make the selection larger or smaller. Drag a corner handle to adjust width and height simultaneously. Shift+drag a corner handle to size proportionally.
   - Position the cursor outside of the bounding box to see the Rotate icon; drag when it appears to rotate the selection. Shift+drag to constrain to straight, 45-degree, or 90-degree angles.
   - Ctrl+drag (⌘+drag on a Mac) a corner point to distort the selection, as shown in Figure 4-4.

2. **Press Return or Enter or double-click in the center of the selection area to confirm the transformation; press Esc to release the transformation and return to the original selection.**

Figure 4-4: Distort, resize, and rotate a selection using the Transform Selection feature.

Feathering

Knowing how to retouch an image means little if you don't know how to make it discreet. If you boost up the color using curves to the CEO's face, do you want it to appear like a pancake has been attached to his cheek? Of course not — that isn't discreet at all (or very wise). That's where feathering comes in. *Feathering* a selection blurs its edges, so as to create a natural-looking transition between the selection and the background of the image.

To feather an image, follow these steps:

1. **Create a selection.**

   For the nonfeathered image shown on top in Figure 4-5, we used the Elliptical Marquee tool to make a selection. We then copied the selection, created a new, blank image, and pasted the selection into the new image.

   To create the feathered image on the bottom in Figure 4-5, we used the Elliptical Marquee tool to select the same area on the original image and went on to Step 2.

2. **Choose Select➪Modify➪Feather.**
3. **In the Feather dialog box that appears, type a value in the Feather Radius text field and then click OK.**

   For example, we entered **20** in the Feather Radius text field. (We then copied the selection, created a new image, and pasted the feathered selection into the new image to create the image on the bottom of Figure 4-5.) Voilà! The edges of the image are softened over a 20-pixel area, as shown on the bottom of Figure 4-5. This technique is also referred to as a *vignette* in the printing industry.

Figure 4-5: The top image doesn't have feathering, while the second has feathering applied.

The results of the feathering depend upon the resolution of the image. A feather of 20 pixels in a 72-ppi (pixels per inch) image will be a much larger area than a feather of 20 pixels in a 300-ppi image. Typical amounts for a nice vignette on an edge of an image would be 20 to 50 pixels. Experiment with your images to find what works best for you.

This feathering effect created a nice soft edge to your image, but it's also useful when retouching images:

1. **Using any selection method, create a selection around a part of an image that you want to lighten.**
2. **Choose Select⇨Modify⇨Feather; in the Feather dialog box that appears, enter 25 in the Feather Radius text field and click OK.**

   If you get an error message stating, No Pixels are more than 50% selected, click OK and create a larger selection.
3. **Choose Image⇨Adjustments⇨Curves.**
4. **Click in the center of the curve to add an anchor point and drag up to lighten the image.**

   This step lightens the midtones of the image.

Notice how the lightening fades out so that there is no definite edge to the correction. You can have more fun like this in Chapter 7 of this minibook, where we cover color correction.

Saving Selections

The term *alpha channel* sounds pretty complicated, but it's simply a saved selection. Depending upon the mode you're in, you already have several channels to contend with. A selection is just an extra channel that you can call on at any time.

To create an alpha channel, follow these steps:

1. **Create a selection that you want to save.**
2. **Choose Select⇨Save Selection.**
3. **Name the Selection and click OK.**

   In the Channels palette is an additional named channel that contains your selection.

To load a saved selection, follow these steps:

1. **Choose Select⇨Load Selection.**

   The Load Selection dialog box appears.

2. **Select your named channel from the Channel drop-down list.**

   If you have an active selection and then choose to load a selection, you have additional options. You can do the following with an active selection when loading a channel by selecting one of the following options:

   - **New Selection:** Eliminate the existing selection and create a new selection based upon the channel you select.
   - **Add To Selection:** Add the channel to the existing selection.
   - **Subtract From Selection:** Subtract the channel from the existing selection.
   - **Intersect With Selection:** Intersect the channel with the existing selection.

3. **Click OK.**

Other Adobe applications, such as InDesign, Illustrator, Premiere, and After Effects, can also recognize alpha channels.

Using the New Vanishing Point Feature

This incredible new feature lets you preserve correct perspective in edits of images that contain perspective planes, such as the sides of a building. You can do so much with this feature, and we provide you with a simple introduction. Try experimenting with multiple planes and copying and pasting items into the Vanishing Point window for even more effects. Follow these steps:

1. **Open a file that you want to apply a perspective filter to.**

   For this example, we used the file named Vanishing Point.psd. You can find the file in Windows OS at C:\Program Files\Adobe\Adobe Photoshop CS3\Samples and on the Mac OS at Applications\Adobe\Adobe Photoshop CS3\Samples.

2. **Create a new blank layer by clicking the Create A New Layer button at the bottom of the Layers palette.**

   If you create a new layer each time you use Vanishing Point, the results appear on a separate, editable layer. You can then use layer features, such as opacity, layer styles, and blending modes. Putting the Vanishing Point results in a separate layer also preserves your original image.

3. **Choose Filter⇨Vanishing Point.**

   A separate Vanishing Point window appears. If you receive an error message about an existing plane, click OK.

   If you're using a sample file from Photoshop, it may or may not have the plane at release time. To help you understand this feature better, you should delete the existing plane by pressing the Delete or Backspace key.

4. **Select the Create Plane tool and define the four corners nodes of the plane surface.**

   Try to use objects in the image to help create the plane.

   After the four corner nodes of the plane are created, the tool automatically is switched to the Edit Plane tool.

5. **Select and drag the corner nodes to make an accurate plane.**

   The plane grid should appear blue, not yellow or red, if it's accurate.

   After creating the plane, you can move, scale, or reshape the plane. Keep in mind that your results depend on how accurately the plane lines up with perspective of the image.

   You can use your first Vanishing Point session to simply creating perspective planes and then click OK. The planes appear in subsequent Vanishing Point sessions when you choose Filter⇨Vanishing Point. Saving perspective planes is especially useful if you plan to copy and paste an image into Vanishing Point and need to have a ready-made plane to target.

6. **Choose the Stamp tool in the Vanishing Point window and then choose On from the Heal drop-down menu in the options bar.**

   You're going to love where this is going. In the example, we simply clone the blue broom, but it should get your brains working about all the ways that you can apply this greatly improved feature.

7. **With the Stamp tool still selected, cross over the middle part of the broom and Alt+click (Option+Click on a Mac) to define it as the source that is to be cloned.**

8. **Without clicking, move toward the back of the perspective plane and click and drag to reproduce the cloned part of the image, in this case the broom.**

   Notice that it's cloned as a smaller version, in the correct perspective for its new location.

9. **Start from Step 7 and clone the broom in front of the dog or clone any region of an image up closer to the front of the perspective pane.**

   The cloned region is now cloned as a larger version of itself.

   You can use the Marquee tool options (Feather, Opacity, Heal, and Move Mode) at any time, either before or after making the selection. When you move the Marquee tool, the Stamp tool, or the Brush tool into a plane, the bounding box is highlighted, indicating that the plane is active.

10. **Click OK.**

    To preserve the perspective plane information in an image, save your document in PSD, TIFF, or JPEG format.

Chapter 5: Using the Photoshop Pen Tool

In this Chapter

- **Putting shape layers to work**
- **Using a path as a selection**
- **Creating clipping paths**

The Pen tool is the ultimate method to make precise selections. You can also use it to create vector shapes and clipping paths (silhouettes). In this chapter, you discover how to take advantage of this super multitasking tool. This chapter also shows you how to apply paths made with the Pen tool as shapes, selections, and clipping paths. If you're interested in the fundamentals of creating paths with the Pen tool in Illustrator, check out Book IV, Chapter 5, where we cover the Pen tool in more detail.

We recommend that you use the Pen tool as much as you can to truly master its capabilities. If you don't use it on a regular basis, it will seem awkward, but it does get easier! Knowing how to effectively use the Pen tool puts you a grade above the average Photoshop user, and the quality of your selections will show it. Read Chapter 9 of this minibook to find out how to use the Pen tool to create layer masks and adjustment layers.

Using Shape Layers

As a default, when you start creating with the Pen tool, Photoshop automatically creates a *shape layer,* which is useful for adding additional elements, but is frustrating if you're attempting to create just a path with the Pen tool. Select the Pen tool and note the default setting on the left side of the Options bar. You can choose from the following options:

- **Shape layers:** Creates a new shape layer, a filled layer that contains your vector path.
- **Paths:** Creates a path only; no layer is created.
- **Fill Pixels:** Creates pixels directly on the image. No editable path or layer is created. This option may not be useful to new users, but some existing users prefer to use this method because it's the only way to access the Line tool from previous versions.

Shape layers can be very useful when the goal of your design is to seamlessly integrate vector shapes and pixel data. A shape layer can contain vector shapes that you can then modify with the same features of any other layer. You can adjust the opacity of the shape layer, change the blending mode, and even apply layer effects to add drop shadows and dimension. Find out how to do this in Chapter 9 of this minibook.

Create a shape layer using any of these methods:

- **Create a shape with the Pen tool.** With the Pen tool, you can create interesting custom shapes and even store them for future use. We show you how in the following section.
- **Use one of the Vector Shape tools shown in Figure 5-1.** Vector shapes are premade shapes (you can even create your own!) that you can create by dragging on your image area with a shape tool.
- **Import a shape from Illustrator.** Choose File⇨Place to import an Illustrator file as a shape layer or path into Photoshop.

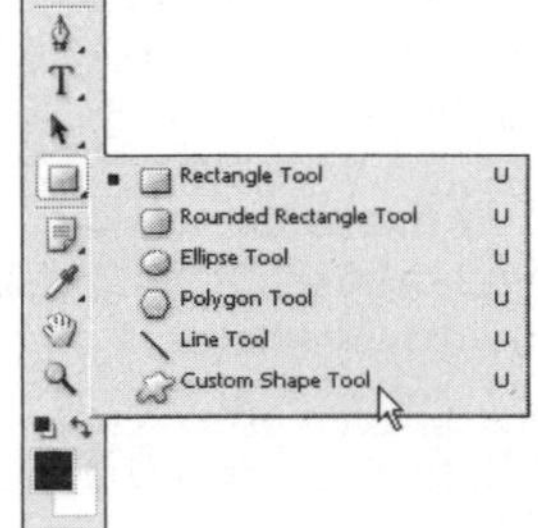

Figure 5-1: The Vector Shape tools.

Creating and using a custom shape

Perhaps you like the wave kind of shape (see Figure 5-2) that has been cropping up in design pieces all over the place.

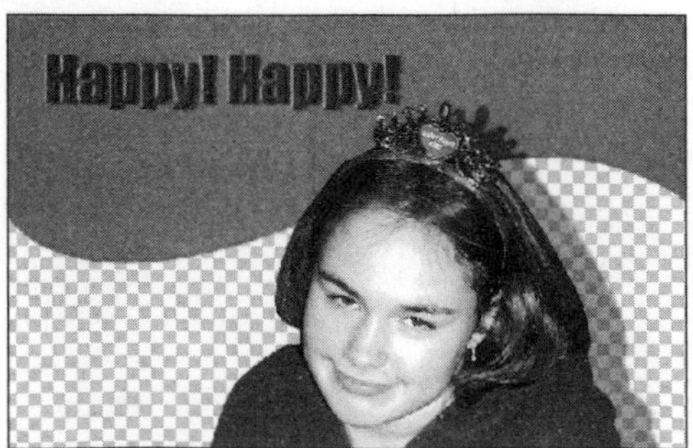

Figure 5-2: A custom wave shape integrated with an image in Photoshop.

Copy and paste shapes right from Illustrator CS3 to Photoshop CS3. Simply select your shape in Adobe Illustrator and choose Edit⇨Copy, then switch to the Photoshop application, and with a document open, choose Edit⇨Paste.

You can create a wavy shape like that, too. With an image or blank document open, just follow these steps:

1. **Click and drag with the Pen tool to create a wavy shape.**

   Don't worry about the size of the shape. The shape is vector, so you can scale it up or down to whatever size you need without worrying about making jagged edges. Just make sure that you close the shape (return back to the original point with the end point).

   As you create the shape, it fills in with your foreground color. Try to ignore it if you can; the next section shows you how to change the fill color, and Chapter 8 of this minibook covers how to change it to a transparent fill.

2. **With the shape still selected, choose Edit⇨Define Custom Shape, name the shape, and click OK.**

   After you have saved your custom shape, you can recreate it at any time. If you don't like the shape, choose Windows⇨ Layers to open the Layers palette and then drag the shape layer you just created to the Trash icon in the lower-right corner of the palette. If you'd like to experiment with your custom shape now, continue with these steps.

3. **Click and hold on the Rectangle tool to access the other hidden vector tools; select the last tool, the Custom Shape Tool.**

   When the Custom Shape tool is selected, a Shape drop-down menu appears on the Options bar at the top of the screen, as shown in Figure 5-3.

   You have lots of custom shapes to choose from, including the one you've just created. If you just saved a shape, yours is in the last square; you have to scroll down to select it.

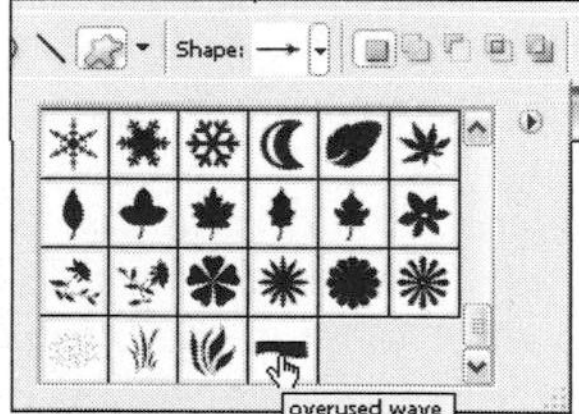

Figure 5-3: A Shape drop-down menu appears in the Vector Shape options toolbar when the Custom Shape tool is active.

4. **Select your custom shape; click and drag in the image area to create your shape.**

   You can make it any size that you want.

5. **To change the shape's size, choose Edit⇨Free Transform Path, press Ctrl+T (⌘+T on a Mac), or grab a bounding box handle and drag.**

   Shift+drag a corner handle to keep the shape proportional as you resize it.

Because a shape is created on its own layer, you can experiment with different levels of transparency and blending modes in the Layers palette. Figure 5-4 shows shapes that are partially transparent. Discover lots of other features you can use with shape layers in Chapter 9 of this minibook.

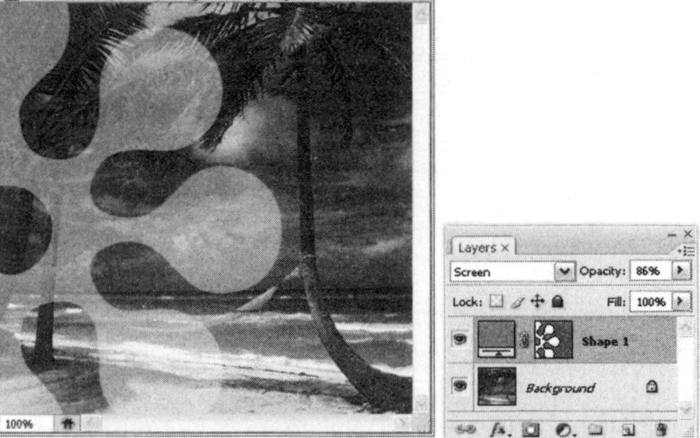

Figure 5-4: Experiment with blending modes and opacity changes on shape layers.

Changing the color of the shape

When you create a shape with a shape tool, the shape takes the color of your present foreground color. To change the color of an existing shape, open the Layers palette by choosing Window⇨Layers; notice that the Vector Shape tool creates a new layer for every shape you make. Creating a new layer is a benefit when it comes to creating special effects because the shape layer is independent of the rest of your image. (Read more about using layers in Chapter 9 of this minibook.)

To change a shape's color, double-click the color thumbnail, on the left in the shape layer. The Color Picker appears, as shown in Figure 5-5. To select a new color, drag the Hue slider up or down or click in the large color pane to select a color with the saturation and lightness that you want to use. Click OK when you're done.

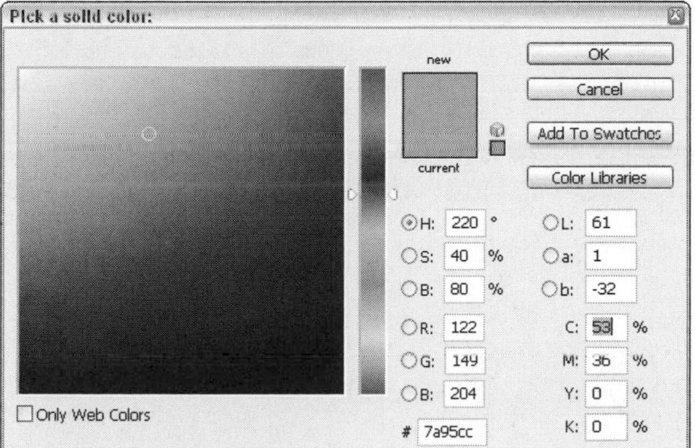

Figure 5-5: Double-click the color Thumbnail on the shape layer to select a new color.

Editing a shape

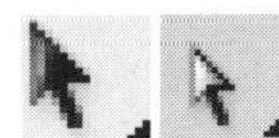

Like Adobe Illustrator, Photoshop provides both a Path Selection tool and a Direct Selection tool. The Direct Selection tool is hidden under the Path Selection tool. To move an entire shape on a layer, choose the Path Selection tool and drag the shape.

To edit the shape, deselect the shape (while using the Path Selection or Direct Selection tool, click outside the shape). Then select the Direct Selection tool. With the Direct Selection tool, click individual anchor points and handles to edit and fine-tune the shape, as shown in Figure 5-6.

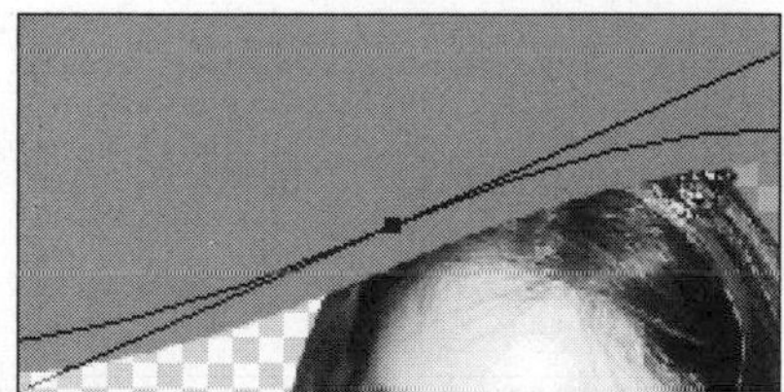

Figure 5-6: Edit individual anchor points with the Direct Selection tool.

Removing a shape layer

Because the Pen tool now has multiple options, you may find yourself unexpectedly creating a shape layer. Delete a shape layer by dragging the layer thumbnail to the Trash icon in the lower-right corner of the Layers palette.

If you want to keep your path but throw away the shape layer, choose Window➪Paths. Then drag the shape vector mask to the New Path icon, as shown in Figure 5-7, which creates a saved path. Now you can throw away the shape layer.

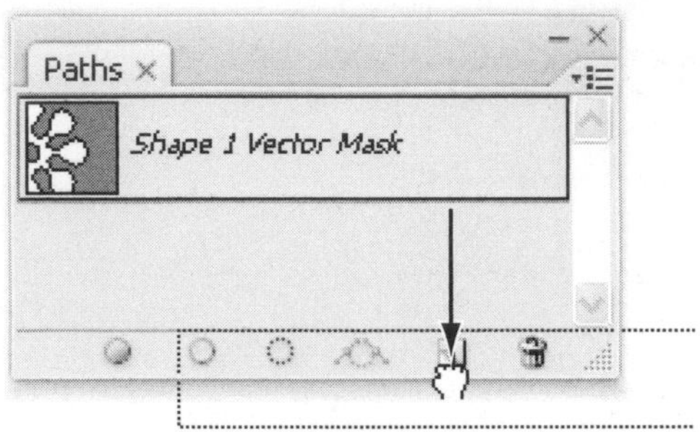

Figure 5-7: Save your path by dragging the shape path to the Create New Path icon before throwing away the shape layer.

Using a Path as a Selection

You can use the Pen tool to create precise selections that would be difficult to create with other selection methods. The Pen tool produces clean edges that print well and can be edited using the Direct Selection tool. Before using the Pen tool, make sure that you click the Paths button on the Options bar.

To use a path as a selection (which is extremely helpful when you're trying to make a precise selection), follow these steps:

1. **Open any file, or create a new blank file.**
2. **Using the Pen tool (make sure that the Paths button is selected on the Options bar or else you will create a Shape layer!), click to place anchor points; drag to create a curved path around the image area that you want selected; and completely close the path by returning to the start point (see Figure 5-8).**

   Use the techniques that we discuss in Book IV, Chapter 4 to perform this step. A circle will appear before you click to close the path.
3. **Choose Window➪Paths.**

Figure 5-8: Make sure that you select the Paths button to create only the pen path, not a shape layer.

In the Paths palette, you can create new and activate existing paths, apply a stroke, or turn paths into selections by clicking the icons at the bottom of the palette (see Figure 5-9).

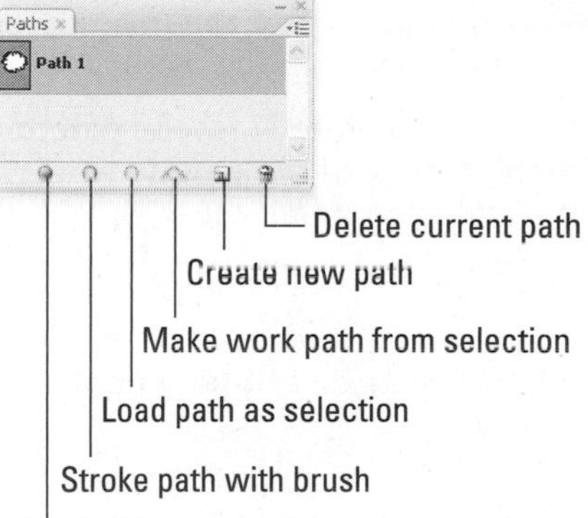

Figure 5-9: The Paths palette and its options.

4. **Click the Load Path As Selection icon.**

   The path is converted into a selection.

Use this quick and easy method for turning an existing path into a selection: Ctrl+click (⌘+click on a Mac) the path thumbnail in the Paths palette.

Clipping Paths

If you want to create a beautiful silhouette that transfers well to other applications for text wrapping (see Figure 5-10), create a clipping path.

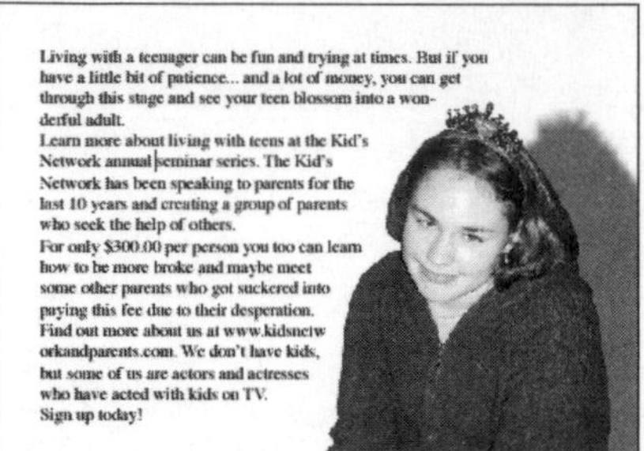

Living with a teenager can be fun and trying at times. But if you have a little bit of patience... and a lot of money, you can get through this stage and see your teen blossom into a wonderful adult.
Learn more about living with teens at the Kid's Network annual seminar series. The Kid's Network has been speaking to parents for the last 10 years and creating a group of parents who seek the help of others.
For only $300.00 per person you too can learn how to be more broke and maybe meet some other parents who got suckered into paying this fee due to their desperation.
Find out more about us at www.kidsnetworkandparents.com. We don't have kids, but some of us are actors and actresses who have acted with kids on TV.
Sign up today!

Figure 5-10: Clipping paths allow you to create silhouettes in other applications.

Creating a clipping path is easy when you have a good path! Just follow these steps:

1. **Use the Pen tool to create a path around the image area that is to be the silhouette.**
2. **In the Paths palette, choose Save Path from the palette menu (click the triangle in the upper-right corner of the palette to access this menu), as shown in Figure 5-11, and then name the path.**

   (If Save Path isn't an option, your path has already been saved; skip to Step 3.)
3. **From the same palette menu, choose Clipping Path.**

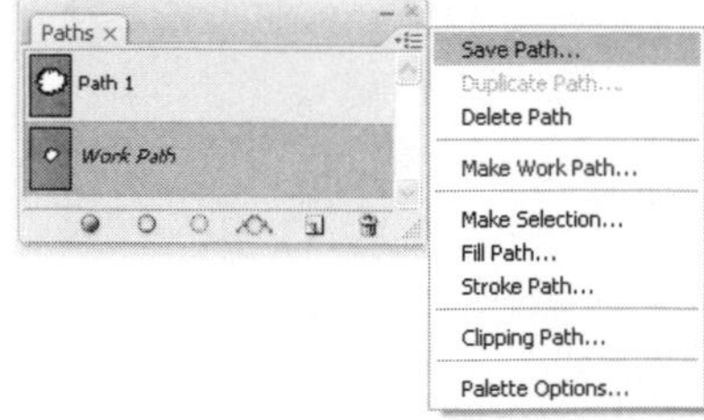

Figure 5-11: Convert your work path to a saved path.

4. **In the Clipping Paths dialog box, choose your path from the drop-down list if it's not already selected; click OK.**

   Leave the Flatness Device Pixels text field blank unless you have a need to change it. The flatness value determines how many device pixels are used to create your silhouette. The higher the amount, the less points are created, thereby allowing for faster processing time. This speed does come at a cost, though; set the flatness value too high, and you may see (you'd have to look really close) straight edges instead of curved edges.

5. **Choose File⇨Save As and in the Format drop-down list, select Photoshop EPS; in the EPS Options dialog box that appears, accept the defaults and click OK.**

   If you get PostScript errors when printing, choose Clipping Path from the palette menu and up the value to 2 pixels in the Flatness Device Pixels text field. Keep returning to this text field and upping the value until the file prints, or give up and try printing your document with another printer.

If you're placing this file in other Adobe applications, such as InDesign, you don't need to save the file as EPS; you can leave it as a Photoshop (`.psd`) file.

Chapter 6: Thinking about Resolution Basics

In This Chapter

- Understanding resolution basics
- Adjusting file size
- Applying the Unsharp Mask filter to an image

Something as important as getting the right resolution for your images deserves its own chapter, but fortunately, the topic isn't all that complex. In this chapter, you discover the necessary resolution for various uses of Photoshop imagery (from printing a high-resolution graphic to e-mailing a picture of your kids to Mom), how to properly increase the resolution, and how to adjust image size.

Having the proper resolution is important to the final outcome of your image, especially if you plan to print that image. Combine the information here with using the correction tools that we show you in the next chapter, and you should be ready to roll with great imagery.

Creating Images for Print

To see and make changes to the present size and resolution of an image in Photoshop, choose Image⇨Image Size. The Image Size dialog box appears.

The Width and Height text fields in the Pixel Dimensions area of the Image Size dialog box are used for on-screen resizing, such as for the Web and e-mail. The Width and Height text fields in the Document Size area show the size at which the image will print. The Resolution text field determines the resolution of the printed image; a higher value means a smaller, more finely detailed printed image.

Before you decide upon a resolution, you should understand what some of the resolution jargon means:

- **dpi (dots per inch):** The resolution of an image when printed.
- **lpi (lines per inch):** The varying dot pattern that printers and presses use to create images (see Figure 6-1). This dot pattern is referred to as the lpi, even though it represents rows of dots. The higher the lpi, the finer the detail, and the less of the dot pattern or line screen you see.
- **Dot gain:** The spread of ink as it's applied to paper. Certain types of paper will wick a dot of ink farther than others. For example, newsprint has a high dot gain and typically prints at 85 lpi; a coated stock paper has a lower dot gain and can be printed at 133–150 lpi and even higher.

Human eyes typically can't detect a dot pattern in a printed image at 133 dpi or higher.

Figure 6-1: The dot pattern used to print images is referred to as lpi (lines per inch).

Deciding the resolution or dpi of an image requires backward planning. If you want to create the best possible image, you should know where it will print *before* deciding the resolution. Communicate with your printer service if the image is going to press. If you're sending your image to a high-speed copier, you can estimate that it will handle 100 lpi; a desktop printer will handle 85 lpi to 100 lpi.

The resolution formula

When creating an image for print, keep this formula in mind:

2 x lpi = dpi (dots per inch)

This formula means that if your image is going to press using 150 lpi, have your image at 300 dpi. To save space, many designers use 1.5 x lpi and get pretty much the same results; you can decide which works best for you.

Changing the resolution

Using the Image Size dialog box is only one way that you can control the resolution in Photoshop. Even though you can increase the resolution, do so sparingly and avoid it if you can. The exception is when you have an image that is large in dimension size but low in resolution, like those that you typically get from a digital camera. You may have a top-of-the-line digital camera that produces 72 dpi images, but at that resolution, the pictures are 28 x 21 inches (or larger)!

To increase the resolution of an image without sacrificing quality:

1. **Choose Image⇨Image Size.**

   The Image Size dialog box appears, as shown in Figure 6-3.

2. **Deselect the Resample Image check box.**

   This way, Photoshop doesn't add additional pixels.

3. **Enter the desired resolution in the Resolution text field.**

   Photoshop keeps the pixel size (the size of the image on screen) the same, but the document size (the size of the image when printed) decreases when you enter a higher resolution.

4. **If the image isn't the size that you need it to be, select the Resample Image check box and type the size in the Width and Height text fields in the Document Size section.**

   Note that it's best to reduce the size of a bitmap image, such as a digital photo, rather than increase it.

   You can also deselect the Resample Image check box and essentially play a game of give and take to see what the resolution will be when you enter the size you want your image printed at in the Width and Height text fields in the Document Size area.

   Images can typically be scaled from 50 to 120 percent before looking jagged (to scale by a percentage, select Percent from the drop-down lists beside the Width and Height text fields). Keep this in mind when placing and resizing your images in a page layout application, such as InDesign.

5. **Click OK when you're finished; double-click the Zoom tool in the toolbox to see the image at actual size on-screen.**

To increase the resolution *without* changing the image size, follow these steps. (This situation isn't perfect because pixels that don't presently exist are created by Photoshop and may not be totally accurate. Photoshop tries to give you the best image, but you may have some loss of detail.)

1. **Choose Image➪Image Size.**
2. **When the Image Size dialog box appears, make sure that the Resample Image check box is selected.**

   Note that Bicubic is selected in the method drop-down list. This method is the best, but slowest, way to reinterpret pixels when you resize an image. Using this method, Photoshop essentially looks at all the pixels and takes a good guess as to how the newly created pixels should look, based upon surrounding pixels.
3. **Enter the resolution that you need in the Resolution text field, click OK, and then double-click the Zoom tool to see the image at actual size.**

Determining the Resolution for Web Images

Did you ever have somebody e-mail you an image, and, after spending 10 minutes downloading it, you discover that the image is so huge that all you can see on the monitor is your nephew's left eye? Many people are under the misconception that if an image is 72 dpi, it's ready for the Web. Actually, pixel dimension is all that matters for Web viewing of images; this section helps you make sense of this.

Most people view Web pages in their browser windows in an area of about 640 x 480 pixels. You can use this figure as a basis for any images you create for the Web, whether the viewer is using a 14-inch or a 21-inch monitor. (Remember, those people who have large monitors set to high screen resolutions don't necessarily want a Web page taking up the whole screen!) If you're creating images for a Web page or to attach to an e-mail message, you may want to pick a standard size to design by, such as 600 x 400 pixels at 72 dpi.

To use the Image Size dialog box to determine the resolution and size for on-screen images, follow these steps:

1. **Have an image open and choose Image➪Image Size.**

   The Image Size dialog box appears.
2. **To make the image take up half the width of a typical browser window, type 300 (half of 600) in the top Width text field.**

   If a little chain link is visible to the right, the Constrain Proportions check box is selected, and Photoshop automatically determines the height from the width that you entered.

3. **Click OK and double-click the Zoom tool to see the image at actual size on-screen.**

   That's it! It doesn't matter whether your image is 3,000 or 30 pixels wide, as long as you enter the correct dimensions in the Pixel Dimension area, the image works beautifully.

Applying the Unsharp Mask Filter to an Image

When you resample an image in Photoshop, it can become blurry. A good practice is to apply the Unsharp Mask filter. This feature sharpens the image based upon levels of contrast, while keeping the areas that don't have contrasting pixels smooth. You do have to set up this feature correctly to get good results. Here is the down-and-dirty method of using the Unsharp Mask filter:

1. **Choose View⇨Actual Pixels or double-click the Zoom tool.**

   When you're using a filter, you want to view your image at actual size to best see the effect.

2. **Choose Filter⇨Sharpen⇨Unsharp Mask.**

   In the Unsharp Mask dialog box that appears, set these three options:

   - **Amount:** The Amount value ranges from 0 to 500. The amount that you choose has a lot to do with the subject matter. Sharpening a car or appliance at 300 to 400 is fine, but do this to the CEO's 75-year-old wife, and you may suffer an untimely death because every wrinkle, mole, or hair will magically become more defined. If you're not sure what to use, start with 150 and play around until you find an Amount value that looks good.
   - **Radius:** The Unsharp Mask filter creates a halo around the areas that have enough contrast to be considered an edge. Typically, leaving the amount between 1 to 2 is fine for print, but if you're creating a billboard or poster, increase the size.
   - **Threshold:** This option is the most important one in the Unsharp Mask dialog box. The Threshold setting is what determines what should be sharpened. If left at zero, you'll see noise throughout the image, much like the grain that you see in high-speed film. Bring it up to 10, and this triggers the Unsharp Mask filter to apply only the sharpening when the pixels are ten shades or more away from each other. The amount of tolerance ranges from 1 to 255. Apply too much, and no sharpening appears; apply too little, and the image becomes grainy. A good number to start with is 10.

To compare the original state of the image with the preview of the Unsharp Mask filter's effect in the preview pane of the Unsharp Mask dialog box, click and hold on the image in the Preview pane; this shows the original state of the image. When you release the mouse button, the unsharp mask is previewed again.

3. **When you've made your choice, click OK.**

   The image appears to have more detail.

Once in a while, stray colored pixels may appear after you apply the Unsharp Mask filter. Get in the habit of choosing Edit➪Fade Unsharp Mask immediately after applying the Unsharp Mask filter. In the Fade dialog box, select the Luminosity blend mode from the Mode drop-down list and then click OK. This step applies the Unsharp Mask filter to the grays in the image only, thereby eliminating sharpening of colored pixels.

New in Photoshop CS3 you can use smart filters. Smart filters allow you to undo, all or some of any filter, including sharpening filters, that you apply to a layer. Find out how by reading Chapter 8 in this minibook.

Chapter 7: Creating a Good Image

In This Chapter

- Understanding the Histogram
- Getting ready to correct an image
- Making a good tone curve
- Discovering adjustment layers

With all the incredible things you can do in Photoshop, you can easily forget the basics. Yes, you can create incredible compositions with special effects, but if the people look greenish, it detracts from the image. Get in the habit of building good clean images before heading into the artsy filters and fun things. Color correction isn't complicated, and if done properly, it will produce magical results in your images. In this chapter, you discover how to use the values you read in the Info palette and use the Curves dialog box to produce quality image corrections.

Reading a Histogram

Before making adjustments, look at the image's *histogram,* which displays an image's tonal values, to evaluate whether the image has sufficient detail to produce a high-quality image. In Photoshop CS3, choose Window➪Histogram to display the Histogram palette.

The greater the range of values in the histogram, the greater the detail. Poor images without much information can be difficult, if not impossible, to correct. The Histogram palette also displays the overall distribution of shadows, midtones, and highlights to help you determine which tonal corrections are needed.

Figure 7-1 shows a good full histogram that indicates a smooth transition from one shade to another in the image. Figure 7-2 shows that when a histogram is spread out and has gaps in it, the image is jumping too quickly from one shade to another, producing a posterized effect. *Posterization* is an effect that reduces tonal values to a limited amount, creating a more defined range of values from one shade to another. Great if you want it, yucky if you want a smooth tonal change from one shadow to another.

So how do you get a good histogram? If you're scanning, make sure that your scanner is set for the maximum amount of colors. Scanning at 16 shades of gray gives you 16 lines in your histogram . . . not good!

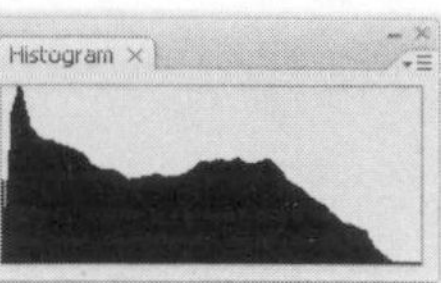

Figure 7-1: A histogram shows lots of information, and this one shows an image that has smooth transitions from one color to another.

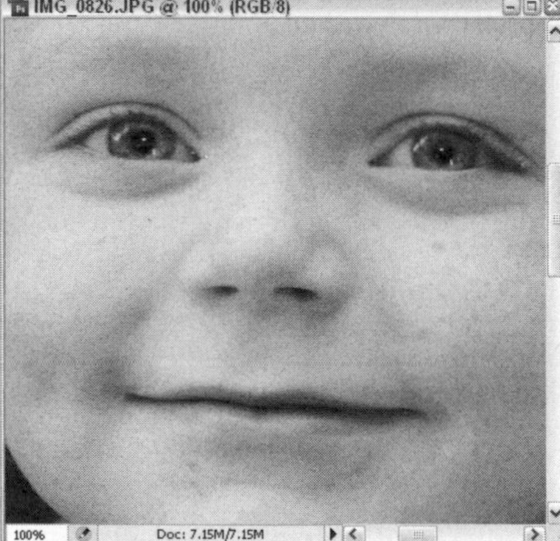

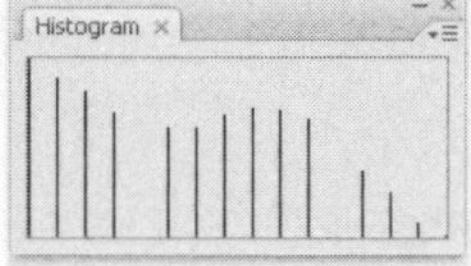

Figure 7-2: A histogram showing little information; the enlarged image shows the lack of smoothness in the gradation of color.

If you have a bad histogram, we recommend that you rescan or reshoot the image. If you have a good histogram to start with, keep the histogram good by not messing around with multiple tone correction tools. Most professionals use the Curves feature . . . and that's it. Curves (choose Image➪Adjustments➪Curves), if used properly, do all the adjusting of levels (brightness and contrast) and color balance, all in one step. You can read more about curves in the section "Creating a Good Tone Curve," later in this chapter.

Figure 7-3 shows what happens to a perfectly good histogram when someone gets a little too zealous and uses the entire plethora of color correction controls in Photoshop. Just because the controls are there doesn't mean that you have to use them.

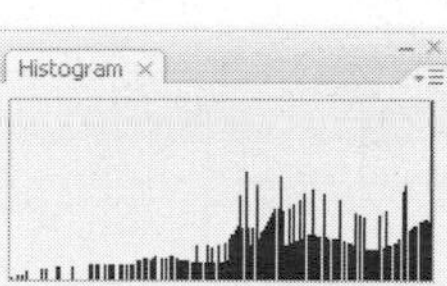

Figure 7-3: Tonal information is broken up as more and more adjustments are made to an image.

If you see a Warning icon appear while you're making adjustments, double-click anywhere on the histogram to refresh the display.

Breaking into key types

Don't panic if your histogram is smashed all the way to the left or right. The bars of the histogram represent tonal values. You can break down the types of images, based upon their values, into three key types:

- **High key:** A very light-colored image, such as the image shown in Figure 7-4. Information is pushed toward the right in the histogram. Color correction has to be handled a little differently for these images to keep the light appearance to them.
- **Low key:** A very dark image, such as the image shown in Figure 7-5. Information is pushed to the left in the histogram. This type of image is difficult to scan on low-end scanners because the dark areas tend to blend together with little definition.

Figure 7-4: A high key image is a light image.

Figure 7-5: A low key image is a dark image.

- **Mid key:** A typical image with a full range of shades would be considered mid key, such as the image shown in Figure 7-6. These images are the most common and easiest to work with. In this chapter, we deal with images that are considered mid key.

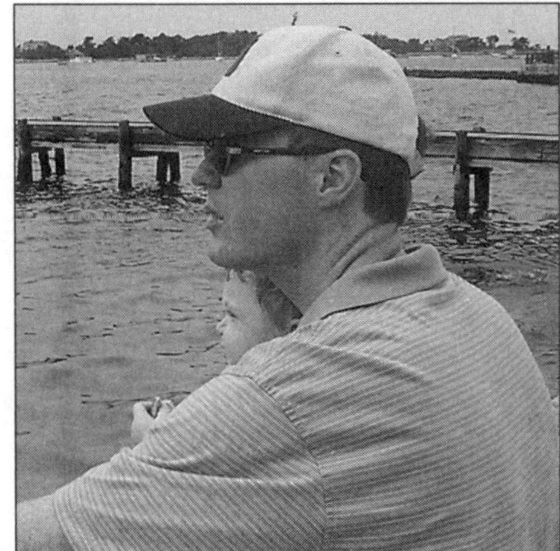

Figure 7-6: A typical image with a full range of values is a mid key image.

Setting up the correction

To produce the best possible image, try to avoid correcting in CMYK mode. If your images are typically in RGB or LAB mode, keep them in that mode throughout the process. Convert them to CMYK only when you're finished manipulating the image.

Don't forget! Press Ctrl+Y (⌘+Y on a Mac) to toggle on and off the CMYK preview so that you can see what your image will look like in CMYK mode without converting it!

Set up these items before starting any color correction:

1. **Select the Eyedropper tool; on the Options bar, change the sample size from Point Sample to 3 By 3 Average in the Sample Size drop-down list.**

   The Eyedropper tool is hidden in the Count Tool if you have Photoshop Extended.

   This setting gives you more accurate readings.
2. **If the Histogram palette isn't already visible, choose Window➪Histogram.**
3. **If the Info palette isn't already visible, choose Window➪Info to show the Info palette so that you can check values.**
4. **Make sure that your color settings are correct.**

   If you're not sure how to check or set up color settings, see Chapter 3 of this minibook.

Creating a Good Tone Curve

A *tone curve* represents the density of an image. To get the best image, you must first find the highlight and shadow points in the image. An image created in less-than-perfect lighting conditions may be washed out or have odd color casts. See Figure 7-7 for an example of an image with no set highlight and shadow. Check out Figure 7-8 to see an image that went through the process of setting a highlight and shadow.

Figure 7-7: The image is murky before defining a highlight and shadow.

To make the process of creating a good tone curve more manageable, we've broken the process into four parts:

- ✦ Finding the highlight and shadow
- ✦ Setting the highlight and shadow
- ✦ Adjusting the midtone
- ✦ Finding a neutral

Even though each part has its own set of steps, you must go through all four parts to accomplish the task of creating a good tone curve (unless you're working with grayscale images, in which case you can skip the neutral part). In this example, an Adjustment layer is used for the curve adjustments. The benefit is that you can turn off the visibility of the adjustment at a later point or double-click the adjustment layer thumbnail to make ongoing edits without destroying your image.

Figure 7-8: The tonal values are opened up after highlight and shadow have been set.

Finding and setting the highlight and shadow

In the noncomputer world, you'd spend a fair amount of time trying to locate the lightest and darkest part of an image. Fortunately, you can cheat in Photoshop by using some of the new features in the Curves palette. Here's how you access the palette:

1. **With an image worthy of adjustment — meaning one that isn't perfect already — choose Window⇨Layer (if the Layers palette isn't already open).**

2. **Click and hold on the Create New Fill Or Adjustment Layer button at the bottom of the Layers palette and select Curves.**

   The Curves palette, shown in Figure 7-9, appears.

Notice the grayed-out histogram behind the image Curve window. The histogram aids you in determining where you need to adjust the image's curve.

If you're correcting in RGB (as you should be!), the tone curve may be opposite of what you think it should be. Instead of light to dark displaying as you'd expect, RGB displays dark to light. Now think about it: RGB is generated with light, and no RGB means that there is no light and you therefore have black. Turn all RGB on full force, and you create white. Try pointing three filtered lights, one red, one green, and one blue. The three lights pointed in one direction really do create white.

If working with RGB confuses you, simply click on the Pigment/Ink% check box, shown in Figure 7-10. The sample in this example uses the curve based upon pigment.

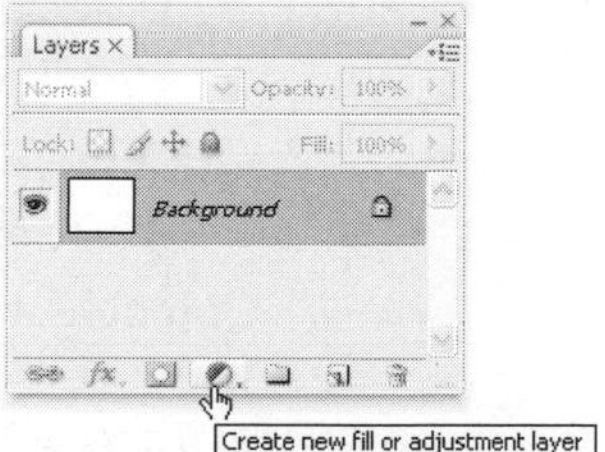

Figure 7-9: You can access the new and improved Curves palette by using the Create New Fill Or Adjustment Layer button.

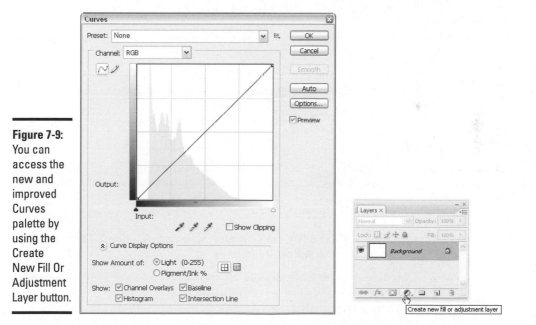

Note that in the new Curves palette, you see a Preset drop-down menu that offers quick fixes using standard curves for certain corrections. These settings are great for quick fixes, but for the best image, you should create a custom curve.

The first thing you need to do in the Curves palette is determine the lightest and darkest part of the image, which is referred to as locating the highlight and shadow:

1. **To help you see where the highlight and shadow are in the image, check the Show Clipping check box.**

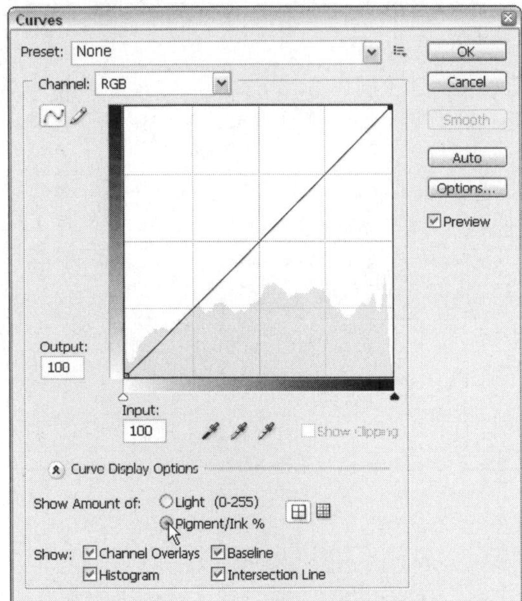

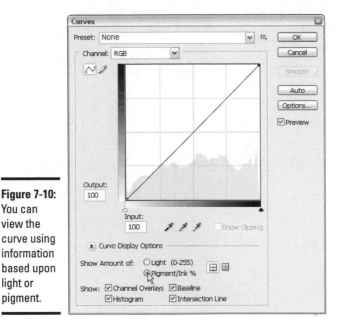

Figure 7-10: You can view the curve using information based upon light or pigment.

2. **Grab the right modify curve slider, shown in Figure 7-11, and slide it until you start to see white appear.**

   Coincidently, the white should appear where you see your histogram (grayed out in the curves palette) begin.

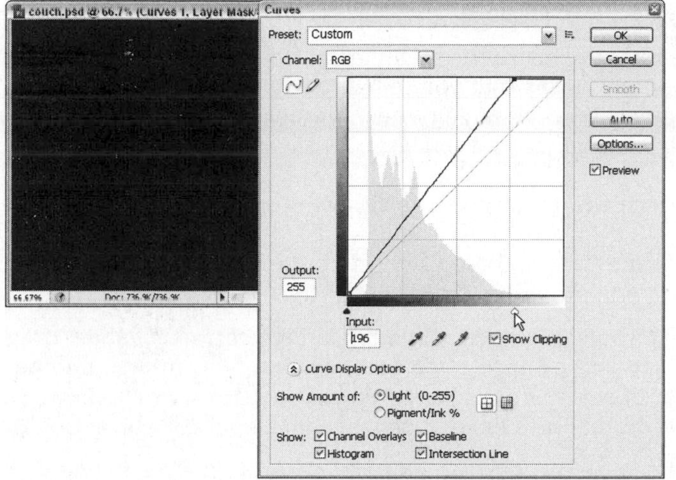

Figure 7-11: Use the clipping tools to locate the highlight of an image.

Book II Chapter 7

Creating a Good Image

3. **Now grab the left modify curve slider and drag it until you see the darker part of the image peak in, as shown in Figure 7-12, and then uncheck the Show Clipping check box.**

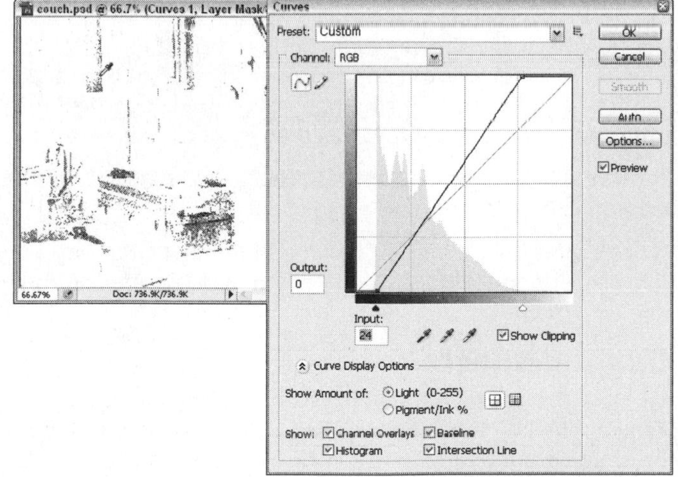

Figure 7-12: Use the clipping tools to locate the shadow of an image.

Adjusting the midtone

You may have heard the statement, "Open up the midtones." This phrase essentially means that you're lightening the midtonal values of an image. In many cases, opening up the midtones is necessary to add contrast and bring out detail in your image.

To adjust the midtones, follow these steps:

1. **In the Curves dialog box, click the middle of the curve ramp to create an anchor point; drag up slightly.**

   The image lightens. (If you're in Pigment/Ink % mode, drag down to lighten the image.) Don't move a dramatic amount and be very careful to observe what is happening in your Histogram palette (which you should always have open when making color corrections).

   Because you set highlight and shadow (see preceding section) and are now making a midtone correction, you see the bars in the histogram spreading out. The spreading of the information is necessary to a point, and it's the reason why you don't click OK until *all steps* have been taken in the Curves dialog box.

2. **To adjust the three-quarter tones (the shades around 75 percent), click halfway between the bottom of the curve ramp and the midpoint to set an anchor point.**

   Use the grid in the Curves dialog box to find it easily. (In Pigment/Ink %, the three-quarter point is in the upper section of the color ramp.) Adjust the three-quarter area of the tone curve up or down slightly to create contrast in the image. Again, keep an eye on your histogram!

3. **If you're working on a grayscale image, your tonal correction is done, and you can click OK.**

   If you're working on a color image, don't click OK; keep the Curves dialog box open for the final step, which is outlined in the next section.

Finding a neutral

The last step in creating a tone curve only applies if you're working on a color image. The key to understanding color is knowing that equal amounts of color create gray. By positioning the mouse cursor over gray areas in an image and reading the values in the Info palette, you can determine what colors you need to adjust.

1. **With your Curves dialog box open, position it so that you can see the Info palette.**

   If the Info palette is buried under another palette or a dialog box, choose Window⇨Info to bring it to the front.

2. **Position your cursor over your image and, in the Info palette, look for the RGB values in the upper-left section.**

   You see color values and then forward slashes and more color values. The numbers before the slash indicate the values in the image before you opened the Curves dialog box; the numbers after the slash show the values now that you have made changes in the Curves dialog box. Pay attention to the values after the slashes.

3. **Position the cursor over something gray in your image.**

   It can be a shadow on a white shirt, a counter top, a road — anything that is a shade of gray. Look at the Info palette. If your image is perfectly color balanced, the RGB values following the forward slashes should all be the same.

4. **If your color isn't balanced, click the Set Gray Point Eyedropper in the Curves dialog box and click the neutral or gray area of the image.**

   The middle eyedropper (Set Gray Point) is a handy way of bringing the location that you click on closer together in RGB values, thereby balancing the colors.

5. **Now you can click OK; if you're asked whether you want to save your color target values, click Yes.**

Curves can be as complex or simple as you make them. As you gain more confidence using them, you can check neutrals throughout an image to ensure that all unwanted color casts are eliminated. You can even individually adjust each color's curve by selecting them from the Channel drop-down list in the Curves dialog box.

When you're finished with color correction, using the Unsharp Mask filter on your image is a good idea. Chapter 5 of this minibook shows you how to use this filter.

Using an Adjustment Layer

You may go through a curve adjustment only to discover that some areas of the image are still too dark or too light. If this is the case, you're better off using an *adjustment layer,* which is a layer that adjusts a selected area of your image, based upon a correction applied on the layer. By using an adjustment layer, you can turn off the correction or change it over and over again with no degradation to the quality of the image. You can apply an adjustment layer by following these steps:

1. **Select the area of the image that needs adjustments.**

   See Chapter 4 of this minibook if you need a refresher on how to make selections in Photoshop.

2. **Choose Select➪Modify➪Feather to soften the selection.**

   The Feather dialog box appears.

3. **Enter a value into the Feather dialog box.**

   If you're not sure what value will work best, enter 15 in the Feather Radius text field and click OK.

4. **If the Layers palette isn't visible, choose Windows➪Layers; click and hold on the Create New Fill Or Adjustment Layer icon and select Curves from the menu that appears.**

5. **In the Curves dialog box, click the middle of the curve ramp to create an anchor point; drag up or down to lighten or darken your selected area and click OK.**

   Notice in the Layers palette (see Figure 7-13) that your adjustment layer, named Curves 2, has a mask to the right of it. The selected area is white; unselected areas are black.

Figure 7-13: You can paint on the Adjustment Layer mask to apply correction to different parts of the image.

6. **With your adjustment layer selected in the Layers palette, use the Brush tool to paint white to apply the correction to other areas of the image; paint with black to exclude areas from the correction.**

   You can even change the opacity using the Brush tool Options bar at the top to apply only some of the correction!

Testing a Printer

If you go through all the work of making color corrections to your images and you still get printed images that look hot pink, it may not be you! Test your printer by following these steps:

1. **Create a neutral gray out of equal RGB values (double-click the Fill Color swatch in the toolbar).**
2. **Create a shape, using your neutral gray as the fill color.**

   For example, you can use the Ellipse tool to create a circle or oval.
3. **Choose File➪Print and click OK to print the image from your color printer.**

If you're seeing heavy color casts, you need to adjust your printer; cleaning or replacing the ink cartridge may fix the problem. Check out Chapter 10 of this minibook for more about printing your Photoshop files.

Chapter 8: Working with Painting and Retouching Tools

In This Chapter

- Using the Swatches palette
- Getting to know foreground and background colors
- Introducing painting and retouching tools
- Discovering blending modes

This chapter shows you how to use the painting and retouching tools in Photoshop. If you're unsure about how good the painting you're about to do will look, create a new layer and paint on that. (See Chapter 9 of this minibook to find out how to create and use layers.) That way, you can delete the layer by dragging it to the Trash icon (at the bottom of the Layers palette) if you decide that you don't like what you have done. Don't forget to make the Eraser tool your friend! You can also repair painting or retouching mistakes by Alt+dragging (Option+dragging on a Mac) with the Eraser tool selected to erase the last version saved or present history state.

Have fun and be creative! Because Photoshop is pixel-based, you can create incredible imagery with the painting tools. Smooth gradations from one color to the next, integrated with blending modes and transparency, can lead from super-artsy to super-realistic effects. In this chapter, you discover painting fundamentals, and we show you how to use retouching tools to eliminate wrinkles, blemishes, and scratches. Don't you wish you could do that in real life?

Using the Swatches Palette

Use the Swatches palette to store and retrieve frequently used colors. The Swatches palette allows you to quickly select colors.

The Swatches palette also gives you access to many other color options. By using the palette menu, you can select from a multitude of different color schemes, such as Pantone or Web-safe color sets. These color systems are converted to whatever color mode in which you're working.

To sample and then store a color for later use, follow these steps:

1. **To sample a color from an image, select the Eyedropper tool in the toolbox and click a color on the image.**

   Alternatively, you can use any of the paint tools (the Brush tool for example) and Alt+click (Option+click on a Mac).

   The color you click becomes the foreground color.

2. **Store the color in the Swatches palette by clicking the New Swatch button at the bottom of the Swatches palette.**

Anytime you want to use that color again, simply click it in the Swatches palette to make it the foreground color.

Choosing Foreground and Background Colors

At the bottom of the toolbox reside the foreground and background color swatches. The *foreground color* is the color that you apply when using any of the painting tools. The *background color* is the color that you see if you erase or delete pixels from the image.

Choose a foreground or background color by clicking the swatch, which opens the Color Picker dialog box. To use the color picker, you can either enter values in the text fields on the right, or you can slide the hue slider.

Pick the hue (color) that you want to start with and then click in the color pane to the left to choose the amount of light and saturation (grayness or brightness) you want in the color. Select the Only Web Colors check box to choose one of the 216 colors in the Web safe color palette. The hexadecimal value used in HTML documents appears in the text field in the lower right of the color picker.

Add To Swatches

New in Photoshop CS3, you can click the Add To Swatches button right in the Color Picker to save a color for future use.

The Painting and Retouching Tools

Grouped together in the toolbox are the tools used for painting and retouching. The arrow in the lower right of a tool indicates that the tool has more related hidden tools; simply click and hold on the tool to see additional painting and retouching tools. In this chapter, we show you how the Spot Healing Brush, Healing Brush, Patch, Red Eye, Brush, Clone Stamp, History Brush, Eraser, and Gradient tools work. You also discover ways to fill shapes with colors and patterns.

Changing the brush

As you click to select different painting tools, note the Brush menu, second from the left, on the Options bar, as shown in Figure 8-1. Click the arrow to open the Brush Picker. You can use the Master Diameter slider to make the brush size larger or smaller, as well as change the hardness of the brush.

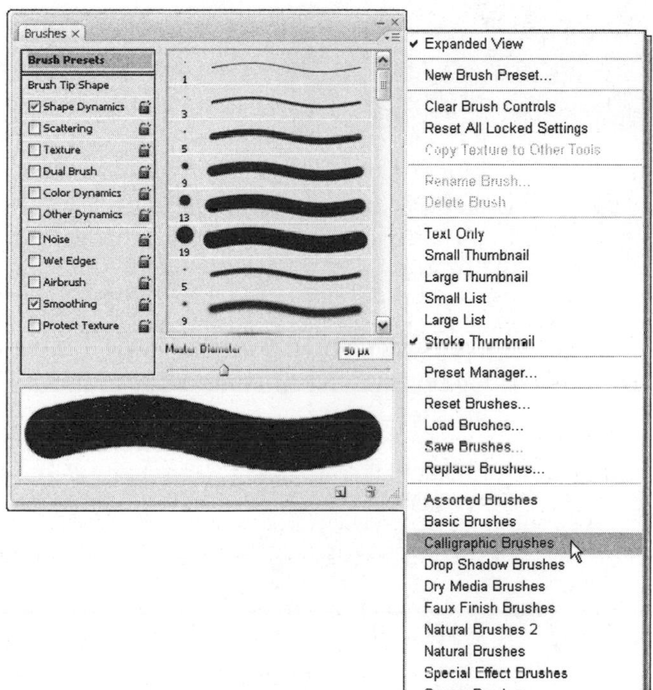

Figure 8-1: The Brushes Preset Picker.

The hardness refers to how "fuzzy" the edges are; a softer brush is more feathered and soft around the edges, while a harder edge would be more definite with a harder edge (see Figure 8-2).

Don't feel like accessing the Brushes palette every time you want to make a change? Press the right bracket] several times to make your brush diameter larger or press the left bracket [to make the brush diameter smaller. Press Shift+] to make the brush harder or Shift+[to make the brush softer.

Figure 8-2: A soft edge (left) as compared to a hard edge (right) brush stroke.

Choose Window⇨Brushes to see a list of Brush presets, plus many more brush options that you can use to create custom brushes. You can also choose other brush libraries using the palette menu (click the triangle in the upper-right corner of the Brushes Preset Picker). When you select an additional library, a dialog box appears, asking whether you want to replace the current brushes with the brushes in the selected library. Click the Append button to keep existing brushes and add the library to the list, or click OK to replace the existing brushes.

Access the Brushes Preset Picker as you're painting by right-clicking (Ctrl+ clicking on a Mac) anywhere in the image area. Double-click a brush to select it; press Esc to hide the Brushes palette.

The Spot Healing Brush Tool

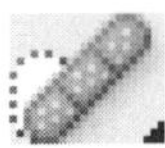

The Spot Healing Brush tool is destined to become everyone's favorite. Who wouldn't love a tool that can remove years from your face and any blemishes, too?

The Spot Healing Brush tool quickly removes blemishes and other imperfections in your images. Click a blemish and watch it paint matching texture, lighting, transparency, and shading to the pixels being healed. The Spot Healing Brush doesn't require you to specify a sample spot. The Spot Healing Brush automatically samples from around the retouched area.

The Healing Brush Tool

You can use the Healing Brush tool for repairs, such as eliminating scratches and dust from scanned images. The difference between the Spot Healing Brush tool (see preceding section) and the Healing Brush tool is that a sample spot is required before applying the Healing Brush. Follow these steps to use this tool:

1. **Select the Healing Brush tool in the toolbox (it's a hidden tool of the Spot Healing Brush tool).**
2. **Find an area in the image that looks good and then Alt+click (Option+click on a Mac) to sample that area.**

   For example, if you're going to eliminate wrinkles on a face, choose a wrinkle-free area of skin near the wrinkle. (Try to keep it relatively close in skin tone.)
3. **Position the mouse cursor over the area to be repaired and start painting.**

   The Healing Brush tool goes into action, blending and softening to create a realistic repair of the area.
4. **Repeat Steps 2 and 3 as necessary to repair the blemish, wrinkles, or scratches.**

The Patch Tool

Hidden behind the Healing Brush tool in the toolbox is the Patch tool. Use the Patch tool to repair larger areas, such as a big scratch or a large area of skin, by following these steps:

1. **Click and hold the Healing Brush tool to select the Patch tool; on the Options bar, select the Destination radio button.**

   You can either patch the source area or the destination. The preference is really up to you. We recommend taking a good source and dragging it over the location of the image that needs to be repaired.
2. **With the Patch tool still selected, drag to create a marquee around the source that you want to use as the patch.**

   The source would be an unscratched or wrinkle-free area.
3. **After you create the marquee, drag the selected source area to the destination that is to be repaired.**

   The Patch tool clones the selected source area as you drag it to the destination (the scratched area); when you release the mouse button, the tool blends in the source selection and repairs the scratched area!

Make the patch look even better by choosing Edit⇨Fade Patch Selection immediately after you apply the patch. Adjust the opacity until there are no tell-tale signs that you made a change.

The Red Eye Tool

So you finally got the group together and shot the perfect image, but red eye took over! *Red eye* is caused by a reflection of the camera's flash in the retina of your photo's subject(s). You see it more often when taking pictures in a dark room because the subject's iris is wide open. If you can, use your camera's red-eye reduction feature. Or, better yet, use a separate flash unit that you can mount on the camera farther away from the camera's lens.

You will love the fact that red eye is extremely easy to fix in Photoshop CS3. Just follow these steps:

1. **Select the Red Eye tool (hidden behind the Spot Healing Brush tool).**
2. **Click a red eye.**

   You should see a change immediately, but if you need to make adjustments to the size or the darkness amount, you can change options in the tool options bar at the top of your work area.

The Brush Tool

Painting with the Brush tool in Photoshop is much like painting in the real world. What you should know are all the nifty keyboard commands that you can use to be much more productive when painting. These shortcuts are really great, so make sure that you try them as you read about them. By the way, the keyboard commands you see in Table 8-1 work on all the painting tools.

Table 8-1 Brush Keyboard Shortcuts

Function	*Windows*	*Mac*
Choose the Brush tool	B	B
Increase brush size	]	]
Decrease brush size	[	[
Harden brush	Shift+]	Shift+]
Soften brush	Shift+[	Shift+[
Sample color	Alt+click	Option+click

Function	Windows	Mac
Switch foreground and background color	X	X
Change opacity by a given percentage	Type a number botwoon 1 and 100	Type a number botwoon1 and 100

If you're really into the brushes, you have lots of great options available in the Brushes palette (choose Window➪Brushes to open the palette).

You have several choices of attributes, most of which have dynamic controls in the menu options that allow you to vary brush characteristics by tilting or applying more pressure to a stylus pen (if you're using a pressure-sensitive drawing tablet), among other things.

Note: A warning sign indicates that you don't have the appropriate device attached to use the selected feature, such as a pressure-sensitive drawing tablet.

The following options are available in the Brushes palette:

✦ **Brush Tip Shape:** Select from these standard controls for determining brush dimensions and spacing.

✦ **Shape Dynamics:** Change the size of the brush as you paint.

✦ **Scattering:** Scatter the brush strokes and control brush tip count.

✦ **Texture:** Choose a texture from pre-existing patterns or your own.

Create a pattern by selecting an image area with the Rectangular Marquee tool. Choose Edit➪Define Pattern, name the pattern, and then click OK. The pattern is now available in the Brush palettes Texture choices.

✦ **Dual Brush:** Use two brushes at the same time.

✦ **Color Dynamics:** Change the color as you paint.

✦ **Other Dynamics:** Change the opacity and flow.

If you've been using Photoshop for several versions, you may notice that with Photoshop CS3, the attributes at the bottom of the Brushes palette aren't necessarily new, but have been moved from their old positions on the Options bar. Here is what these attributes do:

✦ **Noise:** Adds a grainy texture to the brush stroke.

✦ **Wet Edges:** Makes the brush stroke appear to be wet by creating a heavier amount of color on the edges of the brush strokes.

✦ **Airbrush:** Gives airbrush features to the Brush tools (CS3 no longer has a standalone Airbrush tool as in previous versions of Photoshop). You can also turn on the Airbrush feature by clicking the Airbrush button and adjusting the pressure and flow on the Options bar.

If you click and hold with the Brush tool out on the image area, the paint stops spreading. Turn on the Airbrush feature and notice that when you click and hold, the paint keeps spreading, just like with a can of spray paint. You can use the Flow slider on the Options bar to control the pressure.

✦ **Smoothing:** Smoothes the path that you create with the mouse.

✦ **Protect Texture:** Preserves the texture pattern when applying brush presets.

In addition to the preceding options, you can also adjust the jitter of the brush. The *jitter* specifies the randomness of the brush attribute. At 0 percent, an element doesn't change over the course of a stroke; at 100 percent, a stroke will totally vary from one attribute to another. For example, if you select Other Dynamics in the Brushes palette and then change the Opacity Jitter to 100 percent, the opacity will vary from 0 to 100 percent while you're painting.

After going through all the available brush options, you may want to start thinking about how you'll apply the same attributes later. Saving the Brush tool attributes is important as you increase in skill level.

The Clone Stamp Tool

The Clone Stamp tool is used for pixel-to-pixel cloning. It's different from the Healing Brush tool in that it does no automatic blending into the target area. You can use the Clone Stamp tool for removing a product name from an image, replacing a telephone wire that is crossing in front of a building, or duplicating an item.

Here's how you use the Clone Stamp tool:

1. **With the Clone Stamp tool selected, position the cursor over the area that you want to clone and then Alt+click (Option+click on a Mac) to define the clone source.**
2. **Position the cursor over the area where you want to paint the cloned pixels and start painting.**

   Note the cross hair at the original sampled area, as shown in Figure 8-3. As you're painting, the cross hair follows the pixels that you're cloning.

Figure 8-3: A cross hair over the source shows what you are cloning.

When using the Clone Stamp tool for touching up images, it's best to resample many times so as to not leave a seam where you replaced pixels. A good clone stamper Alt+clicks (Option+clicks on a Mac) and paints many times over until the retouching is complete.

The History Brush Tool

Choose Window➪History to see the History palette. You could work for weeks playing around in the History palette, but this section gives you the basics.

At the top of the History palette is a snapshot of the last saved version of the image. Beside the snapshot is an icon noting that it's the present History state.

By default, when you paint with the History Brush tool, it will paint back to the way the image looked at the last saved version, but you can click the empty square to the left of any state in the History palette to make it the target for the History Brush tool.

Use the History Brush tool to fix errors and add spunk to your images.

The Eraser Tool

You may not think of the Eraser tool as a painting tool, but it can be! When you drag on the image with the Eraser tool, it rubs out pixels to the background color. (Basically, it paints with the background color.) If you're dragging with the Eraser tool on a layer, it rubs out pixels to reveal the layer's transparent background. (You can also think of the Eraser tool as painting with transparency.)

The Eraser tool uses all the same commands as the Brush tools. You can make an eraser larger, softer, and more or less opaque. But even better, follow these steps to use the Eraser tool creatively:

1. **Open any color image and apply a filter.**

   For example, we chose Filter➪Blur➪Gaussian Blur. In the Gaussian Blur dialog box that appeared, we changed the blur to 5 and then clicked OK to apply the Gaussian Blur filter.

2. **Select the Eraser tool and press 5 to change it to 50 percent opacity.**

   You can also use the Opacity slider on the Options bar.

3. **Hold down the Alt (Option on a Mac) key to paint back 50 percent of the original image's state before applying the filter; continue painting in the same area to bring the image back to its original state!**

   The original sharpness of the image returns where you painted.

Holding down the Alt (Option on a Mac) key is the key command to erase to the last saved version (or history state) of the image. This tool is incredible for fixing little mistakes, or when you applied cool filters and you want to bring back some of the original image.

The Gradient Tool

Choose the Gradient tool and click and drag across an image area to create a gradient in the direction and length of the mouse motion. A short drag creates a short gradient; a long drag produces a smoother, longer gradient.

Using the Options bar, you can also choose the type of gradient that you want: Linear, Radial, Angle, Reflected, or Diamond.

As a default, gradients are created using the current foreground and background colors. Click the arrow on the gradient button on the Options bar to assign a different preset gradient.

To create a gradient, follow these steps:

1. **Choose the Gradient tool and click the Gradient Editor button on the Options bar.**

   The Gradient Editor dialog box appears. At the bottom of the gradient preview, you see two or more stops. The stops are where new colors are inserted into the gradient. They look like little house icons. Use the stops on the top of the gradient slider to determine the opacity.

2. **Click a stop and click the color swatch to the right of the word Color to open the color picker and assign a different color to the stop.**
3. **Click anywhere below the gradient preview to add more color stops.**
4. **Drag a color stop off the Gradient Editor dialog box to delete it.**
5. **Click on the top of the gradient preview to assign different stops with varying amounts of opacity, as shown in Figure 8-4.**

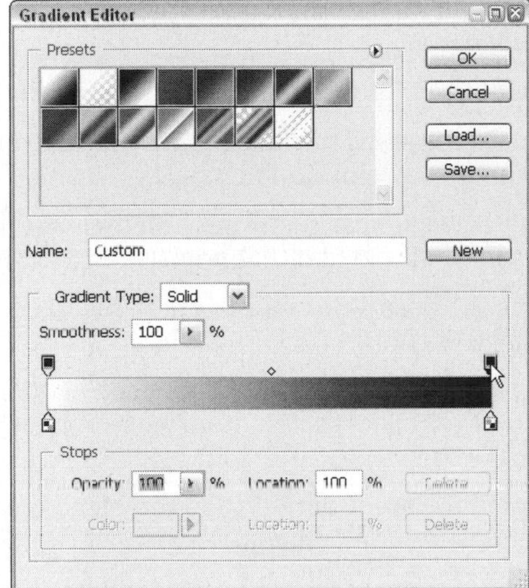

Figure 8-4: Assigning varying amounts of opacity using the stops on top of the gradient slider.

6. **When you're finished editing the gradient, name it and then click the New button.**

   The new gradient is added to the preset gradient choices.
7. **To apply your gradient, drag across a selection or image using the Gradient tool.**

Blending Modes

You can use blending modes to add flair to the traditional opaque paint. Use blending modes to paint highlights or shadows that allow details to show through from the underlying image or to colorize a desaturated image. You access the blending modes for paint tools from the Options bar.

You really can't get a good idea of how the blending mode will work with the paint color and the underlying color until you experiment. (That's what multiple undos are for!) Alternatively, you can copy the image you want to experiment with onto a new layer and hide the original layer; see Chapter 9 of this minibook for more about layers.

The following list describes the available blending modes:

- **Normal:** Paints normally, with no interaction with underlying colors.
- **Dissolve:** Gives a random replacement of the pixels, depending on the opacity at any pixel location.
- **Behind:** Edits or paints only on the transparent part of a layer.
- **Darken:** Replaces only the areas that are lighter than the blend color. Areas darker than the blend color don't change.
- **Multiply:** Creates an effect similar to drawing on the page with magic markers. Also looks like colored film that you see on theatre lights.
- **Color Burn:** Darkens the base color to reflect the blend color. If you're using white, no change occurs.
- **Linear Burn:** Looks at the color information in each channel and darkens the base color to reflect the blending color by decreasing the brightness.
- **Lighten:** Replaces only the areas darker than the blend color. Areas lighter than the blend color don't change.
- **Screen:** Multiplies the inverse of the underlying colors. The resulting color is always a lighter color.
- **Color Dodge:** Brightens the underlying color to reflect the blend color. If you're using black, there is no change.
- **Linear Dodge:** Looks at the color information in each channel and brightens the base color to reflect the blending color by increasing the brightness.
- **Overlay:** Multiplies or screens the colors, depending on the base color.
- **Soft Light:** Darkens or lightens the colors, depending on the blend color. The effect is similar to shining a diffused spotlight on the artwork.
- **Hard Light:** Multiplies or screens the colors, depending on the blend color. The effect is similar to shining a harsh spotlight on the artwork.
- **Vivid Light:** Burns or dodges the colors by increasing or decreasing the contrast.

- **Linear Light:** Burns or dodges the colors by decreasing or increasing the brightness.
- **Pin Light:** Replaces the colors, depending on the blend color.
- **Hard Mix:** Paints strokes that have no effect with other Hard Mix paint strokes. Use this mode when you want no interaction between the colors.
- **Difference:** Subtracts either the blend color from the base color or the base color from the blend color, depending on which has the greater brightness value. The effect is similar to a color negative.
- **Exclusion:** Creates an effect similar to, but with less contrast than, the Difference mode.
- **Hue:** Applies the hue (color) of the blend object onto the underlying objects but keeps the underlying shading or luminosity intact.
- **Saturation:** Applies the saturation of the blend color but uses the luminance and hue of the base color.
- **Color:** Applies the blend object's color to the underlying objects but preserves the gray levels in the artwork. This mode is great for tinting objects or changing their colors.
- **Luminosity:** Creates a resulting color with the hue and saturation of the base color and the luminance of the blend color. This mode is essentially the opposite of the Color mode.
- **Lighter Color:** Compares the total of all channel values for the blend and base color and displays the higher value color.
- **Darker Color:** Compares the total of all channel values for the blend and base color and displays the lower value color.

Painting with color

This section provides an example of using the blending modes to change and add color to an image. A great example of using a blending mode is tinting a black-and-white (grayscale) image with color. You can't paint color in Grayscale mode, so follow these steps to add color to a black-and-white image:

1. **Open an image in any color mode and choose Image⇨Mode⇨RGB.**
2. **If the image isn't already a grayscale image, choose Image⇨Adjustments⇨Desaturate.**

   This feature makes it appear as though the image is black and white, but you're still in a color mode with which you can apply color.

3. **Choose a painting tool (the Brush tool, for example) and, using the Swatches palette, choose the first color that you want to paint with.**
4. **On the Options bar, select Color from the Mode drop-down list and then use the Opacity slider to change the opacity to 50 percent.**

   You could also just type 5.
5. **Start painting!**

   The Color blending mode is used to change the color of the pixels, while keeping the underlying grayscale (shading) intact.

Another way to bring attention to a certain item in an RGB image (like those cute greeting cards that have the single rose in color and everything else in black and white) is to select the item you want to bring attention to. Choose Select⇨Modify⇨Feather to soften the selection a bit (5 pixels is a good number to enter in the Feather Radius text field). Then choose Select⇨Inverse. Now with everything else selected, choose Image⇨Adjustments⇨Desaturate. Everything else in the image looks black and white, except for the original item that you selected.

Filling selections

If you have a definite shape that doesn't lend itself to being painted, you can fill it with color instead. Make a selection and choose Edit⇨Fill to access the Fill dialog box. From the Use drop-down list, you can choose from the following options to fill the selection: Foreground Color, Background Color, Color (to open the color picker while in the Fill dialog box) Pattern, History, Black, 50% Gray, or White.

If you want to use an existing or saved pattern from the Brushes palette, you can retrieve a pattern by selecting Pattern in the Fill dialog box as well. Select History from the Use drop-down list to fill with the last version saved or the history state.

If you would rather use the Paint Bucket tool, which fills based upon the tolerance set on the Options bar, it's hidden in the Gradient tool.

To use the Paint Bucket tool to fill with the foreground color, simply click the item that you want to fill. This technique isn't as exact as using the Fill dialog box, but it's good for filling solid areas quickly.

Saving Presets

All the Photoshop tools allow you to save presets so that you can retrieve them from a list of presets. The following steps show you an example of saving a Brush tool preset, but the same method can be used for all other tools as well:

1. **Choose a brush size, color, softness, or anything!**
2. **Click the Tool Preset Picker button on the left side of the Options bar.**

   The preset menu for that tool appears.
3. **Click the triangle in the upper-right corner to access the fly-out menu and then choose New Tool Preset.**

   The New Tool Preset dialog box appears.
4. **Type a descriptive name in the Name text field (leave the Include Color check box selected if you want the preset to also remember the present color) and then click OK.**

   Your preset is created and saved.
5. **Access the preset by clicking the tool's Preset Picker button and choosing it from the tool's Preset Picker list.**

Each preset that you create is specific to the tool that it was created in, so you can have a crop preset, an eraser preset, and so on. After you get in the habit of saving presets, you'll wonder how you ever got along without them!

Chapter 9: Using Layers

In This Chapter

- Discovering layers
- Using type as a layer
- Implementing layer masks
- Organizing your layers
- Using Smart Objects
- Playing with layer effects

Layers are incredibly helpful in production. By using layers, you can make realistic additions to an image that you can remove, edit, and control with blending modes and transparency. Unfortunately, to show you all the features of layers goes beyond what we can cover in this chapter. This chapter covers layer basics to get you started working with layers in Photoshop. We show you how to create composite images using easy layer features — just enough knowledge to get yourself into a pretty complex mess of layers! Even if you're an experienced Photoshop user, read this chapter to discover all sorts of neat key commands that can help you in your workflow.

If you're a video professional, open some videos in Photoshop Extended CS3. Photoshop Extended automatically creates a Movie layer, and using the timeline, you can do pixel editing frame by frame!

Have fun with layers and don't worry if you mess up; you can always press F12 to revert the image to the state it was in at the last time you saved it.

Creating and Working with Layers

Layers make creating *composite images* (images pieced together from many other individual images) easy because you can separate individual elements of the composite onto their own layers. Much like creating collages by cutting pictures from magazines, you can mask out selections on one image and place them on a layer in another image. When pixel information is on its own layer, you can move it, transform it, correct its color, or apply filters just to that layer, without disturbing pixel information on other layers.

The best way to understand how to create and use layers is to, well, create and use layers. The following steps show you how to create a new, layered image:

1. **Create a new document by choosing File⇨New.**

   The New dialog box appears.

2. **Select Default Photoshop Size from the Preset Sizes drop-down list, select the Transparent option from the Background Contents area, and then click OK.**

   Because you selected the Transparent option, your image opens with an empty layer instead of a white background layer. The image appears as a checkerboard pattern, which signifies that it's transparent.

   If you don't like to see the default checkerboard pattern where there is transparency, choose Edit⇨Preferences⇨Transparency And Gamut (Photoshop⇨Preferences⇨Transparency And Gamut on a Mac). In the Preferences dialog box that appears, you can change the Grid Size drop-down list to None to remove the checkerboard pattern entirely. If you don't want to totally remove the transparency grid, you can change the size of the checkerboard pattern or change the color of the checkerboard.

   When you open an existing document (say a photograph), this image will be your background layer.

3. **Create a shape on the new image.**

   For example, create a red square by using the Rectangular Marquee tool to create a square selection; we then filled the selection with red by double-clicking the Foreground color swatch, selecting a red from the color picker, and clicking in the selection with the Paint Bucket tool (hidden under the Gradient tool).

   After you've selected the color, you can also use the key command Alt+Delete (Option+Delete on a Mac) to fill the selected area with color.

4. **To rename the layer, double-click the layer name (Layer 1) in the Layers palette and type a short, descriptive name.**

   A good practice is to name your layers based on what they contain; for this example, the layer was named the catchy name of "square."

5. **Create a new layer by Alt+clicking (Option+clicking on a Mac) the New Layer button at the bottom of the Layers palette.**

   The New Layer dialog box appears.

6. **Give your new layer a descriptive name and then click OK.**

7. **Create a shape on the new layer.**

We created a circle by using the Elliptical Marquee tool and filling the selection with yellow.

The new shape can overlap the shape on the other layer, as shown in Figure 9-1.

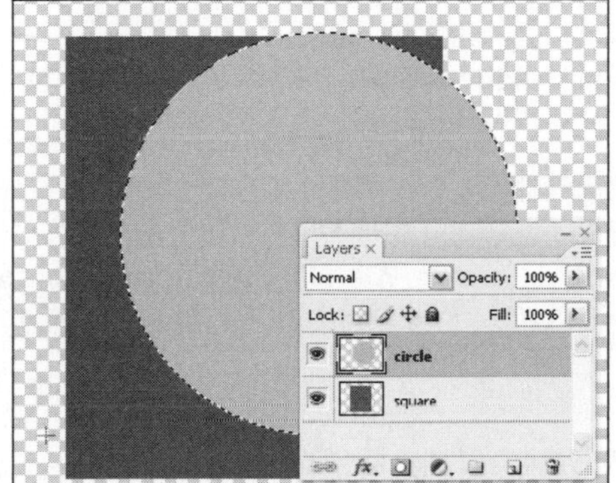

Figure 9-1: The circle overlaps the square.

Duplicating a layer

Perhaps you want to create a duplicate of a layer for your composite. This technique can be helpful for do-it-yourself drop shadows, as well as adding elements to an image, such as more apples in a bowl of fruit.

Alt+drag (Option+drag on a Mac) the square layer to the New Layer button at the bottom of the Layers palette to duplicate it. Again, by holding down Alt (Option on a Mac), you can name the layer as you create it.

Selecting a layer

When you start working with layers, you may find yourself moving or adjusting pixels, only to discover that you accidentally edited pixels on the wrong layer. Select the layer that you plan to work on by clicking the layer name in the Layers palette.

Unlike previous versions of Photoshop, Photoshop CS3 represents a selected layer by simply highlighting the layer in the Layer's palette. Don't bother looking for an indicator paintbrush icon in this version.

Here are some tips to help you select the correct layer:

- ✦ Select the Move tool and then right-click (Ctrl+click on a Mac) to see a contextual menu listing all layers that have pixel data at the point you clicked and to choose the layer that you want to work with.

- Get in the habit of holding down the Ctrl (⌘ on a Mac) key while using the Move tool and when selecting layers. This technique temporarily turns on the Auto Select feature, which automatically selects the top-most visible layer that contains the pixel data that you clicked.
- Press Alt+[(Option+[on a Mac) to select the next layer down from the selected layer in the stacking order.
- Press Alt+] (Option+] on a Mac) to select the next layer up from the selected layer in the stacking order.

Controlling the visibility of a layer

Hide layers that you don't immediately need by clicking the eye icon in the Layers palette. To see only one layer, Alt+click (Option+click on a Mac) the eye icon of the layer you want to keep visible. Alt+click (Option+click on a Mac) the eye icon again to show all layers.

Rearranging the stacking order

Layers are like clear pieces of film lying on top of each other. Change the stacking order of the layers in the Layers palette by dragging a layer until you see a black separator line appear, indicating that you're dragging the layer to that location. You can also use these great commands to help you move a layer:

Command	Windows Shortcut	Mac Shortcut
Move selected layer up	Ctrl+]	⌘+]
Move selected layer down	Ctrl+[	⌘+[

Creating a Text Layer

When you create text in Photoshop, the text is created on its own layer. By having the text separate from the rest of your image, applying different styles and blending modes to customize the type, as well as repositioning the text, are simplified.

To create a text layer, choose the Type tool and click the image area. You can also click and drag to create a text area. The Options bar, shown in Figure 9-2, gives you the controls to change font, size, blending mode, and color of the text.

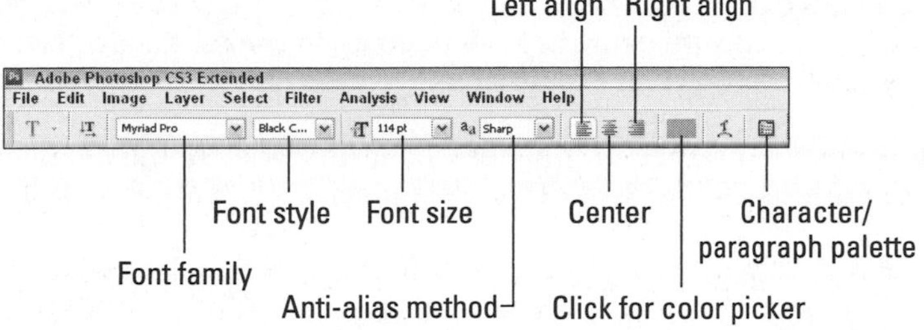

Figure 9-2: The Text tool options.

Warping text

When you click the Create Warped Text button on the Options bar, the Warp Text dialog box appears. This dialog box enables you to apply different types of distortion to your text.

You can still edit text that has been warped. To remove a warp, click the Create Warp Text button again and select None from the Style drop-down list.

Fine-tuning text

For controls such as leading, baseline shift, and paragraph controls, click the Toggle The Character And Paragraph Palettes icon near the right end of the Options bar.

Use the keyboard commands in Table 9-1 to build text in Photoshop. Make sure that you have text selected when you use these shortcuts.

Table 9-1 Helpful Typesetting Key Commands

Function	*Windows*	*Mac*
Increase font size	Shift+Ctrl+>	Shift+⌘+>
Decrease font size	Shift+Ctrl+<	Shift+⌘+<
Increase kerning (cursor must be between two letters)	Alt+→	Option+→
Decrease kerning (cursor must be between two letters)	Alt+←	Option+←
Increase tracking (several letters selected)	Alt+→	Option+→
Decrease tracking (several letters selected)	Alt+←	Option+←
Increase or decrease leading (several lines selected)	Alt+↑ or Alt+↓	Option+↑ or Option+↓

To change the font, drag over the font family name on the Options bar and then press the up-arrow key (↑) to go up in the font list or the down-arrow key (↓) to go down in the font list.

After you're finished editing text, confirm or delete the changes by clicking the buttons on the right of the Options bar.

If you'd rather use key commands to confirm or delete your changes, press the Esc key to cancel text changes; press Ctrl+Enter (⌘+Return on a Mac) to commit text changes (or use the Enter key on the numeric keypad).

Using Layer Masks

In this section, we show you how to create a layer mask from a selection or a pen path. A *layer mask* covers up areas of the image that you want to make transparent and exposes pixels that you want visible. Masks can be based upon a selection that you've created with the selection tools, by painting on the mask itself, or by using the Pen tool to create a path around the object you want to keep visible.

Creating a layer mask from a selection

You need to have two images open to follow these steps where we show you how to create layer masks from a selection:

1. **When combining images, choose Image➪Image Size to make sure that the images are approximately the same resolution.**

   Otherwise, you may create some interesting, but disproportional, effects.

2. **Using the Move tool, click one image and drag it to the other image window.**

   A black border appears around the image area when dropping an image into another image window. By dragging and dropping an image, you automatically create a new layer on top of the active layer.

   Hold down the Shift key when dragging one image to another to perfectly center the new image layer in the document window.

3. **Using any selection method, select a part of the image that you want to keep on the newly placed layer. Choose Select➪ Modify➪Feather to soften the selection (5 pixels should be enough).**

4. **Click the Layer Mask button at the bottom of the Layers palette.**

   A mask is created off to the right of your layer, leaving only your selection visible, as shown in Figure 9-3.

Figure 9-3: A custom mask is created automatically from an active selection on a layer when the Layer Mask button is clicked.

5. **If you click the Layer thumbnail in the Layers palette, the mask thumbnail shows corner edges, indicating that it is activated.**

   While the layer mask is active, you can paint on the mask.

6. **Press** D **to return to the default black-and-white swatch colors in the toolbox.**

7. **Select the Brush tool and paint black while the mask thumbnail is selected to cover up areas of the image that you don't want to see; press** X **to switch to white and paint to expose areas on the image that you do want to see.**

   You can even change the opacity as you paint to blend images in with each other.

To create a smooth transition from one image to another, drag the Gradient tool across the image while the layer mask is selected in the Layers palette.

Creating a vector mask from a pen path

A *vector mask* masks a selection, but it does so with the precision that you can get only from using a path. The following steps show you another, slightly more precise, way to create a layer mask by using a pen path:

1. **Use the Pen tool and click from point to point to make a closed pen path.**

   If you already have a path, choose Windows⇨Paths and click a path to select it.

See Chapter 4 of this minibook for more about working with the Pen tool.

2. **On the Layers palette, click the Layer Mask button and then click it again.**

   Wow! A mask from your pen path! Anything that wasn't contained within the path is now masked out. Use the Direct Selection tool to edit the path, if necessary.

If you no longer want vector mask, drag the thumbnail to the Trash icon in the Layers palette. An alert dialog box appears, asking if you'd like to discard the mask or apply it. Click the Discard button to revert your image back to the way it appeared before applying the mask or click the Apply button to apply the masked area.

Organizing Your Layers

As you advance in layer skills, you'll want to keep layers named, neat, and in order. In this section, we show you some tips to help you organize multiple layers.

Activating multiple layers simultaneously

Select multiple layers simultaneously by selecting one layer and then Shift+clicking to select additional layers. The selected layers are highlighted. Selected layers will move and transform together, making repositioning and resizing easier than activating each layer independently.

Select multiple layers to keep their relative positions to each other and take advantage of alignment features. When you select two or more layers and choose the Move tool, you can take advantage of alignment features on the Options bar (see Figure 9-4). Select three or more layers for distribution options.

New Auto-Align Layers tool

Ever have multiple shots of a group, one with the guy's eyes shut, and the girl looking the other way? Or maybe you like the smile in one better than in another. Using the new auto-alignment feature, you can pull the best parts of multiple images into one "best" image.

To use the new tool, simply have the Move tool active, select multiple layers, and then click the Auto-Align Layers button to the right of the alignment tools. The window you see in Figure 9-5 appears; make your selection and click OK.

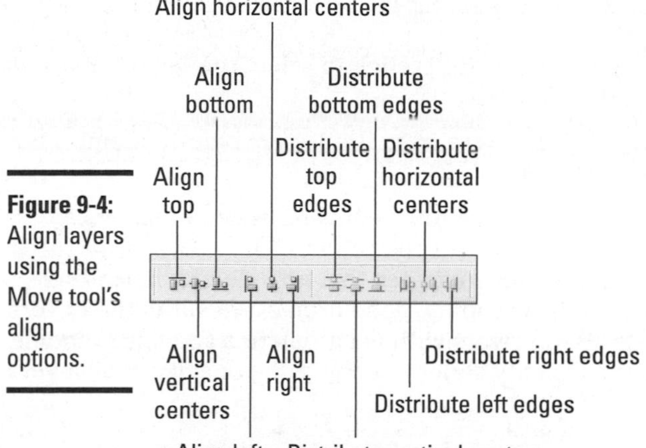

Figure 9-4: Align layers using the Move tool's align options.

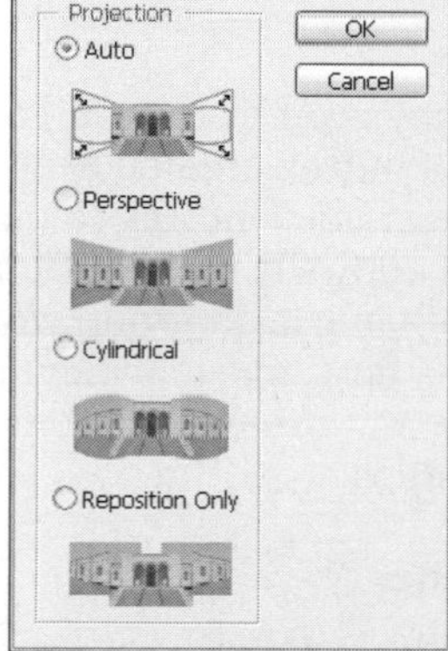

Figure 9-5: The new Auto-Align Layers feature can help create a better composite.

Layer groups

After you start using layers, you'll likely use lots of them, and your Layers palette will become huge. If you find yourself scrolling to navigate from one layer to another, take advantage of *layer groups,* which essentially act as folders that hold layers that you choose. Just like a folder you use for paper, you can add, remove, and shuffle around the layers within a layer set. Use layer sets to organize your layers and make the job of duplicating multiple layers easier.

To create a layer group, follow these steps:

1. **After creating several layers, Shift+click to select the layers that you want to group together in a set.**
2. **Choose New Group From Layers from the Layers palette menu, name the group, and then click OK.**

   That's it. You've created a layer group from your selected layers.

Pass through in the blending mode indicates that no individual blending modes are changed. Using the Blending Mode drop-down list in the Layers palette, you can change all the layers within a group to a specific blending mode, or you can use the Opacity slider to change the opacity of all layers in a group at once.

After you create a layer group, you can still reorganize layers within the group or even drag in or out additional layers. You can open and close a layer group with the arrow to the left of the set name.

Duplicating a layer group

After you've created a layer group, you may want to copy it. For example, you may want to copy an image, such as a button created from several layers topped off with a text layer. The most efficient way to make a copy of that button is to create a layer group and copy the entire group. To copy an image made up of several layers that aren't in a layer group would require you to individually duplicate each layer — how time-consuming!

To duplicate a layer group, follow these steps:

1. **Select a group from the Layers palette.**
2. **From the palette menu, choose Duplicate Group.**

   The Duplicate Group dialog box appears.
3. **For the destination, choose the present document or any open document or create a new document.**

   Be sure to give the duplicated set a distinctive name!
4. **Click OK.**

Using Layer Styles

Layer styles are wonderful little extras that you can apply to layers to create drop shadows, bevel and emboss effects, apply color overlays, gradients, patterns and strokes, and more.

Applying a style

To apply a layer style (for example, the drop shadow style, one of the most popular effects) to an image, just follow these steps:

1. **Create a layer on any image.**

   For example, you could create a text layer to see the effects of the layer styles.

2. **With the layer selected, click and hold the Layer Style button at the bottom of the Layers palette; from the menu options, choose Drop Shadow.**

   In the Layer Style dialog box that appears, you can choose to change the blending mode, color, distance spread, and size of a drop shadow. You should see it has already applied to your text. Position the cursor on the image area and drag to visually adjust the position of the drop shadow.

3. **When you're happy with the drop shadow, click OK to apply it.**

To apply another effect and change its options, click and hold the Layer Style button in the Layers palette and choose the name of the layer style from the menu that appears — Bevel And Emboss, for example. In the dialog box that appears, change the settings to customize the layer style and click OK to apply it to your image. For example, if you choose Bevel And Emboss from the Layer Styles menu, you can choose from several emboss styles and adjust the depth, size, and softness.

Here are some consistent items that you see in the Layer Style dialog box, no matter what effect you choose:

- **Contour:** Use contours to control the shape and appearance of an effect. Click the arrow to open the Contour fly-out menu to choose a contour preset or click the contour preview to open the Contour Editor and create your own edge.
- **Angle:** Drag the cross hair in the angle circle or enter a value in the Angle text field to control where the light source comes from.
- **Global light:** If you aren't smart about lighting effects on multiple objects, global light will make it seem as though you are. Select the Use Global Light check box to keep the angle consistent from one layer style to another.
- **Color:** Whenever you see a color box, you can click it to select a color. This color can be for the drop shadow, highlight, or shadow of an emboss, or for a color overlay.

Creating and saving a style

If you come up with a combination of attributes that you like, click the New Style button in the upper right of the Layer Style dialog box. Name the style, and it's now stored in the Styles palette. After you click OK, you can retrieve the style at any time by choosing Window➪Styles. If it helps, click the palette menu button and choose either Small or Large List to change the Styles palette to show only the name of the styles.

After you've applied a layer style to a layer, the style is listed in the Layers palette. You can turn off the visibility of the style by turning off the eye icon or even throw away the layer style by dragging it to the Layers palette's Trash icon.

Thinking about opacity versus fill

In the Layers palette, you have two transparency options, one for opacity and one for fill. Opacity affects the opacity of the entire layer, including effects. Fill, on the other hand, affects only the layer itself, but not layer styles. Figure 9-6 shows what happens when the Bevel And Emboss style is applied to text and the fill is reduced to 0 percent. It looks like the text was embossed onto the image. You can do lots of neat stuff with the Layer Fill feature!

Figure 9-6: A text layer with styles applied and the fill reduced to 0 percent.

Smart, Really Smart! Smart Objects

Choose File➪Place and place an image, illustration, or even a movie into a Photoshop document and discover that, as always, a new layer is created, but even better than that, a Smart Object is created. The icon in the lower right of the layer thumbnail indicates that this layer is a Smart Object.

What does being a Smart Object mean? It means that you have much more flexibility with the placement of your images. Have you ever placed a logo, to find out later you need it to be three times the size? Resizing is no longer an issue, as the Photoshop Smart Object is linked to an embedded original. If the original is vector, you can freely resize the image over and over again without worrying about poor resolution. Want to change the spelling of your placed Illustrator logo? Just double-click the Smart Object, the embedded original is opened right in Adobe Illustrator, make your changes and save the file, and viola . . . it's automatically updated in the Photoshop file.

What could be better than this? Smart filters, of course. You can apply Smart filters to any Smart Object layer, or even convert a layer to use Smart Filters, by choosing Filters⇨Convert For Smart Filters. Once a layer has been converted to a Smart Object, you can choose filters, any filters, and apply them to the layer. If you want to paint out the effects of the filter on the layer, simply paint with black on the Filter effects thumbnail. Paint with different opacities of black and white to give an artistic feel to the Filter effect, as shown in Figure 9-7. You can even turn off the filters by turning off the visibility on the Filter Effects thumbnail by clicking the eye icon to the left of the Filter Effects Thumbnail.

Figure 9-7: Cover the filter effects by painting on the filter effects thumbnail.

Merging and Flattening the Image

Merging layers combines several selected layers into one layer. *Flattening* is when you reduce all layers to one background layer. Layers can increase your file in size, thereby also tying up valuable processing resources. To keep file size down, you may choose to merge some layers or even flatten the entire image down to one background layer.

Merging

Merging layers is helpful when you no longer need every layer to be independent, like when you have a separate shadow layer aligned to another layer and don't plan on moving it again, or when you combine many layers to create a composite and want to consolidate it to one layer.

To merge layers (in a visual and easy way), follow these steps:

1. **Turn on the visibility of only the layers that you want merged.**
2. **Choose Merge Visible from the Layers palette menu.**

   That's it. The entire image isn't flattened, but the visible layers are now reduced to one layer.

To merge visible layers onto a target (selected) layer that you create while keeping the visible layers independent, do the following: Create a blank layer and select it. Hold down Alt (Option on a Mac) when choosing Merge Visible from the palette menu.

Flattening

If you don't have to flatten your image, don't! Flattening your image reduces all layers down to one background layer, which is necessary for certain file formats, but after you flatten an image, you can't take advantage of blending options or reposition the layered items. (Read more about saving files in Chapter 10 of this minibook.)

If you absolutely must flatten layers, keep a copy of the original, unflattened document for additional edits in the future.

To flatten all layers in an image, choose Layer⇨Flatten Image or choose Flatten Image from the palette menu on the Layers palette.

Chapter 10: Saving Photoshop Images for Print and the Web

In This Chapter

- **Determining the correct file formats for saving**
- **Preparing your images for the Web**
- **Discovering the color table**

A productive workflow depends on you choosing the proper format in which to save your Photoshop files. Without the correct settings, your file may not be visible to other applications, or you may delete valuable components, such as layers or channels. This chapter provides you with the necessary information to save the file correctly for both print and Web. We cover the file format choices before moving on to the proper use of the Save For Web & Devices feature (for saving in the GIF, JPEG, PNG, and WBMP file formats).

Saving files in the correct file format is important not only for file size, but in support of different Photoshop features, as well. If you're unsure about saving in the right format, save a copy of the file, keeping the original in the PSD format (the native Photoshop format). Photoshop alerts you automatically when you choose a format in the Save As or the Save For Web & Devices dialog box that doesn't support Photoshop features. When you choose a format that doesn't support some of the features you've used, such as channels or layers, a yield sign appears when a copy is being made. It's a good idea to save an original backup just in case you need to return to the original file.

Choosing a File Format for Saving

When you choose File➪Save for the first time (or you choose File➪Save As to save a different version of a file), you see at least 18 different file formats that you can choose from in the Save As Type drop-down list. We don't cover each format in this chapter (some are specific to proprietary workflows), but we do show you which formats are best for the typical workflow that you may face.

Creating a PDF presentation

You can create a multipage PDF file or presentation by using Adobe Bridge (choose File⇨Browse). While in Adobe Bridge, choose Tools⇨Photoshop⇨PDF Presentation. In the PDF Presentation dialog box, use the Browse button to choose the files that you want to add to the Source list. You can Ctrl+click (⌘+click on a Mac) to select multiple files and add them to the Source list.

In the output options section, choose Multi-Page or Presentation PDF. If you choose Presentation, you're given the opportunity to set up slide show options, such as timing and transition effects.

Click Save, name the file, and click Save again. The Save Adobe PDF dialog box appears. If you want to see the PDF immediately, make sure that you select the View PDF After Saving check box, choose any other specific options that you want for the PDF (see Book VII for more specifics on PDF settings), and click OK.

Wonderful and easy Photoshop PSD

If you're in an Adobe workflow (you're using any Adobe products), you can keep the image in the native Photoshop PSD format. By choosing this format, transparency, layers, channels, and paths are all maintained and left intact when placed in the other applications.

To maximize compatibility with previous versions of Photoshop and with other applications, choose Edit⇨Preferences⇨File Handling (Photoshop⇨Preferences⇨File Handling on a Mac). Choose Always from the Maximize PSD File Compatibility drop-down list. This choice saves a composite (flattened) image along with the layers of your document.

Leaving the Maximize PSD File Compatibility drop-down list set to Always creates a larger file. If file size is an issue, leave the drop-down list set to Ask, and only use the feature when you need to open the Photoshop file in older versions of Photoshop.

Photoshop EPS

Virtually every desktop application accepts the EPS (Encapsulated PostScript) file format. The EPS format is used to transfer PostScript-language artwork between various applications. It supports vector data, duotones, and clipping paths.

When you choose to save in the EPS format, an EPS Options dialog box appears. Leave the defaults and click OK.

Alter the settings in the EPS Options dialog box *only* if you're familiar with custom printer calibration, or you need to save your image to a specific screen ruling. Screen rulings (lpi) are usually set in a page layout application, such as Adobe InDesign or QuarkXPress.

Photoshop PDF

If compatibility is an issue, save your file in the Photoshop PDF (Portable Document Format) format. PDF files are supported by more than a dozen platforms when viewers use Acrobat or Adobe Reader. (Adobe Reader is available for free at `www.adobe.com`.) What a perfect way to send pictures to friends and family! Saving your file in the Photoshop PDF format supports your ability to edit the image when you open the file by choosing File⇨Open in Photoshop.

TIFF

TIFF (Tagged Image File Format) is a flexible bitmap image format that is supported by most image-editing and page-layout applications widely supported by all printers. TIFF supports layers and channels, but it has a maximum size of 4GB. We hope your files aren't that large!

DCS

The Photoshop DCS (Desktop Color Separation) 1.0 and 2.0 formats are versions of EPS that enable you to save color separations of CMYK or multichannel files. Some workflows require this format, but if you have implemented spot color channels in your image, using the DCS file format is required to maintain them.

Choose the DCS 2.0 format unless you received specific instructions to use the DCS 1.0 format — for example, for reasons of incompatibility in certain workflows.

Saving for the Web and Devices

To access the maximum number of options for the GIF, JPEG, PNG, and WBMP file formats, save your image by choosing File⇨Save For Web & Devices. The Save For Web & Devices dialog box appears, which allows you to optimize the image as you save it. This procedure may sound big, but it's just the process of making the image as small as possible while keeping it visually pleasing.

Saving images for the Web is a give-and-take experience. You may find yourself sacrificing perfect imagery to make the image small enough in size that it can be downloaded and viewed quickly by users. Read the upcoming sections on GIF and JPG formats to see how you can best handle creating Web images.

The following sections describe the differences between GIF, JPEG, PNG, and WBMP. Choose the appropriate format based upon the type of image you're saving.

Having the image size correct before you save the file for the Web is a good practice. If you need to read up on resizing images, see Chapter 6 of this minibook. But generally speaking, you want to resize the image to the right pixel dimensions. Choose Filter⇨Sharpen⇨Unsharp Mask to gain back some of the detail lost when resizing the image and then save the image for the Web.

GIF

Supposedly, the way you pronounce GIF (Graphics Interchange Format) is based on the type of peanut butter you eat. Is it pronounced like the peanut butter brand (Jiff), or with a hard G, like gift? Most people seem to pronounce it like gift (minus the T).

Use the GIF format if you have lots of solid color, such as a logo like the one shown in Figure 10-1.

Figure 10-1: An image with large amounts of solid color is a good candidate for the GIF file format.

The GIF format is not *lossy* (it doesn't lose data when the file is compressed in this format), but it does reduce the file size by using a limited number of colors in a color table. The lower the number of colors, the smaller the file size. If you've ever worked in the Index color mode, you're familiar with this process.

Transparency is supported by the GIF file. But generally, GIFs don't do a good job with anything that needs smooth transitions from one color to another because of its poor support of anti-aliasing. *Anti-aliasing* is the method that Photoshop uses to smooth jagged edges. When pixels transition from one color to another, Photoshop produces multiple color pixels to evenly blend from one pixel to another.

Because anti-aliasing needs to create multiple colors for this effect, GIF files are generally not recommended. In fact, when you reduce a GIF in size, you're more apt to see *banding* because the anti-aliasing can't take place with the limited number of colors available in the GIF format.

You can, of course, dramatically increase the number of colors to create a smoother transition, but then you risk creating monster files that take forever to download.

Saving a GIF

When you choose File⇨Save for Web, you first see the available GIF format options. The GIF options may be more clear to you if you have an image (with lots of solid color) open.

To save a file for the Web as a GIF, follow these steps:

1. **Choose File⇨Save For Web & Devices.**

   The Save For Web & Devices dialog box appears.

2. **At the top, click the 2-Up tab.**

   You see the original image on the left and the optimized image on the right (or top and bottom, depending upon the proportions of your image).

   In the lower portion of the display, you see the original file size compared to the optimized file size, as well as the approximate download time. This time is important! Nobody wants to wait around for a Web page to load; most people won't wait more than ten seconds for the entire Web page to appear, so try to keep an individual image's download time down to five seconds or less. Remember, all the images on a page can add up to one monstrous wait time for the viewer!

   Change the download speed by choosing from the Preview menu (it's the arrow on the upper-right side of the Save For Web & Devices dialog box). The Preview menu isn't labeled, so look for the ToolTip to appear when you hover your cursor over the arrow icon.

3. **Choose GIF 32 No Dither from the Preset drop-down list.**

   You may see a change already. Photoshop supplies you with presets that you can choose from, or you can customize and save your own.

4. **Choose whether you want dithering applied to the image by selecting an option from the Specify The Dither Algorithm drop-down list.**

   This choice is purely personal. Because you may be limiting colors, Photoshop can use dithering to mix the pixels of the available colors to simulate the missing colors. Many designers choose the No Dither option.

Using the color table

When you save an image as a GIF using the Save For Web & Devices dialog box, you see the color table for the image on the right side of the dialog box. The color table is important because it not only allows you to see the colors used in the image, but also enables you to customize the color table by using the options at the bottom of the color table.

You may want to customize your color table by selecting some of your colors to be Web safe and locking colors so that they're not bumped off as you reduce the amount of colors.

To customize a color table, follow these steps:

1. **If your image has only a few colors that you'd like to convert to Web-safe colors, choose the Eyedropper tool from the left of the Save For Web & Devices dialog box and click the color, in the Optimized view.**

   The sampled color is highlighted in the color table.

2. **Click the Web Safe button at the bottom of the color table.**

   A ToolTip appears when you cross over this button with the text; Shifts/Unshift selected colors to web palette.

   A diamond appears, indicating that the color is now Web safe.

3. **Lock colors that you don't want to delete as you reduce the number of colors in the color table.**

   Select a color with the Eyedropper tool or choose it in the color table and then click the Lock Color button. A white square appears in the lower-right corner, indicating that the color is locked.

If you lock 32 colors and then reduce the color table to 24, some of your locked colors will be deleted. If you choose to add colors, those locked colors will be the first to return.

How is the color table created? Based upon a color reduction algorithm method that you choose, the Save For The Web feature samples the number of colors that you indicate. If keeping colors Web safe is important, select the Restrictive (Web) option for the method; if you want your image to look better on most monitors, but not necessarily be Web safe, choose the Adaptive option.

4. **Use the arrows to the right of the Colors combo box or enter a number to add or delete colors from the color table.**

5. **If your image uses transparency, select the Transparency check box.**

   Remember that transparency is counted as one of your colors in the color table.

6. **Select the Interlaced check box only if your GIF image is large in size (25K or larger).**

   Selecting this option causes the image to build in several scans on the Web page, a low-resolution image that pops up quickly to be refreshed with the higher resolution image when it's finished downloading. Interlacing gives the illusion of the download going faster but makes the file size larger, so use it only if necessary.

7. **Click Save.**

   Now the image is ready to be attached to an e-mail message or used in a Web page.

JPEG

JPEG (Joint Photographic Experts Group) is the best format for continuous tone images (those with smooth transitions from one color to another, as in photographs), like the image shown in Figure 10-2.

The JPEG format is lossy, so you should not save a JPEG, open it, edit it, and save it again as a JPEG. Because the JPEG compression causes data to be lost, your image will eventually look like it was printed on a paper towel. Save a copy of the file as a JPEG, keeping the original image in the PSD format if you need to later edit the image, open the original PSD, make your changes, save the PSD, and then save a copy of the edited file as a JPEG.

The JPEG format does *not* support transparency, but you can cheat the system a little by using matting.

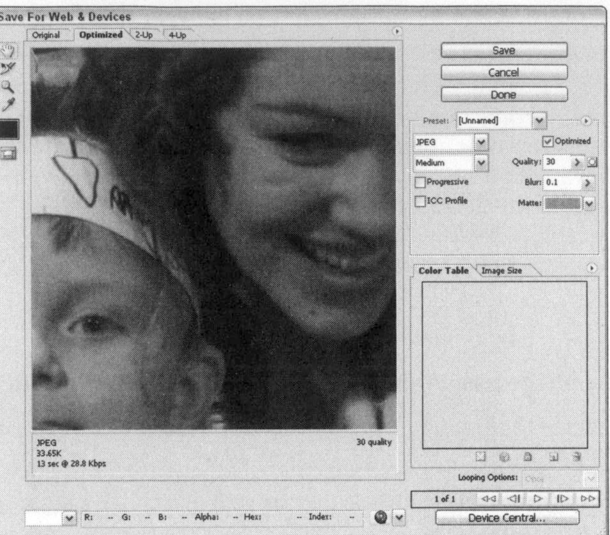

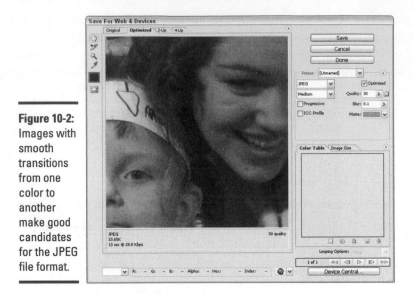

Figure 10-2: Images with smooth transitions from one color to another make good candidates for the JPEG file format.

A good image to save in the JPEG format is a typical photograph or illustration with lots of smooth transitions from one color to the next. To save an image as a JPEG, follow these steps:

1. **Choose File⇨Save For Web & Devices and then click the 2-Up tab to view the original image (left) at the same time as the optimized image (right).**
2. **Choose one of the JPEG preset settings from the Settings drop-down list.**

   You can choose Low, Medium, High, or customize a level in between the presets by using the Quality slider.
3. **Leave the Optimized check box selected to build the best JPEG at the smallest size.**

   The only issue with leaving this check box selected is that some very old browsers won't read the JPEG correctly. (This is probably not an issue for most of your viewers.)
4. **Deselect the ICC Profile check box unless you're in a color-managed workflow and color accuracy is essential.**

   Deselecting the ICC Profile check box dramatically increases the file size, and most people aren't looking for *exact* color matches from an image on the monitor . . . and it's scary if they are!

5. **Use the Blur slider to bring down some detail.**

   It's funny, but one JPEG that's the exact same pixel dimensions as another may vary in file size because the more detailed an image, the more information is needed. So an image of lots of apples will be larger than an image the same size that has a lot of clear blue sky in it. The blur feature does blur the image (surprise!), so you may want to use this for only a Low Source image in Dreamweaver.

6. **(Optional) Choose a matte color from the Matte drop-down list.**

   Because JPEG doesn't support transparency, you can flood the transparent area with a color that you choose from the Matte drop-down list. Choose the color that you're using for the background of your Web page by choosing Other and entering the hexadecimal color in the lower portion of the color picker.

7. **Click Save.**

PNG

PNG (Portable Network Graphics) is almost the perfect combination of JPEG and GIF. Unfortunately, PNG isn't yet widely supported . . . note, as well, that PNG-24 images have file sizes that can be too large to use on the Web.

PNG supports varying levels of transparency and anti-aliasing. This variation means that you can specify an image as being 50 percent transparent, and it will actually show through to the underlying Web page! You have a choice of PNG-8 and PNG-24 in the Save For Web & Devices dialog box. As a file format for optimizing images, PNG-8 doesn't give you any advantage over a regular GIF file.

PNG files are *not* supported by all browsers. In older browsers, a plug-in may be required to view your page. Ouch . . . by choosing PNG, you could shoot yourself in the foot because not all your viewers will be able to view the PNG.

If you're saving a PNG file, you have a choice of PNG-8 or PNG-24. The PNG-8 options are essentially the same as the GIF options; see the "Saving a GIF" section, earlier in this chapter, for details.

PNG-24 saves 24-bit images that support anti-aliasing (the smooth transition from one color to another). They work beautifully for continuous-tone images, but are much larger than a JPEG file. The truly awesome feature of a PNG file is that it supports 256 levels of transparency. In other words, you can apply varying amounts of transparency in an image, as shown in Figure 10-3, where the image shows through to the background.

Figure 10-3: A PNG-24 file with varying amounts of transparency.

WBMP

WBMP is short for Wireless BitMap, a format optimized for mobile computing, has no compression, is one-bit color (just black and white, no shades!), and is one bit deep. WBMP images aren't necessary pretty, but functional (see Figure 10-4). You do have dithering controls to show some level of tone value.

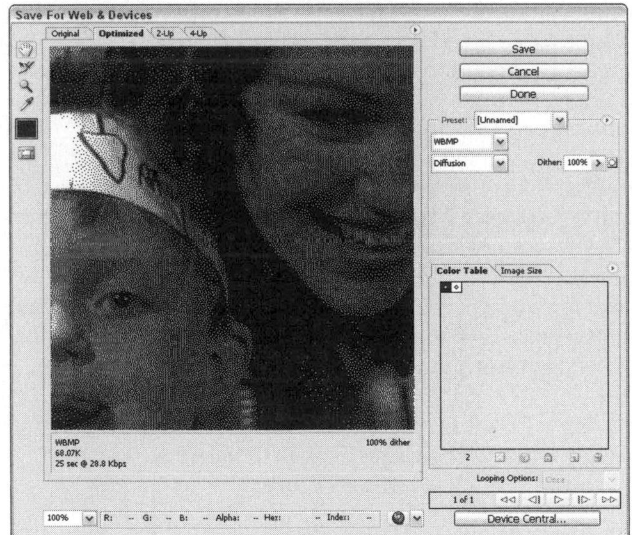

Figure 10-4: The WBMP format supports black and white only.

If you're creating images for mobile devices, you should know that WBMP is part of the Wireless Application Protocol, Wireless Application Environment Specification Version 1.1.

Select the Preview In Default Browser check box at the bottom of the Save For Web & Devices dialog box to launch your chosen Web browser and display the image as it will appear with the present settings. If you haven't set up a browser, click the down arrow and choose Other from the drop-down menu. Browse to locate a browser that you want to preview your image in.

Want to see how your mobile content is going to look on specific devices? Then click the Device Central button in the lower right of the Save For Web & Devices dialog box.

Matte

Matting appears as a choice in the JPEG, GIF, and PNG format options. Matting is useful if you don't want ragged edges appearing around your image. Matting looks for pixels that are greater than 50 percent transparent and makes them fully transparent; any pixels that are 50 percent or less transparent become fully opaque.

Even though your image might be on a transparent layer, there will be some iffy pixels, the ones that aren't sure what they want to be . . . to be transparent or not to be transparent. Choose a matte color to blend in with the transparent iffy pixels by selecting Eyedropper, White, Black, or Other (to open the color picker) from the Matte drop-down list in the Save For Web & Devices dialog box.

Saving Settings

Whether you're saving a GIF, JPG, or PNG file, you probably spent some time experimenting with settings to find what works best for your needs. Save your selected options to reload at a later time by saving the settings. Do so by clicking the arrow to the right of the Preset drop-down list. Choose Save Settings from the menu that appears and give your settings a name. Your named, customized settings then appear in the Settings drop-down list.

Book III

Fireworks CS3

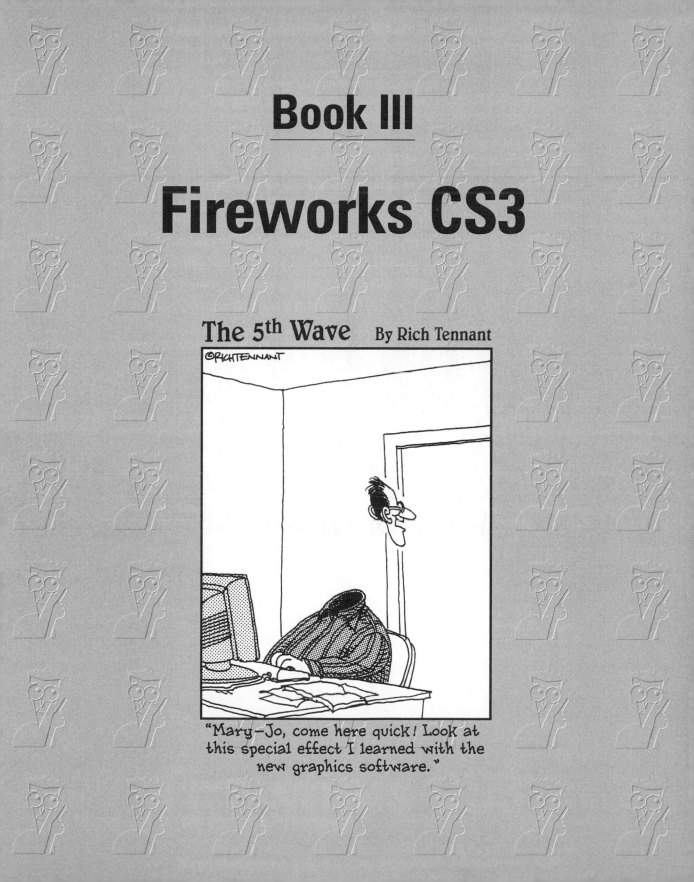

The 5th Wave By Rich Tennant

"Mary-Jo, come here quick! Look at this special effect I learned with the new graphics software."

Chapter 1: Introduction to Fireworks CS3

In This Chapter

- **Understanding the power of Fireworks CS3**
- **Touring the Fireworks CS3 interface**
- **Checking over your work with a preview**
- **Creating a customized work environment**
- **Setting your preferences**
- **Getting help when you need it**

Fireworks CS3 is the latest version of a graphics creation and editing program designed to streamline the process of making images for the Web. In the days before the original version of Fireworks, making graphics for the Web could be a frustrating and time-consuming process involving trial and error. And the results often looked pretty bad.

With products such as Fireworks, all that has changed. This chapter gives you a brief introduction and tour of the product and shows you how to set up Fireworks to fit your working style.

Understanding the Power of Fireworks

You can divide the basic process of making graphics for a Web site into two major parts:

- **Creating the images:** Drawing, importing, and manipulating pictures, as well as designing the overall page layout on the Fireworks canvas
- **Optimizing the images:** Slicing the page layout into pieces, selecting the proper compression format and level for each piece, and exporting the individual pieces

Fireworks has two different tools that make the process of creating graphics for a Web site easier: layers and slices. Layers are a mainstay of graphics development tools, such as Photoshop and Illustrator, and of animation programs, such as Adobe Flash. Layers make creating and editing graphics a simpler proposition. Slices, first introduced in the original version of Fireworks, offer an efficient way to divide a design into individually optimized Web graphics. You can read more about both layers and slices in the following sections.

Making designing easier with layers

We discuss layers in more detail in Book III, Chapter 5, but this section serves as an introduction to the benefits of layers.

Layers act like transparent sheets that you can stack, one on top of the other. You draw a separate element of the image on each transparency. Any area where you haven't put something remains transparent, so layers beneath show through. In a typical file, you may have several text layers and many layers of backgrounds, icons, lines, shapes, and so on.

If you ever make mistakes or change your mind about overall layout, text, or graphical elements, layers can save you much time as you design your site. Suppose that you're painting watercolors on fine paper. If you mess up one part of the image, you often ruin the whole thing because you have only one layer to work with — the paper. Short of cutting a piece out of the paper, you probably can't delete your mistakes. Layers offer a more flexible approach to creating and editing images.

Using layers provides many benefits. Some of the most practical advantages include the following:

- ✦ You can change any element of your design — text, bitmap, or vector shape — without altering or destroying any other element.
- ✦ You can apply effects to layers that are grouped together, decreasing the amount of time needed to edit an image. (Of course, you can also apply effects to individual layers.)
- ✦ You can easily move elements up and down in the stack of layers to change the visual effect on the screen.
- ✦ You can test new designs and effects in a snap because you can very easily hide and show elements of an image.

Creating slices

We discuss slices in more detail in Book III, Chapter 6, but here's an introduction to the concept of slices. Imagine for a moment that you've created your masterpiece design for a new Web site. Your Fireworks file may include a lot of different kinds of imagery, such as the following:

- ✦ Animations
- ✦ Drawings

- Header graphics, such as banners
- Logos
- Navigation buttons
- Photos

Before you can create your Web page, you have to get all these graphics into a Web-friendly format, which is where slices come in. The idea is simple and elegant: Include a special layer in the program that no one can ever remove, in which you can create guides as to how you want the images to be "sliced" into separate, individually optimized, and hyperlinked images. Figure 1-1 shows that special layer, called the *Web Layer,* and some slices in action, including a slice with an attached behavior (see Book III, Chapter 7 for information on behaviors).

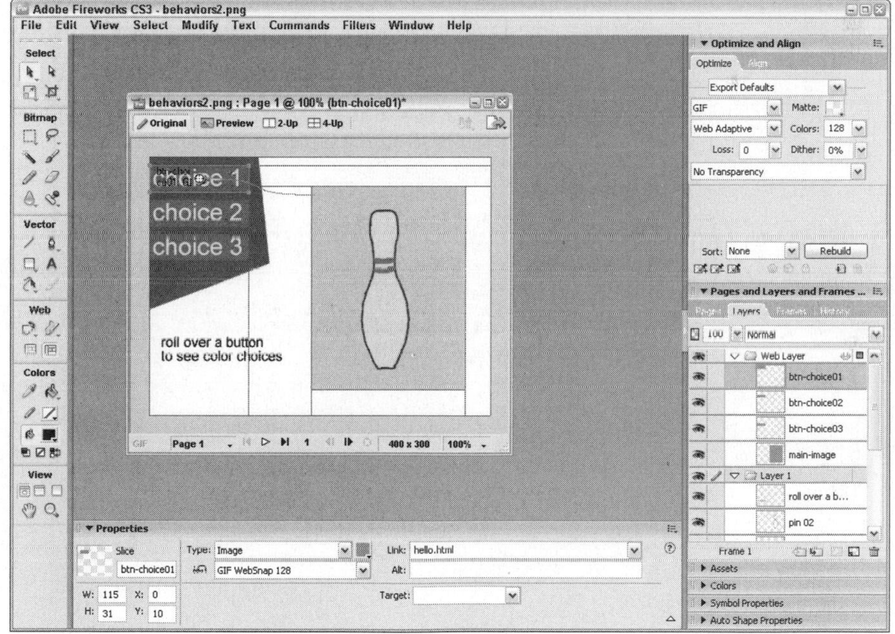

Figure 1-1: The Web Layer and slices.

Slices provide some key advantages over outmoded methods of creating images for the Web:

- You can slice a design into more than one image at a time.
- You can export multiple files in a single procedure.
- You can control exactly where images are sliced, which helps prevent you from making images with overlapping areas.

- You have an increased ability to optimize image size (and thereby reduce download time) by selecting the best optimization method for each slice.

Slices guarantee that the layout of your Web page appears nearly identical on every user's screen to the design that you create in Fireworks. (If you have HTML text on your page, the appearance of that text may vary, depending on which browser and platform the user views your page with.)

Taking a Quick Tour of the Fireworks Interface

The Fireworks interface is set up to make accessing the tools quick and intuitive. When you start Fireworks, it doesn't create a new document automatically; instead, you see the Start page, as Figure 1-2 shows. From the Start page, you get one-click access to

- **Create New:** Click the Fireworks File link to open a new, blank image.
- **Extend:** Click the Fireworks Exchange link to browse to a part of the Adobe Web site that includes a lot of free, cool, downloadable tools and graphical elements created by users like you.

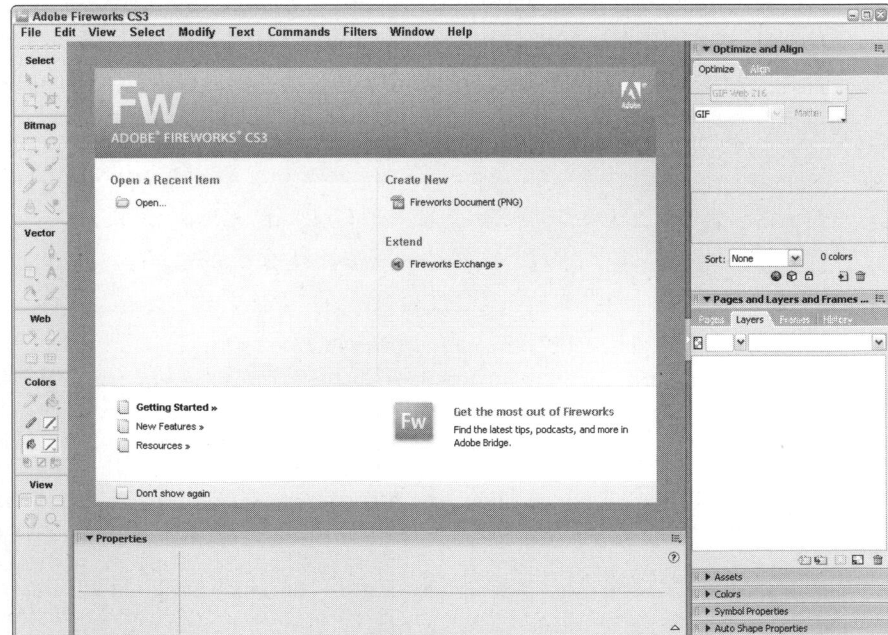

Figure 1-2: The Start page, welcoming you to Fireworks CS3.

✦ **Open a Recent Item:** Just click the filename, or click the Open folder and browse to a file to open the image in Fireworks.

✦ **Information:** Click the Getting Started link, the New Features link, or the Resources link to view basic tips and tutorials. Or click the link to the Fireworks Developer Center, where you can find tutorials, sample files, and feedback from other Fireworks users.

If you don't want the Start page to show up every time you launch Fireworks, select the Don't Show Again check box at the bottom-left corner of the page.

To create a new Fireworks file (called a PNG file), follow these steps:

1. **Choose File⇨New, or click the Fireworks File link on the Start page.**

   The New Document dialog box appears.

2. **Choose the canvas size for your document in the New Document dialog box.**

   The default width and height are 660 x 440 pixels (or the dimensions of the previous file that you created in Fireworks), and the default resolution is 72 pixels per inch. You can enter your own size in the fields provided and change the unit of measurement by selecting one from the drop-down list. Leave the resolution at 72 pixels per inch unless you're designing for some medium other than the Web, such as print.

3. **Select a color for the canvas.**

   The default canvas color is white, but you can choose a custom color by selecting the Custom radio button and then using the eyedropper to choose a color from the color picker. You can also choose to have a transparent background by selecting the Transparent radio button.

4. **Click OK to create your new Fireworks document.**

   When you click OK, your screen looks similar to Figure 1-3.

The Tools panel: A bird's-eye view

The panels along the left side of the screen are parts of the Tools panel, which provides access to all the tools that you use to make and modify your graphics. The Tools panel divides tools into groups based on their function:

✦ **Select:** Contains tools used to select an object, as well as tools used to crop or otherwise manipulate the canvas.

✦ **Bitmap:** Stores tools used to paint, draw, fill, and so on.

✦ **Vector:** Contains tools used to create and manipulate vector graphics. (See Book IV for more on vector graphics.)

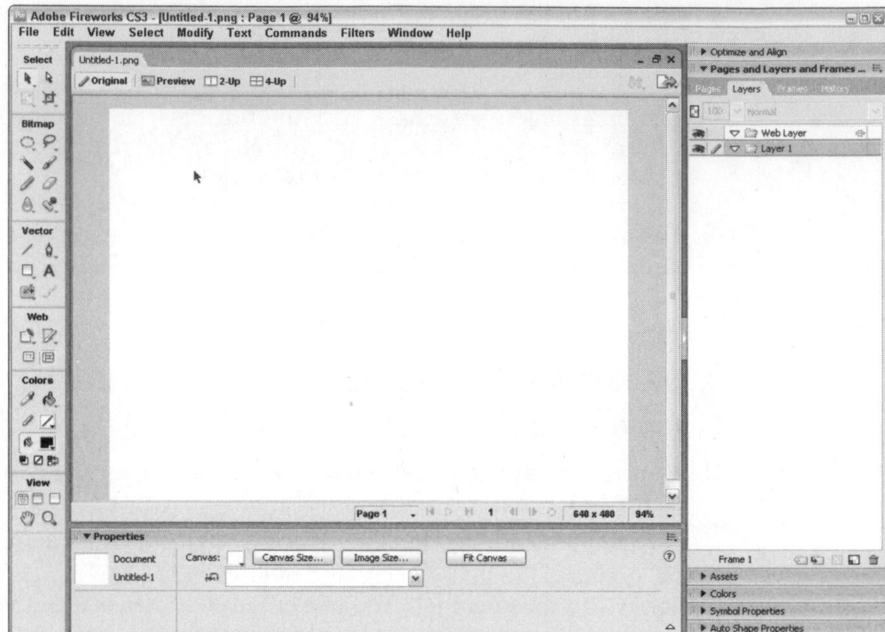

Figure 1-3: The default Fireworks CS3 interface.

- **Web:** Holds tools, such as the Slice tool, that are designed specifically for getting images ready for the Web.
- **Colors:** Stows away tools that control the color(s) of objects.
- **View:** Holds tools that you can use to change your view of the canvas or the screen.

An arrow at the lower-right corner of a tool's icon indicates that the tool has one or more specialized variations. You can click the arrow to activate a pop-up menu that displays icons for the available variations.

The Tools panel: A bug's-eye view

This section gives you the lowdown on the tools that you probably use the most in the Tools panel. A triangle (known as the *flippy*) at the bottom right of the tool icon indicates that related tools are available. Click the icon or the flippy and hold the mouse button down to activate a pop-up menu so that you can choose from all the available tools. When you select a tool, you can also cycle through the related tools by pressing certain keys on your keyboard (for example, select the Marquee tool in the Bitmap section and press M to toggle through the Marquee tool options). The tool tip for each tool includes the key that you can press to cycle through the options on the tool. You can activate the tool tip by hovering the mouse over the tool.

You get to see the tools in action in various chapters of several of the minibooks, but for now, here are the highlights for each of the four key categories of drawing tools:

- **Select:** The following four tools (clockwise from top left) make up the Select section of the Tools panel:
  - **Pointer/Select Behind tool:** Use the Pointer tool to select objects on the canvas by clicking them or clicking and dragging an area that encompasses them. Use the Select Behind tool when you want to click an object on the canvas that other objects cover.
  - **Subselection tool:** Use the Subselection tool to select an individual object from a group.
  - **Crop/Export Area tool:** Click the Crop tool and click and drag to select an area on the canvas to crop an image. When you *crop* an image, you discard everything outside the selected area from your image. After you have selected the area that you want to keep, double-click inside the area to crop. Use the Export Area tool to create a new image from the area that you select. After you have selected the area you want to export, double-click inside the area to bring up the Export Preview window.
  - **Scale/Skew/Distort tool:** This tool is inactive (as indicated by the dimmed icon) until you select an object on the canvas. Click this tool and click and drag the transform handles at the corners of the object to change its size and/or shape.
- **Bitmap:** The following tools (clockwise from top left) make up the Bitmap section of the Tools panel:
  - **Marquee/Oval Marquee tool:** Click the Marquee tool and click and drag to select a rectangular area on the canvas. Hold down the shift key while you click and drag to select a square area. If you want to select an oval area, use the Oval Marquee variation (hold down the shift to select a perfect circle). When you select an area, you select all objects that fall completely within the area.
  - **Lasso/Polygon Lasso tool:** Click the Lasso tool and click and drag on the canvas to select an irregularly shaped area of the canvas. If the shape you want to select is made up of straight lines, use the Polygon Lasso.
  - **Brush tool:** Click this tool to paint on the canvas. See Book III, Chapter 3 for more information about the very versatile Brush tool.
  - **Eraser tool:** Click the Eraser tool to erase a swath through any bitmap object on the canvas. The Eraser tool doesn't work with vector objects in Fireworks.

- **Rubber Stamp/Replace Color/Red Eye Removal tool:** Click this tool to copy a selected area of a bitmap to another spot on the canvas. Alt+click the area that you want to copy (Opt+click on the Mac) and then click and paint where you want the copy to go. Use the Replace Color tool to swap one color for another wherever you click and drag the Replace Color brush on the canvas. Simply click with the Red Eye Removal tool to replace red with black wherever you click the canvas; as you might guess from its name, this tool is designed to fix that annoying byproduct of flash photography, red pupils.
- **Blur/Sharpen/Dodge/Burn/Smudge tools:** Click the Blur tool and click and drag on the canvas to soften the focus of an area of a bitmap image. Use the Sharpen tool to bring a selected area into focus. Click the Dodge tool and click and drag on the canvas to lighten an area of a bitmap image. Click the Burn tool and click and drag to darken an area of a bitmap image. Click the Smudge tool and click and drag on the canvas to smear a part of an image into another part of the image, as if you were finger painting. You can set the parameters for these tools in the Property inspector (explained later in this chapter, in the section "The Property inspector").
- **Pencil tool:** Click the Pencil tool and click and drag to draw single-pixel-width bitmap lines. If you want control over the thickness and texture of the line that you're creating, use the Brush tool.
- **Magic Wand tool:** Click the Magic Wand and click a bitmap to select neighboring areas of solid or similar colors in your image.

✦ **Vector:** The following tools (clockwise from top left) make up the Vector section of the Tools panel:

- **Line tool:** Throw your ruler away! With the Line tool, you can draw a straight line every time. You can adjust the line's thickness, color, and other parameters in the Property inspector.
- **Pen/Vector Path/Redraw Path tool:** Click the Pen tool to create vector graphics by drawing *Beziér* paths. You can use the Pen tool to select points and let Fireworks connect the dots, or you can draw the shape yourself with the Vector Path tool. You can use the Redraw Path tool to change the shape of a vector graphic by clicking and dragging any of the points that define the shape.
- **Text tool:** Click this tool and click the canvas to place and edit text on the canvas. See Book III, Chapter 3 for information on how to make the most of the Text tool.
- **Knife tool:** Click this tool and click and drag a line to cut vector paths in two.
- **Freeform/Reshape Area/Path Scrubber (Additive)/Path Scrubber (Subtractive) tool:** Use the Freeform tool to reshape a vector path by

pushing or pulling the stroke instead of moving the individual points that define it. Use the Reshape Area tool to pull a vector path as if it were taffy. If you have a graphics tablet, use the Path Scrubber tool to change the color, thickness, and various other properties of the vector path. You can set the properties to vary based on variations in the pressure or speed that you use in drawing.

  - **Rectangle/ Ellipse/Polygon/Auto Shape tool:** Create vector shapes by clicking these tools and clicking and dragging on the canvas.

- **Web:** The Web tools allow you to create and show or hide areas that can be used as links on Web pages.
  - Rectangle/Circle/Polygon Hotspot tools: Use these tools to create hotspots (linkable areas) without cutting up the underlying images in "HTML and images" exports.
  - Slice/Polygon Slice tools: Use these tools to "slice" up your canvas into individual images for export.
  - Hide Slices and Hotspots and Show Slices and Hotspots tools. Click the tool on the bottom left of the Web section to hide the Web Layer (the overlays that show where your slices and hotspots are). Click the tool on the right to show the Web Layer.
- **Colors:** The Colors tools allow you to select and apply colors to lines, objects, and anything else on your canvas.
  - **Eyedropper tool:** Click this handy tool to select a color from the swatches in the color picker or from any object on the canvas by clicking when you place the Eyedropper on the color that you want.
  - **Paint Bucket/Gradient tool:** Click this tool and then click a shape on the canvas to fill the shape with a solid color (Paint Bucket) or gradient. For details about gradients, see Book III, Chapter 4.
  - **The Stroke tool:** Click the color box next to the pencil to choose a stroke color. For more information on choosing colors, see Book III, Chapter 3.
  - **The Fill tool:** Click the color box next to the paint bucket to choose a fill color.
  - **The Default Color button:** Click it to give a black stroke and white fill to a selected vector object (or to a vector object you're about to create).
  - **The "None" color button (a white square with a red slash):** Click this tool to delete the color of the selected fill or stroke.
  - **The Swap Stroke and Fill Colors button:** Does just that with a single mouse click.

- **View:** The View buttons offer handy ways to change your view of the Fireworks workspace. You can toggle through the top three View mode buttons by clicking one and pressing the F key on your keyboard.
  - **Standard Screen Mode button:** Click this to work in the default Fireworks view mode.
  - **Full Screen with Menus Mode button:** Click this to maximize the canvas within the space created within the surrounding panels.
  - **Full Screen Mode button:** Click this to view the canvas on a black background, with no Fireworks menus, toolbars, or panels showing.
  - **Hand tool:** Click the hand tool and then click and drag the canvas around in the Document window. This tool is only useful when you can't see the whole canvas in the Document window, either because the canvas is bigger than the Document window, or because you are zoomed in.
  - **Zoom tool:** Click the Zoom tool and click the canvas to zoom in (magnify the view by set increments), centered on where you click. Hold down the Alt key (Option key on the Mac) when you click to zoom out (demagnify).

Across the aisle: The right-side panels

Six key panels appear on the right side of the screen, opposite the Tools panel. Some panels are grouped together by default. These panels include the following:

- **The Optimize and Align panels:** This group of panels lets you set your export options (GIF or JPEG, quality level, and so on) and allows you to align objects in your design. The Align panel is new to Fireworks CS3. See Book III, Chapter 6 for more information about the Optimize panel.

- **The Pages, Layers, Frames, and History panels:** New to Fireworks CS3, the Pages panel gives you easy access to multiple pages if your Fireworks document consists of more than one page. (See Book III, Chapter 2 for information about pages). The Layers panel contains all your layer options and information. The first layer is always the Web Layer, which holds information about the coordinates of the slices. (See Book III, Chapter 6 for more about slices.) The Frames panel gives you access to the Frames area, where you can navigate easily among the frames in your document. You use frames to make button rollovers and animations. (See Book III, Chapter 5 for more details.) The History panel allows you to view a list of your most recent actions.
- **The Assets panel:** This group of panels provides quick access to premade design elements such as button styles and common shapes, plus a way to

centralize and organize links from Web objects to Web pages. Fireworks can actually generate your entire Web page — images, code, and all.

- **The Colors panel:** The Colors panel, via its Mixer and Swatches tabs, offers quick access to the tools that you can use to add and edit colors and gradients to objects on the canvas.
- **The Symbol Properties panel:** Use this panel to edit the values of JavaScript properties of a graphic, animation, or button symbol. See Book III, Chapter 7 for more information about symbols.
- **The Auto Shape Properties panel:** When you select an Auto Shape object on the canvas, you get access to many of its special properties via this panel, including Thickness and Roundness.

The Property inspector

The Property inspector is docked to the bottom of the Document window. This panel changes automatically to reflect the settings for the currently selected tool or object.

The Property inspector allows you to see and adjust the parameters of whatever object or tool you select. If you're working on a text layer, for example, the Property inspector gives you immediate access to and complete control over the font, size, color, and other attributes of the text. When you select a shape, on the other hand, the Property inspector offers you easy access to controls over the shape's size, position on the canvas, color, texture, and more.

TIP

If you ever want to hide all the panels temporarily, press F4 or the Tab key. To make the panels visible, press F4 or the Tab key again.

Viewing and Previewing Your Work

While you work, you view the canvas with Original view selected. The other three view options at the top of the canvas allow you to preview what your optimized images will look like. The views are as follows:

- **Original:** This is the default view in which you create and edit your design.
- **Preview:** This view shows you what the page will look like when it is optimized for the Web, based on your current image optimization settings.
- **2-Up:** This view offers previews of what optimized images will look like, but with a little something extra: a side-by-side comparison of the original image and an optimized version of the image, or two optimization settings.

✦ **4-Up:** By selecting the 4-Up view, you can preview the original image and three different optimization settings at the same time. You can compare how they look and how big the resulting image file is at each setting, as well as how long the image takes to download at a particular Internet connection speed.

Because every image compresses a little differently, you can never predict exactly what an image may look like after you optimize it. The longer you work with Fireworks, the better you get at narrowing the optimization options before you preview; nevertheless, you may find previewing before you export more efficient. For more information about the purpose and art of image optimization, see Book III, Chapter 6.

At the top right of the canvas is a feature that you may have met in the original Fireworks: a Quick Export button. The Quick Export button lets you export files to, and even launch, other applications, such as Dreamweaver, Adobe Flash, Photoshop, and Illustrator. The Quick Export button also gives you export options for Director Shockwave Studio, FreeHand, GoLive, FrontPage, Adobe Flex, and other programs.

Customizing Your Work Environment

During different phases of the design process, you may find that you refer to some panels constantly but other panels not at all. Unless you have a gigantic monitor set to a high resolution, you need to collapse some less frequently used panels to make room for more frequently used ones.

Collapsing and expanding panels

Every panel's name appears at the left on the top title bar in the panel. To the left of the name sits a handy little arrow that points down to indicate that the panel is expanded, or points to the panel name if the panel is collapsed.

You can expand or collapse a panel in two ways:

✦ Click the name of the panel.

✦ Click the arrow to the left of the panel name.

When the panel expands, it makes room for itself by forcing the panels below it down — unless it's a panel on the bottom, in which case it forces the panels above it up. If your monitor doesn't have enough room to show all the panels open at one time, Fireworks collapses the panel directly beneath or above the one that you expand.

If you have a panel expanded but still can't see quite enough of it, you can drag the panel open wider or longer by clicking the left or bottom edge of the panel and dragging it.

In addition to collapsing and expanding panels, you can also open and close panels. Check out Table 1-1, which includes the key commands for closing and opening panels.

Table 1-1 Keyboard Shortcuts for Opening and Closing Panels

Panel	*Keyboard Shortcut (PC)*	*Keyboard Shortcut (Mac)*	*Panel*	*Keyboard Shortcut (PC)*	*Keyboard Shortcut (Mac)*
Tools	Ctrl+F2	⌘+F2	Styles	Shift+F11	Shift+F11
Properties	Ctrl+F3	⌘+F3	Library	F11	F11
Optimize	F6	F6	Color Mixer	Shift+F9	Shift+F9
Layers	F2	F2	Swatches	Ctrl+F9	⌘+F9
Frames	Shift+F2	Shift+F2	Info	Alt+Shift+F12	Opt+Shift+F12
History	Shift+F10	Shift+F10	Behaviors	Shift+F3	Shift+F3

To hide all panels simultaneously, choose Window⇨Hide Panels, or use the keyboard shortcut F4. To hide only the right-side panels, click the button with the arrow on it between the canvas and right-side panels, halfway down the screen.

Moving, docking, and grouping panels

When you open Fireworks for the first time, all the panels are docked and grouped in the default configuration. (Refer to Figure 1-3 to see this default configuration.) However, you can easily undock and move panels and put them in custom groups.

To move a panel, follow these steps:

1. **Click the gripper at the top left of the panel.**

   The gripper is made up of two parallel lines of dots at the top left, on the panel's title bar.

2. **Drag the panel to the spot on the screen where you want it to go.**
3. **Release the mouse button.**

   You now see the panel in the position that you selected, in its own window, as you can see in Figure 1-4.

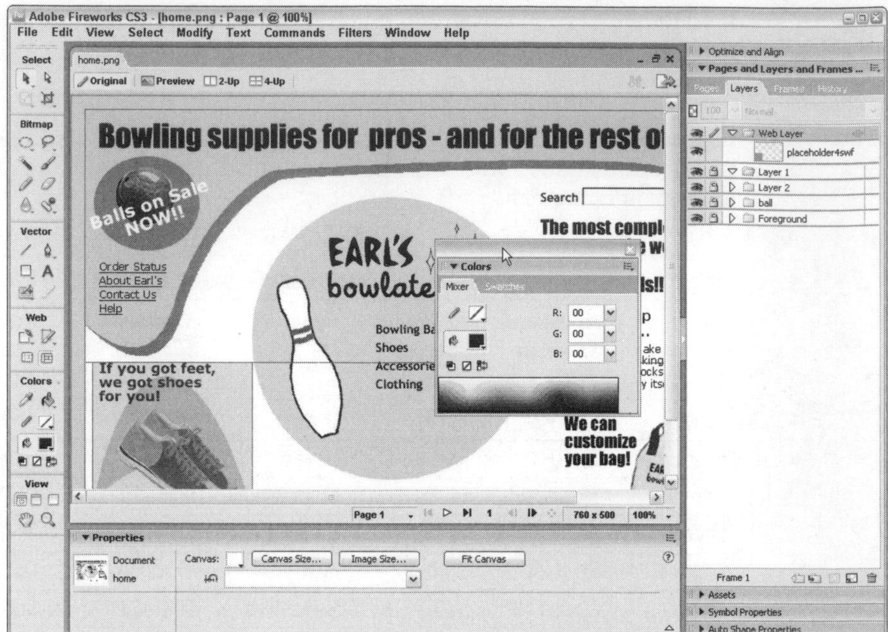

Figure 1-4: The Colors panel, undocked.

When you move a panel, you automatically undock it, but you don't automatically dock it somewhere else when you release the mouse button. The panel remains floating in the Fireworks window until you dock it. To dock a panel, follow these steps:

1. **Place your cursor over the gripper at the top left of the panel.**

   The gripper is made up of two parallel lines of dots at the top left, on the panel's title bar.

2. **Drag the panel to a docking area.**

   A docking area is anywhere along the outer edge of the Document window or adjacent to a docked panel. When you drag the panel over a docking area, a rectangle appears on the screen to give you a preview of the space that the panel occupies if you docked it there.

3. **Release the mouse button.**

   The panel is docked in its expanded state.

Fireworks gives you the option of consolidating or group panels, which provides a nice way to put the panels that you like using together. To group a panel with another panel, follow these steps:

1. **Click the Panel Options icon (the three white lines and triangle) at the top right of the panel that you want to add to a group.**

   The Panel Options menu appears.

2. **Select the Group *name of selected panel* With option.**

   An additional pop-up menu appears.

3. **Choose the panel that you want to group the currently selected panel with.**

   The panel that you add appears as a tab in the panel to which you added it.

Follow these steps to close a panel or panel group:

1. **Click the tab of the panel that you want to separate from the group.**
2. **Click the Panel Options icon at the top right of the panel.**

   The Panel Options menu appears.

3. **Select the Close Panel Group option.**

If you have moved your panels around and docked them to accommodate a particular project or document, you can save your panel arrangement by choosing Window⇨Workspace Layouts⇨Save Current and giving your settings a name. You can then retrieve that layout setup from the same location.

Setting Fireworks Preferences

Setting preferences allows you to customize the way Fireworks handles certain basic functions and displays certain items. To edit Fireworks preferences, choose Edit⇨Preferences (see Figure 1-5) or use the keyboard shortcut Ctrl+U.

As you can see in Figure 1-5, the Preferences dialog box has five tabs:

- ✦ General
- ✦ Editing
- ✦ Launch and Edit
- ✦ Folders
- ✦ Import

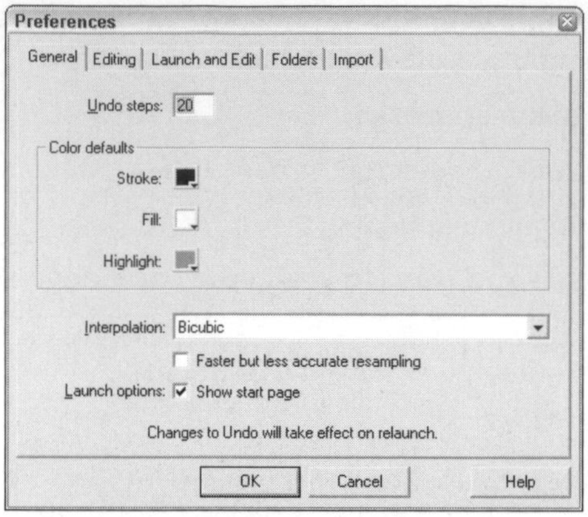

Preferences

General | Editing | Launch and Edit | Folders | Import

Undo steps: 20

Color defaults

Stroke:

Fill:

Highlight:

Interpolation: Bicubic

Faster but less accurate resampling

Launch options: Show start page

Changes to Undo will take effect on relaunch.

OK | Cancel | Help

Figure 1-5: The Preferences dialog box.

Setting General preferences

You can click the General tab in the Preferences dialog box and customize the following settings:

- **Undo Steps:** Set the value from 0 to 999. This setting affects the Edit⇨Undo/Redo command and increases the number of possible steps in the History panel. Be aware, however, that the more Undo steps you allow, the more memory Fireworks requires. You must close and relaunch Fireworks to use the new setting.
- **Color Defaults:** Set the default colors for Stroke (a line or border), Fill (the inside of a shape), and Highlight (the color that indicates what you currently have selected). To apply the changes to the default Stroke and Fill colors in the current document, you have to click the Set Default Stroke/Fill Colors button in the Tools panel.
- **Interpolation:** Choose one of the four methods that Fireworks can use to render a change to the image size:
  - **Bicubic Interpolation:** The default method, which generally yields the highest-quality results
  - **Bilinear Interpolation:** Gives a sharpness level somewhere between Bicubic and Soft
  - **Soft Interpolation:** Blurs the image slightly
  - **Nearest Neighbor Interpolation:** Sharpens edges

  A check box lets you select Faster but Less Accurate Resampling. If working quickly is more important than retaining better image integrity, select this check box. For more details on changing image size, see Book III, Chapter 2.

- **Launch options:** Select this check box if you want to see the Start page when you launch Fireworks; deselect the check box if you don't want to see the Start page.

Editing just the way you want

Select the Edit tab to access these editing preferences in Fireworks:

- **Delete Objects When Cropping:** Leave this check box selected if you want to delete objects and pixels that fall outside the area to which you crop your image.
- **Delete Paths When Converting to Marquee:** Deselect this check box if you want a path to remain on the canvas when you convert it to a marquee.
- **Brush-Size Painting Cursors:** Select this check box if you want the cursor size to represent the size of stroke that you are about to make.
- **Precise Cursors:** Select this check box if you prefer to use cross hairs as a cursor rather than the custom cursors for each tool.
- **Bitmap Option:** Select the Turn Off "Hide Edges" check box if you always want to see the path selection feedback of a selected object.
- **Pen Tool Options:** You have two options here:
  - Select the Show Pen Preview check box if you want Fireworks to show you what your path will look like (before you actually draw the line) based on the position of your cursor.
  - Select the Show Solid Points check box if you want selected points to appear hollow and deselected points to appear solid.
- **Pointer Tool Options:** You have several options here:
  - Select the Mouse Highlight check box if you want an object's selection feedback (the box that indicates that an object has been selected) to activate when you roll the cursor over that object.
  - Select the Preview Drag check box if you want to see an object as you drag it.
  - Select the Show Fill Handles check box if you want to be able to drag handles to change the position, width, skew, and rotation of a gradient fill.
  - Set the value of the Pick Distance option from 1 to 10 to specify how close in pixels your cursor needs to be to an object for you to select it.
  - Set the value of the Snap Distance option from 1 to 10 to specify how close to a grid or guide in pixels an object must be before the object snaps to the grid or guide.

Telling Fireworks how to play with others

You set the Launch and Edit preferences to specify how you want Fireworks to act when it's launched from within other applications in the Adobe Creative Suite 3.

The options are the same whether you choose options under When Editing from External Application or When Optimizing from External Application:

- **Ask When Launching:** Select this option if you want Fireworks to ask you whether to edit the PNG source file when you launch Fireworks from within another application.
- **Always Use Source PNG:** Select this option if you want Fireworks always to find the source PNG for editing an image from within another application.
- **Never Use Source PNG:** Select this option if you never want Fireworks to locate and make available for editing the source file for an image that you are editing from within another application.

In most cases (with Adobe Flash being an exception), if you edit an image by launching Fireworks from within another application, Fireworks attempts to locate the source PNG file for editing, regardless of the Launch and Edit preferences. When you edit the source file, you're editing the *original* file, not a copy of it. If you want to preserve the original, you can use the Save As command to create a new file to work on, with a new name.

Expanding your Folder options

Fireworks comes with its own effects, textures, and patterns, but the application allows you to access additional materials for use in modifying bitmap images. Select the Folders tab to gain access to the following:

- **Photoshop Plug-Ins:** If you have Photoshop plug-ins that you want to be able to use in Fireworks, select the Photoshop Plug-Ins check box. Press the Browse button and use the dialog box to browse to the folder that holds those plug-ins.
- **Textures:** If you have additional textures that you want to access from within Fireworks, select the Textures check box. Press the Browse button and use the dialog box to browse to the folder that has the texture files.
- **Patterns:** If you have additional patterns that you want to access from within Fireworks, select the Patterns check box. Press the Browse button and use the dialog box to browse to the folder that has the pattern files.

If you change these preferences, you need to quit and relaunch Fireworks for the changes to take effect.

You can access the effects, textures, and patterns from the Property inspector when you select an object.

Importing files in a useful form

Thanks to Adobe's purchase of Macromedia, Fireworks is more compatible than ever with Photoshop. Set the Import preferences to tell Fireworks how you want to convert Photoshop (`.psd`) files for editing in Fireworks:

- ✦ **Layers:** You have three options under this heading:
  - **Convert to Fireworks Objects:** Select this option if you want Fireworks to make each Photoshop layer into an object on its own Fireworks layer.
  - **Share Layer Between Frames:** Select this check box if you want to share each layer of the Photoshop file across all Fireworks frames.
  - **Convert to Frames:** Select this option if you want Fireworks to import each Photoshop layer as a Fireworks frame. This option can save you a few steps if the Photoshop file has layers that correspond to animation frames or button states.
- ✦ **Text:** You have two options under this heading:
  - **Editable:** Select this option if you want to edit text layers from the Photoshop file using the Fireworks Text tool. The text may look slightly different in Fireworks, though it's close.
  - **Maintain Appearance:** Select this option if you need the text in Fireworks to look identical to the text in Photoshop but don't have to edit the text.

  If you don't need to preserve any editability from the Photoshop file, select the Use Flat Composite Image check box.

Getting Help

Fireworks offers several forms of assistance to users. If you can't find the answer to your question in this book, several good options are available, as follows:

- ✦ **The Help menu:** This menu offers links to appropriate parts of the Adobe Web site and an indexed, searchable online manual.

  Press F1 to access the online manual at any time when you're using Fireworks. We always go to the online manual first when we need to figure out how to do something in Fireworks.

- **Fireworks tutorials:** You can use either of two basic Fireworks tutorials, one on Graphic Design Basics and the other on Web Design Basics. You can download them from the Web by clicking the Resources link on the Fireworks Start page and then clicking the Tutorials link in the Adobe Fireworks CS3 Documentation section at the top of the page. Then click the Download PDF link to download the appropriate PDF and source files for your platform (PC or Mac). The tutorials are quick, easy, and very helpful to the novice.
- **The installation CD-ROM:** The CD-ROM from which you installed Fireworks contains a couple of searchable, printable PDF files:
  - **Using Fireworks PDF:** Offers the basics
  - **Extending Fireworks PDF:** Describes how you can use JavaScript to control every command and setting in Fireworks

- You can copy the PDFs into the Fireworks folder on your hard drive so that you don't have to rummage around for the installation CD when you have a question that this book and the Help menu can't answer.
- **Tool tips:** Tool tips are built into the Fireworks user interface. Hover the cursor over an interface element to see a brief description of the element's function or capabilities.

If none of these resources gives you an answer to your question, Adobe offers both free Web-based support (including online forums) and fee-based support via e-mail and telephone.

Chapter 2: Fireworks CS3 Basics

In This Chapter

- Creating a new Fireworks document
- Switching the view of your document
- Saving your documents
- Changing a document's size
- Working with pages
- Using master pages
- Understanding color management

In this chapter, we introduce some of the basic processes of working with Fireworks CS3. If you're a regular computer user, many of these processes are already second nature to you. We show you how to create and save a Fireworks document, how to change the magnification of your document, and how to change the size of your document. We also offer an introduction to the concept of Pages, new to Fireworks CS3. Finally, we give you an introduction to some issues regarding the way colors appear on the Web.

Creating a New Document

Before you can start creating or editing cool images with Fireworks, you need to start the program and either create a brand-new blank document or open an existing image that you want to change. You can open Fireworks in several ways:

- Select Fireworks CS3 from the Start menu.
- Click the Fireworks icon in your taskbar or double-click the icon on your desktop, if you have either of those options available.
- Double-click the icon of an existing Fireworks PNG file.
- Double-click the icon of any image associated with Fireworks. (During installation, you can choose which file types you want to associate with Fireworks, including GIFs and JPEGs.)

No matter how you open Fireworks, you can create a new Fireworks document by following these steps:

1. **Choose File⇨New or press Ctrl+N.**

   The New Document dialog box opens, displaying options for the size and background color of your canvas, as well as the resolution of your document, as Figure 2-1 shows you. The settings of the most recently opened Fireworks document determine the default for all these settings. If you want to use those settings, simply click OK. Otherwise, continue with the following steps.

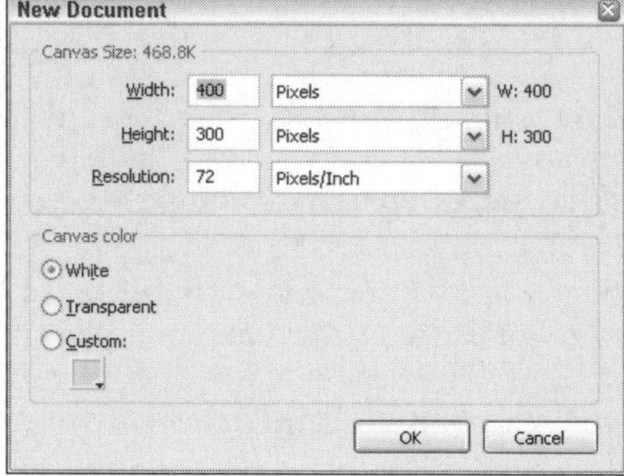

Figure 2-1: Set the canvas size and canvas color in the New Document dialog box.

2. **Type numbers in the Width and Height text fields to set the width and height of your canvas; use the drop-down list to select whether you want the width and height of the canvas measured in pixels, inches, or centimeters.**

   If you're designing for the Web, pixels work best because pixels are the basic display units on computer monitors.

   You can use different units of measurement for the width and height, although doing so would probably be more confusing than helpful.

3. **Set the canvas color.**

   The default canvas color is white. You can also set the canvas to be transparent, which can be useful if you're making a graphic that you want to have a transparent background. If you want your Web page to use a particular color for the background, click the square to use the eyedropper and choose a color from the color picker, as you can see in Figure 2-2.

4. **Click OK.**

   Your canvas opens to the specified size and with the specified background color.

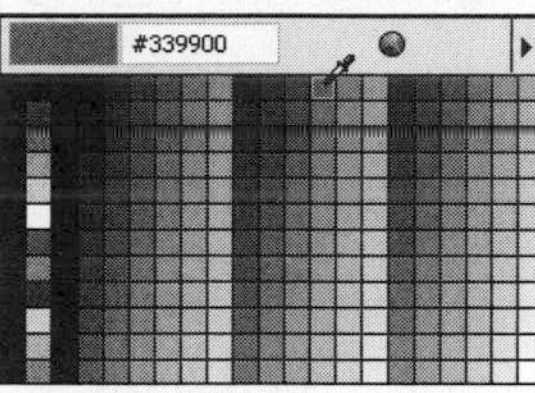

Figure 2-2: Use the color picker to select a custom background color for your canvas.

Changing Views of Your Document

After you start adding stuff to your canvas, you may find that you want to make adjustments too fine to eyeball with the canvas at 100-percent size. Fireworks offers several ways for you to increase and decrease the magnification of your canvas. Changing the magnification doesn't affect your document's size, it just changes your view of it, as if you're looking at your document through a magnifying glass.

To increase the magnification of the canvas so that you can make fine adjustments, use one of the following methods:

- ✦ **Choose View⇨Zoom In or press Ctrl+=.** Repeat as necessary to achieve the view that you want.
- ✦ **Choose View⇨Magnification and then select a magnification percentage greater than 100 percent.** If you use this method, you can select your magnification percentage directly rather than step through each level. Figure 2-3 shows this selection method.
- ✦ **Click the Magnification drop-down list at the bottom-right of the canvas.** Select from the list of preset magnification levels.
- ✦ **Click the Zoom tool in the View section of the Tools panel and then click the canvas.** If you press Ctrl+Z, you can click and drag the Zoom tool to zoom in on the selected area of the canvas.

If your canvas is larger than the window in which you're viewing it, you can decrease the magnification of the canvas so that you can see the entire document by using one of the following methods:

- ✦ **Choose View⇨Zoom Out or press Ctrl+–.** Repeat as necessary to achieve the view you want.
- ✦ **Choose View⇨Magnification and then select a magnification percentage less than 100 percent.** If you use this method, you can select your magnification percentage directly, rather than step through each level.

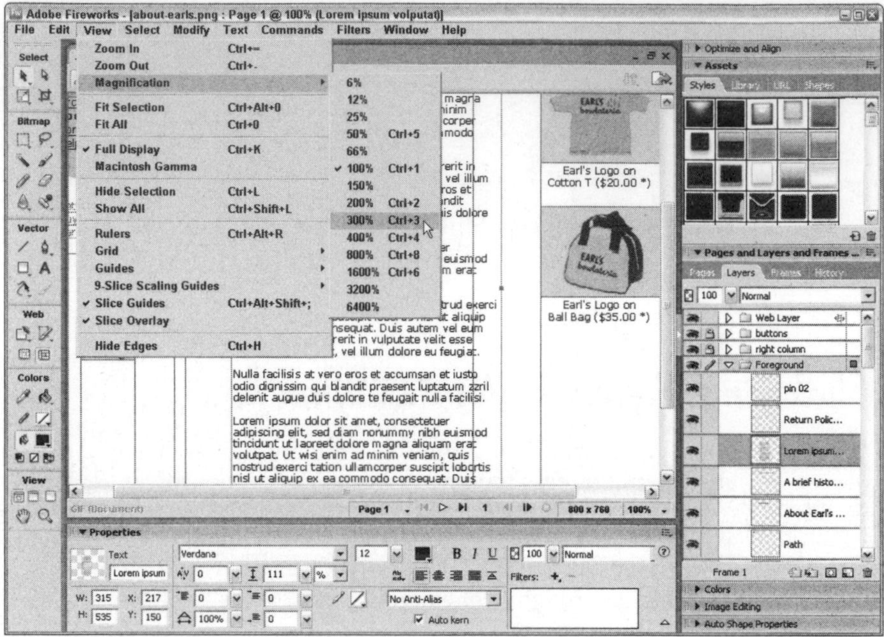

Figure 2-3: Changing the canvas magnification.

✦ **Click the Magnification drop-down list at the bottom of the canvas.** Select from the list of preset magnification levels.

✦ **Click the Zoom tool in the View section of the Tools panel and then hold down the Alt key and click the canvas.** Notice that when you press the Alt key while you have the Zoom tool over the canvas, the plus sign in the tool changes to a minus sign to indicate that you can click to zoom out.

You can access several of the most common magnification levels in one step with the key commands listed in Table 2-1. On a Mac, substitute the Ctrl key with the ⌘ key for all key combinations.

Table 2-1 Magnification Shortcuts

Magnification Percentage	*Key Combination*
50%	Ctrl+5
100%	Ctrl+1
200%	Ctrl+2
300%	Ctrl+3
400%	Ctrl+4
800%	Ctrl+8
1600%	Ctrl+6

Saving Documents

You may have read this advice elsewhere, but it bears repeating: Save early and save often. We can't think of anything worse than working for hours on an image, getting it just perfect, and having a power outage or other mishap wipe out all that work in one cruel second.

Spare yourself the frustration of losing your work and save your documents often by choosing File⇨Save or by pressing Ctrl+S. When you save a file that you create in Fireworks using this method, you save the file in the native Fireworks file format, PNG.

When you open and edit a TIFF, BMP, WBMP, GIF, or JPEG file, you can save as that file type rather than save the edited file as a PNG. To exercise the option, just save by choosing File⇨Save or by pressing Ctrl+S. If you've added Fireworks-specific elements such as slices or frames to your file, a dialog box appears, asking how you want to save the file. If you save the file as its original format, you lose any of those Fireworks-specific features.

You can still use the Undo command after you save, so it never really hurts to save your document. However, if you want to preserve intermediate versions of a document, you can save versions rather than save over your previous work. If you want to try several different approaches to a design but don't want to clog one file with all the approaches, use the Save As command and name the file with a slight variation. (For example, if you named your file `homepage.png`, you can name a second version `homepage_v02.png`.) When you choose Save As, any changes to the file since you last saved it are saved in the new version of the file, not the old one.

To save a version of your document, follow these simple steps:

1. **Choose File⇨Save or press Ctrl+S to save the file in its current state, with its current name.**
2. **Choose File⇨Save As or press Ctrl+Shift+S (⌘+Shift+S on a Mac).**

   The Save As dialog box appears, as you can see in Figure 2-4.
3. **Type a new filename in the File Name text field.**

   If you have already named the file, the current name already appears in the text field, so you need to modify the filename in order to save the current version of the document.
4. **If you're editing a non-PNG file and want to save the file in its original format, use the Save As Type drop-down list to select the format.**
5. **Click Save.**

   The new version of the file is now open and ready for modification.

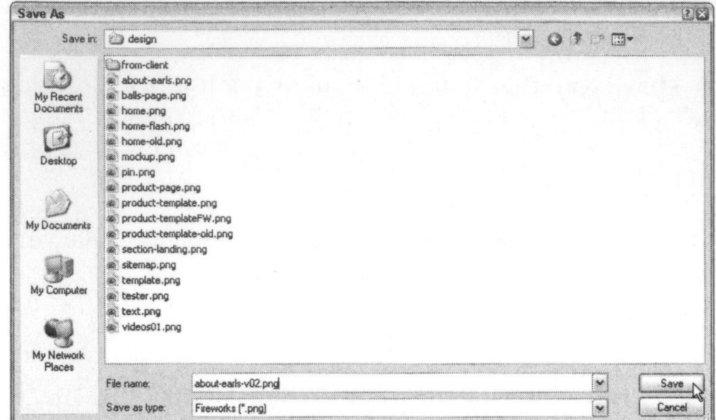

Figure 2-4: Use the Save As command to save versions of your work.

Modifying Document Size

You can modify the size of your Fireworks document in two fundamentally different ways. With these methods, you're changing the actual dimensions of the document, not just the magnification of the canvas:

- **Changing the image size:** When you change the image size, Fireworks re-creates the entire document, including everything on the canvas, at a different height, width, or both.
- **Changing the canvas size:** When you change the canvas size, you don't change the size of the objects on the canvas, you change only the size of the space on which you put the material, as if you cut the top, bottom, or sides off a printed picture (or pasted extra strips on, if you're increasing the canvas size). You can use the crop tool to reduce the canvas size, or you can use a dialog box to increase or reduce the canvas size.

Changing the image size

To change the image size of your document, you use the Image Size dialog box, which you can access by choosing Modify⇨Canvas⇨Image Size or pressing Ctrl+J (no shortcut on the Mac). When you change the image size of your document, you change the dimensions of the canvas and of everything on the canvas. If you shrink your image, Fireworks discards some of the data when it reorders the pixels to make the image smaller.

If you increase the size of your image, Fireworks *interpolates* data, which means that it performs sophisticated calculations to decide what color of pixels to add and where to add them in order to make a larger version of the image. Although Fireworks interpolates smartly, you can't avoid some amount of distortion.

Using the Image Size dialog box, you can choose which method Fireworks uses to interpolate or resample pixels:

- ✦ **Bicubic interpolation:** Bicubic interpolation is the default method and generally gives you the highest-quality results with the widest variety of images by taking an average of the nearest 16 pixels in the original image size to create a new pixel in the resized image.
- ✦ **Bilinear interpolation:** The bilinear method gives a sharpness level somewhere in between Bicubic and Soft.
- ✦ **Soft interpolation:** This method blurs the image slightly. Why would you want to slightly blur the resized image? Because resizing can result in visual inconsistencies, called *artifacts,* in the image. Blurring the image takes the edge off the artifacts, in much the same way that a soft-focus lens makes a starlet's skin look smoother.
- ✦ **Nearest-neighbor interpolation:** This method sharpens edges, so it works best on images that don't have subtle gradients. If you use this method on a bitmap of a sunset, for example, you get *banding* — noticeable stripes of color instead of a smooth blending of colors.

When you shrink your image, Fireworks discards some pixels and replaces a few to smooth out the resized image. If you have a 400 x 300 image that you shrink to 240 x 180, and then you enlarge it back to its original size, the image that you end up with doesn't exactly match the original image. However, as long as you don't make extreme size changes, you may not notice much of a difference.

If the Constrain Proportions check box is selected in the Image Size dialog box, as it is by default, and you change the width in the Pixel Dimensions part of the dialog box, the height in that part of the dialog box updates automatically, as do the width and height in the Print Size part of the dialog box. If you change the image resolution in the Print Size part of the dialog box, the width and height in both Pixel Dimensions and Print Size update automatically.

The Pixel Dimensions and Print Size widths and heights are identical; they're just being measured with different units. (In the Image Size dialog box, you can set Pixel Dimensions and Print Size to use the same units of measurement. See the two sets of steps that follow to find out how.)

To change the image size of your document in order to display the image online, follow these steps:

1. **Choose Modify⇨Canvas⇨Image Size.**

   The Image Size dialog box appears, with the current image size and resolution as the defaults, as you can see in Figure 2-5.

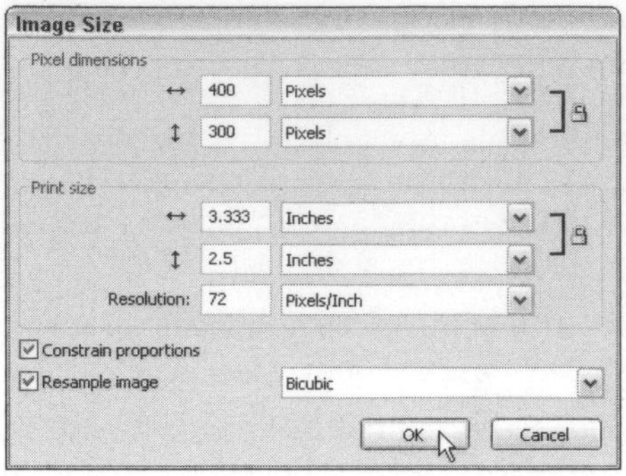

Image Size
Pixel dimensions
↔ 400 Pixels
↕ 300 Pixels
Print size
↔ 3.333 Inches
↕ 2.5 Inches
Resolution: 72 Pixels/Inch
☑ Constrain proportions
☑ Resample image Bicubic
OK Cancel

Figure 2-5: Changing the image size.

2. **Type new numbers in the width and height text fields in the Pixel Dimensions part of the dialog box to set the new width and height for your image; use the drop-down list to select whether you want to change the width and height of the image based on pixels or percentages.**

   If you're designing for the Web, you may want to use pixels because pixels are the standard units of computer monitor display. If you're designing for print, inches or centimeters may work better. If you want your new image to have the same *aspect ratio* (the ratio of width to height, for example, 4:3 for an image that is 400 x 300 pixels) as your current image, leave the Constrain Proportions check box selected. A padlock icon at the right indicates that Fireworks will constrain proportions.

   If you want to stretch or squash everything in your image as if it's being reflected in a funhouse mirror, deselect the Constrain Proportions check box and make sure that the new width and height dimensions don't preserve the aspect ratio of the old width and height. (You can make this change most easily by changing only height or only width.)

   You can use different units of measurement for the width and height, although doing so doesn't really give you any advantages.

3. **Select a method for resampling your image or leave it at the default.**

   You can read more about resampling settings (Bicubic interpolation or Soft interpolation, for example) earlier in this section.

4. **Click OK.**

   The image resizes.

To change the image size of your document for the purpose of printing it, follow these steps:

1. **Choose Modify➪Canvas➪Image Size.**

   The Image Size dialog box appears, with the current image size and resolution as the defaults.

2. **Set the image resolution in the Print Size section of the Image Size dialog box.**

   Computer screen resolution is standardized at 72 dots per inch (dpi). Most printers nowadays print at resolutions of anywhere from 300 dpi to 2400 dpi. If you're designing for the Web and working with a resolution of 72 dpi, changing the resolution here doesn't increase the resolution of any of your bitmaps (that's kind of like trying to focus a photograph after you've already taken it), but it ensures that the printout fills the page properly.

3. **Type new numbers in the width and height text fields in the Print Size part of the dialog box; use the drop-down list to change the measurement units, if you want.**

   If the Constrain Proportions check box is selected, as it is by default, and you want the printed image to have the same aspect ratio as the current image, skip this step and go on to Step 4. You can deselect the Constrain Proportions check box and type new numbers in the Width and Height text fields if you want to stretch or squish your image.

   You can use different units of measurement for the width and height, although doing so doesn't give you any advantages.

4. **Leave the Resample Image check box selected unless you want to change the image size by changing the image resolution.**

   If you change the image resolution, you change the number of pixels per inch.

5. **Click OK.**

   The image resizes.

Changing the canvas size

Making the canvas size smaller is sort of like removing strips from the outside of a drawing or painting. Whatever is on those strips gets discarded with the strips. In other words, when you reduce the canvas size, you essentially crop or cut out a piece of the image.

To reduce the canvas size, follow these steps:

1. **Choose Modify➪Canvas➪Canvas Size.**

   The Canvas Size dialog box opens, as shown in Figure 2-6. The default width and height dimensions when the dialog box opens are the current dimensions of the document.

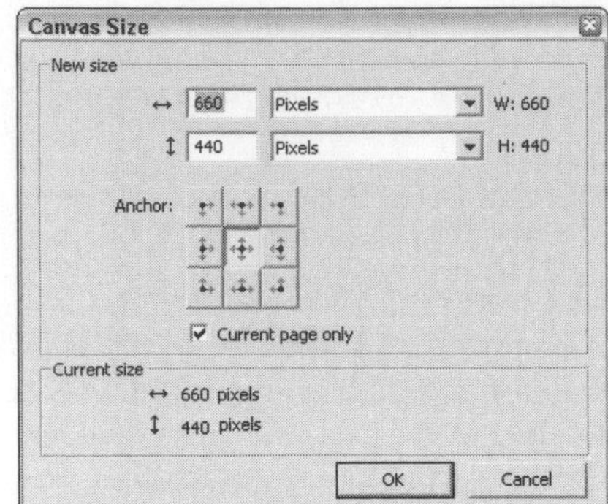

Figure 2-6: Use the Canvas Size dialog box to crop your canvas.

2. **Type new numbers for the width and height in the text fields and select the measurement units for the width and height.**

   You have the choice, as you do elsewhere, of pixels, inches, or centimeters.

3. **Select the anchor area.**

   Because you're cutting off part of your canvas, you have to set the anchor to tell Fireworks which edges of the canvas to discard. You can click

   - **One of the top three squares:** Fireworks preserves the top and cuts off any pixels below the height that you have set in the height text field.
   - **One of the middle three squares:** Fireworks removes the top and bottom of the existing document.
   - **One of the bottom squares:** Fireworks cuts off any pixels above the height that you have set in the height text field.
   - **One of the left three squares:** Fireworks discards any pixels to the right of the width that you have set in the width text field.
   - **One of the middle three squares:** Fireworks chops off the pixels on either side of the width that you have set in the width text field.
   - **One of the right three squares:** Fireworks lops off everything to the left of the width that you have set in the width text field.

4. **If you have a multipage document and want the change to affect all pages in the document, deselect the Current Page Only check box.**

   Otherwise, leave the check box selected

5. **Click OK.**

   The canvas resizes.

If you don't know what dimensions you want your image to have, but you do know which area of the current image you want to keep, you can reduce the canvas size by using the Crop tool. See Book III, Chapter 1 for information about how to use the Crop tool.

Making the canvas size bigger is like sewing extra strips onto the outside edges of a canvas. You add space to the canvas without changing the size of anything already sitting on it.

To increase the canvas size, just follow these steps:

1. **Choose Modify➪Canvas➪Canvas Size.**

   A dialog box opens, showing the current document dimensions.

2. **Type the new width and height in the width and height text fields and select the measurement units for the width and height.**

   You can choose pixels, inches, or centimeters.

3. **Select the anchor area.**

   Because you're adding an area on to your canvas, you have to set the anchor to tell Fireworks where to put the new area. You can click

   - **One of the top three squares:** Fireworks adds the space to the bottom of your current canvas.
   - **One of the middle squares:** Fireworks adds equal space to the top and bottom of your current canvas.
   - **One of the bottom squares:** Fireworks adds space to the top of your current canvas.
   - **One of the left three squares:** Fireworks adds space to the right of your current canvas.
   - **One of the center three squares:** Fireworks adds equal space to the left and right of your current canvas.
   - **One of the right three squares:** Fireworks adds space to the left of your current canvas.

4. **If you have a multipage document and want the change to affect all pages in the document, deselect the Current Page Only check box.**

   Otherwise, leave the check box selected.

5. **Click OK.**

   The canvas resizes.

Organizing Your Document into Pages

Previous versions of Fireworks allowed each PNG file to include only a single page. There was no convenient way to create a multipage document for printing, or to save designs for multiple pages of a Web site in a single Fireworks document. That's all changed with the release of Fireworks CS3.

Now you can use a single Fireworks document to create a hyperlinked set of HTML pages. Each page can have its own canvas size, canvas color, and even resolution.

Adding a page to your document

To add a page to a document you already have open on your desktop, follow these simple steps:

1. **If the Pages panel is not active, press F5.**

   The Pages panel opens on the right, with the current page highlighted.

2. **Click the Panel Options icon at the top right of the Pages panel.**

   The Options menu appears.

3. **Choose New Page.**

   The new page appears, highlighted, in the Pages panel. The new page is active, so any changes you make on the canvas apply to the new page.

Selecting a page in your document

If you have a multipage document and want to move from one page to another, you can select it from the Pages menu at the bottom of the canvas, or just follow these steps:

1. **If the Pages panel is not active, press F5.**

   The Pages panel opens on the right, with the current page highlighted.

2. **In the Pages panel, click the name of the page you want to work on.**

   The page you selected is highlighted in the Pages panel, and the canvas shows the selected page.

Deleting a page from your document

To delete a page from your multipage document, follow these steps:

1. **If the Pages panel is not active, press F5.**

   The Pages panel opens on the right, with the current page highlighted.

2. **In the Pages panel, click the name of the page you want to delete.**

   The selected page is highlighted.

3. **Click the Panel Options icon at the top right of the Pages panel.**

   The Options menu appears.

4. **Select Delete Page.**

   The page disappears from the Pages panel and is deleted from the PNG.

Mastering Master Pages

If there is a design element you want to appear identically on every page of your document (a company logo, for example), you can create a master page with that element and any other objects you want visible on all pages of your document.

When you create a new page in a document with a master page, the new page is automatically linked with the master page — that is, it inherits the canvas size and color, and the resolution, of the master page, as well as any layers and objects in the master page. Whenever the master page changes, all the pages linked to it reflect those changes automatically.

Making a page the master

To make a page in your document the master page, just follow these steps:

1. **Select the page in the Pages panel.**

   The page you selected is highlighted in the Pages panel.

2. **Click the Panel Options icon at the top right of the Pages panel.**

   The Options menu appears.

3. **Select Set As Master Page from the Options menu.**

   The designation "[Master Page]" appears next to the page name in the Pages panel. Any new pages you create will be linked to this page by default.

Master pages cannot have any shared layers. If you have shared layers in a page that you convert to a master page, the shared layers are converted to normal layers.

Linking pages to the master page

If you have existing pages in your document when you create a master page, the existing pages are not automatically linked to the master page. It may look as though they are, because they share the master page's current layers and objects. What they don't do, however, is inherit the canvas size, canvas color, and resolution. So when you update those properties on the master page, the unlinked pages won't inherit the changes. To link a page to the master page, follow these steps:

1. **Select the page you want to link to the master page by clicking it in the Pages panel.**

   The page appears on the canvas and is highlighted in the Pages panel.

2. **Click the Panel Options icon at the top right of the Pages panel.**

   The Options menu appears.

3. **Select Link to Master Page from the Options menu.**

   A link icon appears next to the page in the Pages panel, and the canvas updates with the master page's canvas properties.

Note that you can change a canvas property on a page that's linked to the master page; the page whose canvas property you change simply loses its link to the master page.

Resetting the master page

Resetting the master page of a document doesn't mean changing the master page; it means resetting the document to its default state, that is, without a master page. If you have a master page in your document and don't want to have one any longer, simply select the master page in the Pages panel and choose Reset Master Page from the panel's Options menu.

An Introduction to Color Management

The primary colors of light are Red, Green, and Blue (RGB). All the colors that you see on a computer monitor are made up of varying amounts of those three colors. When you work in Photoshop or Illustrator, you have the option to create your designs using CMYK colors (Cyan, Magenta, Yellow, and Black). CMYK is the process used in traditional offset printing. If you're creating an image that you want to use for printing, be sure to set a resolution of at least 300 dpi in the Image Size dialog box before you put any bitmap objects in your Fireworks document. Better yet, use Photoshop to make the image; you can import the image into Fireworks if you want to deploy it on the Web. (See Book III, Chapter 7 for information about integrating Fireworks and Photoshop, and see Book II for more about how to use Photoshop.)

Because Fireworks is made for Web design, it uses only the RGB color spectrum; all its color options are combinations of red, green, and blue. The following section explains how you use hexadecimal numbers to create different colors using the RGB color spectrum.

Hexadecimal numbers

When you design a Web page, you select a background color and HTML text colors. In HTML, hexadecimal numbers — signified by the pound symbol (#), followed by six digits (from 0 through 9) or letters (A through F) — specify colors. Zero represents the bottom of the scale (zero luminosity) and F represents the top of the scale (full luminosity).

The hexadecimal number's six places operate as three pairs. The first pair represents red, the second pair represents green, and the third pair represents blue. For example, to make the background color for your page white, you write the following code:

```
<BODY bgcolor="#FFFFFF">
```

To make white, you need to set each color to its highest luminosity, which is represented by the pair `FF`. If you want to put black text on your page, you can use the following code:

```
<FONT color="#000000">text</FONT>
```

To make black, you need to set each color to its lowest luminosity, which is represented by the pair `00`. If you don't understand the code in the preceding examples, see Book I, which covers Dreamweaver CS3.

The hexadecimal expression of a pure RGB red is #FF0000; a pure green is #00FF00; and a pure blue is #0000FF. The number of possible colors can boggle the mind: It's in the millions. Historically, only a small subset of those possible colors worked on the Web, though.

Web-safe colors

In the early days of the Web, many computer monitors could display only 256 colors. Because 40 of those colors were reserved for the computer's operating system or were otherwise off limits, that left 216 colors available for use on Web sites: the *Web-safe colors.* When you set your monitor's resolution to the 8-bit display option, your monitor can show only that old set of 256 colors. What happens when you look at an image that has colors that don't fall into that set of 256? Your computer approximates the colors it can't display, by either using a process called dithering or changing the colors to ones that it can display.

Dithering is the process of combining two or more colors to mimic another color. Offset printing uses a similar process to make many colors out of the four CMYK ink colors. If you look at a color image in a newspaper or magazine through a magnifying glass, you see that it's made up of many little colored dots. Viewed from a certain distance, those tiny dots blend together to form what looks like solid colors. For example, you may see orange with your naked eyes, but if you look closely with a magnifying glass, you see alternating yellow and magenta dots on that newspaper or magazine page.

When a computer dithers a color, it patterns two colors to create the illusion of a third color. As with a color photo in a newspaper, this strategy works only to a limited extent. If you look closely, you can see the pattern. If you use the dithered color for a line or some small page element, you may not really notice the dither. If, on the other hand, you select non-Web safe colors for your page background, text colors, or both, people who view your site using a monitor set to 8-bit may have a difficult time trying to read the text on your Web site.

If users have their monitors set to 16-bit and they're looking at a 24-bit color, they get a dithered color also, but the higher resolution of 16-bit versus 8-bit means that the computer can choose closer colors, so the dither doesn't look as obvious.

The more colors that you have in your image, the larger the file size.

So, do you want to use only Web-safe colors when you design your Web site? Isn't that terribly limiting? After all, designers didn't choose the Web-safe colors, and you can find some really ugly ones in the bunch! Not to mention, 8-bit monitors have gone the way of 28Kbps modems — the only place you're likely to see them is at a computer museum!

By all means, go ahead and use non-Web-safe colors. Nowadays, browsers have become more sophisticated, and average computer owners can afford monitors that display at 16-bit and higher. As a result, designers have decided that it's better to allow inconsistency in the realm of display in order to offer higher image quality to better-equipped users.

In keeping with tradition, though, Fireworks still uses the Web-safe color palette as its default in the color picker.

In the next chapter, we get into the nitty-gritty of applying all this color stuff to the real-life situations of choosing colors for page backgrounds, HTML text, and the like.

Chapter 3: Working with Text, Shapes, and Images

In This Chapter

- **Entering and editing text**
- **Creating and changing shapes**
- **Working with bitmaps**

In this chapter, we explore the power that Fireworks CS3 gives you to write and edit text, make and manipulate vector shapes, and create and mutate bitmap images. You may sometimes feel a little overwhelmed by the control that you have with Fireworks. But Fireworks has a limited number of tools, and the concepts behind the tools are simple. And whether you have a clear idea about what you want or you're interested in experimenting, Fireworks suits your needs.

Working with Text

Some of the most important decisions that you make in building your Web site involve how you present text on the screen. In general, a finished Web page has two kinds of text:

- **HTML text:** The text that you see on the Web page that you create with HTML. This type of text is akin to the text in word-processing software, such as Microsoft Word.
- **Graphic text:** The text that's embedded in an image, such as a JPEG or a GIF file. In other words, it's a *picture* of text.

Which method of presenting text works better for you and people viewing your Web site depends largely on the function of the text.

Some advantages of using HTML text include the following:

- HTML text is smaller (in kilobytes) and therefore loads faster in a user's Web browser.
- Visitors can vary the size of the text by changing settings in their browsers.

- Special software and hardware (in the case of Braille) can make HTML text available to visually impaired users via audio or touch.
- Visitors to your site can select, copy, and paste HTML text into e-mails or word-processing documents, which can help spread the word that you're trying to get out via your Web site.

On the downside, HTML text can use only very basic fonts — those fonts that all computers have, notably Arial and Times — and you can present HTML text in only a limited number of ways.

Graphic text, in contrast, is much more visually dynamic than HTML text because it's part of an image. You commonly find graphic text used for buttons and banners, which need to grab the user's attention. Some of the key advantages to using graphic text include the following:

- You can create text using any font that you have installed on your computer.
- You can apply a lot of different effects to text, such as glows and shadows (both conventional drop-shadows and shadow auto shapes). See Book III, Chapter 4 for details. You can also run text along a path — sideways, diagonal, or even curved! We show you how in the "Aligning text along a path" section.
- You have greater control of elements such as *leading* (the spacing between lines of text) and *kerning* (the spacing between letters).

Of course, using graphic text also has drawbacks. Users can't copy and paste text from graphic text, for example. Also, because the graphic text is part of an image, the size (in kilobytes) of the text is larger than that of plain HTML text.

Remember, always use an Alt tag for graphic text. The Alt tag says what the graphic text says, so visually impaired users have access to it.

Regardless of the kind of text that you want to create, Fireworks can help. The following sections show how you can use the Fireworks text-editing tools to create text as part of an image, as well as export text in HTML format.

If you want to include your main HTML text in your Fireworks document, or if you want to use placeholder text that you eventually replace with final HTML text later in Dreamweaver, use the Fireworks text default, 12-point Arial or Verdana, with no anti-alias (smoothing), in your page design. Using one of those settings gives you a good approximation of how the text looks on the HTML page that you make from your design.

Creating text with the Text tool

You can create text with Fireworks in a snap, which really helps you out because you do a lot of text creating when you make images and page mock-ups. To create some text, just follow these three easy steps:

1. **Select the Text tool by clicking the capital A in the Vector section of the Tools panel.**

   An I-shaped pointer appears, as you can see in Figure 3-1.

2. **Move the pointer to the point on the canvas where you want to create the text.**

3. **Click the canvas and type away.**

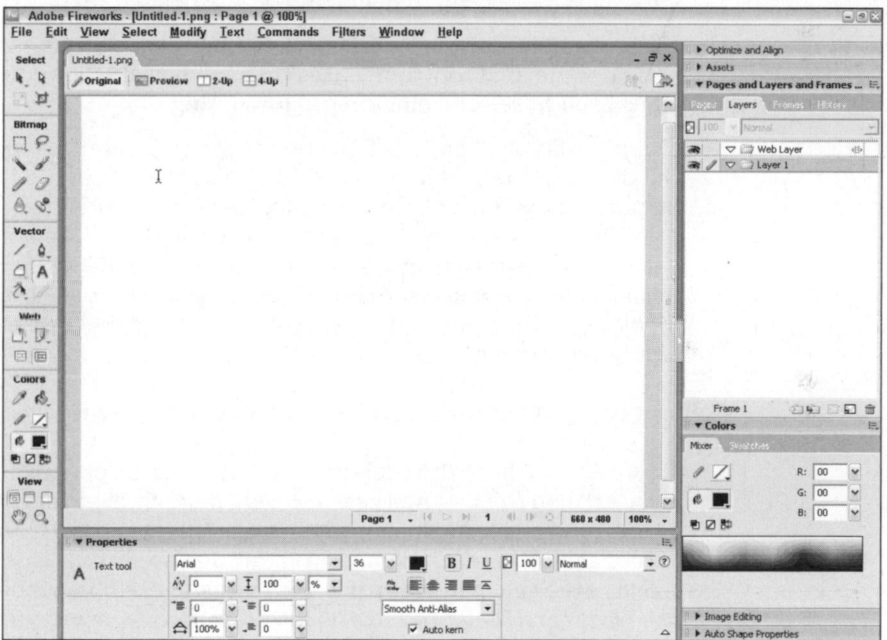

Figure 3-1: Getting ready to enter text.

You can always move the text later, as well as change its font or color. We cover those details later in this chapter.

If the text you want to add already exists in a word-processing program, open the text document, select the applicable text, and copy it. Then select the Text tool in Fireworks, click the canvas, and press Ctrl+V to paste the text. Your text appears in the default font.

If you're pasting text into your Fireworks document, set the width of the text box before you paste the text in. The default Fireworks text box expands outward to the right rather than downward. To set the width of the text box, select the Text tool from the Tools panel and click and drag diagonally on the canvas to create a text box of the right size. If your text is too long to fit in the box that you create, the box expands downward automatically.

Selecting a font and changing its size and smoothness

After you create a snippet of text, you can select it for editing in one of three ways:

- ✦ After selecting the Text tool, select the text that you want to edit by clicking and dragging to highlight just the desired text.
- ✦ Using the Pointer tool, double-click the text that you created. Doing so activates the Text tool and makes the text available for editing. Double-click again to select a single word for editing.
- ✦ Using the Pointer tool, click the text that you created. Doing so selects the entire text box. When you edit the text settings in the Property inspector (see Book III, Chapter 1 for more about the Property inspector), Fireworks applies the changes to all the text in the box. After you select text, the Property inspector switches automatically to show the available text properties that you can apply to your selected text, including bold, italic, various text alignments, and effects such as drop-shadow and glow.

You can change your text to a different font in one of two ways:

- ✦ Choose a font from the drop-down list (the list displaying the default font, Arial on the PC and Geneva on the Mac) in the Property inspector. The drop-down list displays all the fonts that you have in your machine in alphabetical order. As you scroll through the list, the list displays the name of the selected font using the font face itself, so you can quickly see what each font looks like. Figure 3-2 shows you what the Property inspector looks like when you select text.
- ✦ Choose Text⇨Font and then select from the list of fonts that appears on the screen.

If you have tons of fonts and your favorite is way down on the list, you can skip to it by clicking in the scrolling drop-down list in the Property inspector and typing the first letter of the font name. This action jumps you to the first font available with that letter. You can then press the down-arrow key to find the font that you're looking for. Press Enter to apply the font to the selected text.

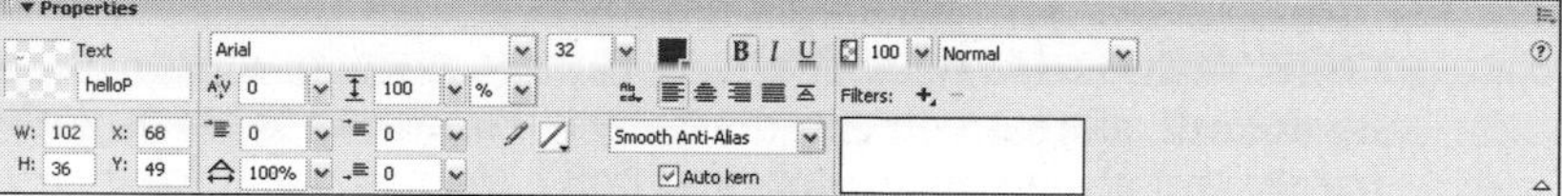

Figure 3-2: The Property inspector puts all your text options within one click.

After you select a font, you can change its size in no time at all. You can change a font size in Fireworks in one of two ways:

✦ **Use the Size field:** The Property inspector contains a field indicating the current size of the font that you're working with. To change the text size, simply type in the text field the point size that you want and press Enter.

✦ **Use the Slider:** Click and hold the arrow at the right of the Size field and then slide it up. The text size increases. Similarly, slide it down and the text size decreases (see Figure 3-3).

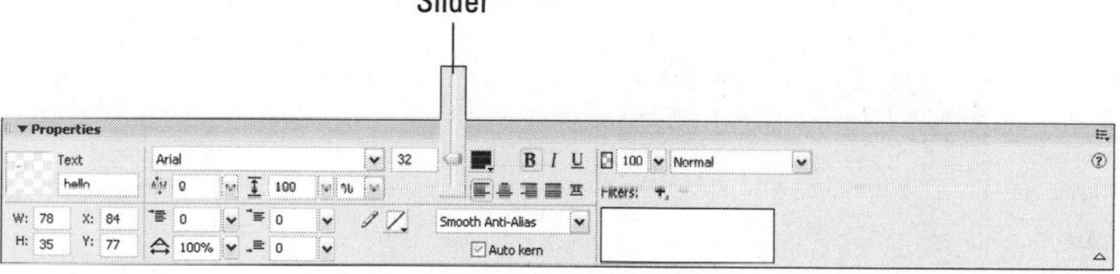

Figure 3-3: Use the handy size slider to set your font size.

If you're creating graphic text (that is, text to be exported in a graphic), you'll probably want to select an anti-alias style from the Anti-Alias select menu. Anti-aliasing is the smoothing of the text's appearance to make it look like a printed typeface.

Because greater levels of anti-aliasing can make text look blurry, you have the following choices of basic anti-aliasing from the Anti-Alias select menu, each of which provides a different method of creating the smoothness:

✦ No Anti-Alias

✦ Crisp Anti-Alias

✦ Strong anti-Alias

✦ Smooth anti-Alias

You can also use System Anti-Alias (the built-in anti-aliasing used by your operating system) or choose a custom level.

Adding a little color

By default, all text you enter initially in Fireworks is black. Although black is handy and always in fashion, you don't want to use it for every occasion. You can pretty easily change the font color in Fireworks. To change your color the basic way, just follow these steps:

1. **Select the Text tool and place the cursor next to the first word that you want to change the color of. Click and drag until you select all the text that you want to make a different color.**

   Alternatively, if you're using the Pointer tool, click the text to select it.

2. **Click the Color box to open the color picker.**

   The color picker appears on-screen, showing only Web-safe colors by default (see Figure 3-4). Your mouse pointer changes to an eyedropper when you roll over the palette. (You can read more about the System Color Picker, which offers other color options, later in this section.) You can move the eyedropper anywhere within the Fireworks window.

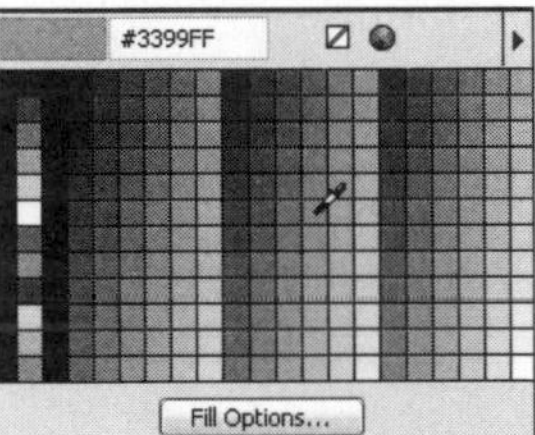

Figure 3-4: Use the eyedropper to choose a color in the color picker.

3. **Using the eyedropper, click a color.**

   The square now becomes the color that you select for your text. More important, your selected text becomes that color as well. If the text appears to be a different color than the square, you still have the text highlighted. Click anywhere on the canvas or click any tool to deselect the text and see the color applied to the text.

If you don't feel like moving your mouse all the way to the bottom of the screen, you can also change the color of your font by using the Colors area of the Tools panel or by using the Colors panel. They work the same way as the color picker in the Property inspector, so feel free to use whichever one you find most convenient.

The color picker contains a number of different views. The default view uses Web-safe color cubes. You can switch views by clicking the right-facing triangle in the top-right corner of the color picker and then selecting a new view from the list that appears. The other views include the following:

✦ **Swatches panel:** Displays your saved colors. If you have any saved colors, they show up here. If not, the panel displays the Web-safe palette.

✦ **Continuous tone:** Shows the colors as they move from lighter to darker, left to right across the color picker. You can find all these colors in the Web-safe color cubes, just arranged differently.

✦ **Windows OS:** Shows the 256 Windows operating system colors.

✦ **Mac OS:** Shows the system colors for the Mac operating system.

✦ **Grayscale:** Provides a range of grays from light to dark. Be warned, though: Only six grayscale colors are Web safe!

What if the color you want isn't in the Web-safe palette? Well, thankfully, Fireworks gives you a number of different coloring options. On the top of the palette, you can find the System Color Picker (the color wheel near the middle of the top of the color picker). You can click the System Color Picker to see your other color options. The System Color Picker offers several other ways for you to choose a color (as you can see in Figure 3-5):

✦ **RGB values:** Red, green, and blue make up all the colors that you can see on-screen.

✦ **Hue, Saturation, and Luminosity values:** A different way of telling the computer how to combine red, green, and blue.

✦ **The color matrix:** A visual representation of the hue (the horizontal axis), saturation (the vertical axis), and luminosity (the extra strip on the right) values.

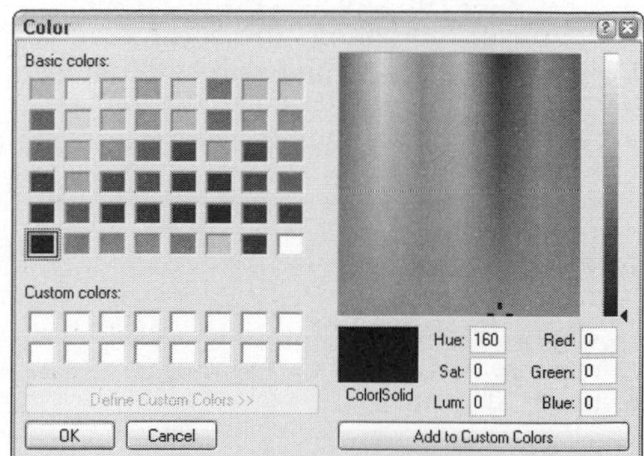

Figure 3-5: The System Color Picker offers more options than the color picker.

Using the color matrix gives you the most flexibility in choosing a color because you can visually pick precisely the color that you want. Here's how you use the color matrix to change the color of selected text:

1. **Select the Text tool and place the cursor next to the first word that you want to change the color of. Click and drag until you select all the text that you want to make a different color.**

   Alternatively, if you're using the Pointer tool, click the text to select it.

2. **Click the Color box to open the color picker.**

3. **From the top middle of the color picker, select the System Color Picker.**

   The Color dialog box appears, as shown in Figure 3-5.

4. **Place your cursor over the color that you want and click the mouse button.**

   You see a cross hair where you click. At the center of the cross hair, you can see the color that you choose. The higher you go in the matrix, the more saturated the color becomes. If you want to make the color darker or lighter, click the shade that you want in the Luminosity bar next to the matrix, or click and move the slider to the right of the shade. At this point, you still haven't changed the color of the text on the canvas.

5. **Click OK to apply the color to your text.**

   The text you selected on the canvas changes to the color that you selected in Step 4.

If you want to use a color frequently, click the Add to Custom Colors button on the lower right after you select your custom color. That way, whenever you need to use that color, you can click its square in the color picker instead of having to remember its RGB values or trying to find it in the color matrix.

Manipulating text

After you type or paste your text, you can change anything about it, from its color to its position on the page. You change the color exactly the same way that you apply the color in the first place, and you can just as easily edit, move, and delete text.

Inserting text

To insert text, just follow these steps:

1. **Choose the Text tool from the Tools panel.**

   An I-beam-shaped cursor appears.

2. **Click the place in the text box where you want to add text.**

   A blinking vertical line indicates where you will insert your new text.

3. **Start typing, or paste text (press Ctrl+V) that you have copied from elsewhere.**

Deleting text

To delete text, do the following:

1. **Choose the Text tool from the Tools panel.**
2. **Click the place in the text box where you want to delete text.**
3. **Click and drag over the text you want to delete.**

   The selected text is highlighted, as shown in Figure 3-6.

4. **Press Delete or cut the text by pressing Ctrl+X.**

   The highlighted text disappears.

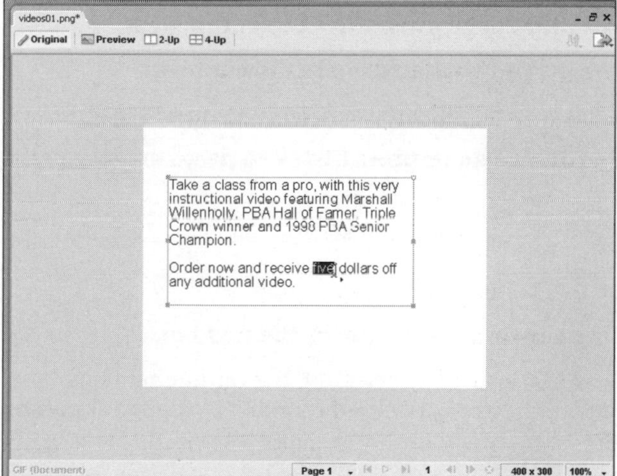

Figure 3-6: Selecting text in a text box.

To delete an entire selection of text, select the Pointer tool and then click the text box that you want to delete. After you select the text box, press the Del key to delete the text box and everything in it.

If you realize that you deleted more than you wanted to, or deleted the wrong chunk of text, press Ctrl+Z to undo the deletion.

Replacing text

To replace text, just follow these steps:

1. **Choose the Text tool from the Tools panel.**
2. **Click the place in the text box where you want to replace text.**
3. **Click and drag over the text you want to replace with other text.**

   The selected text is highlighted (refer to Figure 3-6).
4. **Start typing, or press Ctrl+V to paste in text that you copied from elsewhere.**

Moving text

To move text within a text box, do the following:

1. **Choose the Text tool from the Tools panel.**
2. **Click and drag over the text you want to move.**

   The selected text is highlighted (refer to Figure 3-6).
3. **Choose Edit⇨Cut or press Ctrl+X to cut the text.**
4. **Click where you want to drop in the cut text.**

   A blinking vertical line indicates where you will insert your text.
5. **Choose Edit⇨Paste or press Ctrl+V to paste the text at the insertion point.**

To move a text box, follow these steps:

1. **Choose the Pointer tool.**
2. **Place the cursor anywhere over the text box.**

   If the text box is already selected, the outline remains blue. Otherwise, an outline appears in red to indicate that your cursor is over the text box.
3. **Click anywhere within the text box and, with the mouse button held down, drag to move the text box.**

   Fireworks shows you where you're moving the text.
4. **Release the mouse button when you have the top left of your text where you want it.**

   The text relocates.

Changing text box dimensions

After you move your text box, you may find that the text is too wide, too narrow, too long, or too short to fit in its new position in your design. Do you have to change your text? Not necessarily. Fireworks lets you adjust the dimensions of your text box, which may be all that you need to do.

To change the width or length of a text box, just follow these steps:

1. **Choose the Pointer tool.**
2. **Place the cursor anywhere over the text box.**

   An outline appears in red to indicate that you have rolled the cursor over the text box.
3. **Click anywhere within the text box to select it.**

   The red outline changes to blue to indicate that you have selected the entire text box.
4. **Place the Pointer over one of the resize handles (the squares in the middle of the right or left side, which allow you to change the width of the box, and the squares in the corners, which allow you to change the width and height at the same time).**

   The Pointer (the black arrow) automatically changes to the Subselection tool (the white arrow).
5. **Click a resize handle and drag the box to the width or length that you want.**
6. **Release the mouse button to see the change.**

   If you widen your text box, Fireworks automatically shortens it. If you make your text box narrower, on the other hand, Fireworks makes the text box longer. If you drag the box longer than it needs to be to hold the text, the bottom of the box snaps to the lowest point to which your text reaches at the width that you drag the box to.

Aligning text along a path

Graphic text in Fireworks doesn't have to conform to the straight and narrow — it can hug any curve like a fancy sports car. To align a block of text to a vector path (see the section "Working with Vector Shapes," later in this chapter, for info on vector shapes, paths, and strokes), simply follow these easy steps:

1. **Select the text block and Shift+click the shape or path.**

   Both the text and path have light-blue outlines that show you've selected them.

2. **Choose Text➪Attach to Path or press Ctrl+Shift+Y.**

   The text conforms to the path or shape. The path loses its stroke attributes, and any attributes that you attach to the path after aligning the text (such as color, shadows, and so on) are applied to the text, not the path.

After you have attached text to a path, you can edit the path, and the text follows the edited path. To detach text from a path, simply choose Text➪Detach from Path.

Working with Vector Shapes

Fireworks gives you two ways to draw on your canvas:

✦ **Vector mode:** Uses points, lines, and shapes to define image elements

✦ **Bitmap mode:** Uses pixels to define image elements

Each method has advantages and disadvantages, and which mode you use depends on what you want to do.

If you want to make a shape that you can easily tweak, resize, or export to Flash or Illustrator later, you want to work in vector mode. When you make a simple vector shape in Fireworks, you actually create a mathematical model of a series of points connected by lines. By adding, subtracting, or moving points, you can change the shape without changing any of its other qualities, such as the line (stroke), width, and texture.

Because a simple vector shape is more a mathematical description of an image than an actual image, it has a small data size. Not only that, but a square of a particular color, stroke width, and gradient fill is basically the same data size whether it's 10 x 10 pixels or 1000 x 1000 pixels on-screen. That size consistency becomes important in Flash, in which smaller image data sizes mean faster downloads.

The basic building block of a shape is the path. The *path* by itself is just a set of coordinates; to make the path appear, you need to apply a stroke. A *stroke* in Fireworks is like a brushstroke in a painting. Stroke properties include width, texture, and color. The thicker the brush, the thicker the stroke that it makes. Of course, in Fireworks, you can make strokes with the Pencil and Pen tools, and with other tools as well.

Read on to discover how to create and edit vector shapes.

Making a good old-fashioned line

When you first create a line using the Line tool, it's a straight line (which can be vertical, horizontal, or diagonal). To create a line in Fireworks, just follow these steps:

1. **Click the Line tool in the Vector part of the Tools panel.**
2. **Place your cursor over the spot where you want your line to start.**

   When you have your cursor over the canvas, the cursor becomes a cross hair. The center of that cross hair is your point of contact with the canvas.
3. **Click where you want your line to start and, holding the mouse button down, move your cursor to where you want your line to end.**
4. **Release the mouse button.**

By default, the stroke of your line is 1 pixel in width.

You can access dotted and dashed line stroke options, as well as other options, in the Stroke Category pop-up menu in the Property inspector, as you can see in Figure 3-7.

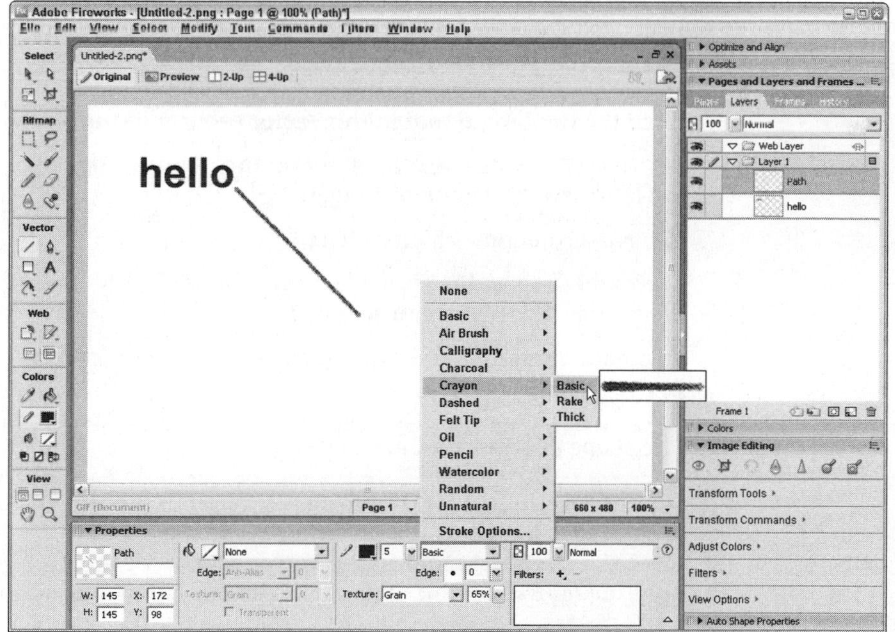

Figure 3-7: Select a stroke option from the Property inspector.

If you hold down the Shift key while you draw a line, you restrict the angle of the line to 45-degree increments.

Making simple shapes

Fireworks has easy-to-use tools for creating rectangles (including squares), ovals (including circles), and polygons. The tools for making all these shapes are grouped with the Rectangle tool in the Vector section of the Tools panel. When you click the Rectangle tool and hold down the mouse button, a pop-up menu displays three basic tools at the top:

- **The Rectangle tool:** Use this tool to create squares and other rectangles.
- **The Ellipse tool:** Use this tool to create round shapes such as circles and other ovals.
- **The Polygon tool:** Use this tool to create many-sided shapes (up to 360 sides). Use the Property inspector to set the number of sides before you draw on the canvas. The slider includes values from 3 to 25; for values greater than 25, you need to type a number in the field. By default, the Polygon tool creates pentagons. Add three sides and you have an octagon, or delete two sides to get a triangle.

See the section "Making complex shapes," later in this chapter, for information on the other options in the Rectangle tool's pop-up menu.

To make a rectangle, follow these steps:

1. **Click the Rectangle tool in the Vector section of the Tools panel.**
2. **Place your cursor over the point on the canvas where you want the top-left corner of your rectangle.**

   The cursor becomes a cross hair.
3. **Click and drag to the spot where you want the bottom-right corner of the rectangle, as you can see in Figure 3-8.**

   To create a square, hold down the Shift key as you drag.
4. **Release the mouse button.**

   The shape appears on the canvas.

To make an oval, follow these steps:

1. **Click the Rectangle tool in the Vector section of the Tools panel and hold the mouse button down until the pop-up menu with the Ellipse tool appears.**

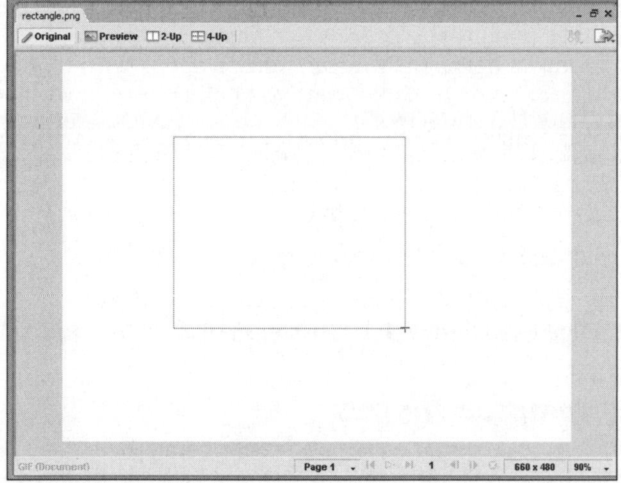

Figure 3-8: Making a rectangle shape.

2. **Place the cursor over the Ellipse tool and release the mouse button.**

   The Ellipse tool is selected.

3. **Place your cursor over the point on the canvas where you want the oval.**

   Your cursor becomes a cross hair.

4. **Click and drag to create the oval.**

   To create a circle, hold down the Shift key as you drag.

An oval doesn't have corners, so you may not be able to get precise placement when you make the shape. But you can easily move the shape, as we describe in the "Editing, moving, and deleting shapes" section, later in this chapter.

You can make an equilateral polygon (a shape in which all sides have equal lengths) by following these steps:

1. **Click the Rectangle tool in the Vector section of the Tools panel and hold the mouse button down until the pop-up menu with the Polygon tool appears.**
2. **Place the cursor over the Polygon tool and release the mouse button.**

   The Polygon tool is selected.

3. **In the Sides text field on the right of the Property inspector, type the number of sides you want the polygon to have, or use the slider next to the Sides text field to set the number of sides.**

By default, the polygon is five sided. If you set the number of sides to three rather than five, you draw a triangle. Set the number of sides to six and you draw a hexagon. You can make a shape with up to 360 sides — just don't expect us to know what you call a polygon with 360 sides!

4. **Place your cursor over the point on the canvas where you want the shape.**

   Your cursor becomes a cross hair.

5. **Click and drag to create the polygon.**

   The Property inspector changes to give you access to various properties of the polygon, including fill options, stroke options, and effects.

Making complex shapes

You can make complex shapes simply by choosing them directly from the Rectangle tool's Auto Shapes pop-up menu, which presents you with icons representing the following choices:

- Arrow
- Beveled Rectangle
- Chamfer Rectangle
- Connector Line
- Doughnut
- L-Shape
- Pie
- Rounded Rectangle
- Smart Polygon
- Spiral
- Star

You can also create an Auto Shape by selecting it from the Insert New Auto Shape pop-up menu in the Auto Shape Properties panel, which by default is the bottom right panel. (Because it is closed by default, click the triangle or panel name to open the panel.) And when you have an Auto Shape selected on the canvas, you can change many of its settings in the Auto Shape Property inspector.

The new Shapes panel, which you can find grouped in the Assets panel, includes shapes such as 3D Box, Talking (a comic strip-type dialog bubble), and Frames (a few picture frames). To place one of these shapes on the canvas, simply click it in the Shapes panel, drag it onto the canvas, and release the mouse button.

If you can't find the kind of shape that you want to make in the Vector Shape tool's pop-up menu or the Shapes panel, you can make a custom, free-form shape. Believe it or not, you can just as easily make odd shapes as regular ones, and you may have more fun doing it!

The main tool that you use to create complex shapes is the Pen tool, which you can find in the Vectors section of the Tools panel. As does the Rectangle tool, the Pen tool comes with some variations, which you can access by clicking and holding the mouse button down on the Pen tool. The pop-up menu for the Pen tool displays the following variations:

- **The Pen tool:** Use the Pen tool to place points on the page; Fireworks connects the dots for you.
- **The Vector Path tool:** Use the Vector Path tool to draw as you do with a felt-tip marker. You can manipulate the path in ways that you can't if you use a bitmap tool (or a real felt-tip marker); see the section "Editing, moving, and deleting shapes," later in this chapter.
- **The Redraw Path tool:** Use the Redraw Path tool to change the length or shape of a path that you've already created.

To make a free-form shape with straight lines, follow these steps:

1. **Click the Pen tool in the Vector section of the Tools panel.**
2. **Place the cursor over the canvas.**

   Your cursor becomes a fountain pen.
3. **Click to make your starting point.**
4. **Move your cursor and click to create a second point.**

   Fireworks connects the dots with a straight line.
5. **Move your cursor and click to create a third point, and, if you want, a fourth, fifth, tenth, or one-hundred-forty-second point.**
6. **If you want a closed shape, click again on your starting point to close the shape. Otherwise, double-click the end point to make an open shape.**

You may initially have some problems making curved lines with the Pen tool. If you know a few things about the Pen tool, you can much more easily use it to make curved lines. First of all, you can make two kinds of points with the Pen tool. Which kind of point you make determines whether the line connecting the dots is straight or curved:

- **Corner points:** These points anchor straight lines.
- **Curve points:** These points anchor curved lines.

If you simply click in various spots to make the shape, you automatically make corner points. To make a free-form shape with curved lines, as in the one shown in Figure 3-9, do the following:

1. **Click the Pen tool in the Vector section of the Tools panel.**
2. **Place the cursor over the canvas.**

   Your cursor becomes a fountain pen.
3. **Click to make your starting point.**
4. **Move your cursor and click a second point. Keeping the mouse button held down, move your cursor.**

   Point handles (solid circles at both ends of a line that has the selected point in the middle) appear, which tells you that you have made a curve point. As you move the mouse, Fireworks previews the curve between the first and second points.
5. **Release the mouse button to make the curve.**

   Fireworks joins your first and second points.
6. **Move your cursor and click and drag to create as many curved lines as you want.**
7. **If you want a closed shape, click again on your starting point to close the shape. Otherwise, double-click the end point to make an open shape.**

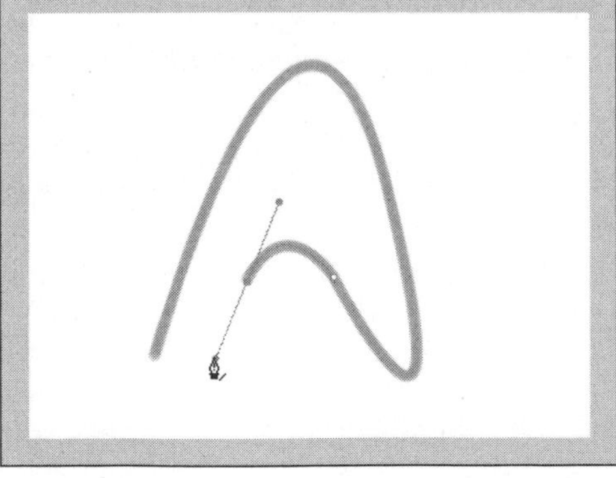

Figure 3-9: Making a complex, curved shape.

Editing, moving, and deleting shapes

You can alter a simple shape nearly as easily as you can make one. If you make a shape using any of the tools grouped with the Rectangle, Ellipse, or Polygon tool, Fireworks thinks of the shape as a group of points. If you want to edit the shape, first you need to ungroup the points so that you can move them.

To change the shape of a straight-sided simple shape (a shape with nothing but corner points, such as a rectangle), follow these steps:

1. **Click the Subselection tool (the white arrow) in the top of the Tools panel.**
2. **Click anywhere on the line defining the shape.**

   All the points, and the guide lines connecting them, are highlighted.
3. **Choose Modify➪Ungroup or press Ctrl+Shift+G (⌘+Shift+G on a Mac) to ungroup the points.**

   The shape remains selected.
4. **Click and drag any point in the shape to the new location that you want.**

   You can also delete a point by clicking it and pressing the Backspace or Delete key.

If you want to edit a complex shape (such as the one in Figure 3-9), you can use the Subselection tool to alter any of the curves:

1. **Select the Subselection tool (the white arrow) from the top of the Tools panel.**
2. **Click anywhere on the line defining the shape.**

   All the points, and the guide lines connecting them, are highlighted.
3. **If the shape is grouped, choose Modify➪Ungroup or press Ctrl+ Shift+G (⌘+Shift+G on a Mac) to ungroup the points.**

   When points are grouped, they're locked together and can't be manipulated individually.
4. **Click and drag a curve point to its new location or click a curve point to make it active, and then click and drag one of the point handles to change the shape of the curve.**

Moving a shape is a piece of cake. Here's how:

1. **Click the Pointer tool (the black arrow) in the top of the Tools panel.**
2. **Click anywhere on the line defining the shape and, keeping the mouse button held down, drag the shape to the location that you want.**

   WARNING!

   You can also use the Subselection tool to move a shape, but you have to be careful not to click a handle. If you click and drag a point handle, you move the point rather than the whole shape. If you change the shape by mistake, press Ctrl+Z to undo the change.

Deleting a shape is simple; just follow these steps:

1. **Click the Pointer tool (the black arrow) or the Subselection tool (the white arrow) from the top of the Tools panel.**
2. **Click anywhere on the line defining the shape.**
3. **Press the Delete or Backspace key.**

   If you want to cut the shape and paste it somewhere else (in your current document or in a different document), press Ctrl+X to remove the shape and Ctrl+V to paste it in your desired new location.

Splitting shapes

If you ever want to split one shape into two shapes, you can call upon the services of the Knife tool. You have access to the Knife tool only when you select an ungrouped shape. When you don't have an ungrouped shape selected, the Knife tool is grayed out in the Tools panel.

To split an ungrouped shape, follow these steps:

1. **Click the Pointer tool (the black arrow) at the top of the Tools panel.**
2. **Click anywhere on the line defining the shape that you want to split.**

   All the points, and the guide lines connecting them, are highlighted. Just as important, the Knife tool in the Vector section of the Tools panel becomes available. (If the Knife tool remains grayed out, press Ctrl+Shift+G (⌘+Shift+G on a Mac) to ungroup the shape and make the Knife tool available.)
3. **Select the Knife tool from the Vector section of the Tools panel by clicking it or pressing the Y key.**

   When you move your cursor over the canvas, your cursor becomes a blade.
4. **Click and drag the cursor over the guide lines where you want the shape to split, as you can see in Figure 3-10.**

   New points show where you made the cut. You now have two shapes. If you want to move or edit either of the new shapes, select the shape that you want with the Subselect tool.

If you hold down the Shift key while dragging, you can constrain the split to 45-degree angles.

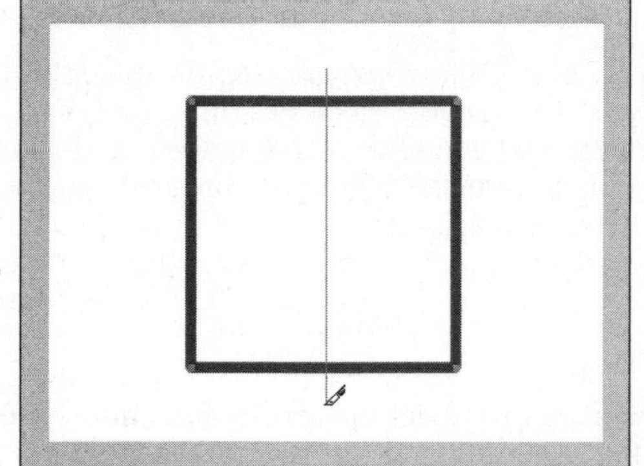

Figure 3-10: Splitting a square into two pieces.

Adding a little color to your shapes

You can think of your shapes as having two parts: the path that defines the outside (which can have a stroke or not) and the whole of the inside (which can be empty or filled). The most basic stroke for a shape is a solid color; likewise, the most basic inside for a filled shape is a solid color.

You can get pretty fancy with both strokes and fills (adding gradients, textures, and more, which you can read about in Book III, Chapter 4). However, we start with the basics: adding solid colors to strokes and fills.

Adding color to the stroke

The initial default color of strokes in Fireworks is black. So, when you add color to the stroke, you're really changing the stroke's color from black to the color that you choose. Whatever you last selected as the stroke color becomes the new default.

To add or change the color of your stroke, just follow these steps:

1. **Click the Pointer tool (the black arrow) or Subselection tool (the white arrow) in the Tools panel.**
2. **Click anywhere in the stroke.**

   The stroke is highlighted to show that you selected it.
3. **Click the color box next to the Pencil icon in the Stroke part of the Property inspector.**

   The pointer assumes the shape of an eyedropper, and the Fireworks color picker appears. You can choose a color from the color picker or place the eyedropper anywhere in the Fireworks window to select a color.

4. **Click to select the color that the tip of the eyedropper is over.**

   The stroke changes color. To find out more about the color picker, see the "Adding a little color" section, earlier in this chapter.

If your stroke is only 1 pixel wide, the highlight obscures the line, and you can't see your change immediately. Don't worry, though. Just click anywhere on the canvas except in the shape that you just changed; you do this to deselect the shape so that you can see it. (You can also deselect the shape by pressing Ctrl+D.

To remove a stroke from a path, select the stroke and choose None from the Stroke Category pop-up menu in the Stroke part of the Property inspector.

Adding a fill color to the inside of the shape

Fills in Fireworks are empty by default. So when we say that you add color to the fill, you really add color to the fill! Just as with adding color to a stroke, after you know how to add a color to the fill, you also know how to change the fill's color.

To add a fill color to your shape, or to change the color that your shape currently has, just follow these steps:

1. **Click the Pointer tool (the black arrow) in the Tools panel.**
2. **Click anywhere in the shape.**

   The stroke highlights to show that you selected the shape.
3. **Click the square with the red line through it (next to the Paint Bucket icon) in the Fill part of the Property inspector.**

   The pointer assumes the shape of an eyedropper, and the Fireworks color picker pops up. You can choose a color from the color picker or place the eyedropper anywhere in the Fireworks window to select a color.
4. **Select a color.**

   To get the goods on the color picker, see the "Adding a little color" section, earlier in this chapter.

To remove an existing fill from your shape, follow the preceding steps, but at Step 4, click the Transparent button (the square with the red line through it at the top middle of the color picker).

Want to add a gradient or texture fill to your shape? See the section on adding gradients and textures to shape fills and bitmap selections in Book III, Chapter 4. Trying to turn your shape into a button symbol? See Book III, Chapter 7 for the basics on using symbols in Fireworks CS3.

Working with Bitmap Images

Vector images are compact and versatile, but they can't handle the complexity of photographic images or illustrations. In a photographic image, any given pixel can be a completely different color than any of the pixels around it, so each pixel's color must be defined individually. That makes bitmaps big from a file-size perspective, but for photos on your Web site, bitmaps are the only way to go.

Fireworks offers an array of useful tools for making and manipulating bitmap images. You may use the bitmap tools to draw in Fireworks, but you probably want to use bitmap mode mostly when you need to place and tweak imported images, such as photographs.

Exploring the bitmap drawing tools

The main bitmap drawing tools in Fireworks are the Brush and Pencil tools. You can use those tools somewhat interchangeably. Each tool has an amazing amount of flexibility, so although you can start drawing with them quickly, getting comfortable with their full capabilities may take some time.

Most of the flexibility of the tools centers around the concept of *tips.* In the real world, the sharper a pencil, the thinner a line it draws. The thicker the end of a paintbrush, the thicker the line it makes, and the kind of bristles it has affects the texture of the line it makes. The same results hold true with the tools in Fireworks.

In Fireworks, however, each tool has its own unique tip (though all those tools are really just variations of the Pencil and Brush tools) to form a stroke category, as the following list describes:

- **Basic:** Hard Line, Hard Rounded, Soft Line, Soft Rounded
- **Air Brush:** Basic, Textured
- **Calligraphy:** Bamboo, Basic, Quill, Ribbon, Wet
- **Charcoal:** Creamy, Pastel, Soft, Textured
- **Crayon:** Basic, Rake, Thick
- **Dashed:** Basic Dash, Dash Double, Dash Triple, Dotted, Hard Dash, Heavy Dash
- **Felt Tip:** Dark Marker, Highlighter, Light Marker, Thin
- **Oil:** Bristle, Broad Splatter, Splatter, Strands, Textured Bristle
- **Pencil:** 1-Pixel Hard, 1-Pixel Soft, Colored Pencil, Graphite
- **Watercolor:** Heavy, Thick, Thin

- **Random:** Confetti, Dots, Fur, Squares, Yarn
- **Unnatural:** 3D, 3D Glow, Chameleon, Fluid Splatter, Outline, Paint Splatter, Toothpaste, Toxic Waste, Viscous Alien Paint

The tips run the gamut from basic to out of this world. Figure 3-11 shows you strokes made with three of the more complex tips. After you're familiar with the default stroke settings, you may want to customize the tips. The Edit Stroke dialog box offers you an amazing amount of control over stroke parameters such as ink amount, flow rate, shape, and sensitivity. To open the Edit Stroke dialog box, choose Stroke Options from the Stroke Category pop-up menu of the Property inspector and click Advanced. See the Fireworks Help files for further details, or feel free to experiment!

If you have a pressure-sensitive graphics tablet, you can set your drawing speed and pressure to modify how you place the stroke on the canvas. Just enter the settings that you want in the Sensitivity tab of the Edit Stroke dialog box.

Figure 3-11: Lines made with three exotic brush stroke tips.

To draw a line or shape using the Brush or Pencil tool, follow these steps:

1. **Select the Brush or Pencil tool from the Bitmap area of the Tools panel.**

   When you place your pointer over the canvas, the pointer takes the shape of a cross hair. The default tip for the Brush tool is also the default tip for the Pencil tool: 1-Pixel Hard.

2. **Select a color from the color picker in the tool's Property inspector.**

   To find out more about the color picker, see the "Adding a little color" section, earlier in this chapter.

3. **Select a tip from the Stroke Category pop-up menu.**

   Each specialized tip has its own default edge size and texture.

4. **Click and drag on the canvas to make your line or shape.**

   The wider the brush, the more pronounced the effect of a fancy tip. See Book III, Chapter 4 for more information on customizing the brush edge and texture.

Inserting a bitmap image

You probably need to insert an existing bitmap image into a Fireworks document often if you're designing a Web page, whether the bitmaps are pictures of your products or pictures of your family.

To insert a bitmap image into your document, you can drag and drop the image onto the canvas from your desktop or a folder, or you can import the image. To import a bitmap image, follow these steps:

1. **Choose File⇨Import or press Ctrl+R.**

   The Import dialog box appears.

2. **Navigate to the folder containing the image that you want to insert.**
3. **Double-click the filename, or click the filename and click OK.**

   The Import dialog box closes, revealing the canvas. The cursor changes into the Insertion Pointer — a right angle.

4. **Align the Insertion Pointer with the top-left point on your canvas where you want the inserted image to go.**
5. **Click to place the image.**

Selecting areas in a bitmap image

Fireworks allows you to select areas within an image in several different ways. If you've used Photoshop before, the Marquee tool, Lasso tool, and Magic Wand tool probably look familiar. In case you're new to these tools, the following sections give you a brief rundown.

Using the Marquee tool

The Marquee tool has two guises, which you can access by clicking and holding the Marquee tool until the pop-up menu appears:

- **The Marquee tool:** Use this tool to make rectangular selections.
- **The Oval Marquee tool:** Use this tool to make oval-shaped selections.

To select a rectangular or oval part of your bitmap, simply follow these steps:

1. **Select the Marquee tool or the Oval Marquee tool from the Bitmap part of the Tools panel.**

   When you move your pointer over the canvas, your pointer becomes a cross.

2. **Place the center of the pointer over one corner of the area that you want to select.**

3. **Click and drag diagonally over the area that you want to select.**

   A flashing marquee marks the selected area; the marquee is rectangular if you selected the Marquee tool and oval if you selected the Oval Marquee tool.

You can convert any vector shape on the canvas to a marquee by selecting it and choosing Modify⇨Convert Path to Marquee. Then just select an edge style and click OK. The path becomes a marquee. Depending on how your preferences are set, the path itself may disappear from the canvas (see Book III, Chapter 1 for details on setting your Preferences).

Using the Lasso tool

The Lasso tool has two guises, which you can access by clicking and holding the Lasso tool until the pop-up menu appears:

- **The Lasso tool:** Use this tool to make a free-form selection area by "drawing" the area.
- **The Polygon Lasso tool:** Use this tool to select a polygonal area by clicking points on the perimeter of the area.

To select an irregular area of your bitmap, follow these steps:

1. **Select the Lasso tool from the Bitmap part of the Tools panel.**

   When you place your pointer over the canvas, the pointer becomes a lasso.

2. **Place the bottom tip of the pointer over the spot on the canvas where you want your selection to start.**

3. **Click and drag to create an outline of the area you want to select, as Figure 3-12 shows you.**

   You have to close the outline to make the selection. When you have your pointer over the spot where you started your selection, a little filled square appears at the bottom right of the pointer. Click to close the selection shape.

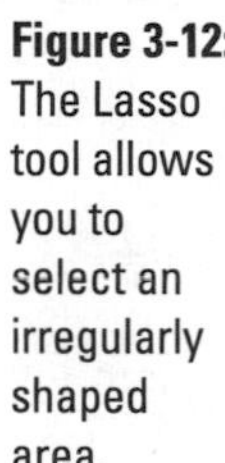

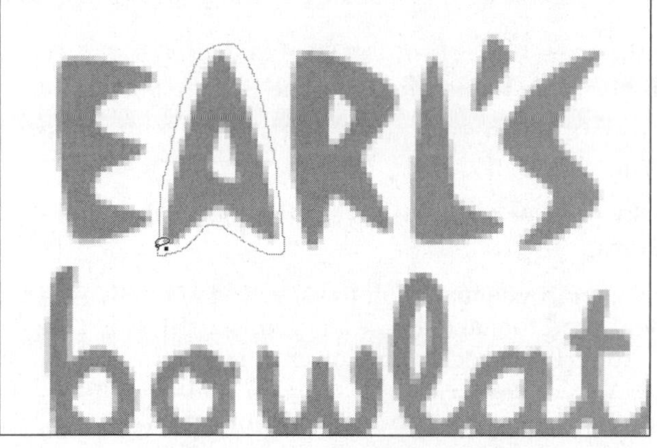

Figure 3-12: The Lasso tool allows you to select an irregularly shaped area.

To select a polygonal area of your bitmap, follow these steps:

1. **Select the Polygon Lasso tool from the Bitmap part of the Tools panel.**

   When you place your pointer over the canvas, the pointer becomes a lasso.

2. **Place the bottom tip of the pointer over the spot on the canvas where you want your selection to start.**

3. **Click to establish the first point of the area that you want to select.**

4. **Move your cursor to the second point of the area that you want to select; click it.**

   Fireworks connects the points with a straight line.

5. **Place your cursor and click all points making up the polygonal selection.**

   You have to close the outline to make the selection. Double-click to close the selection from the last-placed point to the first-placed point. Or, when you have your pointer over the first-placed point (a little filled square appears at the bottom right of the pointer), click to close the selection shape.

Using the Magic Wand

The third bitmap selection tool is known as the Magic Wand tool. The Magic Wand tool selects an area of solid color or of similar colors. (You can set the wand's sensitivity level so that it selects areas of more similar or less similar colors.)

To select a contiguous area of similar color in your bitmap, follow these steps:

1. **Select the Magic Wand tool from the Bitmap section of the Tools panel.**

   When you place your pointer over the canvas, the pointer takes the form of a magician's wand.

2. **Place the pointer over the part of the image that you want to select and click.**

   A blinking marquee marks off the selected area. If you select too much area, you need to make the wand more sensitive. Set the Tolerance level in the Property inspector to a lower number. If you don't select enough area, set the Tolerance level to a higher number (up to 255, at which setting you probably select your entire bitmap).

Editing bitmaps: The basics

Fireworks allows you to manipulate bitmaps in all kinds of crazy and interesting ways, but naturally, it also allows you to do common everyday image-altering as well.

Perhaps the most basic bitmap editing tasks that you can do are cropping, resizing, rotating, and distorting an image, which you can read about in Book III, Chapter 4, along with basic filtering operations, such as Blurring, Sharpening, and making color adjustments.

No introductory chapter on bitmap editing is complete, though, without a quick look at the Eraser tool. As you may expect, the Eraser tool is the anti-brush. The Brush tool adds a line, shape, or pattern to a bitmap. The Eraser tool removes a line of pixels from a bitmap.

To erase pixels from your bitmap, follow these steps:

1. **Select the Eraser tool from the Bitmap part of the Tools panel.**

   The Eraser tool defaults to a circle, though you can make it square shaped by clicking the square shape in the Property inspector.

2. **In the Property inspector, type a size in the Size text field or use the handy slider to set the width of the Eraser.**

   The range goes from 1 to 100.

3. **Select the circle shape or square shape by clicking on one or the other.**

4. **Set the Edge by typing a number or using the slider.**

The range goes from 0 to 100. Setting to 0 gives a hard edge to your Eraser (it removes a single pixel at a time), and setting to 100 gives a fuzzy edge to the erased area.

5. **Set the Opacity of the Eraser by typing a number or using the slider.**

   The range goes from 1 to 100 percent. If you set the Opacity to 100 percent, the Eraser clears all the erased pixels entirely (except at the edges, if you set an edge of greater than 0). If you set the opacity to less than 100 percent, the Eraser creates a translucent effect, allowing whatever you have under the bitmap to show through. The lower the opacity setting, the more the image underneath shows through.

6. **Click and drag on your image with the Eraser tool to rub out those unwanted pixels.**

The pixels disappear as you drag the cursor over them.

Chapter 4: Transforming Text, Shapes, and Images

In This Chapter

- **Scaling your images**
- **Distorting and skewing text and graphics**
- **Rotating and flipping graphics and text**
- **Adding gradients, textures, and patterns**
- **Using filters**
- **Using Photoshop Live Effects**

In the course of laying out the pages of your Web site, you may want to change the size or color of an image so that it fits more naturally into your design. In this chapter, we show you how to manipulate images, or parts of images, to create effects from subtle to extreme.

Scaling Graphics

When we talk about *scaling graphics,* we're talking about changing the size of a bitmap or vector shape on the canvas, not changing the size of your overall image (that is, everything on the whole of your canvas). To find out how to change the canvas size, see Book III, Chapter 2. You can change the size of an image element or selected part of an image element in two ways:

- **Use the Scale tool:** Click and drag the image object or selection. Use this option if you want to figure out the proper size of the image by eyeballing it.
- **Change the numbers in the Property inspector:** Type numbers in the width and height boxes. Use this option if you have exact dimensions in mind for your image.

You can use both methods fairly simply, and you get identical results (whether you drag an object to a specific width or type that width into the Property inspector, the resized object looks the same).

When you scale or resize a bitmap, the new version of the image will suffer some degradation. The more extreme the change in size, the more glaring will be the degradation. One of the advantages of vectors is that they can be scaled and resized without suffering any degradation.

Using the Scale Transformation tool

You can change the size of an object, either retaining its proportions or distorting it, by using the Scale tool. To change the size of an object by using the click-and-drag method, follow these instructions:

1. **Click the Pointer tool or Subselection tool from the Select section of the Tools panel and then click the object you want to resize.**

   For more information on selecting image objects or parts of image objects, see Book III, Chapter 3.

2. **Select the Scale tool — it looks a bit like a baseball diamond — from the Select section of the Tools panel or choose Modify⇨Transform⇨Scale.**

   A box with eight handles and a center point overlays the selected object. You can also select the Scale tool by clicking the arrow next to Transform Tools in the Image Editing panel.

3. **Click and drag one of the handles to scale the object in one of two ways:**

   - **To scale the object while retaining its proportions:** Click one of the corner handles (make sure that the cursor looks like a double-sided arrow) and drag the object to the desired size.
   - **To scale the object and distort its proportions:** Click and drag the middle handle on either the left or right side of the box around the object (make sure that the cursor looks like a double-sided arrow) to change the object's width, or click and drag the center handle on either the top or bottom of the box around the object (make sure that the cursor looks like a double-sided arrow) to change the object's height.

     By default, Fireworks continues to display the original box around the object, but it adds a version of the box with a dotted line to show the new dimensions as you drag (see Figure 4-1).

     When the cursor looks like a three-quarter circle with an arrow, you can rotate the image rather than resize it. See the "Rotating graphics" section, later in this chapter, for details on rotating images.

4. **Release the mouse button.**

   Fireworks redraws the image to your selected size.

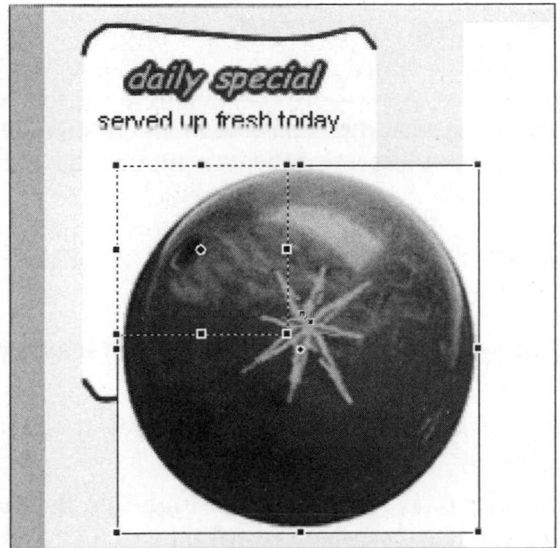

Figure 4-1: Resizing an image using the click-and-drag method.

5. **Click and drag to reposition the image, if necessary.**

   The cursor changes into a four-pointed arrow when you place it over the redrawn image, which indicates that you can move the image. (See Figure 4-2.) You can remove the transform handles by double-clicking the image, which also changes the tool to the Pointer tool.

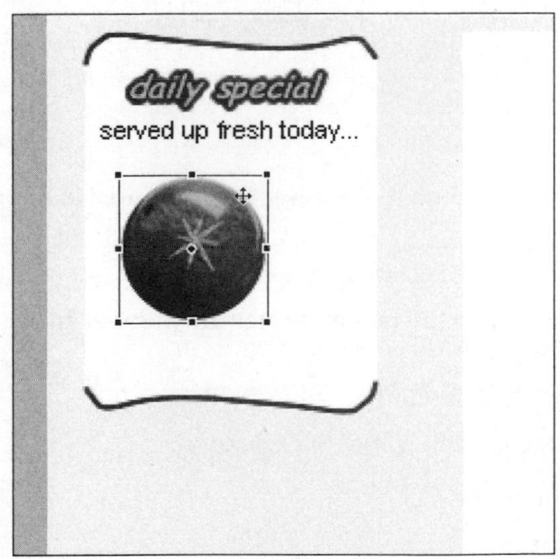

Figure 4-2: The cursor becomes a four-pointed arrow to indicate that you can move the object by dragging it.

Resizing by entering numerical values

Sometimes you have a space with a defined width and height into which you want to place images of that exact width and height. If the images aren't already sized to fit that space, and you have calculated the exact proportions or aren't worried about distorting the images, use the following method to resize the images.

To change the width, height, or both of an image by typing in a new value for the width and/or the height, just follow these steps:

1. **Using the Pointer tool or Subselection tool, click the object you want to resize.**

   See Book III, Chapter 3 for more information on selecting image objects or parts of image objects.

2. **In the Property inspector, double-click or highlight the number in the Width field, as Figure 4-3 shows you, and type in a new number.**

   If you can't see the Width and Height fields, your Property inspector may be collapsed. To expand the panel, click the downward-pointing arrow at the bottom-right corner of the panel. If you can't see the Property inspector on-screen, press Ctrl+F3 to open it.

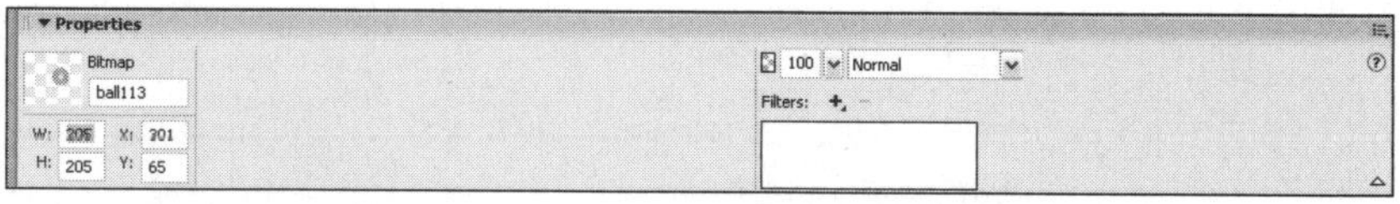

Figure 4-3: Adjusting the width of a selected object.

3. **If you don't want to change the height, press Enter to implement the width change.**

   Fireworks redraws the selection at the new width.

4. **If you want to change the height, select the number in the Height field and type a new value.**

5. **Press Enter or click in another value field.**

   Fireworks updates the height of the selection.

Distorting and Skewing Images and Text

Changing the width but not the height of an image object, or changing the object's height but not the width, distorts the object along one axis. What if you want to stretch one corner of an object but leave the rest of the object more or less intact, or perform some other unusual stretching or shrinking? You have the Distort and Skew tools at your disposal — they're just hiding behind the Scale tool. To access the Distort and Skew tools, click and hold the Scale tool in the Select section of the Tools panel and select one of the tools from the menu that pops up, or select the Scale tool and press Q on your keyboard until the tool you want appears.

What's the difference between skewing and distorting? Skewing is actually a particular kind of distortion:

- **Distorting:** Stretching or shrinking one or more sides of an image object.
- **Skewing:** Distorting an image object by stretching or shrinking two of its four sides while leaving the other two the same, or stretching or shrinking three of the four sides of the object's bounding box at once but not changing the dimensions of the fourth side. Skewing can create the illusion of perspective.

The Distort tool is far more versatile than the Skew tool:

- You can use the Distort tool to resize along one axis, in which case you scale the object.
- You can use the Distort tool to stretch or shrink three sides of an object simultaneously, in which case you skew the object.
- You can use the Distort tool to create more complex forms of image manipulation by both scaling and skewing the object, for example.

Distorting an image

To distort an object by using the Distort tool, follow these steps:

1. **Click the Pointer tool or Subselection tool in the Tools panel and then click the object that you want to distort.**
2. **Select the Distort tool from the Tools panel or choose Modify⇨Transform⇨Distort.**

   If you want to select the tool from the Tools panel, click and hold on the Scale tool in the Select section of the Tools panel and select the Distort tool from the pop-up menu. A box with eight handles and a center point overlays the selected object.

You can also select the Distort tool from the Image Editing panel by clicking the arrow next to Transform Tools and selecting Distort from the options that appear.

3. **Click and drag any handle.**

   By default, Fireworks continues to display the original box around the object, but it adds a version of the box with a dotted line to show the new dimensions as you drag, as you can see in Figure 4-4. The cursor becomes a double-sided arrow as you place it over a center or middle handle.

   When you try to drag handles too far (if you try to drag a middle-left handle above the top-left handle, for example), the dotted line stretches to wherever you drag the handle, but when you release the mouse button, the image snaps to the farthest allowable point in the direction you dragged. In short, a handle can't cross other handles.

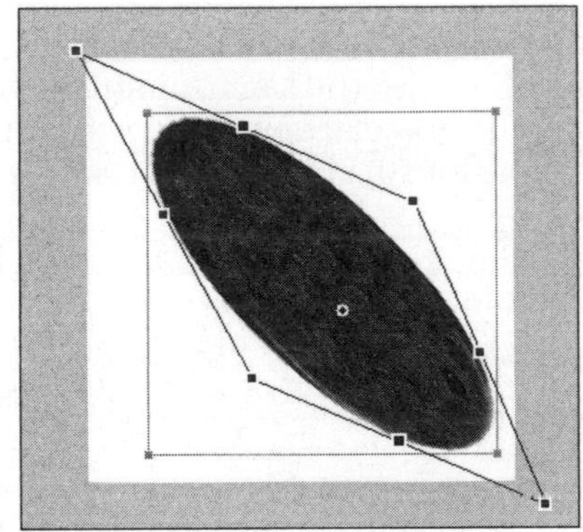

Figure 4-4: Distorting an image to create a weird effect.

4. **Click and drag any other handles.**

   You can stretch and squash the image by dragging as many handles as many times as you want.

5. **Press Enter or double-click anywhere on the canvas.**

   Fireworks updates the selection.

Skewing an image

To skew an image, follow these simple steps:

1. **With the Pointer tool or Subselection tool, click the object that you want to skew.**

2. **Select the Skew tool from the Tools panel or choose Modify⇨Transform⇨Skew.**

   If you want to select the tool from the Tools panel, click and hold on the Scale tool in the Select section of the Tools panel and select the Skew tool when the pop-up menu displays the Skew and Distort tools. A box with eight handles and a center point overlays the selected object.

   You can also select the Skew tool from the Image Editing panel by clicking the arrow next to Transform Tools and selecting Skew from the options that appear.

3. **Click and drag any handle:**
   - **The center handles:** On the top and bottom, these handles can skew a side of the image left or right.
   - **The middle handles:** The handles on the left and right can skew a side of the image up or down.
   - **The corner handles:** These handles behave differently, depending on whether you drag them along the left-right axis or the up-down axis. However, no matter which axis you drag along, the handles spread the selected side of the image along that axis. For example, if you select the top-left corner and drag up, the bottom-left corner stretches down proportionally.

   By default, Fireworks continues to display the original box around the object, but it adds a version of the box with a dotted line to show the new dimensions as you drag, as shown in Figure 4-4. The cursor becomes a double-sided arrow as you place it over a center or middle handle. The arrow indicates in which directions you can drag the handle.

4. **Press Enter or double-click anywhere on the canvas.**

   Fireworks updates the selection, the transformation handles disappear, and the tool reverts to the Pointer tool.

Distorting and skewing text

In Fireworks, you can distort text as easily as you can distort images. To distort the text in a text box while leaving the text editable, just follow these steps:

1. **Click the Pointer tool or Subselection tool in the Tools panel and then click the text box that you want to distort.**

   You can also select the text box using the Text tool, but you can't distort only part of the text in a text box. You can, however, Shift+click two text boxes and distort them together.

2. **Select the Distort tool from the Tools panel or choose Modify⇨Transform⇨Distort.**

   If you want to select the tool from the Tools panel, click and hold on the Scale tool in the Tools panel and select the Distort tool from the pop-up menu. A box with eight handles and a center point overlays the selected text box.

   You can also select the Distort tool from the Image Editing panel by clicking the arrow next to Transform Tools and selecting Distort from the options that appear.

3. **Click and drag any handle.**

   By default, Fireworks continues to display the original box around the object, but it adds a version of the box with a dotted line to show the new dimensions as you drag. The cursor becomes a double-sided arrow as you place it over a center or middle handle.

   When you try to drag handles too far (if you try to drag a middle-right handle above the top-right handle, for example), the dotted line stretches to wherever you drag the handle, but when you release the mouse button, the image snaps to the farthest allowable point in the direction that you dragged. In short, a handle can't cross other handles.

4. **Click and drag any other handles.**

   You can stretch, squash, and drag as many handles as many times as you want.

5. **Press Enter or double-click anywhere on the canvas.**

   Fireworks updates the selection, as Figure 4-5 shows you.

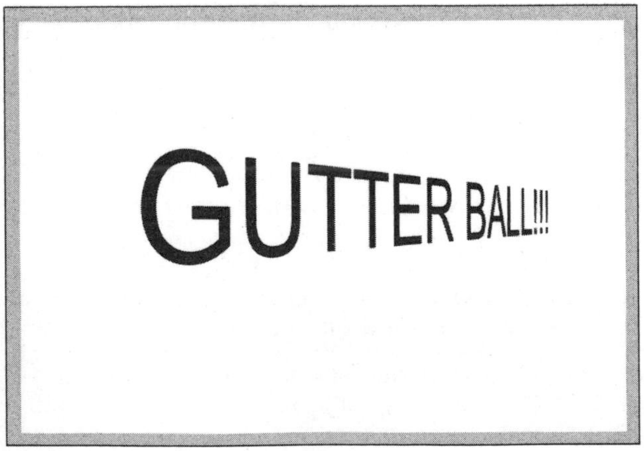

GUTTER BALL!!!

Figure 4-5: Distorting a text box can give the illusion of perspective to text.

To skew a text box, follow these simple steps:

1. **Using the Pointer tool in the Tools panel, click the text box.**

   You can also select the text box by using the Text tool, but either way, you can't distort only a part of the text in a text box.

2. **Select the Skew tool from the Tools panel or choose Modify➪Transform➪Skew.**

   If you want to select the tool from the Tools panel, click and hold on the Scale tool in the Tools panel and select the Skew tool when the pop-up menu displays the Skew and Distort tools. A box with eight handles and a center point overlays the selected text box.

   You can also select the Skew tool from the Image Editing panel, by clicking the arrow next to Transform Tools and selecting Skew from the options that appear.

3. **Click and drag any handle:**

   - **The center handles:** On the top and bottom, these handles can skew a side of the text left or right.
   - **The middle handles:** The handles on the left and right can skew a side of the text up or down.
   - **The corner handles:** These handles behave differently, depending on whether you drag them along the left-right axis or the up-down axis. However, no matter which axis you drag along, they spread the selected side of the text along that axis. For example, if you select the top-left corner and drag up, the bottom-left corner stretches down proportionally.

4. **Press Enter or double-click anywhere on the canvas.**

   Fireworks updates the selection, the transformation handles disappear, and the tool reverts to the Pointer tool.

You can align text along a vector shape or path. See Book III, Chapter 3 to find out more about aligning text.

Rotating and Flipping Graphics and Text

As is the case with resizing, Fireworks allows you to rotate and flip everything on the canvas simultaneously, but it also allows you to select individual graphic elements (image objects) and rotate or flip them independently.

Rotating graphics

You can rotate a graphic in two ways:

- **Rotate a preset amount:** Fireworks offers a quick way to rotate a graphic either 90 or 180 degrees around its center point.
- **Rotate any amount:** You can click and drag to rotate an image around its center point, or even move the point and rotate the image around a point not at the image's center.

To rotate a graphic by 90-degree increments, follow these steps:

1. **Select the object by using the Pointer tool or Subselection tool.**

   For more information on selecting image objects or parts of image objects, see Book III, Chapter 3.

2. **Choose how you want to rotate the object:**

   - **To rotate the object 180 degrees (turning it upside down):** Choose Modify➪Transform➪Rotate 180 Degrees.
   - **To rotate a graphic 90 degrees clockwise (to turn it sideways to the right):** Choose Modify➪Transform➪Rotate 90 Degrees CW, or press Ctrl+Shift+9.
   - **To rotate a graphic 90 degrees counterclockwise (to turn it sideways to the left):** Choose Modify➪Transform➪Rotate 90 Degrees CCW, or press Ctrl+Shift+7.

Rotating an object freehand requires a couple of extra steps, but it gives you much finer control over the degree of rotation. To rotate an object any amount around its center axis, just follow these steps:

1. **Select the object by clicking the Pointer tool or Subselection tool and clicking the object on the canvas.**
2. **Choose Modify➪Transform➪Free Transform (or Scale, Skew, or Distort).**

   You can also use the keyboard shortcut Ctrl+T to access the Free Transform command. When you're rotating an object, it doesn't matter which tool you choose.

3. **Place your cursor over the canvas.**

   The cursor changes into a rounded arrow, as you can see in Figure 4-6.

4. **Click and drag the cursor in any direction.**

   If you drag down or to the right, the image rotates clockwise; if you drag up or to the left, the image rotates counterclockwise.

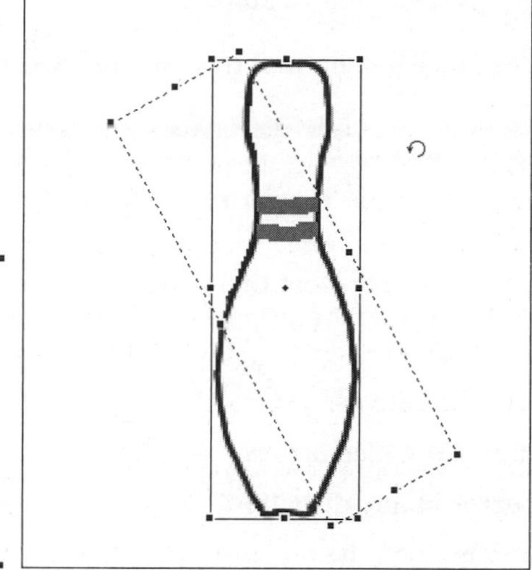

Figure 4-6: Rotating a bowling pin image object so that it appears to be falling.

If you hold down the Shift key while rotating your graphic, you restrict the angle of the rotation to 15-degree increments.

5. **Press Enter or double-click anywhere on the canvas.**

   Fireworks updates the selection, the transformation handles disappear, and the tool reverts to the Pointer tool.

Rotating text

In Fireworks, you can rotate text essentially the same way that you rotate a graphic. To rotate a text box in 90-degree increments, follow these steps:

1. **Click the Pointer tool or Subselection tool in the Tools panel and then click the text box.**

   You can also select the text box by using the Text tool, but either way, you can't rotate only a part of a text box.

2. **Choose how you want to rotate the text:**

   - **To rotate the text box by 180 degrees (turning it upside down):** Choose Modify➪Transform➪Rotate 180 Degrees.
   - **To rotate a text box 90 degrees clockwise (to turn it sideways to the right):** Choose Modify➪Transform➪Rotate 90 Degrees CW, or press Ctrl+Shift+9.
   - **To rotate a text box 90 degrees counterclockwise (to turn it sideways to the left):** Choose Modify➪Transform➪Rotate 90 Degrees CCW, or press Ctrl+Shift+7.

To rotate text freehand, follow these simple steps:

1. **Use the Pointer tool or Subselection tool to select the text box that you want to rotate.**

   You can rotate only the entire text box.

2. **Choose Modify⇨Transform⇨Free Transform (or Scale, Skew, or Distort).**

   You can also use the keyboard shortcut Ctrl+T to access the Free Transform command. When you're rotating a text box, it doesn't matter which tool you choose.

3. **Place your cursor over the canvas.**

   The cursor changes into a rounded arrow.

4. **Click and drag the cursor in any direction.**

   If you drag down or to the right, the text box rotates clockwise; if you drag up or to the left, the text box rotates counterclockwise.

5. **Press Enter or double-click anywhere on the canvas.**

   Fireworks updates the selection, the transformation handles disappear, and the tool reverts to the Pointer tool.

Flipping images

Fireworks lets you flip images vertically and horizontally. You can do both manipulations in a snap.

To flip an image horizontally (making it a mirror image of what it was originally) or vertically (turning it upside down), follow these steps:

1. **Select the object you want to flip.**

2. **Choose Modify⇨Transform⇨Flip Horizontal to make a mirror image of the object; choose Modify⇨Transform⇨Flip Vertical to turn the object upside down.**

   Depending on which choice you make, your selection either flips horizontally, as Figure 4-7 shows you, or vertically, as you can see in Figure 4-8.

Flipping text

Fireworks lets you flip text boxes vertically and horizontally. Both manipulations are a piece of cake.

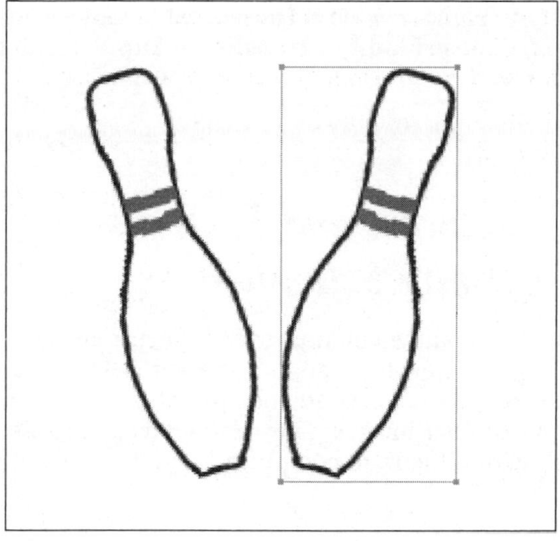

Figure 4-7: The left image of the bowling pin has been duplicated, moved, and flipped horizontally to make the image of the bowling pin on the right.

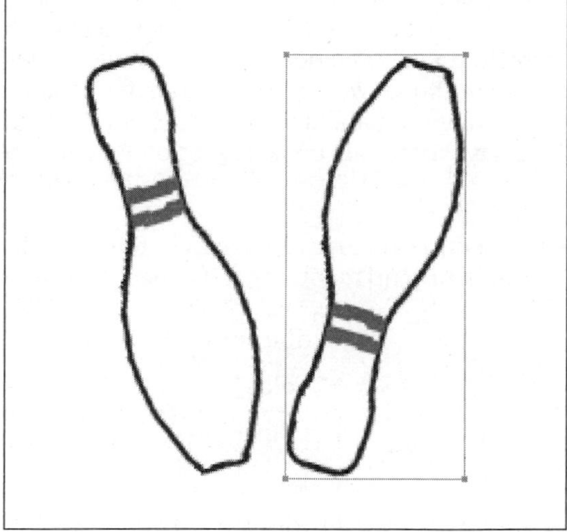

Figure 4-8: The left image of the bowling pin has been duplicated, moved, and flipped vertically to make the image of the bowling pin on the right.

Follow these steps to flip a text box horizontally (making it a mirror image of what it was originally) or vertically (turning it upside down):

1. **Select the text box that you want to flip with the Pointer tool or Subselection tool.**

   You can also select the text box using the Text tool, but either way, you can't distort only a part of a text box.

2. **Choose Modify⇨Transform⇨Flip Horizontal to make a mirror image of the text box; choose Modify⇨Transform⇨Flip Vertical to turn the text upside down.**

   Your selection flips horizontally or vertically.

Adding Gradients, Textures, and Patterns to Shape Fills and Bitmap Selections

In Book III, Chapter 3, we show you how to fill a vector shape with a color. In this section, you find out how to treat your shape to a fancier filling: a gradient, a pattern, and (or) a texture. Gradients, patterns, and textures can add the illusion of depth to your images. They also increase the file size of your images because they're difficult to compress, so you may want to use them sparingly.

Introducing gradients

A gradient is a subtle blend of one color into another. A classic example of a gradient in nature is a sky at sunset (or sunrise, if you ever wake up that early). Near the horizon, the sky is a deep, bright orange; straight up, the sky is a dark blue. In between those two colors is a bunch of transitions: from bright orange to pale orange to pale blue to dark blue. The transitions are so subtle, it's difficult to say where one color leaves off and another begins. That's a gradient.

Fireworks ships with a wonderful array of useful gradient patterns, which you can access through a pop-up menu in the Property inspector:

- Linear
- Radial
- Rectangle
- Cone
- Contour
- Satin
- Starburst
- Folds
- Ellipse
- Bars
- Ripples
- Waves

The fact that this page is in black and white doesn't do these gradients justice compared to what they look like in full color, but you can still get a pretty good idea of the variety of the gradients by checking out Figure 4-9.

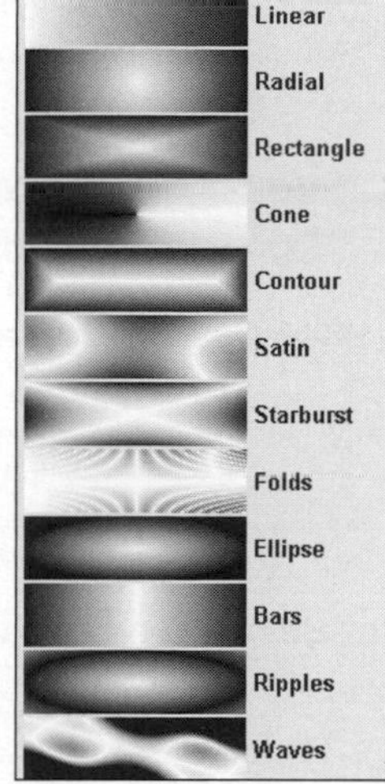

Figure 4-9: Fireworks ships with these gradient patterns.

You can choose any colors to make your gradients, but Fireworks also has the following handy preset gradient options:

- Blue, Yellow, Blue
- Cobalt Blue
- Copper
- Emerald Green
- Pastels
- Red, Blue
- Red, Green, Blue
- Silver
- Spectrum
- Violet, Orange
- White, Black
- Black, White
- Blue, Red, Yellow

To add a preset gradient fill to a vector shape, follow these steps:

1. **Select the Pointer tool or Subselection tool and click the shape.**
2. **Click and hold the Fill Categories box next to the Paint Bucket icon in the Property inspector.**
3. **Choose Gradient.**
4. **Select a gradient type from the menu (see Figure 4-10).**

   The default colors for gradients are black and white. If you want those colors for your gradient, congratulations! You're done! If not, continue to the next step.

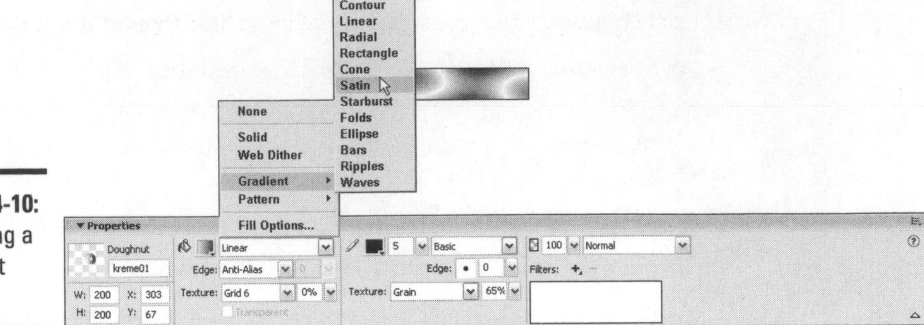

Figure 4-10: Selecting a gradient type.

5. **Click the Fill Color box next to the Paint Bucket icon in the Property inspector.**

   A pop-up window, like the one in Figure 4-11, appears:

   - At the bottom of the pop-up window, you can see a preview pane, which shows what the gradient pattern will look like when you apply it to the shape. (Figure 4-11 shows the selected pattern, Cone.)
   - In the middle of the window lies the Preset drop-down list, from which you can choose preset colors for your gradient.
   - At the top of the window, you can find a simpler preview strip that shows color but not pattern information. Above and below that strip are sliders. The sliders above give you control over the opacity of each color in the gradient; the sliders below give you control over the amount of each color in the gradient.

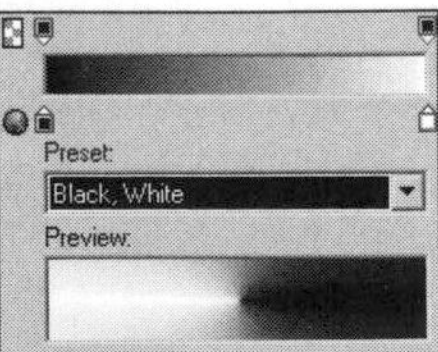

Figure 4-11: The gradient pop-up window has controls for color and opacity, a list of gradient presets, and a Preview pane.

6. **Select preset colors for your gradient from the Preset drop-down list.**

   The preview panes and the selected shape update.

   Different presets have different numbers, or instances, of colors. The Cobalt Blue preset, for example, creates its opalescent glow with two instances each of three colors.

7. **Click anywhere outside the pop-up window to make the window disappear.**

You have to go through a number of steps to add a user-defined gradient fill to a vector shape, but you can make the process as simple or complex as you want. Just follow these steps:

1. **Select the Pointer tool or Subselection tool and click the shape.**
2. **Click and hold the Fill Categories box next to the Paint Bucket icon in the Property inspector.**
3. **Select a gradient type from the pop-up menu (refer to Figure 4-10).**

   The default colors for gradients are black and white.

4. **Click the Fill Color box next to the Paint Bucket icon in the Property inspector.**

   A pop-up window appears (which you can see in Figure 4-11).

5. **Click the left color slider, as Figure 4-12 shows you.**

   When you place the cursor over a slider, the cursor becomes a solid black arrow with no stem. When you click and release the slider, the color picker pops up. To get the lowdown on the color picker, see Book III, Chapter 3.

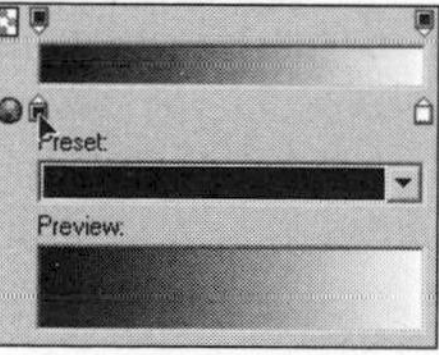

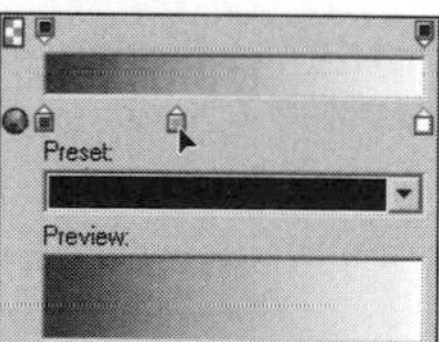

Figure 4-12: Left: Picking the first color for the gradient. Right: Adding a color.

6. **Select a color from the color picker.**

   Your cursor is an eyedropper in the color picker.

7. **If you want more than two colors in your gradient, click anywhere between the two default color sliders. If not, skip to Step 12.**

   Your cursor becomes an arrow with a small plus sign (+) when you move it between the existing color sliders. After you click, a new slider appears, and your cursor becomes a solid black arrow with no stem until you move it off the new slider.

   By default, the color of the new slider is the color in the strip directly above where you clicked.

8. **If you want to change the color of the new slider, click it and release.**

   When you click and release, the color picker pops up.

9. **Select a color by using the eyedropper.**
10. **If you want, move the new color slider left or right to change where the new color blends with the other colors.**
11. **If you want more than three colors in your gradient, repeat Steps 7 through 10.**
12. **Click the right color slider.**
13. **Select a color by using the eyedropper.**
14. **If you want, move any of the sliders horizontally to adjust where their respective colors fall in the gradient.**
15. **If you want, adjust the opacity of the entire gradient or vary the opacity of different parts of the gradient.**

    By default, the opacity of both ends is set to 100 percent (no background shows through). You can add and adjust opacity sliders just as you can color sliders, and they work in more or less the same way.

    When you click an opacity slider, a pop-up window displays a slider that goes from 0 percent at the left (no gradient shows in front of the background) to 100 percent at the right.

16. **Click anywhere outside the pop-up window to make it disappear.**

After you add a gradient fill to your shape, you can rotate, skew, move, and change the width of the gradient. See the Fireworks Help files (found in the Help menu) for details.

To remove a color slider or opacity slider (you must have at least two colors to make a gradient, of course), click and drag it up out of the gradient pop-up window. When you release the mouse button, the slider disappears, and you have a less complex gradient fill.

Follow these steps to add a gradient fill to a bitmap selection:

1. **Using the appropriate Tool from the Bitmap section of the Tools panel, select the part of the bitmap image that you want to fill.**

   In most cases, the Magic Wand tool works best for this job. For more information on selecting parts of image objects, see Book III, Chapter 3.

2. **Click the Color box next to the Paint Bucket icon in the Colors section of the Tools panel.**

   The color picker appears.

3. **Click the Fill Options button at the bottom of the color picker.**

   A new pop-up window appears in place of the color picker.

4. **Select a gradient pattern from the drop-down list.**
5. **Follow Steps 4 through 6 in the steps that describe adding a preset gradient fill to a vector shape, or Steps 4 through 6 in the steps that describe adding a user-defined gradient fill to a vector shape, both of which you can find a little earlier in this section.**
6. **Click the Paint Bucket tool.**
7. **Click anywhere in the selected area to apply the gradient fill.**

Adding patterns

You get Fireworks CS3 already loaded with a dizzying array of patterns with names like Bubbles, Flames, Moon, and three varieties of Oil Paint. Fireworks has so many patterns, we don't have room to list them all here. As with gradients, Fireworks shows you a preview of each pattern as you roll over its name with your mouse. How do you get to the pattern names? Just follow these steps to add a pattern to a vector shape:

1. **Select the Pointer tool or Subselection tool and click the shape that you want to add a pattern to.**
2. **Click and hold the Fill Categories box next to the Paint Bucket icon in the Property inspector.**
3. **Choose Pattern.**
4. **Select a pattern type from the menu.**

   Each pattern appears in a preview window next to its name as you roll over the name. When you release the mouse button, the pop-up menu disappears and the pattern is applied to your shape.

Adding textures

You can add textures to your fills and bitmap selections even more easily than you can add gradients. You can even have fills with both a gradient and a texture, or with both a pattern and a texture, though combining gradients or patterns with textures often diminishes the graphic power of both in a given image.

Fireworks ships with more than 50 textures. To add a texture to a vector shape, follow these steps:

1. **Click the Pointer tool or Subselection tool and click the shape.**

   If the shape is transparent, you need to add a color or gradient fill. If the shape has a transparent fill (no fill), the Texture list box is inactive.

2. **Click and hold the arrow in the Texture drop-down list.**

   You can find this list under the Edge drop-down list in the Property inspector.

3. **Select a texture from the drop-down list.**

   The drop-down list displays the built-in textures. If you have additional textures on your computer, select Other from the list and browse to the texture you want to use.

   When you release the mouse button, the texture is applied to the shape fill with the default opacity of 50 percent.

4. **Type a value or drag the slider in the Amount of Texture field (next to the Texture drop-down list) to set the opacity of the texture.**

   You don't see any of the texture with a setting of 0, and a setting of 100 shows the texture at full (100 percent) opacity.

Adjusting Color Information and More with Filters

Fireworks has plenty of useful presets and defaults for the novice user, and enough tweakability to satisfy almost any professional. Pros especially appreciate the amount of control Fireworks gives users in the area of color adjustment. Blend modes offer another way to adjust the color information of objects. You can find out more about blending modes in Book III, Chapter 5.

You can accomplish many of the effects that we describe in the following sections in two basic ways:

- **Using Photoshop Live Effects:** These effects, formerly known simply as Live Effects, act a bit like putting on a pair of sunglasses. You don't change the colors of whatever you're looking at; you put something between you and the object that changes the appearance of the object. You can turn Photoshop Live Effects off and on without changing the pixels that make up the object to which you apply the effects. If you change the object in your Web page design later or repurpose it elsewhere, perhaps with different effects applied, you can use Photoshop Live Effects to apply nondestructive changes to the object in a particular PNG file. *Nondestructive* means that the object itself is unchanged, but how the object appears on-screen changes. You can apply Photoshop Live Effects only to whole objects, not to parts of objects.

And now in Fireworks CS3, you can apply Photoshop Live Effects to whole layers simultaneously. Also, Layer Effects applied in Photoshop can be edited in Fireworks.

- **Using Filters:** You can think of this method as *destructive* because it alters the pixels in the bitmap. This approach is like making everything you see yellow by painting everything yellow. Though the process is destructive, it isn't permanent — as long as you have the Undo command available.

We show you how to use the Filters method in the following sections.

Fine-tuning your colors

We touch briefly on the color adjustment tools at the end of Book III, Chapter 3, but here we go into a bit more detail. The color adjustment controls available from the Filters menu are as follows:

- **Auto Levels:** In theory, an optimal image has an even distribution of dark tones, medium tones, and light tones. Auto Levels sets levels automatically so that shadows, midtones, and highlights are evenly distributed in your image.
- **Brightness/Contrast:** Controls the overall luminosity of a selection and the contrast of color shades within a selection.
- **Curves:** Offers a way to modify very specific colors without affecting others.
- **Hue/Saturation:** Controls the tones and intensities of colors within a selection.
- **Invert:** Allows you to reverse the colors in a selection to make something that looks like a photographic negative.
- **Levels:** As with curves, the Levels filter allows you to modify colors, but it does so by letting you adjust shadows, midtones, and highlights of one of the three individual color channels (red, green, or blue) or all channels together.

To change the brightness or contrast of a graphic or selection, just follow these steps:

1. **Select a graphic or part of a graphic.**

   For more information on selecting image objects or parts of image objects, see Book III, Chapter 3.

2. **Choose Filters⇨Adjust Color⇨Brightness/Contrast.**

   A dialog box with separate sliders for brightness and contrast appears.

3. **If you want to lighten or darken your selection, click and drag the Brightness slider.**

   The default position is at the center. You can drag left down to –100 units to darken the selection, or you can drag right up to 100 units to lighten the selection. If the Preview check box is selected, as it is by default, you can see the change to your selection when you release the mouse button.

4. **If you want to alter the relationship between the dark and light pixels in your selection, click and drag the Contrast slider.**

   The default position is at the center. You can drag left down to –100 units to reduce the contrast in the selection, or you can drag right up to 100 units to increase the contrast in the selection. If the Preview check box is selected, as it is by default, you can see the change to your selection when you release the mouse button.

5. **Click OK.**

All colors on a computer monitor are formed from the combination of the three color channels: red, green, and blue. You can change the curves for the individual color channels or for the combination of all channels. You can make curve adjustments for bitmaps only, not shapes. If you want to adjust the color of a vector shape using curve values, convert it to a bitmap first (select the object and choose Flatten Selection from the Options menu in the Layers panel). To change the curve of the RGB channels, follow these steps:

1. **Select a graphic or part of a graphic.**

   For more information on selecting image objects or parts of image objects, see Book III, Chapter 3.

2. **Choose Filters⇨Adjust Color⇨Curves.**

   A dialog box with a grid appears, as you can see in Figure 4-13. The grid's horizontal axis shows the original brightness of the pixels in your selection. The grid's vertical axis shows the new brightness of the pixels.

3. **Choose a channel from the Channel drop-down list.**

   Your choices are RGB (all channels), Red, Green, or Blue.

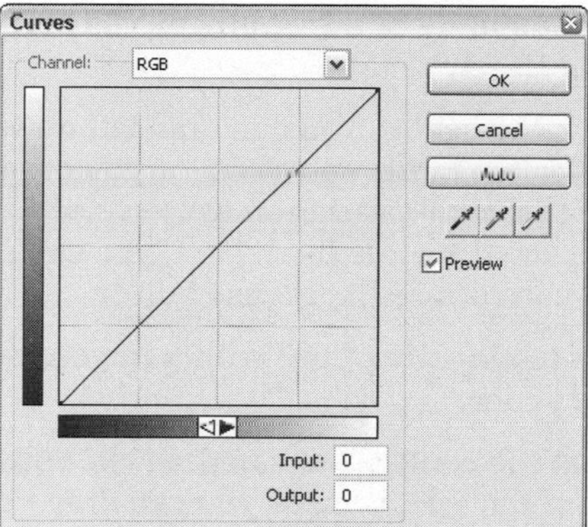

Figure 4-13: The default setting in the Curves dialog box is a diagonal line.

4. **Click anywhere along the line in the grid and drag to adjust the curve.**

   When you click the line, Fireworks generates a handle automatically. The end points always remain where they start, but you can add handles anywhere else on the line and drag them to new points. You can delete handles by dragging them up out of the dialog box. You can type a numerical value into the Input and Output text fields instead of dragging the line, if you prefer.

   If the Preview check box is selected, as it is by default, you can see the changes when you release the mouse button after dragging a handle.

   Clicking the Auto button restores the line to its original setting.

5. **Click OK.**

Follow these steps to change the hue, saturation, and (or) lightness of a graphic or selection:

1. **Select a graphic or part of a graphic.**

   For more information on selecting image objects or parts of image objects, see Book III, Chapter 3.

2. **Choose Filters➪Adjust Color➪Hue/Saturation.**

   A dialog box with separate sliders for Hue, Saturation, and Lightness pops up.

3. **If you want to change the basic color of your selection, click and drag the Hue slider.**

   The default position is at the center. You can drag left down to –180 degrees, or you can drag right up to 180 degrees. (You can think of the slider as a flattened circle, the way a map of the Earth is a flattened globe.) If the Preview check box is selected, as it is by default, you can see the change to your selection when you release the mouse button.

4. **If you want to alter the intensity of the colors in your selection, click and drag the Saturation slider.**

   The default position is at the center. You can drag left down to –100 units to reduce the color saturation in the selection, or you can drag right up to 100 units to increase the color saturation in the selection. If the Preview check box is selected, as it is by default, you can see the change to your selection when you release the mouse button.

5. **If you want to alter the luminosity of the colors in your selection, click and drag the Lightness slider.**

   The default position is at the center. You can drag left down to –100 units to reduce the lightness of the selection, or you can drag right up to 100 units to increase the lightness of the selection. A setting of –100 gives you black, and a setting of 100 gives you white. If the Preview check box is selected, as it is by default, you can see the change to your selection when you release the mouse button.

6. **Click OK.**

If you want to change the hue, saturation, or both of black or white pixels, select the Colorize check box and then make your adjustments.

To invert the colors of a graphic or any selection, follow these steps:

1. **Select a graphic or part of a graphic.**

   For more information on selecting image objects or parts of image objects, see Book III, Chapter 3.

2. **Choose Filters⇨Adjust Color⇨Invert, or use the key command Ctrl+Alt+Shift+I (⌘+Opt+Shift+I on a Mac).**

   The colors of your selection are inverted, as in a photographic negative.

The Levels command lets you make color corrections to an image or selection by altering the balance of highlights, midtones, and shadows. You call the graphical representation of the distribution of shades a *histogram.*

To adjust the levels of an image or image selection, follow these steps:

1. **Select a graphic or part of a graphic.**

   For more information on selecting image objects or parts of image objects, see Book III, Chapter 3.

2. **Choose Filters⇨Adjust Color⇨Levels.**

   The Levels dialog box appears, as Figure 4-14 shows you.

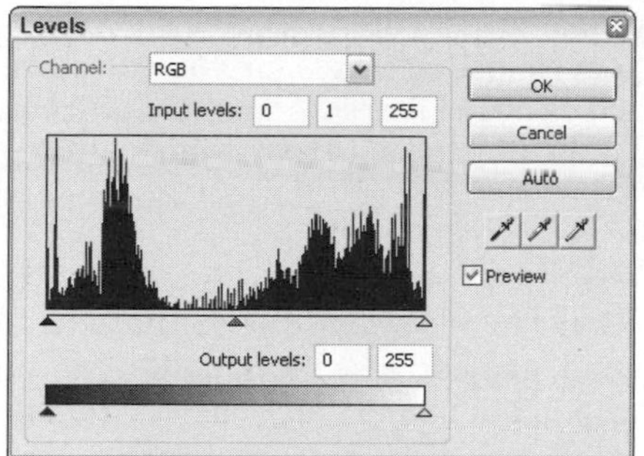

Figure 4-14: The Levels dialog box includes a histogram.

3. **Choose a channel from the Channel drop-down list.**

   Your choices are RGB (all channels), Red, Green, or Blue.

4. **Click and drag the Input shadows slider (the black triangle at the left under the histogram) to adjust the blacks in the selected image.**

   You can't drag the shadows slider farther right than the midtones slider because shadows must always be darker than midtones. The slider scale goes from 0 (no brightness, which is black) to 255 (full brightness, which is white). The midtones slider moves automatically when you move the shadows slider.

5. **Click and drag the Input midtones slider (the gray triangle in the middle under the histogram) to adjust the midtones (grays).**

   You can't drag the midtones slider farther left than the shadows slider or farther right than the highlights slider. The midtones slider's scale goes from 0 to 10.

   Dragging the midtones slider to the right generally darkens the selection, and dragging it to the far left can create something resembling a posterization effect, in which transitions between colors happen abruptly rather than smoothly.

6. **Click and drag the Input highlights slider (the white triangle at the right under the histogram) to adjust the whites in your image.**

   You can't drag the highlights slider farther left than the midtone slider because highlights must be lighter than midtones.

7. **Click and drag the Output shadows and highlights sliders as needed.**

   You can move these sliders past each other. Moving the darkness slider all the way to the right and the lightness slider all the way to the left inverts the colors in the selection.

8. **Click OK.**

   If you click Cancel, your adjustments aren't implemented. If you click the Auto button, Fireworks sets the optimal color balance automatically.

To let Fireworks set the optimal levels automatically, you can click the Auto buttons in the Curves and Levels dialog boxes, or you can select a graphic or part of a graphic and then choose Filters⇨Adjust Color⇨Auto Levels or press Ctrl+Alt+Shift+A (PC only; no Mac shortcut equivalent).

Blurring and sharpening

Blurring a graphic or selection can add a sense of softness to an image; sharpening, on the other hand, can add a sense of solidity or hyper-reality to an image. Note that the Sharpen command can't correct a blatantly out-of-focus photo; nothing can.

To blur an image or part of an image using Fireworks presets, simply follow these steps:

1. **Select a graphic or part of a graphic.**

   For more information on selecting image objects or parts of image objects, see Book III, Chapter 3.

2. **Choose Filters⇨Blur⇨Blur.**

   For a more pronounced effect, choose Filters⇨Blur⇨Blur More. You can also click Filters on the Image Editing panel and choose Blur or Blur More from the list that appears.

3. **Click OK.**

You can also use the Blur tool from the Bitmap section of the Tools panel to "paint" a blur across your image. If you want to blur multiple small parts of an image, you may find the Blur tool more effective.

If you want more control over the amount of blur in your image, you can employ the Gaussian Blur filter by following these steps:

1. **Select a graphic or part of a graphic.**

   For more information on selecting image objects or parts of image objects, see Book III, Chapter 3.

2. **Choose Filters⇨Blur⇨Gaussian Blur.**

   The Gaussian Blur dialog box appears.

3. **Click and drag the slider to set the radius of the blur.**

   The radius can be set from 0.1 (hardly noticeable blur) to 250.0 (nearly total blur).

4. **Click OK.**

You can get other blur filters as well, including Motion, Radial, and Zoom, each with its own properties and settings. Experiment to find the filter that gives you the effect you're looking for.

To sharpen an image or selection by using Fireworks presets, just follow these steps:

1. **Select a graphic or part of a graphic.**

   For more information on selecting image objects or parts of image objects, see Book III, Chapter 3.

2. **Choose Filters⇨Sharpen⇨Sharpen.**

   For a more pronounced effect, choose Filters⇨Sharpen⇨Sharpen More.

3. **Click OK.**

If you want more control over the amount and manner of the sharpening, you can use the Unsharp Mask filter. This filter works by strengthening the contrast between adjacent pixels, which makes edges between areas of color more sharply defined. Actually, all the Sharpen filters work this way, but with Unsharp Mask, you can create your own settings for three aspects of the sharpening process:

- **Sharpen Amount:** Determines the amount of contrast introduced between adjacent pixels
- **Pixel Radius:** Determines the size of the area around each pixel that gets sharpened
- **Threshold:** Determines which pixels get sharpened, based on the existing contrast levels in the selection or image

Follow these steps to sharpen an image or selection, using the Unsharp Mask filter:

1. **Select a graphic or part of a graphic.**

   For more information on selecting image objects or parts of image objects, see Book III, Chapter 3.

2. **Choose Filters⇨Sharpen⇨Unsharp Mask.**

   The Unsharp Mask dialog box pops up.

3. **Click and drag the Sharpen Amount slider.**

   The slider goes from 1 percent (not very much) to 500 percent (very strong contrast).

4. **Click and drag the Pixel Radius slider.**

   The slider goes from 0.1 (hardly noticeable) to 250.0 (very strong effect).

5. **Click and drag the Threshold slider.**

   The slider goes from 0 (change all pixels) to 255 (change no pixels).

6. **Click OK.**

Using the other filters: Convert to Alpha and Find Edges

The Convert to Alpha filter makes your selection transparent. The lighter the pixel, the more transparent it becomes. White pixels, for example, seem to disappear, allowing the background to show through fully. Black pixels, on the other hand, remain black and completely opaque.

To convert a selection to Alpha, follow these simple steps:

1. **Select a graphic or part of a graphic.**

   For more information on selecting image objects or parts of image objects, see Book III, Chapter 3.

2. **Choose Filters⇨Other⇨Convert to Alpha.**

   The selection is converted.

3. **Click anywhere on the canvas or press Ctrl+D to deselect your selection.**

The Find Edges filter makes a photograph look like a line drawing by greatly simplifying the color information in the image.

To use the Find Edges filter, just follow these steps:

1. **Select a graphic or part of a graphic.**

   For more information on selecting image objects or parts of image objects, see Book III, Chapter 3.

2. **Choose Filters⇨Other⇨Find Edges.**

   The selection takes on the appearance of a line drawing.

3. **Click anywhere on the canvas or press Ctrl+D to deselect your selection.**

Adding shadows to objects

You can add several kinds of shadows to objects in Fireworks CS3. Two of the most useful shadows are

- **Drop shadows:** Create the illusion that text or objects are floating above the surface of the canvas.
- **Shadow auto shapes:** Adjust shadow auto shapes as if changing the position of the light source that's making the text or object cast a shadow.

To add a drop shadow to an object, simply select the object and click the + (Plus) button next to Filters in the Properties panel. Then choose Shadow and Glow⇨Drop Shadow. You can edit various properties of the drop shadow by clicking the Information button (the white, italic *i* in a blue circle in the Filters section of the Properties panel). To add a shadow auto shape to an object, select the object and choose Commands⇨Creative⇨Add Shadow. You can edit the offsets and width of the auto shape using the Auto Shape Properties panel.

Adding Photoshop Live Effects

NEW TO CS3

With Fireworks CS3, you now have a new set of options for effects such as drop shadows, glows, bevels, and the like: Photoshop Live Effects. The new effects include the following:

- **Drop Shadow:** Makes an object appear to be floating above other objects.
- **Inner Shadow:** Adds dark pixels inside an object to make it appear as though you can see through it to its shadow on a surface below.
- **Outer Glow:** Adds a halo around the outside edges of an object.
- **Inner Glow:** Adds a halo to the inside edges of an object.
- **Bevel and Emboss:** Adds shading to make an object appear to be sticking up from or sinking below the surface of the canvas.
- **Satin:** Adds shading to an object to give it the shiny appearance of satin.
- **Color Overlay:** Adds a layer of color of adjustable opacity over an object.
- **Gradient Overlay:** Adds one of five types of gradient to the inside of an object.
- **Pattern Overlay:** Adds a pattern inside an object.
- **Stroke:** Adds a line to the edges of an object. You can choose the color, thickness, and position of the line.

Many of the Photoshop Live Effects duplicate image-transforming effects of their namesake filters. But Photoshop Live Effects have two important differences from Filters:

- ✦ Live Effects are nondestructive (they don't change the object to which they're applied; instead, they change the object's appearance).
- ✦ Live Effects can be applied to layers, not just objects.

To apply a Drop Shadow Live Effect to an object, follow these steps:

1. **Select an object by clicking it on the canvas or in the Layers panel.**

   The object is highlighted on the canvas and in the Layers panel.

2. **Click the + (plus) button in the Filters section of the Properties panel and click Photoshop Live Effects at the bottom of the menu that appears.**

   The Photoshop Live Effects window appears.

3. **Click the check box next to the words Drop Shadow.**

   The drop shadow appears on the canvas, as shown in Figure 4-15.

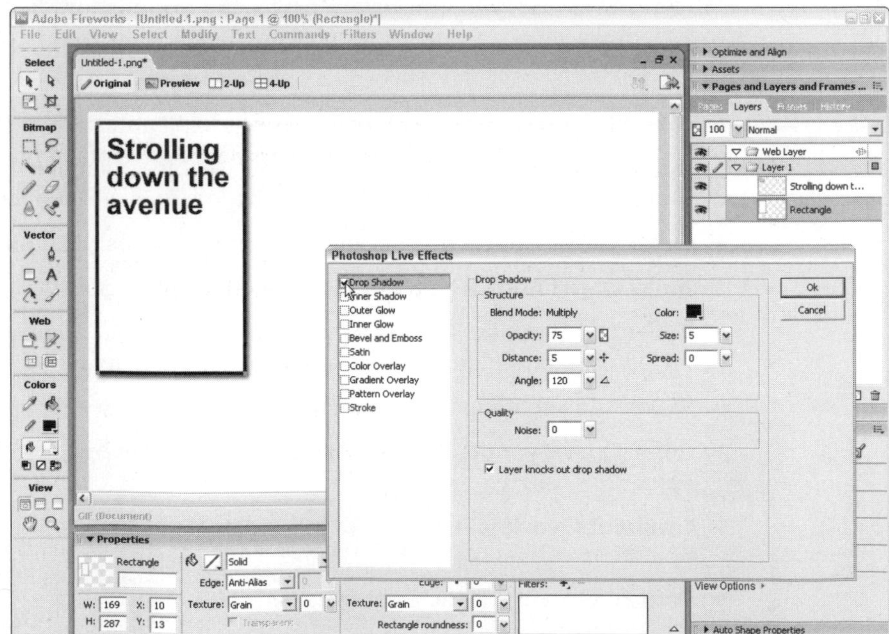

Figure 4-15: Drop Shadow is selected in the Photoshop Live Effects window.

4. **Select the opacity of the shadow by typing a number in the Opacity text field or clicking the arrow next to the text field and dragging the slider that appears.**

   The values range from 0 at the bottom of the slider (totally transparent) to 100 at the top of the slider (completely opaque).

5. **Select a distance by entering a number in the Distance text field or clicking the arrow next to the text field and dragging the slider that appears.**

   The range of numbers available is 0 to 250, from the bottom of the slider to the top. The higher the number, the higher above the surface of the canvas the object appears to float.

6. **Select an angle by typing a number in the Angle text field or clicking the arrow next to the text field and clicking and dragging the control that appears.**

   The angle control sets the position of the light source that is causing the object to cast a shadow. The range of values is –180 to 180. A positive value makes the shadow fall below the object, and a negative value makes the shadow fall above the object.

7. **Select a color for the shadow by clicking the Color square and clicking a square in the color picker.**

   For more information on the color picker, see Book III, Chapter 3. The default color for drop shadows is black.

8. **Select a size by entering a number in the Size text field or clicking the arrow next to the text field and dragging the slider that appears.**

   The range of values is from 1 at the bottom of the slider (thin shadow) to 250 at the top of the slider (wide shadow).

9. **Select a spread by entering a number in the Spread text field or clicking the arrow next to the text field and dragging the slider that appears.**

   The range of values is from 0 at the bottom of the slider (shadow appears diffuse) to 100 at the top of the slider (shadow appears to have solid edges).

10. **Select a Noise value in the Quality section by entering a number in the Noise text field or clicking the arrow next to the text field and dragging the slider that appears.**

    The range is from 0 at the bottom of the slider (no noise, a smooth shadow) to 100 at the top of the slider (lots of noise, a grainy shadow).

11. **Leave the Layer Knocks Out Drop Shadow check box selected if you want the object to obscure the shadow beneath it.**

    Otherwise, if your object has an opacity of less than 100% and you want to see the shadow through the object, click the box to deselect it.

Adding a Photoshop Live Effect to a Layer

To add a Photoshop Live Effect to an entire layer (that is, to all objects on that layer, as shown in Figure 4-16), simply click the layer name in the Layers panel and then follow the preceding Steps 2–11.

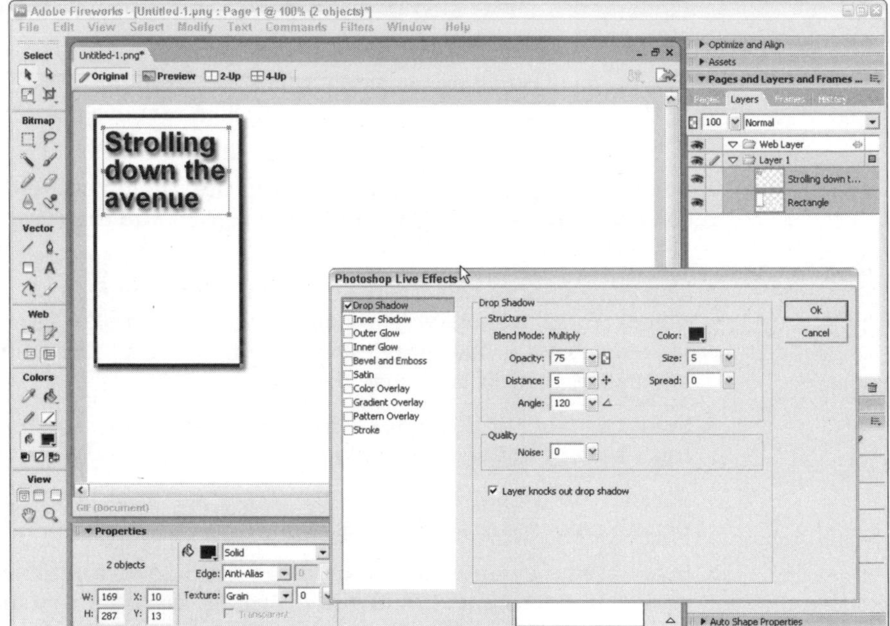

Figure 4-16: The effect is applied to both objects on the layer.

Turning a Live Effect On and Off

To turn a Live Effect off, follow these steps:

1. **Select the object or layer that has the Live Effect applied by clicking the object or layer on the canvas or in the Layers panel.**

   The object or all the objects in the layer highlight on the canvas and in the Layers panel.

2. **Select the check box next to Photoshop Live Effects in the Filters section of the Properties panel.**

   The check mark changes to a red X and the effect no longer appears on the canvas.

To turn the Live Effect back on, simply click the red X next to the Photoshop Live Effects in the Filters section of the Properties panel.

Editing an existing Live Effect

To edit an existing Photoshop Live Effect on an object, click the object on the canvas or in the Layers panel and then double-click Photoshop Live Effects in the Filters section of the Properties panel. The Photoshop Live Effects window appears.

If the effect is turned off when you double-click Photoshop Live Effects, it is turned on automatically when you adjust your Live Effects settings and click OK in the Photoshop Live Effects window.

Chapter 5: The Power of Layers and Frames

In This Chapter

- **Managing layers and sublayers**
- **Using layers to mask images**
- **Using the Web Layer**
- **Working with objects**
- **Managing frames**
- **Using frames to create rollovers and animated GIFs**

Everything that you put on your canvas in Fireworks CS3 — everything that you draw, type, paste, or import — exists in a layer. And every layer exists in a frame. Initially, you may think this concept seems simple enough, but it's more involved than it first appears. Frames can share layers, and a single layer can contain a single object (a bitmap, shape, or text) or multiple objects. A large file can actually get pretty complex; it can have dozens of bitmaps, shapes, and text blocks. *Layers* give you a way to organize your Fireworks PNG images so that you can easily turn groups of objects on or off (make the groups of objects visible or hide them), put objects on top of or beneath other objects, lock groups of objects so that you can't modify them, and find objects easily.

Users of Photoshop will be delighted to find that with this new release, Fireworks files can now be organized into hierarchical layers, which gives you finer control over the objects in your PNGs. This style of organization also removes a major hassle to working with Photoshop files, because previous versions of Fireworks did not preserve Photoshop's hierarchical layer structure.

Frames, on the other hand, offer a way to organize layers so that you can export multiple states of buttons (different versions of the button, such as those versions that appear when the user rolls over or clicks the button) and animated GIFs quickly and easily.

The *Web Layer,* the repository for slices and hotspots, is always the top layer, as shown in Figure 5-1. You create slices in the Web Layer in order to cut your page design into individual images. After you slice images, you can optimize, export, and place them in HTML pages, where you can hyperlink them. You create hotspots in the Web Layer to make images that you can export for your Web page along with some HTML code that specifies areas in the image that you want hyperlinked. You can make the Web Layer visible or invisible, and you can lock and unlock it, but you can't delete it.

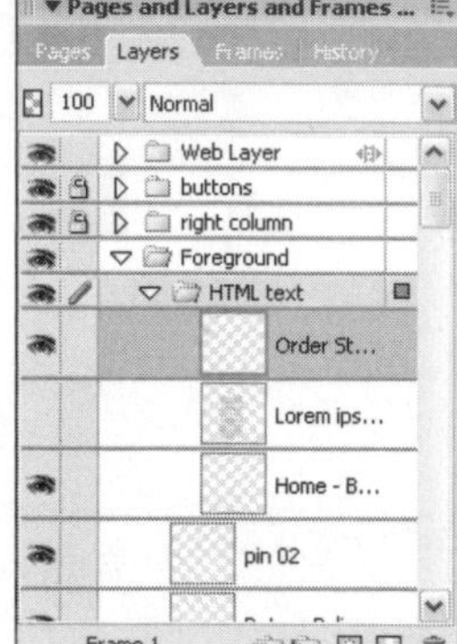

Figure 5-1: The Layers panel displays a stack of layers in their collapsed states.

Managing Layers

You can think of a layer as a transparent folder that holds "files" (image objects and text objects). (Check out the little folder icons next to the layer names in Figure 5-1.) You can copy or move the individual objects to other layers, delete them, name them, rename them, and so on. The power of layers comes from the fact that you can group objects into layers. Then you can copy, move, name, and delete whole groups of objects simultaneously. And you can make everything in a layer visible or invisible with one click of the mouse. Sublayers offer a deeper level of organization, which comes in handy if you have lots of objects and you want to be able to organize them so that you can quickly turn on and off elements of your design.

Take a closer look at the Layers panel. Looking left to right at an unexpanded layer, you can see the following across five columns:

✦ **The Show/Hide layer button:** An eye appears in this column when the layer is visible on the canvas. When the layer is invisible on the canvas, the column is empty. Click in the column to toggle the layer's visibility on the canvas off and on. When you export images from your PNG, only visible objects are exported.

✦ **The Lock/Unlock button:** If you click this column of a collapsed layer, a lock appears, indicating that you can't edit any of the objects on that layer. If you click the layer name (in the fourth column) or turn on the Show/Hide layers button (in the second column), a pencil appears in the third column, indicating that the layer is unlocked and active. If the layer is unlocked and active, you can edit the objects in the layer. You can have only one layer active at a time, though you can unlock or lock any number of layers simultaneously. You can, of course, make individual objects visible or invisible, and locked or unlocked.

- **The Expand/Collapse button:** A right-pointing arrow in the box indicates that you can expand the layer. A downward-pointing arrow in the box indicates that you can collapse the layer. Click the arrow to toggle between expanded and collapsed views of the layer.
- **The layer name:** By default, Fireworks names each layer for the order in which you created it. The first layer is called Layer 1, the second layer is called Layer 2, and so on. (To find out how to give the layer a more meaningful name, check out the "Renaming a layer" section, later in this chapter.) When the layer is active, the layer name is highlighted in the Layers panel and the folder icon to the left of the name appears open.

  NEW TO CS3

  The sublayer name is indented slightly to denote its sublayer status (see Figure 5-1, in which "HTML text" is a sublayer of the "Foreground" layer). From here on, we often use the term *layer* to apply to both layers and sublayers except when the two function differently.
- **The layer status:** When the layer is active, a box appears in the fifth column. The box's fill color corresponds to the color of the outlines around the selected object on the canvas and in the Layers panel.

Adding and deleting layers and sublayers

When you add a new layer to your PNG, the new layer always gets added above the currently selected layer. You can add a layer or sublayer in three easy ways:

- **Click the New/Duplicate Layer button (the folder with the plus sign on it) or New Sub Layer button (the folder with the right-angled arrow) at the bottom middle of the Layers panel.**
- **Choose Edit⇨Insert⇨Layer (there's no menu item for sublayers in the Insert menu).**
- **Choose New Layer or New Sub Layer from the Layer panel's Options menu (the bulleted list icon at the right of the panel's title bar).**

In either case, the new layer appears in the Layers panel, with the layer's default name highlighted. The newly created layer or sublayer is active until you click another layer or sublayer, or an object on the canvas that resides in another layer or sublayer.

To delete a layer or sublayer, click it in the Layers panel and drag it to the Delete button (the garbage can icon) at the bottom right of the Layers panel. You can also click the layer and then click the Delete button in the Layers panel.

Making a layer active

You can have only one layer or sublayer active at a time. However, you can have many objects on a layer ready to edit at the same time, which can come in handy when you want to move several objects the same amount and in the same direction. To change any object in a layer, you need to make the layer active, as follows:

- ✦ **Make a layer active:** Click an object on the canvas that's in that layer or click the name of that layer in the Layers panel.
- ✦ **Make a layer inactive, but not locked:** Click an object on the canvas that's not in that layer, or click the name of another layer in the Layers panel.

Sometimes when you have an object from one layer selected and you click an object on another layer to make it active, the item that you're trying to select doesn't highlight. Why not? Look closely: You have selected a new layer, just not the one that you want. Often you find yourself in this position if you have a very large object on the bottom layer of your file; when you try to click something in front of it, Fireworks thinks you're trying to click the large object on the bottom layer, so it highlights that object rather than the smaller object (the one that you're trying to select) in front of it. Luckily, you can just click the object that you want to select in the Layers panel to make it active, or you can lock the layers that are "in the way" so that you can click the object on the canvas.

To select multiple neighboring objects or layers in the layers panel, simply click the first object or layer that you want to select and then Shift+click the last one. All the objects and layers in between are also selected.

Expanding and collapsing layers

Because files can contain many layers, and layers can contain many objects, and you have only so much room for the Layers panel, Fireworks lets you expand and collapse a layer as you need:

- ✦ **Expand a layer:** Click the right-facing arrow in the third column of that layer. Each object in that layer appears on its own line below the layer name. Each object has its own Show/Hide button, as well as a thumbnail of the object and a name.
- ✦ **Collapse a layer:** Click the downward-facing arrow. If the layer is active, it remains so until you click another layer or an object on the canvas that resides on another layer.

Figure 5-2 shows the Layers panel with some layers collapsed and some layers expanded to show the objects they contain. Several layers are locked, and the layer called "shapes" is active, as indicated by the pencil icon.

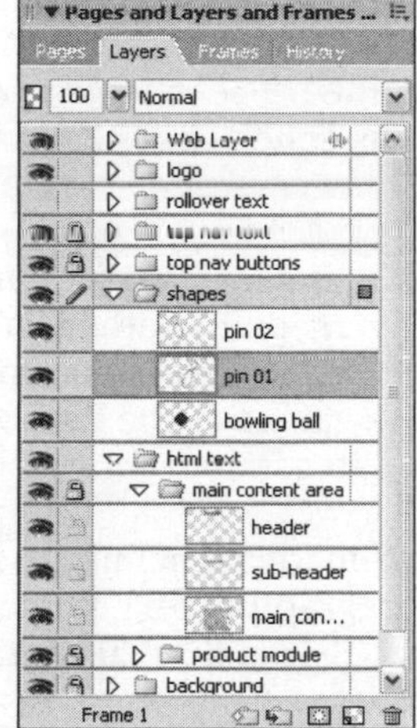

Figure 5-2: The object "pin 01" is selected.

Making a layer visible or invisible on the canvas

The more complicated your designs get, the more you *show* and *hide* layers, making them visible or invisible. Luckily, you can show and hide layers easily, as follows:

- **Make a layer visible (show a layer):** Click in the first column or the name column of the Layers panel.
- **Make a layer invisible (hide a layer):** Click the Hide Layer button (the eye icon) in the first column.

If you export your design as images (so that you can use the images in a Web page), objects on hidden/invisible layers don't export. In other words, what you see on the canvas when you export is what you get in your exported images folder.

Locking and unlocking a layer

Sometimes when you have many overlapping objects, selecting some objects without selecting others can get difficult. To prevent accidentally moving or deleting objects, you can lock the layer that they're on.

- **Lock a layer:** Click in the second column. If the column is blank when you click in it, the lock appears. If the column has a pencil in it, the pencil changes to a lock, and the pencil appears in an adjacent layer, if you have one.
- **Unlock a layer:** Click the lock in that layer. You don't automatically make a layer active by unlocking it.

Renaming a layer

By default, each nontext layer is named for the order in which you created it. The first layer is called Layer 1, the second is called Layer 2, and so on (the numbering scheme extends to sublayers).

If you have only a couple of layers in your document, that naming scheme may work just fine. If you have dozens of layers, on the other hand, you probably want to place similar objects together on layers and then name the layers. By doing so, you can tell with a quick glance at the Layers panel where the objects are.

When you add text to a layer, Fireworks automatically names the layer based on the text that you enter. If you enter a paragraph of text, you don't have to remember the whole thing; Fireworks uses only the first 20 characters of text for the layer name.

To rename a layer from its default name, just follow these simple steps:

1. **Double-click the layer name.**

   A simple dialog box appears. The current name is highlighted in the text field.

2. **Type a new name.**

   You don't need to click in the text field because the current layer name is already highlighted. If you want to keep part of the current name, use your mouse to select the part of the name that you want to replace or remove and type over or delete it.

3. **If you have multiple frames in your document and you want this layer to be visible in the other frames, select the Share Across Frames check box (this doesn't apply to sublayers, which inherit the sharing property of the layer they're part of).**

   Otherwise, move on to Step 4.

4. **Press the Enter key.**

   The dialog box closes, and your layer has a new name.

Moving a layer in front of or behind other layers

As you add layers to your PNG file, they stack up. Figure 5-3 illustrates the relationship between objects, their position on the canvas, and their position in the Layers panel. The before part (on the top) of Figure 5-3 shows the bowling ball in front of both pins, and in the Layers panel, the object named "bowling ball" is above the "pin" objects. The after part (on the bottom) of Figure 5-3 shows the large pin in front of the bowling ball. The ball, in turn, is in front of a smaller bowling pin. In the Layers panel, the ball object is between the pin objects.

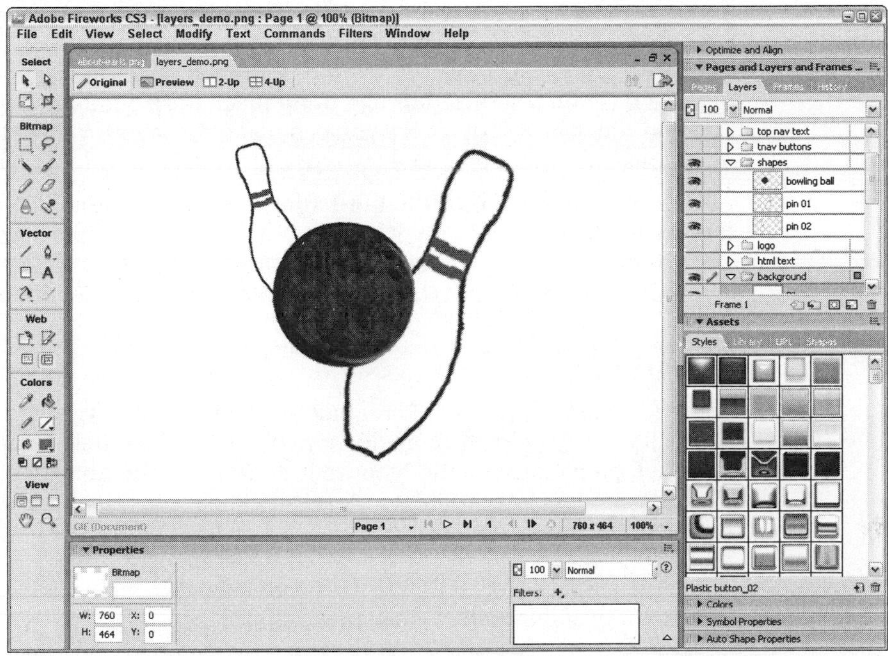

Figure 5-3: Moving a layer in the Layers panel, before (top) and after (bottom).

You can change the order of a layer or object in one of two ways:

- **Move a layer or object in front of another:** Click the name column of the layer or object and drag it up. A black horizontal line appears when you roll over a spot where you can place the layer or object. Release the mouse button to drop the layer or object in its new location.
- **Move a layer or object behind another:** Click the name column of the layer or object and drag it down. A black horizontal line appears when you roll over a spot where you can place the layer or object. Release the mouse button to drop the layer or object in its new location.

Merging layers

Sometimes in the process of creating a PNG document, you find that you need all the objects you've made, but you don't need them to be on so many layers. If, on the other hand, you want to move all the objects in one layer to another, and you have quite a few objects in each layer, you probably want to merge the layers.

To merge all the objects on one layer into a single bitmap object in the layer immediately underneath, follow these steps:

1. **Click in the name column of the layer in the Layers panel.**

   Make sure that all the objects in the layer are highlighted. (If they're not, you may have clicked an object in the layer rather than the layer itself.)

2. **If necessary, drag the layer so that it's on top of the layer that you want to merge it into.**

   You use the Merge Down command in Step 3, so you need to make sure the two layers are one on top of the other.

3. **Click the Options menu icon (it looks like a bulleted list) at the top right of the Layers panel and select Merge Down.**

   The selected layer merges into the one below it. The objects in the upper layer are combined into a single bitmap object in the new layer.

   You can't edit text in the new object, and vector shapes in the new object are now bitmaps.

You can also use the key command Ctrl+E to merge a layer into the one below it, or choose Modify➪Merge Down.

To merge all the visible layers together into one, do the following:

1. **Click in the name column of any layer in the Layers panel.**
2. **Choose Modify➪Flatten Layers.**

   Your document now has a single layer. Each object remains separate from the others.

Using Layers for Masking

A *mask* is a layer that you create specifically to let some areas of an image show while you keep other areas hidden. Fireworks uses two kinds of masks — bitmap masks and vector masks (you can use text as a vector mask). Both kinds of masks have one thing in common — what they do: When you lay a mask over an image, the mask blocks out parts of the image and lets other parts show through. The shape of the mask determines which parts show through and which are blocked out, as Figure 5-4 shows you.

Figure 5-4: This figure was created by masking a beach with a photo of a dog.

When you use a *bitmap mask,* the grayscale values of the mask determine what, and how much, shows through. The lighter the pixel, the more the object or objects beneath show through. The darker the pixel, the less the stuff underneath shows through.

A *vector mask,* on the other hand, uses the shape outline of the vector object like a cookie cutter. However, Fireworks gives you a lot more flexibility than you have with a real cookie cutter! For example, you can *anti-alias* (smooth out jagged edges) and even *feather* (blur) the edges of your mask, or you can change the size of your mask at any time after you've created it.

Fireworks offers many ways to create masks. We cover the basics here, but you can always refer to the Fireworks Help files if you want to explore masks in more depth.

Creating a bitmap mask

To make a bitmap mask using an existing bitmap, follow these steps:

1. **If you want to mask multiple objects, group them by selecting them and using the key command Ctrl+G.**
2. **Select the object you want to use to make the mask.**

   You can select multiple objects to make a mask by Shift+clicking them, but if you do, Fireworks automatically makes a vector mask, not a bitmap mask. See the section "Creating a vector mask," later in this chapter, if you want to make a vector mask that uses multiple bitmap objects.
3. **Choose Edit⇨Cut or press Ctrl+X.**

   Cut? That's right. We have you paste the shape in Step 5.
4. **Select the layer, object, or group you want to be visible through the mask by selecting it in the Layers panel or on the canvas.**

   The layer, object, or group is highlighted.
5. **Choose Edit⇨Paste as Mask.**

   All the parts of the masked image that fall outside the masking object disappear. In the Layers panel, the mask icon shows up in the third column, and a link icon and thumbnail of the mask shape show up next to the thumbnail of the masked image.
6. **If it's not already selected, select Alpha channel in the Property inspector.**

   When the mask is selected in the Layers panel, the Property inspector offers two options for a bitmap mask: Mask to Alpha Channel and Mask to Grayscale (the default), as Figure 5-5 shows you. Mask to Alpha Channel uses the transparency of the mask bitmap, and Mask to Grayscale uses the brightness of the pixels in the mask bitmap.

Figure 5-5: You can change the Mask setting in the Property inspector.

You can think of bitmaps as having four channels: Red, Green, Blue, and Alpha. The Red, Green, and Blue channels describe the amount of each of those colors in every pixel in the bitmap. The Alpha channel contains information about the level of transparency of each pixel in the bitmap.

You can hide a mask temporarily by clicking it in the Layers panel and then choosing Disable Mask from the Layers panel's Options menu (the bulleted list icon at the top right of the panel). The mask icon disappears from the Show/Hide object column and a red X appears over the mask, indicating that the mask is disabled. To re-enable the mask, simply click it.

To make a bitmap mask by creating an empty mask and modifying it, follow these steps:

1. **Select the object you want to mask by clicking it on the canvas or in the Layers panel.**
2. **Click the Mask button at the bottom of the Layers panel or choose Modify⇨Mask⇨Reveal All.**

   The Mask icon is the rectangle with a dotted circle inside. Reveal All means that the mask you made is completely transparent until you modify it.
3. **Select a paintbrush or other drawing tool and draw on top of the bitmap.**

   Wherever you draw, the mask blocks the image behind.

What if you want to do the opposite — reveal what's underneath only where you draw? Easy! Just follow these steps:

1. **Select the object you want to mask by clicking it on the canvas or in the Layers panel.**
2. **Choose Modify⇨Mask⇨Hide All.**

   Hide All means that the mask you made is completely opaque until you modify it, so when you first apply the mask, it looks as though your masked object has disappeared.
3. **Select any color other than black.**

   Because the opaque areas of the mask appear black, you have to draw the areas that you want to show through by using any other color.
4. **Select a paintbrush or other drawing tool and draw on top of the bitmap.**

   Wherever you draw, the mask reveals the image behind.

You can delete a mask by clicking it in the Layers panel and then choosing Delete Mask from the Layers panel's Options menu (the bulleted list icon at the top right of the panel). When you delete a mask, a dialog box appears to give you the option to apply the mask before deleting it, which changes the masked image.

Creating a vector mask

To make a vector mask, such as the one shown in Figure 5-6, follow these steps:

1. **Select a text block or vector shape by clicking the shape on the canvas or in the Layers panel.**

   The object is highlighted on the canvas and in the Layers panel.

2. **Drag the shape or text over the object or objects you want to mask.**

   The layer with the shape doesn't have to be on top of the layers with the objects you want to mask, but you can position the shape more easily if you can see it!

3. **Choose Edit⇨Cut or press Ctrl+X.**

   You paste the shape in Step 5, so you need to cut it here.

4. **Select the layer or object you want to be visible through the mask by clicking it in the Layers panel or on the canvas.**

   The layer or object is highlighted.

Figure 5-6: A vector star-shaped mask with bevels and drop shadows added to make the image "pop."

5. **Choose Edit⇨Paste as Mask.**

   All the parts of the masked image that fall outside the mask shape or text disappear. In the Layers panel, the mask icon shows up in the third column, and a link icon and thumbnail of the mask shape appear next to the thumbnail of the masked image, as shown in Figure 5-7.

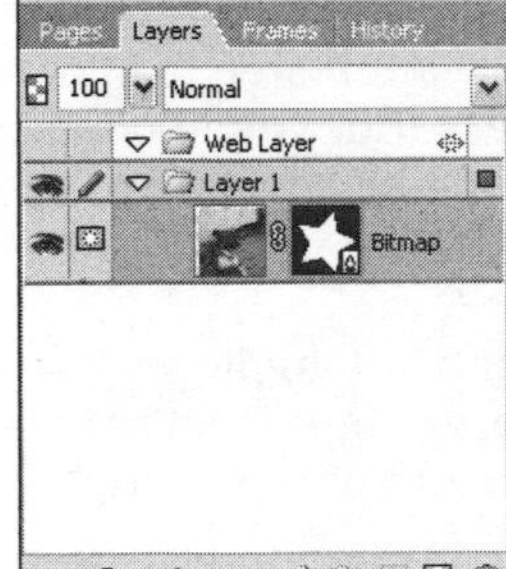

Figure 5-7: An active mask in the Layers panel.

Using the Web Layer

The Web Layer was the greatest innovation of the original version of Fireworks, and even if it no longer seems revolutionary, it's still as handy a feature as you come across in making Web pages. The Web Layer lets you cut your page layout into *slices,* which are pieces of your layout that end up as individual images on your Web page, held in place by HTML or CSS. The Web Layer also lets you name and optimize each slice individually, which means that you can find the best balance of file size and image quality for each piece of your layout. Just as important, because it's a repository for slice information, the Web Layer lets you save slice coordinates, dimensions, and optimization settings along with everything else in your PNG file.

You never have to leave the Fireworks application to ready your images for the Web, and you don't have to write down or remember your image size, placement, and optimization settings if you ever need to remake an image. The Web Layer also lets you see at a glance where your slices are, which helps you re-create your page design in HTML. For details about slices and image optimization (including when to use GIFs and when to use JPEGs), see Book III, Chapter 6.

Standard HTML pages are built on a grid system of cells organized into rows and columns. The rows and columns make up a *table.* You can have multiple tables on a Web page, and you can even have tables within tables within tables. You can set the height of each row and the width of each column individually, but you can't make a round cell or a triangular table.

If you use Fireworks to make your HTML, each slice that you make in your PNG ends up as an image that fills a table cell in your Web page. Using Dreamweaver, you can combine multiple images in a single cell in your HTML code, but Fireworks isn't made to work that way.

Think of your Web page design as a rectangular sheet cake. You can make the decorations on top of the cake all kinds of shapes, but when you cut the cake, you probably make rectangular slices, cutting right through text, slicing a single icing rose into four pieces, and so on. You ignore the design on the surface of the cake because you're more interested in slicing the cake quickly and controlling the size of each piece. But you may make a few specially cut pieces if somebody really wants the blue rose near the top or the exclamation points from the text that says, "Happy Birthday!!!"

When you're cutting up a Web page, you want certain pieces to remain intact (a corporate logo or a navigation button, for example), but other objects fit the HTML grid structure better if you slice them into pieces or include them with other objects on a single piece. If you have an object with round edges, you need to slice it into rectangles so that you can reconstruct it on a Web page, as with the bowling ball shown in Figure 5-8. You re-create the bowling ball in HTML as three stacked rectangles. The middle slice in Figure 5-8 is selected, so its name and image compression type appear at the top left of the slice.

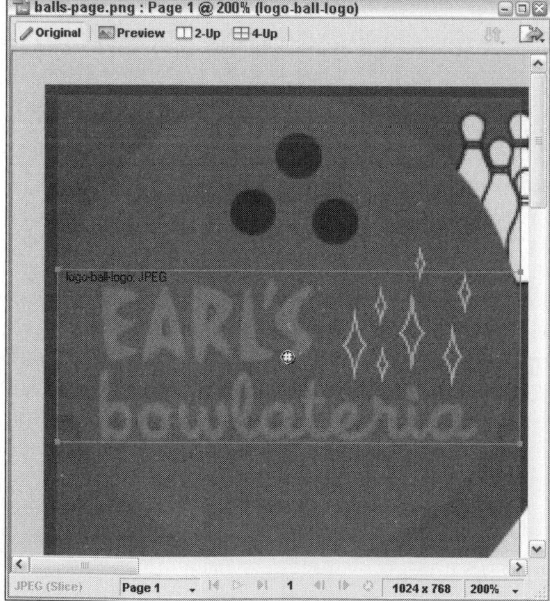

Figure 5-8: A bowling ball divided into multiple slices so that it can be reconstituted on a Web page.

Cutting your objects with the Slice tool

The Slice tool, which you can find in the Web section of the Tools panel, looks like a utility knife on a green square with red lines on each side. When you employ the Slice tool, the slices you create are added automatically to the Web Layer.

To make a slice in your PNG file, follow these steps:

1. **Select the Slice tool from the Web section of the Tools panel.**
2. **Click and drag diagonally on the canvas to make a rectangle.**

   The slice shows up as a green overlay on the canvas.

Slicing your canvas more exactly with the Polygon Slice tool

The Slice tool has a partner "hidden" behind it in the toolbar: the Polygon Slice tool, which you can get to by clicking and holding the Slice tool until the pop-up menu containing the Polygon Slice tool appears, or by clicking the Slice tool and pressing K on your keyboard.

You can probably guess that the Polygon Slice tool lets you make nonrectangular slices. But wait! Didn't we say that slices and images have to be rectangular? The short answer is that the Polygon Slice tool doesn't create a nonrectangular slice — it creates a rectangular slice with a *polygonal hotspot* (a polygonal area that you can hyperlink in combination with some HTML code) inside.

So what's the difference between a polygonal hotspot made by the Polygon Slice tool and one made by the Polygon Hotspot tool? The Polygon Hotspot tool doesn't make a slice, it just makes an irregularly shaped linkable area in a slice. (A slice may contain many hotspots, each linked to a different page.) The Polygon Slice tool, on the other hand, makes both hotspots and slices. If you have a map of the United States, and you want each state to link to its own HTML page, use the Polygon Hotspot tool to make linked areas in the shape of each state. (For more information on the Polygon Hotspot tool, see Book III, Chapter 6.) If you just have a few irregularly shaped buttons, you can use the Polygon Slice tool to make a linkable image.

To make a polygonal slice, follow these steps:

1. **Select the Polygon Slice tool from the Slice tool menu in the Web area of the Tools panel.**

   If the regular Slice tool is showing, click and hold the Slice tool button to reveal the pop-up menu so that you can select the Polygon Slice tool.

2. **Click a series of points to make a polygonal shape.**

   Fireworks automatically draws straight lines to connect each point to the last. You don't need to click the first spot to close the shape.

You can make a polygon slice to match any vector shape by using the Insert Polygon Slice command. Simply select the shape and choose Edit⇨Insert⇨Polygon Slice, or press Alt+Shift+P.

Working with Objects

In the world of Fireworks, an *object* is any self-contained bitmap, vector shape, or text block that can appear on the canvas. The object may include blank space, and you can make a single object out of many objects (as you do when you merge layers, which you can read about in the section "Merging layers," earlier in this chapter). In general, you want to leave anything in your design that you may want to edit individually as a single object.

Renaming an object in the Layers panel

By default, each object is named for its type (path, bitmap, and so on), but you can individually rename them. As with layers, being able to name objects in the Layers panel becomes crucial as you add more elements to your design. The Layers panel does contain thumbnails of each object, but if you have multiple similar objects in several places on the canvas, you may want a way to tell the objects apart in the Layers panel.

To rename an object, double-click the current name of the object in the Layers panel and type a new name in the text field that appears. Press Enter or click outside the text field to save the new name. Renaming an object makes it active. When the object is active, the line around the icon is highlighted and the column's background becomes gray (light blue on a Mac).

Moving an object between layers

You may want to move an object from the layer it was originally created on to a different layer. For example, you may want an object to be stacked on top of or under other items on the canvas and have other objects in the layer remain exactly where they are. Luckily, you can move an object from one layer to another in a snap.

To move an object from one layer to another, click the name column of the object in the Layers panel and drag it to a new location. A black horizontal line appears when you roll over a spot where you can place the object. Release the mouse button to drop the object in its new location.

Setting an object's opacity/transparency

You can set each object's transparency independently by using the slider near the top left of the Layers panel. By default, objects are completely opaque, and the opaque object completely blocks out whatever objects are underneath it, as in Figure 5-3. You can make the objects on a layer semi-transparent, which allows the objects underneath to show through by an adjustable amount.

The extreme ends of the Opacity/Transparency scale are 100 percent opaque (which can also be thought of as 0 percent transparent) and 0 percent opaque (100 percent transparent). When you add an object to the canvas, its default opacity of 100 shows up at the top left of the Layers panel and in the object's Property inspector.

To adjust the transparency of a layer, follow these simple steps:

1. **Click the name column of the object that you want to adjust or click the object on the canvas to select the object.**

   The object is highlighted on both the canvas and in the Layers panel.

2. **Click and drag the Opacity/Transparency slider to adjust how opaque you want the object to be.**

   The Opacity/Transparency slider is the button with the downward-pointing arrow located near the top left of the Layers panel, next to the Opacity text field. (You can find an identical slider in the Property inspector.)

3. **Release the mouse button when you get to the setting you want.**

You can also type a number from 0 to 100 into the text field next to the slider to set the object's transparency. Remember to press the Enter key to apply the new setting.

Fireworks can do a few fancier tricks with opacity. For example, you can set an opacity gradient to make some parts of your object more transparent than others. See the following section for more information on this topic.

Blending

Blending one object with another involves varying the transparency of the top object so that some of the bottom object shows through. But blending in Fireworks involves more than just adjusting opacity. With Fireworks CS3, you can choose from a whopping 47 blending modes, in conjunction with the Opacity control and the colors of your objects, to produce different blending effects. Some of the most common blending modes are listed in Table 5-1.

Table 5-1	Blending Modes
Mode	*What It Does*
Normal	The default blending mode. Actually, no blending goes on at all.
Darken	Replaces pixels of the top object that are lighter than the pixels in the object underneath with the darker pixels from below.
Multiply	Multiplies the value of each pixel of the top object with each pixel of the objects underneath, which generally results in a darker color.
Lighten	Replaces pixels of the top object that are darker than the object underneath with the lighter pixels from the object below.
Screen	Divides the value of each pixel of the bottom object by each pixel of the object on top and produces a lighter color.
Difference	Subtracts the darker color from the color with more brightness, regardless of which is on top.
Hue	Replaces the luminance and saturation of a pixel on top with those values of the pixel underneath.
Saturation	Replaces the hue and luminance of a pixel on top with those values of the pixel underneath.
Color	Replaces the luminance of a pixel on top with that of the pixel underneath, but keeps the hue and saturation of the top pixel the same.
Luminosity	Replaces the hue and saturation of the pixel on top with those values of the pixel underneath, leaving the luminance of the pixel on top.
Invert	Changes the colors of the pixels in the object underneath to their opposites, regardless of the colors of the object on top.
Tint	Adds gray to the areas of overlap.
Erase	Removes all pixels in the overlapping areas, leaving a hole in the canvas. Any objects underneath the object with a blend mode of Erase become invisible where the objects overlap.

Additionally, Fireworks CS3 debuts seven blend modes inherited from Photoshop CS2:

- ✦ Dissolve
- ✦ Linear Burn
- ✦ Linear Dodge
- ✦ Vivid Light
- ✦ Linear Light
- ✦ Pin Light
- ✦ Hard Mix

See your Fireworks documentation for details, or better yet, experiment! Seeing what the blending modes do by choosing different ones and changing their settings is much more worthwhile than reading technical explanations of what they're doing — and it's more fun!

Layers can have blending modes, but the blending mode settings of individual objects on the layer override the settings of the layer that they're on. So different objects on the same layer can have individualized blend settings. The blending mode of a *group* of objects, however, overrides the blending modes of individual objects within the group. Removing the blending mode of the group restores the blending modes of the individual objects.

To blend an existing object with whatever is under it, just follow these steps:

1. **Select the object you want to blend by clicking it on the canvas or in the Layers panel.**
2. **Select a blending mode from the drop-down list at the top-right of the Layers panel.**

   When you release the mouse button, the blend mode takes effect.
3. **If you want, adjust the transparency of the object by typing a value between 1 and 100 in the Opacity text field next to the blending mode list or by using the Opacity/Transparency slider between the Opacity text field and the blending mode list.**

The blended object affects (or is affected by) any objects that you put under the blended object where both objects overlap.

You can also establish a blend's opacity and mode *before* you create an object. You do so by setting the properties of a drawing tool in the Property inspector, as you can see in Figure 5-9. (***Note:*** Not all tools permit you to set the object properties before you create the object.) Your settings apply every time you use that tool. Remember, blend settings of individual objects override the blend settings of the layer the objects are on.

To set the blend before you draw, follow these steps:

1. **Press Ctrl+D or choose Edit⇨Deselect to make sure that you don't have any objects selected.**

   If you have an object selected, you may accidentally change its blending mode when you're trying to set a blending mode for the object you're about to create.
2. **Select a drawing tool, such as the Brush tool.**

   You can't change the blending mode of some tools from the default, which is Normal.
3. **Select a color for the tool.**

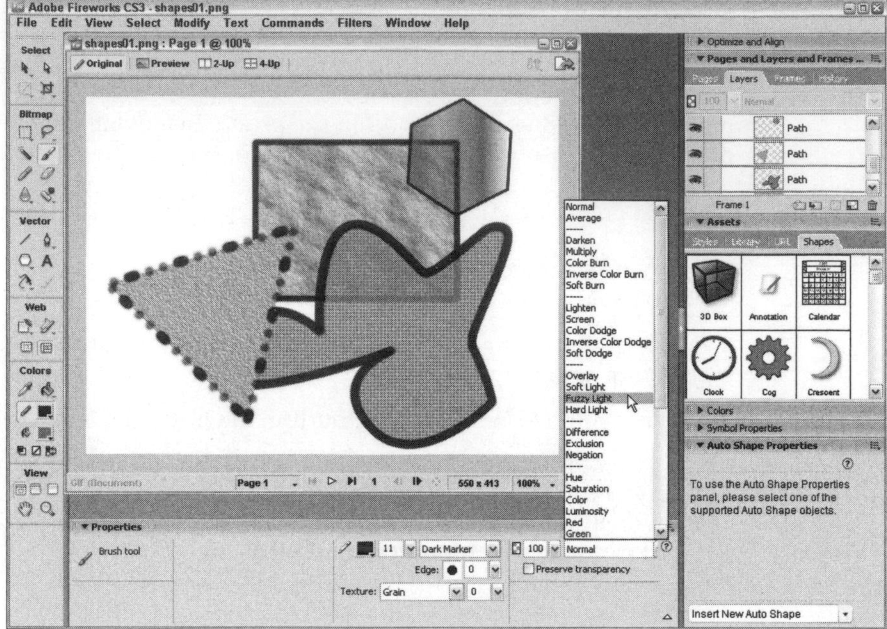

Figure 5-9: You can set a tool's blending mode by using the tool's Property inspector.

See the section on adding color in Book III, Chapter 2 if you don't know how to select a color for the tool. You can always change the color of the object later, but that can get complicated, especially if you have a special blending mode and opacity set.

4. **Select a blending mode from the drop-down list in the tool's Property inspector.**

5. **If you want, set an opacity for the tool by typing a value in the Property inspector's Opacity text field.**

   You can also set the opacity by dragging the Property inspector's Opacity/Transparency slider (the button with the downward-pointing arrow between the Opacity text field and the blending mode list).

6. **Use the tool to make your vector shape or bitmap.**

   The tool's blend and opacity settings remain in effect until you change them. After you create an object, you can always adjust its blend and opacity settings. You may want to create a new layer (see the section "Adding and deleting layers and sublayers," earlier in this chapter) before making a new object. If you don't make a new layer, remember that the object's blend settings override the layer's blend settings.

Managing Frames

Given all that you can do with layers, you may be wondering why you need these things called "frames." *Frames* are essentially sets of layers that let you do two things that layers alone can't accomplish:

- ✦ Export multiple button states (different versions of the button, such as those versions that appear when the user rolls over or clicks the button) simultaneously
- ✦ Create and export animated GIFs (files that contain multiple GIF images displayed in sequence)

You can think of layers as stacked one on top of the other; you may want to think of frames, on the other hand, as a series, each following the previous in the same location but at a later time, like a flip book. Each frame is distinct from the others. A given frame may share layers or objects with other frames, but the shared layers or objects usually change from one frame to the next (the objects are a different color, have a different effect applied to them, or are at different coordinates). These differences make up multiple button states or animated GIFs.

The Frames panel (see Figure 5-12) displays frames in much the same way as the Layers panel displays layers, except that the Frames panel doesn't show the objects contained within each frame.

As with layers, you can duplicate, add, and delete frames. You must have at least two frames in your Fireworks PNG file in order to export buttons with rollover states or animated GIFs.

Adding frames

By default, your Fireworks PNG has a single frame, which contains all the layers in the file. To add a frame to your file, just follow these steps:

1. **Click the Options menu (the bulleted list icon) at the top right of the Frames panel and choose Add Frames or Duplicate Frame from the menu.**

   Choose Duplicate Frame if you want to copy the objects in the current frame to the new frames. Choose Add Frames if you want to add empty frames to your file. Either the Add Frames or Duplicate Frame dialog box (which you can see in Figure 5-10) appears, both of which have identical parameters.

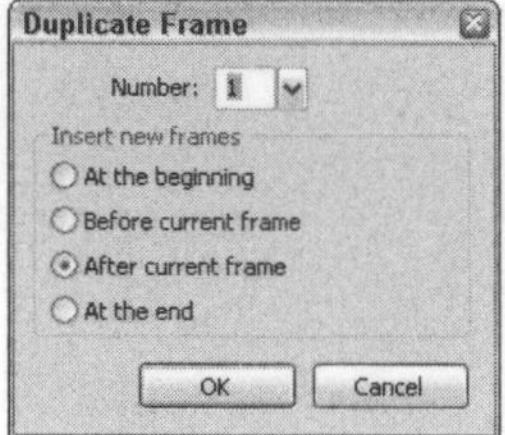

Figure 5-10: The Duplicate Frame dialog box.

2. **Enter a number or click the arrow next to the text field to use a slider to set the number of frames that you want to add:**

   - For a simple rollover, you want one additional frame, for a total of two frames in your file.
   - If you want your button to have an on state as well as a highlight (rollover) and normal state, you want two additional frames, for a total of three frames.
   - If you want a highlight-while-on state, you want three additional frames, for a total of four frames.

   The slider goes from 0 to 10, but you can type in values higher than 10.

   If your animated GIF has more than 20 frames, the file size may be too large for you to use. For complicated animations, you're better off using Flash (see Book V for more information on Flash CS3).

3. **Select one of the options for where you want to add the new frames in reference to the current one.**

   You have the following options:

   - **At the Beginning:** The first new frame becomes Frame 1 and the remaining frames are numbered sequentially, regardless of how many frames you currently have in your document, and regardless of which frame is currently active.
   - **Before Current Frame:** The frames are added before the currently active frame.
   - **After Current Frame:** The frames are added after the currently active frame.
   - **At the End:** The new frames are the last frames, no matter how many frames you already have or which frame is currently active.

4. **Click OK.**

Deleting and editing frames

To delete a frame, click the frame in the Frames panel and drag it to the garbage can icon at the bottom right of the Frames panel. To delete multiple frames simultaneously, Shift+click all the frames in the Frames panel that you want to delete and, while the frames are highlighted, click the garbage can icon at the bottom right of the Frames panel.

You can select a frame for editing in two ways:

- **Click the frame in the Frames panel.**
- **Click and hold the frame indicator at the bottom left of the Layers panel.** A drop-down list appears, giving you easy access to all the frames in your document. Simply select the frame that you want to edit.

Renaming frames

You can easily rename frames: Double-click the frame's name in the Frames panel and type the new name in the text field that appears.

Using Frames to Create Rollovers and Animated GIFs

Now that you know how to make and manage frames, you're ready to use them! In this section we cover how to create rollovers and animated GIFs, both of which can add interest to your Web site.

Creating a rollover

Creating a button rollover really just involves making two (or three or even four) versions, or *states,* of a button graphic, each on its own frame. Dreamweaver lets you generate rollover code pretty easily, but you can also have Fireworks make the rollover code along with the HTML. (See Book I for much more about Dreamweaver.)

To make a simple button rollover, follow these steps:

1. **Make a button, or set of buttons, using the processes outlined in Book III, Chapters 3 and 4.**

   The button can have text or an icon, it can have a shape or bitmap under the text or icon, and it can be any shape or size you like (but you probably want to keep it on the small side to limit file size and leave room on your page for content). For easy housekeeping, if you're creating a navigation bar, keep all the buttons for which you want to have additional states on the same layer.

2. **Disable sharing across frames by double-clicking the layer and deselecting the Share Across Frames check box.**

   By default, objects on layers aren't shared across frames, so you may be able to skip this step. If a layer is shared across frames, changes to any objects in that layer appear in all frames. If a layer is shared across frames, the Shared icon (which resembles a ladder or strip of film with arrows on both sides) appears to the right of the layer name in the Layers panel.

3. **Add one frame after the current frame by clicking the New/Duplicate Frame button in the Frames panel or by choosing Add Frames from the Frames panel's Options menu (the bulleted list icon at the top right of the panel).**

4. **In Frame 2, edit the objects that make up your button to create a highlighted rollover state.**

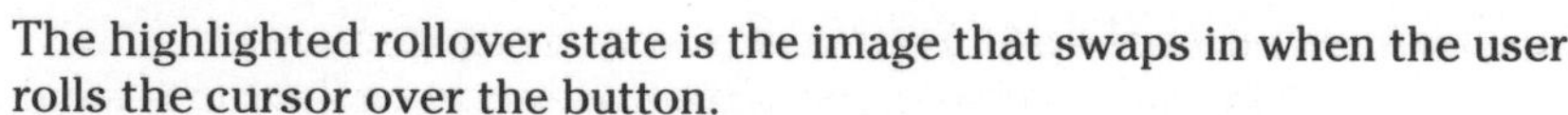

   The highlighted rollover state is the image that swaps in when the user rolls the cursor over the button.

   You can make the text a different color or add a glow to it, or you can make the vector shape or bitmap a different color. You have too many options to mention here, really. Just make sure that the user can notice the difference when he or she moves a cursor over the button.

5. **Make a slice overlaying the button graphic.**

   See Book III, Chapter 6 for details on making slices, or just check out the "Cutting your objects with the Slice tool" section, earlier in this chapter.

6. **Click and release the mouse button in the middle of the slice to access the Add Behavior pop-up menu and choose the Add Simple Rollover behavior.**

   When a slice is active, you can see the Target icon in the middle of the slice. When you place your cursor over the target, it becomes a hand.

If you want to test the rollover, click the Preview tab at the top of the canvas to make the Preview pane active. Place your cursor over your button in the Preview pane to see the Rollover behavior in action. Next, move the cursor off the button to see the button return to its normal state; the change from the rollover state back to the normal state is part of a Simple Rollover.

You can add an on state (for when the user is on the Web page that the button represents) and a highlight-while-on state (for when the user rolls over the button on the Web page that the button represents). You add these states by repeating Steps 3 and 4 in the previous list, and you can add more behaviors via the Behaviors panel. See Book III, Chapter 7 for further details.

Creating an animated GIF

You may find that you can most easily create an animated GIF by building one frame, duplicating it, editing that frame, duplicating it, and so on. Fireworks has a display mode called onion skinning, which you may find especially handy for building animated GIFs. With onion skinning turned on, as Figure 5-11 shows you, you can see the frame you're working on, plus dimmed versions either of the next frame, the previous and next frames, or all frames. That setup can greatly help you pace your animation to get the illusion of smooth motion.

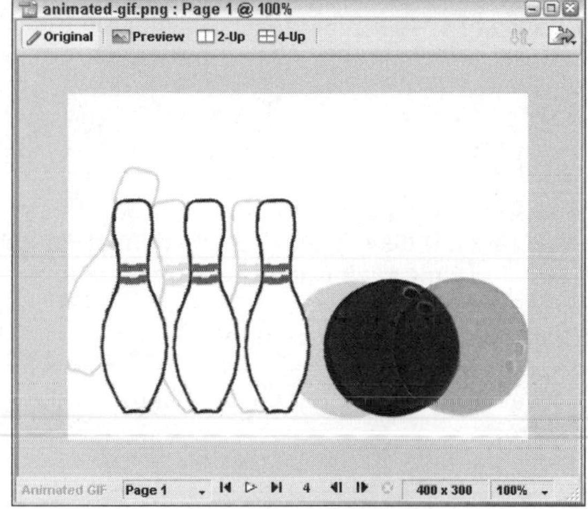

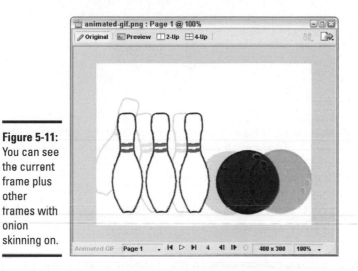

Figure 5-11: You can see the current frame plus other frames with onion skinning on.

To activate onion skinning, just follow these steps:

1. **Click the Onion Skinning button (the downward-pointing pentagon) at the lower left of the Frames panel.**

   The Onion Skinning menu pops up.

2. **Select one of the four options:**

   - **Show Next Frame:** Select the Show Next Frame option if you already have your frames set up and want to check frames two at a time.
   - **Before and After:** Select the Before and After option if you want to see the previous and next frames, as well as the current frame.
   - **Show All Frames:** Select the Show All Frames option to see all the frames simultaneously.

- **Custom:** Select the Custom option if you want to set the number of frames to be visible simultaneously and to customize their transparencies.

3. **Leave the Multi-Frame Editing option selected if you want to be able to edit the objects in the visible but not current frames.**

   Use the Select Behind tool to select objects in frames other than the current one.

When you duplicate a frame, you duplicate the objects in it. When you edit an object in a frame, though, you change only that instance of it. In our bowling ball animation, which you can see in Figure 5-11, we rotated the ball (as well as moved it left) in each frame to give the illusion that the ball is rolling. If we want to, we can make the ball a different color in each frame, as well.

Setting the frame rate

The frame rate is the speed at which each frame follows the previous frame. You can use the same rate all the way through the animation, or you can set individually the amount of time each frame stays on-screen.

To set a constant frame rate, follow these steps:

1. **Click the first frame and Shift+click the last frame in the Frames panel to select all the frames.**

   All the frames are highlighted.

2. **Double-click the frame delay column (the column on the right) of any frame in the Frames panel.**

   The Frame Delay dialog box appears.

3. **Type a number in the Frame Delay text field to set the amount of time in hundredths of a second that you want each frame to remain on-screen.**

   If you want the frames to stay on-screen for more than a second, you need to type a number over 100. For example, if you type 350, each frame stays on-screen for 3.5 seconds. You don't get much of an illusion of motion at that frame rate, however! The less time that you have each frame on-screen, the more frames of your animation appear each second. The more frames per second, the smoother the animation looks. But the more frames you have in your animation, the bigger the file.

4. **Press Enter.**

To change the amount of time one frame stays on-screen, follow these steps:

1. **Double-click the frame delay column (the column on the right) of any frame in the Frames panel.**

   The Frame Delay dialog box appears.

2. **Type a new number in the Frame Delay text field to set the amount of time in hundredths of a second that you want the frame to remain on-screen.**

3. **Press Enter.**

To loop or not to loop

Fireworks lets you loop your animation, which causes it to automatically start over at the beginning after playing the last frame. You can have the GIF loop indefinitely, you can set it to play once (stopping at the last frame), or you can make it play a designated number of times and then stop on the last frame.

The default for animated GIFs is to loop endlessly. To make a GIF that stops at the final frame, just follow these steps:

1. **Click the GIF Animation Looping button (the oval with an arrow) at the bottom of the Frames panel.**

   The Looping pop-up menu appears.

2. **Select the number of times you want the animation to repeat, or select No Looping if you want it to play only once.**

   Because you're setting the amount of times you want it to repeat, if you select 1, that means that the animation plays twice through and stops. After you have made your choice, the choice appears next to the Loop button, as you can see in Figure 5-12.

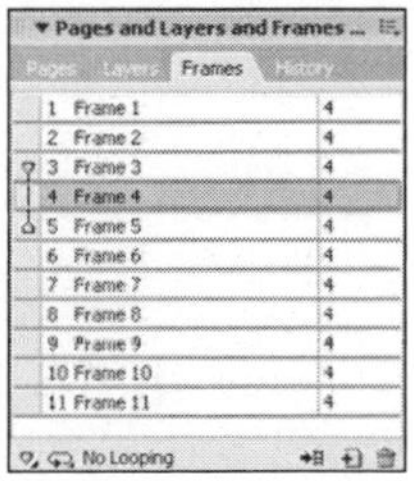

Figure 5-12: The Frames panel shows the frames' settings.

The Frames panel, which you can see in Figure 5-12, shows what mode of onion skinning is on, if any, and on which frames (first column); it also shows the frame name (second column), frame delay (third column), and looping information (bottom).

Previewing animated GIFs

You can preview animated GIFs in the Preview pane (click Preview at the top of the canvas to view the Preview pane) or in the Original pane. You have access to these controls in the order that they appear from left to right at the bottom of the pane, as follows:

- Go to First Frame
- Play/Stop
- Go to Last Frame
- Go Back One Frame
- Go Forward One Frame

The animation plays at the frame rate that you have set for it (see the section "Setting the frame rate," earlier in this chapter), and, conveniently, you can adjust the frame rate in the Frames panel without leaving the Preview pane. Your animation loops in the Preview pane even if you don't have it set to loop for export. Onion skinning is not visible in the Preview pane.

Chapter 6: Slicing Up Content for the Web

In This Chapter

- ✓ **Creating, using, and editing slices**
- ✓ **Making your images Web ready**
- ✓ **Getting a sneak preview of your slices**
- ✓ **Fitting hotspots to your slices**
- ✓ **Exporting your images for the Web**

After you design your page, you need to figure out how to translate your design to the Web. If you're planning to export HTML as well as images from Fireworks and don't want to mess with the code afterward, you don't have to. When you want to make changes to the Web page, you can do so in Fireworks and then re-export the HTML and images.

Of course, you can also export all the images from Fireworks but generate the HTML code in Dreamweaver. Regardless of your Web-coding skill level or your site maintenance needs, you probably want to slice and optimize your images, and you can do so easily with Fireworks. The following section explains the whys and hows of slicing your design in Fireworks; for more information on image optimization, see the "Optimizing Your Images for the Web" section, later in this chapter.

Exploring the Advantages of Using Slices

When you slice a page layout, such as the one in Figure 6-1, you want to *optimize* (reduce the file size of) your images so that you can reconstruct your design with HTML in such a way as to balance image quality with download time.

Slicing your design offers two advantages:

- **Individually optimized images:** You can compress each sliced image by a different amount by using the most appropriate method, giving you maximum control over the balance between image quality and file size.

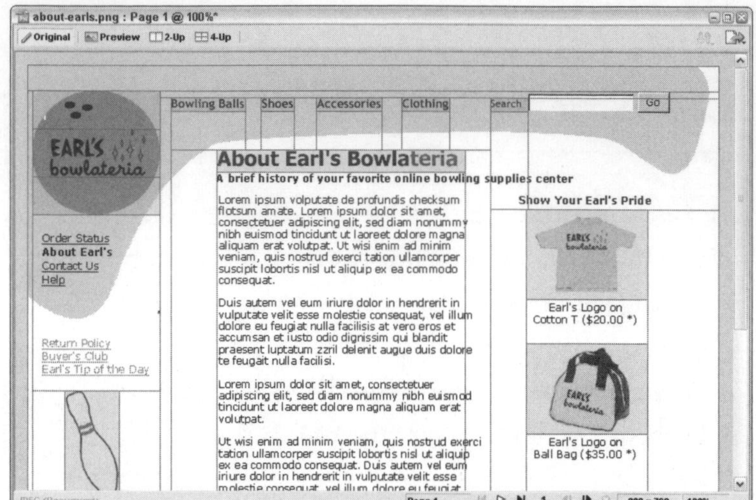

Figure 6-1: This layout is sliced into exportable images

- ✦ **Gradual download:** The browser displays each sliced image as it downloads to the user's computer, so the page appears to build gradually. Users find watching this process much more interesting than staring at a blank screen waiting for a complete page to load all at one time!

When you use slices in combination with frames, you gain other advantages (for more on frames, see Book III, Chapter 5). You can export multiple images simultaneously from a single slice, which is the easiest way to make buttons that change based on user actions. (See the "Exporting Images" section, later in this chapter, for the details on exporting multiple images from a single slice.)

You can easily make a Web page with a single image, but that page may take too long to download because the image file is so large. That's where slices come in. Although you don't have a minimum or maximum number of slices that you can make on a page, you don't want to make too many slices. Having many teeny-weeny images can give you a page that loads *too* gradually. You need to find a good balance.

Every image tag in a Web page's HTML code results in a call to the Web site's host server. The more images that you have on your page, the more requests for images the browser has to make, and the more images the server has to send. That process can feel like having a waiter bring you a salad one piece of lettuce at a time — with you having to request each piece!

Creating and Editing Slices

In Book III, Chapter 5, we cover the basics of how to make a slice, but here we give you some more details. So you don't have to flip back to the previous chapter, here's a reminder on how to make a slice in your Fireworks PNG file:

1. **Select the Slice tool from the Web section of the Tools panel.**
2. **Click and drag diagonally on the canvas to make a rectangle.**

   The slice shows up as a green overlay on the canvas.

The default appearance of the slice is as a bright-green, semitransparent overlay. You can change the default color of slices in the Preferences settings if you need to make the underlying images easier to see. You can also change the color of an individual slice in the Property inspector when you have the slice selected. Changing a slice color doesn't affect the underlying image in any way.

One handy feature of the Slice tool is its snap feature. If you have navigation buttons on the left side of your page, you may want the buttons all to be the same width to simplify your HTML. When you have a single slice made for your first button and you click and drag to make the slice for the second button, Fireworks snaps to the identical width when you have your cursor within a few pixels of it. Of course, you can also make sure they're the same width by typing a value into the width text field, or by copying and pasting the slice.

Naming a slice

When you name a slice, you're doing more than making it easy to identify in the Layers panel — you're also naming the image for export. For that reason, when you name a slice, you want to avoid using spaces or any special characters that are illegal in filenames (Windows filenames cannot contain the following characters: \ / : * ? " < > |).

To name or rename a slice, just follow these steps:

1. **Double-click the current name of the slice in the Layers panel.**

   A text field pops up, as you can see in Figure 6-2. By default, slices are named "Slice." If you don't see the slices, you may have to expand the Web Layer by clicking the triangle at the left.

2. **Type a new name for the slice.**
3. **Press Enter.**

When you select a slice, the Property inspector gives you access to the slice's name, dimensions, position on the page, and more. You can also change the name of the slice in the Property inspector rather than in the Layers panel.

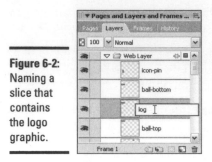

Figure 6-2: Naming a slice that contains the logo graphic.

Moving a slice

You may find that you need to move a slice. For example, if you move some elements in your design a few pixels one way or the other, the image underlying the slice may shift enough that you need to adjust the slice's position. You can choose between three basic ways of moving a slice:

- ✦ Move a slice by clicking and dragging the slice. (In most cases, you probably want to use this method.)
- ✦ Use the arrow keys to move a slice.
- ✦ Change the X and Y coordinates of the slice in the Property inspector.

If you overlap slices on the canvas, the overlapped area appears only in the image created from one of the slices — the one that appears higher in the Layers panel.

To move a slice using the click-and-drag method, just follow these steps:

1. **Click the slice on the canvas.**

   You can click anywhere on the slice except the corners and the center. Clicking a corner or the center of a slice gives you special options to add behaviors (see Book III, Chapter 7 for the lowdown on behaviors).

2. **Hold down the mouse button and drag the slice to its new location.**

If you want finer control when you move a slice, you can use the arrow keys to move a slice as follows:

1. **Select the slice by clicking it on the canvas or in the Layers panel.**
2. **Press the appropriate arrow key.**

   Each time you press an arrow key, the slice moves by one pixel. If you hold down the Shift key and then press an arrow key, the slice moves by ten pixels.

Sometimes when you want to line something up along one axis, you can most easily line it up by selecting slices and typing the new X or Y coordinates for each slice. The top-left corner of the canvas always has the coordinates (0, 0), and coordinates are expressed in the form (X, Y), with X representing the horizontal coordinate and Y representing the vertical coordinate. If your design is 800 pixels wide and 600 pixels high, the bottom-right corner has the coordinates (800, 600).

A slice's coordinates denote the position of its top-left corner on the canvas.

To move a slice when you know the exact pixel coordinates to which you want to move it, follow these steps:

1. **Select the slice by clicking it on the canvas or in the Layers panel.**

   The Property inspector changes to give you access to slice parameters.

2. **If you want to change the slice's horizontal position, type a numerical value in the Property inspector text field labeled X: and press Enter.**

   Your slice shifts left if you type in a lower number; the slice shifts right if you type in a higher number.

3. **If you want to change the slice's vertical position, type a numerical value in the Property inspector text field labeled Y: and press Enter.**

   Your slice shifts up if you type in a lower number; the slice shifts down if you type in a higher number.

Resizing a slice

Sometimes after you make a slice, you decide that you need to resize the underlying image. After you resize the image, you may want to resize the slice. You may also need to resize a slice if you draw the slice quickly and don't make it big enough. As with moving a slice, you can resize a slice by clicking and dragging or by typing new values.

To resize two dimensions of a slice simultaneously by using the click-and-drag method, follow these steps:

1. **Click a corner of the slice.**

   You have to click a handle at one of the corners to resize the slice. If you click anywhere inside the slice (except the exact center) and drag, you move the slice rather than resize it.

2. **Drag the handle on the corner of the slice to the new location that you want.**

If you want to change only the height, click and drag the top or bottom border of the slice. If you want to change only the width, click and drag the left or right border of the slice. When your cursor is over the border, it changes into the Resize cursor, two parallel lines with an arrow pointing outward from each line, as you can see in Figure 6-3.

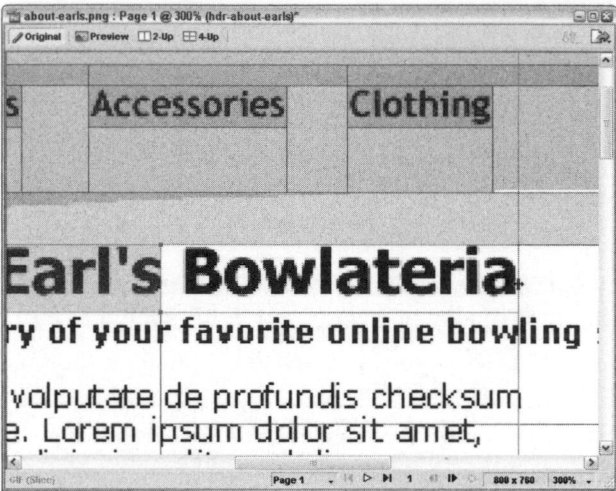

Figure 6-3: Dragging the right edge of a slice to make it wider.

When you're creating slices, their edges snap to edges of already created slices, so if you don't want that, you may find getting the edge of a slice where you want it difficult. You can zoom in until you reach a magnification at which you can resize the slice so that it doesn't snap to the edge of the other slice, or you can use the text fields in the Property inspector to change the selected slice's dimensions.

To resize a slice by typing new values, follow these steps:

1. **Select the slice by clicking it on the canvas or in the Layers panel.**

   The Property inspector changes to give you access to the slice's parameters.

2. **If you want to change the slice's width, type a new numerical value in the text field labeled W: and press Enter.**

   If you increase the width, you add pixels to the right side of the slice. If you decrease the width, you take pixels away from the right side of the slice.

3. **If you want to change the slice's height, type a new numerical value in the text field labeled H: and press Enter.**

   If you increase the height, you add pixels to the bottom of the slice. If you decrease the height, you take pixels away from the bottom of the slice.

Duplicating a slice

If you have a series of buttons, each of which you want to be the same width and height, you can make one slice and duplicate it as many times as you need. Of course, you also need to move each duplicated slice to overlay a different button and name each slice according to the button it overlays. To duplicate a slice, just follow these steps:

1. **Select the slice by clicking it on the canvas or in the Layers panel.**
2. **Choose Edit⇨Duplicate or press Ctrl+Alt+D (⌘+Opt+D on a Mac).**

   A duplicate slice appears on top of, but slightly offset from, the slice that you duplicated.

   If you clone the slice instead of duplicating it (choose Edit⇨Clone or press Ctrl+Shift+D), the new slice appears directly on top of the old one.

   You can also copy and paste a slice, though that's essentially the same as cloning, except that it takes an extra step!
3. **Move the slice to its proper location.**

   See the "Moving a slice" section, earlier in this chapter, for instructions.

Optimizing Your Images for the Web

To understand the process of optimization, you need to know about image compression. When you *compress* an image, you reduce its file size by reducing the amount of data in the file. The two main types of image compression are

- ✦ **Lossy:** Some data is discarded from the image to make the file smaller.
- ✦ **Lossless:** The data in the image is described in a more efficient way, which makes the file smaller.

The two main compression methods used to format images for the Web are

- ✦ **JPEG:** A lossy method, best used for photographs, gradients, and other complex images that have many colors.
- ✦ **GIF:** A generally lossless method, best used for images with large areas of flat color, such as company logos. GIF images can have transparent backgrounds.

Not sure which compression method you want to use for a particular slice? The Preview panes come in handy for this job. You can use a Preview pane any time that you have slices. They show you what the image looks like at your chosen compression setting (or settings). See the section, "Previewing Slices," later in this chapter, for the details.

You can deal with compression by making a setting when you first make the slice and making the fine adjustments later. It doesn't really matter, though. You can just leave each slice at the default setting until you're ready to export.

Working with the options in the Optimize panel

By default, the Optimize panel sits at the top right of the Fireworks window. You can't see it on-screen; choose Window➪Optimize or press F6 to open it. Figure 6-4 shows the Optimize panel as it appears when you expand it and select a slice.

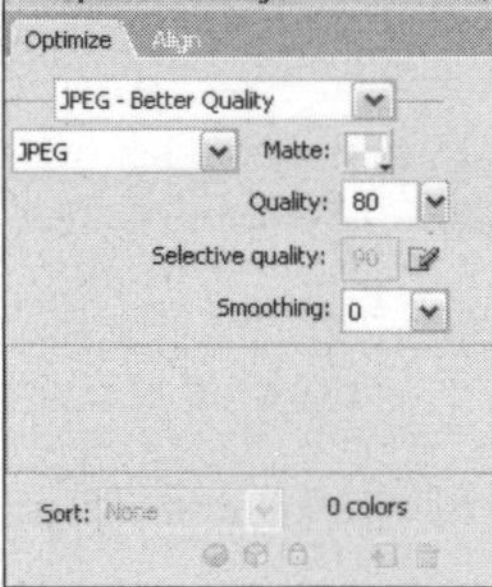

Figure 6-4: The Optimize panel with a default JPEG setting selected.

The top drop-down list displays a saved setting. A *saved setting* is a group of optimization options that includes the export file format and options appropriate to the selected export file format. (The upcoming sections "Making a JPEG" and "Making a GIF" tell you about the main export file formats — JPEG and GIF — and the options specific to each.)

Under the Saved Settings drop-down list, you can find the Export File Format drop-down list. If you use a default setting from the Saved Settings drop-down list, Fireworks automatically shows the file format in the lower list. Otherwise, you have to select the export file format. We look only at JPEGs and GIFs in this book because those file formats are by far the most common Web formats, but Fireworks can export other formats as well.

We discuss the options displayed in the Optimize panel in the next two sections, "Making a JPEG" and "Making a GIF." The Options menu icon (the bulleted list icon) at the top right of the Optimize panel provides access to the Options menu, which offers its own set of choices. The items in the Options menu vary, depending on the file type that you select in the Export File Format drop-down list.

When you have JPEG selected, the Options menu offers the following:

- **Save Settings:** This option lets you preserve your current compression settings as a preset, which you can then select from the Saved Settings drop-down list in the Optimize panel. You may find presets (custom or not) useful for *batch processing* images (automating the export of multiple images that use the same settings).
- **Delete Settings:** This option does what you probably expect — deletes your custom compression settings.

  This option deletes *all* the settings.
- **Optimize to Size:** This handy option lets you set a target file size for your slice. Fireworks then makes the appropriate compression settings to produce a file of your specified size.
- **Export Wizard:** The Export Wizard walks you through the steps of exporting an image with a series of dialog boxes.
- **Progressive JPEG:** If you have this option selected when you export a slice, your JPEG contains two versions of your image. The first is a low-resolution version of the image that loads relatively quickly to a browser. The second, which fills in over the first, is a higher-resolution version. Although you need a shorter amount of time for this type of image to become visible, you have a longer overall download time.

  If you need your JPEG to be large (in terms of width and height) *and* of high quality, consider exporting it as a progressive JPEG.

  Flash can't dynamically import progressive JPEGs, so if you want to link to a JPEG from an SWF file without embedding the graphic in the Flash movie, make sure you don't export the graphic as a progressive JPEG.
- **Sharpen JPEG Edges:** Select this option if you need to make image clarity a priority (if, for example, you have small text in the image). Clarity makes for larger file sizes.
- **Remove Unused Colors:** When this option is selected, as it is by default, Fireworks removes any color from the image's palette that the image doesn't use. Smaller palettes mean smaller file sizes.

- **Show Swatch Feedback, Load Palette, Save Palette:** These options apply to 8-bit graphics (including GIFs; JPEGs are a 24-bit format). Custom palettes are sets of colors to which you can limit images. See the Fireworks Help files or online resources for further details.
- **Help, Group Optimize With, Close Panel Group:** These options don't relate only to JPEGs. See Book III, Chapter 1 for more information about general panel options.

When you have GIF selected from the Export File Format drop-down list, the Options menu makes some JPEG-specific options unavailable but offers the following GIF-specific (8-bit graphic specific) options:

- **Interlaced:** An interlaced GIF is similar to a progressive JPEG. A low-resolution version of the graphic loads first (and fast), and the image slowly transitions until it's at its maximum resolution. As with progressive JPEGs, the image loads faster initially, but the final version of the image doesn't load as quickly as it would if you hadn't interlaced it. (You can also export an interlaced PNG, which downloads in stages the way an interlaced GIF does but has the larger file size of an uncompressed image.)
- **Remove Unused Colors:** When this option is selected, as it is by default, Fireworks removes any color from the image's palette that the image doesn't use. Smaller palettes mean smaller file sizes.

For information about the default GIF settings, see the section "Making a GIF," later in this chapter.

Under the Optimize panel name, you can find the Saved Settings drop-down list, which offers seven default settings (two for JPEGs and five for GIFs). You can read about the GIF default settings in "Using the default GIF settings," later in this chapter. You can choose between two default settings for JPEGs:

- **JPEG — Better Quality:** Makes a high-quality image, which results in a bigger file size and a longer download time.
- **JPEG — Smaller File:** Makes a small file, with a corresponding loss in image quality.

The rest of the parameters in the Optimize panel vary based on what export file format you choose. You can find out about them in the following sections, "Making a JPEG" and "Making a GIF."

Making a JPEG

Because JPEG is a lossy compression method, you want a fair amount of control over just how much data gets discarded from your image. The higher the amount of compression, the lower the image quality — but also the smaller the file size and consequently the faster the download time. Fireworks gives you a few options so that you can maximize image quality while minimizing file size. See "Previewing Slices" in this chapter for information on how to find out, before you export, what the image will look like and how big the file will be.

Using the default JPEG settings

You can easily use a default setting on a slice. Just follow these steps:

1. **Select the slice by clicking it on the canvas or in the Layers panel.**
2. **Select either JPEG — Better Quality or JPEG — Smaller File from the Settings drop-down list in the Optimize panel.**

   The Image Type, Quality, and Smoothing drop-down lists update according to the setting that you choose.

Using custom JPEG settings

To make or edit a custom JPEG setting, follow these steps:

1. **Select the slice by clicking it on the canvas or in the Layers panel.**
2. **Select JPEG from the Export File Format drop-down list in the Optimize panel.**
3. **Type a number in the Quality text field or use the slider (click the button next to the text field with the downward-pointing arrow to activate the slider) to set the image quality.**

   You can enter any whole number from 0 to 100, with 0 representing the lowest quality and 100 the highest.

   If you need a part of your image to be a higher quality than the rest, follow the following set of instructions, which describe using the Selective Quality option.
4. **Set the smoothing, if you need to.**

   Smoothing blurs the image a little, reducing its quality but also reducing its file size. You can type or select any whole number from 1 to 8, with 1 representing the least blurring and 8 representing the most blurring. If you don't want smoothing, leave it at its default setting, 0.

The Selective Quality option in the Optimize panel lets you compress different parts of your image by different amounts. In some cases, you can use Selective Quality as a great alternative to cutting a photograph into different slices set at different compression levels.

Here's how to use the Selective Quality option:

1. **Click the Original button at the top left of the canvas if you aren't already viewing the Original pane.**
2. **Use a Selection tool to select the area of the image that you want to compress differently than the rest of the image.**

   If the Web Layer is visible, you'll need to click the Eye icon to make the slice invisible in order to select an area.
3. **Choose Modify⇨Selective JPEG⇨Save Selection as JPEG Mask.**

   Your JPEG mask shows up as a pink overlay (which may look gray when it's on top of the slice's green overlay), and the Selective Quality field in the Optimize panel becomes active.
4. **Select JPEG from the drop-down list in the Optimize panel, if it's not already selected.**
5. **Click the Selective Quality button (the pencil and paper) in the Optimize panel.**

   The Selective JPEG Settings dialog box, shown in Figure 6-5, appears.

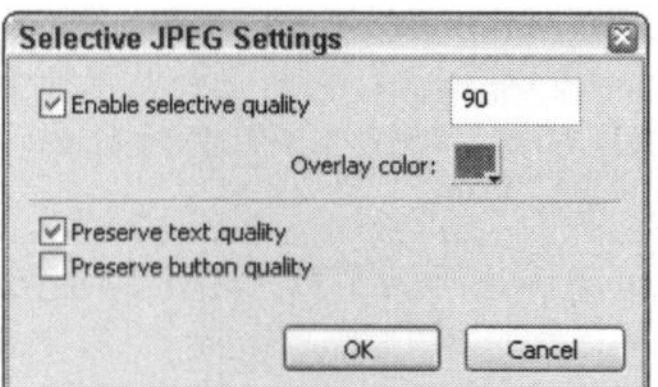

Figure 6-5: The Selective JPEG Settings dialog box offers a few simple options.

6. **Make sure that the Enable Selective Quality check box is selected in the Selective JPEG Settings dialog box (it's selected by default).**
7. **Type a number from 0 to 100 in the text field.**

   Zero represents the lowest quality; 100 represents the highest quality. Typically, the number you input in the Selective Quality text field is higher than the number in the main JPEG Quality text field (see the set of steps that precedes this set).
8. **Change the overlay color if you don't like the default overlay color.**

   The overlay color doesn't affect the exported image, only how the PNG file appears on-screen when you view it in Fireworks.

9. **Select the Preserve Text Quality check box if you want to preserve the quality of any text within your selection, regardless of the overall compression settings.**

   You can use this handy shortcut with or without a JPEG mask.

10. **Select the Preserve Button Quality check box if you want to preserve the quality of any buttons within your selection, regardless of the overall compression settings.**

11. **Click OK or press Enter.**

Making a GIF

Okay, when we say that the GIF compression method is generally lossless, we mean this: You can make lossless GIFs, but you can also make lossy GIFs if you need to. GIFs compress image data in a couple of ways:

- **By keeping track of the data more efficiently:** GIFs group adjacent pixels of the same color in each row of the image, so the pixels can be described as a group rather than as individual pixels. The fewer colors that you have in each row, and the more pixels of the same color that are together in a line, the better GIF compression works.
- **By limiting the number of colors in an image:** You can create custom *palettes* (sets of colors) or use the specialized built-in palettes that Fireworks offers. If you compress your image with a palette that doesn't contain all the colors in the image, Fireworks substitutes colors from the palette, effectively reducing the number of colors in the GIF, as compared to the source image.

  Sometimes you can simulate the appearance of the lost color by dithering two colors from the palette. You can find out more about dithering in the section on Web-safe colors in Book III, Chapter 2.

Using the default GIF settings

Fireworks offers several default Saved Settings for GIFs (available from the Saved Settings drop-down list at the top of the Optimize panel):

- **GIF Web 216:** This setting limits the colors in your GIF to the basic Web-safe palette.
- **GIF Web Snap 256:** This setting limits the number of colors in your GIF to 256 while snapping any colors close in appearance to Web-safe colors to the Web-safe palette.
- **GIF Web Snap 128:** This setting limits the colors in your GIF to 128 while snapping any colors close in appearance to Web-safe colors to the Web-safe palette.

- **GIF Adaptive 256:** This setting limits the colors in your GIF to the 256 most common in the GIF. Other colors are changed to the closest color in the palette. This setting gives you the highest-fidelity GIF version of your image.
- **Animated GIF Web Snap 128:** This setting is the same as GIF Web Snap 128 but is for animated GIFs.

Using custom GIF settings

To make a basic GIF that doesn't use a Fireworks default setting, just follow these steps:

1. **Select a slice by clicking it on the canvas or in the Layers panel.**
2. **Select GIF from the Export File Format drop-down list in the Optimize panel.**

   The Optimize panel (see Figure 6-6) displays the setting for a top navigation button. Transparency appears as a checkerboard pattern in the palette. And because you are creating a custom setting, the Saved Settings field is blank.

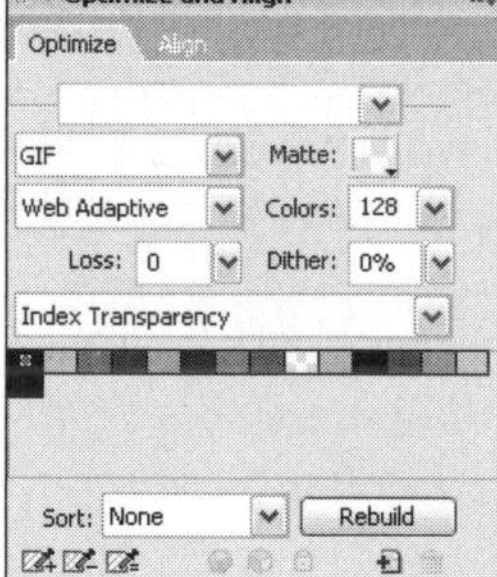

Figure 6-6: A button's settings in the Optimize panel.

3. **Set the compression mode by selecting one from the Indexed Palette drop-down list (right below the Export File Format drop-down list).**

   Palettes are sets of colors. For GIFs, the palettes may contain no more than 256 colors. For Web images, choose from the top four: Adaptive; Web Adaptive; Web 216; and Exact.

   For more information about these palettes, see the Fireworks Help files, which you can access via the Fireworks Help menu.

4. **Type a number in the Colors text field or use the drop-down list to set the number of colors in your palette, if you're not compressing by using the Web 216 or Exact settings.**

   The fewer colors that you have in your palette, the smaller the file size of your image. If you have fewer colors in the palette than in your image, however, Fireworks has to substitute colors, which deteriorates image quality. If your image has more than 256 colors, you may get better results using a JPEG setting.

5. **If you have more colors in your image than in your palette, and if you prefer dithering to straight one-for-one color substitutions, type a percent in the Dither text field or use the slider (click the button next to the text field with the downward-pointing arrow to activate the slider) to set a percentage from 1 to 99.**

   The more you dither, the fewer colors you need in your palette. Unfortunately, dithering can look pixelated up close and increases the file size.

Making a transparent GIF

To make a GIF with transparent areas, which allow the HTML page background color or background image to show through, follow these steps:

1. **Select a slice by clicking it on the canvas or in the Layers panel.**
2. **Select GIF from the Export File Format drop-down list in the Optimize panel, if GIF isn't already selected.**
3. **Select Index Transparency from the Transparency drop-down list.**

   The default is No Transparency. Even when you don't have a background in your PNG file, you still need to select Index Transparency to make a GIF with transparent pixels. Otherwise, your GIF will have a solid white background.

4. **Click the eyedropper button with the equal sign (=) to select a color in the palette or on the canvas that you want to make transparent.**

   The three transparency eyedropper buttons are at the bottom left of the Optimize panel. The selected color becomes transparent in the palette in the Optimize panel. If you're viewing a Preview pane, the transparency appears (or disappears, we should say) on the canvas.

5. **Use the eyedropper with the plus sign (+) to select additional colors that you want to make transparent.**

   You can use the eyedropper with the minus sign (–) to restore opacity to a color that you make transparent, if you need to.

Previewing Slices

You can optimize your slices as you make them, or you can make all your slices first and then optimize them all at one time. Either way, if you're having trouble deciding on the best method or amount of compression to use on a slice, you can use one of the three Preview panes to help you make an informed decision. Just click one of the following buttons at the top of the canvas:

- **Preview:** This view shows a single version of your canvas, in which you can see what your slices will look like and how big their file sizes will be at your current compression settings. Click a slice to preview it.
- **2-Up:** This view puts two versions of your canvas side by side, so you can compare the original image with a compressed version of the image, or you can compare two compressed versions to each other. Click a slice on either side to preview it on both sides.
- **4-Up:** This view divides the work area into quadrants, so you can compare three compression settings simultaneously to the original image. Click a slice in any quadrant to preview the settings in all quadrants.

In the Preview panes, slices that aren't currently selected look slightly pale, as though you're looking at them through a fogged-up window. Selected slices look as they will when you export them, given their current settings (including transparencies, which appear as checkerboards), as you can see in Figure 6-7.

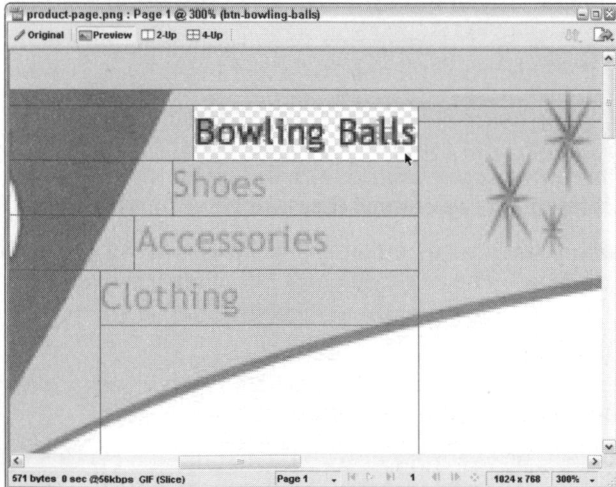

Figure 6-7: The checkerboard behind the Bowling Balls button indicates that the slice's background is transparent.

The Preview pane

You can select the Preview pane by clicking the Preview button at the top left of the image's window, right above the canvas.

The Preview pane previews more than just the appearance of your image; it also shows you the image's projected file size *and* the amount of time it takes for a file that size to download at a particular download speed. (The default is 56 Kbps, or the approximate speed of a dial-up modem.)

In Figure 6-7, you can see the file size, export file format, and download time stats at the bottom left, below the canvas. Because a 56 Kbps modem can download at a rate of 5K per second, and this image is a little over 0.5K, the download time shows as 0 sec (less than 1 second).

When you change the settings in the Optimize panel, the size and download time information at the bottom of the Preview pane update automatically. The Optimize panel works the same way, whether you're looking at a Preview pane or the default Original pane.

The 2-Up view

You can select the 2-Up view simply by clicking the 2-Up button at the top left of the image's window, above the canvas.

The 2-Up view sets two versions of the canvas side by side. At the bottom of each pane, you can find an indicator of which view is in the pane and some of its vital statistics. In Figure 6-8, the pane on the right shows what the image would look like as a JPEG with the settings as shown at the bottom of the pane, and the pane on the left shows what the image would look like if exported as a GIF with the settings as shown at the bottom of the pane.

You can click in either pane to select the slice and then adjust its settings in the Optimize panel. You can set the magnification of both panes several ways:

- You can use the Magnifying tool in the View section of the Tools panel.
- You can choose Zoom In, Zoom Out, or a preset Magnification setting from the View menu.
- You can select a zoom setting from the drop-down list at the bottom right of the window.

To toggle between an optimized setting and the original image, click the indented button at the left just below the canvas. A pop-up menu allows you to select Original (No Preview) or Export Preview.

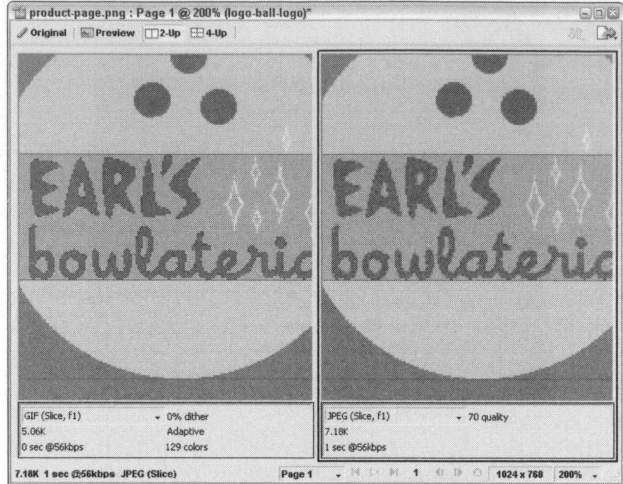

Figure 6-8: Comparing two possible compression settings side by side in the 2-Up view.

You can use the Hand tool from the View section of the Tools panel to move the canvas (select the Hand tool and then click and drag on the canvas) or just hold down the spacebar while you click and drag (whatever tool you're using becomes the Hand tool automatically). When you move the canvas in one pane, the canvas also moves in the other pane.

To select a different slice than the one currently selected, click the Pointer tool from the Tools panel and then click a slice in either pane or in the Layers panel. The slice becomes active in both panes simultaneously.

The 4-Up view

You can select the 4-Up view by clicking the 4-Up button at the top left above the canvas. When you first open the 4-Up view, the top-left quadrant displays the Original view, and the other three panes have identical compression settings. To change the settings in one pane, click in the pane to select it and then change its settings in the Optimize panel. In fact, you use the concept, properties, and processes of the 4-Up view just as you use those of the 2-Up view; you just get two extra panes.

Figure 6-9 shows the 4-Up view. Comparing the three compression settings, it seems that the one that best balances visual quality with file size is the GIF pane at the bottom right.

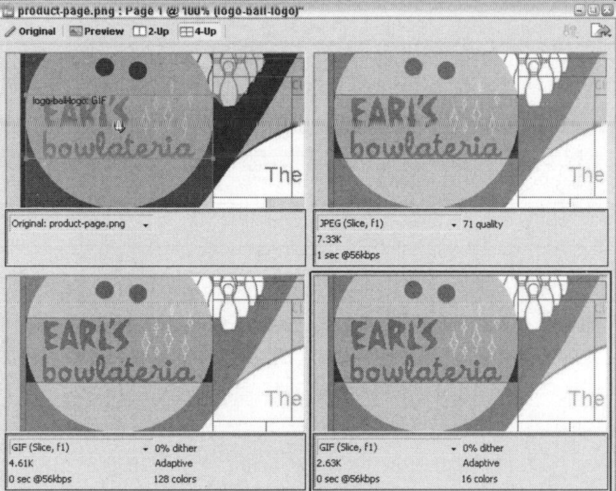

Figure 6-9: Comparing three possible compression settings using the 4-Up view.

Relating Hotspots and Slices

Slices can only be rectangular, which works fine if you have rectangular buttons. But what if you want to create nonrectangular HTML links to other Web pages? You have two choices:

- **Use the Polygon Slice tool to make a polygonal slice.** This choice works best if the area that you want to use as a hyperlink is fairly isolated from other slices. See Book III, Chapter 5 for details on the Polygon Slice tool.
- **Use a Hotspot tool to draw hotspots on an image.** Fireworks creates the underlying image, plus an image map. An *image map* is some HTML code representing coordinates for hyperlinked polygonal hotspots. Hotspots are areas on an image that you code to respond to user actions.

Typically, the hotspots are hyperlinked to Web pages. In Figure 6-10, the bowling ball can be linked to a page about bowling balls, and the pin can be linked to a page with a list of bowling alleys. Don't use hotspots more than you need to so that you don't add too much code to your HTML or tax the user's processor with too many instructions.

If you're not familiar with Web page coding, don't worry. You don't need to know all the ins and outs of HTML to make an image map — Fireworks takes care of that for you. You just have to create hotspots in the shapes that you want and export HTML with your images. See Book III, Chapter 7 for details on exporting HTML.

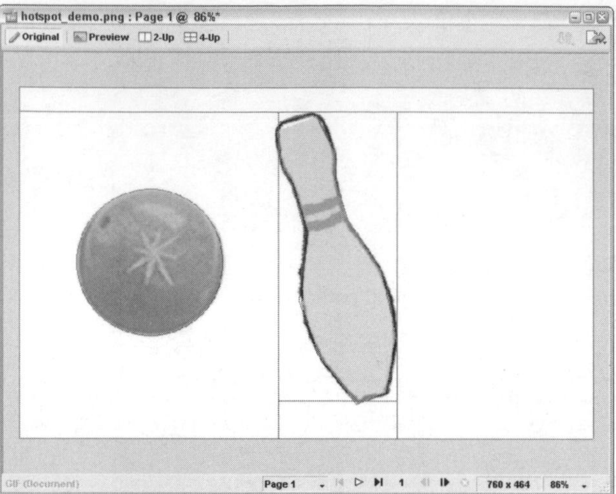

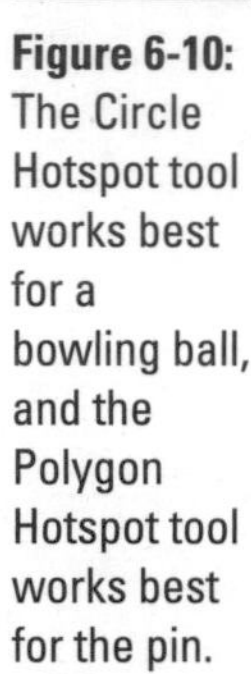

Figure 6-10: The Circle Hotspot tool works best for a bowling ball, and the Polygon Hotspot tool works best for the pin.

Exporting Images

You can export images in two ways: one by one or all at one time. You can have Fireworks generate HTML at the same time that you export your images, or you can export the images only and write the code yourself in Dreamweaver (Book I describes how to use Dreamweaver). (Fireworks generates a less efficient code than code that you write in Dreamweaver, and you may find editing the Fireworks code more difficult than in Dreamweaver.)

Exporting a single image

To export a single image, follow these steps:

1. **Right-click a slice and select Export Selected Slice from the contextual menu.**

   An Export dialog box appears, with default values set for exporting a single image.

2. **Navigate to the folder into which you want to put your image.**
3. **Leave the Save as Type setting at the default, Images Only.**
4. **If you need to, rename the image.**

   If you want the filename to be the same as the slice name, you don't need to rename the image.

5. **Leave the Slices setting at the default, Export Slices.**
6. **Leave the Selected Slices Only and Current Frame Only check boxes selected.**
7. **Click the Save button.**

Exporting multiple image slices

To export all the image slices in a PNG file simultaneously, if you plan to write the HTML yourself, follow these steps:

1. **Choose File⇨Export or press Ctrl+Shift+R.**

   The Export dialog box appears, with default values set for exporting multiple images and HTML, as shown in Figure 6-11.

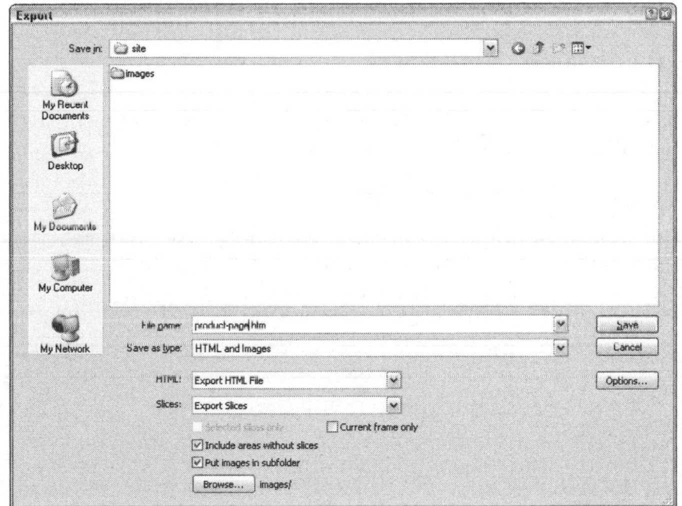

Figure 6-11: The Export dialog box set to export HTML and images.

2. **Select Images Only from the Save as Type drop-down list.**

   The options below the Save as Type drop-down list update to reflect your selection.
3. **Leave the Slices setting at the default, Export Slices.**
4. **Deselect the Include Areas without Slices check box if you need only the sliced images to build your HMTL page.**

5. **If you have rollover images that you want to export, deselect the Current Frame Only check box if it's selected.**

   Remember, it takes multiple frames to make rollover images.

6. **Click the Save button.**

Exporting an animated GIF

When you save the file as an animated GIF, you also get a Flash SWF option beyond the default Images Only option in the Save as Type drop-down list. Although that option does let you make some additional settings, if you want the ultimate format of the animation to be an SWF file rather than a GIF file, you probably want to open the PNG file in Flash and export from there. Why? Because Flash offers more powerful authoring and editing tools, many more export parameters than Fireworks, and ActionScript for adding complex interactivity to your animation.

To export an animation as an animated GIF (not a Flash SWF movie), follow these simple steps:

1. **Select Animated GIF in the Optimize panel's Export File Format drop-down list.**
2. **Choose File➪Export or press Ctrl+Shift+R.**

   The Export dialog box appears, with default values set for exporting animated GIFs.

3. **Navigate to the folder into which you want the GIF to go.**
4. **Leave the default Images Only setting in the Save as Type drop-down list.**
5. **Click Save.**

You can do much more with the Export function than we cover in this section. For information on exporting HTML and other export options, see the section about advanced export functions in Book III, Chapter 7.

Chapter 7: Advanced Fireworks CS3 Tools

In This Chapter

- **Applying styles**
- **Working with symbols**
- **Using advanced export options**
- **Creating image maps and advanced button rollovers**
- **Making your pages interactive with behaviors**
- **Creating a slideshow**

Fireworks CS3, like all the applications in the Adobe CS3 suite, is deep and rich. In this chapter, we introduce some of the application's more advanced capabilities, such as the following:

- **Adding pizzazz to your design by applying visual styles to objects (including text blocks).** You can create your own styles or use one of the vast array that comes with Fireworks.
- **Increasing productivity by including reusable symbols in your designs.** Symbols are much more than just pictures; they can contain multiple frames (animation symbols) and multiple frames plus behaviors (button symbols).
- **Exporting HTML code with JavaScript/CSS.** *JavaScript* is a coding language that you can use to make elements of your Web page change based on user feedback, among other things; *CSS,* which stands for Cascading Style Sheets, offers a different method of coding pop-up menus or arranging graphics and text on a Web page. If you add behaviors to your Fireworks PNG, you add either JavaScript or CSS to the HTML that Fireworks generates — you choose which type of code gets added when you export the HTML.
- **Creating image maps with hotspots.**
- **Setting up button behaviors that go beyond simple rollovers.** (See Book III, Chapter 5 for instructions on how to create simple button rollovers.)
- **Using the Image Swap behavior to make an image on your Web page change when the user rolls over a separate image.**

Adding Styles to Objects

Styles are your shortcuts to creating eye-catching designs. Typically, they combine various combinations of strokes, fills, and effects. You can make your own styles, edit the ones that come with Fireworks to create custom styles, or just apply the styles straight out of the box. We don't have space here to explore all the aspects of styles, but we can give you a big head start by showing you how to use them.

To apply a style to a bitmap or vector object, follow these steps:

1. **Select an object by clicking it on the canvas or in the Layers panel.**

   The object highlights on the canvas and in the Layers panel.

2. **If it isn't already open, open the Styles panel by pressing Shift+F11 (PC only) or clicking the Styles tab in the Assets panel.**

   All the available styles appear in a grid.

3. **Click a style in the Styles panel.**

   The object inherits the attributes of the style, as shown in Figure 7-1.

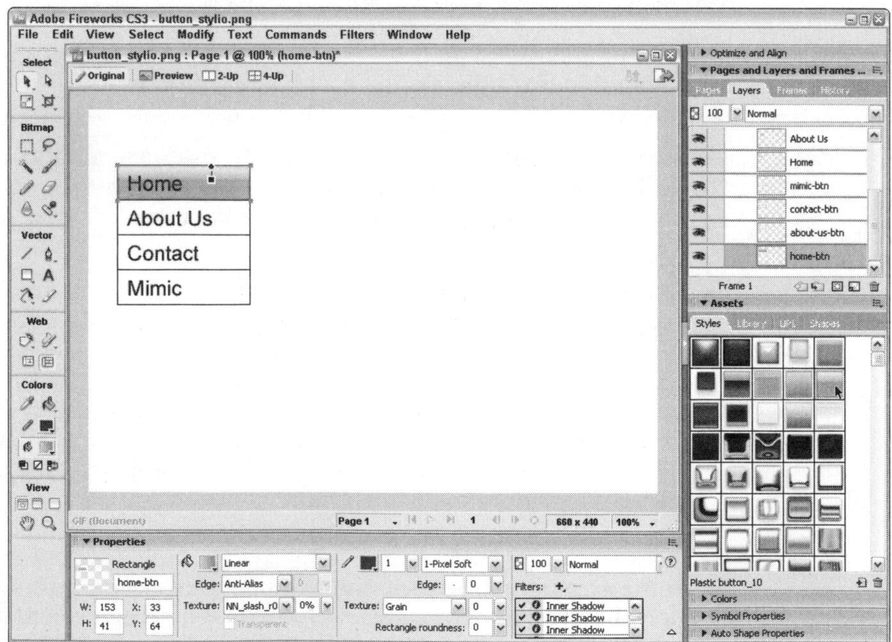

Figure 7-1: Style Plastic button_10 is applied to the Home button.

You can edit any of the properties of the styled object using the Properties panel. Just be aware that you will not be editing the underlying style. If you make edits you like and want to apply them to other objects in your design (or in future designs), make sure that the styled object is selected and select New Style from the Assets options menu. A New Style window appears, in which you can name the style and preserve whichever attributes you wish.

Using (And Reusing) Symbols

Symbols are reusable elements that can be stored centrally in a library and used as "instances" multiple times in a single document or in many documents. Any edits you make to a symbol will update all the instances of that symbol on the canvas. Fireworks has three types of symbols:

- **Graphic:** Bitmap or vector objects, which may have filters and effects applied
- **Animation:** Motion graphics with multiple frames
- **Button:** Graphics with button behaviors attached

Figure 7-2 shows all three button types in the Library panel. The selected 2-State Button is previewed at the top of the panel. Click the play button (the white triangle at the right of the preview window) to preview a button symbol's behavior or an animation symbol's motion.

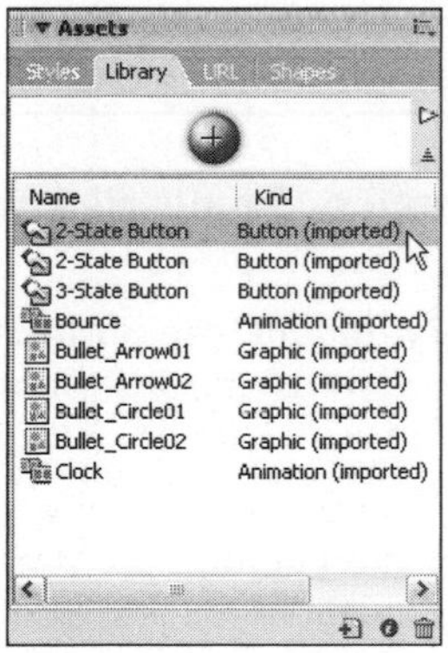

Figure 7-2: Selecting a 2-State Button in the Library panel.

Fireworks ships with many symbols, including buttons, animations, bullet and flow diagram graphics, and Flex component graphics. You can create, edit, and delete symbols, and you can import and export them as well. We don't have space to describe all the things you can do with symbols, but we get you started by showing you how to add an instance of a Fireworks CS3 prepackaged button symbol to your design.

To gain access to a premade symbol, you must import it into your library. To import a symbol, follow these steps:

1. **If the Library panel isn't already open, press F11 to open it, or click the Library tab in the Assets panel.**
2. **Select Import Symbols from the Assets panel Options menu.**

   The Open window appears. The Options menu is located at the top right of the Assets panel.
3. **Navigate to the folder containing the button symbols and double-click the symbol you want to import.**

   The Import Symbols window appears, with the selected symbol highlighted. If you want to see the symbol before you import it, single-click it and you'll see it in the Preview section of the Open window.
4. **Click Import.**

   The Import Symbols window disappears, and the symbol appears in the Library panel.

To add an instance of a button symbol to the canvas, follow these steps:

1. **If the Library panel isn't already open, press F11 (PC only) to open it, or click the Library tab in the Assets panel.**
2. **Click a 2-State Button symbol name in the Library panel and drag it to the canvas. Let go of the mouse button when the symbol is where you want it on the canvas.**

   The symbol appears on the canvas (and in the preview pane at the top of the Library panel).
3. **If you want to be able to resize the button, double-click the button symbol on the canvas to edit it.**

   The 2-State Button window appears. By default, the button graphic says "Button" on it. We're assuming that you want your button to say something different, such as "Home." If so, be sure to read "Editing a button symbol instance," later in this chapter.

   You can edit many of the properties of the symbol, but remember: When you edit the symbol, you change all associated instances of it on the canvas.
4. **Select the 9-Slice Scaling Guides Enable check box.**

   Dotted blue lines show where the 9-slice guides will go. See "Scaling with 9-slice," later in this chapter, for the lowdown on 9-slice scaling.

5. **Click Done.**

   The 2-State Button window closes. The button appears on the canvas, with slice, frame, and behavior settings automatically configured.

After you have the button symbol instance on the canvas, chances are you'll want to change the text on the button. To edit an instance of a symbol on the canvas, follow these easy steps:

1. **Double-click the button symbol on the canvas to edit it.**

   The 2-State Button window appears. By default, the button graphic says "Button" on it. We're assuming that you want your button to say something different, such as "Home." If so, be sure to read "Editing a button symbol instance," later in this chapter.

2. **Double-click the text on the button and type or paste new text.**

   The text behaves just as it would on the canvas (see Figure 7-3 in the following section).

3. **Click anywhere in the 2-State Button window to deselect the text.**

   A warning dialog box appears, asking whether you want to update the text in the other button states.

4. **To make the Down state of the button say the same thing as the Up (default) state, click Yes.**

   The dialog box closes and the button is updated. If, for some reason, you want the Down state of the button to say something different than the Up state, click No, click the Down tab, and edit the text as you did in Step 2.

5. **If you want to resize the button, select the 9-Slice Scaling Guides Enable check box.**

   Dotted blue lines show where the 9-slice guides will go. See "Scaling with 9-slice," later in this chapter, for the lowdown on 9-slice scaling.

6. **Click Done.**

   The 2-State Button window closes.

Editing a button symbol instance

You can edit a button symbol, and you may want to do it so that you can customize the button's look wherever it appears. But when you want to make several buttons from the same symbol, each of which has its own text, you need to edit each instance of the button on the canvas. The look of the button will remain consistent with the symbol, and each instance of the button will remain attached to the symbol (so that if you edit the symbol itself, all the instances will update). To edit a button symbol instance on the canvas, follow these steps:

1. **Click the button symbol instance on the canvas.**

   All the points, and the guidelines connecting them, appear in light blue, and the instance is highlighted in the Layers panel. The button instance's properties appear in the Properties panel. You may have to make the Web layer inactive in order to select the instance (to do so, click the eye icon at the left of the Web Layer in the Layers panel).

2. **Name the slice by entering text in the top-left text field in the Properties panel.**

   The text you enter will be used to name the exported image.

3. **Change the text on the button by entering what you want the button to say in the Text text field of the Properties panel and press Enter.**

   The button updates on the canvas.

4. **If you plan to export HTML from Fireworks, enter a URL in the Link text field and Alt text in the Alt text field.**

   Figure 7-3 shows how the Properties panel might look if you were planning to export HTML along with images.

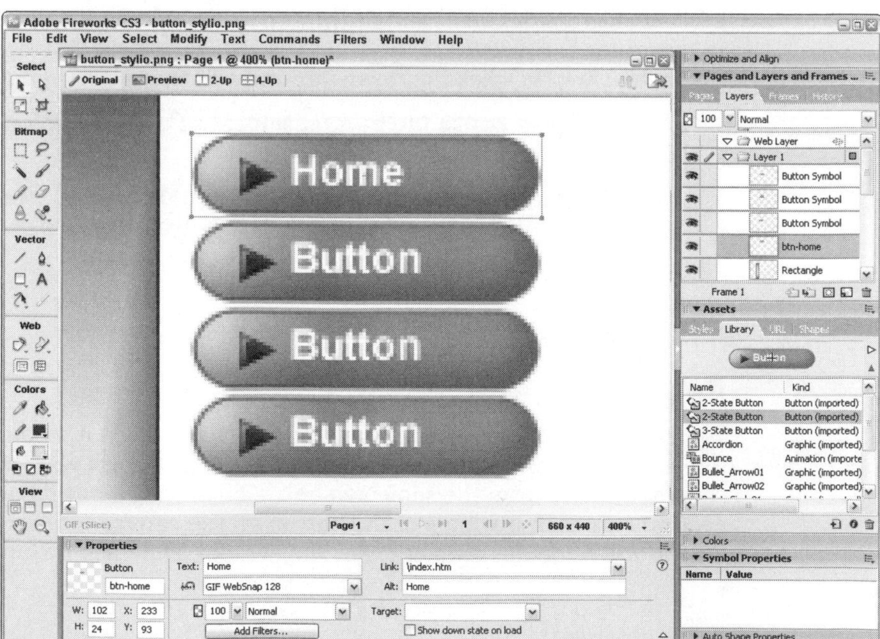

Figure 7-3: Using the Properties panel to edit a button instance.

Scaling with 9-slice

If you want to resize an object that has a style applied to it, or just has a gradient or filter effect such as inner glow or emboss, Fireworks CS3 offers you the option to scale the object using the new 9-slice method. The 9-slice feature allows you to scale the object up or down without distorting its geometry. For example, if your button has a gradient and you want to stretch the button but maintain the integrity of the gradient, you'll want to scale with 9-slice.

To scale a button using the 9-slice feature, follow these simple steps:

1. **Double-click the symbol in the library.**

   The Convert to Symbol dialog box appears. If you don't have the Library panel open, press Shift+F11 to open it (PC only).

2. **If the Enable 9-Slice Scaling Guides check box is not selected, click the check box to select it.**

   It is not selected by default, unless you selected it when you originally imported the symbol.

3. **Click the Edit button.**

   The Button Editor window appears, showing the button with the 9-slice guides, as shown in Figure 7-4.

Figure 7-4: Editing a 2-State Button symbol.

4. **Align the 9-slice guides to protect the areas of the button you don't want scaled.**

   The slice in the center, with the plus (+) sign in it, is the part that will get scaled.

5. **Click Done.**

   The Button Editor window disappears, and the first instance of the button on the canvas has the blue points and guidelines on it, along with a blue plus (+) sign in the middle.

6. **Choose Modify➪Transform➪Scale.**

   The points and guidelines turn black. You can also choose Free Transform (or press Ctrl+T).

7. **Click on a point and drag away from the center of the button object. Release the mouse button when the button has reached the size you want.**

   The button is scaled, but its edges have not been distorted, as shown in Figure 7-5. Hold down the Alt key (PC) or Option key (Mac) while dragging to resize equally from the center of the button.

Figure 7-5: 9-slice scaling leaves the button ends intact while stretching its middle.

Using Advanced Export Options

In Book III, Chapter 6, we describe how to export images, but not how to export HTML or other types of files. If you're designing a Web page and you have behaviors or hotspots in your Fireworks PNG file, you want to export HTML along with your images because the HTML and JavaScript or CSS code make hotspots and behaviors work in Web pages.

When you want to export any type of file from Fireworks, you first have to choose File⇨Export or press Ctrl+Shift+R to bring up the Export dialog box, which you can see in Figure 7-6. The Save as Type drop-down list in the Export dialog box offers access to an array of extra options:

✦ **HTML and Images:** Exports HTML (or other Web language) code, as well as images.

✦ **Images Only:** Exports images at your chosen optimization settings.

✦ **Dreamweaver Library (.lbi):** Exports Library items, as well as images. (*Library items* are snippets of HTML code that you can use in Dreamweaver to make site maintenance easier.)

✦ **CSS Layers (.htm):** Allows you to export layers, frames, or slices as Cascading Style Sheet layers, so Fireworks generates both images and CSS-based HTML code, placing each layer, frame, or slice in its own CSS layer (or *div*). (For information about working with CSS in Dreamweaver, see Book I, Chapter 5.)

✦ **Director (.htm):** Exports either layers or frames as images that you can import into Director for use in Shockwave movies. (Director is not part of the CS3 suite, so we don't cover it in this book.)

✦ **Layers to Files:** Exports each layer in the current frame as a separate image file, which you may find useful if you're planning to use the layers to build an animation in another application.

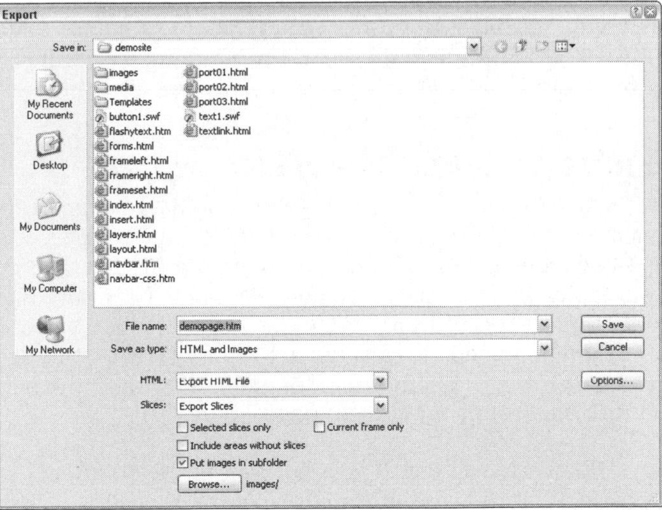

Figure 7-6: The Export dialog box offers different options, depending on which option you choose.

- **Frames to Files:** Exports each frame as a separate image file, which you may find useful if you're planning to use the frames to build an animation in another application.
- **Lotus Domino Designer:** Exports either the top four layers, the top four frames, or the first four frames of each slice as separate files. Domino is an IBM Web-based collaboration tool.

- **MXML and Images:** Exports code and images for building Rich Internet Applications using Adobe Flex.

Using the Save As command offers you additional formats not available through the Export command, including the following:

- **Flash SWF:** Exports an SWF file, which you can view via the Flash browser plug-in and import into Flash. Flash is a much more flexible authoring tool for SWFs. See Book III for a wealth of information about Flash.
- **Illustrator 8:** Exports either the current frame, leaving layers intact, or exports a document in which frames are converted to layers. Book IV covers Illustrator.
- **Photoshop PSD:** Exports the PNG as a layered Photoshop document (PSD). You can choose to maintain editability over text layers and effects, which may result in variations in appearance between the two files, or to maintain the appearance by giving up editability over text and effects. Remember, your PNG's Web Layer doesn't get exported. See Book II for much more about Photoshop.

Although you may want to export any of these types of files, we focus on the HTML and Images option in the following sections. You will probably use this option the most.

Readying your PNG for HTML export

If you're using Fireworks to generate your HTML code, you probably have buttons in your design that you want linked to other pages on your site. Or perhaps you have one or more hotspots in your PNG and you want those hotspots to link to other pages on your Web site. Naturally, Fireworks makes it easy for you to add URLs to create the hyperlinks for buttons and hotspots. You just need to plan ahead: Prepare HTML document names (`about-us.htm` or `contact.htm`, for example) for all the pages to which you want to link from your current page.

To add a URL to an existing slice or hotspot in the document's Web layer (see Book III, Chapter 6 for information on creating slices), just follow these steps:

1. **Select the slice or hotspot by clicking it on the canvas or in the Layers panel (if you need to, open the Layers panel by pressing F2; you also can expand the panel by clicking the panel name).**

   The Property inspector is updated to show information about the selected slice or hotspot.

2. **Click in the Link text field in the Property inspector.**

   If you have added links to other slices or other hotspots, those links appear as drop-down list choices in the Link text field.

3. **Type a URL.**

   If you're linking to a page on your own site and you have all your HTML pages in the same folder, simply type the name of the HTML document (for example, index.htm or help.htm). You have to type the name of the document exactly as it appears. (If you type `index.htm` but your home page is actually `index.html`, the link doesn't work.)

   If you're linking to a page not on your site, include the complete URL (such as `http://catalog.dummies.com/booksanddownloads.asp`).

4. **Press Enter or click anywhere on the canvas.**

Exporting HTML with your images

If you want, you can tell Fireworks to generate the HTML along with the optimized images for your Web page and make that the end of it. If you plan to make any changes to the HTML in Dreamweaver or another HTML editor, however, you can set some options to control the way Fireworks sets up tables in the HTML it generates, which can make your Web page maintenance a little easier down the line.

To export HTML and images that you plan not to update, or that you plan to update in Fireworks rather than Dreamweaver, follow these steps:

1. **Set up a folder structure for your Web site on your hard drive.**

   You need a master folder that holds every file for your site. Inside the master folder, you may want to put an images folder, which can hold all your images, keeping them separate from the HTML documents. You can have your HTML documents and image files all mixed together in the master folder, but if you have many images, you can find and work with all the files much more easily if you create a separate folder for the images.

2. **Check to make sure that all the right layers are visible (or not visible) in your PNG file.**

   Remember, the exported image files include only visible layers and objects. If you don't see it on-screen now, it won't be exported. See Book III, Chapter 5 for details on making layers visible/invisible.

3. **In Fireworks, choose File⇨Export or press Ctrl+Shift+R.**

   The Export dialog box appears.

4. **Navigate to the Web site's master folder.**

   If you haven't created a master folder for your Web site, you can create a folder by clicking the standard Windows Create New Folder icon to the right of the Save In drop-down list.

5. **Type a name for your page in the File Name text field if the default isn't what you want to name your HTML page.**

   The default HTML file extension in the Adobe CS3 suite is `.htm`, but you can also use `.html`.

6. **Select HTML and Images from the Save as Type drop-down list.**

   The options below this drop-down list update to reflect your choice.

7. **Select Export HTML File from the HTML drop-down list.**

   If you select Copy to Clipboard rather than Export HTML File, Fireworks exports the code to a temporary location (your computer's Clipboard), from which you can paste the code into an existing document. If you select Copy to Clipboard, you can simply open any type of text document and press Ctrl+V to paste the HTML into the file.

   Export HTML File has myriad options available. See the following section, "Setting the export HTML file options," for more information.

8. **Select Export Slices from the Slices drop-down list.**

   If you haven't made slices in your PNG file but you have placed guides in the file, you can select the Slice Along Guides option, and Fireworks cuts up your design based on the guides.

9. **Leave the Current Frame Only check box deselected unless you have multiple frames in your document, at least one of which you do not want to export.**

10. **Leave the Include Areas without Slices option selected unless you have a plan to deal with areas you didn't slice.**

    If you're using a background image, for example, or you want to use transparent spacer GIFs, you may not need images from the nonsliced areas — if you have any.

11. **Select the Put Images in Subfolder check box if you want to export your images to a folder inside your site's master folder.**

    You need to decide when you export where you want your images to live, because your HTML document will include links to the images. You express the links as pathnames to the images relative to the location of the HTML document.

12. **Click the Save button.**

    The HTML file is saved to your site's master folder, and the images are saved either to that same folder or to a folder within that folder, as you specify in Step 11.

Setting the export HTML file options

When you click the Options button in the Export dialog box, the HTML Setup dialog box opens, as you can see in Figure 7-7. In the HTML Setup dialog box, you can view and modify the default settings that determine the structure of the exported HTML document.

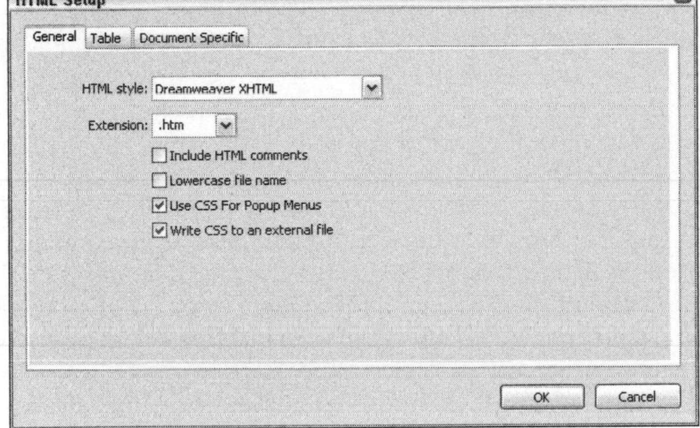

Figure 7-7: The HTML Setup dialog box opens when you click Options in the Export dialog box.

You can access settings on the three tabs in the HTML Setup dialog box:

- ✦ **General:** Lets you change the default HTML style (different HTML editors have different styles of writing and displaying the code) and file extension. With Fireworks CS3, the new default is Dreamweaver XHTML (eXtensible HyperText Markup Language, the latest version of HTML).

  You can also choose whether you want Fireworks to put comments in the HTML document. (*Comments* are notes in the HTML source code that typically contain information about the structure of the code, such as "<!— –Left navigation starts here —>." The browser doesn't display comments. If you want to be able to launch and edit entire tables from Dreamweaver, be sure that you select the Include HTML Comments check box.) Select the Lowercase File Name check box if you want to make the names of the HTML file and all exported images all lowercase, even if you name images with uppercase and lowercase letters in your PNG. Select the Use CSS For Popup Menus check box if you want the pop-up menus in your file to be exported as CSS code rather than JavaScript. If you select this check box, an additional option becomes available. Select the Write CSS to an External File check box if you want to keep the CSS code in a separate file from the HTML.

- **Table:** Lets you customize the way Fireworks sets up tables. In the default, Fireworks puts a 1-pixel-high spacer row at the top and a 1-pixel-wide spacer column on the right to hold the design in place. You can choose to have Fireworks nest tables (put one table inside another) instead. You can also tell Fireworks to re-create parts of your design that lack objects as cells with background-transparent spacer GIFs in the HTML, to leave the cell empty, or to put in a nonbreaking space. A *spacer GIF* is a one-pixel-by-one-pixel transparent image that you can set to any height and width in your HTML to hold open an otherwise empty table cell.
- **Document Specific:** Lets you customize image naming based on table structure, image function, or both. For example, for slices with multiple frames, Fireworks appends `_f2`, `_f3`, and so on, to the filename. If the images from Frame 2 of your PNG are buttons in their rollover state, you may want to have Fireworks append `-o` or `-over` to the filename. If you want all images to have identical Alt tags, enter the desired word or phrase in the Default ALT Tag text field (see Book I, Chapter 2 for details on Alt tags). If your PNG file contains a nav bar image (see the "Creating advanced button rollovers" section, later in this chapter), you can select the Export Multiple Nav Bar HTML Files check box if you want Fireworks to generate separate HTML files for each button in the navigation bar. The Include Areas without Slice Objects check box is selected by default; leave it selected to get the most consistent results. Select the UTF-8 Encoding check box if you want to use multiple character sets (Hebrew and English, for example) in your HTML.

The Set Defaults button on the Document Specific tab lets you save any new settings you make, which you may find particularly useful if you like to use a specific naming convention for button rollovers and on states. When you adjust the Document Specific settings to your liking and click the Set Defaults button, your adjusted settings become the new default Document Specific settings.

Setting Up Image Maps and Button Rollovers

Fireworks writes image maps and JavaScript into the HTML code you export, provided that you have hotspots (which Fireworks uses to make image maps) or behaviors (which Fireworks uses to make JavaScript) in your PNG. The following sections outline how to set up image maps (which let you make several distinct hyperlinks from a single image) and complex button behaviors (which make the button image change based on a user action, such as rolling the mouse over the image or clicking the image).

Fireworks can show slices and hotspots overlapping, but you don't want to overlap them. Fireworks doesn't export any part of a slice that's under another slice. (The slice on top includes the overlapped area; the slice underneath is cut off.) Likewise, whichever hotspot is on top in the Layers panel overrides the hotspot underneath.

Creating image maps with hotspots

The three hotspot tools let you create hotspots shaped like rectangles, circles, or polygons. You can also use the Polygon Slice tool to create a hotspot, although as a rule, you should use the hotspot tools unless you're making a single, isolated hotspot. (For more information on the Polygon Slice tool, see Book III, Chapter 6.)

To create a circular or rectangular hotspot using a hotspot tool, just follow these steps:

1. **Select a hotspot tool from the Web section of the Tools panel.**

   Click and hold on the Rectangle Hotspot tool to access the pop-up menu containing the Circle Hotspot tool, if you need to.

2. **Click and drag over the area you want to make a hotspot.**
3. **Type a URL in the Link text field in the Property inspector and press Enter.**

   The URL should be an HTML document name (`about-us.htm`, for example) or pathname (`/aboutus/staff.htm`, for example) for the page you want the hotspot to link to. You can add URLs as you make the hotspots, or you can create all your hotspots and then select each one and add a URL in the Property inspector.

4. **Make as many more hotspots as you need by repeating Steps 1 through 3.**

When you create hotspots using the Polygon Slice tool, you're actually making rectangular images with linked areas inside. As a result, Fireworks makes a separate image map for each slice. That approach works fine if you're making only one polygonal slice, but if you're making several adjacent hotspots, you may want to use the Polygon Hotspot tool or make your image map in Dreamweaver. (See Book III, Chapter 6 for information about how to use the Polygon Slice tool, and Book I, Chapter 6 for information on creating hotspots using Dreamweaver.)

You only have to do a little more to make a polygonal hotspot rather than a rectangular or circular hotspot. To make a polygonal hotspot, just follow these steps:

1. **Select the Polygon Hotspot tool from the Web section of the Tools panel.**

   Click and hold on the Rectangle Hotspot tool to access the pop-up menu containing the Polygon Hotspot tool.

2. **Click the canvas to establish the first point of your polygon.**
3. **Click a second point.**

   Fireworks draws a line connecting the points.

4. **Continue to click until you have drawn the shape that you want.**

   You don't need to click again on the first point to close the shape. You may want to avoid making hotspots that have more than six or seven points, because the more points that you make, the more code you need to reproduce your hotspot as an image map. The polygonal hotspot for the bowling pin in Figure 7-8 sacrifices perfect coverage of the pin to make a simpler shape, which means less code.

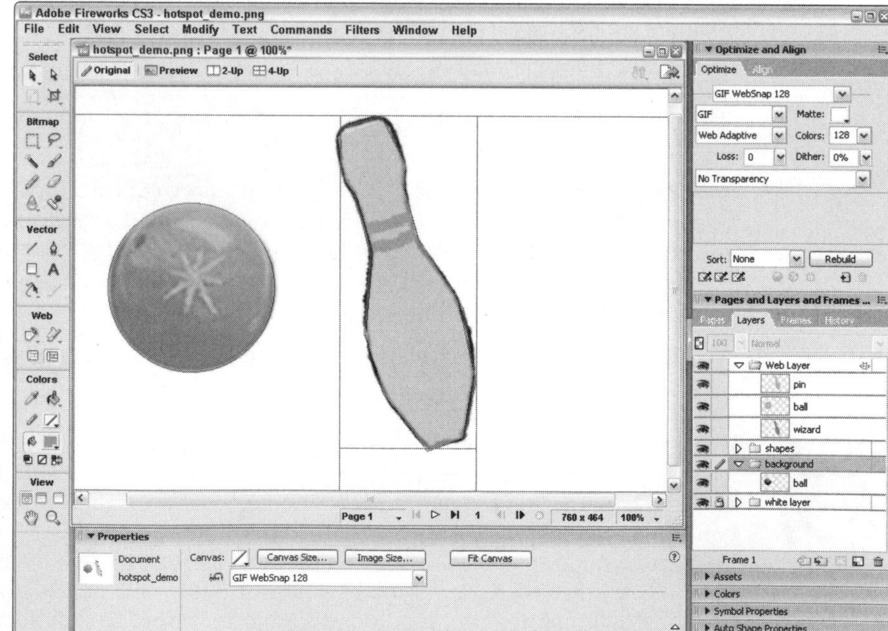

Figure 7-8: The Circle Hotspot tool covers the bowling ball; the Polygon Hotspot tool works best for the pin.

5. **Type a URL in the Link text field in the Property inspector and press Enter.**

   The URL should be an HTML document name (`aboutus.htm`, for example) or pathname (`/aboutus/staff.htm`, for example) for the page you want the hotspot to link to. You can add URLs as you make the hotspots, or you can create all of your hotspots and then select each one and add a URL in the Property inspector.

6. **Click the Polygon Hotspot tool and then deselect the last hotspot that you made by pressing Ctrl+D or choosing Select⇨Deselect.**

   Deselecting ensures that you don't inadvertently add an extra point to your Polygon hotspot.

When it comes time to export your images, you need to export HTML as well as images in order to get the image map that Fireworks makes from your hotspots. See the "Exporting HTML with your images" section, earlier in this chapter, for more details.

Dreamweaver has its own tool for creating hotspots and image maps. You can also use that tool to edit hotspots and image maps generated by Fireworks. See Book I, Chapter 6 for more details.

Creating advanced button rollovers

In Book III, Chapter 5, we discuss how to use frames in conjunction with text and drawing tools to make the images (one per frame for each button) for a simple button rollover. If you plan to use Dreamweaver to generate the rollover code, that chapter provides all the information you need.

If you want to export the rollover code for a 2-State Button (normal and rollover/highlight) from Fireworks, you need to add a behavior to the slice by taking these steps:

1. **Right-click the slice for which you want to create rollover code, or select the slice and click the behavior handle (the round icon) in the center of the selected slice.**

   A contextual menu appears.

2. **Choose Add Simple Rollover.**

You can also add rollover behavior to a button by using the Behavior panel, as follows:

1. **If the Behavior panel is not currently open, choose Window⇨Behaviors or press Shift+F3.**

2. **Click the Add Behavior (+) button at the top left of the Behaviors panel.**

   A menu appears.

3. **Choose Simple Rollover from the menu.**

You have set up a behavior that swaps the image in Frame 1 with the image in Frame 2 when a user rolls a cursor over the button on your Web page. The behavior also swaps the image back when the user moves the cursor off the button.

If you want to check out your rollover in action without building your Web page, click the Preview button at the top of the canvas and move your cursor over the slice.

Your button can have up to four states. Fireworks uses the image in Frame 1 for the normal, default state; Frame 2 for the Rollover state; Frame 3 for the Down state; and Frame 4 for the Over While Down state. If you want to include a Down state for your button, and you have a third frame in your PNG with the image for an additional button state, follow the preceding steps to add a Rollover state and then do the following:

1. **Click the Add Behavior button at the top left of the Behaviors panel.**

   A menu appears.

2. **Choose Set Nav Bar Image from the menu.**

   The Set Nav Bar Image dialog box appears.

3. **Click OK.**

   Now, when a user clicks the button in your exported HTML, the button changes from the rollover state to the down state.

   Figure 7-9 shows what the Behaviors panel looks like after you add the Simple Rollover and Set Nav Bar Image behaviors. You can use the add behavior (+) button to add a behavior and use the remove behavior (–) button to remove a behavior from a slice.

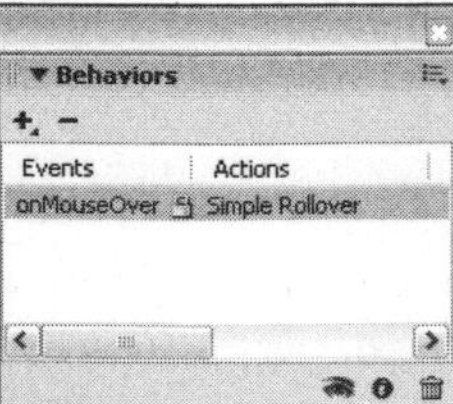

Figure 7-9: The Behaviors panel shows the action(s) assigned to a slice.

If the 3-State Button is linking to another page, adding a Down state doesn't give you much bang for your buck because the linked page may appear in the browser window before the user even has a chance to notice that the button changed.

You may want to include an Over While Down state for your button (sort of an extra rollover) if you're using the Down state of the button to indicate the current page. If so, check in the Frames panel to make sure that you have a fourth frame with the image for an extra button state, add the Rollover and Set Nav Bar Image behaviors by using the steps earlier in this section, and then perform the following steps:

1. **Double-click the Set Nav Bar Image line in the Behaviors panel.**

   The Set Nav Bar Image dialog box appears.

2. **Select the Include Over While Down State (Frame 4) check box.**

   If the button is for the current page, select the Show Down Image upon Load check box, as well.

3. **Click OK.**

   Select the Export Multiple Nav Bar HTML Files check box on the Document Specific tab of the HTML Setup dialog box if you want Fireworks to generate separate HTML files for each button in the nav bar (see the "Setting the export HTML file options" section, earlier in this chapter, for more information).

Bringing Interactivity to Your Pages with Behaviors

Fireworks can generate JavaScript that does more than merely change the state of a button. For instance, you can set a behavior that swaps one image for another image elsewhere on the page when you roll over a button or hotspot. You can also use Fireworks to generate pop-up menus, which you can export as either JavaScript or CSS code.

The Swap Images behavior

A button rollover is an *image swap* — you exchange the image for one button state with the image for another state. But you can roll over a button and have a different image on the page swap. For example, you can set up a rollover behavior for two or more buttons to show different color choices for a product, so when the user rolls over a button for color choices, the image of the product changes to show the appropriately colored version. If you want the image swap and page download to happen quickly, limit the number of images that you want to swap and limit the file size of each swapped image.

To add the Swap Image behavior to a trigger slice and target slice, create the frames, images, and slices. (See Book III, Chapter 3 to learn how to create images, Book III, Chapter 5 for information on frames, and Book III, Chapter 6 for information on slices.) Then, follow these steps:

1. **Click the slice that you want to use to trigger the image swap.**

   You can click the slice either on the canvas or in the Layers panel.

2. **Click the Add Behavior (+) button at the top left of the Behaviors panel (if the Behaviors panel isn't visible, press Shift+F3).**

   A menu appears.

3. **Choose Swap Image.**

   The Swap Image dialog box, which you can see in Figure 7-10, appears.

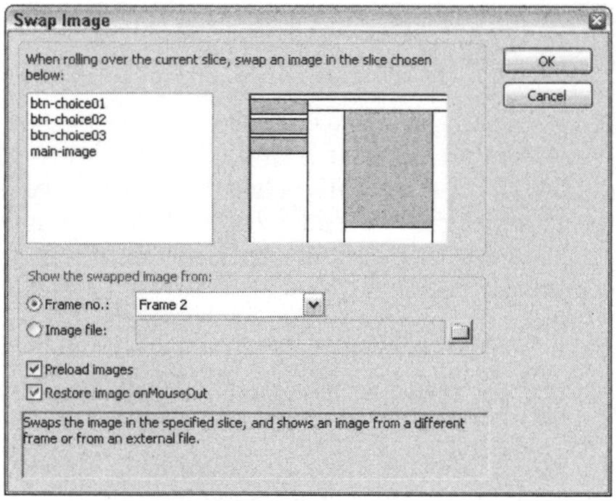

Figure 7-10: The Swap Image dialog box lets you choose by name or position on the page.

4. **Select the targeted slice by clicking its name (in the box on the left) or by clicking its representation (in the box on the right).**

   When you click in either box, both boxes update to show your selection.

5. **Using the Frame No. drop-down list, select the frame number that you want the rollover to trigger.**

   The drop-down list shows all the frames in your PNG file.

   You can also select the Image File radio button and navigate to an existing image file outside your PNG to swap in. But for the rollover to work correctly in all browsers, the default target image and swapped target image have to be the same height and width.

6. **Leave the Preload Images and the Restore Image onMouseOut check boxes selected.**

Preloading the swapped image ensures the user doesn't experience a delay when he or she rolls over the button that triggers the swap. You make a trade-off with preloading because the Web page takes longer to load initially.

Restoring the image to default prevents the swapped image from "sticking." If you want the swapped image to remain in place until the user rolls over another button, deselect the Restore Image onMouseOut check box.

7. **Click OK.**

A line on the canvas from the center of the trigger slice to the target slice shows that one slice triggers a behavior in the other, as you can see in Figure 7-11.

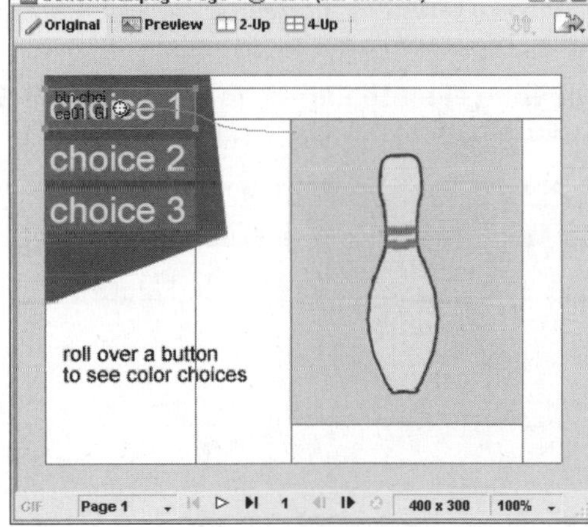

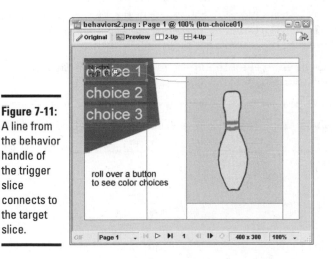

Figure 7-11: A line from the behavior handle of the trigger slice connects to the target slice.

You can have multiple buttons trigger a rollover in the same slice, and you can have a single button trigger rollovers in multiple slices. Of course, the more big rollovers you have on the page, the longer the page takes to load. On the other hand, rollovers give useful feedback (and instant gratification) to the user, and Fireworks makes producing them a snap.

Generating pop-up menus

You can cram a lot of navigation into a small space by using a pop-up menu because pop-up menus appear only when a user rolls over a button or hotspot. Fireworks lets you specify many of the parameters of a menu's appearance. To start with, you can choose whether the links in your pop-up menu are made of text or images. In a nutshell, that choice boils down to this:

- **Linked images:** This option makes for a slower download but gives you more control over the appearance of the text because the text is graphic.
- **Linked text:** This option ensures faster download but gives you less control over the appearance of the text because the text is HTML.

You can also customize the position of the menu relative to the slice that triggers it, the color of the text and cell background for both normal and rollover states, and more. In fact, you have so many options, we can't cover them all here! After you have the basics, though, you can explore all the options by using the Fireworks Help files (select the Help menu at the top right of the Fireworks menu bar) or just by experimenting.

To make a basic, one-level pop-up menu with linked text, follow these steps:

1. **Select a slice by clicking it on the canvas or in the Layers panel (if you need to, open the Layers panel by pressing F2; you also can expand the panel by clicking the panel name).**
2. **Click the Add Behavior (+) button at the top left of the Behaviors panel (if the Behaviors panel isn't visible, press Shift+F3).**

   A pop-up menu appears.
3. **Choose Set Pop-up Menu from the Add Behaviors pop-up menu.**

   The Pop-up Menu Editor, which you can see in Figure 7-12, appears, with the Content tab active by default.

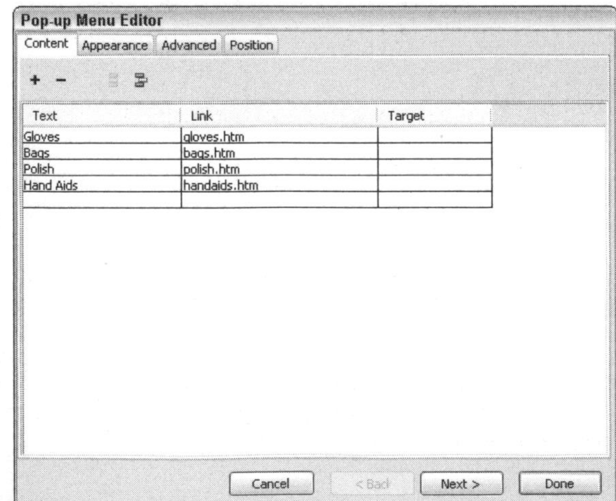

Figure 7-12: The Content tab of the Pop-up Menu Editor, with a few items added.

4. **Click under the Text column of the Pop-up Menu Editor and type the text as you want it to appear in your menu.**

5. **Press Tab or click under the Link column of the Pop-up Menu Editor and type or select the URL or filename for the page you want your text linked to.**

   If you have any existing links already on your page, they appear in a drop-down list in the Link column.

6. **If you want the link to open in a new window or different frameset, tab over to or click in the Target column to set the target for the link.**

   If you simply want the linked page to open in the user's current browser window, leave this column blank (refer to Figure 7-12). For information on other Target options, see the discussion of links in Book I, Chapter 2, or the discussion of frames in Book I, Chapter 4.

7. **Repeat Steps 4 through 6 for each item in your menu.**

   You can add rows to the list of menu items by clicking the Add Menu button (the plus sign at the top left) or by pressing the Tab key until a text field appears in the Text column.

8. **Click the Next button at the bottom of the Pop-up Menu Editor.**

   The Appearance tab becomes active.

9. **For the Cells option, make sure that the HTML radio button (the default selection) is selected.**

   If you want to use images rather than HTML text, you need to select the Image radio button. Each navigation item is in its own table cell.

10. **Select Vertical Menu or Horizontal Menu from the drop-down list.**

    If you select Vertical Menu, menu items will be stacked vertically in a single column. If you select Horizontal Menu, menu items will appear in a horizontal row.

11. **Select the font face, size, style, and alignment.**

    Of course, you don't need to do this step if you're using graphics rather than HTML text.

12. **Select the text color and cell background color for the Up (normal) state by clicking the Text and Cell color swatches and clicking when the eyedropper is on the color you want in the color picker that pops up.**

    If you don't want to use the defaults, click the color boxes to open the color picker. At the bottom of the dialog box, you can see a preview of your menu, as shown in Figure 7-13.

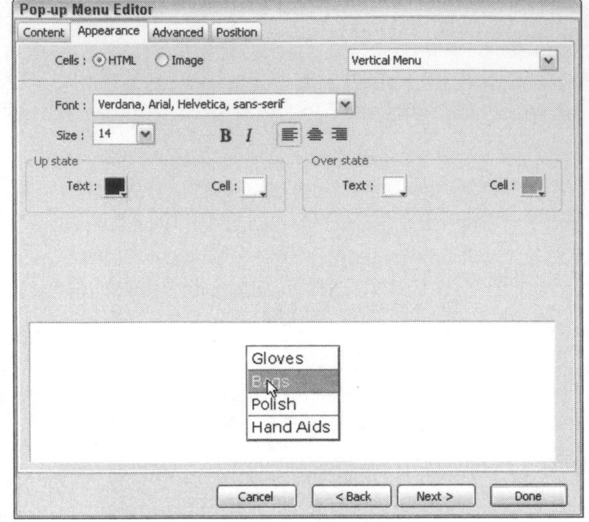

Figure 7-13: The preview shows what the menu looks like after you change each parameter.

13. **Select the text color and cell background color for the Over (rollover) state by clicking the Text and Cell color swatches and clicking when the eyedropper is on the color you want in the color picker that pops up.**

    If you don't want to use the defaults, click the color boxes to open the color picker. At the bottom of the dialog box, you can see a preview of your menu.

14. **Click the Next button at the bottom of the Pop-up Menu Editor.**

    The Advanced tab becomes active.

15. **Adjust any of the parameters in the Advanced tab as needed.**

    You can preview all the following settings at the bottom of the dialog box, except Menu Delay:

    - **Cell Width and Cell Height:** By default, Fireworks sets the cell width and cell height automatically, based on the content, but you can select Pixels from the drop-down list and type in a custom width and/or height.
    - **Cell Padding and Cell Spacing:** *Cell padding* is the space between the edges of the cells and the text within the cells. The default Cell Padding setting is 3 pixels. *Cell spacing* is the space between the edge of one cell and the edge of an adjacent cell. The default Cell Spacing setting is 0.
    - **Text Indent:** *Text indent* is the number of pixels from the left (in a vertical menu) or from the top (in a horizontal menu) to the text, not

including the gaps introduced by cell padding and cell spacing. The default Text Indent setting is 0.

- **Menu Delay:** Menu delay is the amount of time your menu stays on-screen after the user's mouse rolls off the menu. You adjust it in milliseconds (ms), or thousandths of a second. The default, 1000 ms, equals one second.
- **Pop-up Borders:** You can turn on or off the border of your pop-up menu (and you can adjust its width if you have the border on), and you can customize the colors that make up the border.

16. **Click the Next button at the bottom of the Pop-up Menu Editor.**

    The Position tab becomes active.

17. **Click a Menu Position icon.**

    The X and Y coordinates, which represent the top-left corner of the menu relative to the slice, update. You can type your own values for the X and Y coordinates if you want to customize them.

18. **Click Done.**

The Preview pane that you access at the top of your canvas doesn't let you see the pop-up menu in action. To preview your pop-up menu in action, you have to choose File➪Preview in Browser or press F12 (PC only). You can use any Web browser installed on your computer to preview your menu, as long as you have JavaScript enabled on that browser.

Pop-up menus are a tricky business because their appearance can vary in different browsers. Be sure to test all your target browsers to make sure that they display the menus in a way you find acceptable.

When you make a slice active that has a pop-up menu behavior attached, you see an outline on the canvas in Fireworks in which the pop-up menu will appear when the user rolls over the slice.

To edit the pop-up menu, click the behavior handle (the round icon in the middle of the slice, visible when you select the slice) and choose Edit Pop-up Menu, or double-click the behavior's name in the Behaviors panel.

Creating a Slideshow for the Web

You can now create a Flash-based Web slideshow without leaving Fireworks. You can choose settings for image size, length of time each image appears on-screen, transition type, and more. There are so many customization options, we don't have space for all the details here. Instead, we offer the quickest route to a working Web slideshow.

To create a slideshow, follow these steps:

1. **Choose Commands⇨Create Slideshow.**

   The Create Slideshow window appears.

2. **Click the plus (+) button in the Albums section to create an Album.**

   The Files to Process window appears. (We're assuming that you have not already created an Album. If you have, however, then instead click the Open an Existing AlbumBook link at the top left of the Create Slideshow window.)

3. **Click the Ellipse button (the one with the ". . ." on it).**

   The Open window appears.

4. **Navigate to the folder that contains the images you want to use in your slideshow and click to select the images. When you have selected all the images you want to add, click Done.**

   Hold down the Shift key while you click to select multiple files. When you click Done, the window disappears.

5. **Click OK in the Files to Process window.**

   The album title and the folder name appear in the Albums section of the Create Slideshow window. By default, the album title matches the name of the folder containing the images.

6. **Click the title or folder name of the album you just created.**

   The title and folder name of the album are highlighted in green, and the images appear in the images section.

7. **Click Slideshow Properties.**

   The Slideshow Properties panel slides open, as shown in Figure 7-14.

8. **Type a number or use the arrows to set an Interval for the slideshow.**

   The number you enter sets the number of seconds each slide appears on-screen.

9. **Select a transition effect from the Type pop-up menu by clicking the arrow at the right and clicking an effect. Next, enter a number for the amount of seconds you want each transition to take.**

   If you want the slides to appear one after the other without any transitional effect, deselect the Use Transition check box.

10. **If you don't want your slideshow to start with the first image as listed in the Images section of the window, enter the number of the image you'd like to appear first in the First Image field.**

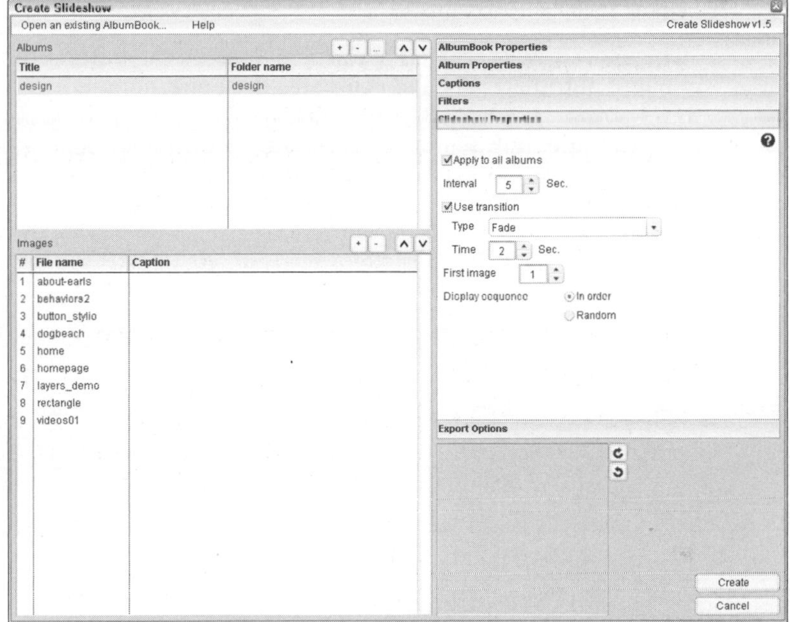

Figure 7-14: Editing the settings in the Slideshow Properties section of the Create Slideshow window.

By default, the slideshow starts with the image numbered 1, as shown in the Images section.

11. **Select either In Order or Random to set how the slideshow will cycle through the images in the album.**

12. **If you want a caption to appear under an image, click in the Caption column of the image and type a caption.**

    If you do this for one image, you'll probably want to do it for all of them.

13. **Click each image to view it in the Preview window. Click the Rotate 90 Degrees Clockwise or Rotate 90 Degrees Counter-Clockwise button, if necessary.**

14. **Click Export Options to set how and where the slideshow will go.**

    You must enter an Export path. You can click the Ellipse (. . .) button to navigate to a folder. Click the question mark (?) icon to view descriptions of all the options.

15. **Click AlbumBook Properties and choose a player from the Player pop-up menu.**

    The image directly below the menu shows a thumbnail of what the selected player looks like.

16. Click Create.

The slideshow is created. Fireworks does all the batch-processing of the images automatically and generates the code.

The Create Slideshow feature offers more options and capabilities than we can show you here. Feel free to experiment, or try using the online Help files for further information.

Book IV

Illustrator CS3

"Are you using that 'clone' tool again?!"

Book IV: Illustrator CS3 441

Chapter 1: What's New in Adobe Illustrator CS3?

In This Chapter

- **Working in the new streamlined interface**
- **Going live with color**
- **Integrating Flash**
- **Drawing with new tools**
- **Easily erasing vector paths**
- **Getting to know the Isolation mode**
- **Using the new cropping tool**

Yes, Adobe has done it again — an even better Adobe Illustrator, and you can discover the best new features in this chapter. This chapter breezes through the new features to open your eyes to exciting new work methods. Don't forget to look for references to where you can get more in-depth knowledge in other locations of this book.

Integrated Interface

As you may guess, Adobe Illustrator follows the other products in the suite with its similar interface, which makes it easy for you to set up efficient workspaces and keep just the tools you need handy.

The user experience is noticeably different right away. As you launch Adobe Illustrator CS3, a splash screen appears, asking whether you're opening an existing document or if you're creating a new print, Web, mobile device, video, CMYK, RGB, or template file. By selecting the appropriate selection, you'll have the correct tools and preferences set up from the beginning.

Just like many of the other CS3 applications, you now have a space-saving one-column toolbar that you can switch back to two by clicking on the gray bar at the top of the toolbar and a palette system that you can collapse to icons (see Figure 1-1).

Figure 1-1: The space-saving interface in Adobe Illustrator CS3.

Live Color

Gain your color confidence! Live Color allows for complete color exploration in addition to timesaving features to apply color schemes to your Illustrator objects. If you've ever been frustrated by having to color objects individually, you're sure to appreciate the new, interactive way to create and apply color schemes.

Live Color includes the Color Guide panel (see Figure 1-2), which includes features that allow you to save color groups without affecting your artwork.

Use the Color Guide to find compelling colors and save them to color groups in your Swatches panel. You can create color schemes based on 23 classic color-harmony rules, such as Complementary, Analogous, Monochromatic, and Triad, or you can create custom harmony rules. Even if you've gone through art school, using Live Colors beats trying to figure out a color scheme on your own. (Read more about Live Color in Chapter 9 of this minibook.)

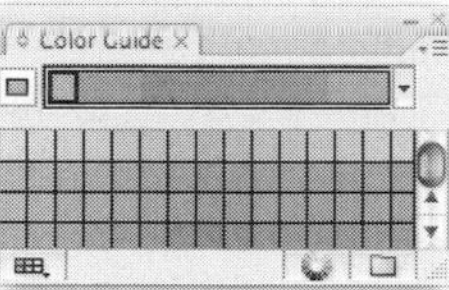

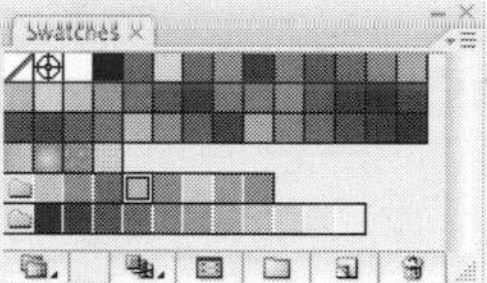

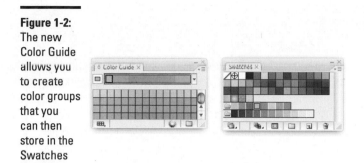

Figure 1-2: The new Color Guide allows you to create color groups that you can then store in the Swatches panel.

Flash Integration

Flash is vector, and Illustrator is *vector,* which means illustrations created in these applications are composed of mathematically created line and curve segments. Why can't they be better friends? Well, in this version, they're great buddies. Not only do you have the ability to do simple tasks like cut and paste from Adobe Illustrator directly into Flash files, but you also can transfer Illustrator layers and grouping structures along with all object names. (Read more about Flash integration with the CS3 products in Book V on Flash.)

Vector graphics

Vector graphics are made up of lines and curves defined by mathematical objects called *vectors.* Because the paths (the lines and curves) are defined mathematically, you can move, resize, or change the color of vector objects without losing quality in the graphic.

Vector graphics are resolution-independent; that is, they can be scaled to any size and printed at any resolution without losing detail. On the other hand, bitmap graphics have a predetermined amount of pixels creating them, so you can't scale (resize) them easily — if you scale them smaller, you throw out pixels; if you scale them bigger, you end up with a blocky, jagged picture.

(continued)

(continued)

The following figure shows the differences between an enlarged vector graphic on the left (notice the smooth edges) and an enlarged bitmap graphic on the right (note the jagged edges). Many companies have their logos created as vectors to avoid problems with scaling: A vector graphic logo maintains its high-quality appearance at any size.

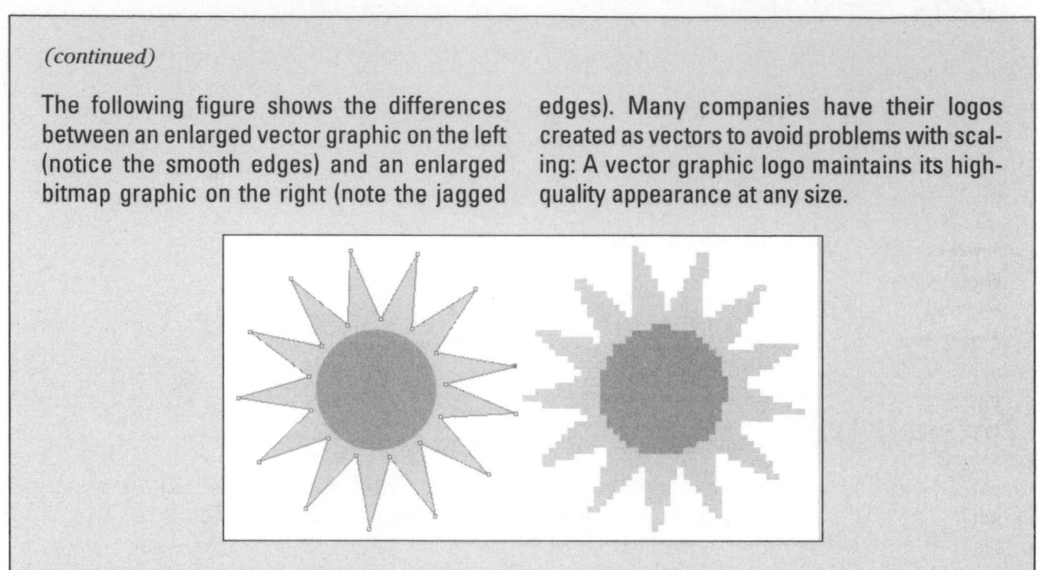

Improved Drawing Controls

Illustrator drawing tools have long been the industry standard for power and versatility, but they've also always been a little unnatural and tedious to those who are new to using vector drawing tools. Now, in Adobe CS3, the drawing tools have been improved to allow you to work faster and get better results, starting with Point selection: Simply move your cursor over an anchor point (with the direct selection tool), and it's enlarged to help you see it better.

The control panel has gained additional tools to help you change curved corners to rounded curves, or back again. You can also connect and remove anchor points quickly with the improved path controls shown in Figure 1-3.

Figure 1-3: New tools in the control panel help edit paths.

Read more about improved performance and how to use the drawing tools in Chapter 5 of this minibook.

Erase It Away

If you're an experienced Illustrator user, you'll really appreciate the new Eraser tool. It lets you erase as easily as you create, even reconnecting paths as you erase over shapes and paths. You can make the eraser larger or smaller by double-clicking the Eraser tool and changing the options in the Eraser Tool Options window, shown in Figure 1-4.

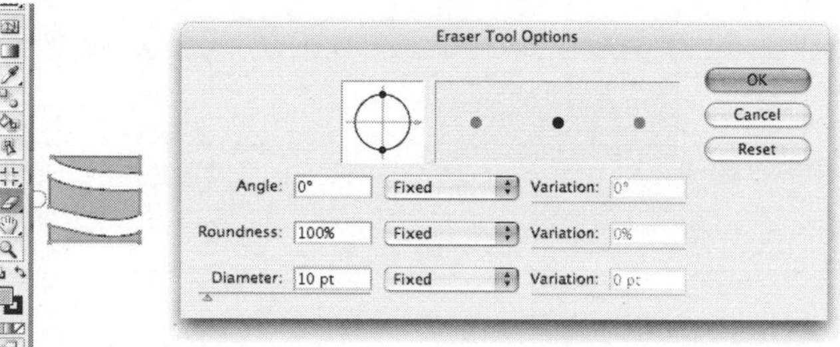

Figure 1-4: The new Eraser tool makes it easy to take away shapes and paths, just where you want.

Isolation Mode

Those of you who build a little more than text art and the occasional logo will appreciate the new Isolation mode that allows you to take selected objects into a mode that protects other artwork. Isolation mode is truly essential if you work on complex artwork and spend a lot of time grouping, hiding, locking, and restacking layers to access objects for editing.

To use this new mode, just use the Selection tool to double-click any grouped set of objects. The rest of your artwork becomes inaccessible, as shown in Figure 1-5. This feature is truly a timesaver!

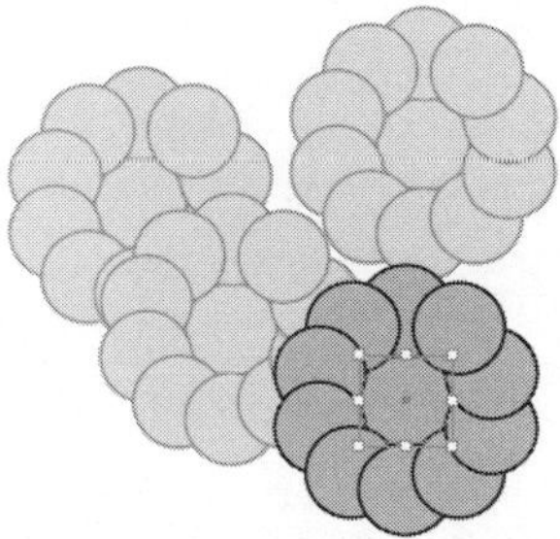

Figure 1-5: Double-click a group using the Selection tool to enter the Isolation mode.

New Cropping Tool

Use the new cropping tool with a powerful option to get just what you need in your Illustrator document. When the new Crop Area tool is selected, options appear in the Control panel for measure as well as Presets that you can choose from. Want even more control? Double-click the Crop Area tool for additional options, shown in Figure 1-6.

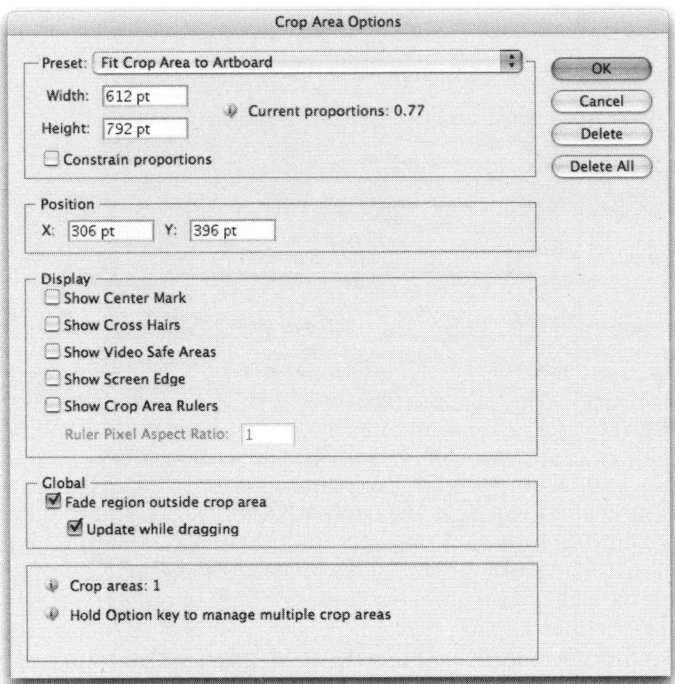

Figure 1-6: The Crop Area tool options.

Chapter 2: Discovering Illustrator CS3

In This Chapter

- Knowing when to use Illustrator
- Opening documents
- Creating new documents
- Checking out the tools
- Getting to know the palettes
- Changing views
- Zooming in and out

Adobe Illustrator goes hand in hand with the other Adobe products but serves its own unique purpose. Adobe Illustrator creates single-page artwork, not lengthy documents with repeated headers, footers, and page numbers, such as documents created in InDesign, and not artwork created out of pixels, such as images edited or created in Photoshop. Illustrator is generally used to create logos, illustrations, maps, packages, labels, signage, Web art, and more.

Deciding When to Use Illustrator CS3

So how do you draw the line and decide when to create graphics in Illustrator rather than Photoshop? By using Illustrator, you gain the following benefits:

- ✦ Illustrator can save and export graphics into most file formats. By choosing to save or export, you can create a file that can be used in most other applications. For instance, Illustrator files can be saved as `.svg`, `.bmp`, `.tiff`, `.pdf`, `.jpg`, and even as a Flash `.swf` file, to name a few.
- ✦ Illustrator files are easily integrated into other Adobe applications. You can save Illustrator files in their native format and open or place them in other Adobe applications, such as InDesign, Photoshop, Dreamweaver, and Flash. You can also save Adobe Illustrator artwork in the `.pdf` format

(Acrobat Portable Document Format). This format allows anyone using the free Acrobat Reader software to open and view the file, but editing capabilities are still maintained when the file is later opened in Illustrator.

- Illustrator is resolution-independent. Resolution of Illustrator vector artwork isn't determined until output. In other words, if you print to a 600-dpi (dots per inch) printer, the artwork is printed at 600 dpi; print to a 2,400-dpi printer, and the artwork will print at 2,400 dpi. Illustrator graphics are very different from the bitmap images you create or edit in Photoshop, where resolution is determined upon creation of the artwork.
- Illustrator has limitless scalability, which means that you can create vector artwork in Illustrator and scale it to the size of your thumb or the size of a barn, and it will still look good. See the "Vector graphics" sidebar in Chapter 1 of this minibook for more information.

Opening an Existing Document

To familiarize yourself with the basics of Illustrator and what the work area looks like, jump right in by opening an existing document in Illustrator. If you don't have an Illustrator file already created, you can open one of the sample files that is packaged with the Illustrator application. For example, you can open the file named `Cheshire Cat.ai` in the Sample Art folder. The path to the file is C:\Programs\Adobe\Adobe Illustrator CS3\Cool Extras\Sample Files\Sample Art (Applications\Adobe Illustrator CS3\ Cool Extras\Sample Files\Sample Art\ on a Mac).

When you launch Illustrator CS3 for the first time, a Welcome screen appears, giving you various options. Click the Open icon and then browse to locate a file to open. (Note that you can uncheck the Don't Show Again check box to not see the Welcome screen at launch.)

If your preferences have been changed from the original defaults, the Welcome screen may not appear. To open a file in that case, choose File➪Open and select the file in the Open dialog box. The Open dialog box is used to open existing Adobe Illustrator files, or even files from other Adobe applications.

Use File➪Open to open PDFs in Illustrator as well as many other file formats.

Creating a New Document

To create a new document in Illustrator, follow these steps:

1. **Choose File➪New.**

The New Document dialog box appears, as shown in Figure 2-2. This dialog box enables you to determine the new document's profile, size, units of measurement, color mode, and page orientation.

2. **Enter a name for your new file in the Name text field.**

   You can determine the name of the file now or when you save the document later.

3. **Choose a New Document Profile from a drop-down list.**

   Selecting the correct profile sets up preferences, such as resolution and colors, correctly. Select the Advanced tab to see what changes are selected for each profile and change them if necessary.

4. **Set the size of the document page by choosing from the Size drop-down list or by typing measurements in the Width and Height text fields.**

   The size can be set from several standard sizes available in the Size drop-down list, or you can enter your own measurements in the Width and Height text fields. Note that several Web sizes are listed first, followed by other typical paper sizes.

5. **Select the type of measurement that you're most comfortable with by choosing from the Units drop-down list.**

   Note that your selection sets all measurement boxes and rulers to the increments you choose: points, picas, inches, millimeters, centimeters, or pixels.

6. **Pick the orientation for the artboard.**

   The *artboard* is your canvas for creating your artwork in Illustrator. You can choose between Portrait (the short sides of the artboard at the top and bottom) and Landscape (the long sides of the artboard on the top and bottom).

7. **When you're finished making your selections, click OK.**

   An Illustrator artboard appears.

Don't worry if document size and color mode need to be changed at a later point. You can change them by choosing File➪Document Setup and making changes in the Document Setup dialog box.

Taking a Look at the Document Window

To investigate the work area and really get familiar with Illustrator, open a new document and take a look around. In the Illustrator work area, you have a total of 227 inches in width and height to create your artwork in.

That's great, but it also leaves enough space to lose objects, too! The following list explains the areas that you'll work with as you create artwork in Illustrator:

- **Imageable area:** The space inside the innermost dotted lines, which marks the printing area on the page. Many printers can't print all the way to the edges of the paper, so the imageable area is determined by the printer that you have selected in the Print dialog box. To turn off or on this dotted border, choose View⇨Hide/Show Page Tiling.

  You can move the imageable area around on your page by using the Page tool. See the nearby sidebar, "The Page tool," for more on this tool.
- **Edge of the page:** The page's edge is marked by the outermost set of dotted lines.
- **Nonimageable area:** The space between the two sets of dotted lines representing the imageable area and the edge of the page. The nonimageable area is the margin of the page that can't be printed on.
- **Artboard:** The area bounded by solid lines that represents the entire region that can contain printable artwork. By default, the artboard is the same size as the page, but it can be enlarged or reduced. The U.S. default artboard is 8.5 x 11 inches, but it can be set as large as 227 x 227 inches. You can hide the artboard boundaries by choosing View⇨Hide Artboard.

The Page tool

Use the Page tool to move the printable area of your page to a different location. For example, if you have a printer that can print only on paper that is 8.5 x 11 inches or less, but you have a page size of 11 x 17, you can use the Page tool (a hidden tool accessed by holding down the mouse button on the Hand tool) to indicate what part of the page you want to print. Follow these steps to use the Page tool:

1. **When adjusting page boundaries, choose View⇨Fit in Window so that you can see all of your artwork.**
2. **Hold down on the Hand tool to select the hidden Page tool.**

   The pointer becomes a dotted cross when you move it to the active window.
3. **Position the mouse over the artboard and click and drag the page to a new location.**

   As you drag, the Page tool acts as if you were moving the page from its lower-left corner. Two gray rectangles are displayed. The outer rectangle represents the page size, and the inner rectangle represents the printable area of a page. You can move the page anywhere on the artboard; just remember that any part of a page that extends past the printable area boundary isn't printed.

✦ **Scratch area:** The area outside the artboard that extends to the edge of the 227-inch square window. The scratch area represents a space on which you can create, edit, and store elements of artwork before moving them onto the artboard. Objects placed onto the scratch area are visible on-screen, but they don't print. However, objects in the scratch area will appear if the document is saved and placed as an image in other applications.

Basically, the rules regarding the work area are simple: If you're printing directly from Adobe Illustrator, make sure that you choose the proper paper size and printer in the Print dialog box. Open the Print dialog box by choosing File⇨Print. If you're creating artwork for another application, such as for a document you're creating in InDesign, the boundaries have no effect on what appears in the Illustrator file. Everything in Illustrator's scratch area will appear in the other application.

Becoming Familiar with the Tools

As you begin using Adobe Illustrator, you'll find it helpful to be familiar with its tools. Tools are used to create, select, and manipulate objects in Illustrator. The tools should be visible as a default, but if not, you can access them by choosing Window⇨Tools.

Table 2-1 lists the tools that we show you how to use throughout this minibook. Hover the cursor over the tool in the toolbox to see the name of the tool appear in a ToolTip. In parentheses on the ToolTip (and noted in the second column of Table 2-1) is the keyboard command that you can use to access that tool. When you see a small triangle at the lower-right corner of the tool icon, you know that it contains additional hidden tools. Select the tool and hold the mouse button to see any hidden tools.

Table 2-1 Illustrator CS2 Tools

Icon Covered	*Tool/Keyboard Command*	*What It Does*	*Chapter in This Minibook*
	Selection Tool (V)	Activates objects	3
	Direct Selection (A)	Activates individual points or paths	3
	Group Selection (A)	Selects grouped items	3

(continued)

Table 2-1 *(continued)*

Icon Covered	*Tool/Keyboard Command*	*What It Does*	*Chapter in This Minibook*
	Magic Wand (Y)	Selects based upon similarity	3
	Lasso (Q)	Selects Freehand	3
	Pen (P)	Creates paths	5
T	Type (T)	Creates text	6
	Line Segment (/)	Draws line segments	5
	Shape Tool (M)	Creates shape objects	4
	Paint Brush (B)	Creates paths	5
	Pencil (N)	Creates paths	5
	Rotate (R)	Rotates objects	10
	Scale (S)	Enlarges or reduces objects	10
	Warp (Shift+R)	Warps objects	10
	Free Transform (E)	Transforms objects	10
	Symbol Sprayer (Shift+S)	Applies Symbol instances	11
	Graph Tool (J)	Creates graphs	11

Icon Covered	Tool/Keyboard Command	What It Does	Chapter in This Minibook
	Mesh (U)	Creates a gradient mesh	11
	Gradient (G)	Modifies gradients	11
	Eyedropper (I)	Copies and applies attributes	9
	Blend (W)	Creates transitional blends	11
	Live Paint Bucket (K)	Applies color to strokes and fills	9
	Live Paint Selection (Shift+L)	Selects Live Paint Areas Tool	8
	Slice Tool (Shift K)	Creates HTML slices	13
	Crop Area Tool (Shift+O)	Crops multiple areas	1
	Eraser Tool (Shift+E)	Erases vector paths	3
	Scissors (C)	Cuts paths	5
	Hand (H)	Navigates on the page	2
	Zoom (Z)	Increases and decreases the on-screen view	2

Checking Out the Panels

The new standardized interface is a great boost for users as Illustrator's panel system is similar to all the other products in Adobe's Creative Suites. This consistency makes working and finding tools and features easier.

When you first open Illustrator, you'll notice the one-column toolbar and the panels that have been reduced to icons on the right. To select a panel, click the appropriate icon, and the Fill panel appears.

How do you know which icon brings up which panel? Good question. If you're hunting around for the appropriate panels, you can do one of three things.

- **Choose Window and select the named panel from a list.**
- **Position your mouse on the left side of the icons, when you see the double arrow icon, click and drag to the left.** The panel names appear.
- **Click the Expand dock gray bar at the top of the icons.** The panels expand so that you can see their contents and names. See Figure 2-1 to see the panels in iconic and expanded views.

The panels that you see as a default are docked together. To *dock* a palette means that, for organizational purposes, the panel is attached in the docking area.

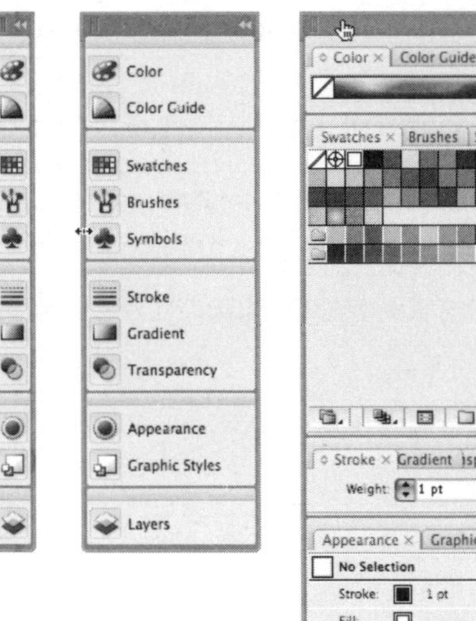

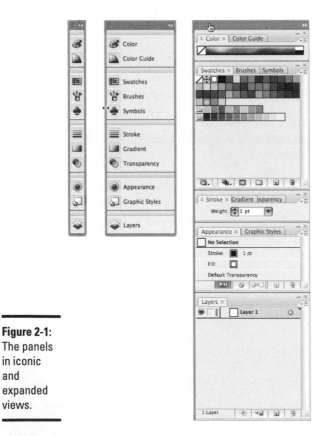

Figure 2-1: The panels in iconic and expanded views.

You can arrange panels to make them more helpful for production. You may choose to have only certain panels visible while working. Here's the low-down on using Illustrator's panels:

✦ To see additional options for each panel, click the Show Options button on the upper-right side of the panel (see Figure 2-2.)

Figure 2-2: Each panel has additional options available.

✦ To move a panel group, click and drag above the tabbed panel name.

✦ To rearrange or separate a panel from its group, drag the panel's tab. Dragging a tab outside the docking area creates a new separate panel window.

✦ To move a tab to another palette, drag the tab to that palette.

Look out for those panels — they can take over your screen! Some panels, but not all, can be resized. Panels that you can resize have an active lower-right corner (denoted by three small lines in the corner). To change the size of a panel, drag the lower-right corner of the panel (on a Mac, drag the size box at the lower-right corner of the panel).

As you become more efficient, you may find it helpful to reduce the clutter on your screen by hiding all panels except those that are necessary for your work. Save your own panel configuration by choosing Window➪Workspace➪Save Workspace. Choose Window➪Workspace➪[Basic] to return to the default workspace.

Changing Views

When you're working in Illustrator, precision is important, but you also want to see how the artwork really looks. Whether for the Web or print, Illustrator offers several ways in which to view your artwork:

✦ **Preview and Outline views:** By default, Illustrator shows the Preview view, where you see colors, stroke widths, images, and patterns as they should appear when printed or completed for on-screen presentation.

Sometimes this view can become a nuisance, especially if you have two thick lines and you're trying to create a corner point by connecting them. At times like this, or whenever you want the strokes and fills reduced to the underlying structure, choose View➪Outline. You now see the outline of the illustration, as shown in Figure 2-3.

Figure 2-3: Preview mode (left) and Outline mode (right).

✦ **Pixel view:** If you don't want to be surprised when your artwork appears in your Web browser, use the Pixel view. This view, shown in Figure 2-4, maintains the vectors of your artwork, but gives you a view showing how the pixels will appear when the image is viewed on-screen, as if on the Web.

Figure 2-4: See how your artwork translates into pixels in the Pixel view.

Pixel view is great for previewing what your text will look like on-screen — some fonts just don't look good as pixels, especially if the text is small. Using Pixel view, you can go through several different fonts until you find one that is more readable as pixels.

✦ **Overprint view:** For those of you in print production, the Overprint preview can be a real timesaver. Choose View➪Attributes to bring up the Attributes palette, which you can use to set the fill and stroke colors to overprint. This view creates additional colors when printing and aids printers when trapping abutting colors.

Trapping is the slight overprint of a lighter color into a darker color to correct for press *misregistration.* When several colors are printed on one piece, the likelihood that they'll be perfectly aligned is pretty slim! Setting a stroke to Overprint on the Window➪Attributes palette is one solution. With overprint selected, the stroke is overprinted on the touching colors. This mixing of color produces an additional color, but is less obvious to the viewer than a white space created by misregistration. Select Overprint to see the result of overprinting in Overprint view in Figure 2-5.

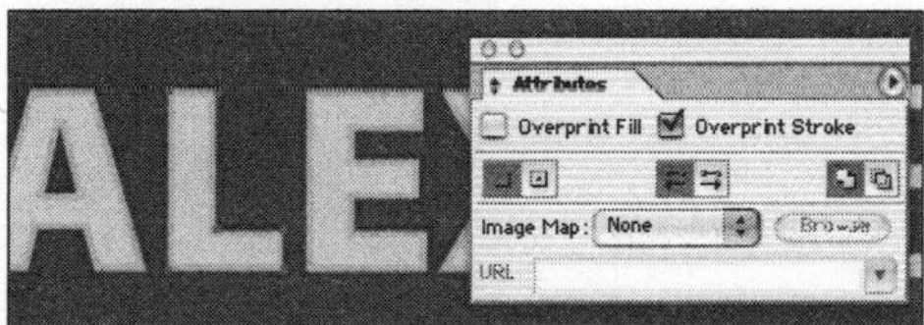

Figure 2-5: Overprint view.

Navigating the Work Area with Zoom Controls

You can navigate the work area efficiently by using the Hand tool and the various zoom controls. You can change the magnification of the artboard in several ways, including using menu items, the Zoom tool, and keyboard commands. Choose the method you feel most comfortable with:

✦ **Hand tool:** Scroll around the document window by using the scrollbars or the Hand tool. The Hand tool gives you the ability to scroll by dragging. You can imagine you're pushing a piece of paper around on your desk when you use the Hand tool.

  Hold down the spacebar to temporarily access the Hand tool while any tool (except the Type tool) is selected. Holding down the spacebar while the Type tool is selected only gives you spaces!

✦ **View menu:** Using the View menu, you can easily select the magnification that you want from a choice of four: Zoom In, Zoom Out, Fit In Window (especially useful when you get lost in the scratch area), and Actual Size (gives you a 100-percent view of your artwork).

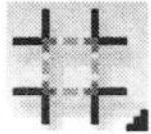

✦ **New Crop Area tool:** Using the new Crop Area tool you can define crop areas interactively for print or export. You can choose preset formats and define multiple crop areas.

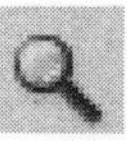

✦ **The Zoom tool:** Using the Zoom tool, you can click the document window to zoom in; to zoom out, Alt+click (Option+click on a Mac). Double-click with the Zoom tool to quickly resize the document window to 100 percent. Control what is visible when using the Zoom tool by clicking and dragging over the area that you want zoomed into.

✦ **Keyboard shortcuts:** If you're not the type of person who likes to use keyboard shortcuts, you may change your mind about using them for magnification. They make sense and are easy to use and remember. Table 2-2 lists the most popular keyboard shortcuts to change magnification.

The shortcuts in Table 2-2 require a little coordination to use, but they give you more control in your zoom. While holding down the keys, drag from the upper-left to the bottom-right corner of the area you want to zoom to. A marquee appears while you're dragging; when you release the mouse button, the selected area zooms up to the size of your window! The Zoom Out command doesn't give you that much control; it simply zooms back out, much like the commands in Table 2-2.

Table 2-2 Magnification Keyboard Shortcuts

Command	*Windows Shortcut*	*Mac Shortcut*
Actual Size	Ctrl+1	Replace+1
Fit in Window	Ctrl+0 (zero)	Replace +0 (zero)
Zoom In	Ctrl++ (plus)	Replace ++ (plus)
Zoom Out	Ctrl+– (minus)	Replace +– (minus)
Hand tool	Spacebar	Spacebar

Table 2-3 Zoom Keyboard Shortcuts

Command	*Windows Shortcut*	*Mac Shortcut*
Zoom In to Selected Area	Ctrl+spacebar+drag	Replace +spacebar+drag
Zoom Out	Ctrl+Alt+spacebar	Replace+Option+spacebar

Chapter 3: Using the Selection Tools

In This Chapter

- Anchor points, the bounding boxes, and selection tools
- Working with selections
- Grouping and ungrouping selections
- Constraining movement and cloning objects

You've probably heard the old line, "You have to select it to affect it." This statement is so true. When you're ready to apply a change to an object in Illustrator, you must have that object selected, or Illustrator won't know what to do. You'll sit there clicking a color swatch over and over again, and nothing will happen. Although making selections may sound simple, it can become more difficult when working on complicated artwork.

Getting to Know the Selection Tools

Before delving into the world of selecting objects in Illustrator, you must know what the selection tools are. In this section, we take you through a quick tour of anchor points (integral to the world of selections), the bounding box, and, of course, the selection tools (yes, there are more than one).

Anchor points

To understand selections, you must first understand how Illustrator works with *anchor points.* Anchor points act like handles and can be individually selected and moved to other locations. Essentially, the anchor points are what you use to drag objects or parts of objects around the workspace. After you've placed anchor points on an object, you can then create strokes or paths from the anchor points.

You can select several anchor points at the same time (Figure 3-1) or only one (Figure 3-2). Selecting several anchor points at once enables you to move the entire object without changing the anchor points in relationship to one another. You can tell which anchor points are selected and active because they appear as solid boxes.

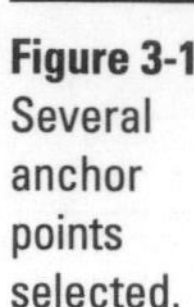

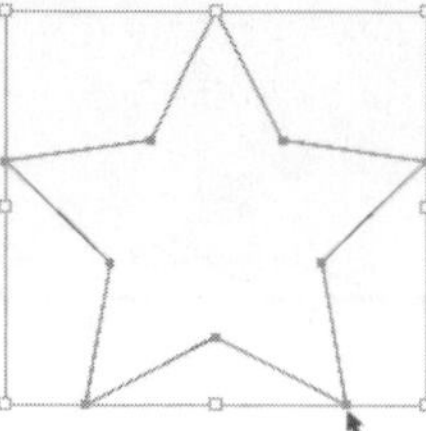

Figure 3-1: Several anchor points selected.

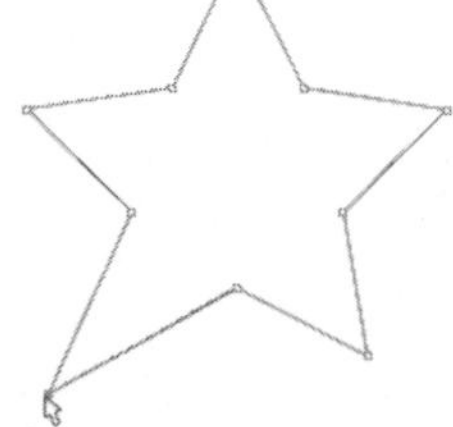

Figure 3-2: One anchor point selected.

Bounding box

As a default, Illustrator shows a bounding box when an object is selected with the Selection tool (a bounding box is shown in Figure 3-1). This feature can be helpful if you understand its function, but confusing if you don't know how to use it.

By dragging on the handles, you can use the bounding box for quick transforms, such as scaling and rotating. To rotate, you pass the mouse cursor (without clicking) outside a handle until you see a rotate symbol, and then drag.

If the bounding box bothers you, you can turn off the feature by choosing View➪Hide Bounding Box.

Selection tools

Illustrator CS3 offers three main selection tools:

- **Selection tool:** Selects entire objects or groups. This tool activates all anchor points in an object or group at the same time, allowing you to move an object without changing its shape.
- **Direct Selection tool:** Selects individual points.
- **Group Selection tool:** Hidden in the Direct Selection tool in the toolbox, you use this tool to select items within a group. This tool adds grouped

items as you click an object in the order in which objects were grouped. This selection tool will become more useful to you as you find out about grouping objects in Illustrator.

You can select an object with the Selection tool using one of three main methods:

- ✦ Click the object's path.
- ✦ Click an anchor point of the object.
- ✦ Drag a marquee around part or all of the object's path. (In the later section, "Using a marquee to select an object," we discuss using the marquee method.)

Use the Magic Wand selection tool to select objects with like values, such as fill and stroke colors, based upon a tolerance, and stroke weight. Change the options of this tool by double-clicking the Magic Wand tool.

Use the Lasso tool to click and drag around anchor points that you want to select.

Working with Selections

After you have an understanding about the basics of selections, you probably will be anxious to jump in and start with the selecting. So in this section, we introduce you to the basics: making a selection, working with anchor points and the marquee, making multiple selections, and, of course, saving your work.

When we give you Ctrl key combinations, you should press the ⌘ key if you're using a Mac (unless we note otherwise).

Creating a selection

To work with selections, you need to actually have something on the page in Illustrator. Use the following techniques to make a selection:

1. **Create a new page in Adobe Illustrator (any size or profile is okay).**

   Alternatively, you can open an existing illustration; see Chapter 2 of this minibook for instructions.

2. **If you're starting from a new page, create an object to work with.**

   For example, select the Rectangle tool and click and drag from the top left to the lower right to create a shape.

Exact size doesn't matter, but make it large enough that you can see it. To start over, choose Edit⇨Undo or press Ctrl+Z.

As a default, all shapes start out having a black stroke and a white fill (see Figure 3-3). If yours is not black and white, press D, which changes the selected object to the default colors.

Figure 3-3: Create a rectangle to practice using the Selection tools.

3. **Using the Selection tool, click the object to make sure that it's active.**

   Note that all anchor points are solid, indicating that all anchor points are active, as shown in Figure 3-4. As a default, you see many additional points that you can use to transform your selected object.

Figure 3-4: All anchor points activate with the Selection tool.

4. **Click and drag the rectangle to another location.**

   All anchor points travel together.

5. **When completed, deactivate your selection.**

   You can use one of these three methods:

   - Choose Select⇨Deselect.
   - Ctrl+click anywhere on the page.
   - Press Ctrl+Shift+A.

Selecting an anchor point

When you have a selection to work with (see the preceding numbered list), you can deselect all the active anchor points and then make just one anchor point active. Just follow these steps:

1. **Make sure that the object isn't selected by choosing Select➪Deselect.**
2. **Select the Direct Selection tool (the white arrow) from the toolbox.**
3. **Click one anchor point.**

   Only one anchor point (the one you clicked) is solid, and the others are hollow, as shown in Figure 3-5.

Figure 3-5: Only the selected anchor point becomes active when selected with the Direct Selection tool.

4. **Click and drag that solid anchor point using the Direct Selection tool.**

   Only that one anchor point moves.

New in Illustrator CS3, an anchor point actually enlarges when you cross over it using the Direct Selection tool. This enlargement is a big break for those who typically have to squint to see where the anchor points are positioned.

Using a marquee to select an object

Sometimes it's easier to surround what you want selected by dragging the mouse to create a marquee. Follow these steps to select an object by creating a marquee:

1. **Choose the Selection tool.**
2. **Click outside the object (we use a rectangle in this example) and drag over a small part of it, as shown in Figure 3-6.**

   The entire object becomes selected.

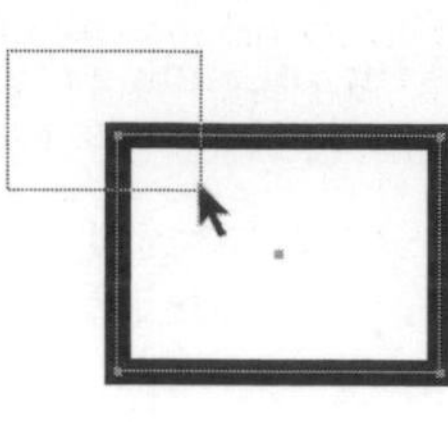

Figure 3-6: Selecting an entire object with a marquee and the Selection tool.

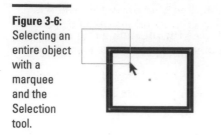

You can also select just one anchor point in an object by using the marquee method:

1. **Make sure that the object isn't selected by choosing Select⇨Deselect and then choose the Direct Selection tool.**
2. **Click outside a corner of the object and drag over just the anchor point that you want to select.**

   Notice that only that anchor point is active, which can be a sight-saver when you're trying to select individual points (see Figure 3-7).

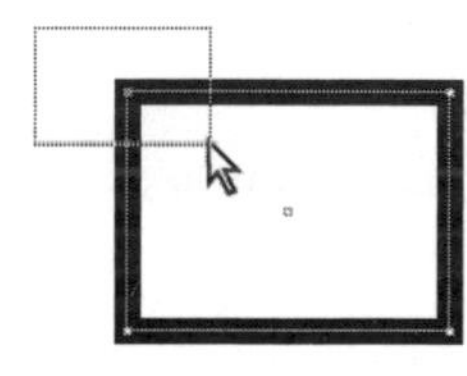

Figure 3-7: Selecting individual anchor points with a marquee and the Direct Selection tool.

You can use this method to cross over just the two top points or side anchor points to activate multiple anchor points as well.

Selecting multiple objects

If you have multiple items on your page, you can select them by using one of the following methods:

✦ Select one object or anchor point and then hold down the Shift key and click another object or anchor point. Depending on which selection tool you're using, you'll either select all anchor points on an object (Selection tool) or additional anchor points only (Direct Select tool).

  You can use the Shift key to deactivate an object as well. Shift+click a selected object to deselect it.

✦ Choose Select➪All or press Ctrl+A.

✦ Use the marquee selection technique and drag outside and over the objects. When you use this technique with the Selection tool, all anchor points in the objects are selected; with the Direct Selection tool, only the points that you drag over are selected.

Saving a selection

Spending way too much time trying to make your selections? Illustrator comes to the rescue with the Save Selection feature. After you have a selection that you may need again, choose Select➪Save Selection and name the selection. It now appears at the bottom of the Select menu. To change the name or delete the saved selection, choose Select➪Edit Selection. This selection is saved with the document.

Grouping and Ungrouping

Keep objects together by grouping them. The Group function is handy in a situation when you're creating something from multiple objects, such as a logo. With the Group function, you can make sure that all the objects that make up the logo stay together when you move, rotate, scale, or copy it. Just follow these steps to create a group:

1. **If you aren't already working with an illustration that contains a whole bunch of objects, create several objects on a new page, anywhere and any size.**

   For example, select the Rectangle tool and click and drag on the page several times to create additional rectangles.

2. **Select the first object with the Selection tool and then hold down the Shift key and click a second object.**
3. **Choose Object➪Group or press Ctrl+G.**
4. **Choose Select➪Deselect and then click one of the objects with the Selection tool.**

   Both objects become selected.

5. **While the first two objects are still selected, Shift+click a third object.**
6. **With all three objects selected, choose Object➪Group again.**

   Illustrator remembers the grouping order. To prove that, deselect the group by choosing Select➪Deselect and switch to the Group Selection tool. (Hold down the mouse button on the Direct Selection tool to access the Group Selection tool.)
7. **Using the Group Selection tool, click the first object, and all anchor points become active. Click again on the first object, and the second object becomes selected. Click yet again on the first object, and the third object becomes selected.**

   This tool activates the objects in the order that you grouped them. After you've grouped the objects together, you can now treat them as a single object.

To Ungroup objects, choose Object➪Ungroup or use the key command Ctrl+Shift+G. In a situation where you group objects twice (because you added an object to the group, for example), you would have to choose Ungroup twice.

Using the Isolation mode

Now in Illustrator you can take advantage of the Isolation mode, which allows you to easily select and edit objects in a group without disturbing other parts of your artwork. Simply double-click a group, and it opens in a separate Isolation mode, where all objects outside of the group are dimmed and inactive. Do the work that you need to on the group and exit out of the Isolation mode by clicking on the arrow to the left of Group in the upper right of the window, as shown in Figure 3-8.

Figure 3-8: The Isolation mode allows you to edit group contents without disturbing other artwork.

Manipulating Selected Objects

In the following list, you can discover a few other cool things that you can do with selected objects:

- **Moving selected objects:** When an object is selected, you can drag it to any location on the page, but what if you only want to nudge it a bit? To nudge an item one pixel at a time, select it with the Selection tool and press the left-, right-, up-, or down-arrow key to reposition the object. Hold down the Shift key as you press an arrow key to move an object by ten pixels at a time.
- **Constraining movement:** Want to move an object over to the other side of the page without changing its alignment? Constrain something by selecting an object with the Selection tool and dragging the item and then hold down the Shift key before you release the mouse button. By pressing the Shift key mid-drag, you constrain the movement to 45-, 90-, or 180-degree angles!
- **Cloning selected objects:** Use the Selection tool to easily clone (duplicate) an item and move it to a new location. To clone an item, simply select it with the Selection tool and then hold down the Alt key (Option key on a Mac). Look for the cursor to change to two arrows (see Figure 3-9) and then drag the item to another location on the page. Notice that the original object is left intact and that a copy of the object has been created and moved.

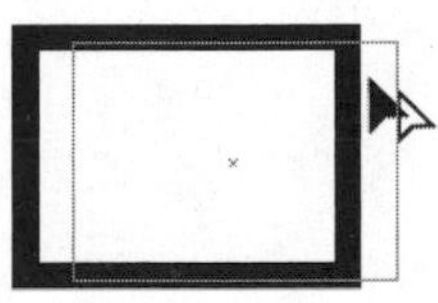

Figure 3-9: Look for the double arrow before dragging to clone the selected object.

- **Constraining the clone:** By Alt+dragging (Option+dragging on a Mac) an item and then pressing Shift, you can clone the item and keep it aligned with the original. ***Remember:*** Don't hold down the Shift key until you're in the process of dragging the item; otherwise, pressing Shift will deselect the original object.

After you've cloned an object to a new location, try this neat trick where you create multiple objects equally apart from each other using the Transform Again command: Choose Object⇨Transform⇨Transform Again, or press Ctrl+D to have another object cloned the exact distance as the first cloned object (see Figure 3-10). We discuss transforms in more detail in Chapter 10 of this minibook.

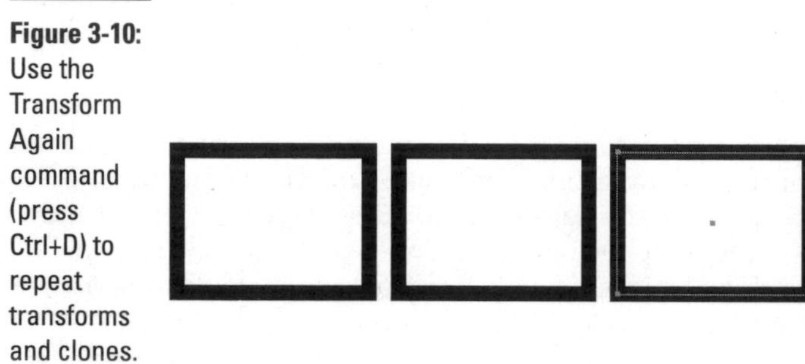

Figure 3-10: Use the Transform Again command (press Ctrl+D) to repeat transforms and clones.

✦ **Using the Select menu:** Using the Select menu, you can gain additional selection controls, such as Select⇨Inverse, which allows you to select one object and then turn your selection inside out. Also, the Select⇨Select Same options allow you to select one object and then select additional objects on the page based upon similarities in Color, Fill, Stroke, and other special attributes.

Chapter 4: Creating Basic Shapes

In This Chapter

- Introducing rectangles, ellipses, stars, and polygons
- Resizing shapes after creation
- Creating shapes

Shapes, shapes, shapes . . . they're everywhere in Illustrator. Basic shapes, such as squares, circles, polygons, and stars, are used in all types of illustrations. With the right know-how and the right shape tools, you can easily create these shapes exactly the way you want. In this chapter, we show you how to use these tools to control a shape's outcome, create shapes based on precise measurements, and change the number of points a star has.

The Basic Shape Tools

As a default, the only visible shape tool in the toolbox is the Rectangle tool. Click and hold down that tool, and you have access to the Rounded Rectangle, Ellipse, Polygon, and Star tools, shown in Figure 4-1. (Although you see the Flare tool, it's not a basic shape.)

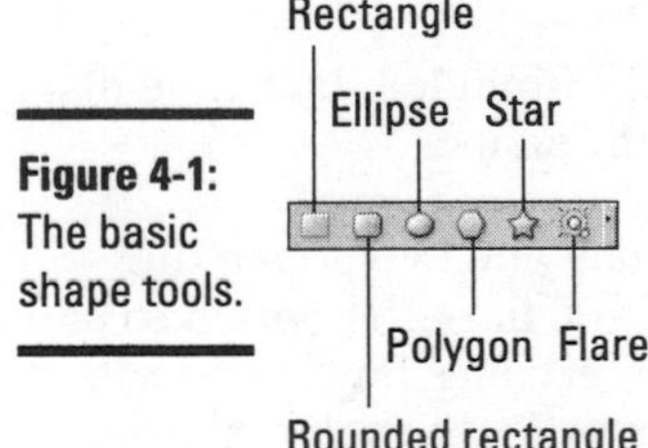

Figure 4-1: The basic shape tools.

You can tear off this tool set so that you don't have to find the hidden shapes in the future. Click and hold on the Rectangle tool and drag to the arrow on the far right. Wait until you see the pop-up hint (Tearoff) and then release the mouse button. These tools are now in a free-floating toolbar that you can drag to another location.

Creating rectangles and ellipses

Rectangles and ellipses are the most fundamental shapes that you can create (see Figure 4-2). To create a rectangle shape freehand, select the Rectangle tool and simply click the page where you want the shape to appear. Then drag diagonally toward the opposite side, drag it the distance that you want the shape to be in size, and release the mouse button. You can drag up or down. You do the same to create an ellipse with the Ellipse tool.

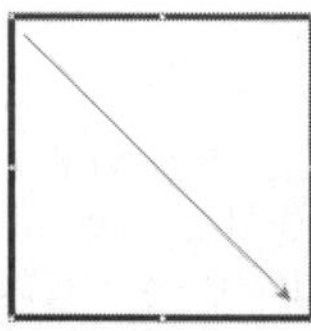

Figure 4-2: Click and drag diagonally to create a rectangle or ellipse.

After you create the shape, adjust its size and position by using the Selection tool. Reposition the shape by clicking the selected object and dragging. Resize the object by grabbing a handle and adjusting in or out. To adjust two sides together, grab a corner handle. To resize your shape proportionally, Shift+drag a corner handle.

Using the Rounded Rectangle tool

You can create the rounded rectangle by using one of two methods:

- ✦ Freehand clicking and dragging to create the rounded rectangle shape.
- ✦ Clicking once on the artboard to bring up the Rounded Rectangle dialog box, where you can enter values to define the shape.

The difference between these two methods is that when you open the Rounded Rectangle dialog box (see Figure 4-3), you have the option to enter a value in the Corner Radius text field, which determines how much rounding is applied to the corners of the shape. The smaller the value, the less rounded the corners will be; the higher the value, the more rounded. Be careful; you can actually round a rectangle's corners so much that it becomes an ellipse!

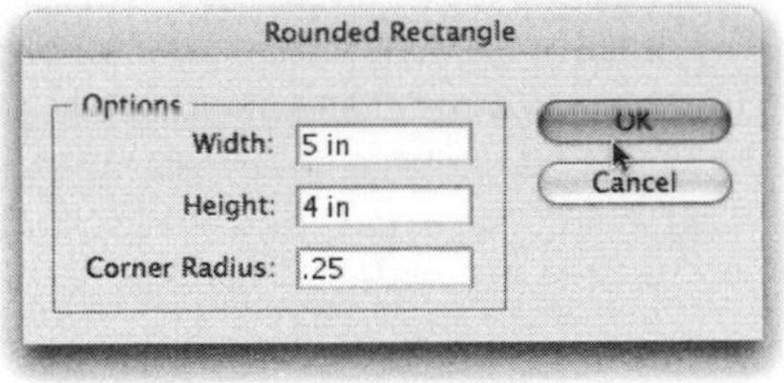

Figure 4-3: Select the Rounded Rectangle tool and click once on the artboard to customize the size.

Using the Polygon tool

You create stars and polygons in much the same way as the rectangles and ellipses. Select the Polygon tool and click and drag from one corner to another to create the default six-sided polygon shape. You can also select the Polygon tool and click once on the artboard to change the Polygon tool options in the Polygon dialog box.

You can change the polygon shape by entering new values in the Radius and Sides text fields, as shown in Figure 4-4. The radius is determined from the center to the edge of the polygon. The value for the number of sides can range from 3 (making triangles a breeze to create) to 1000. Whoa . . . a polygon with 1,000 sides would look like a circle unless it was the size of Texas!

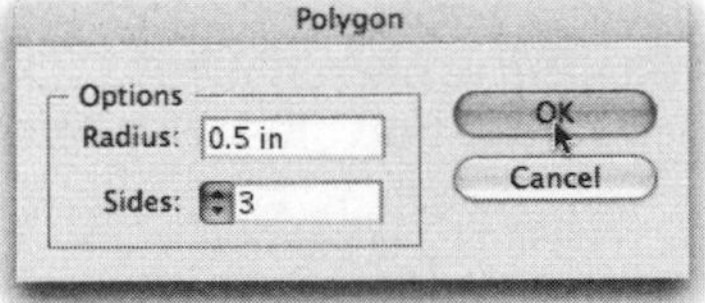

Figure 4-4: Creating a polygon shape.

Using the Star tool

To create a star shape, select the Star tool from the toolbox. (Remember that it may be hiding under other shape tools.) If you click once on the artboard to bring up the Star dialog box, you see three text fields in which you can enter values to customize your star shape:

- ✦ **Radius 1:** Distance from the outer points to the center of the star.
- ✦ **Radius 2:** Distance from the inner points to the center of the star.
- ✦ **Points:** Number of points that make up the star.

The closer together the Radius 1 and Radius 2 values are to each other, the shorter the points on your star. In other words, you can go from a starburst to a seal of approval by entering values that are close in the Radius 1 and Radius 2 text fields, as shown in Figure 4-5.

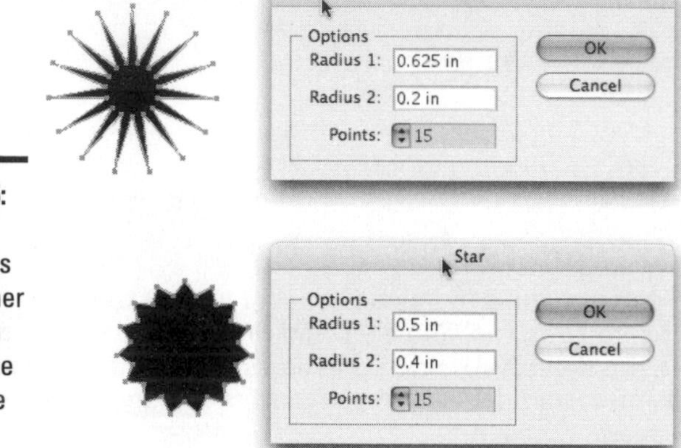

Figure 4-5: Radius 1 and Radius 2 are farther from each other in the star on the bottom.

Resizing Shapes

You often need a shape to be an exact size (for example, 2 x 3 inches). After you create a shape, the best way to resize it to exact measurements is to use the Transform panel, shown in Figure 4-6. Have your object selected and then choose Window⇨Transform to open the Transform panel. Note that on this panel, you can enter values to place an object in the X and Y fields, as well as enter values in the Width and Height text fields to determine the exact size of an object.

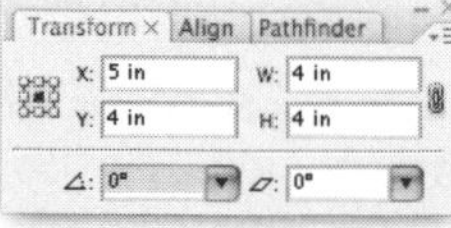

Figure 4-6: Use the Transform panel to precisely set the size of a shape.

In many of the Adobe Illustrator panels, you may see measurement increments consisting of points, picas, millimeters, centimeters, or inches, which can be confusing and maybe even intimidating. But you can control which measurement increments to use.

Show Rulers by choosing View➪Show Rulers or press Ctrl+R. Then right-click (Ctrl+click on a Mac) on the ruler to change the measurement increment to an increment you're more familiar with. The contextual menu that appears allows you to change the measurement increment right on the document.

Alternatively, you can simply type the number followed by a measurement extension into the Width and Height text fields in the Transform palette (refer to Figure 4-6), and the measurement converts properly for you. Table 4-1 lists the extensions that you can use.

Table 4-1 Measurement Extensions

Extension	*Measurement Unit*
" or in	Inches
pt	Points
mm	Millimeters
cm	Centimeters
p	Picas

If you don't want to bother creating a shape freehand and then changing the size, select the shape tool and click your page. An options dialog box specific to the shape you're creating appears, in which you can type values into the width and height text fields.

If you accidentally click and drag, you end up with a very small shape on your page. If this happens, don't fret. Simply get rid of the small shape by selecting it and pressing the Delete key, and then try again.

Tips for Creating Shapes

The following are simple tips to improve your skills at creating basic shapes in Illustrator:

- ✦ Press and hold the Shift key while dragging with the Rectangle or Ellipse tool to create a perfect square or circle. This trick is also helpful when you're using the Polygon and Star tools — holding down the Shift key constrains them so that they're straight (see Figure 4-7).

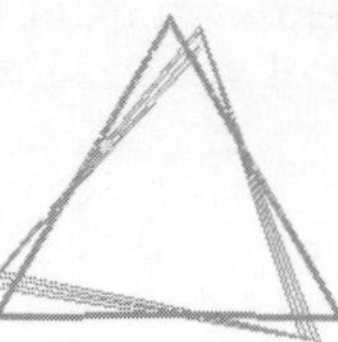

Figure 4-7: Use the Shift key to constrain a shape as you create it.

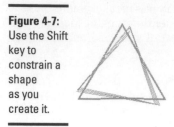

✦ Create a shape from the center out by holding down the Alt (Option on a Mac) key while dragging (see Figure 4-8). Hold down Alt+Shift (Option+ Shift on a Mac) to pull a constrained shape out from the center.

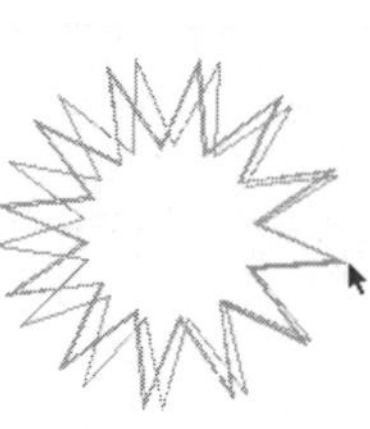

Figure 4-8: Hold down the Alt (Option on a Mac) key when making a shape to create it from a center point.

✦ When creating a star or polygon shape by clicking and dragging, if you keep the mouse button down, you can then press the up- or down-arrow key to interactively add points or sides to your shape.

Creating advanced shapes

At times, it may be much easier to use advanced tools in Illustrator to create unique shapes. The Pathfinder panel is an incredible tool that allows you to combine, knock out, and even create shapes from other intersected shapes.

You use the Pathfinder panel, shown in Figure 4-9, to combine objects into new shapes. To use the Pathfinder panel, choose Window➪Pathfinder.

Across the top row of the Pathfinder panel are the Shape Modes, which let you control the interaction between selected shapes. You can choose from the shape modes listed in Table 4-2.

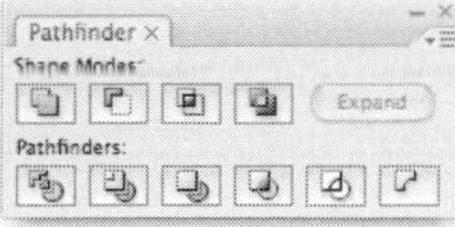

Figure 4-9: You use the Pathfinder panel to combine objects into new shapes.

Table 4-2 Shape Modes

Button	*Mode*	*What It Does*
	Add To Shape Area	Essentially unites the selected shape into one.
	Subtract from shape area	Cuts out the topmost shape from the underlying shape.
	Intersect shape areas	Uses the area of the topmost shape to clip the underlying shape as a mask would.
	Exclude overlapping shape areas	Uses the area of the shape to invert the underlying shape, turning filled regions into holes and vice versa.

If you like the Exclude Overlapping Shapes effect, you can also get a similar effect by selecting several shapes and selecting Object➪Compound Path➪Make. This command takes the topmost shapes and "punches" them out of the bottom shape.

The shapes remain separate so that you can still adjust them, which is great if you like to tweak your artwork (but it drives some people crazy). You can turn the results of the Shape Modes into one shape by either pressing the Expand button after selecting the shape mode or holding down the Alt key (Option key on a Mac) when selecting a Shape Mode.

Using the Pathfinders

The Pathfinders are the buttons at the bottom of the Pathfinder panel. They also let you create new shapes out of overlapping objects. Table 4-3 offers a summary of what each Pathfinder does.

Table 4-3 The Pathfinders

Button	*What It Does*
	Does exactly that. Create some overlapping shapes, select them, and then press the Divide button on the Pathfinder panel. All the shapes divide into their own shape. This tool is actually very useful tool when you're trying to create custom shapes.
	Removes the part of a filled object that is hidden.
	Removes the part of a filled object that is hidden. Also removes any strokes and merges any adjoining or overlapping objects filled with the same color.
	Deletes all parts of the artwork that fall outside the boundary of the topmost object. It also removes any strokes. If you want your strokes to remain when using this feature, you need to select them and choose Object⇨Path⇨Outline Stroke.
	Divides an object into its shape's line segments, or edges. Useful for preparing artwork that needs a trap for overprinting objects.

Chapter 5: Using the Pen Tool and Placing Images

In This Chapter

- Familiarizing yourself with the Pen tool
- Creating paths, closed shapes, and curves
- Creating template layers
- Placing images in Illustrator CS3

You've seen illustrations that you know are made from paths, but how do you make your own? In this chapter, we show you how to use the Pen tool to create paths and closed shapes.

The Pen tool requires a little more coordination than other Illustrator tools. Fortunately, Adobe Illustrator CS3 includes new features to help make using the Pen tool a little easier. After you master the Pen tool, the possibilities for creating illustrations are unlimited. Read this chapter to build your skills with the most popular feature in graphic software, the Bézier curve.

Pen Tool Fundamentals

You can use the Pen tool to create all sorts of things, such as straight lines, curves, and closed shapes, which you can then incorporate into illustrations:

- **Bézier curve:** Originally developed by Pierre Bézier in the 1970s for CAD/CAM operations, the Bézier curve (shown in Figure 5-1) became the underpinnings of the entire Adobe PostScript drawing model. A *Bézier curve* is one that you can control the depth and size of by using direction lines.
- **Anchor points:** You can use anchor points to control the shape of a path or object. Anchor points are automatically created when using shape tools. You can manually create anchor points by clicking from point to point with the Pen tool.
- **Direction lines:** These lines are essentially the handles that you use on curved points to adjust the depth and angle of curved paths.

Figure 5-1: The depth and direction of the Bézier curves are controlled by direction lines.

- **Closed shape:** When a path is created, it becomes a closed shape when the start point joins the endpoint.
- **Simple path:** A *path* consists of one or more straight or curved segments. Anchor points mark the endpoints of the path segments.

In the next section, we show you how to control the anchor points.

Creating a straight line

A basic function of the Pen tool is to create a simple path. You can create a simple, straight line with the Pen tool by following these steps:

1. **Before you start, press D or click the small black-and-white color swatches at the bottom of the toolbox.**

   You revert back to the default colors of a black stroke and a white fill. With black as a stroke, you can see your path clearly.

2. **Click the Fill swatch, located at the bottom of the toolbox, to make sure that the Fill swatch is in front of the Stroke swatch, and then press the forward slash (/) key to change the fill to None.**

   The trick of pressing D to change the foreground and background colors to the default of black and white also works in Photoshop and InDesign.

3. **Open a new blank page and select the Pen tool.**

   Notice that when you move the mouse over the artboard, the Pen cursor appears with an X beside it, indicating that you're creating the first anchor point of a path.

4. **Click the artboard to create the first anchor point of a line.**

   The X disappears.

Don't drag the mouse, or you'll end up creating a curve instead of a straight segment.

5. **Click anywhere else on the document to create the ending anchor point of the line.**

   Illustrator creates a path between the two anchor points. Essentially, the path looks like a line segment with an anchor point at each end (see Figure 5-2).

Figure 5-2: A path connected by two anchor points.

To make a correction to a line you created with the Pen tool (as described in the preceding steps), follow these steps:

1. **Choose Select⇨Deselect to make sure that no objects are currently selected.**
2. **Select the Direct Selection tool from the toolbox.**

   Notice that in Illustrator CS3, Adobe has been kind and added a feature that enlarges the anchor point when you pass over it with the Direct Selection tool.
3. **Click to select one anchor point on the line.**

   Notice that the selected anchor point is solid and the other is hollow. Solid indicates that the anchor point you clicked is active while the hollow one is inactive.
4. **Click and drag the anchor point with the Direct Selection tool.**

   The selected anchor point moves, changing the direction of the path while not affecting the other anchor point. And that's it.

Use the Direct Selection tool (shortcut to select this tool is A) to make any corrections to paths. Make sure that only the anchor point you want to change is active. If the entire path is selected, all anchor points are solid. If only one anchor point is selected, all but that one point will be hollow.

Creating a constrained straight line

In this section, we show you how to create a real straight line, meaning one that is on multiples of a 45-degree angle. Illustrator makes it easy; just follow these steps:

1. **Select the Pen tool and click anywhere on the artboard to place an anchor point.**
2. **Hold down the Shift key and click another location to place the ending anchor point.**

   Notice that when you're holding the Shift key, the line snaps to a multiple of 45 degrees. ***Remember:*** Release the mouse button before you release the Shift key, or else the line will pop out of alignment.

Creating a curve

In this section, you discover how to use the Bézier path to create a curved segment. We won't guarantee that you'll love it — not at first anyway. But after you know how to use a Bézier path, you'll likely find it useful. To create a Bézier path, just follow these steps:

1. **Starting with a blank artboard, select the Pen tool and click anywhere on the artboard to place the first anchor point.**
2. **Now click someplace else to place your ending anchor point, but don't let go of the mouse button. Drag the cursor until a direction line appears.**

   If you look real close, you see that anchor points are square, and the direction lines have circles at the end, as shown in Figure 5-3.

Figure 5-3: Click and drag with the Pen tool to create a curved path.

3. **Drag the direction line closer to the anchor point to flatten the curve; drag farther away from the anchor point to increase the curve, as shown in Figure 5-4.**
4. **Release the mouse button when you're happy with the curve.**

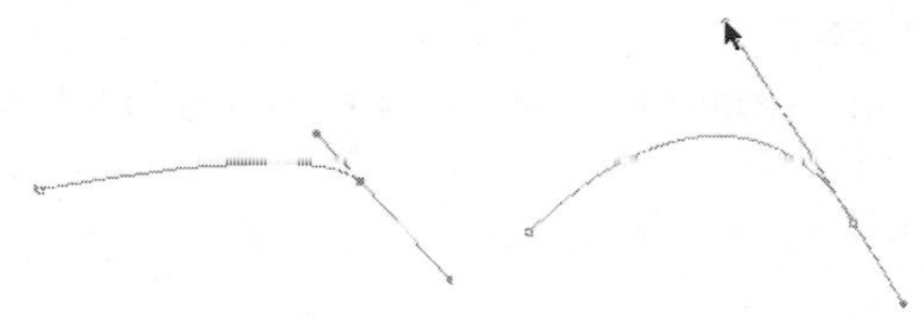

Figure 5-4: The directional lines determine how the curve appears.

What you have created is an open path, a path that doesn't form a closed shape. We show you how to reconnect to the starting point of the path to make a closed shape in the next section.

To alter a curved segment after you've created it, follow these steps:

1. **Choose Select⇨Deselect to make sure that no objects are currently selected.**
2. **Choose the Direct Selection tool and click the last anchor point created.**

   If they're not already visible, the direction lines appear.

   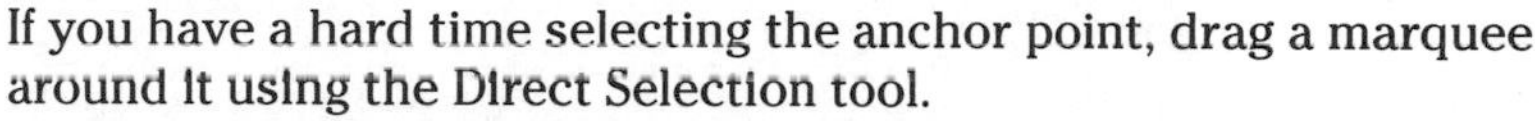

   If you have a hard time selecting the anchor point, drag a marquee around it using the Direct Selection tool.
3. **Click precisely at the end of one of the direction lines; drag the direction line to change the curve.**

Reconnecting to an existing path

Creating one segment is fine if you just want a line or an arch. But if you want to create a shape, you need to add more anchor points to the original segment. If you want to fill your shape with a color or a gradient, you need to close it, meaning that you need to eventually come back to the starting anchor point.

To add segments to your path and create a closed shape, follow these steps:

1. **Create a segment (straight or curved).**

   We show you how in the preceding sections of this chapter.

   You can continue from this point, clicking and adding anchor points until you eventually close the shape. For this example, you deselect the path so that you can discover how to continue adding to paths that have already been created. Knowing how to edit existing paths is extremely helpful when you need to make adjustments to artwork.

2. **With the Pen tool selected, move the cursor over an end anchor point on the deselected path.**
3. **To connect your next segment, click when you see the Pen icon with a forward slash.**

   The forward slash indicates that you're connecting to this path.
4. **Click someplace else to create the next anchor point in the path; drag the mouse if you want to create a curved segment.**
5. **Click to place additional anchor points, dragging as needed to curve those segments.**

   Remember that you want to close this shape, so place your anchor points so that you can eventually come back around to the first anchor point.

   Figure 5-5 shows a shape that is a result of several linked anchor points.

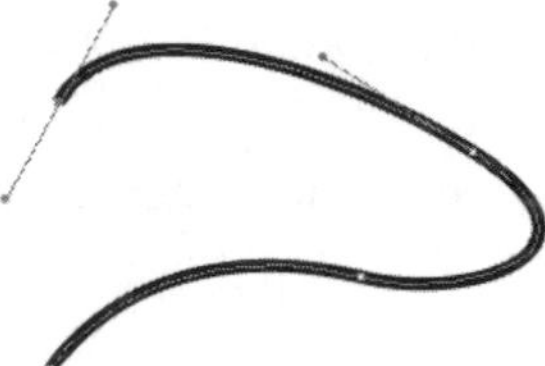

Figure 5-5: Adding more anchor points to create a shape.

6. **When you get back to the first anchor point, move the cursor over it and click when the close icon (a small hollow circle) appears, as shown in Figure 5-6.**

   The shape now has no end points.

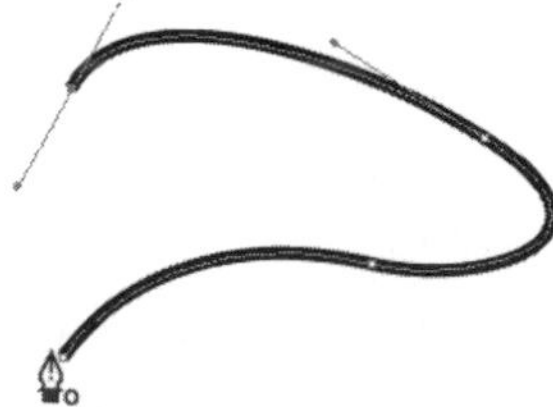

Figure 5-6: Click when the close path icon appears.

Controlling the curves

After you feel comfortable creating curves and paths, you need to take control of those curves so that you can create them with a greater degree of precision. The following steps walk you through the manual method for changing direction of anchor points, as well as reveal helpful keyboard commands to make controlling paths a little more fluid. At the end of this section, we introduce you to new tools that may also want to take advantage of to help you get control of the Pen tool.

To control a curve, follow these steps:

1. **Create a new document and then choose View⇨Show Grid to show a series of horizontal and vertical rules that act as guides.**

   If it helps, use the Zoom tool to zoom in to the document.

2. **Using the Pen tool, click an intersection of any of these lines in the middle area of the page to place your initial anchor point and drag upward.**

   Let go, but don't click when the direction line has extended up to the horizontal grid line above it, as shown in Figure 5-7a.

3. **Click to place the second anchor point on the intersection of the grid directly to the right of your initial point; drag the direction line down to the grid line directly below it, as shown in Figure 5-7b.**

   TIP: If you have a hard time keeping the direction line straight, hold down the Shift key to constrain it.

4. **Choose Select⇨Deselect to deselect your curve.**

   Congratulations! You've created a controlled curve. In these steps, we created an arch that is going up, so we first clicked and dragged up. Likewise, to create a downward arch, you must click and drag down. Using the grid, try to create a downward arch like the one shown in Figure 5-7c.

(a)

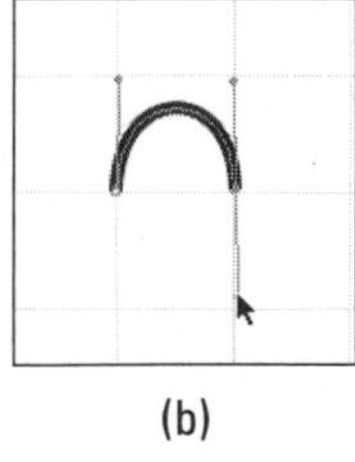

(b)

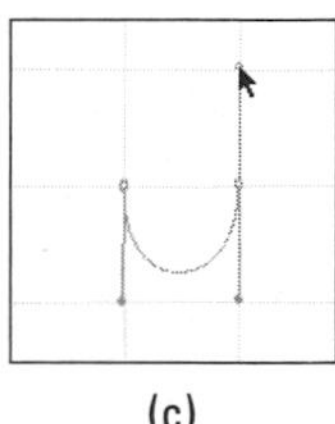

(c)

Figure 5-7: Creating a controlled Bézier Curve.

Creating a corner point

To change directions of a path from being a curve to a corner, you have to create a *corner point,* as shown on the right in Figure 5-8. A corner point has no direction lines and allows for a sharp direction change in a path.

You can switch from the Pen tool to the Convert Anchor Point tool to change a smooth anchor point into a corner point, but that process is a bit time consuming. An easier way is to press the Alt (Option on a Mac) key (the Pen tool temporarily changes into the Convert Anchor Point tool) while clicking the anchor point.

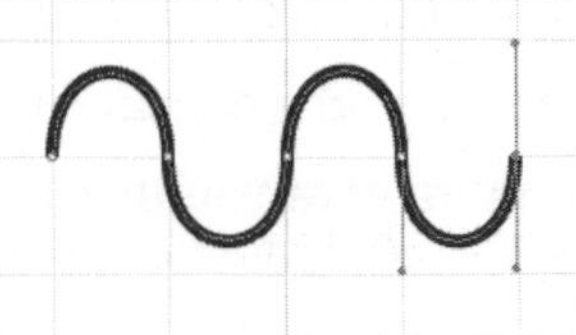

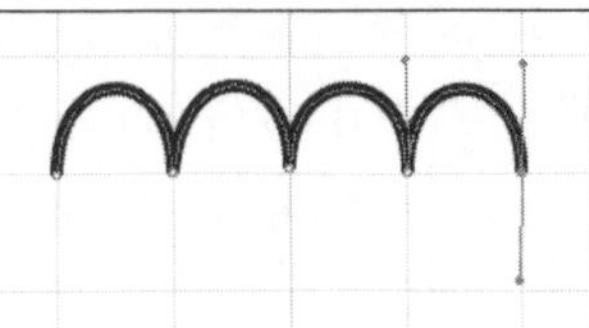

Figure 5-8: Smooth versus corner points.

To change a smooth anchor point into a corner point using the shortcut method, follow these steps:

1. **Create an upward arch.**

   We show you how in the preceding section, "Controlling the curves" (refer to Figure 5-8b).

2. **Hold down the Alt (Option on a Mac) key and position the cursor over the last anchor point (the last point that you created with the Pen tool).**

3. **When the cursor changes to a caret (that's the Convert Anchor Point tool), click and drag until the direction line is up to the grid line above, as shown on the left in Figure 5-9.**

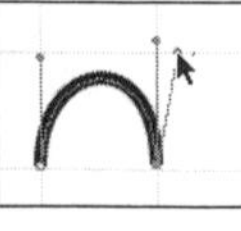

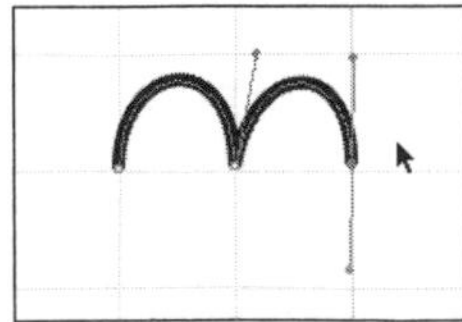

Figure 5-9: Converting a smooth anchor point to a corner point.

4. **Release the Alt (Option on a Mac) key and the mouse button, move the cursor to the grid line to the right, and click and drag down.**

The Hidden Pen Tools

Hold down on the Pen tool icon in the toolbox to access additional tools: the Add Anchor Point, Delete Anchor Point, and Convert Anchor Point tools, shown in Table 5-1. In the preceding section, we show you how to create a corner point with the shortcut method, by pressing the Alt (Option on a Mac) key to access the Convert Anchor Point tool. You may feel more comfortable switching to that tool when you need to convert a point, but switching tools can be more time-consuming.

Table 5-1 The Hidden Pen Tools

Icon	*Tool*
	Pen
	Add Anchor Point
	Delete Anchor Point
	Convert Anchor Point

Even though you can use a hidden tool to delete and add anchor points, Illustrator automatically does this as a default when you're using the Pen tool. When you move the cursor over an anchor point with the Pen tool, a minus icon appears. To delete that anchor point, simply click. Likewise, when you move the cursor over a part of the path that doesn't contain anchor points, a plus icon appears. Simply click to add an anchor point.

If you prefer to use the tools dedicated to adding and deleting anchor points, choose Edit (Windows) or Illustrator (Mac)⇨Preferences⇨General; in the Preferences dialog box that appears, select the Disable Auto Add/Delete check box. Then, when you want to add or delete an anchor point, select the appropriate tool and click on the path.

So what's new in CS3?

Some tools have been added to the control panel in Illustrator CS3, and you can take advantage of them to do many of the Pen tool functions you do manually. To tell you the truth, using keyboard modifiers to switch your Pen tool is probably still faster, but some of you who may be resistant to contorting your fingers while trying to create a path may appreciate these new tools.

In order to see the new tools, select the Pen tool and start creating a path. Notice that the control panel has a series of buttons available, as shown in Figure 5-10.

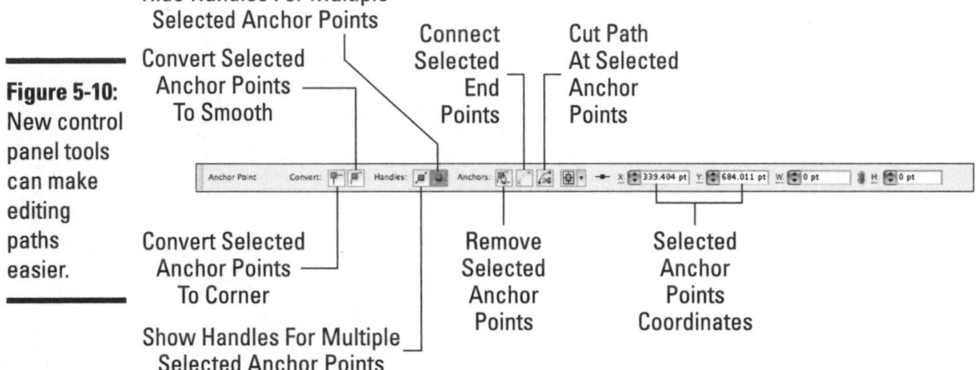

Figure 5-10: New control panel tools can make editing paths easier.

Using the new Eraser tool

The Eraser tool is a tool both new and old users will love! The Eraser tool allows you to quickly remove areas of artwork as easily as you erase pixels in Photoshop by stroking with your mouse over any shape or set of shapes.

New paths are automatically created along the edges of your erasure, even preserving the smoothness of your erasure as you see in Figure 5-11.

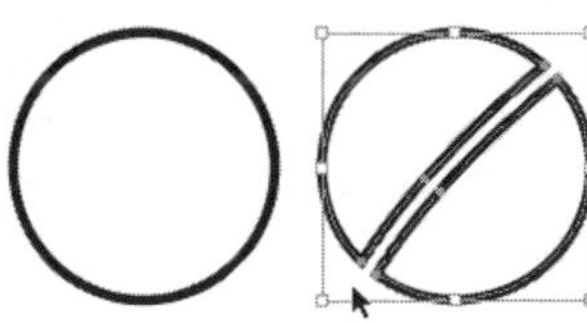

Figure 5-11: Use the new Eraser tool to delete sections of a path.

By double-clicking the Eraser tool, you can define the diameter, angle, and roundness of your eraser and even set Wacom (digitizing) tablet interaction parameters, such as Pressure and Tilt (see Figure 5-12).

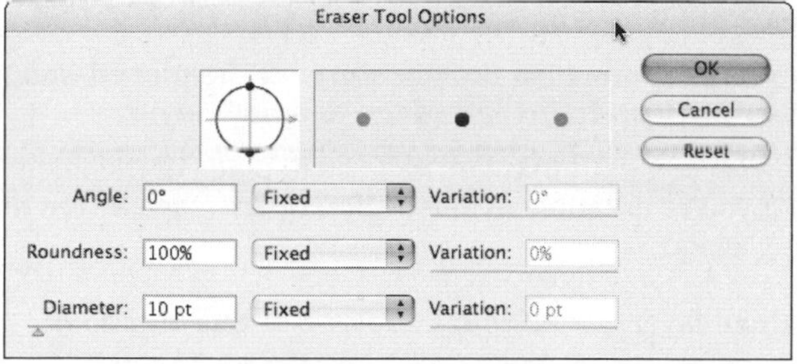

Figure 5-12: Double-click the Eraser tool to set various tool options.

If you want to erase more than a single selected object, use Isolation Mode to segregate grouped objects for editing. Remember that to enter Isolation mode, you simply double-click a group of items. You can then use the eraser on all objects in that group at once without disturbing the rest of your design.

Tracing Artwork

You can use a template layer to trace an image manually. A *template layer* is a locked, dimmed layer that you can use to draw over placed images with the Pen tool, much like you'd do with a piece of onion skin paper over the top of an image.

Just follow these steps to create a template layer:

1. **Take a scanned image or logo and save it in a format that Illustrator can import from your image-editing program, such as Photoshop.**

   Typically, you save the image as an `.eps`, `.tif`, or native `.psd` (Photoshop file).

2. **Choose File⇨Place to open the Place dialog box.**

3. **In the Place dialog box, locate the saved image; then select the Template check box and click Place.**

   Note that the Template check box may be in a different location depending upon your platform, but it's always located at the bottom of the dialog box.

   Selecting the Template check box tells Illustrator to lock down the scanned image on a layer. Essentially, you can't reposition or edit your image.

   After you click Place, a template layer is automatically created for you, and another layer is waiting for you to create your path. The newly created top layer is like a piece of tracing paper that has been placed on top of the scanned image.

4. **Re-create the image by tracing over it with the Pen tool.**
5. **When you're done, turn the visibility off the placed image by clicking the Visibility icon to the left of the template layer.**

   You now have a path that you can use in place of the image, which is useful if you're creating an illustration of an image or are digitally re-creating a logo.

For more about layers, check out Chapter 8 of this minibook.

Keep practicing to get yourself more comfortable with clicking and dragging, flowing with the direction line pointing the way that you want the path to be created; everything will fall into place.

Using Live Trace

Use the Live Trace feature, introduced in Illustrator CS2, to automatically trace raster images into vector paths. This does work great in many instances, but is definitely not a "magic pill" for getting your images re-created as vectors. For example, a logo with many precise curves and straight lines isn't a good candidate for this feature, but a hand-drawn illustration, clip art, or other drawing works well.

Here are the steps that you want to take to use Live Trace.

1. **Choose File⇨Place and place a scan or raster illustration that you want to convert to vector paths.**
2. **Immediately after placing, you see that the control panel now has some additional buttons available, as shown in Figure 5-13.**

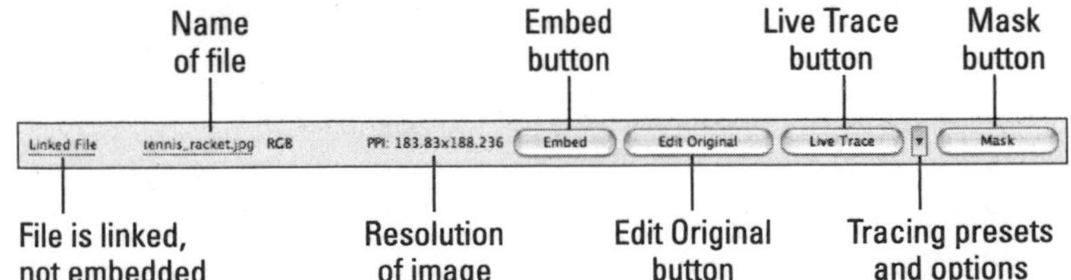

Figure 5-13: The Live Trace Control panel features.

3. **You can either press the Live Trace button to automatically trace based upon default settings or, better yet, click and hold on the Tracing presets and options arrow and choose a more appropriate setting.**

Choose Tracing Options from the very bottom of the Tracing options and presets drop-down menu to customize settings.

4. **After you select the settings you're happy with, you can either use the Live Paint features to color in the work or press the Expand button in the Control panel to expand the trace object to vector paths that can be edited.**

   See Chapter 9 of this minibook for more information on painting fills and strokes.

Other Things You Should Know about Placing Images

In the preceding section, you discover how to place an image as a template. But what if you want to place an image to be utilized in your illustration file? Simply choose File➪Place.

Click once on an image to see the Link check box. If you keep the check box selected, the image is linked to the original file. This is good if you plan on referencing the file several times in the illustration (saves file space) or if you want to edit the original and have it update the placed image in Illustrator. This option is usually checked by those in the prepress industry who want to have access to the original image file. Just remember to send the image with the Illustrator file if it's to be output or used someplace other than on your computer.

If you uncheck the Link check box, the image is embedded into the Illustrator file. This option does keep the filing system cleaner, but doesn't leave much room to edit the original image at a later point. There are certain instances, such as when you want an image to become a Symbol (see Chapter 11 of this minibook), that the image will have to be embedded, but most functions work with linked and unlinked files.

Using Photoshop Layer Comps

Layer Comps are a feature in Photoshop that allow you to set the visibility, appearance, and position of layers. It's a great organizational tool that you can now take advantage of in other Adobe products. Read more about Photoshop in Book II.

You can place a `.psd` (Photoshop) image that has saved Layer Comps from Photoshop and choose which layer comp set you want visible while placing in Adobe Illustrator CS3.

Chapter 6: Using Type in Illustrator

In This Chapter

- ✔ **Introducing the Type tools**
- ✔ **Getting to know text areas**
- ✔ **Manipulating text along paths and within shapes**
- ✔ **Assigning font styles**
- ✔ **Discovering the Character and Paragraph panels**
- ✔ **Using the new control panel for text controls**
- ✔ **Saving time with text utilities**

One of Illustrator's strongest areas is manipulating text. Whether you're using Illustrator to create logos, business cards, or type to be used on the Web, you have everything you need to create professional text.

In this chapter, you meet the Type tools and discover a few basic (and more advanced) text-editing tricks that you can take advantage of. You then discover other text tools, such as the Character and Paragraph panels. You end the chapter by getting a quick-and-dirty lowdown on the Illustrator text utilities. These utilities can save you loads of time, so don't skip this section.

Working with Type

You can do all sorts of cool things with type, from the simplest tasks of creating a line of text and dealing with text overflow to more complicated tricks, such as placing text along paths and wrapping text around objects.

Figure 6-1 shows the Type tools with an example of what you can do with each one. Click and hold the Type tool to see the hidden tools. The different tools give you the ability to be creative and also accommodate foreign languages.

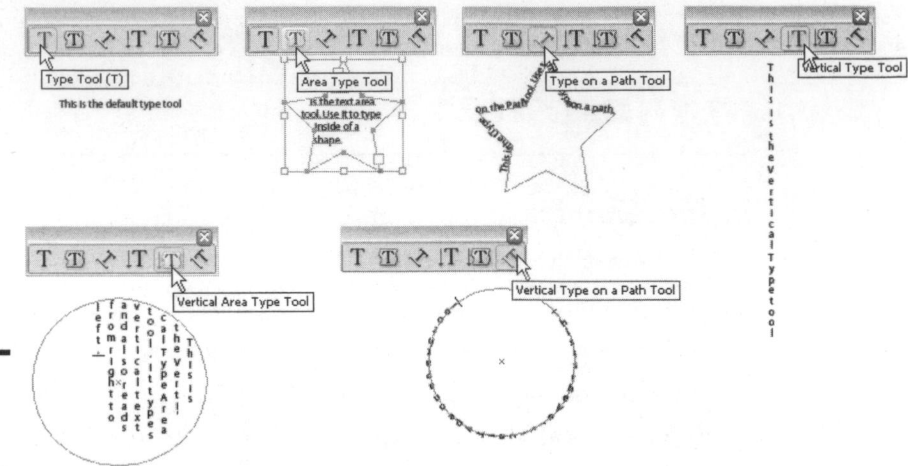

Figure 6-1: The Type tools.

Creating text areas

A *text area* is a region that you define. Text, when inserted in this region, is constrained within the shape. To create a text area, click and drag with the Type tool.

As you create and finish typing in a text area, you may want to quickly click and drag a new text area elsewhere on your artboard. Unfortunately, if you're on the Type tool, Illustrator doesn't allow you to do so. You have two options to address this problem:

- Choose Select➪Deselect and then create another area.
- Hold down the Ctrl key (or, as always unless otherwise noted, ⌘ on a Mac) to temporarily access the Selection tool, and click. When you release the Ctrl key, you'll still be on the Type tool, and you can then create a new text area.

Creating a line of text

To create a simple line of text, select the Type tool and click the artboard. A blinking insertion point appears. You can now start typing. Using this method, the line of type goes on forever and ever (even beyond the end of the Scratch area) until you press Enter (Return on a Mac) to start a new line of text. This excess length is fine if you just need short lines of text, say for callouts or captions, but it doesn't work well if you're creating a label or anything else that has large amounts of copy.

Many new users click and drag an ever-so-small text area that doesn't allow room for even one letter. If you do this, switch to your Selection tool, delete the active type area, and then click to create a new text insertion point.

Flowing text into an area

Select the Type tool and then drag on the artboard to create a text area. The cursor appears in the text area; text you type automatically flows to the next line when it reaches the edge of the text area. You can also switch to the Selection tool and adjust the width and height of the text area using the handles.

Need an exact size for a text area? With the Type tool selected, drag to create a text area of any size. Then choose Window➪Transform to view the Transform panel. Type an exact width in the W text field and exact height in the H text field.

Dealing with text overflow

Watch out for excess text! If you create a text area that's too small to hold all the text you want to put into it, a red plus sign appears in the lower-right corner, as shown in Figure 6-2.

When Illustrator indicates to you that you have too much text for the text area, you have several options:

- ✦ Make the text area larger by switching to the Selection tool and dragging the handles.
- ✦ Make the text smaller until you don't see the overflow indicated.
- ✦ Link this text area to another, which is called *threading* and is covered later in this chapter in the "Threading text into shapes" section.

Figure 6-2: The plus icon notes that text is overflowing.

Indicates text doesn't fit inside text area

Creating columns of text with the Area Type tool

The easiest and most practical way to create rows and columns of text is to use the area type options in Adobe Illustrator. This feature lets you create rows and columns from any text area. You can just have rows, or you can just have columns (much like columns of text in a newspaper), or even both.

1. **Select the Type tool and drag to create a text area.**
2. **Choose Type⇨Area Type Options.**

   The Area Type Options dialog box appears, as shown in Figure 6-3. At the end of this section, we provide a list explaining all the options in the Area Type Options dialog box.

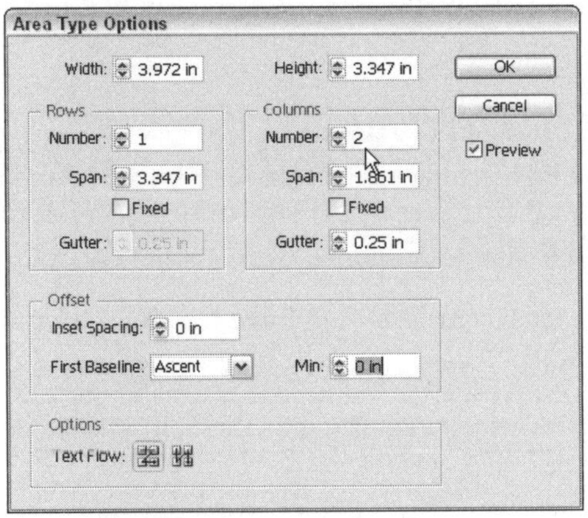

Figure 6-3: The Area Type Options dialog box lets you create columns of text.

3. **Enter the desired width and height in the Width and Height text fields.**

   The Width and Height text fields contain the height and width of your entire text area. For example, we entered 325 pt in the Width text field and 250 pt in the Height text field.

4. **In the Columns area, enter the number of columns you want to create in the Columns Number text field, the span distance in the Columns Span text field, and the gutter space in the Columns Gutter text field.**

   We entered **2** to create two columns in the Columns Number text field.

The *span* specifies the height of individual rows and the width of individual columns. The *gutter* is the space between the columns and is automatically set for you.

5. **Click OK.**

When you create two or more columns of text using the Area Type Options dialog box, text flows to the next column when you reach the end of a column, as shown in Figure 6-4.

This is what happens when you overflow text from one column to another. Using the Area Type Options you can easily create columns or even rows of text.
I am going to just blather on now to fill in copy until it overflows, my kids get embarrassed when i use their names in screen shots, so here we go. Kelly is a sweet teenager and acts just like one, Alex is just about the cutest thirteen year old you can find. Grant is only 4, but acts like he is thirty. We love Elizabeth very much, but pity the man she will marry.

Figure 6-4: One column of text flows into the next.

The following is a breakdown of the other options available in the Area Type Options dialog box (refer to Figure 6-3):

- **Width and Height:** The present width and height of the entire text area.
- **Number:** The number of rows and/or columns that you want the text area to contain.
- **Span:** The height of individual rows and the width of individual columns.
- **Fixed:** Determines what happens to the span of rows and columns if you resize the type area. When this check box is selected, resizing the area can change the number of rows and columns but not their width. Leave this option deselected if you want to resize the entire text area and have the columns automatically resize with it.
- **Gutter:** The empty space between rows or columns.
- **Inset Spacing:** The distance from the edges of the text area.
- **First Baseline:** Where you want the first line of text to appear. The Ascent option is the default and starts your text normally at the top. If you want to put a fixed size in, such as 50 pts from the top, select Fixed from the drop-down list and enter 50 pt in the Min text field.
- **Text Flow:** The direction in which you read the text as it flows to another row or column. You can choose to have the text flow horizontally (across rows) or vertically (down columns).

Threading text into shapes

Create custom columns of text that are in different shapes and sizes by threading closed shapes together. This technique works with rectangles, circles, stars, or any closed shape and can lead to some creative text areas.

1. **Create any shape, any size.**

   For this example, we've created a circle.

2. **Create another shape (it can be any shape) someplace else on the page.**

3. **Using the Selection tool, select one shape and Shift+click the other to make just those two shapes active.**

4. **Choose Type⇨Threaded Text⇨Create.**

   A threading line appears, as shown in Figure 6-5, indicating the direction of the threaded text.

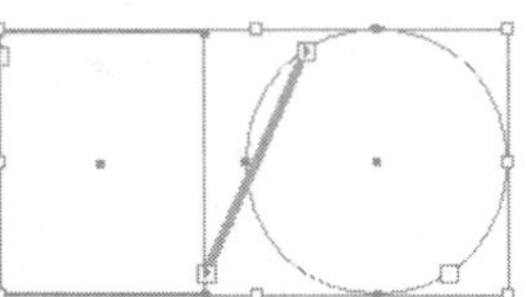

Figure 6-5: Threaded text areas flow from one area to another.

5. **Select the Type tool, click the top of the shape to start the threading, and start typing.**

   Continue typing until the text flows over into the other shape.

If you don't want the text to be threaded anymore, choose Type⇨Threaded Text⇨Remove Threading, which eliminates all threading from the text shapes. To remove one or more shapes from the threading but not all the shapes, select the shape you want to remove from the threading and choose Type⇨Threaded Text⇨Release Selection.

Wrapping text

Wrapping text isn't quite the same as wrapping a present — it's easier! A *text wrap* forces text to wrap around a graphic, as shown in Figure 6-6. This feature can add a bit of creativity to any piece.

Figure 6-6: The graphic is forcing the text to wrap around it.

Follow these steps to wrap text around another object or group of objects:

1. **Select the wrap object.**

   This is the object that you want the text to wrap around.

2. **Make sure that the wrap object is on top of the text you want to wrap around it by choosing Object⇨Arrange⇨Bring to Front.**

   If you're working in layers (which we discuss in Chapter 8 of this minibook), make sure that the wrap object is on the top layer.

3. **Choose Object⇨Text Wrap⇨Make.**

   An outline of the wrap area is visible.

4. **Adjust the wrap area by choosing Object⇨Text Wrap⇨ Text Wrap Options.**

   The Text Wrap Options dialog box appears, as shown in Figure 6-7, giving you the following options:

   - **Offset:** Specifies the amount of space between the text and the wrap object. You can enter a positive or negative value.
   - **Invert Wrap:** Wraps the text on the inside of the wrap object instead of around it.

5. **When you've finished making your selections, click OK.**

If you want to change the text wrap at a later point, select the object and choose Object⇨Text Wrap⇨Text Wrap Options. Make your changes and click OK.

If you want to unwrap text from an object, select the wrap object and choose Object⇨Text Wrap⇨Release.

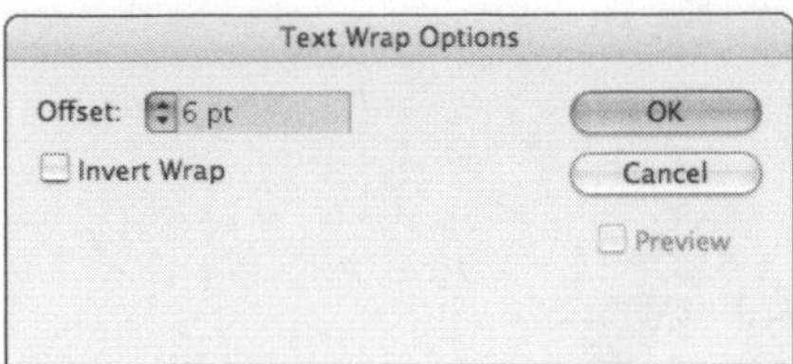

Figure 6-7: Adjust the distance of the text wrap from the object and where the text starts using Text Wrap Options.

Outlining text

Illustrator gives you the opportunity to change text into outlines or artwork. Basically, you change the text into an object, so you can no longer edit that text by typing. The plus side is that it saves you the trouble of sending fonts to everyone who wants to use the file. Turning text into outlines makes it appear as though your text was created with the Pen tool. You want to use this tool when creating logos that will be used frequently by other people or artwork that you may not have control over.

To turn text into an outline, follow these steps:

1. **Type some text on your page.**

   For this example, just type a word (say, your name) and make sure that the font size is at least 36 pts. You want to have it large enough to see the effect of outlining it.

2. **Switch to the Selection tool and choose Type⇨Create Outlines.**

   You can also use the keyboard command Ctrl+Shift+O (⌘+Shift+O on a Mac).

   The text is now grouped together in outline form.

3. **If you're being creative, or just particular, and want to move individual letters, use the Group Select tool or choose Object⇨Ungroup to separate the letters, as shown in Figure 6-8.**

When you convert type to outlines, the type loses its hints. *Hints* are the instructions built into fonts to adjust their shape so that your system displays or prints them in the best way based on the size. Without hints, letters like lowercase *e* or *a* might fill in as the letter forms are reduced in size.

Make sure that the text is the approximate size that it might be used at before creating outlines. Because the text loses the hints, try not to create outlines on text smaller than 10 pts.

Figure 6-8: Letters become shapes when converted to outlines.

Putting text on a path, in a closed shape, or on the path of a shape

Wow — that's some heading, huh? You've probably seen text following a swirly path or inside some shape. Maybe you think accomplishing such a task is too intimidating to even attempt. In this section, we show you just how easy these things are! There are Type tools dedicated to putting type on a path or a shape (refer to Figure 6-1), but we think you'll find that the key modifiers we show you in this section are easier to use.

Creating text on a path

Follow these steps to put type on a path:

1. **Create a path using the Pen, Line, or Pencil tool.**

   Don't worry if it has a stroke or fill applied.

2. **Select the Type tool and simply cross over the start of the path.**

3. **Look for an I-bar with a squiggle to appear (it indicates that the text will run along the path) and click.**

   The stroke and fill of the path immediately change to None.

4. **Start typing, and the text runs on the path.**

5. **To reposition where the text falls on the path, choose Window➪Type➪Paragraph and change the alignment in the Paragraph panel.**

   Alternatively, switch to the Selection tool and drag the I-bar that appears, as shown in Figure 6-9, to move the text freehand.

Figure 6-9: Using the Selection tool, you can click and drag the I-bar and adjust the text.

Flip the text to the other side of a path by clicking and dragging the I-bar under or over the path.

Creating text in a closed shape

Putting text inside a shape can add spunk to a layout. This feature allows you to custom-create a closed shape with the shape tools or the Pen tool and flow text into it. Follow these steps to add text inside a shape:

1. **Create a closed shape — a circle or oval, for example.**
2. **Select the Type tool and cross over the closed shape.**
3. **When you see the I-bar swell or become rounded, click inside the shape.**
4. **Start typing, and the text is contained inside the shape.**

Text on the path of a closed shape

Perhaps you want text to run around the edge of a shape instead of inside it. Follow these steps to have text created on the path of a closed shape:

1. **Create a closed shape, such as a circle.**
2. **Select the Type tool and cross over the path of the circle.**
3. **Don't click when you see the I-bar swell up; hold down the Alt (Option on a Mac) key instead.**

   The icon now changes into the squiggle I-bar that you see when creating text on a path.
4. **When the squiggle line appears, click.**
5. **Start typing, and the text flows around the path of the shape, as shown in Figure 6-10.**

Figure 6-10: By holding down the Alt or Option key, you can flow text around a closed shape.

To change the origin of the text or move it around, use the alignment options in the Paragraph panel or switch to the Selection tool and drag the I-bar to a new location on the path.

You can drag the I-bar in and out of the shape to flip the text so that it appears on the outside or inside of the path.

Assigning Font Styles

After you have text on your page, you'll often want to change it to be more interesting than the typical 12-pt Times font. Formatting text in Illustrator isn't only simple, but you can do it multiple ways. In the following list, we name and define some basic type components (see Figure 6-11):

- **Font:** A complete set of characters, letters, and symbols of a particular typeface design.
- **X height:** The height of type, based on the height of the small x in that type family.
- **Kerning:** The space between two letters. Often used for letters in larger type that need to be pulled closer together, like "W i." Kern a little to get the i to slide in a little closer to the W, maybe even going into the space that the W takes, as shown in Figure 6-12. Kerning doesn't distort the text; it only increases or decreases the space between two letters.

Figure 6-11: Components of type.

Figure 6-12: The letters before kerning (left) and after.

- **Tracking:** The space between multiple letters. Designers like to use this technique to spread out words by increasing the space between letters. Adjusting the tracking doesn't distort text; it increases or decreases the space between the letters, as shown in Figure 6-13.

AGI TRAINING

A G I   T R A I N I N G

Figure 6-13: A headline with tracking set at zero (top) and at 300 (bottom).

Pretty good tracking and kerning has already been determined in most fonts. You don't need to bother with these settings unless you're trying to tweak the text for a more customized look.

- **Baseline:** The line that type sits on. The baseline doesn't include descenders, type that extends down, like lowercase *y* and *g*. You adjust the baseline for trademark signs or mathematical formulas, as shown in Figure 6-14.

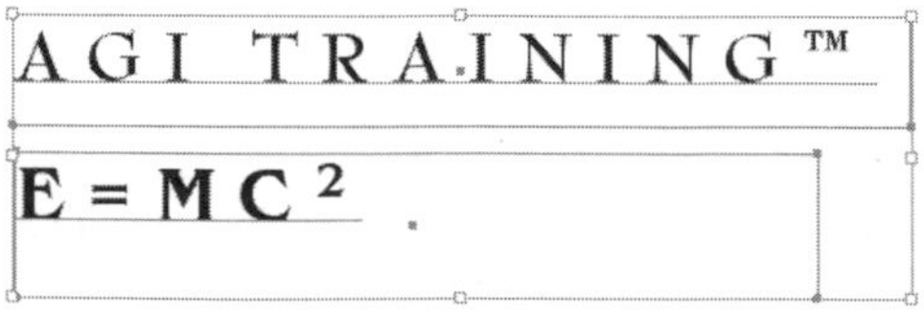

A G I   T R A I N I N G ™

E = M C ²

Figure 6-14: Adjust the baseline for text characters that need to be above or below the baseline.

The Keyboard shortcuts for type shown in Table 6-1 work with Adobe Illustrator, Photoshop, and InDesign.

Table 6-1 Keyboard Shortcuts for Type

Command	*Windows*	*Mac*
Align left, right, or center	Shift+Ctrl+L, R, or C	Shift+⌘+L, R, or C
Justify	Shift+Ctrl+J	Shift+⌘ +J
Insert soft return	Shift+Enter	Shift+Return
Reset horizontal scale to 100%	Shift+Ctrl+X	Shift+ ⌘ +X
Increase/decrease point size	Shift+Ctrl+> or <	Shift+ ⌘ +> or <
Increase/decrease leading	Alt+↑ or ↓	Option+↑ or ↓
Set leading to the font size	Double-click the leading icon in the Character panel	Double-click the leading icon in the Character panel
Reset tracking/kerning to 0	Alt+Ctrl+Q	Option+⌘ +Q
Add or remove space (kerning) between two characters	Alt+→ or ←	Option+→ or ←
Add or remove space (kerning) between characters by 5 times the increment value	Alt+Ctrl+→ or ←	Option+ ⌘+→ or ←
Add or remove space (kerning) between selected words	Alt+Ctrl+\ or Backspace	Option+ ⌘ +\ or Backspace
Add or remove space (kerning) between words by 5 times the increment value	Shift+Alt+Ctrl+\ or Backspace	Shift+Option+ ⌘ +\ or Backspace
Increase/decrease baseline shift	Alt+Shift+↑ or ↓	Option+Shift+↑ or ↓

Using the Character Panel

To visualize changes that you're making to text and to see characteristics that are already selected, choose Window⇨Type⇨Character or press Ctrl+T, which brings up the Character panel. Click the triangle in the upper-right corner to see a panel menu of additional options. Choose Show Options, and additional type attributes appear, such as baseline shift, underline, and strikethrough.

Pressing Ctrl+T is a toggle switch to either show or hide the Character panel. If you don't see the Character panel appear at first, you may have hidden it by pressing the keyboard shortcut. Just try it again.

The following list explains the options in the Character panel (see Figure 6-15):

✦ **Font:** Pick the font that you want to use from this drop-down list.

In this version, you can select the font name in the Character panel or control panel and press the up or down arrow key to automatically switch to the next font above or below on the font list. Do this while you have text selected to see the text change live!

✦ **Set Font Style:** Pick the style (for example, bold, italic, or bold italic) from this drop-down list. The choices here are limited by the fonts that you have loaded. In other words, if you have only Times regular loaded in your system, you won't have the choice to bold or italicize it.

✦ **Type Size:** Choose the size of the type in this combo box. Average readable type is 12 pt; headlines can vary from 18 pts and up.

✦ **Leading:** Select how much space you want between the lines of text in this combo box. Illustrator uses the professional typesetting method of including the type size in the total leading. In other words, if you have 12 pt and want it double-spaced, set the leading at 24 pts.

✦ **Kerning:** Use this combo box by placing the cursor between two letters. Increase the amount by clicking the up arrow or by typing in a value to push the letters further apart from each other; decrease the spacing between the letters by typing in a lower value, even negative numbers, or by clicking the down arrow.

✦ **Tracking:** Use the Tracking combo box by selecting multiple letters and increasing or decreasing the space between all of them at once by clicking the up or down arrows or by typing in a positive or negative value.

✦ **Horizontal Scale:** Distorts the selected text by stretching it horizontally. Enter a positive number to increase the size of the letters; enter a negative number to decrease the size.

✦ **Vertical Scale:** Distorts the selected text vertically. Enter a positive number to increase the size of the letters; enter a negative number to decrease the size.

Using horizontal or vertical scaling to make text look like condensed type often doesn't give good results. When you distort text, the nice thick and thin characteristics of the typeface also become distorted and can produce weird effects.

✦ **Baseline Shift:** Use baseline shift for trademark signs and mathematical formulas that require selected letters to be moved above or below the baseline.

- **Character Rotation:** Rotate just the selected text by entering an angle in this text field or by clicking the up or down arrows.
- **Rotate:** Choose to rotate your selected text on any angle.
- **Underline and Strikethrough:** Finally! This simple text attribute was noticeably missing from previous versions, but now a type style you can choose.
- **Language:** Choose a language from this drop-down list. ***Note:*** The language you specify here is used by Illustrator's spell checker and hyphenation feature. We discuss these features in the later section, "Text Utilities: Your Key to Efficiency."

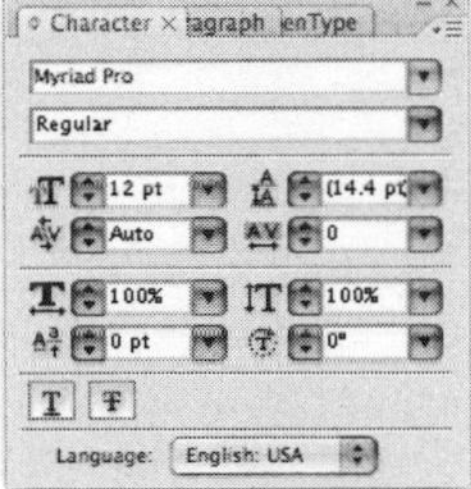

Figure 6-15: The Character panel with additional options showing.

Using the Control Panel

Try and get used to using the control panel to quickly access your type tools and type panels. Note in Figure 6-16 that, when you have active text, hyperlinked text buttons allow you to quickly access panels, such as the Character and Paragraph panels. You can also use this control panel as a quick and easy way to select fonts, size, alignment, color, and transparency.

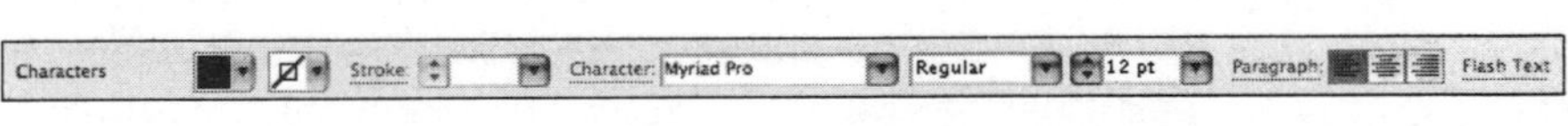

Figure 6-16: Access type functions quickly using the control panel across the top of your Illustrator document.

Using the Paragraph Panel

Access the Paragraph panel quickly by clicking the Paragraph hyperlink in the control panel or by choosing Window⇨Type⇨Paragraph. In this panel are all the attributes that apply to an entire paragraph, including alignment and indents, which we discuss in this section, and also hyphenation, which we discuss later in this chapter. For example, you can't flush left one word in a paragraph. When you click the Flush Left button, the entire paragraph flushes left. To see additional options in the Paragraph panel, click the triangle in the upper-right of the panel (the panel menu) and choose Show Options.

Alignment

You can choose any of the following alignment methods by choosing the appropriate button on the Paragraph panel:

- **Flush Left:** All text is flush to the left with a ragged edge on the right. This is the most common way to align text.
- **Center:** All text is centered.
- **Flush Right:** All text is flush to the right and ragged on the left.
- **Justify With The Last Line Aligned Left:** Right and left edges are both straight, with the last line left-aligned.
- **Justify With The Last Line Aligned Center:** Right and left edges are both straight, with the last line centered.
- **Justify With The Last Line Aligned Right:** Right and left edges are both straight, with the last line right-aligned.
- **Justify All Lines:** This method is called *forced justification,* where the last line is stretched the entire column width, no matter how short it is. This alignment is used in many publications, but it can create some awful results.

Indents

You can choose from the following methods of indentation:

- **First Line Indent:** Indents the first line of every paragraph. In other words, every time you press the Enter (Return on a Mac) key, this spacing is created.

  To avoid first-line indents and space after from occurring, say if you just want to break a line in a specific place, create a line break or soft return by pressing Shift+Enter (Shift+Return on a Mac).

- **Right Indent:** Indents from the right side of the column of text.
- **Left Indent:** Indents from the left side of the column of text.

Use the Eyedropper tool to copy the character, paragraph, fill, and stroke attributes. Select the text that you want to, select the Eyedropper tool, and click once on the text with the attributes you want to apply to the selected text.

By default, the Eyedropper affects all attributes of a type selection, including appearance attributes. To customize the attributes affected by these tools, double-click the Eyedropper tool to open the Eyedropper dialog box.

Text Utilities: Your Key to Efficiency

After you have text in an Illustrator document, you may need to perform various tasks within that text, such as searching for a word to replace with another word, checking your spelling and grammar, saving and creating your own styles, or changing the case of a block of text. You're in luck, because Illustrator provides various text utilities that enable you to easily and efficiently perform all these otherwise tedious tasks. In this section, we give you a quick tour of these utilities.

Find And Replace

Generally, artwork created in Illustrator isn't text heavy, but the fact that Illustrator has a Find And Replace feature can be a huge help. Use the Find And Replace dialog box (choose Edit⇨Find And Replace) to search for words that need to be changed, such as changing Smyth to Smith, or to locate items that may be difficult to find otherwise. This feature works pretty much like all other search and Replace methods.

Spell checker

Can you believe there was a time when Illustrator didn't have a spell checker? Thankfully, it does now — and its simple design makes it easy to use.

To use the spell checker, choose Edit⇨Check Spelling, and then click the Start button in the dialog box that appears. The spell checker works much like the spell checker in Microsoft Word or other popular applications: When a misspelled word is found, you're offered a list of Replacements. You can either choose to fix that instance, all instances, ignore the misspelling, or add your word to the dictionary.

If you click the arrow to the left of Options, you can set other specifications, such as whether you want to look for letter case issues or have the spell checker note repeated words.

Note: The spell checker uses whatever language you specify in the Character panel. We discuss this panel in the earlier section, "Using the Character Panel."

If you work in a specialized industry that uses loads of custom words, save yourself time by choosing Edit⇨Edit Custom Dictionary and then add your own words. We recommend that you do so before you're ready to spell check a document so that the spell checker doesn't flag the custom words later (which slows you down).

The Hyphenation feature

Nothing is worse than severely hyphenated copy. Most designers either use hyphenation as little as possible or avoid it altogether by turning off the Hyphenation feature.

Here are a few things that you should know about customizing your hyphenation settings if you decide to use this feature:

- **Turning the Hyphenation feature on/off:** Activate or deactivate the feature in the Hyphenation dialog box (see Figure 6-17); access this dialog box by choosing Window⇨Type⇨Paragraph, clicking the arrow in the upper-right of the Paragraph panel to access the panel menu, and then choosing Hyphenation from the list of options that appears. If you're not going to use the Hyphenation feature, turn it off by deselecting the Hyphenation check box at the top of the Hyphenation dialog box.

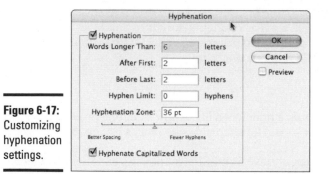

Figure 6-17: Customizing hyphenation settings.

- **Setting specifications in the Hyphenation dialog box:** Set specifications in the dialog box that determine the length of words to hyphenate, how many hyphens should be used in a single document, whether to hyphenate capitalized words, and how words should be hyphenated. The Before Last setting is useful, for example, if you don't want to have a word such as "liquidated" hyphenated as "liquidat-ed." Type 3 in the Before Last text field, and Illustrator won't hyphenate words if it leaves only two letters on the next line.

✦ **Hyphenation Limit and Hyphenation Zone:** They're not diets or worlds in another dimension. The Hyphenation Limit setting enables you to limit the number of hyphens in a row. So, for example, type 2 in the Hyphenation Limit text field so that there are never more than two hyphenated words in a row. The Hyphenation Zone text field enables you to set up an area of hyphenation based upon a measurement. For example, you can specify 1 inch to allow for only one hyphenation every inch. You can also use the slider to determine whether you want better spacing or fewer hyphens. This slider works only with the Single-line composer (the default).

The Find Font feature

If you work in production, you'll love the Find Font feature, which enables you to list all the fonts in a file that contains text and then search for and Replace fonts (including the font's type style) by name. You do so from the Find Font dialog box (see Figure 6-18), accessed by choosing Type⇨Find Font. Select the font that you want to Replace from the Fonts in Document list. Next, select a font from the Replace with Font From list. Note that the font must already appear in the document. Click the Change button to Replace the font (or click the Change All button to Replace all instances of the font) and then click OK. That's it!

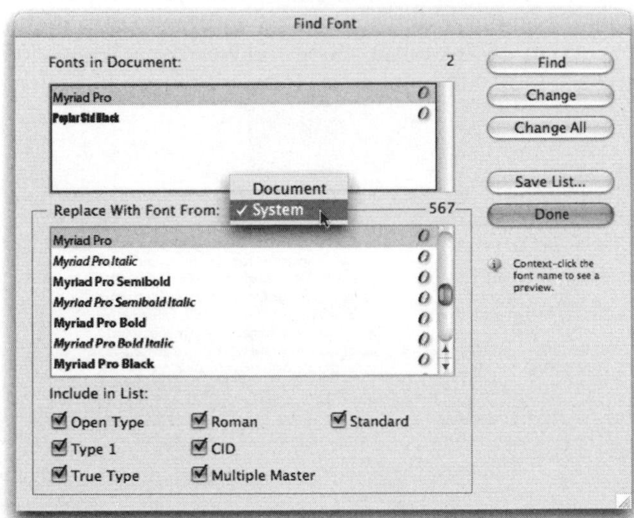

Figure 6-18: Use the Find Font dialog box to find and replace typefaces.

This cool feature enables you to Replace fonts with fonts from the current working document or from your entire system. Select System from the Replace with Font From drop-down list to choose from all the fonts loaded in your system.

The Change Case feature

Doesn't it drive you crazy when you type an entire paragraph before discovering that you somehow pressed the Caps Lock key? Fix it fast by selecting the text, choosing Type⇨Change Case, and then choosing one of the following:

- **Uppercase:** Makes the selected text all uppercase.
- **Lowercase:** Makes the selected text all lowercase.
- **Title Case:** Capitalizes the first letter in each word.
- **Sentence Case:** Capitalizes just the first letter in the selected sentence(s).

In Illustrator CS3, you use the same type engine used by InDesign for high-quality text control. As a default, you're working in what is referred to as a single-line composer. Select Single or Every Line composer from the Paragraph panel menu.

The different options include

- **Single-Line Composer:** Useful if you prefer to have manual control over how lines break. In fact, this method had been in place in the past. The single-line composer doesn't take the entire paragraph into consideration when expanding letter space and word spacing, so justified text can sometimes look odd in its entire form (see Figure 6-19).

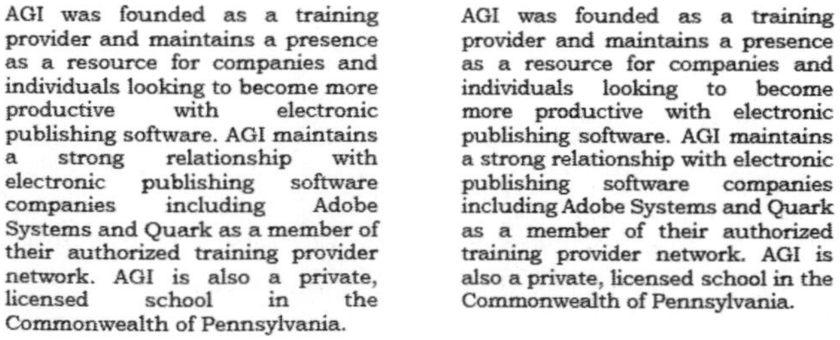

AGI was founded as a training provider and maintains a presence as a resource for companies and individuals looking to become more productive with electronic publishing software. AGI maintains a strong relationship with electronic publishing software companies including Adobe Systems and Quark as a member of their authorized training provider network. AGI is also a private, licensed school in the Commonwealth of Pennsylvania.

AGI was founded as a training provider and maintains a presence as a resource for companies and individuals looking to become more productive with electronic publishing software. AGI maintains a strong relationship with electronic publishing software companies including Adobe Systems and Quark as a member of their authorized training provider network. AGI is also a private, licensed school in the Commonwealth of Pennsylvania.

Figure 6-19: A paragraph created using the Single-Line Composer (left) and using the Every-Line Composer (right).

✦ **Every-Line Composer:** The every-line composer is a very professional way of setting text; many factors are taken into account as far as spacing is concerned, and spacing is based on the entire paragraph. Using this method, you see few spacing issues that create strange effects, such as the ones on the left of Figure 6-19.

Text styles

A *text style* is a saved set of text attributes, such as font, size, and so on. Creating text styles keeps you consistent and saves you time by enabling you to efficiently implement changes in one step instead of having to select the text attributes for each instance of that style of text (say a heading or caption). So when you're finally happy with the way your headlines appear and the body copy looks or when your boss asks whether the body copy can be a smidgen smaller (okay . . . a smidgen?), you can confidently answer, "Sure!"

If you've created styles, changing a text attribute is simple. What's more, the change is applied at once to all text that uses that style. Otherwise, you'd have to make the attribute change to every occurrence of body text, which could take a long time if your text is spread out.

Illustrator offers two types of text styles:

✦ **Character styles:** Saves attributes for individual selected text. If you want just the word "New" in a line of text to be red 20 pt Arial, you can save it as a character style sheet. Then, when you apply it, the attributes apply only to the selected text (and not the entire line or paragraph).

✦ **Paragraph styles:** Saves attributes for an entire paragraph. A span of text is considered a paragraph until it reaches a hard return or paragraph break. Note that pressing Shift+Enter (Shift+Return on a Mac) is considered a soft return, and paragraph styles will continue to apply beyond the soft return.

There are many ways to create character and paragraph styles, but we show you the easiest and most direct methods.

Creating character styles

Create a character style when you want individual sections of text to be treated differently from other text in the paragraph. So instead of manually applying a style over and over again, you create and implement a character style. To do so, open a document containing text and follow these steps:

1. **Set up text with the text attributes you want included in the character style in the Character and Paragraph panels and then choose Window⇨Type⇨Character Styles.**

The Character Styles panel opens.

2. **Select the text from Step 1 and Alt+click (Option+click on a Mac) the New Style button (dog-eared page icon) at the bottom of the Character Styles panel.**
3. **In the Character Styles Options dialog box that appears, name your style and click OK.**

   Illustrator records what attributes have already been applied to the selected text and builds a style for them.
4. **Now create another text area by choosing Select⇨Deselect and using the Type tool to drag out a new text area.**

   We discuss using the Type tool in the earlier section, "Creating text areas."
5. **Change the font and size to something dramatically different from your saved style and type some text.**
6. **Select some (not all) of the new text and then Alt+click (Option+click on a Mac) the style name in the Character Styles panel.**

   You Alt+click (Option+click on a Mac) to eliminate any attributes that weren't a part of the saved style. The attributes of the saved character style are applied to the selected text.

When creating a new panel item (any panel) in Adobe Illustrator, InDesign, or Photoshop, we recommend that you get in the habit of Alt+clicking (Option+clicking on a Mac) the New Style button. This habit allows you to name the item (style, layer, swatch, and so on) while adding it to the panel.

Creating a paragraph style

Paragraph styles include attributes that are applied to an entire paragraph. What constitutes a paragraph is all text that falls before a hard return (you create a hard return when you press Enter [Return on a Mac]), so this could be one line of text for a headline or ten lines in a body text paragraph.

To create a paragraph style, open a document that contains text or open a new document and add text to it; then follow these steps:

1. **Choose Window⇨Type⇨Paragraph Styles to open the Paragraph Styles panel.**
2. **Find a paragraph of text that has the same text attributes throughout it and put your cursor anywhere in that paragraph.**

   You don't even have to select the whole paragraph!

3. **Alt+click (Option+click on a Mac) the Create New Style button (the dog-eared icon at the bottom of the Paragraph panel) to create a new paragraph style; give your new style a name.**

   Your new style now appears in the Paragraph Styles panel list of styles.

4. **Create a paragraph of text elsewhere in your document and make its attributes different from the text in Step 2.**

5. **Put your cursor anywhere in the new paragraph and Alt+click (Option+click on a Mac) your named style in the Paragraph Styles panel.**

   The attributes from the style are applied to the entire paragraph.

Updating styles

When you use existing text to build styles, reselect the text and assign the style. In other words, if you put the cursor in the original text whose attributes were saved as a style, it doesn't have a style assigned to it in the Styles panel. Assign the style by selecting the text or paragraph and clicking the appropriate style listed in the Styles panel. By doing so, you ensure that any future updates to that style will apply to that original text, as well as to all other instances.

To update a style, simply select its name in either the Character or Paragraph Styles panel. Choose Options from the panel menu, which you access by clicking the arrow in the upper-right corner of the panel. In the resulting dialog box (see Figure 6-20), make changes by clicking the main attribute on the left and then updating the choices on the right. After you do so, all tagged styles are updated.

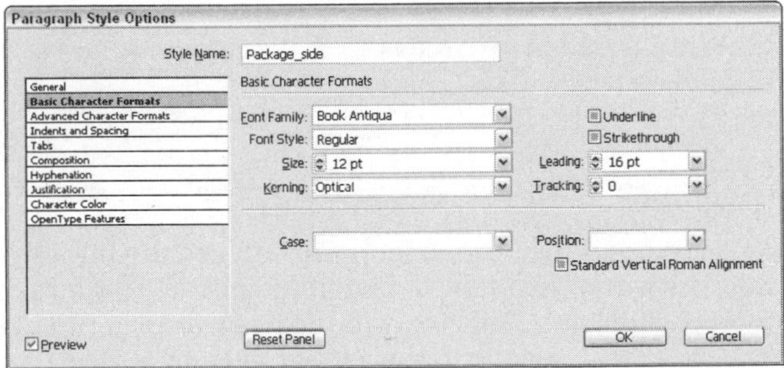

Figure 6-20: Updating a paragraph style.

Documents created in older versions of Adobe Illustrator (Version 10 or earlier) contain what is called *legacy text,* which is text using the older text engine. When these files are opened, you see a warning dialog box, such as the one you see in Figure 6-21.

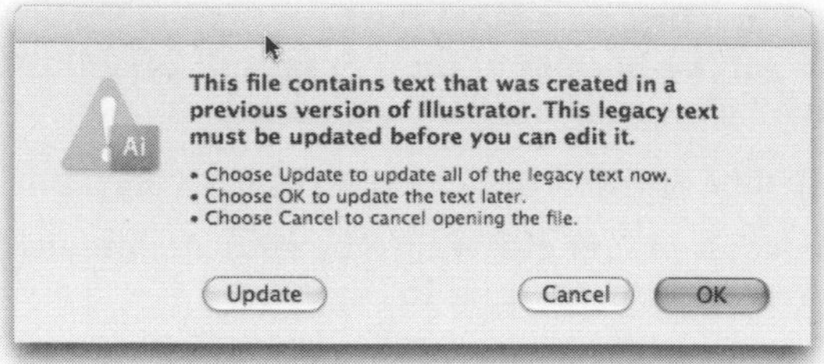
Ai
This file contains text that was created in a previous version of Illustrator. This legacy text must be updated before you can edit it.
• Choose Update to update all of the legacy text now.
• Choose OK to update the text later.
• Choose Cancel to cancel opening the file.
Update
Cancel
OK

Figure 6-21: Legacy text warning. Click OK, not Update!

Understand that if you click the Update button, any text on the document will most likely reflow, causing line breaks, leading, and other spacing to change.

Click the OK button to update the file after it's opened to lock down the text. If necessary, you can use the Type tool to click a selected text area to update only the contained text. Another Warning dialog box appears that gives you the opportunity to Update the selected text, copy the Text Object, or cancel the text tool selection. This method is the best way to see what changes are occurring so that you can catch any spacing issues right off the bat. See Figure 6-22 for samples of the three options in the warning dialog window.

tia della minestrone, i ravioli, e la farinata.
La città all'ovest della Liguria é San
Remo, che é accanto al Monaco. San
Remo é famosa per il museo di pasta e la festa di musica. La città
all'est della Liguria é La
Spezia, che é conosciu-
ta per una base
navale. La Spezia é
vicino à Carrara, il
posto dové
Michelangelo prese
la sua marma.
Da Genova si
andrà in barca alle
Cinque Terre, una zona
che non é possibile rag-

noce, e il pesce. E anche la regione nattia
della minestrone, i ravioli, e la farinata.
La città all'ovest della Liguria é San
Remo, che é accanto al Monaco. San
Remo é famosa per il museo di pasta e la
festa di musica. La città all'est della Liguria é La Spezia, che é conosciuta
per una base navale. La
Spezia é vicino à Carrara, il
posto dové Michelan-
gelo prese la sua
marma.
Da Genova si andrà
in barca alle Cinque
Terre, una zona che non
é possibile raggiungere in
machina; si deve andare o in
barca o in treno. Le Cinque Terre

noce, e il pesce. E anche la regione nattia
della minestrone, i ravioli, e la farinata.
La città all'ovest della Liguria é San
Remo, che é accanto al Monaco. San
Remo é famosa per il museo di pasta e la
festa di musica. La città all'est della Liguria é La Spezia, che é conosciuta
per una base navale. La
Spezia é vicino à Carrara, il
posto dové Michelan-
gelo prese la sua
marma. dové
Da Genova si andrà
in barca alle Cinque
Terre, una zona che non
é possibile raggiungere in
machina; si deve andare o in
barca o in treno. Le Cinque Terre

Figure 6-22: Original text (left), updated text (middle), and text object copied (right).

REMEMBER

If you choose to Copy the Text Object, you can use the underlying locked copy to adjust the new text flow to match the old. Throw away the legacy text layer by clicking and dragging it to the trash icon in the Layers panel, or click on the visibility Eye icon to the left of the Legacy Text layer to hide it when you are finished.

Chapter 7: Organizing Your Illustrations

In This Chapter

- ✔ **Setting up the ruler**
- ✔ **Placing paths and shapes**
- ✔ **Rearranging, hiding, and locking objects**
- ✔ **Masking objects**

You can know all the neat special effects in Illustrator, but if you don't have a strong foundation on the organization of your artwork, you can fall flat on your face when it comes to getting some features to work. In this chapter, we focus on a few tricks of the trade.

Setting Ruler Increments

Using rulers to help you accurately place objects in your illustration sounds pretty simple (and it is), but not knowing how to effectively use the rulers in Illustrator can drive you over the edge.

To view rulers in Illustrator, choose View⇨Show Rulers or press Ctrl+R (⌘+R on a Mac). When the rulers appear, they'll be in the default setting of points (or whatever measurement increment was last set up in the preferences).

You can change the rulers' increments to the measurement system that you prefer in the following ways:

- ✦ Create a new document and select your preferred measurement units in the New Document dialog box.
- ✦ Right-click (Ctrl+click on a Mac) the horizontal or vertical ruler and pick a measurement increment.
- ✦ Choose Edit⇨Preferences⇨Units And Display Performance (Illustrator⇨Preferences⇨Units And Display Performance on a Mac) to bring up the Preferences dialog box.

Be *very* careful with this dialog box. Change ruler units only by using the General tab of the Preferences dialog box. If you change the units of measurement in the Stroke and Type tabs, you can end up with 12-*inch* type instead of that dainty 12-*point* type you were expecting! ***Remember:*** Setting the General Preferences changes the preferences for all future documents.

✦ Choose File➪Document Setup to change measurement units only for the document that you're working on.

Using Guides

Guides can make producing accurate illustrations much easier, and they can even go away when you're done with them. You can use two kinds of guides in Illustrator:

✦ **Ruler guides:** Straight-line guides that are created by clicking the ruler and dragging out to the artboard.

✦ **Custom guides:** Guides created from Illustrator objects, such as shapes or paths. Great for copying the exact angle of a path and replicating it, as shown in Figure 7-1.

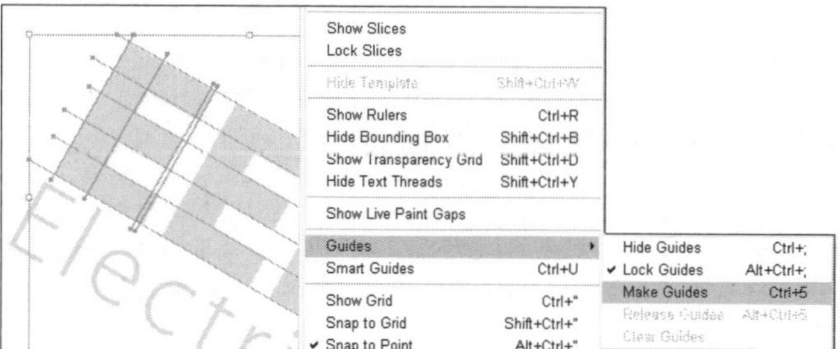

Figure 7-1: Turn your selected paths and shapes into custom guides.

Creating a ruler guide

A ruler guide is the easiest guide to create. Click anywhere on the vertical or horizontal ruler and drag it to the artboard to create a ruler guide, as shown in Figure 7-2. By default, the horizontal ruler creates horizontal guides (no kidding), and the vertical ruler creates vertical guides. You can Alt+drag (Option+drag on a Mac) to change the orientation of the guide. The vertical ruler then creates a horizontal guide, and the horizontal ruler then creates a vertical guide.

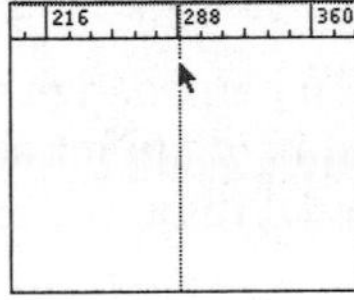

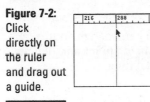

Figure 7-2: Click directly on the ruler and drag out a guide.

Creating a custom guide

Create a custom guide by selecting a path or shape and choosing View➪Guides➪Make Guides. Whatever is selected turns into a nonprinting guide. Changing a path into a guide isn't permanent. Choose View➪Guides➪Release Guides to turn guides back into paths.

Using the Transform Panel for Placement

Placing shapes and paths precisely where you want them can be difficult for those with even the most steady of hands. Save yourself aggravation by using the Transform panel to perform such tasks as scaling and rotating objects. On a more practical note, however, the Transform panel also enables you to type in *x, y* coordinates. This way, you can position your objects exactly where you want them.

In Adobe Illustrator and InDesign, the *Reference Point Indicator* icon is on the left side of the Transform panel. Click the handle of the Reference Point Indicator icon to change the point of reference. If you want to measure from the upper-left corner, click the indicator on the handle in the upper left. Want to know exactly where the center of an object is? Click the center point in the indicator. The point of reference is the spot on the object that falls at the *x, y* coordinates:

- ✦ **X coordinate:** Sets the placement of the selected object from left to right.
- ✦ **Y coordinate:** Sets the placement of the selected object from top to bottom.

Did you ever notice that Adobe Illustrator, which is based on PostScript, considers the lower-left corner the zero point? This can be confusing at first. You can change the ruler origin if it really drives you crazy by following the steps in the next section.

Changing the Ruler Origin

In Adobe Illustrator, InDesign, and Photoshop, you can change your *ruler origin.* This action helps define your measuring starting point and defines the part of the page that will print if you use manual tiling.

To change the ruler origin, follow these steps:

1. **Move the pointer to the upper-left corner of the rulers where the rulers intersect, as shown in Figure 7-3.**

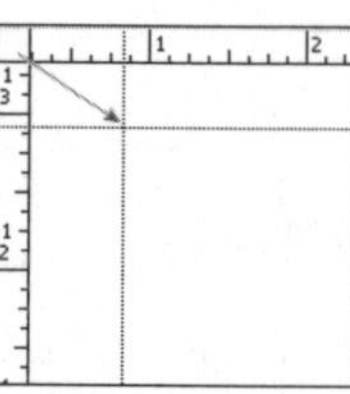

Figure 7-3: Click and drag where the rulers intersect to change the start origin of your ruler.

2. **Drag the pointer to where you want the new ruler origin.**

   As you drag, a cross hair in the window and in the rulers indicates where the new ruler origin will be placed.

You can put the original ruler origin back in place by double-clicking the ruler intersection.

Thinking about Object Arrangement

Just like stacking paper on your desk, new objects in Illustrator are placed on top of the existing objects. Change this order by using the Object➪Arrange choices.

The easiest choices are to bring an object to the front or send it to the back. The results of sending forward or backward can be a little unnerving if you don't know exactly in what order objects were created. Figure 7-4 shows an illustration that we rearranged using four of the available choices. Figure 7-5 shows the result of each choice.

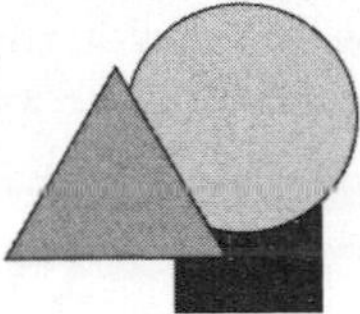

Figure 7-4: The objects in their original positions.

To change the stacking order, select the object(s) whose placement you want to change and then choose one of the following:

- **Object⇨Arrange⇨Bring To Front:** Brings the selected object(s) to the top of the painting order. In Figure 7-5a, the square is brought in front by using the Bring To Front command.
- **Object⇨Arrange⇨Bring Forward:** Brings the selected object(s) in front of the object created just before it, or one level closer to the front. In Figure 7-5b, the square is pulled up in front of the circle with the Bring Forward command.
- **Object⇨Arrange⇨Send Backward:** Moves the selected object(s) so that it falls under the object created just before it, or one level further to the back. In Figure 6-5c, the triangle is sent backward so that it's just under the circle.
- **Object⇨Arrange⇨Send To Back:** Pushes the selected object(s) to the bottom of the painting order. In Figure 7-5d, the triangle is placed on the bottom using the Send To Back command.

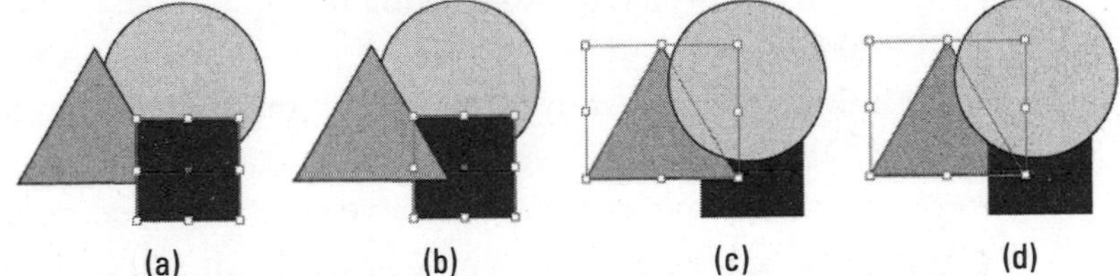

Figure 7-5: Rearranging objects.

Hiding Objects

Seasoned Illustrator users love the Hide command. Use it when the object that you want to select is stuck behind something else, or when you need to select one object and another keeps activating instead.

A good opportunity to use the Hide command is when you're creating text inside a shape. In Chapter 6 of this mini-book, we show you that as soon as you turn a shape into a text area, the fill and stroke attributes turn into None. Follow these steps to hide a shape:

1. **Create a shape.**

   For this example, we created a circle.

2. **Click the Fill color box at the bottom of the Illustrator toolbox and then choose Window⇨Swatches.**

   The Swatches panel appears.

3. **In the panel, choose a color for the fill.**

   We've chosen yellow here. The stroke doesn't matter; we've set it to None.

   When changing your shape into a text area, the color you've chosen is going to disappear. To have the colored shape remain, you have to cheat the system.

4. **With your colored shape selected, choose Edit⇨Copy; alternatively, you can press Ctrl+C (⌘+C on a Mac).**

   This step makes a copy of your shape.

5. **Choose Edit⇨Paste In Back or press Ctrl+B (⌘+B on a Mac).**

   This step puts a copy of your shape exactly in back of the original.

6. **Choose Object⇨Hide or press Ctrl+3 (⌘+3 on a Mac).**

   The copy of the shape is now hidden; what you see is your original shape.

7. **Switch to the Type tool by selecting the tool in the toolbox or pressing T.**

8. **With the cursor, cross over the edge of the shape to change it to the Area Type tool.**

   The Area Type tool enables you to type into a shape.

9. **When you see the type insertion cursor swell up (as shown in Figure 7-6), click the edge of the shape.**

   The insertion point is now blinking inside the shape, and the fill and stroke attributes of the shape have been changed to none.

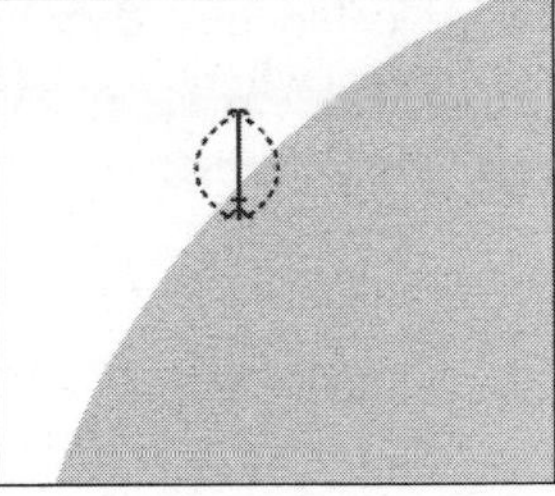

Figure 7-6: The type insertion tool as it appears when positioned on the edge of a shape.

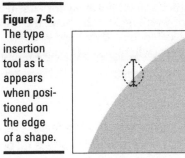

10. **Type some text (see Figure 7-7).**

Figure 7-7: Type directly into the shape.

11. **When you're finished entering text, choose Object⇨Show All or press Ctrl+Alt+3 (⌘+Option+3 on a Mac).**

Your colored shape reappears with the text in the middle of it (see Figure 7-8).

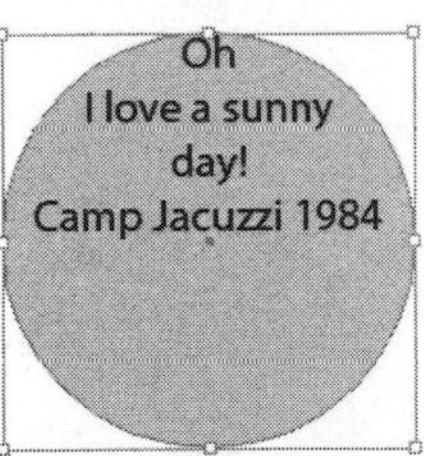

Figure 7-8: The hidden shape reappears exactly where it was before the Hide command was used.

Use the Hide command anytime you want to tuck something away for later use. We promise that anything hidden in Illustrator won't be lost. Just use the Show All command, and any hidden objects are revealed, exactly where you left them. Too bad the Show All command can't reveal where you left your car keys!

Locking Objects

Locking items is handy when you're building an illustration. Not only does the Lock command lock down objects that you don't want to make changes to, but it also drives anyone who tries to edit your files crazy! In fact, we mention locking mainly to help preserve your sanity. There will be many times you need to make simple adjustments to another designer's artwork and you just can't, unless the objects are first unlocked. You can lock and unlock objects as follows:

- **Lock an object:** Choose Object⇨Lock or press Ctrl+2 (⌘+2 on a Mac) to lock an object so that you can't select it, move it, or change its attributes.
- **Unlock an object:** Choose Object⇨Unlock All or press Ctrl+Alt+2 (⌘+Option+2 on a Mac). Then you can make changes to it.

You can also lock and hide objects with layers. See Chapter 8 in this minibook for more information about using layers.

Creating a Clipping Mask

Creating a clipping mask may sound complex, but it's actually easy and brings together some of the items that we talk about in this chapter, such as arranging objects. A *clipping mask* allows a topmost object to define the selected shapes underneath it. It's similar to you cutting a hole in a piece of paper and peering through it to the objects below, except that with a clipping mask, the area around the defining shape is transparent (see Figure 7-9).

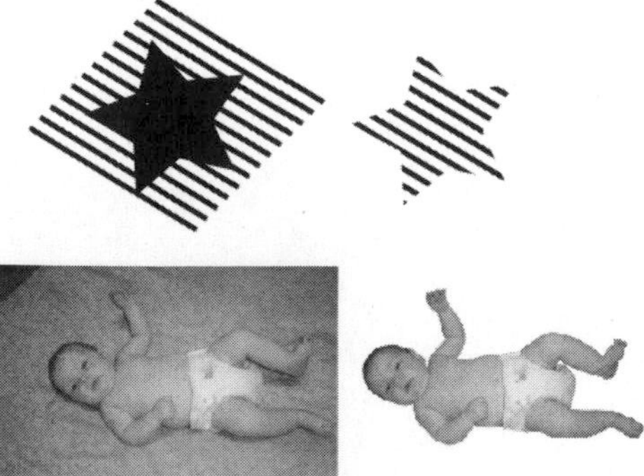

Figure 7-9: Examples of items using the clipping mask feature.

You may remember what a film mask looks like. It's black to block out the picture and clear where you want to view an image, as shown in Figure 7-10.

Figure 7-10: An illustration of a conventional film mask.

The clipping mask feature uses the same principal as the conventional film mask, but the clipping mask is a whole lot easier to create and modify. To create a clipping mask, follow these steps:

1. **Choose File⇨Place to place an image.**

   Masks work with objects created in Illustrator, as well as those placed (scanned or otherwise imported into Illustrator), but an example using a single placed image is less complicated.

2. **Create the item that you want to use as a mask by creating a shape or a closed path with the Pen tool.**

   For example, in Figure 7-11, the circle is the mask. (The photo underneath it is the placed image from Step 1.) The circle is placed where the mask will be created. It doesn't matter what the shape's color, fill, and stroke are because these automatically change to None when you create a mask.

   Note: When creating a clipping mask, make sure that the object to be used as a mask is a closed shape and is at the top of the stacking order.

Figure 7-11: The shape that is to become the mask is positioned over the object, in this case an image.

3. **Using the Selection tool, select the placed image and the shape.**

   Shift+click to add an object to the selection.

4. **Choose Object➪Clipping Mask➪Make.**

   Ta-da! The clipping mask is created. The masked items are grouped together, but you can use the Direct Selection tool to move around the image or the mask individually.

5. **To turn off the clipping mask, choose Object➪Clipping Mask➪Release.**

You can also use text as a mask. Just type a word, make sure that it is positioned over an image or other Illustrator object(s), select both the text and the object, and then choose Object➪Clipping Mask➪Make.

Chapter 8: Using Layers

In This Chapter

- Working with layers
- Putting something on a layer
- Locking and putting away layers

This chapter shows you just how simple it is to use layers and how helpful layers can be when you're producing complex artwork. Layers are similar to clear pages stacked on top of your artwork: You can place content (text, shapes, and so on) on a layer, lift up a layer, remove a layer, hide and show layers, or lock a layer so that you can't edit the content on it. Layers are an incredible feature that can help you:

- ✦ Organize the painting (stacking) order of objects.
- ✦ Activate objects that would otherwise be difficult to select with the Selection or Direct Selection tool.
- ✦ Lock items that you don't want to reposition or change.
- ✦ Hide items until you need them.
- ✦ Repurpose objects for artwork variations. For example, business cards use the same logo and company address, but the name and contact information change for each person. In this case, placing the logo and company address on one layer and the person's name and contact information on another layer makes it easy to create a new business card by just changing the name of the person.

Many Illustrator users don't take advantage of layers. Maybe these users don't understand the basic functions of layers, or maybe they think that layers are much more complicated than they really are. By reading this chapter, you'll be able to take advantage of layers in Illustrator.

Unlike in Photoshop, layers in Illustrator don't add an incredible amount of size to the file.

Creating New Layers

When you create a new Illustrator document, you automatically have one layer to start with. To understand how layers work, create a new file and then follow these steps to create new layers and put objects on them:

1. **If the Layers panel isn't already visible, choose Window➪Layers.**

   The Layers panel appears. In Illustrator CS3, you see new layer color bars to help identify selected objects and the layer they're on, as shown in Figure 8-1.

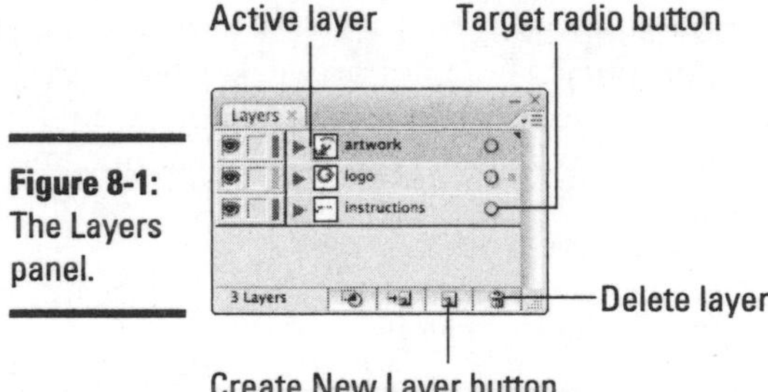

Figure 8-1: The Layers panel.

2. **Create a shape anywhere on the artboard.**

   It doesn't matter what size the shape is, but make sure that it has a colored fill so that you can see it easily. For this example, we created a rectangle.

3. **Click the Fill pop-up menu in the control panel and select any color for the shape, as shown in Figure 8-2.**

   The Fill pop-up menu is the swatch with an arrow in the upper left of the control panel.

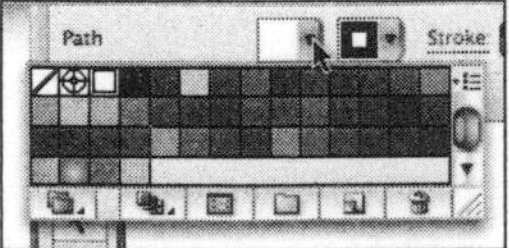

Figure 8-2: Select any color from the Color drop-down panel in the control panel.

The blue handle color that appears on the active shape matches the blue-color bar you see on the left side of the layer name and the small selection square to the right of the radio button. The small selection square on the right disappears if you choose Select➪Deselect. You use that square to see what layer a selected object is on.

Also, notice now that you've added a shape to this layer, and an arrow appears to the left of the layer name. This arrow indicates that you now have a *sublayer,* which is essentially a layer within a layer. Click the arrow to expand the layer and show any sublayers nested under it; sublayers are automatically created as you add objects, which helps when you're trying to make difficult selections.

4. **To make a new layer, Alt+click (Option+click on a Mac) the Create New Layer button at the bottom of the Layers panel.**

   The Layer Options window appears (see Figure 8-3), and you can use it to name a layer and change the selection color. You don't have to hold down the Alt or Option key when making a new layer, but if you don't, you won't have the opportunity to name the layer as you create it.

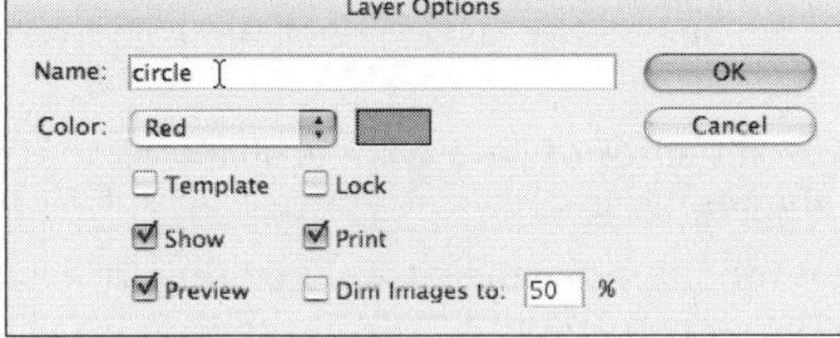

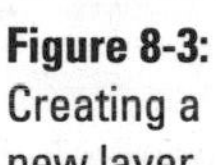

Figure 8-3: Creating a new layer.

5. **Enter a name for the new layer in the Name text field and click OK.**

   In this case, we used the name *circle* because it's the shape that we add in the next step.

   A new layer is added to the top of the stack in the Layers panel.

6. **Make a shape on the new layer and overlap the shape you created in Step 2 (see Figure 8-4).**

   For this example, we created a circle.

7. **Change the fill color for your new shape.**

   Check out the selection handles? They change to a different color, indicating that you're on a different layer. The different colors of the handles are for organizational purposes only and don't print.

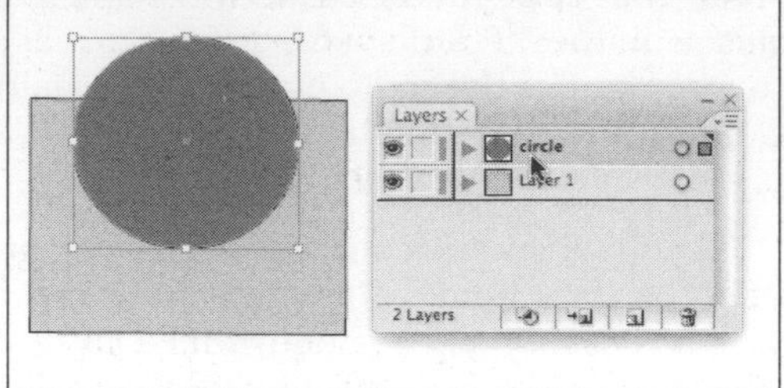

Figure 8-4: A circle on the second layer overlapping the square on the underlying layer.

8. **Just to be different, this time choose New Layer from the panel menu.**

   The Layer Options dialog box appears.

9. **(Optional) In the Layer Options dialog box, change the color of the selection handles by selecting an option from the Color drop-down list.**

   You can also hide or lock the contents of the layer.

10. **Enter a name for this new layer in the Name text field, click OK, and then create a shape on it.**

    For this example, we named the layer "star" and used the Star tool to create a star.

11. **Again, change the fill color of your newest shape so that it's different from the other shapes.**

12. **Use the Selection tool to move the new shape (in our case, the star) so that it overlaps the others slightly.**

13. **Rename the original layer (Layer 1) by double-clicking the layer's name in the Layers panel, typing a new name, and then pressing Enter (Return on a Mac).**

    In our case, it would make sense to rename the original layer as "rectangle" (that's nice and descriptive). You can open up the Options dialog box for any existing layer by choosing Options For Layer (Named Layer) from the panel menu in the Layers panel.

Congratulations! You've created new layers and now have a file that you can use to practice working with layers.

Using Layers for Selections

When you have a selected object on a layer, a color selection square appears to the right of the named layer. If you click the radio button directly to the right of the name, all objects are selected on that layer.

Sublayers each have their own radio button as well. If you have sublayers visible, you can use this same technique to select objects that may be buried behind others.

If you think that you'll be selecting sublayers frequently, double-click the default name and type a more descriptive name.

Changing the Layer Stacking Order

In Chapter 7 of this minibook, we tell you about the Object➪Arrange feature in Illustrator; with layers, this process gets just a little more complicated. Each layer has its own *painting order,* the order in which you see the layers. To move a layer (and thereby change the stacking order of the layers), click and drag that layer until you see the black insertion line where you want the layer to be moved.

As you add shapes to a layer, a sublayer is created, and it has its own little stacking order that is separate from other layers. In other words, if you choose to send an object to the back, and it's on the top layer, it will only go to the back of that layer, and still be in front of any objects on layers beneath.

Understanding how the stacking order affects the illustration is probably the most confusing part about layers. Just remember that for an object to appear behind everything else, it has to be on the bottom layer (and at the bottom of all the objects in that bottom layer); for an object to appear in front of everything else, it has to be on the topmost layer.

Moving and Cloning Objects

To move a selected object from one layer to another, click the small color selection square to the right of the layer's radio button, drag it to the target layer, and release. That's all there is to moving an object from one layer to another.

You can also *clone* items — that is, make a copy of it as you move the copy to another layer. Clone an object by Alt+dragging (Option+dragging on a Mac) the color selection square to another layer. A plus sign appears as you drag (so you know that you're making a clone of the object). Release when you get to the cloned object's target layer.

Hiding Layers

On the Layers panel, notice that to the left of each layer is an eye icon. This is a visibility toggle button. Simply clicking this icon hides the layer (the eye disappears, denoting that this layer is hidden). Click the empty square (where the eye icon was) to show the layer again.

Alt+click (Option+click on a Mac) an eye icon to hide all layers but the one you click; Alt+click again on the eye icon to show all the layers again.

Ctrl+click (⌘+click on a Mac) the eye icon to turn just the selected layer into Outline view mode. In Outline view, all you see are the outlines of the art-work with no stroke widths or fill colors. The rest of your artwork remains in Preview mode, with strokes and fills visible. This technique is pretty tricky and helpful when you're looking for stray points or need to close paths. Ctrl+click (⌘+click on a Mac) back on the eye icon to return the layer to Preview mode.

Locking Layers

Lock layers by clicking the empty square to the right of the Visibility (eye) icon. A padlock icon appears so that you know the layer is now locked. Locking a layer prevents you from making changes to the objects on that layer. Click the padlock to unlock the layer.

Chapter 9: Livening Up Illustrations with Color

In This Chapter

- Using the Swatch and Color panels
- Working with strokes and fills
- Saving and editing colors
- Creating and using color libraries
- Using Live Color and the Color Guide
- Assigning Pantone colors
- Discovering patterns
- Employing gradients
- Exploring the Live Trace feature
- Using the Live Paint feature

This chapter is all about making your brilliant illustrations come alive with color. Here, we show you how to create new and edit existing colors, save custom colors that you create, create and use patterns and gradients, and even apply color attributes to many different shapes.

Choosing a Color Mode

Every time that you create a new file, you choose a profile. This profile determines, among other things, which color mode your document will be created in. Typically, anything related to Web, mobile, and video is in RGB mode, and the print profile is in CMYK. You can also simply choose Basic CMYK or Basic RGB. Here are the differences between the color modes:

- **CMYK (Cyan, Magenta, Yellow, and Black):** This mode is used if you're taking your illustration to a professional printer and the files will be separated into cyan, magenta, yellow, and black plates for printing.
- **RGB (Red, Green, Blue):** Use this mode if your final destination is the Web, mobile device, video, color copier or desktop printer, or screen presentation.

The decision that you make affects the premade swatches, brushes, styles, and a slew of other choices in Adobe Illustrator. This all helps you to avoid sending an RGB color to a print shop. Ever see how that turns out? If your prepress person doesn't catch that the file isn't CMYK and sends an RGB file as separations (cyan, magenta, yellow, and black) to a printer, you can end up with a black blob instead of your beautiful illustration.

You can change the color mode at any time without losing information by choosing File⇨Document Color Mode.

Using the Swatches Panel

Accessing color from the control panel is probably the easiest way to make color choices, as using the Fill and Stroke drop-down menus allow you to quickly access the Swatches palette, as shown in Figure 9-1, and at the same time make sure that the color is actually applying to either the fill or stroke. How many times have you mixed up colors and assigned the stroke color to the fill or vice versa?

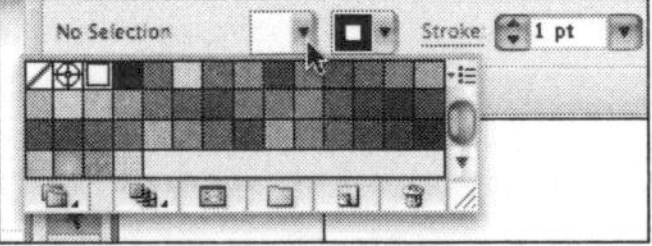

Figure 9-1: Quickly access Swatches from the control panel.

You can also access the Swatches panel, which you open by choosing Window⇨Swatches. Although limited in choice, its basic colors, patterns, and gradients are ready to go. You can use the buttons at the bottom of the Swatches panel (shown in Figure 9-2) to quickly open color libraries, select what kinds of colors to view, access Swatch options, create color Groups, add new swatches, and delete selected swatches.

You may notice some odd color swatches — for example, the cross hair and the diagonal line.

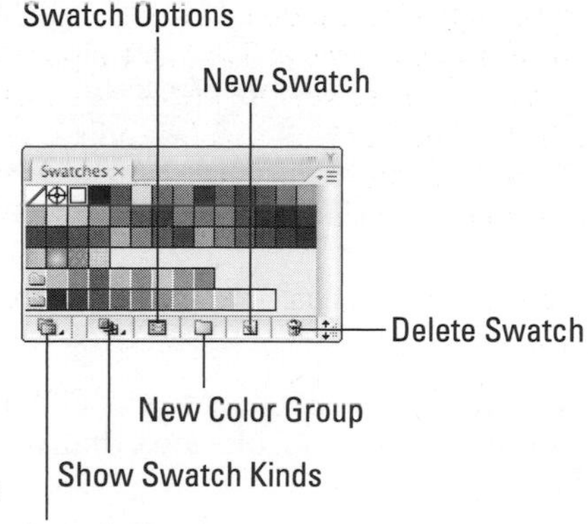

Figure 9-2: Use the buttons at the bottom of the Swatches palette to quickly access color options.

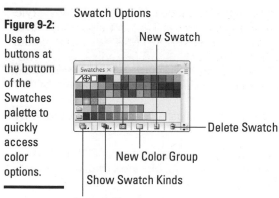

The cross hair represents the Registration color. Only use this swatch when creating custom crop marks or printer marks. It looks black, but it's actually created from 100 percent of all colors. This way, when artwork is separated, the crop mark appears on all color separations.

The diagonal line represents None. Use this option if you want no fill or stroke.

Applying Color to the Fill and Stroke

Illustrator objects are created from *fills* (the inside) and *strokes* (border or path). Look at the bottom of the toolbox for the Fill and Stroke color boxes. If you're applying color to the fill, the Fill color box must be forward in the toolbox. If you're applying color to the stroke, the Stroke color box must be forward.

Table 9-1 lists keyboard shortcuts that can be a tremendous help to you when applying colors to fills and strokes.

Table 9-1 Color Keyboard Shortcuts

Function	*Keyboard Shortcut*
Switch the Fill or Stroke color box position	X
Inverse the Fill and the Stroke color boxes	Shift+X
Default (black stroke, white fill)	D

(continued)

Table 9-1 *(continued)*

Function	*Keyboard Shortcut*
None	/
Last color used	<
Last gradient used	>
Color Picker	Double-click the Fill or Stroke color box

Try this trick: Drag a color from the Swatches panel to the Fill or Stroke color box. This action applies the color to the color box that you dragged to. It doesn't matter which is forward!

To apply a fill color to an existing shape, drag the swatch directly to the shape. Select a swatch, hold down Alt+Shift+Ctrl (Option+Shift+⌘ on a Mac), and drag a color to a shape to apply that color to the stroke.

Changing the Width and Type of a Stroke

Access the Stroke panel by clicking the Stroke Hyperlink in the control panel. In the Stroke panel, you can choose *caps* (the end of a line), *joins* (the end points of a path or dash), and the *miter limit* (the length of a point). The Stroke panel also enables you to turn a path into a dashed line.

As you can see in Figure 9-3, you can choose, in the Stroke panel options, to align the stroke on the center (default) of a path, the inside of a path, and the outside of a path. Figure 9-4 shows the results.

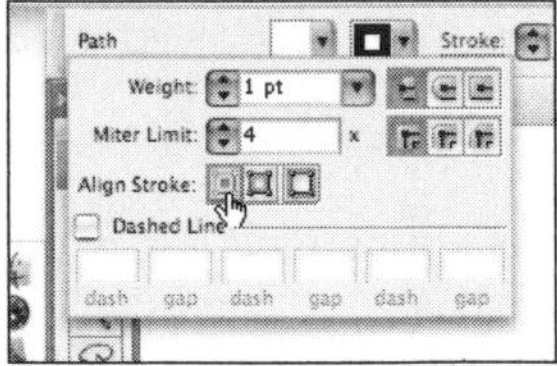

Figure 9-3: The Align Stroke options in the Stroke panel.

This feature is especially helpful when stroking outlined text. See Figure 9-5 to compare text with the traditional centered stroke, as compared to the new option for aligning the stroke outside of a path.

Figure 9-4: The Align Stroke options affect the placement of the stroke on a path.

Figure 9-5: The Align Stroke feature is especially important when stroking text.

You can't adjust the alignment of a stroke on text unless you change it to outlines first. Select the Selection tool and choose Type⇨Create Outlines to enable the Align Stroke options.

You can also customize the following aspects of a stroke in the Stroke panel:

✦ **Cap Options:** The endpoints of a path or dash.

- **Butt Cap:** Click this button to make the ends of stroked lines square.
- **Round Cap:** Click this button to make the ends of stroked lines semicircular.
- **Projecting Cap:** Click this button to make the ends of stroked lines square and extend half the line width beyond the end of the line.

✦ **Join Options:** How corner points appear.

- **Miter Join:** Click this button to make stroked lines with pointed corners.
- **Round Join:** Click this button to make stroked lines with rounded corners.
- **Bevel Join:** Click this button to make stroked lines with squared corners.

✦ **Dashed Lines:** Regularly spaced lines, based upon values you set.

To create a dashed line, specify a dash sequence by entering the lengths of dashes and the gaps between them in the Dash Pattern text fields (see Figure 9-6). The numbers entered are repeated in sequence so that after you've set up the pattern, you don't need to fill in all the text fields. In other words, if you want an evenly spaced dashed stroke, just type the same number in the first and second text fields, and all dashes and spaces will be the same length (say, 12 pts). Change that to 12 in the first text field and 24 in the next, and now you have a larger space between the dashes.

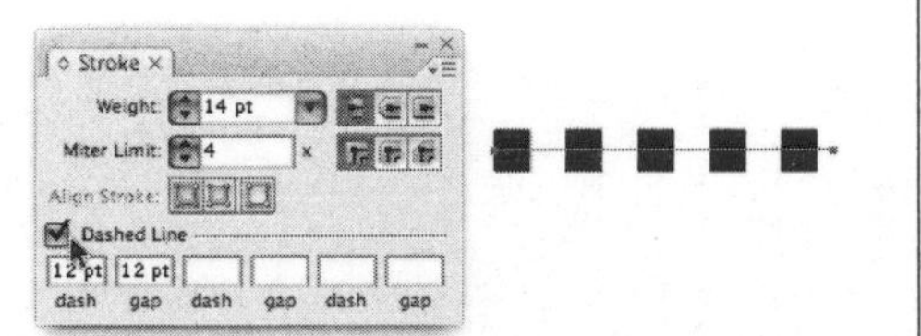

Figure 9-6: Setting up a dashed stroke.

Using the Color Panel

The Color panel (access it by choosing Window➪Color) offers another method for choosing color. It requires you to custom pick a color using values on the color ramp. As a default, you see only the *color ramp* — the large color well spanning the panel. If you don't see all the color options, choose Show Options from the Color panel's panel menu (click the triangle in the upper-right corner to access the panel menu).

Ever want to create tints of a CMYK color but aren't quite sure how to adjust the individual color sliders? Hold down the Shift key while adjusting the color slide of any color and watch how all colors move to a relative position at the same time!

As shown in Figure 9-7, the panel menu offers many other choices. Even though you may be in the RGB or CMYK color mode, you can still choose to build colors in Grayscale, RGB, HSB (Hue Saturation Brightness), CMYK, or Web Safe RGB. Choosing Invert or Complement from the panel menu takes the selected object and inverses the color or changes it to a complementary color. You can also choose the Fill and Stroke color boxes in the upper-left corner of the Color panel.

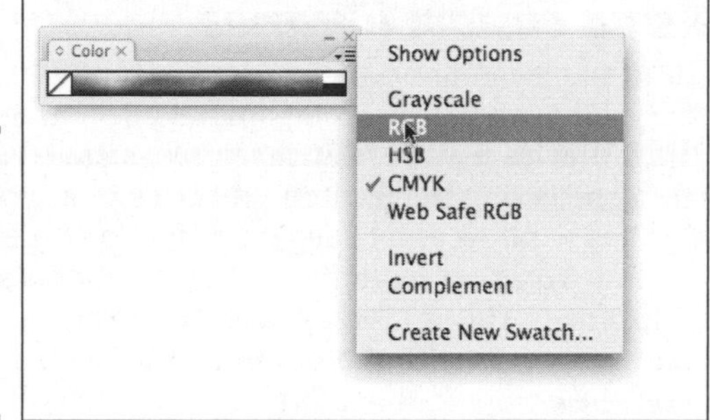

Figure 9-7: Available color models are available in the Color panel.

You see the infamous cube and exclamation point in the Color panels in most of Adobe's software. The cube warns you that the color you have selected isn't one of the 216 nondithering, Web-safe colors, and the exclamation point warns you that your color is not within the CMYK print gamut. In other words, if you see the exclamation point in the Color panel, don't expect that really cool electric blue you see on-screen to print correctly — it may print as dark purple!

Click the cube or exclamation point symbols when you see them to select the closet color in the Web safe or CMYK color gamut.

Saving Colors

Saving colors not only keeps you consistent, but it makes edits and changes to colors easier in the future. Any time you build a color, drag it from the Color panel to the Swatches panel to save it as a color swatch for future use. You can also select an object that uses the color and click the New Swatch button at the bottom of the Swatches panel (refer to Figure 9-2 to see this button). To save a color and name it at the same time, Alt+click (Option+click on a Mac) the New Swatch icon. The New Swatch dialog box opens, where you can name and edit the color if you want. By double-clicking a swatch in the Swatches panel, you can open the options at any time.

A color in the Swatches panel is available only in the document in which it was created. Read the next section on custom libraries to see how to import swatches from saved documents.

Building and using custom libraries

When you save a color in the Swatches panel, you're essentially saving it to your own custom library. You can use Swatches panels from one document to another by using the Libraries feature. Retrieve colors saved in a document's Swatches panel by selecting the Swatch Libraries menu button at the bottom of the Swatches window and dragging down to Other Library. You can also access swatch libraries, including other documents, by choosing Window⇨Swatch Libraries⇨Other Library. Locate the saved document and choose Open. A panel appears with the document name, as shown in Figure 9-8. You can't edit the colors in this panel. To use the colors in this panel, double-click a swatch or drag a swatch to your current document's Swatches panel.

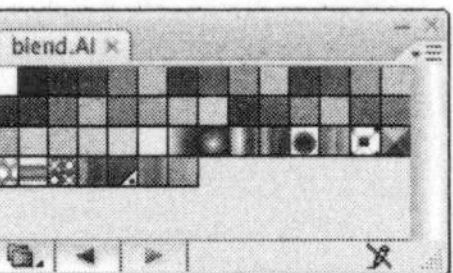

Figure 9-8: An imported custom swatch library.

You can also click the Swatch Libraries button to access color libraries for Pantone colors, Web colors, and some neat creative colors, such as jewel tones and metals.

Using the Color Guide and Color Groups

Perhaps you failed at color in art class or just don't feel that you're one of those people who picks colors that look good together. In Illustrator CS3, you can use the Color Guide to find colors and save them to organized color groups in your Swatches panel. You can create color schemes based on 23 classic color-harmony rules, such as Complementary, Analogous, Monochromatic, and Triad, or you can create custom harmony rules.

Sounds complicated, doesn't it? Fortunately, all you have to do is choose a base color and then see what variations you come up with according to rules you choose. Give it a try:

1. **Choose Window⇨Color Guide.**

   The Color Guide panel appears, as shown in Figure 9-9.

2. **Select a color from your Swatches palette.**

   Immediately, the Color Guide kicks in to provide you with colors that are related to your original swatch.

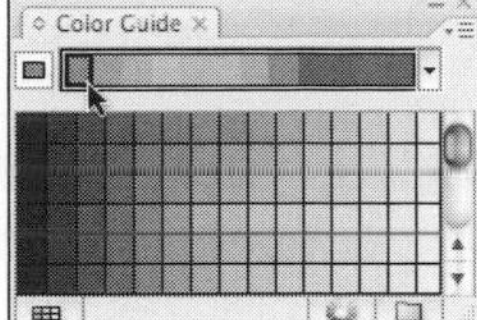

Figure 9-9: The Color Guide helps to identify related colors.

3. **Change the Harmony Rules by selecting the Edit Colors button at the bottom of the Color Guide panel.**

   The Live Color panel, shown in Figure 9-10, appears.

   You could spend days experimenting in the Live Color window, but for the scope of this book you will delve into changing simple harmony rules. To do this, click on the Harmony Rules arrow to the right of the color bar. A drop-down menu appears with many choices as to how you want colors selected, see Figure 9-11. Choose a Color Harmony.

4. **Save your color selection as a color group by clicking the New Color Group icon.**

   If you like, you can rename the color group by double-clicking the group name in the Color Group section of the Live Color window.

5. **Click OK.**

   The Color group is added to the Swatches panel.

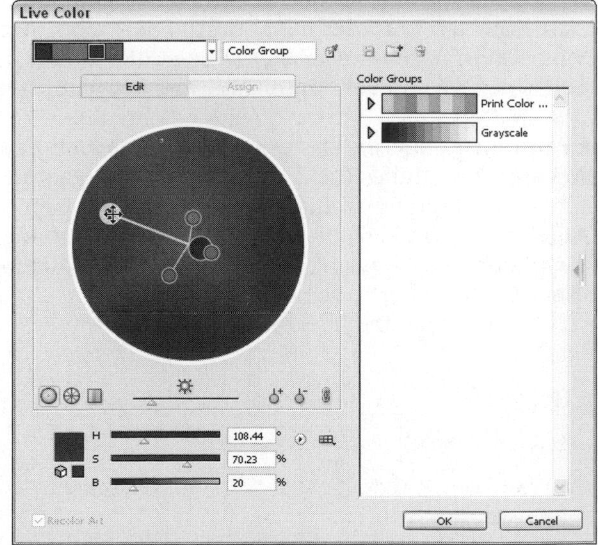

Figure 9-10: The Live Color dialog box allows you to choose and save color groups.

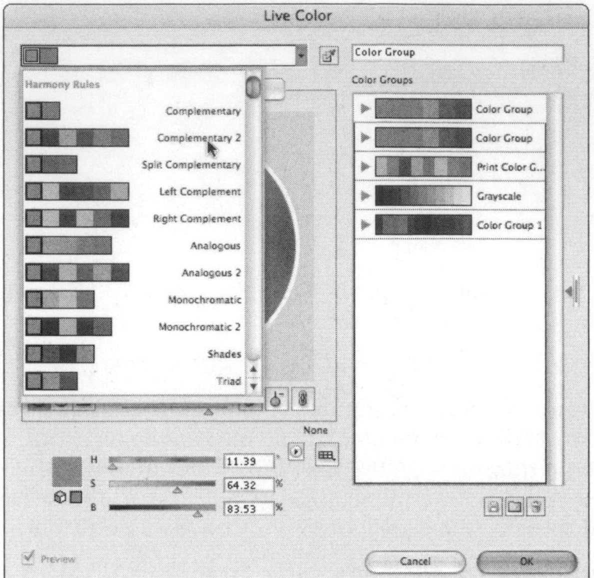

Figure 9-11: Selecting a Harmony Rule.

You don't have to go through the Live Color window in order to save a group of colors. You can Ctrl+click (⌘+Click on a Mac) to select multiple colors and then click the New Color Group button at the bottom of the Swatches panel.

Adding Pantone colors

If you're looking for the typical Pantone Matching System-numbered swatches, click the Swatch Libraries menu button at the bottom of the Swatches panel. From the drop-down list, choose Color Books and then Pantone solid coated, or whatever Pantone library you want to access.

Colors for the Pantone numbering system are often referred to as PMS 485, or PMS 201, or whatever number the color has been designated. You can locate the numbered swatch by typing the number into the Find text field of the Pantone panel, as shown in Figure 9-12. When that number's corresponding color is highlighted in the panel, click it to add it to your Swatches panel. Many users find it easier to see colored swatches by using the List View. Choose List View from the panel options menu.

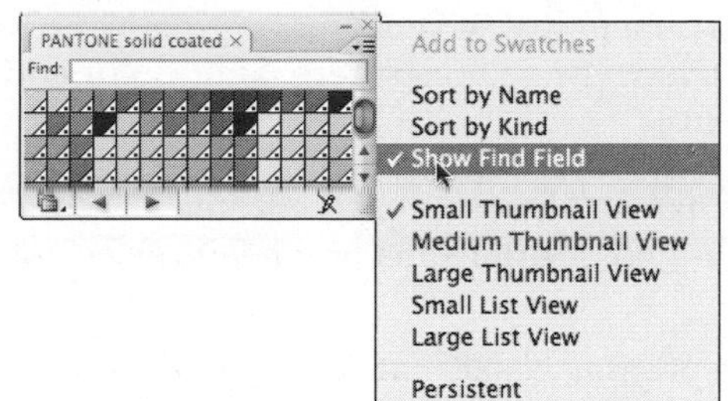

Figure 9-12: Use the Find Field to locate PMS colors.

Editing Colors

Edit colors in the Swatches panel by using the Swatch Options dialog box (shown in Figure 9-13), which you access by double-clicking the color or by choosing Swatch Options from the Swatches panel menu.

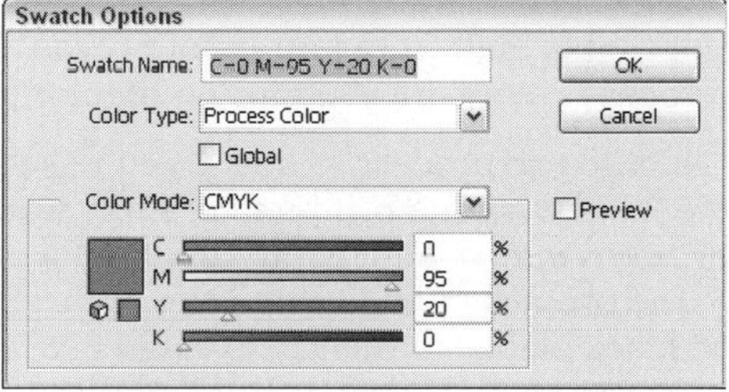

Figure 9-13: Edit a color swatch in the Swatch Options window.

Use the Swatch Options dialog box to

- **Change the color values:** Change the values in a color by using the sliders or by typing values into the color text fields. Having the ability to enter exact color values is especially helpful if you were given a color build to match. Select the Preview check box to see results as you make the changes.
- **Use global colors:** If you plan on using a color frequently, select the Global check box. If the Global check box is selected and you use the swatch throughout the artwork, you only have to change the swatch options one time, and all instances of that color are updated.

One important option to note in the Swatch Options dialog box is the Color Type drop-down list. You have two choices here: Spot Color and Process Color. What's the difference?

- **Spot color:** A color that isn't broken down into the CMYK values. Spot colors are used for 1–2 color print runs or when precise color matching is important.

  Suppose that you're printing 20,000 catalogs and decide to run only two colors, red and black. If you pick spot colors, the catalogs have to go through the press only two times: once for black and once for red. If the red were a process color, however, it would be created out of a combination of cyan, magenta, yellow, and black inks, and so the catalogs would need to go through the press four times in order to build that color. Plus, if you went to a print service and asked for red, what color would you get? Fire-engine red, maroon, or a light and delicate pinkish-red? But if the red you pick is PMS 485, your printer in Lancaster, Pennsylvania, can now print the same color of red on your brochure as the printer doing your business cards in Woburn, Massachusetts.

- **Process color:** A color that is built from four colors (cyan, magenta, yellow, and black). Process colors are used for multicolor jobs.

  For example, you'd want to use process colors if you're sending an ad to a four-color magazine. The magazine printers certainly want to use the same inks they're already running, and using a spot color would require another run through the presses in addition to the runs for the cyan, magenta, yellow, and black plates. In this case, you'd take any spot colors created in corporate logos and such and convert them to process colors.

Choose the Spot Colors option from the Swatches panel menu to choose whether you want Spot colors changed to Lab or CMYK values:

- Choose Lab to get the best possible CMYK conversion for the actual spot color when using a color-calibrated workflow.
- Choose CMYK (default) to get the manufacturer's standard recommended conversion of spot colors to process. Results can vary depending upon printing conditions.

Building and Editing Patterns

Using patterns can be as simple or complicated as you want. If you become familiar with the basics, you can take off in all sorts of creative directions. To build a simple pattern, start by creating the artwork that you want to use as a pattern on your artboard — polka dots, smiley faces, wavy lines, whatever. Then select all the components of the pattern and drag them to the Swatches panel. That's it, you made a pattern! Use the pattern by selecting it as the fill or stroke of an object.

You can't use patterns in artwork that is then going to be saved as a pattern. If you have a pattern in your artwork and try to drag it into the Swatches panel, Illustrator will kick it back out with no error message. On a good note, you can drag text right into the Swatches panel to become a pattern.

You can update patterns that you created or patterns that already reside in the Swatches panel. To edit an existing pattern, follow these steps:

1. **Click the pattern swatch in the Swatches panel and drag it to the artboard.**
2. **Deselect the pattern and use the Direct Selection tool to change its colors or shapes or whatever.**

   Keep making changes until you're happy with the result.
3. **To update the pattern with your new edited version, use the Selection tool to select all pattern elements and Alt+drag (Option+drag on a Mac) the new pattern over the existing pattern swatch in the Swatches panel.**
4. **When a black border appears around the existing pattern, release the mouse button.**

   All instances of the pattern in your illustration are updated.

If you want to add some space between tiles, as shown in Figure 9-14, create a bounding box using a rectangle shape with no fill or stroke (representing the repeat that you want to create). Send it behind the other objects in the pattern and drag all objects, including the bounding box, to the Swatches panel.

Figure 9-14: A pattern with a transparent bounding box.

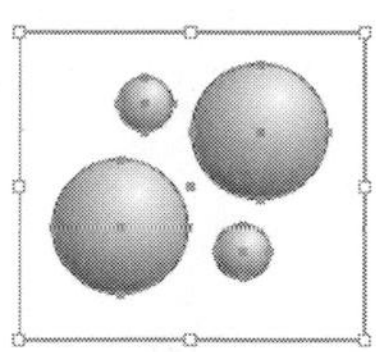

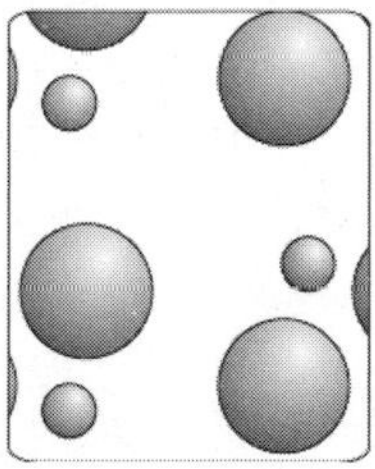

We cover transformations in detail in Chapter 10 of this minibook, but some specific transform features apply to patterns. To scale a pattern, but not the object that it's filling, double-click the Scale tool. In the Scale dialog box that appears, type the value that you want to scale, but deselect all options except for Patterns, as shown in Figure 9-15. This works for the Rotate tool as well!

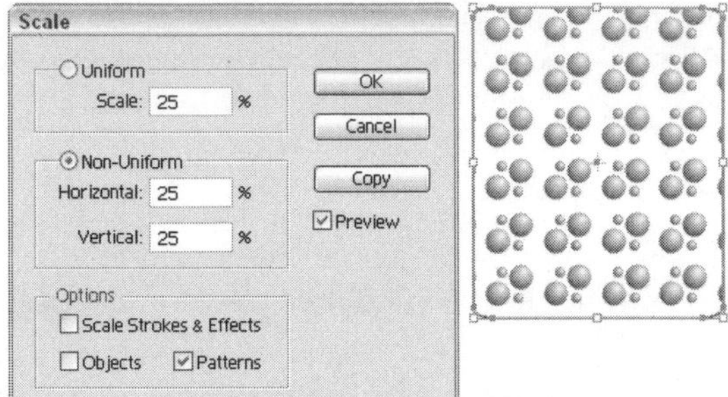

Figure 9-15: Choose to scale or rotate only the pattern, not the object that the pattern is assigned to.

Working with Gradients

Create gradients for nice smooth metallic effects or just to add dimension to illustrations. If you're not sure which swatches are considered gradients, choose Gradient from the Show Swatch Kinds button at the bottom of the Swatches panel.

Once applied, you can access the Gradient panel (shown in Figure 9-16) by choosing Window⇨Gradient. Choose Show Options from the Gradient panel menu to see more options.

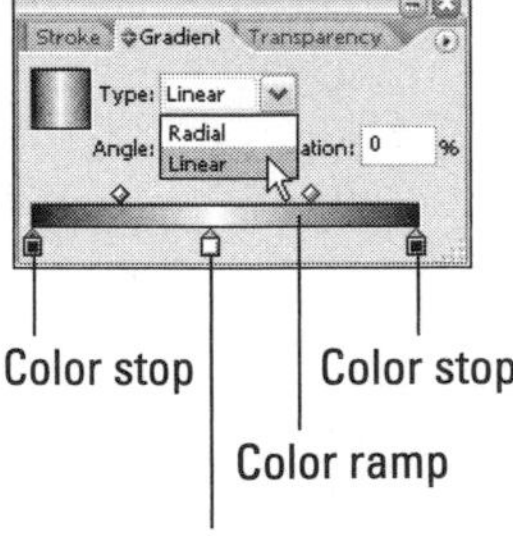

Figure 9-16: The Gradient panel.

On the Gradient panel, use the Type drop-down list to choose a Radial gradient (one that radiates from the center point) or a Linear gradient (one that follows a linear path).

Use the Gradient tool to change the direction and distance of a gradient blend as follows:

1. **Select an object and apply any existing gradient from the Swatches panel to its fill.**
2. **Choose the Gradient tool (press G) and drag in the direction that you want the gradient to go.**

   Drag a long path for a smooth, long gradient. Drag a short path for a short, more defined gradient.

To create a new gradient, follow these steps:

1. **With the Gradient panel options visible, click the gradient box at the bottom of the panel.**

   Two color stops appear, one on each end.
2. **Activate a color stop by clicking it.**

   When a color stop is active, the triangle on the top turns solid.
3. **Choose Window⇨Color to access the Color panel and then click the triangle in the upper-right corner to open the panel menu; choose RGB or CMYK colors.**
4. **Click the color ramp (across the bottom) in the Color panel to pick a random color (or enter values in the text fields to select a specific color) for the active color stop in the Gradient panel.**

   Repeat this step to select colors for other color stops.

To add additional color stops, click beneath the gradient slider and then choose a color from the Color panel. You can also drag a swatch from the Swatches panel to add a new color to the gradient. To remove a color stop, drag it off the Gradient panel.

Copying Color Attributes

Wouldn't it be great if you had tools that could record all the fill and stroke attributes and apply them to other shapes? You're in luck — the Eyedropper tool can do just that! Copy the fill and stroke of an object and apply it to another object using the Eyedropper tool as follows:

1. **Create several shapes with different fill and stroke attributes, or open an existing file that contains several different objects.**
2. **Select the Eyedropper tool and click a shape that has attributes you want to copy.**
3. **Alt+click (Option+click on a Mac) another object to apply those attributes.**

Not only is this technique simple, but you can change the attributes that the Eyedropper applies. Do so by double-clicking the Eyedropper tool; in the dialog box that appears, select only the attributes that you want to copy.

The Live Trace feature

If you're looking for good source art to use to experiment with color, look no further than your own sketches and scanned images. You can automatically trace bitmap images using a variety of settings that range from black-and-white line art to vector art with multitudes of color that can be extracted from your image.

To use the Live Trace feature, follow these steps:

1. **Choose File⇨Place and select an image that you want to trace.**

   The file you place can be a logo, sketch, or even an image. Notice that after you place the image, the control panel offers additional options.
2. **Click the arrow to the right of the Live Trace button.**

   This drop-down list provides Live Trace presets that may help you better trace your image.
3. **Scroll to the bottom and choose Tracing Options.**

   The Tracing Options window appears.
4. **Check the Preview check box and experiment with the various settings, as shown in Figure 9-17.**
5. **When you find the setting that works best for your image, choose Trace.**

You can return to the Tracing Options window and change settings over and over again, until you find the best one.

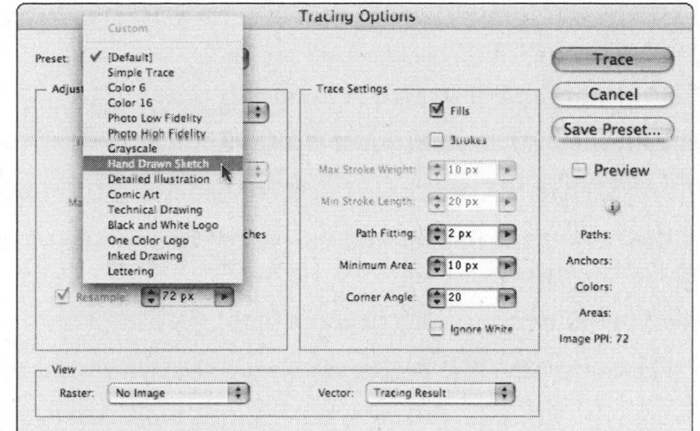

Figure 9-17: Turn bitmap artwork into vector using the Live Trace feature.

The Live Paint Feature

Painting made easy! Don't worry about filling closed shapes, or letting fills escape out of objects with gaps into unwanted areas. With the Live Paint feature, you can create the image you want and fill in regions with color. The Live Paint bucket automatically detects regions composed of independent intersecting paths and fills them accordingly. The paint within a given region remains live and flows automatically if any of the paths are moved. If you want to give it a try, follow this nifty little exercise to put together an example to experiment with.

1. **Using the Ellipse tool, create a circle on your page.**

   Make it large enough to accommodate two or three inner circles.

2. **Press the letter D (just D, nothing else).**

   As long as you're not on the Type tool, you revert back to the default colors of a black stroke and a white fill.

3. **Double-click the Scale tool and enter** 75% **in the Uniform Scale text box.**

4. **Press the Copy button and then click OK.**

   You see a smaller circle inside the original.

5. **Press Ctrl+D (⌘+D on a Mac) to duplicate the transformation and create another circle inside of the last one.**

6. **Choose Select⇨All or press Ctrl+A (⌘+A on a Mac) to activate the circles you just created.**
7. **Make sure that the Fill swatch is forward.**

   The Fill swatch is at the bottom of the toolbar.
8. **Use the Swatches or Color panel and choose any fill color.**
9. **Select the Live Paint Bucket tool and move the cursor over the various regions of the circles.**

   See how the different regions become highlighted?
10. **Click when you have the region activated that you want to fill.**

    Now try it with other fill colors in different regions, as shown in Figure 9-18.

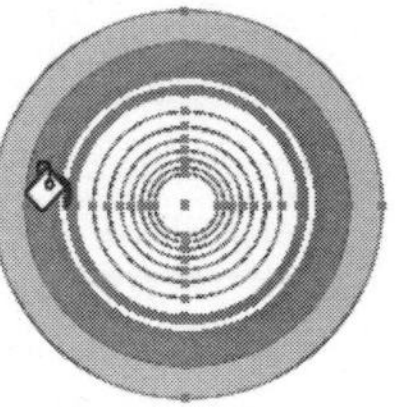

Figure 9-18: Experience newfound freedom when you paint objects with the Live Paint feature.

Got Gaps?

A companion feature to the new paint bucket is support for Gap Detection. With this feature, Illustrator is able to automatically and dynamically detect and close small to large gaps that may be part of the artwork. You can determine whether you want paint to flow across region gap boundaries by using the Gap Options dialog box under Object⇨Live Paint⇨Gap Options, as shown in Figure 9-19.

When you save a file with the Live Paint feature back to an older version of Illustrator, it's best to select the occurrences of Live Paint and choose Object⇨Expand. When the Expand window appears, leave the options at their default and click OK. This setting breaks down the Live Paint objects to individual shapes, which older versions can understand.

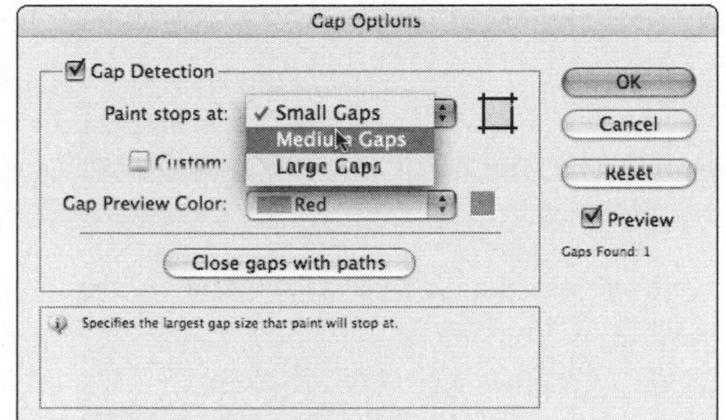

Figure 9-19: The Gap Options dialog box.

Chapter 10: Using the Transform and Distortion Tools

In This Chapter

- Discovering transformation methods
- Putting the Transform tools to work
- Becoming familiar with the Liquify tools
- Distorting, warping, and otherwise reshaping objects

Transformations that you can give to objects in Illustrator include scaling, rotating, skewing, and distorting. In this chapter, we show you how to use the general transform tools as well as some of the neat Liquify and Envelope Distort features available in Illustrator.

Working with Transformations

With just the Selection tool, you can scale and rotate a selected object. Drag the bounding box handles to resize the object (as shown in Figure 10-1) or get outside a handle, and then, when the cursor changes to a flippy arrow (a curved arrow with arrowheads on both ends), drag to rotate the object.

Figure 10-1: Use the bounding box to resize or rotate a selected object.

If you want to scale proportionally, hold down the Shift key as you drag to resize. To rotate an object at 45-degree increments, hold down the Shift key while you're rotating.

When you use the bounding box to rotate a selection, the bounding box rotates with the object, but its handles show the object's original orientation, as shown in Figure 10-2. This can help you to keep track of the original placement but can also interfere when you're building additional artwork. To reset the bounding box so that it's straight at the new orientation, choose Object➪Transform➪Reset Bounding Box.

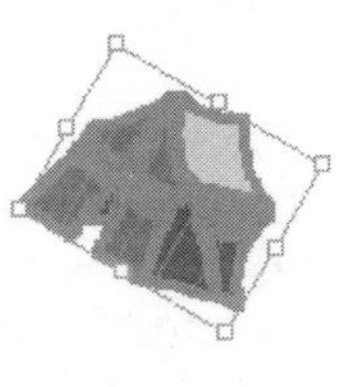

Figure 10-2: The bounding box shows the original placement angle and can reset to that angle.

When you scale, rotate, or use any other type of transformation in Illustrator, the final location becomes the *zero point*. In other applications, such as InDesign, you can rotate an object by any number of degrees (45 degrees, for example) and later enter 0 for the rotation angle in the Transform palette or in the Rotate dialog box to return the object to its original position. With Illustrator, if you enter 0 for the rotation angle to return a rotated object to its original position, the object will not change its position. To return the object to the previous position in Illustrator, you have to enter the negative of the number you originally entered to rotate the object, so you would enter –45 for the degree of rotation in this example.

Transforming an object

The Rotate, Reflect, Scale, and Shear tools all use the same basic steps to perform transformations. Read on for those basic steps, and then follow through some individual examples of the most often used transform tools. The following sections show five ways to transform an object: one for an arbitrary transformation and four others for exact transformations based on a numeric amount that you enter.

Arbitrary transformation method

This method is arbitrary, meaning that you're eyeballing the transformation of an object — in other words, you don't have an exact percentage or angle in mind, and you want to freely transform the object until it looks right. Just follow these steps:

1. **Select an object, and then choose a transform tool (the Rotate, Reflect, Scale, or Shear tool).**
2. **Click once on the artboard.**

   Be careful where you click because the click determines the point of reference, or *axis point,* for the transformation, as shown in Figure 10-3.

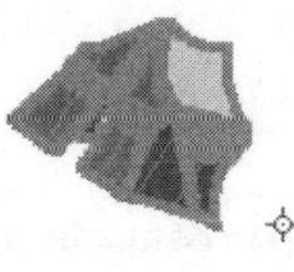

Figure 10-3: The first mouse click creates the point of reference, or axis point for the transformation.

3. **Drag in one smooth movement.**

   Just drag until you get the transformation that you want.

Hold down the Alt (Option on a Mac) key when dragging to clone a newly transformed item while keeping the original object intact. This is especially helpful when you're using the Reflect tool.

Exact transformation methods

In the following methods, we show you how to perform transformations using specific numeric information:

- **Exact transformation method 1:** Using the tool's dialog box
  1. **Select an object and then choose the Rotate, Reflect, Scale, or Shear tool.**

2. **Double-click the transform tool in the toolbox.**

   A dialog box specific to your chosen tool appears. For this example, we selected and then double-clicked the Rotate tool to bring up the Rotate dialog box.

3. **Type an angle, scaled amount, or percentage in the appropriate text field.**

4. **Check preview to see the effect of the transformation before you click OK; click the Copy button instead of OK to keep the original object intact and transform a copy.**

- **Exact transformation method 2:** Using the reference point

  1. **Select an object, and then choose the Rotate, Reflect, Scale, or Shear tool.**

  2. **Alt+click (Option+click on a Mac) where you want the reference point to be.**

  3. **In the appropriate transform tool dialog box that appears, enter your values and click OK or the Copy button to apply your transformation.**

     This is the best method to use if you need to rotate an object an exact amount on a defined axis.

- **Exact transformation method 3:** Using the Transform menu

  1. **Select an object, and then choose a transform option from the Object⇨Transform menu.**

     The appropriate transform dialog box appears.

  2. **Enter your values and click OK or the Copy button.**

- **Exact transformation method 4:** Using the Transform palette

  Select an object and choose Window⇨Transform to access the Transform palette, as shown in Figure 10-4.

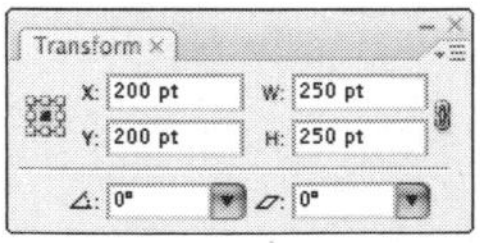

Figure 10-4: The Transform palette allows you to enter values.

Transform ×
X: 200 pt W: 250 pt
Y: 200 pt H: 250 pt
⊿: 0° ▱: 0°

While using this palette is probably the easiest way to go, it doesn't give you the option of specifying where you want your reference point to be or some other options that apply to the individual transform tools.

Using the Transform tools

In this section, we show you how to use some of the most popular transform tools to create transformations.

The Reflect tool

Nothing is symmetrical, right? Maybe not, but objects that are not symmetrically created in Illustrator can look pretty off kilter. Using the Reflect tool, you can reflect an object to create an exact mirrored shape of it; just follow these steps:

1. **Open a new document in Illustrator and type some text or create an object.**

   If you want to reflect text, make sure that you use at least 60-point type so that you can easily see what you're working with.

2. **Select the Reflect tool (hidden under the Rotate tool) and click the object; if you're using text, click in the middle of the text's baseline, as shown on the right in Figure 10-6.**

   This step sets the reference point for the reflection.

3. **Alt+Shift+drag (Option+Shift+drag on a Mac) and release when the object or text is reflecting itself, as shown on the right in Figure 10-5.**

   This step not only clones the reflected object or text, but also snaps it to 45-degree angles.

Figure 10-5: Setting the reference point (left); the completed reflection (right).

Reflect Reflect

The Scale tool

Using the Scale tool, you can scale an object proportionally or non-uniformly. Most people like to be scaled non-uniformly, maybe a little taller, a little thinner, but on with the topic. Follow these steps to see the Scale tool in action:

1. **Create a shape and give it no fill and a 5-point black stroke.**

   For this example, we created a circle. See Chapter 4 of this minibook if you need a reminder on how to do this.

2. **Select your shape and double-click the Scale tool.**

   The Scale dialog box appears.

3. **Type a number in the Scale text field (in the Uniform section) and click the Copy button.**

   We entered 125 in the Scale text field to increase the size of the object by 125 percent.

4. **Press Ctrl+D (⌘+D on a Mac) to repeat the transformation as many times as you want.**

   Each time you press Ctrl+D, the shape is copied and sized by the percent you entered in the Scale text field. This is especially handy with circles and creates an instant bull's-eye!

To experiment with the Scale tool, create different shapes in Step 1 and enter different values in Step 3. Remember that if you type 50% in the Scale text field, the object is made smaller; go over 100% — say to 150% for example — to make the object larger. Leaving the Scale text field at 100% has no effect on the object.

The Shear tool

The Shear tool enables you to shear an object by selecting an axis and dragging to set a shear angle, as shown in Figure 10-6.

Figure 10-6: Create perspective using the Shear tool.

The axis will always be the center of the object unless you use method 1 or method 2 from the earlier section, "Exact transformation methods." Use the Shear tool in combination with the Rotate tool to give an object perspective.

The Reshape tool

The Reshape tool enables you to select anchor points and sections of paths and adjust them in one direction. You determine that direction by dragging an anchor point with the Reshape tool selected.

The Reshape tool works differently from the other transform tools. To use it, follow these steps:

1. **Select just the anchor points on the paths that you want to reshape. Deselect any points that you want to remain in place.**
2. **Select the Reshape tool (hidden under the Scale tool) and position the cursor over the anchor point that you want to modify; click the anchor point.**

   If you click a path segment, a highlighted anchor point with a square around it is added to the path.
3. **Shift+click more anchor points or path segments to act as selection points.**

   You can highlight an unlimited number of anchor points or path segments.
4. **Drag the highlighted anchor points to adjust the path.**

The Free Transform tool

You use the Free Transform tool pretty much like you use the bounding box. (See the earlier section, "Working with Transformations.") This tool is necessary only if you choose View⇨Hide Bounding Box but want free transform capabilities.

Creating Distortions

Bend objects, make them wavy, gooey, or spiky — you can do all of these things by creating simple to complex distortions with the Liquify tools and Envelope Distort features.

The Liquify tools

The Liquify tools can accomplish all sorts of creative or wacky (depending on how you look at it) distortions to your objects. You can choose from seven Liquify tools. Even though we define these for you in Table 10-1, you really need to experiment with these tools to understand their full capabilities. Here are some tips:

- A variety of Liquify tools are available by holding down the mouse button on the default selection, the Warp tool. If you use them frequently, drag to the arrow at the end of the tools and release when you see the ToolTip for Tearoff. You can then position the tools anywhere in your work area.
- Double-click any of the Liquify tools to bring up a dialog box specific to the selected tool, as shown for the Warp tool in Figure 10-8.
- When a Liquify tool is selected, the brush size appears. Adjust the diameter and shape of the Liquify tool by holding down the Alt (Option on a Mac) key while dragging the brush shape smaller or larger. Add the Shift key to constrain the shape to a circle.

Table 10-1 The Liquify Tools

Tool Icon	*Tool Name*	*What It Does*
	Warp tool	Molds objects with the movement of the cursor. Pretend that you're pushing through dough with this tool.
	Twirl tool	Creates swirling distortions within an object.
	Pucker tool	Deflates an object.
	Bloat tool	Inflates an object.
	Scallop tool	Adds curved details to the outline of an object. Think of a seashell with scalloped edges.
	Crystallize tool	Adds many spiked details to the outline of an object, like crystals on a rock.
	Wrinkle tool	Adds wrinkle-like details to the outline of an object.

Using the Envelope Distort command

Use the Envelope Distort command to arch text and apply other creative distortions to an Illustrator object. To use the Envelope Distort command, you can either use a preset warp (the easiest method) or a grid or a top object to determine the amount and type of distortion. In this section, we discuss all three methods.

Using the preset warps

Experimenting is a little more interesting if you have a word or object selected before trying the different warp presets. To warp an object or text to a preset style, follow these steps:

1. **Select the text or object that you want to distort, and then choose Object⇨Envelope Distort⇨Make With Warp.**

   The Warp Options dialog box appears.

2. **Choose a warp style from the Style drop-down list and then specify any other options you want.**
3. **Click OK to apply your distortion.**

Note: If you want to experiment with warping, but also want to revert back to the original at any time, choose Effect⇨Warp. Find out more about exciting Effects that you can apply to objects in Chapter 12 of this minibook.

Reshaping with a mesh grid

You can also assign a grid to the objects to give you the ability to drag different points and create your own custom distortion, as shown in Figure 10-7.

Figure 10-7: Create your own custom distortion using a mesh grid.

Follow these steps to apply a mesh grid:

1. **Select the text or object that you want to distort, and then choose Object⇨Envelope Distort⇨Make With Mesh.**

   The Envelope Mesh dialog box appears.

2. **Specify the number of rows and columns that you want the mesh to contain and then click OK.**
3. **To reshape the object, drag any anchor point on the mesh grid with the Direct Selection tool.**

To delete anchor points on the mesh grid, select an anchor point with the Direct Selection tool and press the Delete key.

You can also use the Mesh tool to edit and delete points when using a mesh grid on objects.

Reshaping an object with a different object

To form letters into the shape of an oval or distort selected objects into another object, use this technique:

1. **Create text that you want to distort.**
2. **Create the object that you want to use as the envelope (the object to be used to define the distortion).**
3. **Choose Object⇨Arrange to make sure that the envelope object is on top, as shown in Figure 10-8.**

Figure 10-8: Position the shape over the text.

4. **Select the text and Shift+click to select the envelope object.**
5. **Choose Object⇨Envelope Distort⇨Make with Top Object.**

The underlying object is distorted to fit the shape of the top (envelope) object.

Chapter 11: Working with Transparency and Special Effects Tools

In This Chapter

- **Finding out about the Gradient Mesh tool**
- **Getting to know the Blend tool**
- **Using the Symbol Sprayer Brush tools**
- **Discovering transparency, blend modes, and opacity masks**

This chapter is full of neat things that you can do using some of the more advanced features in Adobe Illustrator. These special effects tools can help you create art that really makes an impact: Discover how to make your art look like a painting with the Gradient Mesh tool, create morph-like blends with the Blend tool, become a pseudo-graffiti artist by trying out the Symbol Sprayer tool, and see what's underneath objects by using transparency!

The Mesh Tool

If you're creating art in Illustrator that requires solid colors or continuous patterns, you can achieve those results quite easily. But what if you're working on something that requires continuous tones, like a person's face? In that case, you'd turn to the very handy Mesh tool, which enables you to create the impression that you used paint and paintbrushes to create your illustration. Choose to blend one color into another and then use the Mesh tool to adjust where the blends occur and how dramatic the blends should be.

The Mesh tool can be as complex or simple as you want. Create intense illustrations that look like they were created with an airbrush, or just use it to give an object dimension, like the objects shown in Figure 11-1.

We show you how to create a gradient mesh two different ways: First by clicking (which gives you a little more freedom to put mesh points where you want them) and then by manually setting the number of rows and columns in the mesh (which is a more precise method).

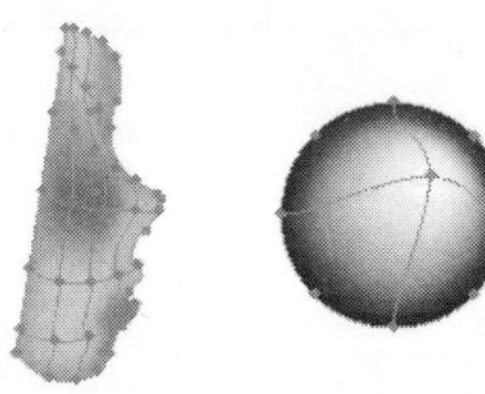

Figure 11-1: Illustrations can be as complex or simple as you want using the Mesh tool.

You can change the color in mesh points by choosing the Direct Selection tool and either clicking a mesh point and picking a fill color, or by clicking in the center of a mesh area and choosing a fill. Each gives you a very different result, as shown in Figure 11-2. To add a mesh point without changing to the current fill color, Shift+click anywhere in a filled vector object.

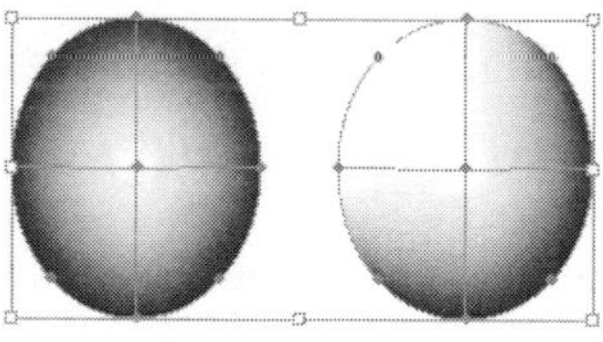

Figure 11-2: Whether you select the mesh point (left) or area in between the mesh points (right) changes the painting result.

To create a gradient mesh by clicking, follow these steps:

1. **Deselect all objects by choosing Select⇨Deselect.**
2. **Select a fill color that you want to apply as a mesh point to an object.**

   For example, if you have a red circle and you want a shaded white spot, choose white for your fill color.

3. **Select the Mesh tool (keyboard shortcut is U) and click anywhere in a filled vector object.**

   The object is converted to a mesh object.

4. **Click the object as many times as you want to add additional mesh points.**

To create a gradient mesh by setting the number of rows and columns, follow these steps:

1. **Select a bitmap or filled vector object.**
2. **Choose Object⇨Create Gradient Mesh.**

   The Create Gradient Mesh dialog box appears.

3. **Set the number of rows and columns of mesh lines to create on the object by entering numbers in the Rows and Columns text fields.**
4. **Choose the direction of the highlight from the Appearance drop-down list.**

   The direction of the highlight determines in what way the gradient flows (see Figure 11-3); you have the following choices:

   * **Flat:** Applies the object's original color evenly across the surface, resulting in no highlight.
   * **To Center:** Creates a highlight in the center of the object.
   * **To Edge:** Creates a highlight on the edges of the object.

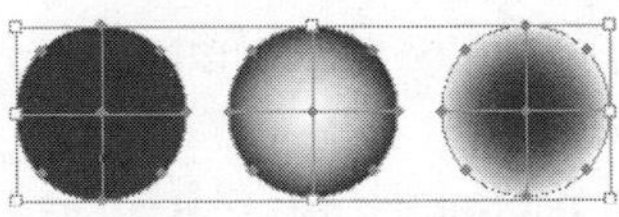

Figure 11-3: Choose a highlight direction for the gradient mesh.

5. **Enter a percentage of white highlight to apply to the mesh object in the Highlight text field.**
6. **Click OK to apply the gradient mesh to the object.**

The Blend Tool

Use the Blend tool (located in the main Illustrator toolbox) to transform one object to another to create interesting morphed artwork or to create shaded objects. With the Blend tool, you can give illustrations a rendered look by blending from one color to another, or you can create an even amount of shapes from one point to another. Figure 11-4 shows examples of what you can do with this tool.

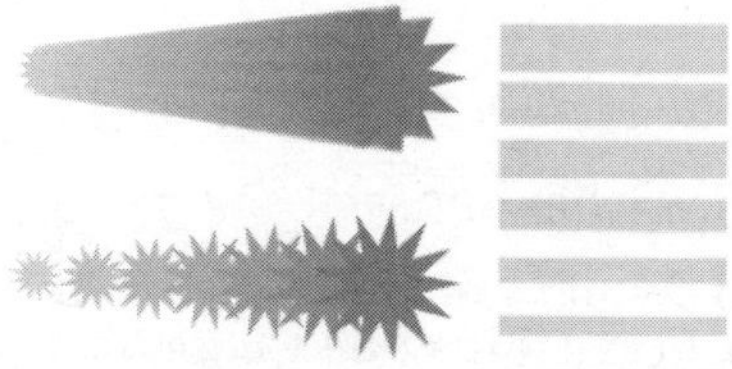

Figure 11-4: Samples of objects using the blend feature.

Creating a blend isn't difficult, and as you get used to it, you can take it farther and farther, creating incredibly realistic effects with it. Follow these steps to create a simple blend from one sized rectangle to another, creating an algorithmic stripe pattern (a rectangle of one height blended to a rectangle of another height):

1. **Create a shape.**

   Size doesn't really matter for this example; you just want to make sure that you can see a difference in shapes when you blend. We're using a rectangle that's roughly 4 x 1 inches.

2. **Give your shape a fill and assign None to the stroke.**

   You can use other settings here, but we recommend keeping it simple if you're still new to working with blends.

3. **With the Selection tool, click the rectangle and Alt+drag (Option+drag on a Mac) toward the bottom of the artboard to clone your shape; press the Shift key before you release the mouse button to make sure that the cloned shape stays perfectly aligned with the original shape.**

4. **Reduce the cloned shape to about half its original height by using the Transform panel (if the Transform panel isn't visible, choose Window⇨Transform).**

   Alternatively, you can hold down the Shift key and drag the bottom-middle bounding box handle, as shown in Figure 11-5.

5. **In the Swatches panel (choose Window⇨Swatches), change the cloned shape's fill to a different color, but keep the stroke at None.**

   Changing the color just helps you see the blend effect a little better.

Figure 11-5: Reduce the size of the cloned shape.

6. **With the Blend tool, click the original shape and then click the cloned shape.**

   As a default, the Blend tool creates a smooth blend that transitions from one color to another, as shown in Figure 11-6. To change the blend effect, you need to experiment with the Blend Options dialog box.

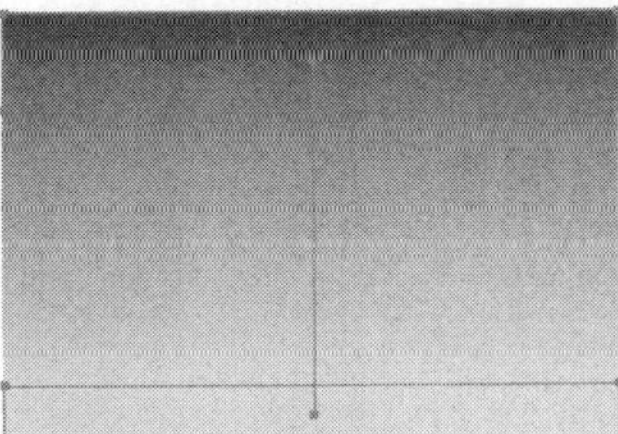

Figure 11-6: A smooth transition is created from one rectangle to the other.

You can change the way that a blend appears by using the Blend Options dialog box, which you access by choosing Object⇨Blend⇨Blend Options. From the Spacing drop-down list, change the blend to one of the following options:

- **Smooth Color:** The blend steps are calculated to provide the optimum number of steps for a smooth transition.
- **Specified Steps:** You can determine the number of steps in a blend by typing a number in the text field to the right of the drop-down list.
- **Specified Distance:** You control the distance between the steps in the blend by typing a number in the text field to the right of the drop-down list.

You can also choose between two orientation options: Align To Page (orients the blend perpendicular to the X-axis of the page) or Align To Path (orients the blend perpendicular to the path). You will probably not see a difference when changing orientation unless you have edited the blend path.

You can easily access the Blend tool options by selecting a Blended object and double-clicking the Blend tool in the toolbox.

If you're feeling adventurous, try changing a smooth blend (such as the one you create in the preceding steps) into a logarithmic blend. In the Blend Options dialog box, choose Specified Steps from the Spacing drop-down list and change the value to 5. This change creates the blend in five steps instead of the 200 plus steps that may have been necessary to create the smooth blend.

Here are a few more tips to help you become more comfortable using blends:

- ✦ You can blend between an unlimited number of objects, colors, opacities, or gradients.
- ✦ Blends can be directly edited with tools, such as the Selection tools, the Rotate tool, or the Scale tool.
- ✦ A straight path is created between blended objects when the blend is first applied. You can switch to the Direct Selection tool and edit the blend path by dragging anchor points.
- ✦ You can edit blends that you created by moving, resizing, deleting, or adding objects. After you make editing changes, the artwork is automatically reblended.

The Symbol Sprayer Tool

The Symbol Sprayer tool is a super tool that you must experiment with to understand its full potential. In a nutshell, however, what it does is work like a can of spray paint that, instead of spraying paint, sprays *symbols* — objects that, in Illustrator, can be either vector- or pixel-based. Each individual symbol is an *instance.*

Illustrator comes with a library of symbols ready for use in the Symbols panel (if the Symbols panel isn't visible, choose Window➪Symbols Panel). Use this panel as a storage bin or library to save repeatedly used artwork or to create your own symbols to apply as instances in your artwork, like blades of grass or stars in the sky. You can then use the Symbolism tools, described in Table 11-1, to adjust and change the appearance of the symbol instances.

Table 11-1 The Symbolism Tools

Button	*Tool Name*	*What It Does*
	Symbol Sprayer	Creates a set of symbol instances.
	Symbol Shifter	Moves symbol instances around. It can also change the relative paint order of symbol instances.
	Symbol Scruncher	Pulls symbol instances together or apart.
	Symbol Sizer	Increases or decreases the size of symbol instances.
	Symbol Spinner	Orients the symbol instances in a set. Symbol instances located near the cursor spin in the direction you move the cursor.
	Symbol Stainer	Colorizes symbol instances.
	Symbol Screener	Increases or decreases the transparency of the symbol instances in a set.
	Symbol Styler	Enables you to apply or remove a graphic style from a symbol instance.

Press the Alt (Option on a Mac) key to reduce the effect of the Symbolism tool. In other words, if you're using the Symbol Sizer tool, you click and hold to make the symbol instances larger; hold down the Alt (Option on a Mac) key to make the symbol instances smaller.

You can also selectively choose the symbols that you want to effect with the Symbolism tools by activating them in the Symbols panel. Ctrl+click (⌘+click on a Mac) multiple symbols to change them at the same time.

Just about anything can be a symbol, including placed objects and objects with patterns and gradients. If you're going to use placed images as symbols, however, choose File⇨Place and deselect the Linked check box in the Place dialog box.

To create a symbol, select the object and drag it into the Symbols panel or click the New Symbol button at the bottom of the Symbols panel. Yes, it's that easy. Then use the Symbol Sprayer tool to apply the Symbol instance on the artboard by following these steps:

1. **Select the symbol instance in the Symbols panel.**

   Either create your own symbol or use one of the default symbols supplied in the panel.

2. **Drag with the Symbol Sprayer tool, spraying the symbol on the artboard (see Figure 11-7).**

   And that's it. You can increase or reduce the area affected by the Symbol sprayer by pressing the bracket keys. Press] repeatedly to enlarge the application area for the symbol or [to make it smaller.

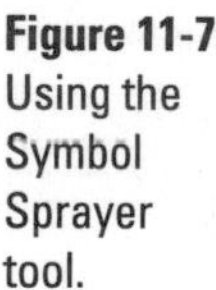

Figure 11-7: Using the Symbol Sprayer tool.

Note that you can access all sorts of Symbol Libraries from the Symbols panel menu. Find 3D, nature, maps, flowers, and even hair and fur symbol collections by selecting Open symbol library.

Want to store artwork that you frequently need to access? Simply drag the selected object(s) into the Symbols panel, or Alt+click (Option+click on a Mac) the New Symbol button to name and store the artwork. Retrieve the artwork later by dragging it from the Symbols panel to the artboard. In fact, you can drag any symbol out to your artboard to change or use it in your own artwork. To release the symbol back into its basic elements, choose Object⇨Expand. In the Expand dialog box, click OK to restore the defaults.

Transparency

Using transparency can add a new level to your illustrations. The transparency feature does exactly what its name implies: It changes an object to make it transparent so that what's underneath that object is visible to varying degrees. You can use the Transparency panel for simple applications of transparency to show through to underlying objects, or you can use transparency for more complex artwork using *opacity masks*, masks that can control the visibility of selected objects.

Choosing Window⇨Transparency brings up the Transparency panel where you can apply different levels of transparency to objects. To do so, create an arrangement of objects that intersect, select the topmost object, and then change the transparency level of the object in the Transparency panel, either by moving the Opacity slider or by entering a value of less than 100 in the Opacity text field.

Blend modes

A *blend mode* determines how the resulting transparency will look. So to achieve different blending effects, you choose different blend modes from the Blend Mode drop-down list in the Transparency panel.

Truly, the best way to find out what all these modes do is to create two shapes that are overlapping and start experimenting. Give the shapes differently colored fills (but note that many of the blending modes don't work with black and white fills). Then select the topmost object and change the blending mode by selecting an option from the Blend Mode drop-down list in the Transparency panel. You'll see all sorts of neat effects and probably end up picking a few favorites.

We define each blend mode in the following list (but we'll say it again, the best way to see what each one does is to apply them — so start experimenting!):

- ✦ **Normal:** Creates no interaction with underlying colors.
- ✦ **Darken:** Replaces only the areas that are lighter than the blend color. Areas darker than the blend color don't change.
- ✦ **Multiply:** Creates an effect similar to drawing on the page with magic markers. Also looks like colored film you see on theater lights.
- ✦ **Color Burn:** Darkens the base color to reflect the blend color. If you're using white, no change occurs.

- **Lighten:** Replaces only the areas darker than the blend color. Areas lighter than the blend color don't change.
- **Screen:** Multiplies the inverse of the underlying colors. The resulting color is always a lighter color.
- **Color Dodge:** Brightens the underlying color to reflect the blend color. If you're using black, there is no change.
- **Overlay:** Multiplies or screens the colors, depending on the base color.
- **Soft Light:** Darkens or lightens the colors, depending on the blend color. The effect is similar to shining a diffused spotlight on the artwork.
- **Hard Light:** Multiplies or screens the colors, depending on the blend color. The effect is similar to shining a harsh spotlight on the artwork.
- **Difference:** Subtracts either the blend color from the base color or the base color from the blend color, depending on which has the greater brightness value. The effect is similar to a color negative.
- **Exclusion:** Creates an effect similar to, but with less contrast than, the Difference mode.
- **Hue:** Applies the hue (color) of the blend object onto the underlying objects, but keeps the underlying shading, or luminosity.
- **Saturation:** Applies the saturation of the blend color, but uses the luminance and hue of the base color.
- **Color:** Applies the blend object's color to the underlying objects but preserves the gray levels in the artwork. This is great for tinting objects or changing their color.
- **Luminosity:** Creates a resulting color with the hue and saturation of the base color and the luminance of the blend color. This is essentially the opposite of the Color mode.

Opacity masks

Just like in Photoshop, you can use masks to make more interesting artwork in Illustrator. Create an opacity mask from the topmost object in a selection of objects or by drawing a mask on a single object. The mask uses the grayscale of the object selected to be the opacity mask. Black areas are totally transparent; shades of gray are semi-transparent, depending on the amount of gray; and white areas are totally opaque. Figure 11-8 shows the effect of an opacity mask.

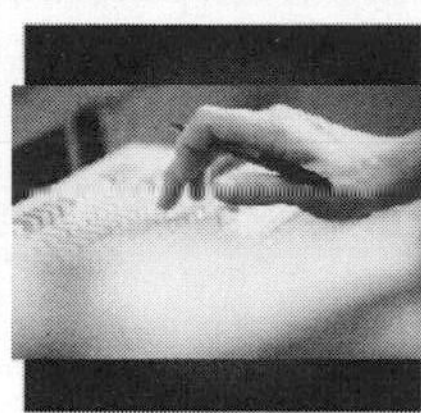

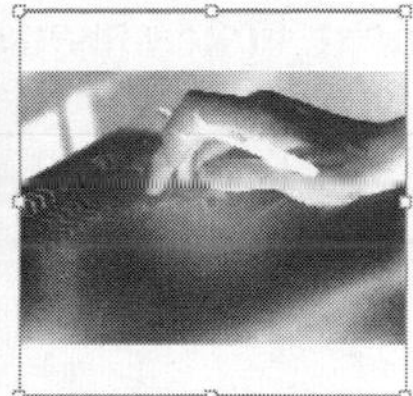

Figure 11-8: An opacity mask takes the topmost object and masks underlying objects.

To create an opacity mask, follow these steps:

1. **Open the Transparency panel menu (click the arrow in the upper-right corner to access this menu) and choose Show Thumbnails.**

   Also, be sure that the Blend Mode drop-down list is set to Normal.

2. **Create a shape anywhere on the artboard or open a document that has artwork on it.**

   We're using a rectangle, but the shape doesn't matter. Make sure that the artwork has a fill. A solid color will help you see the effect.

3. **Open the Symbols panel (choose Window⇨Symbols Panel) and drag a symbol to the artboard.**

   For this example, we're using the butterfly symbol.

4. **With the Selection tool, enlarge your symbol so that it fills your shape (see image on the left in Figure 11-9).**

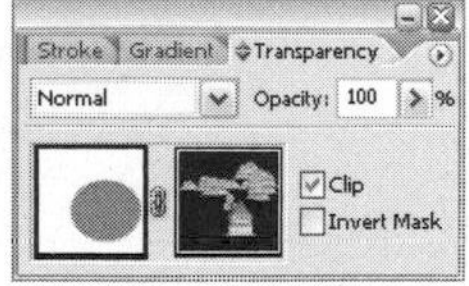

Figure 11-9: Creating an opacity mask.

5. **Select both the symbol and the shape and then choose Make Opacity Mask from the Transparency panel menu.**

   The symbol turns into a mask, showing varying levels of the underlying box through, depending on the original color value. To delete an Opacity mask, choose Release Opacity Mask from the Transparency panel menu.

Click the right thumbnail (this is the mask) in the Transparency panel, and a black border appears around it, indicating that it's active. You can move the items on the mask, or even create items to be added to the mask. It works just like the regular artboard, except that anything done on the mask side will only be used as an opacity mask. To work on the regular artboard, click the left thumbnail.

Chapter 12: Using Filters and Effects

In This Chapter

- **Applying filters and effects**
- **Getting to know the Appearance panel**
- **Discovering graphic styles**
- **Making artwork 3D**
- **Playing with additional fills and strokes**

Filters and effects give you the opportunity to do jazzy things to your Illustrator objects, such as adding drop shadows and squiggling artwork. You can even use Photoshop filters right in Illustrator. In this chapter, we explain the difference between filters and effects (it's a very big difference); show you how to apply, save, and edit filters and effects; and give you a quick tour of the Appearance panel (your trusty sidekick when performing these tasks).

Working with Filters and Effects

Filters apply permanent changes to artwork. After you use the filter, the only way to remove the change is to undo your actions or choose Object⇨Expand and take it apart. This process can be messy and not near as much fun as using an effect that is dynamically connected to the object. *Effects* are very different in that you can apply, change, and even remove effects at any time with the Appearance panel (Window⇨Appearance).

In Figure 12-1, we applied the drop shadow filter when the shape was a rectangle; then we applied the roughen filter. Notice that the drop shadow has no interaction with the original artwork.

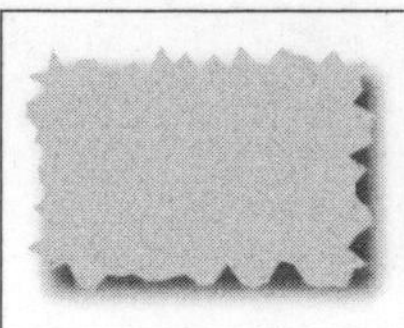

Figure 12-1: A rectangle with the Drop Shadow and Roughen filter applied.

In contrast, in Figure 12-2, we applied the Roughen effect, and the rectangle's drop shadow changed to look like the new shape. In the Appearance panel, you can double-click an effect to change it, or even drag it to the Trash icon in the lower-right corner of the Appearance panel to remove it.

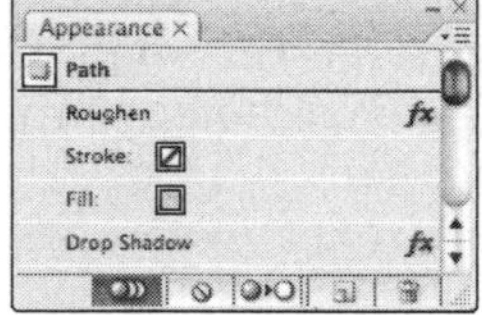

Figure 12-2: A rectangle with the Drop Shadow and Roughen effect applied, and the Appearance panel.

Understanding the Appearance panel

You can apply multiple effects to one object and even copy the effects to multiple objects. This is when a good working knowledge of the Appearance panel is necessary. If it isn't visible, choose Window➪Appearance to show the Appearance panel, as shown in Figure 12-3.

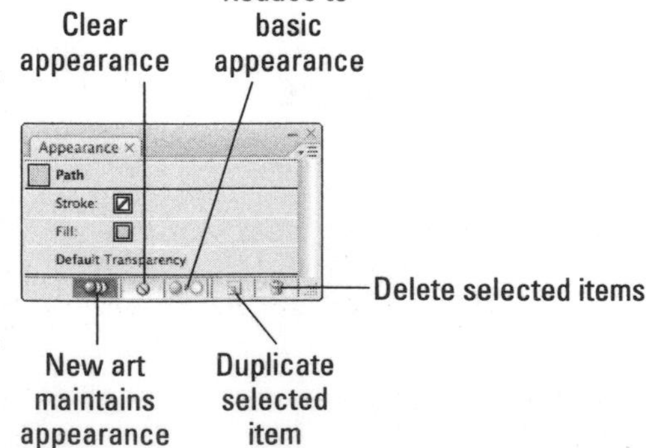

Figure 12-3: Discover how useful the Appearance panel can be.

To turn off effects so that they aren't automatically applied to any future objects, use any one of three buttons at the bottom of the Appearance panel:

- **New Art Maintains Appearance:** With the New Art Maintains Appearance button selected, your new art maintains the effects that you have applied to the present object.

  Click this button to switch to New Art Has Basic Appearance so that when you create the next object, colors are maintained, but just a single fill and stroke are created.
- **Clear Appearance:** Click this button if you have a selected object and want the Fill and Stroke color boxes to be set to None.
- **Reduce To Basic Appearance:** If you have a selected object and discover that you applied unwanted effects, click this button to reduce it back to a single fill and stroke.

As a default, if you have no effects applied, you see only a fill and a stroke listed in the Appearance panel. As you add effects, they're added to this list. You can even add more strokes and fills to the list. Why would you do that? Because you can do incredible things with additional fills and strokes (which we show you in the upcoming section "Applying an effect.")

Applying a filter

If effects are so great, why even use filters? Well, nothing can be all good. If you have lots of RAM (Random Access Memory) and you don't mind running through a few extra steps before printing (see Chapter 13 of this minibook), effects are the way to go. Most people don't mind, but you should see the alternative as well. Plus, some very useful Color filters are available that don't exist as effects — for example, filters that take a full color illustration and change it to grayscale.

If you generally work in the CMYK color mode, you will come across filters and effects that are grayed out. You can apply these filters and effects only in the RGB color mode. Choose File⇨Document Color Mode and change the document to RGB to use them.

Filters aren't dynamically linked to the original object that they were created from.

To apply the Add Arrowhead Filter, follow these steps (which essentially just add arrowheads to a path and are pretty straightforward):

1. **Create a new document, choose any color mode, and draw a path in your document.**

   If you haven't mastered the Pen tool yet (see Chapter 5 of this minibook), use the Pencil tool.

2. **To make it clear what is happening with the arrowheads, give the path a 3-pt stroke and make sure that there's no fill.**

   Using a 3-pt stroke enables you to see the stroke a little easier.

3. **Choose Filter➪Stylize➪Add Arrowheads.**

   Make sure that you choose the top Stylize menu item.

   The Add Arrowheads dialog box appears (see Figure 12-4).

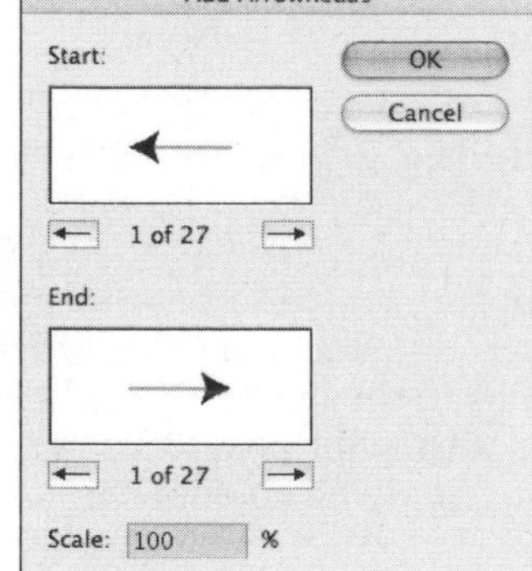

Figure 12-4: Use the Add Arrowheads Filter to create arrows.

4. **Choose to add an arrowhead to both the start and the end of the path by using the arrow keys to scroll through the selection.**

   Note that the Start arrowhead (top of Add Arrowhead dialog box) will be placed on the first point you created; the End arrowhead (bottom of the dialog box) will be placed on the last point you created.

5. **Choose the size of the arrowhead by typing a number in the Scale text field.**

   You can go anywhere from 1 to 1,000 percent, but typically an arrow is set at 50 percent. There is no preview available, but this scales the arrowhead relative to the selected line stroke weight.

Note that if you used the Arrowhead effect instead of the Filter, the arrowhead would dynamically be linked to the stroke. Scaling and changing direction occur automatically as the stroke weight and direction are updated. See the next section for more information on effects.

Applying an effect

To apply the Add Arrowheads effect, choose Effects➪Stylize➪Add Arrowheads. Use the same settings that we describe in the preceding step list and then reposition some of the anchor points on the path by using the Direct Selection tool to see how the arrowhead applied with the effect moves with the direction of the path; the filter keeps the arrowhead in its original position.

Different from filters, the items under the Effect menu are dynamically linked to the object that they were applied to. Effects can be scaled, modified, and even deleted from the original object with no harm done to the original object.

Creating a drop shadow is a quick and easy way of adding dimension and a bit of sophistication to your artwork. The interaction between the object with the drop shadow and the underlying objects can create an interesting look. To add the Drop Shadow effect to an illustration, follow these steps:

1. **Select the object(s) that are to have the drop shadow applied.**
2. **Choose Effect⇨Stylize⇨Drop Shadow.**
3. **In the Drop Shadow dialog box that appears, select the Preview check box in the upper-right corner.**

   You now see the drop shadow applied as you make changes.
4. **Choose from the following options (see Figure 12-5):**
   - **Mode:** Select a blending mode from this drop-down list to choose how you want your selected object to interact with the objects underneath. The default is Multiply, which works well — the effect is similar to coloring with a magic marker.
   - **Opacity:** Enter a value or use the drop-down list to determine how opaque or transparent the drop shadow should be. If it's too strong, choose a lower amount.
   - **Offset:** Enter a value to determine how close the shadow is to the object. If you're working with text or small artwork, smaller values (and shorter shadow) look best. Otherwise, the drop shadow may look like one big indefinable glob.

     The X Offset shifts the shadow from left to right, and the Y Offset shifts it up or down. You can enter negative or positive numbers.
   - **Blur:** Use blur to control how fuzzy the edges of the shadow are. A lower value makes the edge of the shadow more defined.
   - **Color and Darkness:** Select the Color radio button to choose a custom color for the drop shadow. Use Darkness to add more black to the drop shadow. Zero percent is the lowest amount of black, and 100 percent is the highest.

     As a default, the color of the shadow is based upon the color of your object, sort of . . . the Darkness option has a play in this, also. As a default, the shadow is made up of the color in the object if it's solid. Multicolored objects have a gray shadow.

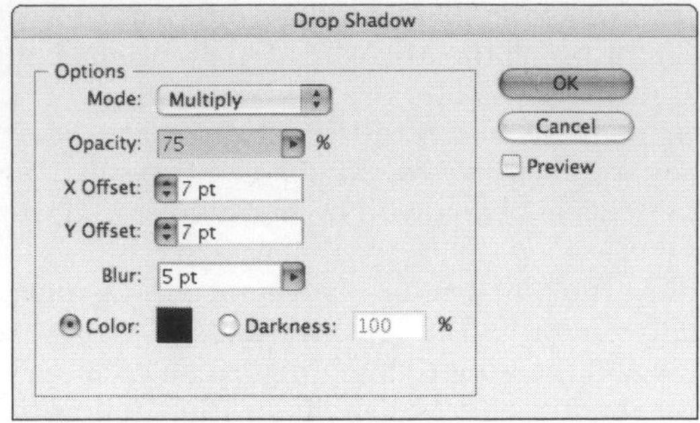

Figure 12-5: The Drop Shadow effect dialog box gives the effect's options and preview.

Saving Graphic Styles

A *graphic style* is a combination of all the settings you choose for a particular filter or effect in the Appearance panel. By saving this information in a graphic style, you store these attributes so that you can quickly and easily apply them to other objects later.

Choose Window⇨Graphics Styles; in the panel that appears are thumbnails of many different styles that Adobe has provided to you as a default. Click any of these graphic styles to apply the style to an active object. Look at the Appearance panel as you click different styles to see that you're applying combinations of attributes, including effects, fills, and strokes (see Figure 12-6).

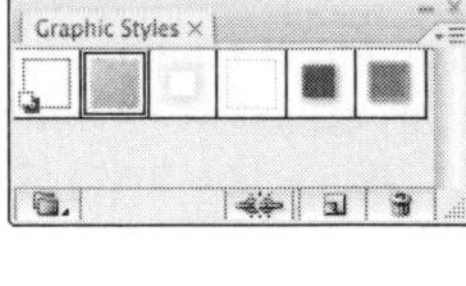

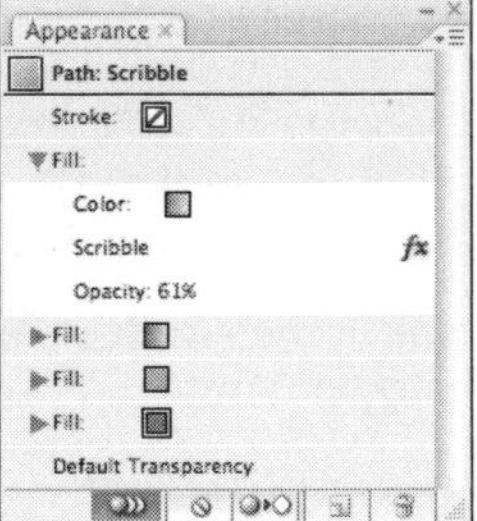

Figure 12-6: The Graphic Styles palette stores combinations of effects and other attributes for future use.

Find more styles by choosing the Graphic Styles panel menu (click the arrow in the upper-right corner of the panel) and selecting Open Graphic Style Library.

You can store attributes as a graphic style in several ways; we show you two easy methods. If you have a combination of attributes already applied to an object, store them by doing one of the following:

- ✦ With the object selected, Alt+click (Option+click on a Mac) the New Graphic Style button at the bottom of the Graphic Style panel. Alt+clicking (Option+clicking on a Mac) allows you to name the style as it is added.
- ✦ Drag the selected object right into the Graphic Style panel. The panel stores its attributes, but you have to double-click the new style to name it.

After you store a graphic style, simply select the object that you want to apply the style to and then click the saved style in the Graphic Styles panel.

Creating 3D Artwork

All the effects in Illustrator are great, but this new feature is really swell. Not only can you add dimension by using the 3D effect, you can also *map artwork* (that is, wrap artwork around a 3D object) and apply lighting to the 3D object. This means that you can design a label for a jelly jar and actually adhere it to the jar to show the client!

Here are the three choices for the 3D effect:

- ✦ **Extrude & Bevel:** This uses the z-axis to extrude an object. For example, a square becomes a cube.
- ✦ **Revolve:** Uses the z-axis and revolves a shape around it. You can use this to change an arc into a ball.
- ✦ **Rotate:** Rotates a 3D object created with the Extrude & Bevel or Revolve effects, or you can rotate a 2D object in 3D space. You can also adjust a 3D or 2D object's perspective.

To apply a 3D effect, you need to create an object appropriate for the 3D effect. Extrude & Bevel works great with shapes and text. If you want to edit an object that already has a 3D effect applied to it, double-click the 3D effect in the Appearance panel.

To apply a 3D effect, follow these steps:

1. **Select the object that you want to apply the 3D effect to.**

   For this example, we're choosing Extrude & Bevel.

2. **Choose Effect⇨3D⇨Extrude & Bevel.**

   Options for your chosen 3D effect appear. The Extrude & Bevel Options dialog box is shown in Figure 12-7.

3. **Select the Preview check box in the dialog box so that you can see results as you experiment with these settings.**

4. **Click the Preview pane (which shows a cube in Figure 12-7) and drag to rotate your object in space.**

   It makes selecting the right angle fun, or you can choose the angle from the Position drop-down list above the preview. This is called positioning the object in space.

   You should never rotate a 3D object with the Rotate tool, unless you want some very funky results; use the Preview pane in this dialog box instead.

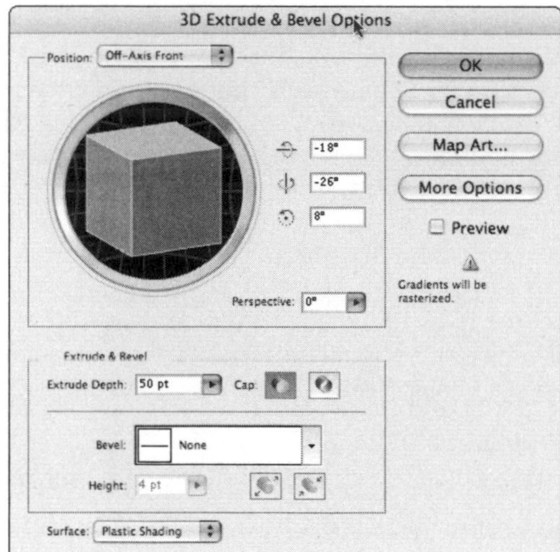

Figure 12-7: The Extrude & Bevel Options dialog box.

5. **If you want, use the Perspective drop-down list to add additional perspective to your object.**

6. **In the Extrude And Bevel section of the 3D Effects dialog box, choose a depth for your object and a cap.**

   The cap determines whether your shape has a solid cap on it or whether it's hollow, as shown in Figure 12-8.

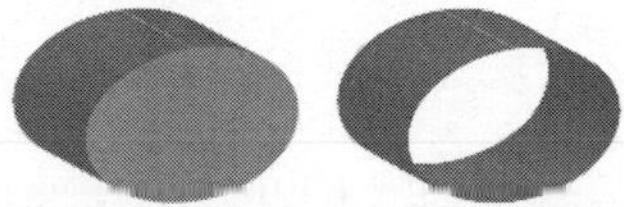

Figure 12-8: Cap on (left) and cap off (right).

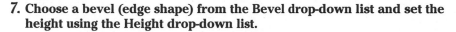

7. **Choose a bevel (edge shape) from the Bevel drop-down list and set the height using the Height drop-down list.**

   You have a choice of two ways to apply the bevel:

   - **Bevel Extent Out:** The bevel is added to the object.
   - **Bevel Extent In:** The bevel is subtracted from the object.

8. **Choose a rendering style from the Surface drop-down list or click the More Options button for in-depth lighting options, such as changing the direction or adding additional lighting.**

9. **Click the Map Art button.**

   The Map Art dialog box opens. Use this dialog box to apply artwork to a 3D object.

10. **Using the Surface arrow buttons, select which surface you want the artwork applied to and then choose the symbol from the Symbols drop-down list, as shown in Figure 12-9.**

    The result is shown on the bottom in Figure 12-9.

Keep the following points in mind when mapping artwork:

✦ An object must be a symbol to be used as mapped artwork. You would simply need to select and drag the artwork that you want mapped to the Symbols panel to make it a selectable item in the Map Art dialog box.

✦ The light gray areas in the Preview pane are the visible areas based upon the object's present position. Drag and scale the artwork in this pane to get the artwork where you want it.

✦ Shaded artwork (the check box at the bottom of the dialog box) looks good but can take a long time to render.

Note: All 3D effects are rendered at 72 dpi (low resolution) so as not to slow down processing speed. You can determine the resolution by choosing Effect⇨Document Raster Effects Settings, or when you save or export the file. You can also select the object and choose Object⇨Rasterize. After the object is rasterized, it can no longer be used as an Illustrator 3D object, so save the original!

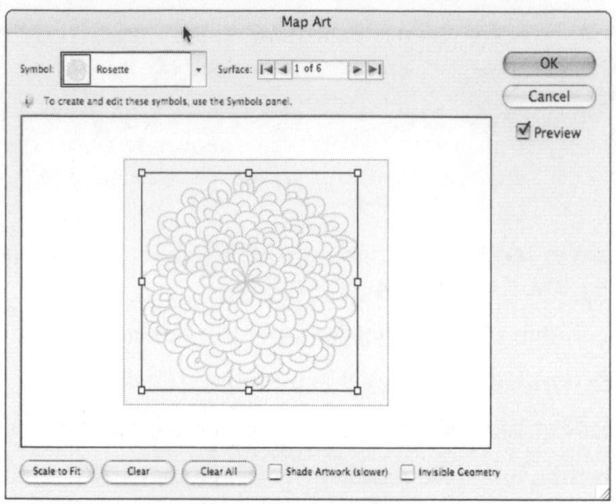

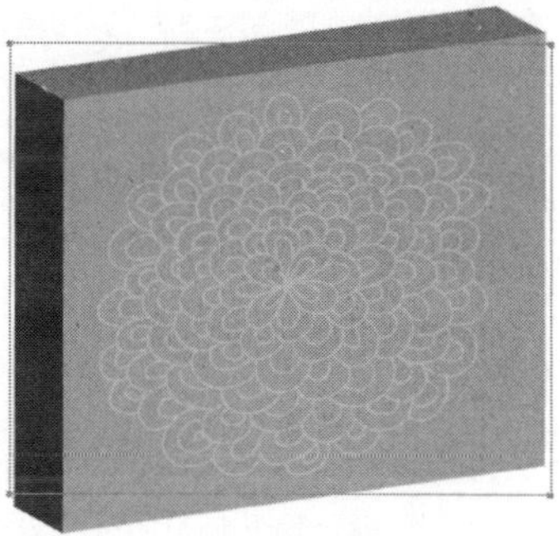

Figure 12-9: In the Map Art dialog box, you can select a surface and apply a symbol to it.

Using the panel menu in the Appearance panel, you can add more fills and strokes. With this feature, you can put different colored fills on top of each other and individually apply effects to each one, creating really interesting and creative results.

Just for fun, follow along to see what you can do to a single object with the Appearance panel:

1. **Create a star shape.**

   It doesn't matter how many points it has, or how large it is, just make it large enough to work with.

2. **Use the Window⇨Swatches panel to fill it with yellow and give it a black stroke.**

3. **Use Window⇨Stroke to make the stroke 1 pt or choose 1 from the Stroke drop-down menu in the control panel.**

   Notice that in the Appearance panel, the present fill and stroke are listed. Even in the simplest form, the Appearance panel helps track basic attributes. You can easily take advantage of the tracking to apply effects to just a fill or a stroke.

4. **Click Stroke in the Appearance panel.**
5. **Choose Effect⇨Path⇨Offset Path and in the Offset Panel dialog box that appears, change the Offset to –5pt and select the Preview check box.**

   Notice that the stroke moves into the fill instead of on the edge.

6. **Change the offset to something that works with your star shape and click OK.**

   Depending on the size of your star, you may want to adjust the amount of offset up or down.

7. **From the panel menu of the Appearance panel, choose to add an additional fill to the star shape.**

   This may sound ridiculous, but you can create some super effects with multiple fills.

8. **Click Fill in the Appearance panel (the top one) and choose Effect⇨Distort and Transform⇨Twist.**
9. **In the Twist dialog box that appears, type 45 into the Angle text field and select the Preview check box.**

   Notice how only the second fill is twisted? Pretty neat, right?

10. **Click OK to exit the Twist dialog box.**
11. **Select the top Fill from the Appearance panel again.**

    You always have to be sure that they're selected before doing anything that is meant to change just a specific fill or stroke.

12. **Then, using the Transparency panel (choose Window⇨Transparency), choose 50% from the Opacity slider or simply type 50% in the Opacity text field.**

    Now you can see your original shape through the new fill!

13. **With that top fill still selected, change the color or choose a pattern in the Swatches palette for a really different appearance.**

    You could go on for hours playing around with combinations of fills and strokes. Hopefully, this clicks, and you can take it further on your own.

Chapter 13: Using Your Illustrator Images

In This Chapter

- Saving Illustrator files
- Exporting files to other programs
- Preparing art for the Web
- Flattening transparency
- Printing from Illustrator

So you have beautiful artwork, but you aren't sure how to get it off your screen. You could have a party and invite all interested clients to stand around your monitor and ooh and ah, or you could actually share or sell your artwork by putting it on the Internet or printing it.

In this chapter, we show you how to use your illustrations in a variety of workflows, from using Illustrator files in page layout programs, to exporting files for Photoshop (and other programs) and the Web. Hopefully, this chapter can help you really use your artwork and understand the saving and flattening choices available in Adobe Illustrator.

Saving and Exporting Illustrator Files

In this section, we show you how the general choices in the Save As dialog box (choose File➪Save As) differ and the benefits of each.

If you need a particular file format that is not listed in the regular Save As dialog box, choose File➪Export for additional choices. Using the File Export command, you can choose to save your files in any of the formats in Table 13-1.

Table 13-1	Available File Formats
File Format	*Extension*
BMP	`.bmp`
Targa	`.tga`
PNG	`.png`
AutoCAD Drawing	`.dwg`
AutoCAD Interchange File	`.dxf`
Enhanced Metafile	`.emf`
Flash	`.swf`
JPEG	`.jpg`
Macintosh PICT	`.pct`
Photoshop	`.psd`
TIFF	`.tif`
Text Format	`.txt`
Windows Metafile	`.wmf`

Many of these formats *rasterize* your artwork, meaning that they'll no longer maintain vector paths and the benefits of being vector. Scalability is not limited, for example. If you think that you may want to edit your image again later, be sure to save a copy of the file and keep the original in the `.ai` format.

The native Adobe Illustrator file format

If your workflow can handle it, the best way to save your file is as a native Illustrator `.ai` file. By workflow, we mean that you're working with Adobe applications such as Adobe InDesign for page layout, Adobe Dreamweaver for Web page creation, Adobe Photoshop for photo-retouching, and Adobe Acrobat for cross-platform documents.

Understanding when it's best to use the `.ai` format is important. Saving your illustration as an `.ai` file ensures that your file is editable; it also ensures that any transparency is retained, even if you use the file in another application.

To save and use a file in the native Illustrator format, follow these steps:

1. **Make an illustration with transparency (50 percent transparent, for example) in Adobe Illustrator and choose File⇨Save As.**

2. **Select Adobe Illustrator Document (`.ai`) from the Save As Type drop-down list, give the file a name, and click Save.**
3. **Leave the Illustrator Native Options at the defaults and click OK.**

After you follow the preceding steps to prepare your Illustrator file, you can use the illustration in other Adobe applications:

- **Adobe Acrobat:** Open the Acrobat application and choose File➪Open. Locate the `.ai` file. Native Illustrator files open in Acrobat when you open them from within the Acrobat application.
- **Adobe InDesign:** Choose File➪Place. This method supports transparency created in Adobe Illustrator. (However, copying and pasting from Illustrator to InDesign does *not* support transparency.) See Figure 13-1.

Figure 13-1: Choose to place an Illustrator file into InDesign to support transparency, even over InDesign text.

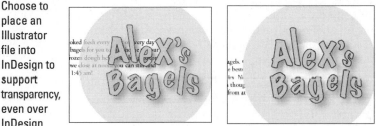

- **Adobe Photoshop:** Choose File➪Place. By placing an Illustrator file into Adobe Photoshop, you automatically create a Photoshop Smart Object. You can scale, rotate, and even apply effects to the Illustrator file and return to the original illustration at any time. Read more about Smart Objects in Photoshop in Chapter 9 of the Photoshop CS3 minibook.

  If you really want to go crazy with an Illustrator file in Photoshop, when you save the file in Illustrator, choose File➪Export and select the Photoshop (`.psd`) format from the Save As Type drop-down list. Choose a resolution from the options window. If you used layers, leave the Write Layers option selected.

  In Photoshop, choose File➪Open, select the file that you just saved in Illustrator as a `.psd`, and click Open. The file opens in Photoshop with the layers intact.

- **Adobe Flash:** New integration features built into Adobe Illustrator CS3 allow you to cut and paste directly into Adobe Flash CS3. If you Choose Edit⇨Copy from Adobe Illustrator, you can then switch to Adobe Flash CS3 and choose Edit⇨Paste. The Paste dialog box appears.
- **Adobe Dreamweaver:** By choosing File⇨Save for Web & Devices, you can choose to save your Illustrator document in the `.gif`, `.jpg`, `.png`, `.swf`, `.svg`, or `WBMP` format. You can then insert these formats into Dreamweaver by choosing Insert⇨Image in Adobe Dreamweaver.

Select the Image button from the Insert panel in Dreamweaver. When the Select Image Source dialog box appears, navigate to the location which you saved your optimized file. Select it and click Choose. If your file is located out of the root folder for the site you're working on, an alert window appears, offering the opportunity to save the file with your other site assets.

Saving Illustrator files back to previous versions

When saving an `.ai` or `.eps` file, you can choose a version from the Version drop-down menu. Keep in mind that any features specific to newer versions of Illustrator will not be supported in older file formats, so make sure that you save a copy and keep the original file intact. Adobe helps you understand the risk of saving back to older versions by putting a warning sign next to the version drop-down menu and showing you specific issues with the version you have selected in the Warnings window.

The EPS file format

EPS is the file format that most text editing and page layout applications accept; EPS supports vector data and is completely scalable. The Illustrator `.eps` format is based on PostScript, which means that you can reopen an EPS file and edit it in Illustrator at any time.

To save a file in Illustrator as an EPS, follow these steps:

1. **Choose File⇨Save As and select EPS (Encapsulated PostScript File) from the Save As Type drop-down list.**
2. **From the Version menu, choose the Illustrator version you're saving to.**
3. **In the EPS Options dialog box that appears (shown in Figure 13-2), choose the preview from the Format drop-down list:**
   - **TIFF (8-bit Color):** A color preview for either Mac or PC.
   - **TIFF (Black & White):** A low-resolution black-and-white preview.

4. **Select either the Transparent or Opaque option, depending on whether you want the non-image areas in your artwork to be transparent or opaque.**

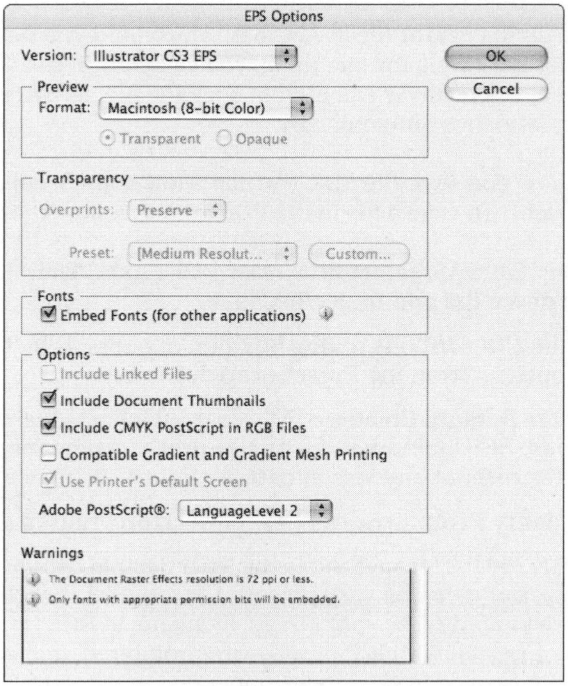

Figure 13-2: The EPS Options dialog box allows you to choose a preview, as well as other important settings.

5. **Set your Transparency Flattening settings.**

   These settings are grayed out if you haven't used transparency in the file. (See the "Flattening Transparency" section, later in this chapter, for more about this setting.)

6. **Leave the Embed Fonts (For Other Applications) check box selected to leave fonts you used embedded in the EPS file format.**

7. **In the Options section, leave the Include CMYK PostScript In RGB Files check box selected.**

   If you don't know which Adobe Postscript level you want to save to, leave it at the default.

8. **Click OK to save your file as an EPS.**

The PDF file format

If you want to save your file in a format that supports over a dozen platforms and requires only the Acrobat Reader, available as a free download at `www.adobe.com`, choose to save in the PDF format.

If you can open an Illustrator file in Acrobat, why would you need to save a file in the PDF format? Well, for one thing, you can compress a PDF down to a smaller size; also, the receiver can double-click the file, and Acrobat or Acrobat Reader launches automatically.

Depending on how you save the PDF, you can allow some level of editability in Adobe Illustrator. To save a file in the PDF format, follow these steps:

1. **Choose File⇨Save As; select Illustrator PDF (`.pdf`) from the Save As Type drop-down list and then click Save.**
2. **In the Adobe PDF Options dialog box that appears, select one of the following options from the Preset drop-down list:**
   - **Illustrator Default:** Creates a PDF file in which all Illustrator data is preserved. PDF files created with this preset can be reopened in Illustrator without any loss of data.
   - **High Quality Print:** Creates PDFs for desktop printers and proofers.
   - **PDF/X-1a:2001:** This method is the least flexible delivery of PDF content data, but it can be very powerful. It requires that the color of all objects be in CMYK or spot colors. Elements in RGB or Lab color spaces or tagged with ICC profiles are prohibited. It also requires that all fonts used in the job be embedded in the supplied PDF file.
   - **PDF/X-3:2002:** This method of creating a PDF has slightly more flexibility than the X-1a:2001 method in that color managed workflows are supported elements in Lab, and attached ICC source profiles may also be used.
   - **PDF/X-4:2007:** This preset is based on PDF 1.4, which includes support for live transparency. PDF/X-4 has the same color management and *International Color Consortium* (ICC) color specifications as PDF/X-3. You can open PDF files created with PDF/X-4 compliance in Acrobat 7.0 and Reader 7.0 and later.
   - **Press Quality:** Creates a PDF file that can be printed to a high-resolution output device. The file will be large, but it will maintain all the information that a commercial printer or service provider needs

to print your file correctly. This option automatically converts the color mode to CMYK, embeds all fonts used in the file, prints at a higher resolution, and uses other settings to preserve the maximum amount of information contained in the original document.

- **Smallest File Size:** Creates a low-resolution PDF suitable for posting on the internet or sending via e-mail.

Before creating an Adobe PDF file using the Press preset, check with your commercial printer to find out what the output resolution and other settings should be.

- **Standard:** Don't pick a PDF/X standard unless you have a specific need or have been requested to. Through the Standard drop-down menu, you can select the type of PDF/X file you want to create.
- **Compatibility:** Different features are available for different versions, such as the ability to support layers in Version 6 or higher. If you want the most compatible file type choose Acrobat 5 (PDF 1.4). But if you want to take advantage of layers or need to preserve spot colors, you must choose Acrobat 6 or higher.

3. **Click Save PDF to save your file as a PDF.**

If you want to be able to reopen the PDF file and edit it in Illustrator, make sure that you leave the Preserve Illustrator Editing Capabilities check box selected in the Adobe PDF Options dialog box.

In the Adobe PDF Options dialog box, to the left of the preset choices are options that you can change to customize your settings. Scan through them to see how you can change resolution settings and even add printer's marks. Take a look at Book VII on Acrobat to find out more about the additional PDF options.

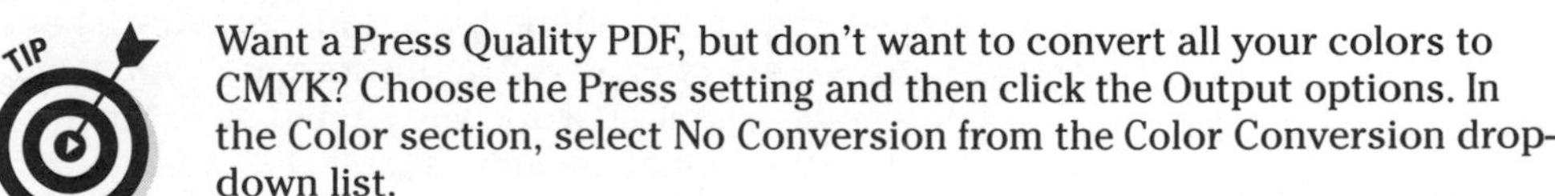

Want a Press Quality PDF, but don't want to convert all your colors to CMYK? Choose the Press setting and then click the Output options. In the Color section, select No Conversion from the Color Conversion drop-down list.

Saving Your Artwork for the Web

If you need to save artwork for the Web, there is no better feature than Save For Web. The Save For Web dialog box gives you a preview pane where you can test different file formats before you actually save the file.

To save an Illustrator file that you intend to use in a Web page, just follow these steps:

1. **Choose File➪Save For Web & Devices.**

   The Save For Web & Devices dialog box appears, showing your artwork on the Optimized tab.

2. **Choose a tabbed view: Original, Optimized, 2-Up, or 4-Up.**

   As a default, you see the artwork in the Optimized view, which previews the artwork as it will appear based upon the settings on the right. The 2-Up view is probably the best choice because it shows your original image versus the optimized version.

3. **Choose a setting for your file from the options on the right.**

   If you want to make it easy on yourself, choose a preset from the Preset drop-down list. Keep in mind these points:

   - GIF is generally used for artwork with spans of solid color. GIF is not a lossy format. You can make your artwork smaller by reducing the number of colors in the image — hence the choices, such as GIF 64 No Dither (64 colors). The lower the amount of colors, the smaller the file size. You can also increase or decrease the number of colors in the file by changing the preset values in the Color text field or by using the arrows to the left of the Color text field.
   - Dithering tries to make your artwork look like it has more colors by creating a pattern in the colors. It looks like a checkerboard pattern up close and even far away, as shown in Figure 13-3. It also makes a larger file size, so why use it? Most designers don't like the effect and choose the No Dither option.
   - JPEG is used for artwork that has subtle gradations from one shade to another. Photographs are often saved in this format. If you have drop shadows or blends in your artwork, you should select this format. JPEG is a lossy file format, meaning that it will reduce your image to a lesser quality and can create odd artifacts in your artwork. You have choices such as High, Medium, and Low in the Settings drop-down list. Make sure that you choose wisely. You can also use the Quality slider to tweak the compression.

Figure 13-3: An example of dithering.

- PNG-8 is very similar to a GIF file format. Unless you have a certain reason for saving as PNG-8, stick with the GIF file format.
- PNG-24 supports the best of two formats. Not only does the PNG format support the nice gradients from one tonal value to another (like JPEG), but it also supports Transparency (like GIFs). Not just any old transparency, if you make an object 50% transparent in Adobe Illustrator, then choose to save it, using Save For Web & Devices, as a PNG-24 file with the Transparency check box checked, the image will show through to any other objects underneath it on its destination page.
- The SWF graphic file format is a version of the Adobe Flash Player vector-based graphics format. Because a SWF file is vector-based, its graphics are scalable and play back smoothly on any screen size and across multiple platforms. Using the Save For Web & Devices dialog box, you can save your image directly to SWF from Adobe Illustrator. With the SWF choice, you can preview and make decisions as to how you want to export to the file, as well as make decisions about how layers should be exported.
- Scalable Vector Graphics (SVG) is an emerging Web standard for two-dimensional graphics. SVG is written in plain text and rendered by the browser, except that in this case, it's not just text that is rendered but also shapes and images, which can be animated and made interactive. SVG is written in XML (Extensible Markup Language). You can choose to save Scalable Vector Graphics out of Adobe Illustrator using the Save For Web & Devices dialog box.
- Use the Wireless Application Protocol Bitmap Format (WBMP) format for bitmap images for mobile devices.

4. **When you're satisfied with your chosen settings, save your file by clicking Save.**

When saving illustrations for the Web, you should keep the following points in mind, which will make the whole process much easier for you and anyone who uses your illustrations:

✦ **Keep it small.** Don't forget that if you're saving illustrations for a Web page, many other elements will be on that page. Try to conserve on file size to make downloading the page quicker for viewers using dial-up connections. Most visitors won't wait more than 10 seconds for a page to download before giving up and moving on to another Web site.

As you make your choices, keep an eye on the file size and the optimized artwork in the lower-left corner of the preview window. On average, a GIF should be around 10K and a JPEG around 15K. These rules aren't written in stone, but please don't try to put a 100K JPEG on a Web page!

You can change the download time by selecting the panel menu in the upper-right corner of the Save For Web & Devices dialog box and choosing Optimize to File Size to input a final file size and have Illustrator create your settings in the Save For Web & Devices dialog box.

- **Preview the file before saving it.** If you want to see the artwork in a Web browser before saving it, click the Preview In Default Browser button at the bottom of the Save For Web & Devices dialog box. The browser of choice appears with your artwork in the quality and size in which it will appear. If you have no browser selected, click and hold down the Preview In Default Browser button to choose Other and then browse to locate a browser that you want to use for previewing. Close the browser to return to the Save for Web & Devices dialog box.
- **Change the size.** Many misconceptions abound about size when it comes to Web artwork. Generally, most people view their browser windows in an area approximately 700 x 500 pixels. Depending on the screen resolution, this may cover the entire screen on a 14-inch monitor, but even viewers with 21-inch monitors with a high resolution often don't want to have their entire screen covered with a browser's window, so they still have a browser window area of around 700 x 500 pixels. When choosing a size for your artwork, use proportions of this amount to help you. For example, if you want an illustration to take up about a quarter of the browser window's width, you should make your image about 175 pixels wide (700÷4 = 175). If you notice that the height of your image is over 500 pixels, you should whittle the height down in size as well, or your viewers will have to scroll to see the whole image (and it will probably take too long to download!).

  Use the Image Size tab to input new sizes. As long as the Constrain Proportions check box is selected, both the height and width of the image will be changed proportionally. Click the Apply button to change the size but do not close the Save For Web & Devices dialog box.
- **Finish the save.** If you aren't finished with the artwork, but you want to save the settings, hold down the Alt (Option on a Mac) key and click the Remember button. (When you're not holding down the Alt or Option key, the Remember button is the Done button.) If you're finished, click the Save button and save your file in the appropriate location.

Flattening Transparency

You may find that all those cool effects that you put into your illustration don't print correctly. When you print a file that has effects such as drop shadows, cool gradient blends, and feathering, Illustrator turns transparent areas that overlap other objects into pixels and leaves what it can as vectors — this process is called *flattening.*

So what actually is flattening? Look at Figure 13-4 to see the difference between the original artwork (on the left) and the flattened artwork (on the right). Notice that in Figure 13-4, when the artwork was flattened, some of the areas turned into pixels. But at what resolution? This is why you want to know about flattening, so that you can determine the quality of art yourself — before getting an unpleasant surprise at the outcome.

Figure 13-4: Artwork before and after flattening applied.

Flattening a file

If you've taken advantage of transparency or effects using transparency (which we discuss in Chapter 11 of this minibook), follow these steps to get the highest quality artwork from your file:

1. **Make sure that you've created the artwork in the CMYK mode.**

   You can change the document's color mode by choosing File➪Document Color Mode.

2. **Choose Effects➪Document Raster Effects Settings.**

   The Document Raster Effects Settings dialog box appears, as shown in Figure 13-5.

3. **Choose the resolution that you want to use by selecting an option in the Resolution area.**

   As a default, the rasterization setting is the Screen (72 ppi) option, which is fine for the screen. Select the Medium (150 ppi) option for printers and copiers and select the High (300 ppi) option for press.

4. **Choose whether you want a white or transparent background.**

   If you select the Transparent option, you create an alpha channel. The alpha channel is retained if the artwork is exported into Photoshop.

5. **You can generally leave the items in the Options section deselected:**

   - The Anti-Alias check box applies anti-aliasing to reduce the appearance of jagged edges in the rasterized image. Deselect this option to maintain the crispness of fine lines and small text.
   - The Create Clipping Mask check box creates a mask that makes the background of the rasterized image appear transparent. You don't need to create a clipping mask if you select the Transparent option for your background.
   - The Add Around Object text field adds the specified number of pixels around the rasterized image.

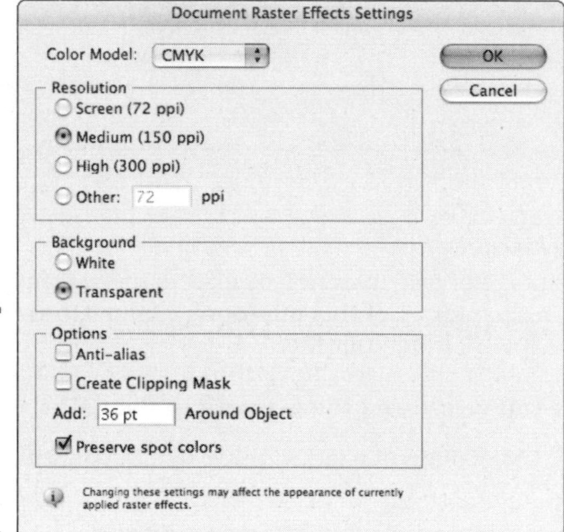

Figure 13-5: Choosing the quality of your rasterized artwork.

6. **Click OK.**

   The next step is to set the transparency options in the Document Setup dialog box.

7. **Choose File➪Document Setup➪Transparency.**

   The Export And Clipboard Transparency Flattener Settings options appear. From the Preset drop-down list, select the Low, Medium, High, or Custom option. Select the Low option for on-screen viewing, the Medium option for printers and copiers, or the High option for press. Choose the Other option if you want to control more of the settings yourself.

8. **Click OK.**

If you find yourself customizing the settings on a regular basis, choose Edit⇨Transparency Flattener Presets to create and store your own presets.

You can apply the flattening in several ways. Here are three simple methods.

- ✦ Select the object(s) that require flattening and choose Object⇨Flatten Transparency. Choose one of the default settings or a custom preset that you created from the Preset drop-down list and click OK.
- ✦ Choose File⇨Print and select Advanced from the list of print options on the left. Choose a preset from the Overprint and Transparency Flattener options. If you used the Attributes panels to create overprints (for trapping used in high-end printing), make sure that you preserve the overprints.

  Note: Overprints will not be preserved in areas that use transparency.
- ✦ Choose File⇨Save As and choose Illustrator EPS. In the Transparency section of the EPS Options dialog box, choose a flattening setting from the Preset drop-down list. If your Transparency options are grayed out, you have no transparency in your file.

Using the Flattener Preview panel

Want to preview your flattening? Use the Flattener Preview panel by choosing Window⇨Flattener Preview.

The Flattener Preview panel doesn't apply the flattening, but it gives you a preview based upon your settings. Click the Refresh button and choose Show Options from the panel menu. Test various settings without actually flattening the file. Experiment with different settings, and then save your presets by selecting Save Transparency Flattener Preset from the panel menu. The saved settings can be accessed in the Preset drop-down list in the Options dialog boxes that appear when you save a file as an EPS or in the Document Setup dialog box.

Click the Refresh button after making changes to update the preview.

Zoom in on the artwork by clicking in the preview pane. Scroll the artwork in the preview pane by holding down the spacebar and dragging. Zoom out by Alt+clicking (Option+clicking on a Mac).

Printing from Illustrator

Printing from Illustrator gives you lots of capabilities, such as printing composites to separations and adding printer's marks.

To print your illustration, follow these steps:

1. **Choose File⇨Print.**
2. **In the Print dialog box that appears, select a printer if one isn't already selected.**
3. **If the PPD isn't selected, choose one from the PPD drop-down list.**

   A *PPD* is a printer description file. Illustrator needs this to determine the specifics of the PostScript printer you're sending your file to. This setting lets Illustrator know whether the printer can print in color, the size paper it can handle, and the resolution, as well as many other important details.
4. **Choose from other options as follows:**

   Use the General options area to pick what pages to print. In the Media area, select the size of media that you're printing to. In the Options area, choose whether you want layers to print and any options specific to printing layers.
5. **Click the Print button to print your illustration.**

And that's it. Printing your illustration can be really simple, but the following list highlights some basic things to keep in mind as you prepare your illustration for printing:

- **Printing a composite:** A *composite* is the full-color image, where all the inks are applied to the page (and not separated out onto individual pages, one for cyan, one for magenta, one for yellow, and one for black). To make sure that your settings are correct, click Output in the print options pane on the left side of the Print dialog box and select Composite from the Mode drop-down list.
- **Printing separations:** To separate colors, click Output in the print options pane on the left side of the Print dialog box; from the Mode drop-down list, choose the Separations (Host-Based) option. Select the

In-RIP Separations option only if your service provider or printer asks you to. Other options to select from are as follows:

- The resolution is determined by your PPD, based upon the dpi in the printer description. You may have only one option available in the Printer Resolution drop-down list.
- Select the Convert Spot Colors to Process check box to make your file 4-color.
- Click the printer icons to the left of the listed colors to turn off or on the colors that you want to print.

✦ **Printer's marks and bleeds:** Click Marks And Bleeds in the print options pane on the left side of the Print dialog box to turn on all printer's marks, or just select the ones that you want to appear.

Specify a bleed area if you're extending images beyond the trim area of a page. If you don't specify a bleed, the artwork will stop at the edge of the page and not leave a trim area for the printer.

After you've created a good set of options specific to your needs, click the Save Preset button at the bottom of the Print dialog box. Name your preset appropriately; when you want to use that preset, select it from the Print Preset drop-down list at the top of the Print dialog box for future print jobs.

Book V

Flash CS3

"How's it going? You get a handle on that Lasso function yet?"

Book V: Flash CS3 603

Chapter 1: Introduction to Adobe Flash CS3

In This Chapter

- Getting to know Adobe Flash CS3 and vector graphics
- Investigating basic moviemaking principles
- Creating a Flash document file
- Exploring the Adobe Flash CS3 interface
- Viewing movies and setting preferences in Adobe Flash CS3
- Getting help

If you're creating a Web site, you don't really need Adobe Flash CS3. So, when and why do you use Flash? You use it when you want your Web site to make greater use of animation, sound, and interactive graphics. Adobe Flash CS3 Professional is an exceptionally powerful product that can be used to create rich Internet applications. Developing those kinds of applications goes beyond the scope of this book. This book is designed to give you an introductory look at Flash's basic capabilities. For more in-depth coverage on Adobe Flash CS3 Professional, you should check out *Flash CS3 For Dummies,* by Ellen Finkelstein and Gurdy Leete (Wiley Publishing, Inc.).

Understanding What Flash Is and How It Works

If someone asks you what Flash is, you can quickly say, "It's a Web animation program." But that statement, although true, doesn't do justice to Flash's wide-ranging capabilities.

Seeing what Flash can do

Flash is a rich program. Only your creativity limits what you can do with Flash. The following list points out Flash's major features and may help you decide whether you want to use Flash on your Web site:

- Animate text and graphics, including changing their color and visibility.
- Create your own graphics or import graphics from another program, such as Adobe Illustrator CS3 or Adobe Fireworks CS3.

- Design Web buttons, still or animated, that link users to other pages or sites or perform other programmed actions.
- Add sound and video to your Web site.
- Add interactivity to your site by letting viewers choose where they go and what they see or hear. You can also create forms for viewers to fill out, poll viewers' interests, and customize a site for each viewer.
- Design more compelling advertisements for your business that you run online.
- Create a user interface, including scrollbars, check boxes, list boxes, forms, and more.

You can design an entire Web site using Flash. For example, you can use Flash buttons to create your menu and place the content of your Web site on the Timeline. (The *Timeline* is the collection of frames and layers that make up a Flash movie and is covered in more detail in Book V, Chapter 5.) Flash gives you complete artistic freedom when designing your site, as compared to designing in HTML, which you may find limiting. For example, HTML significantly limits your placement of objects. On the other hand, when using Flash, you need to be careful that the site displays quickly and that users can easily navigate it. Also, updating your content and connecting to a database to retrieve content is more complex and time consuming with Flash.

Creating content for a Web site in Flash

Using Flash has two components. First, you create the Flash document and publish it to a format that a browser can read. Then, you (or others) view the Flash content in a browser. To create Flash content, follow these basic steps:

1. **Create your Flash animation in Flash and save it as a Flash document.**

   This document has an `.fla` extension. (Chapters 2 through 6 and Chapter 8 in Book V explain the features that Flash offers for creating Flash documents.)

2. **Use the Publish command in Flash to save your `.fla` file as a Flash movie.**

   The Flash movie has an `.swf` extension, and you often hear it called an SWF file. When you publish the movie, Flash also generates the HTML code that you need to insert the SWF file into your Web page. See Book V, Chapter 7 for a detailed description of how to add Flash movies to your Web page.

3. **Insert the HTML code into your Web page (or create a new Web page and add the HTML code).**

   The HTML code refers to the SWF file.

After taking these three steps, you simply follow the procedures that you use for any Web site — uploading the HTML and SWF files.

Using Flash on a Web site

To view a Flash movie, you need the Flash Player. Flash Player 9 is the latest player as of this writing. After you have the Flash Player installed, your browser automatically uses the player to display the Flash animation. You can download the Flash Player for free from the following Web site:

```
www.adobe.com/flashplayer/
```

Although the vast majority of people who access your Web site have the Flash Player on their computers already, you may want to include a button or link on your Web site that connects to this Adobe URL so that people can easily find and download the player if they need it.

Comparing Bitmaps and Vector Graphics

Most graphics that you see on a Web site are bitmap files that are reduced in file size so that they can be displayed as `.gif` or `.jpg` files. A *bitmap* is a graphic image that's made up of many tiny dots (bits) that are very close together. The various colored dots create the pattern that your eyes see as a picture. When the dots are displayed on a computer screen, they're called pixels. To get a bitmap graphic into Flash, you import it. See Book V, Chapter 3 for more details about importing graphics.

Bitmap graphics can create very large file sizes (although compression can make the files smaller). Large file sizes mean that your Web page takes longer to display in a Web browser. Bitmaps also don't scale very well. If you need to enlarge a bitmap, you start to see the individual dots, which give you a grainy graphic image.

Flash creates vector graphics. Unlike bitmaps, *vector graphics* are defined by equations that specify location, direction, and color. The equations result in small file sizes, and that small size provides a faster display on your Web site. And you can easily scale vector graphics. No matter how large or small you make your graphic, it always looks clear. Finally, with vector graphics, you can easily transform an image such as a circle into another image, such as a triangle.

You can't create all graphics by using vectors. Photographs and other complex designs usually need bitmaps to display them in all their glory. Often, you use a combination of bitmap and vector graphics to complete your Web site.

Exploring Basic Moviemaking Principles

Flash uses a classic moviemaking structure, which contains the following components:

- **The Stage:** The Stage contains all your content, which includes graphics and text.
- **Frames:** A frame represents a small unit of time, such as $\frac{1}{12}$ of a second. Each frame contains a tiny section of the animation.
- **The Timeline:** The Timeline contains all the frames. You use the Timeline to manipulate your content over time and thus create the animation.
- **Layers:** Layers are collections of linear frames that are all on the same level. Layers can be moved up or down to change the position of objects on the Stage relative to each other.
- **Scene:** Scenes are discreet collections of layers, and are a great tool to help you organize your movie.

The Stage

The Stage, shown in Figure 1-1, is a simple rectangle on which you place all your content. You change the content on the Stage from frame to frame to create animation. You generally use the drawing and editing tools in the Tools panel to draw and edit the content on the Stage. In this respect, Flash is a graphic program like many others. You can create text, circles, lines, and so on, and you can specify the color of the objects that you create. When you publish your movie, you can save the graphics in standard Web site bitmap formats — JPEG, GIF, and PNG.

In the section "Setting document properties," later in this chapter, we explain how to specify the size and color of the Stage.

The Timeline and frames

You can think of the Timeline (refer to Figure 1-1) as the frames in a film reel. The difference is that Flash's Timeline is electronic, rather than on film. Each frame covers a specific period of time. The default frame rate is 12 frames per second (fps). You use the frames in the Timeline to control the flow of the animation. You click a frame to make it current. By specifying which frames contain animation, you determine when animation starts and stops. Book V, Chapter 5 explains more about working with the frames in the Timeline.

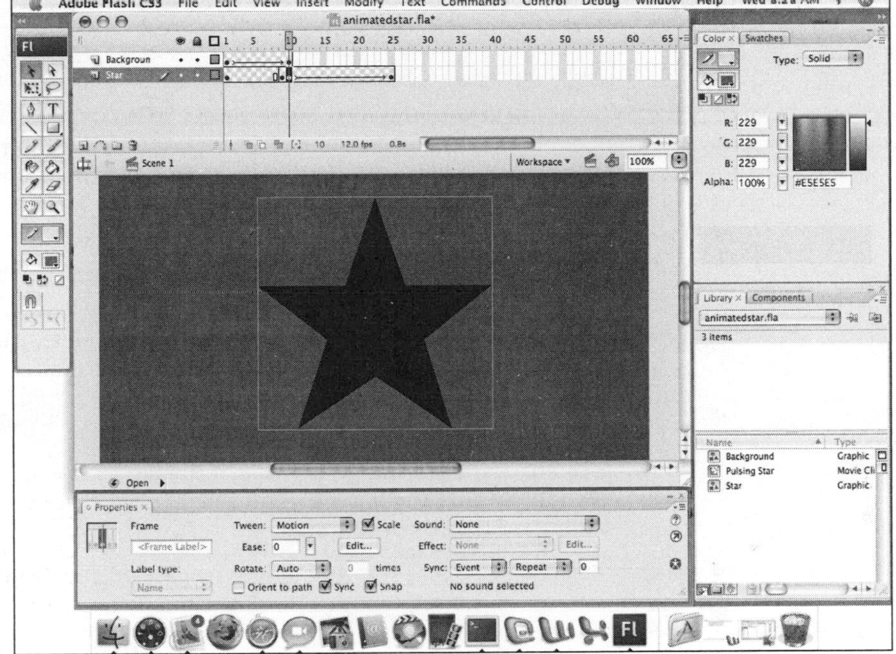

Figure 1-1: The main screen contains everything that you need to create great animations.

Layers

In Figure 1-1, you can see the Layer list to the left of the Timeline. Layers are covered in Book V, Chapter 4, but for now you should understand that you can separate the content on the Stage into layers. Layers help organize your content so that your graphics and animations don't "bump" into each other. You should also use separate layers for sounds and other interactive elements in your movie.

Scenes

A scene is simply a way to organize the Timeline. You can use the default Scene 1 (choose File⇨New to create a new Flash movie) and have just one scene for your entire movie. However, when your animations become more complex, adding scenes can help you keep track of your movie structure. You can find out more about scenes in Book V, Chapter 5.

Taking a Quick Tour of the Flash Interface

The Flash interface exists to help you create animation. Although the interface has several components, and you have many options for customizing those components, don't be intimidated! You'll soon find it easy to use. Refer to Figure 1-1 to see one way of viewing the interface.

Menus

Most of the commands that you use in Flash appear on the toolbar. The following list gives you a summary of the menu items and their main features:

- **File:** Open, close, and save files; import and export files; print a Flash document; publish documents (to create SWF movie files); and close Flash
- **Edit:** Undo and redo actions; cut, copy, and paste; delete, duplicate, and select objects on the Stage; copy and paste frames from the Timelines; edit symbols (which you can read about in Book V, Chapter 3); set preferences; and create keyboard shortcuts
- **View:** Zoom in and out, change how Flash displays objects and text, choose which parts of the screen you want to display, and snap objects to pixels on the Stage or other objects
- **Insert:** Insert symbols, insert and delete frames on the Timeline, insert layers, and create animation (see Book V, Chapter 5 to find out how to create animation)
- **Modify:** Edit layers, scenes, the Stage, symbols, frames, and graphic objects on the Stage
- **Text:** Format text
- **Commands:** Create automated tasks that you can use repeatedly on a variety of objects
- **Control:** Play and rewind animation, test movies and scenes, activate some interactive features, and mute sounds
- **Window:** Display panels and toolbars
- **Help:** Get help on Flash and ActionScript

Most of the menu commands are discussed in detail in the rest of this book.

Table 1-1 lists some of the commonly used keyboard shortcuts for the menu commands. After you get used to them, you may find using them easier (and faster) than using the menu. In the section "Creating your own keyboard shortcuts," later in this chapter, we explain how you can make keyboard shortcuts for your particular needs.

You may want to photocopy Table 1-1 and post it near your computer.

For a Mac, replace the Ctrl key with the ⌘ key.

Table 1-1 **Handy Keyboard Shortcuts**

Menu Command	*Keyboard Shortcut*
File➪New	Ctrl+N
File➪Open	Ctrl+O
File➪Save	Ctrl+S
File➪Import	Ctrl+R
Edit➪Undo	Ctrl+Z
Edit➪Redo	Ctrl+Y
Edit➪Cut	Ctrl+X
Edit➪Copy	Ctrl+C
Edit➪Paste	Ctrl+V
Edit➪Paste in Place	Ctrl+Shift+V
Edit➪Copy Frames	Ctrl+Alt+C
Edit➪Paste Frames	Ctrl+Alt+V
View➪Hide Panels	F4
Insert➪Convert to Symbol	F8
Insert➪New Symbol	Ctrl+F8
Insert➪Frame	F5
Insert➪Keyframe	F6
Modify➪Group	Ctrl+G
Modify➪Break Apart	Ctrl+B
Control➪Play	Enter
Control➪Rewind	Ctrl+Alt+R
Control➪Test Movie	Ctrl+Enter
Window➪Align	Ctrl+K
Window➪Color Swatches	Ctrl+F9
Window➪Actions	F9
Window➪Library	Ctrl+L or F11

Timeline

The Timeline doesn't tell you *what* is happening; it tells you *when* something is happening. But the Timeline does give you clues about the content of your animation. Figure 1-2 shows a Timeline with plenty of action. (Book V, Chapter 5 tells you all about using the Timeline to create animation.)

If the Timeline isn't displayed, choose View⇨Timeline. Each layer has its own Timeline so that you can see the sequence of events separately for each layer. (See Book V, Chapter 4 for more information about the Timeline, layers, and the Layer list.) The Timeline (see Figure 1-2) has the following features:

- **Layer list:** The Layer list helps you organize your content.
- **Insert a layer:** Use the New Layer button to add a new layer.
- **Insert Layer Folder:** This creates a folder that you can add layers into for easy management.
- **Delete a layer:** Use the Delete Layer button to delete a layer.
- **Playhead:** The playhead indicates the current frame.
- **Current frame:** The Current Frame box also displays the current frame.
- **Frame rate:** The Frame Rate box displays the current *frame rate,* which is the number of frames that play per second in an animation.
- **Elapsed seconds:** The Elapsed Seconds box displays the number of seconds that have passed from the beginning of the movie to the current frame, at the current frame rate.
- **Action:** A small *a* in a frame indicates that the frame contains ActionScript to control the animation.
- **Keyframe with no content:** A *keyframe* is a frame that contains a change in the animation. If you insert a keyframe but don't put anything in that keyframe, the Timeline displays an unfilled circle.
- **Keyframe with content:** When a keyframe contains any object, the Timeline displays a filled circle.
- **Sound:** When you insert sound into an animation, the sound's wave appears on the Timeline.
- **Motion tween:** A *motion tween* is motion animation that Flash calculates automatically from the first and last keyframes. The Timeline shows motion tweens in light blue.
- **Shape tween:** A *shape tween* is shape (morphing) animation that Flash calculates automatically. The Timeline shows shape tweens in light green.

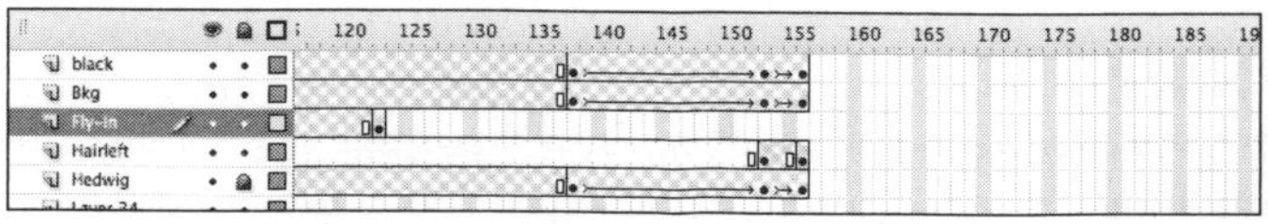

Figure 1-2: Check out the Timeline.

The Tools panel

The Tools panel includes all the tools that you need to create and edit graphics. The Tools panel contains the following sections:

- **Tools:** Select, draw, and edit graphic objects and text
- **View:** Pan and zoom
- **Colors:** Specify the color of lines and fills
- **Options:** Specify options for the buttons in the Tools section

Figure 1-3 shows the Tools panel in detail, and you can also see the options for the Brush tool. See Book V, Chapter 2 for further explanation about the Tools panel.

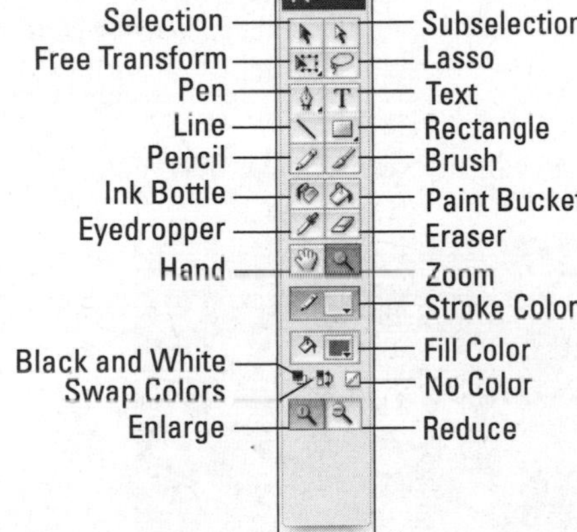

Figure 1-3: Use the Tools panel to create graphics, view your drawing, and specify colors.

Getting Organized with Panels

You use panels to specify settings (such as colors) or to view information about objects. You can access the panels from the Window menu, and panels also have their own Options menus. Click the menu icon in the upper-right corner of a panel to display its Options menu.

You can organize the Flash screen for your convenience. For certain tasks, you may want one group of panels open; for other tasks, you may want a different group available, or none at all. Follow these guidelines when working with panels:

- **Save panel layouts:** If you like to work with certain panels open most of the time, you can save panel configurations. Just display the panels that you want and choose Window➪Workspace➪Save Current. Type a name for the layout and click OK. The next time that you want to see that layout, choose Window➪Workspace➪*YourLayoutName* (you can choose a layout name that makes sense to you).
- **Dock:** You can dock the panels at the edge of the screen so that they don't cover up the Stage. To dock a panel, drag it by its *header* to the right or bottom of the screen until it displays a rectangular border. (See Figure 1-4.) To undock a panel, drag the tab for that panel away from the edge of the screen.
- **Hide/Display panels:** Press F4 to toggle hiding and displaying all the panels.

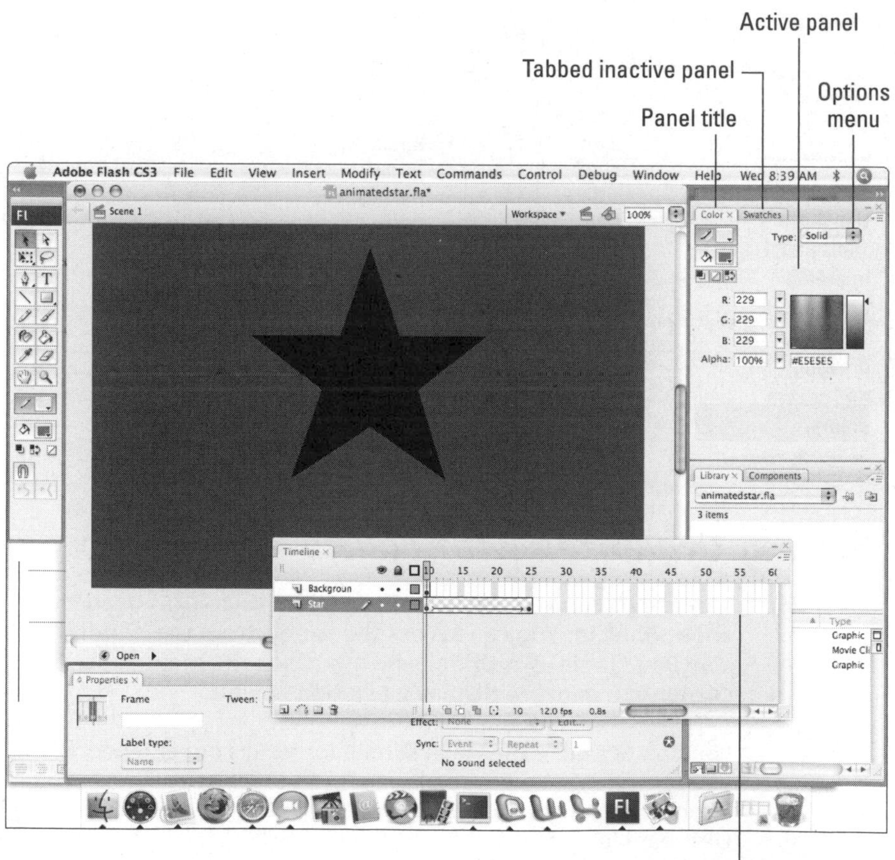

Figure 1-4: Use panels to specify settings and display information about objects.

You can find more information about specific panels throughout this minibook. For example, Chapter 2 includes a discussion of colors as well as the panels that you need to use to create and work with colors.

The Properties panel

The Properties panel is a special panel that you use almost all the time. The Properties panel is *context sensitive,* which means that it changes depending on what you're doing. For example, if you're working with text, you see all the possible text properties, as Figure 1-5 shows you. If you select a rectangle, you see the properties of that shape. Usually, you keep the Properties panel open at the bottom of the screen, either expanded or collapsed. The Properties panel has its own special Expand/Collapse arrow at its lower-right corner that you use to display additional properties.

Figure 1-5: The Properties panel lets you inspect and change the properties of your objects.

To set the properties of an object, select the object and enter the properties in the appropriate boxes of the Properties panel. You can find specific details about the Properties panel (for example, the size of the fonts you're using in your movie) throughout the rest of this minibook in the context of the topics of each chapter.

Library

Every Flash document file has its own Library. Whenever you import a graphic, video, or sound, Flash saves it in the Library. If you save a graphic object as a symbol (see Book V, Chapter 3 for a description of how to do this), the object goes in the Library as well. The Library stores every object that you may use again. These objects all have names so that you can easily find them.

To use an object from the Library, click the keyframe on the Timeline where you want the object to appear and then drag the object from the Library onto the Stage. (Keyframes are explained in Book V, Chapter 5.) You can drag an object from the Preview window or from the item's listing. Figure 1-6 shows a Library with several types of objects.

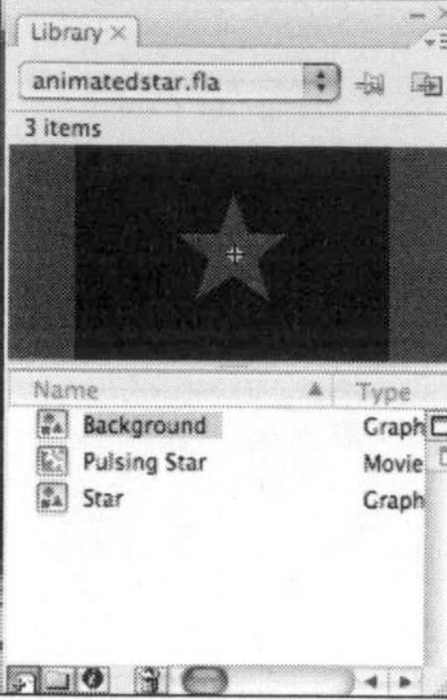

Figure 1-6: The Library contains named objects that are saved with a Flash document file.

To keep your Library from becoming overwhelming, use the following Library tools:

- **Use folders:** Organize your Library items into folders. To create a new folder, click the New Folder icon. Then drag items onto the folder's name. Double-click a folder to expand or collapse it.
- **Sort:** You can alphabetize Library items by any column. Click the heading of the column. To reverse the sort order, click the Sort Order icon.
- **Rename:** Double-click any item and type a new name.
- **Delete:** Select an item and click the Delete (Trashcan) icon. Flash warns that you can't undo this action.
- **Update:** If a sound, video, or bitmap file that you have imported has changed, you can update the Library to use the latest version of that file. Click the menu icon in the upper-right corner of a panel to display its Options menu and then choose Update.

You're not limited to using items in your current document's Library. You can open a Library from any Flash document and drag any of its items into your movie. Choose File⇨Import⇨Import to Library and choose the file. The new Library opens as a stacked panel on your current Library panel.

To see some sample Library items, choose Window⇨Common Libraries. You can find a good assortment of sounds and symbols that come with Flash.

Viewing the Stage

As you work, you often need to zoom in to see part of the Stage more closely or zoom out to see the entire Stage. You may also want to *pan* — to move the display in any direction.

At the upper-right corner of the Timeline, you can find the Zoom drop-down list, as Figure 1-7 shows you. Click the arrow to set the zoom percentage; choose a higher zoom setting to see objects on the Stage more clearly.

Figure 1-7: Zooming in.

You can also zoom in and out by using the Zoom tool in the View section of the Tools panel, which you can see in Figure 1-8. Follow these steps to use the Zoom tool:

1. **Choose the Zoom tool.**

   The Options section displays the plus and minus icons.

2. **Choose the plus icon if you want to zoom in or the minus icon if you want to zoom out.**
3. **Click anywhere on the Stage to zoom in or out.**

To pan, choose the Pan tool in the View section of the Tools panel and drag on the Stage in any direction. You can also use the scrollbars to pan.

If you're not in the Text tool, you can hold down the spacebar to turn the cursor into the Grabber hand, which enables you to move the stage all around your window in any direction.

Figure 1-8: The View section of the Tools panel.

Setting Movie and Flash Preferences

Flash offers you many opportunities to customize the way it looks and functions. You may want to take a look at these features to make your work flow as smoothly as possible.

Setting document properties

One of the first things you do when you start a movie is to set the size and color of the Stage, along with other properties that apply to the entire Flash document. You can adjust these settings using the Properties panel or the Document Properties dialog box. To use the Properties panel, follow these steps:

1. **Choose Window⇨Properties⇨Properties to display the Properties panel, if it isn't already open.**

   If the Properties panel isn't expanded, click its title bar to expand it.

2. **Click the Stage to make sure that no other object is selected.**

   The Properties panel looks like the one shown in Figure 1-9.

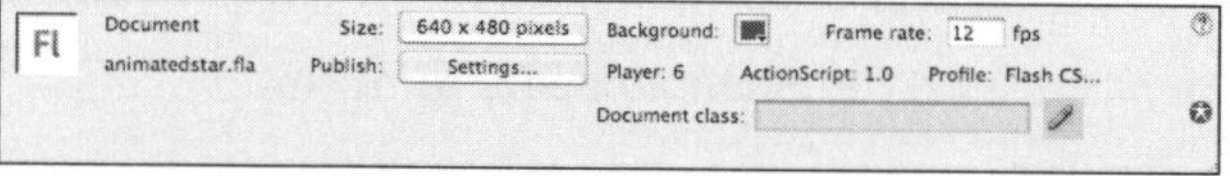

Figure 1-9: The Properties panel when no objects are selected.

3. **To change the Stage size, click the Size button.**

   The Document Properties dialog box, shown in Figure 1-10, opens.

4. **Add a title and description for your document in the appropriate fields.**

5. **Type the new width and height of the Stage in the Dimensions text fields.**

6. **To change the frame rate (the speed at which Flash plays the frames), type a new number in the Frame Rate text field.**

   The default is 12 frames per second (fps).

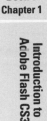

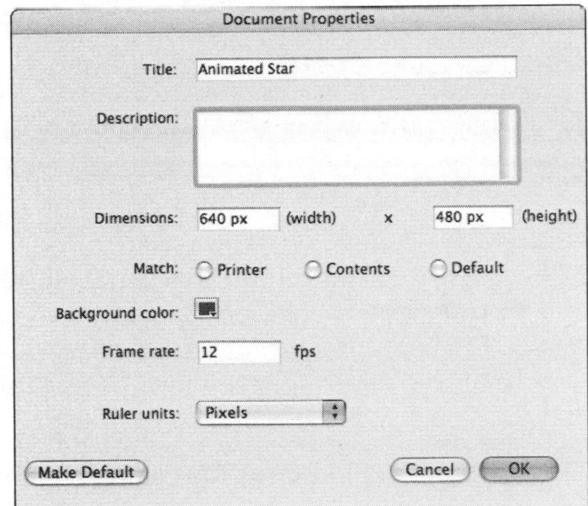

Figure 1-10: The Document Properties dialog box.

7. **To change the Stage color, click the Background Color box. Choose a new color from the color picker.**

   For more about colors, see Book V, Chapter 2.

8. **Click OK.**

To get the smallest possible Stage size, put all your objects at the upper-left corner of the Stage.

Creating your own keyboard shortcuts

You can change any shortcut or create your own. To create shortcuts, choose Edit⇨Keyboard Shortcuts (Flash⇨Keyboard Shortcuts on the Mac) to open the Keyboard Shortcuts dialog box, as shown in Figure 1-11 (which shows the shortcuts for a Mac).

You can't change the default set of shortcuts that comes with Flash. However, you can create a duplicate set of the defaults and modify them. Give the duplicate set a new name, such as MyShortcuts.

The following buttons, located at the top of the Keyboard Shortcuts dialog box, can help you manage your shortcuts:

- **Duplicate Set:** Duplicates a shortcut set
- **Rename Set:** Renames a set of shortcuts
- **Export Set as HTML:** Saves your preferences as an HTML file
- **Delete Set:** Deletes a set of shortcuts

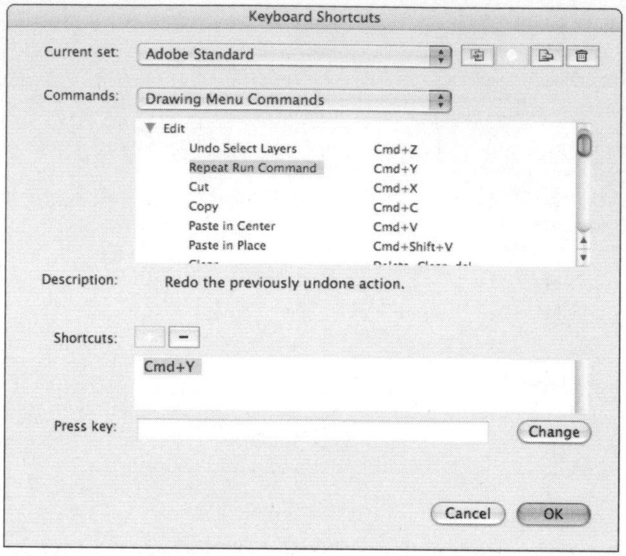

Figure 1-11: Use the Keyboard Shortcuts dialog box to customize shortcuts.

After you have selected a new set of shortcuts from the Commands drop-down list of the Keyboard Shortcuts dialog box, choose the types of commands that you want to change. You can change any of the following types of commands by selecting their name from the Commands drop-down list:

- **Drawing Menu Commands:** Commands from the Drawing menu
- **Drawing Tools Commands:** Tools in the Drawing toolbox
- **Test Movie Menu Commands:** The menu that appears when you choose Control⇨Test Movie
- **Actions Panel Commands:** Commands that control the look and function of the Actions panel

Click the plus sign (+) on the list of commands (not all commands have the plus sign) to display all the commands and their current shortcuts. To create a new shortcut, follow these steps:

1. **Choose the command that you want.**
2. **Click the Add Shortcut button (+).**

   Flash adds a new shortcut.
3. **Press the key (for example, A) for the shortcut that you want to use.**

You must press a modifier key (such as Ctrl or Shift) in conjunction with the shortcut key. If you want to create a shortcut that's already assigned, that command appears. You can decide to override the shortcut, or you can choose another key for your shortcut.

- To change that predefined shortcut, click Change.
- If you don't want to use that shortcut, with the `<empty>` value selected on the Shortcuts list, click Remove Shortcut.

4. **To change another shortcut, repeat Steps 1 through 3.**
5. **Click OK.**

Getting Help

If you need more help than you can find in this book, use Flash's Help system and tutorials, both of which come with the product.

To open Help, choose Help➪Using Flash. The opening screen looks like Figure 1-12.

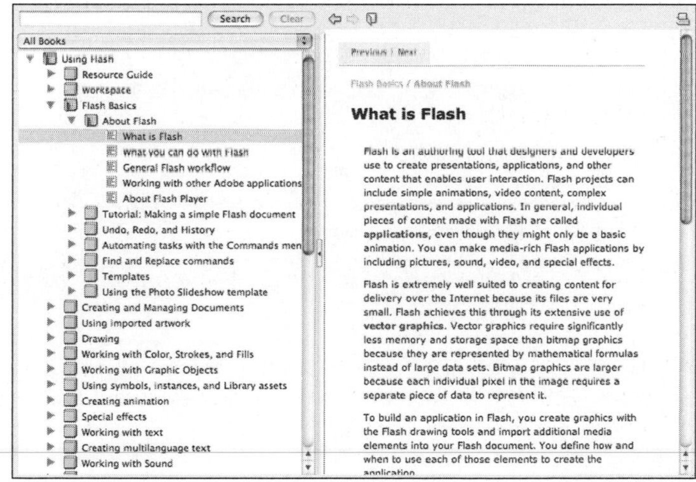

Figure 1-12: Use the Help feature when you have a question.

Chapter 2: Using the Graphics Tools

In This Chapter

- **Understanding when to use the Flash tools**
- **Creating shapes and text**
- **Changing shapes and text to fit your needs**
- **Adding some color**

This chapter shows you how to use the drawing and editing tools in Adobe Flash CS3 to create graphics and text. To produce great animation, you need great graphics.

Choosing When to Use the Flash Tools

Book V, Chapter 1 explains the difference between vector and bitmap graphics. Use the Flash drawing tools when you want to create vector graphics for fast download times.

To create more detailed graphics, you may want to use Illustrator CS3 because it has more advanced creation and editing tools. You may also want to use this program to edit existing bitmaps. On the other hand, you may have bitmaps, such as a photograph or complex logo, that you can get only as a bitmap. To use any bitmap, import it. (See Book V, Chapter 3 for the scoop on importing graphics.)

Creating Shapes and Text

You use the Tools panel to create shapes and text in Flash. See Figure 2-1 for the details of the Tools panel. The Tools section of the Tools panel offers many tools for creating and editing images. Most tools have options that specify how the tool works.

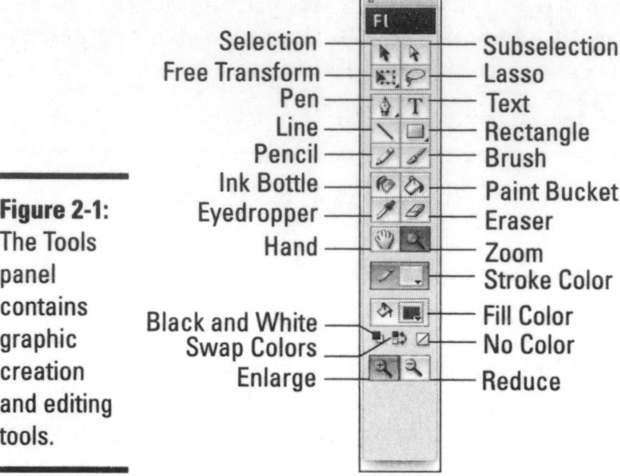

Figure 2-1: The Tools panel contains graphic creation and editing tools.

When creating shapes in Flash, you need to keep in mind what happens when two or more shapes touch:

- **If the shapes are the same color:** They combine. You can use this technique to create complex shapes.
- **If the shapes are different colors:** The top shape replaces and cuts out the overlapping part of the bottom shape.
- **If you use the Pencil or Line tool to intersect any other shape:** The line and other shape are cut at their intersection.

If you don't see the Tools panel, choose Window⇨Tools or press Ctrl+F2 to make it visible.

Line tool

The Line tool draws straight lines. You can continue to draw connected lines to create any shape you want.

To draw a line, follow these steps:

1. **Choose the Line tool from the Tools section of the Tools panel.**
2. **From the Properties panel, choose a color by clicking the Stroke Color box.**

   If the Properties panel isn't visible, choose Window⇨Properties (or press Ctrl+F3) to make it appear.

   You can also find the Stroke Color box in the Colors section of the Tools panel. A *stroke* is another word for a line or the outline of any shape in Flash.

3. **Type a stroke weight (width) in the Stroke Height box of the Properties panel or click the arrow next to the point size box and use the vertical slider to choose a stroke weight.**
4. **Choose a stroke style from the Stroke Style box of the Properties panel.**

   To create a custom stroke style, click the Custom button in the Properties panel.
5. **Click the Stage where you want to start the line and drag (while holding the mouse button down) to the ending point.**
6. **Release the mouse button.**

To constrain the line to multiples of 45 degrees, press Shift while dragging.

Oval tool

An oval has both a stroke (outline) and a fill color. Use the Oval tool to draw ellipses and circles, following these steps:

1. **Choose the Oval tool from the Tools section of the Tools panel.**
2. **From the Properties panel, choose a stroke color by clicking the Stroke Color box and choosing a color.**

   If the Properties panel isn't visible, choose Window➪Properties to make it appear.

   You can also find the Stroke Color box in the Colors section of the Tools panel. As with the Line tool, you can also set a stroke weight and style.
3. **From the Properties panel, choose a fill color by clicking the Fill Color box.**
4. **Click the Stage where you want the upper-left portion of the oval to be and drag (while holding the mouse button down) diagonally to the lower right.**
5. **Release the mouse button.**

To create a circle, press Shift as you drag the mouse.

Rectangle tool

As does an oval, a rectangle has both a stroke and a fill. You can draw rectangles and squares with the Rectangle tool by following these steps:

1. **Choose the Rectangle tool from the Tools section of the Tools panel.**
2. **From the Properties panel, choose a stroke color by clicking the Stroke Color box and choosing a color.**

If the Properties panel isn't visible, choose Window➪Properties to make it appear.

You can also find the Stroke Color box in the Colors section of the Tools panel. As with the Line tool, you can also set a stroke weight and style.

3. **From the Properties panel, choose a fill color by clicking the Fill Color box.**
4. **To draw a rectangle with rounded corners, click the Rounded Rectangle Radius button (the button with the curved black line and the little blue semi-square underneath it) in the Options section of the Tools panel, type a radius, and press Enter.**

   The larger the number entered in the Corner Radius field, the softer the curve of the rectangle's edges.
5. **Click the Stage where you want the upper-left corner of the rectangle to be and drag (while holding the mouse button down) diagonally to the lower right.**
6. **Release the mouse button.**

To create a square, press Shift as you drag the mouse.

In case you want to have greater control over an object, Flash CS3 now has Rectangle and Oval Primitive tools. Select one of these from the Rectangle Tools panel, and you can create objects just as you would with the regular oval and rectangle tools. After you've created an object, you can use the Properties panel to manipulate it, as well as use the Selection and Subselecttools to transform the object, as shown in Figure 2-2.

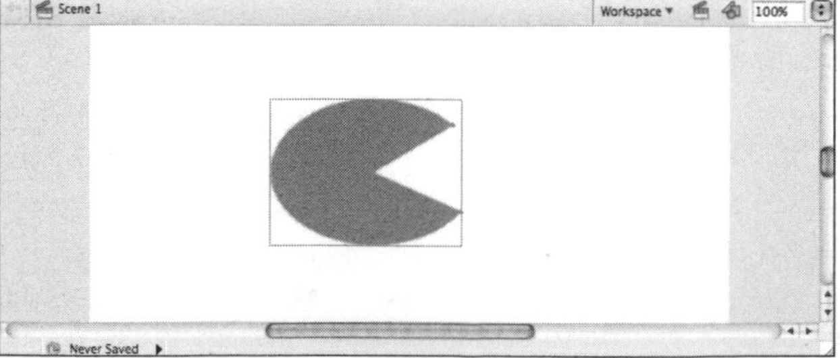

Figure 2-2: Look familiar? The Oval Primitive tool gives you tremendous flexibility over an object without committing it to the Library as a symbol.

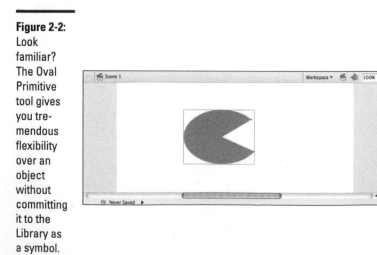

PolyStar tool

In addition to the Rectangle tool, Flash includes a tool for creating other kinds of polygons. To use the PolyStar tool, follow these steps:

1. **Click and hold down the Rectangle button in the Tools section of the Tools panel.**
2. **Click the PolyStar icon from the menu that appears.**
3. **In the Properties panel, click the Options button.**
4. **Select a style of polygon from the Style drop-down list.**

   The Polygon option creates a true polygon and the Star option creates a multipointed star.
5. **Enter the number of sides for the polygon or star.**

   The larger the number of sides, the closer to a circle a polygon looks. For the star, having more points creates a starburst-like effect.
6. **Enter a value for the star point size.**

   The larger the star point size, the more dull the star becomes, making it look closer to a circle.

Pencil tool

The Pencil tool works somewhat like a real pencil. You can draw artistic shapes with it. To draw with the Pencil tool, follow these steps:

1. **Choose the Pencil tool from the Tools section of the Tools panel.**
2. **From the Properties panel, choose a stroke color by clicking the Stroke Color box and choosing a color.**

   If the Properties panel isn't visible, choose Window⇨Properties to make it appear.

   You can also find the Stroke Color box in the Colors section of the Tools panel. As with the Line tool, you can also set a stroke weight and style.
3. **Click the Pencil Mode button in the Options section of the Tools panel, and from the pop-up menu, choose one of the following:**
   - **Straighten:** Straightens wiggly lines and changes sloppy rectangles, ovals, and triangles to perfect ones
   - **Smooth:** Smoothes out curved lines
   - **Ink:** Slightly smoothes and straightens, but mostly leaves your drawings the same

4. **Click the Stage where you want the drawing to start and drag on the Stage.**

   You can draw angles and curves.

5. **Release the mouse button.**

To constrain each line segment to 90-degree angles, press Shift as you drag the mouse. To refine how the options work, choose Edit⇨Preferences and click the Editing tab. Use the Smooth Curves and Recognize Shapes drop-down lists to edit the options described previously. When you're done, click OK.

Pen tool

You can use the Pen tool to draw straight lines and curves. The Pen tool offers the greatest editing control and the most control over curves. Using the Pen tool takes some practice (as most users will no doubt be using either a mouse or a trackpad), but soon you'll can find it very flexible.

Follow these steps to work with the Pen tool:

1. **Choose the Pen tool from the Tools section of the Tools panel.**
2. **From the Properties panel, choose a stroke color by clicking the Stroke Color box and choosing a color.**

   If the Properties panel isn't visible, choose Window⇨Properties to make it appear.

   You can also find the Stroke Color box in the Colors section of the Tools panel. As with the Line tool, you can set a stroke weight and style.

3. **You can draw either straight segments or curves, as follows:**
   - **To draw a straight segment:** Click the start point and click the end point. Don't drag. Click additional points to add segments. Double-click to finish.
   - **To draw a curve:** Click the start point and move the mouse in the desired direction that you want the next point of your shape to be; then, click and drag your mouse in the direction that you want to create the curve. Let go of the mouse to lock that portion of the shape and continue clicking and dragging to create additional curves. Double-click to finish.

To close a figure, place the cursor near the start point until you see a small circle and then click. Press Shift as you draw to constrain the lines or curves to 45-degree angles.

Brush tool

The Brush tool fills areas with a brushlike effect. You can vary the shape and width of the stroke. The Brush tool creates fills, so you use the Fill Color button to set the color. To draw with the Brush tool, follow these steps:

1. **Choose the Brush tool from the Tools section of the Tools panel.**
2. **From the Properties panel, choose a fill color by clicking the Fill Color box and choosing a color.**

   If the Properties panel isn't visible, choose Window➪Properties to make it appear.

   You can also find the Fill Color box in the Colors section of the Tools panel.
3. **Choose a brush mode by clicking the Brush Mode button in the Options section of the Tools panel and choosing one of the following options:**
   - **Paint Normal:** Paints wherever you brush, including over other objects on the same layer (see Book V, Chapter 4 for more details on layers)
   - **Paint Fills:** Fills enclosed and blank areas, but doesn't cover strokes
   - **Paint Behind:** Paints blank areas of the Stage, but doesn't cover fills or strokes
   - **Paint Selection:** Fills in a selected area
   - **Paint Inside:** Paints inside any enclosed area where you start your brush or on the Stage if you don't start in an enclosed area; doesn't cover strokes
4. **Choose a brush size by clicking the Brush Size drop-down list in the Options section of the Tools panel.**
5. **Choose a brush shape by clicking the Brush Shape drop-down list.**

   If you have a pressure-sensitive pen and tablet, you see a pressure button in the Options section. You can then dynamically vary the width of the brush according to how much pressure you put on the pen as you draw.
6. **Click the start point and then drag to draw with the brush.**

Press Shift as you draw to constrain your shapes to 90-degree angles.

If you want your gradient fill to be independent of the background fill, make sure that you don't have the Lock Fill option button selected. If, however, you're creating more than one stroke and you want it to appear as though the gradient is in the background and being applied to both strokes, select the Lock Fill option button.

Paint Bucket tool

The Paint Bucket tool fills enclosed shapes. You can create the enclosed shape with many of the other tools in the Tools panel. You can also use the Paint Bucket tool to change the color of existing fills. To fill an enclosed area, follow these steps:

1. **Choose the Paint Bucket tool from the Tools section of the Tools panel.**
2. **From the Properties panel, choose a fill color by clicking the Fill Color box and choosing a color.**

   If the Properties panel isn't visible, choose Window⇨Properties to make it appear.

   You can also find the Fill Color box in the Colors section of the Tools panel.
3. **Click the Gap Size button in the Options section of the Tools panel, and from the pop-up menu, select an option if you need to fill in a shape that isn't completely enclosed.**

   You can choose from Don't Close Gaps to Close Large Gaps.
4. **Click inside the enclosed area to fill the shape.**

Ink Bottle tool

The Ink Bottle tool outlines an existing shape or changes the color of an existing stroke (outline). Follow these steps to use the Ink Bottle tool:

1. **Select the Ink Bottle tool from the Tools section of the Tools panel.**
2. **From the Properties panel, choose a stroke color by clicking the Stroke Color box and choosing a color.**

   If the Properties panel isn't visible, choose Window⇨Properties to make it appear.

   You can also find the Stroke Color box in the Colors section of the Tools panel. You can set a stroke weight and style as well.
3. **Click anywhere on the shape.**

   If the shape has no stroke outline, Flash adds a stroke. Otherwise, Flash changes the shape's color, width, and style to the settings that you choose.

Text tool

Sooner or later, you may need to explain what all those animations that you've created mean, so you'll probably need some text. Flash offers many text options, both simple and advanced. To create text, follow these steps:

1. **Choose the Text tool from the Tools section of the Tools panel.**
2. **In the Properties panel, which you can see in Figure 2-3, specify the font, size, color, and other properties.**

   If the Properties panel isn't visible, choose Window⇨Properties to make it appear.

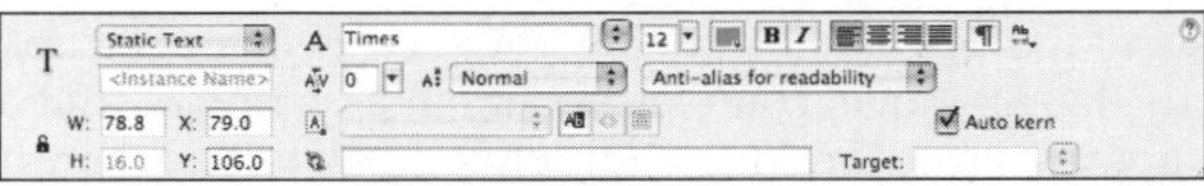

Figure 2-3: Use the Properties panel to set the properties of your text.

3. **Click the Stage and start typing, as follows:**
   - To specify the width of the text area (when creating a paragraph), click at the upper-left corner where you want the text to start and drag to the right margin.
   - To create text that expands as you type (for a single line of text), just click.

You can specify the following text properties in the Properties panel:

✦ **Text type:** Use the Text Type drop-down list to specify one of the following types of text:

   - **Static:** Regular text.
   - **Input:** Text that users type in their browser. You can use input text to make your Web site interactive. Use input text for forms or to enable users to set values that affect the animation.
   - **Dynamic:** Text that you display from another source, such as another Web site, another movie (SWF) file, or an external file. You can use this type of text for weather, sports scores, and so on.

- **Font:** The font or typeface. Select from the drop-down list.
- **Font size:** Type a number or use the vertical slider to choose a size.
- **Color:** Click the Text (fill) Color box to choose a color.
- **Bold/Italic:** Click the Bold button or the Italic button to make the text bold or italic.
- **Justify:** Click one of the Justify buttons to make the text justified to the left, center, or right, or full justified (justified to reach both the left and right margins).
- **Character spacing:** Adjust the *tracking,* the spacing between a series of letters.
- **Character position:** Select Superscript to create text above the normal position or Subscript to create text that appears below the normal position. For normal text, just keep it at Normal.
- **Auto Kern:** *Kerning* is the spacing between two specific letters. You may adjust the kerning of certain letters, such as A and V, that appear to be too far apart. Select the Auto Kern check box to turn kerning on; deselect it to turn kerning off.
- **Aliasing:** By default, all text is *anti-aliased,* or smoothed. If you want the text to appear jagged, select Bitmap from the available options in this drop-down list. You can also customize the thickness and sharpness of the anti-alias by selecting the Custom Anti-Alias option.
- **Format:** Click the Format button to open the Format Options dialog box, where you can set paragraph formatting, as follows:
  - **Indent:** The indentation of the first line of a paragraph.
  - **Line Spacing:** The spacing between lines, measured in points. If your text is 18 points, for example, set a line spacing of 18 points to double-space the text.
  - **Margins:** You can set the pixel width for both the right and left margins.

Click the Expand/Collapse arrow next to the Properties tab for more advanced text options.

Modifying Shapes and Text

If you create something on a computer, you inevitably have to change it. Sometimes you change your mind, and other times you just need to make adjustments to get the effect that you want.

Selection tool

Before you can change an object, you need to select it. To select an object or group of objects, choose the Selection tool (the dark arrow at the top left of the Tools panel) and use one of the following techniques:

- ✦ **To select one object:** Click the object.
- ✦ **To select an object and its stroke:** Double-click the object. (Double-clicking doesn't work with symbols. See Book V, Chapter 3 for more about symbols.)
- ✦ **To select a portion of an object:** Click and drag covering only the portion of the object you want to move. This technique works only for objects that are not symbols.
- ✦ **To select several objects that don't touch:** Click away from the objects and drag diagonally to create a bounding box around the objects that you want to select. Flash selects all objects that are completely inside the box.

See the section "Reshaping with the Selection tool," later in this chapter, for information on reshaping objects by using the Selection tool.

The Selection tool has a Snap button in the Options section of the Tools panel. When you click this button, objects that you move snap to other objects so that you can attach two objects precisely. The Snap option also snaps new objects that you create to existing objects.

Lasso tool

You can also select your objects by lassoing 'em. Use the Lasso tool when you want to select a number of objects but can't get them in a rectangular bounding box. You can drag the mouse and create a free-form shape or use straight-line segments by following these steps:

1. **Choose the Lasso tool from the Tools panel.**
2. **Choose the type of lassoing that you want:**
   - **To lasso free-form:** Click anywhere on the Stage, drag around the objects that you want to select, and then release the mouse button.
   - **To lasso with straight-line segments:** Choose the Polygon Mode button from the Options section of the Tools panel. Click anywhere on the Stage and continue to click at each segment's end point. Double-click to finish.

Moving and copying objects

You can move and copy objects on the Stage in many ways. The best method depends on the circumstances and your personal preferences. Move and copy objects using the following methods:

- **Select and drag:** Use the Selection tool to select an object. Then move the cursor over the object until you see the four-arrow cursor. Click and drag to move the object. Press and hold Ctrl while you drag to copy the object.
- **Arrow keys:** Select an object and use the arrow keys to move the object one pixel at a time in the direction of the arrow.
- **Properties panel:** Select an object and open the Properties panel. Click the Expand/Collapse arrow at the lower-right corner to display the expanded panel. Use the X and Y text fields to set a new location for the object.
- **Cut, copy, and paste:** Select an object; then press Ctrl+X to move (cut) it or Ctrl+C to copy it. If you want to paste the object somewhere else, click another layer or frame. Then press Ctrl+V to paste the object.

Eraser tool

To delete any object, select it and press Delete. However, to erase part of an object, use the Eraser tool, following these steps:

1. **Choose the Eraser tool from the Tools panel.**
2. **Select the eraser size and shape from the Eraser Shape pop-up menu in the Options section of the Tools panel.**
3. **To specify how the Eraser tool works, choose an option from the Eraser Mode pop-up menu:**
   - **Erase Normal:** Erases anything that you drag across.
   - **Erase Fills:** Erases only fills.
   - **Erase Lines:** Erases only strokes.
   - **Erase Selected Fills:** Erases only selected fills.
   - **Erase Inside:** Erases only fills where you first click. Use this option to erase only fills inside an enclosed area, leaving other fills alone.
4. With the Faucet option (in the Options section of the Tools panel) deselected, click on the portion of the object (the fill or the stroke) on the Stage to erase.

To erase an entire fill, select the Faucet option (in the Options section of the Tools panel) and click the fill. This method is the same as selecting a fill and pressing Delete, as though the faucet washes away all the color.

Reshaping with the Selection tool

You can reshape and modify objects using the Selection tool when the objects aren't selected. You can reshape both end points (including corners) and middles (whether straight or curved), as Figure 2-4 shows you, in a couple of ways:

- **End points:** Place the cursor over the end point of a line or curve segment. You see a small corner shape near the cursor. Click on that point and drag to a new location on the Stage to change the location of the end point.
- **Middles:** Place the cursor over the middle of any line or curve segment. You see a small curved shape near the cursor. Click on that point and drag to a new location on the Stage to reshape the segment.

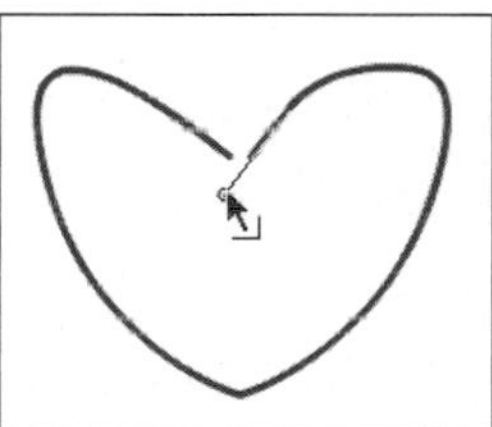

Figure 2-4: Reshape end points and middles of fills and lines with the Selection tool.

Subselect tool

The Subselect tool looks like the Selection tool, but the Subselect tool is a white (rather than black) arrow. Both the Selection tool and the Subselect tool reshape objects, but the Subselect tool uses a more sophisticated technique. When you use the Subselect tool, the shape displays anchor points that you can move or delete. When you click an anchor point, *tangent lines* — lines that are parallel to the curve at the anchor point — appear and enable you to change the direction of the curve. You can reshape strokes or fills that you created with the following tools:

- Pen
- Pencil
- Line
- Oval
- Rectangle
- Brush

To reshape objects with the Subselect tool, follow these steps:

1. **Choose the Subselect tool from the Tools panel.**
2. **Click a stroke or the edge of a fill to display the anchor points.**
3. **Drag any anchor point to modify the shape.**
4. **To change the direction of a curve, select its anchor curve and then drag the tangent line's handles (the dots at either end of the tangent line).**

To delete an anchor, select the object and then click the anchor point that you want to delete. The anchor point turns dark. Then press Delete.

Free Transform tool

The Free Transform tool is the heavyweight of editing tools — it can do almost anything. To use this tool, choose it from the Tools panel and select an object. The object displays a special bounding box that includes handles and a central transformation point, as you can see in Figure 2-5.

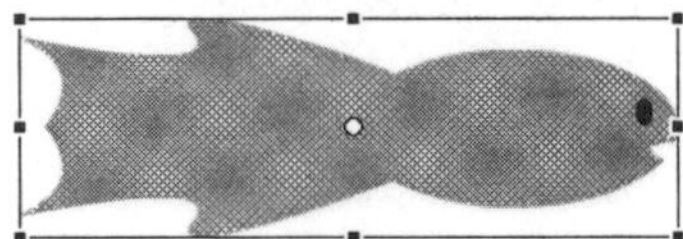

Figure 2-5: The bounding box of the Free Transform tool.

You can use the Free Transform tool in the following ways:

- **Move:** Place the cursor over the object. When you see the four-arrow cursor, click and drag.
- **Rotate:** Place the cursor just outside (but not on) any corner handle. When you see a circular arrow cursor, click and drag.
- **Scale while maintaining proportion:** Place the cursor on any corner handle. When you see a broken two-arrow cursor, click and drag inward or outward while holding down the Shift key.
- **Scale either the height or width:** Place the cursor on any side handle. When you see a two-arrow cursor, click and drag inward or outward.
- **Skew (slant either horizontally or vertically):** Place the cursor anywhere on the bounding box, but not on a handle. When you see the parallel line cursor, click and drag in any direction.

- **Move the transformation point:** Place the cursor on the transformation point at the center of the bounding box. When you see a small circle cursor, click and drag in any direction. Flash uses the transformation point as a base for rotation and scaling.
- **Taper:** Choose the Distort option of the Free Transform tool from the Options section of the Tools panel. Place the cursor on any corner handle and press Shift as you click and drag inward or outward. (See Figure 2-6 for an example of tapering.)

Figure 2-6: Tapering the fish makes its back end wider.

- **Distort:** Choose the Distort option of the Free Transform tool from the Options section of the Tools panel. Click and drag any handle to distort the bounding box. (See Figure 2-7 for an example of distortion.) ***Note:*** The Distort option works on shapes, but not on symbols (see Book V, Chapter 3 for more on symbols), text, or groups. (You can find out more about groups in the "Grouping" section, later in this chapter.)

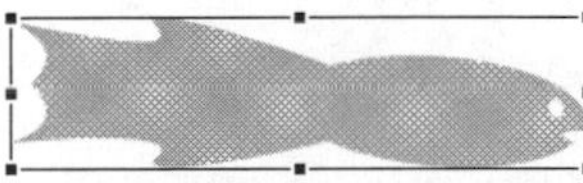

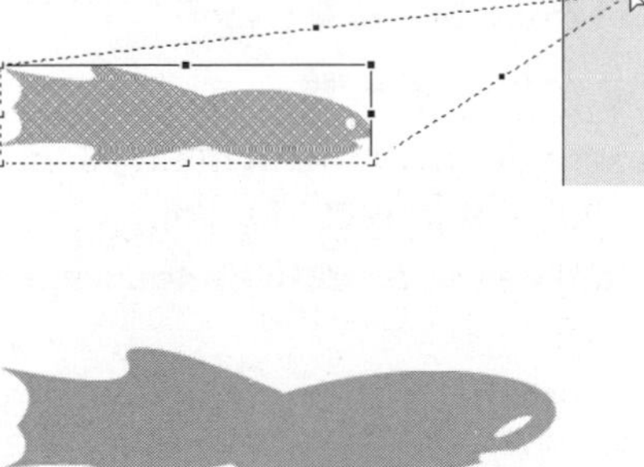

Figure 2-7: Distort the upper-right corner of the goldfish and it looks more like a shark.

✦ **Warp:** Choose the Envelope option of the Free Transform tool from the Options section of the Tools panel. Drag any anchor point or tangent line handle to warp the bounding box.

The Envelope option, which you can see in Figure 2-8, works on shapes, but not on symbols, text, or groups.

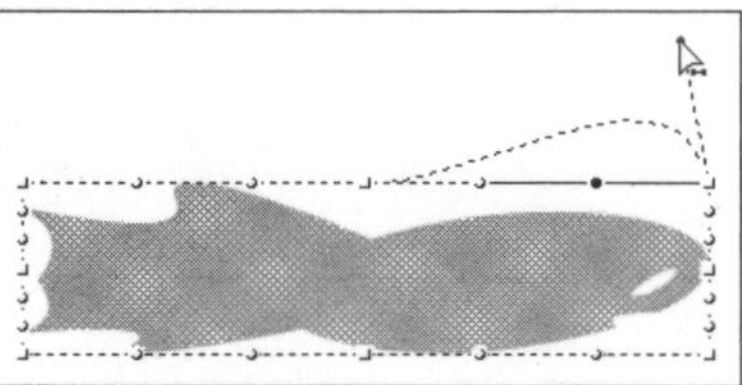

Figure 2-8: Fine-tune shapes by using the Envelope option of the Free Transform tool.

When you select an object — for example, a circle — with the Free Transform tool, you may notice that the tool selects the object, but not the stroke around the object. To select both the object and its stroke, click the Free Transform tool and drag it around the entire object. This tool creates one bounding box for both the fill and the stroke.

Straightening and smoothing with the Selection tool

You can straighten lines and smooth curves with the Selection tool. Both processes reduce the number of changes in direction. You can repeat the process until Flash can't straighten or smooth anymore. Follow these steps to straighten lines and smooth curves:

1. **Choose the Selection tool from the Tools panel.**
2. **Select the shape that you want to modify.**
3. **To straighten, click the Straighten button in the Options section of the Tools panel. To smooth, click the Smooth button.**
4. **Continue to click the Straighten or Smooth button until you like the result.**

Optimizing curves

A process called *optimizing curves* is similar to smoothing curves. Optimizing a curve reduces the number of individual elements that the curve contains and can help reduce the size of your Flash document file. Follow these steps to optimize curves:

1. **Choose the Selection tool from the Tools panel.**
2. **Using the Selection tool, select the object that you want to optimize.**
3. **Choose Modify⇨Shape⇨Optimize.**

   The Optimize Curves dialog box appears, as shown in Figure 2-9. You can select Use Multiple Passes for a slower, more thorough approach. If you select the Show Totals Message check box, the amount of optimization appears after you close the dialog box.

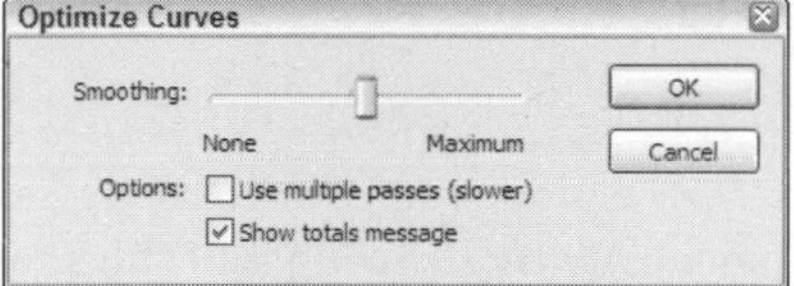

Figure 2-9: The Optimize Curves dialog box.

4. **Choose the amount of smoothing by using the slider in the dialog box.**
5. **Click OK.**

Carefully check the results after optimizing. Sometimes small objects disappear! If you don't like the results, choose Edit⇨Undo and try again with a different Smoothing setting.

Softening edges

To create a soft look around the edges of a shape, follow these steps:

1. **Choose the Selection tool from the Tools panel.**
2. **Using the Selection tool, select a shape.**
3. **Choose Modify⇨Shape⇨Soften Fill Edges.**

   The Soften Fill Edges dialog box opens, as you can see in Figure 2-10.

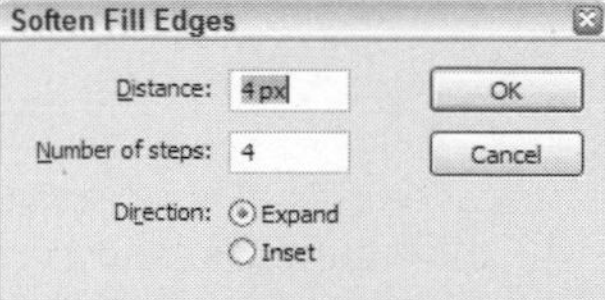

Figure 2-10: The Soften Fill Edges dialog box.

4. **In the Soften Fill Edges dialog box, set the distance.**

   The default distance is the width of the softened part of the edge, in pixels.

   Flash uses the units that you set in the Document Properties dialog box to measure the distance. Choose Modify➪Document to change the measurement units.

5. **Enter the number of steps, that is, the number of concentric rows in the softened edge.**
6. **Select Expand or Inset.**

   The Expand option creates the softened edges outside the shape. The Inset option creates the softened edges within the shape.

7. **Click OK.**

Flipping

You can make symmetric shapes easily by drawing half the shape, copying it, and flipping the copy either vertically or horizontally. You can then move the two shapes together, as Figure 2-11 shows you. To flip an object, follow these steps:

1. **Choose the Selection tool from the Tools panel.**
2. **Using the Selection tool, select the object.**
3. **Choose Modify➪Transform➪Flip Vertical or Flip Horizontal.**

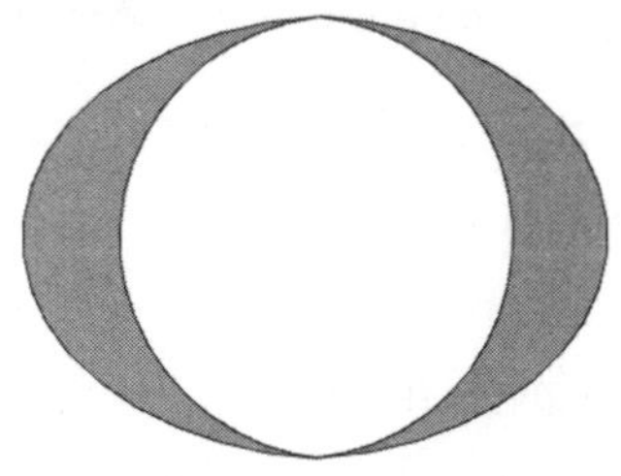

Figure 2-11: Create this shape by copying the crescent, flipping it horizontally, and then moving the two shapes together.

Transferring properties with the Eyedropper tool

The Eyedropper tool transfers stroke and fill properties from one object to another. To transfer properties, follow these steps:

1. **Choose the Eyedropper tool from the Tools panel.**
2. **Select a stroke or fill.**

   If you select a stroke, the Ink Bottle tool activates. If you select a fill, the Paint Bucket tool activates.
3. **Click another stroke or fill.**

   Flash transfers the properties of the stroke or fill to the second object.

Grouping

You often want to work with several objects at one time. Instead of having to select all the objects each time you want to move or copy them, you can group them and work with them as one object. To group objects, select them and choose Modify⇨Group (or press Ctrl+G).

You can edit one element of the group by following these steps:

1. **Choose the Selection tool from the Tools panel.**
2. **Double-click the group.**

   Flash dims other objects on the Stage.
3. **Edit any element of the group.**
4. **To return to regular editing, double-click any blank area on the Stage with the Selection tool.**

   Alternatively, you can choose Edit⇨Edit All to return to regular editing.

To ungroup objects, select the group and choose Modify⇨Ungroup (or press Shift+Ctrl+G).

Breaking objects apart

You can break apart text into letters and then break apart the letters into shapes. After you break apart letters into shapes, you can edit them like any other shape. You can also break apart symbols (see Book V, Chapter 3), groups, and bitmaps. (See the section "Working with bitmap fills," later in this chapter, for more information.)

Aligning objects

To get a professional look, you may want to make sure that objects are properly aligned and equally distributed. To align and distribute objects, follow these steps:

1. **Choose the Selection tool from the Tools panel.**
2. **Using the Selection tool, select the objects.**
3. **Choose Window⇨Align.**

   The Align panel, which you can see in Figure 2-12, appears.

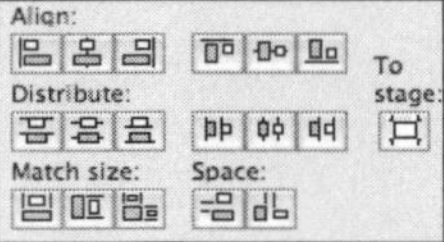

Figure 2-12: Use the Align panel to align and equally space objects, such as buttons for your Web site.

4. **Choose the options that you want in the Align panel, as follows:**
   - Use the top row to align the selected objects horizontally or vertically.
   - Use the middle row to evenly distribute objects horizontally or vertically by their edges.
   - Use the Match Size buttons to match the size of selected objects by width, height, or both.
   - Use the Space buttons to distribute objects by the spaces between them.
   - Use the To Stage button to align or distribute objects relative to the Stage.

To center an object on the Stage, click the To Stage button on the Align panel. Then click the middle Align Vertical and Align Horizontal buttons. However, if you haven't panned or scrolled your display, you can use a quicker method — just cut and paste the object. Flash pastes the object at the center of the display.

Working with Colors

By default, Flash works with a Web-safe palette of 216 colors. These colors probably appear the same in all browsers. However, you can create your own colors. You can also design gradients that vary from one color to another. Or you may want to try the technique of filling objects with bitmap images (which is explained in the "Working with bitmap fills" section, later in this chapter).

Creating solid colors

You can create a solid color when you need to take more artistic license than the standard Web-safe palette allows. Follow these steps to create a solid color:

1. **Choose Window⇨Design Panels⇨Color Mixer.**

   The Color Mixer panel, which you can see in Figure 2-13 with the Solid option active, opens.

   You can specify colors using the RGB (Red, Green, Blue) or HSB (Hue, Saturation, Brightness) system. You can see the current system by the letters that are next to the text fields in the panel. In Figure 2-13, you can tell that the RGB system is active because the text fields are labeled R, G, and B. To choose a different system, click the menu icon in the upper-right corner of the panel to open the panel's Options menu and choose the color system that you want. You can also use the color space in the panel to specify a color.

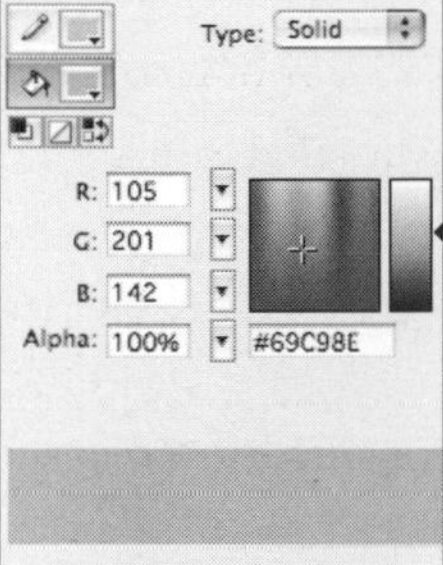

Figure 2-13: The Color Mixer panel is the place to create new colors.

2. **Select Solid from the Fill Style drop-down list.**
3. **Click the Stroke Color or Fill Color icon (to the left of the Stroke or Fill box), depending on whether you want to change a stroke or a fill.**

   You can use this color later for either a stroke or a fill if you save the color as a swatch, as Step 6 explains how to do.

4. **Type the color specifications in the text fields, or click a color in the color space and use the slider to make the color lighter or darker.**
5. **Use the vertical slider next to the Alpha field or text field to set the transparency of the color.**

   A higher alpha percent is more opaque.
6. **To save the color, create a color swatch by clicking the Options menu icon in the upper-right corner of the panel and choosing Add Swatch.**

You can now see your new color displayed in the Stroke Color or Fill Color box in the Properties panel and in the Colors section of the Tools panel. You can use any of the tools to work with that color. If you add a color swatch, you can continue to use that color later by choosing it from the color palette that opens when you click the Stroke Color or Fill Color box.

Creating gradients

Gradients blend one color (lighter with darker) or many colors in either a linear or radial (circular) pattern. Gradients give the appearance of shading and three dimensions. To create a gradient, follow these steps:

1. **Choose Window⇨Design Panels⇨Color Mixer.**

   The Color Mixer panel opens.
2. **From the Type drop-down list, select Linear or Radial to specify the type of gradient that you want to create, as shown in Figure 2-14.**

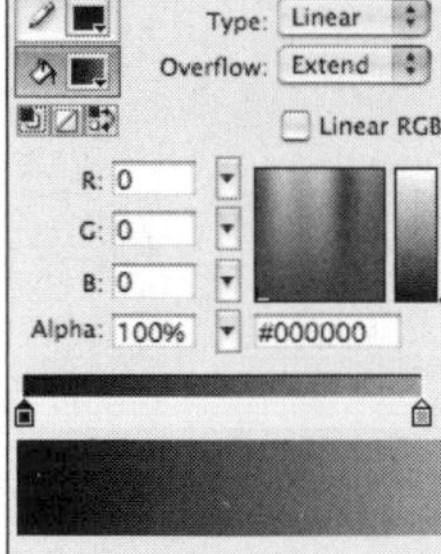

Figure 2-14: Use the Color Mixer panel to create gradients.

3. **Choose a pointer underneath the horizontal gradient bar.**

   The pointer becomes black when you select it so that you know it's active.

4. **Use one of the following methods to select a color for that pointer:**
   - Click the Fill Color box and choose a color.
   - Specify a color using one of the methods of creating a new color discussed in the preceding section.
   - Use the color space to specify a color.
5. **Repeat Steps 3 and 4 for all the pointers.**

   You add a pointer when you want to add a new color to the gradient. Three pointers result in a three-color gradient. To add a pointer, click just beneath the gradient bar where you want the pointer to appear. To delete a pointer, drag it off the gradient bar.
6. **To save the gradient, click the menu icon in the upper-right corner of the Color Mixer panel and choose Add Swatch from the Options menu that appears.**

Editing fills

After you create your gradient or bitmap fills, you may decide that you want to change them. (You can find out about bitmap fills in the following section.) To edit a fill, follow these steps:

1. **Choose the Gradient Transform tool from the Tools panel.**

   If this is the first time you've used the tool, you first need to click and hold down the Free Transform tool. You'll see the Gradient Transform tool pop up beneath your cursor. While still holding the mouse down, drag over the Gradient Transform tool to select it.
2. **Click a gradient or bitmap fill.**

   Flash places a boundary and editing handles around the fill, which vary with the type of fill, as you can see in Figure 2-15.

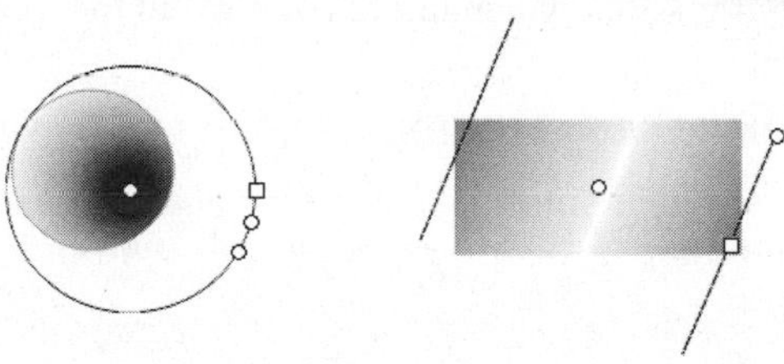

Figure 2-15: When you edit a fill, you see an editing boundary around the fill.

3. **Make one or more of the following changes:**
   - **Move the fill's center:** Drag the small circle at the center of the fill.
   - **Change the fill's width or height:** Drag the square handle inward or outward.
   - **Rotate a fill:** Drag the circle on the editing boundary (the endmost circle for a radial gradient).
   - **Scale a bitmap fill:** Drag the corner square boundary inward or outward.
   - **Scale a radial gradient:** Drag the middle circular handle on the editing boundary inward or outward.
   - **Skew a bitmap fill:** Drag a circular handle on the top or side.

Working with bitmap fills

You can create a fill with a bitmap that you have imported. (See Book V, Chapter 3 for more on importing graphics.) To create a fill with a bitmap image, follow these steps:

1. **Choose File⇨Import.**

   The Import dialog box appears.
2. **Choose the bitmap file that you want and click Open.**

   The bitmap appears on the Stage.
3. **Choose Modify⇨Break Apart.**

   This action selects the entire image as a fill rather than as a single color when you use the eyedropper (in Step 5).
4. **Choose the Eyedropper tool from the Tools section of the Tools panel.**
5. **Click the bitmap image.**

   The Paint Bucket tool is activated, and the Fill Color button (in the Colors section of the Tools panel and in the Properties panel) displays the bitmap image.
6. **Click the object that you want to fill.**

   You may have to move the bitmap image that you imported if it covers your object. The bitmap is *tiled* — repeated throughout the filled area.

Chapter 3: Working with Symbols

In This Chapter

- Understanding the importance of symbols
- Getting graphic with graphic symbols
- Animating with movie clip symbols
- Making your site interactive with button symbols

A *symbol* is any object or group of objects, an animation, or a Web button. You give the symbol a name and save it in the Library. (See Book V, Chapter 1 for a discussion of the Library.) In this chapter, you can find out about symbols and how to use them.

Appreciating the Importance of Symbols

You need to know about symbols if you want to work in Adobe Flash CS3. The following are the three types of symbols:

- **Graphic:** The simplest type of symbol, and a useful way to save groups of objects that you want to reuse. You can animate graphic symbols.
- **Movie clip:** A little movie that you put inside your big movie. You can apply ActionScript, Flash's programming language, to a movie clip or within a movie clip to specify how it functions. The movie clip has its own Timeline, and you generally insert the movie clip on the Timeline of the main Flash movie to let it play. You can place, or *nest,* movie clips inside each other. You may find movie clips useful for building complex animation and an interactive Web site.
- **Button:** You use buttons when you want your site viewers to click to go to another page or create some other effect. You use ActionScript to specify what happens when a viewer clicks a button.

The rest of this chapter explains how to create and work with graphic, movie clip, and button symbols.

Symbols are the building blocks of complex graphics and animation in your Flash documents. Symbols have the following qualities:

- ✦ You can easily use symbols repeatedly by dragging them from the Library onto the Stage. Each time that you drag something from the Library onto the Stage, you create an *instance* of the symbol. You can resize individual instances.
- ✦ Symbols reduce your file size (for faster browser display) because Flash only stores the symbol definition once and remembers one object rather than many.
- ✦ Most animation requires symbols (or text or grouped objects).
- ✦ Symbols keep their integrity, so you can put other objects in front of them or behind them without the objects being joined or cut out.

Working with Graphic Symbols

You usually create a graphic symbol from objects that you've already created. For example, you may have a background that consists of a sky, grass, flowers, and the sun. Saving these objects as a symbol reduces file size and ensures that if you copy or move the background, all its components come along for the ride.

Working with instances of symbols

When you drag a symbol from the Library, the copy on the Stage is called an *instance.* You can have many instances of one symbol in a Flash document. You can change an instance so that it differs from its original symbol, and the original symbol in the Library remains intact. To change an instance, follow these steps:

1. **Select the instance by clicking it on the Stage with the Selection tool.**

   Remember that changing an individual instance doesn't change the symbol itself.

2. **Use the Properties panel to do one or more of the following:**

   - Change the brightness, color, or transparency by selecting an option from the Color drop-down list. Select Advanced from the Color drop-down list to change both color and alpha (transparency) at the same time.
   - Change an instance's type (graphic, movie clip, or button) by selecting an option from the Symbol Behavior drop-down list.

3. **Use the Free Transform tool (or other editing tools) in the Tools panel to rotate, scale, or skew the instance.**

Creating graphic symbols

To create a graphic symbol from existing objects, follow these steps:

1. **Using the Selection tool from the Tools section of the Tools panel, select the objects that you want to convert to a symbol.**
2. **Choose Modify➪Convert to Symbol or press F8.**

   The Convert to Symbol dialog box appears, as shown in Figure 3-1.

Figure 3-1: Convert an object to a symbol.

3. **In the Name text field, enter a name for the symbol.**

   Some people start the names of their symbols with a code that indicates the type of symbol. For example, you can start your graphic symbols with gr_ and then add the name of the symbol. Classifying your symbols in this way automatically alphabetizes them by their type and helps to keep clear which type of symbol you're using.

4. **Select Graphic from the Behavior list of symbol types.**
5. **Click OK.**

   The objects that you selected are now one object, surrounded by a selection border. The symbol is also stored, automatically, in the Library.

You can achieve the same result by creating an empty symbol and then adding your objects. Follow these steps to do so:

1. **Choose Insert➪New Symbol to open the Create New Symbol dialog box.**

   The Create New Symbol dialog box is the same as the Convert to Symbol dialog box (refer to Figure 3-1).

2. **In the Name text field, enter a name for the symbol.**
3. **Select Graphic from the Behavior list of symbol types.**

4. **Click OK.**

   You now find yourself in symbol-editing mode and are no longer on the main Timeline.

5. **Draw the objects for your graphic symbol.**

   All these objects become part of your symbol.

   Note the cross hairs in the middle of the screen. This is the registration point. Generally, this is the center point of your symbol. If you move your object away from that registration point, the symbol will act differently when you animate it. For example, if you make a square and put the registration point at the top left, when you rotate the object it will rotate the square around that point in the top left.

6. **Choose Edit⇨Edit Document to exit symbol-editing mode and return to the main Timeline.**

   The symbol is now in the Library and disappears from the screen.

Using graphic symbols

To insert an instance of a symbol, drag it from the Library onto the Stage. You can drag from the symbol's icon in the Library list or from its preview at the top of the Library window.

You can also use a graphic symbol (and any other type of symbol) from another Flash document file by following these steps:

1. **Choose Import⇨Import to Library.**

   This step opens the Import to Library dialog box, where you can browse for Flash files.

2. **Choose the file that contains the symbol that you want.**
3. **Click the Open button.**

   Flash opens another Library window.

4. **Drag symbols from the new Library window onto the Stage.**

Editing graphic symbols

If you change the original symbol, every instance of the symbol that you've inserted also changes. This feature can save you a lot of time if you need to change the shape of all your buttons, for example. To edit a symbol, follow these steps:

1. **Select any instance of the symbol on the Stage.**

Although you start by selecting an instance of the symbol, when you edit it on the Stage, as Step 2 describes, you're editing the symbol, not the instance.

2. **Right-click the symbol instance and choose one of the following:**
   - **Edit in Place:** This option lets you edit a symbol while still viewing other objects on the Stage. The other objects are dimmed so that you can distinguish them from the symbol.
   - **Edit:** If you select this option, you perform your edits in symbol-editing mode, which lets you edit a symbol separately from the main Stage and Timeline. You see only the symbol.
   - **Edit in New Window:** This option opens a new window, where you edit the symbol. You see only the symbol.
3. **Edit the symbol by changing its color, shape, or effects.**
4. **Choose Edit⇨Edit Document to return to the main Timeline, or if you chose Edit in New Window, click the window's Close button.**

   You see all the instances of the symbol change to reflect the edits.

To return to individual objects, you can break apart any instance of a symbol. Select the instance and choose Modify⇨Break Apart.

Creating and Working with Movie Clip Symbols

You can use movie clips for a number of reasons and in a number of different ways:

- ✦ Use a movie clip to create animation that you want to insert or load onto the main Timeline.
- ✦ Use a movie clip whenever you need to control its functioning with ActionScript. (For more information on ActionScript, see Book V, Chapter 8.) For example, you can use ActionScript to control the size or color of a movie clip. You can also put ActionScript inside a movie clip to tell the movie to stop at a certain frame.
- ✦ You can use movie clips to create interface elements, such as check boxes, radio buttons, and scrollbars. This type of movie clip is called a *component* (you can read more about components in Book V, Chapter 8).
- ✦ You can also use movie clip symbols whenever you want to insert animation into the main Timeline but keep the original movie in the Library for reuse. Figure 3-2 shows a movie clip in symbol-editing mode that will be an animation of a bouncing ball. If you want several bouncing balls on your Web site, you can drag the movie clip onto the Stage as many times as you want.

You can create a movie clip symbol from scratch or convert animation that you've created on the main Timeline to a movie clip. To create a movie clip symbol from scratch, follow these steps:

1. **Choose Insert⇨New Symbol to open the Create New Symbol dialog box.**

   Make sure that no objects are selected when you perform this step.

2. **In the Name text field, enter a name for the symbol.**
3. **Select Movie Clip from the Behavior list of symbol types.**
4. **Click OK.**

   You now find yourself in symbol-editing mode and are no longer on the main Timeline. In Figure 3-2, you can see the movie clip icon and the name of the movie clip, Bouncing Ball, just below the layer list.

5. **Create the objects or animation for your movie clip symbol.**
6. **Choose Edit⇨Edit Document (or press Ctrl+E) to exit symbol-editing mode and return to the main Timeline.**

   The symbol is now in the Library and disappears from the screen.

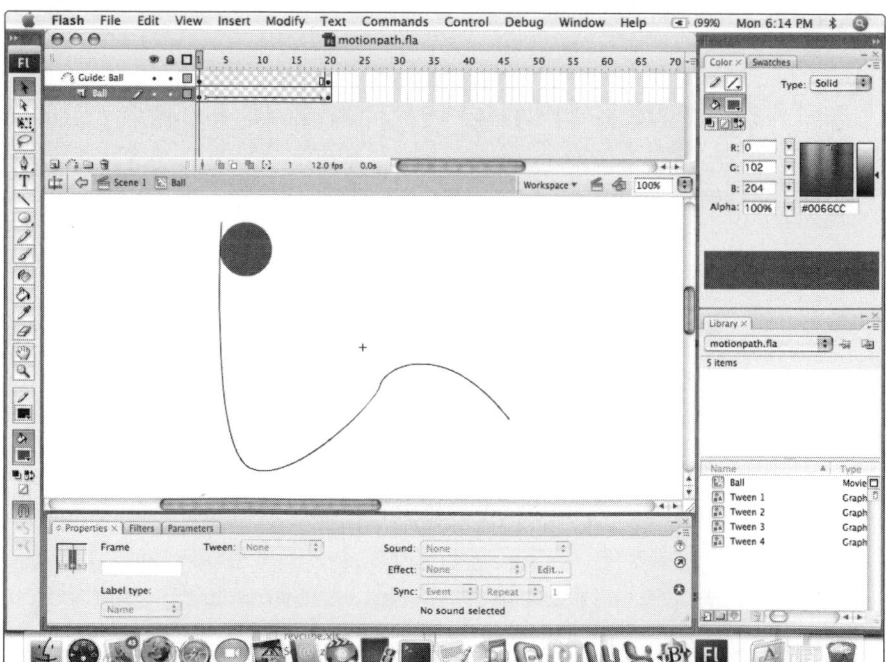

Figure 3-2: Creating a symbol in symbol-editing mode.

Sometimes you create some animation on the main Timeline and later realize that you need to turn that animation into a movie clip. Follow these steps to create a movie clip from an animation:

1. **On the layer listing, click the first layer on the list, press Shift, and then click the last layer.**

   All the layers are now selected. See Book V, Chapter 4 for coverage of layers.

2. **Choose Edit⇨Copy.**
3. **Make sure that no single objects on an individual frame are selected and choose Insert⇨New Symbol.**

   The New Symbol dialog box appears.

4. **In the Name text field, enter a name for the symbol.**
5. **Select Movie Clip from the Behavior list of symbol types.**
6. **Click OK to close the dialog box and enter symbol-editing mode.**
7. **Click the first frame of the Timeline.**

   This is the Timeline for the movie clip, not the whole movie.

8. **Choose Edit⇨Paste in Center.**

   The frames are copied into the active layer.

9. **Choose Edit⇨Edit Document to return to the main Timeline of the movie and exit symbol-editing mode.**

   The movie clip symbol is now saved in the Library.

10. **Delete the original animation by selecting all the layers (as you did in Step 1) and choosing Edit⇨Timeline⇨Remove Frames.**

You can drag a movie clip onto the Stage just like a graphic symbol. You also edit a movie clip in the same way that you edit graphic symbols. See the section "Working with Graphic Symbols," earlier in this chapter, for detailed steps.

Working with Button Symbols

Buttons are a major component of Web sites. You can use buttons as links to move to other pages and sites, and some buttons trigger more complex actions, such as stopping music or starting an animation.

A button has the following *states,* which you define when you create the button:

- **Up:** The appearance of the button when the mouse cursor isn't over the button.
- **Over:** The appearance of the button when the mouse cursor is over the button, but not clicking it.
- **Down:** The appearance of the button when the cursor clicks the button.
- **Hit:** The area of the button that responds to the mouse. This area is invisible. The Hit state is often the same as the Down state because it just defines the active area of the button.

You may want to use the common technique of designing a button that changes color or size when you pass the cursor over the button and then changes again when you click it. This technique provides feedback that the button has responded to the user. Figure 3-3 shows a button's four states.

Figure 3-3: The four button states: Up, Over, Down, and Hit. Each state has a slightly different fill.

Creating simple button symbols

Creating a button involves designing the look of the button for the first three states and the size of the button for the Hit state. Often, you add text to the graphic so that people know what the button is for. Follow these steps to create a button:

1. **Choose Insert⇨New Symbol.**

   The Create New Symbol dialog box appears.

2. **In the Name text field, type a name for the button.**
3. **From the list of behaviors, select Button and click OK.**

You now see the Button Timeline. The dot in the Up frame indicates that the frame is a keyframe. (See Book V, Chapter 5 for more information on keyframes.) The Up frame is active.

4. **Draw the button for the Up state.**

   You can create the graphic with Flash's drawing tools, an imported graphic, or an instance of a symbol.

   Place the graphic for all the button states at the center of the display. (Book V, Chapter 2 explains how to center objects.) If the button images aren't all in the same place, the button shifts when the viewer passes the cursor over or clicks the button.

5. **Click the Over frame and choose Insert⇨Timeline⇨Keyframe.**

   The graphic that you created for the Up state in Step 4 is still on the Stage.

6. **Draw the button for the Over state.**

   Use the graphic for the Up state and change it (or leave it the same, if you want), or delete the graphic and draw a new one in its place.

7. **Click the Down frame and choose Insert⇨Timeline⇨Keyframe.**
8. **Create the graphic for the Down state (as in Step 6).**
9. **Click the Hit frame and choose Insert⇨Timeline⇨Keyframe.**
10. **Create the shape that defines the active area of the button.**

    You want this shape to completely cover all the graphics of the other states. Usually, you need only a rectangle or circle. If you ignore the Hit frame, Flash uses the boundary of the objects in the Up frame.

    If you use text for the button, viewers have to hit the letters precisely, unless you create a hit area around the text.

11. **Choose Edit⇨Edit Document to return to the regular Timeline.**

To place a button on the Stage, use the Selection tool to drag the button from the Library to create an instance of the symbol. To edit a button, double-click it in the Library.

Adding pizzazz to buttons

Buttons don't have to be simple. You can make your buttons more interesting in the following ways:

✦ **Add a sound:** You add a sound to a button's Timeline in symbol-editing mode in the same way that you add a sound to a frame on the main Timeline. See Book V, Chapter 6 for information on adding sounds.

- **Add animation:** Create a movie clip symbol, as you can read about in the section "Creating and Working with Movie Clip Symbols," earlier in this chapter. Click the keyframe of the button's Timeline that you want to contain the movie clip; for example, click the Over keyframe. Delete any existing graphic and drag a movie clip symbol that contains animation from the Library onto the screen.
- **Add interactivity:** In order for the button to do something, it needs some ActionScript. Drag an instance of the button onto the Stage and select that instance by clicking it with the Selection tool. Then use the Actions panel to add ActionScript to the button.

Testing buttons

After you create a button, you should drag an instance of it onto the Stage and test it. To test simple buttons, follow these steps:

1. **Choose Control⇨Enable Simple Buttons.**
2. **Pass the cursor over the button and click it to see whether the effects work.**
3. **To select the button by clicking it, choose Control⇨Enable Simple Buttons again to disable the button.**

If your button contains movie clips, you need to test the entire movie to test the button. Choose Control⇨Test Movie and test the button. To close the movie window, click its Close button.

Chapter 4: Making Your Life Easier with Layers

In This Chapter

- **Getting familiar with layers**
- **Adding depth to your work with layers**
- **Getting what you need from your layer options**
- **Organizing your layers in folders**

You can use layers to organize your Adobe Flash document. Layers are an important part of creating a movie for the following reasons:

- **Layers keep objects from bumping into each other.** If you draw two circles and overlap them, they either merge or one creates a cut-out of the other. However, if you put the two circles on two separate layers, they each remain whole.
- **Each animated object needs its own layer.** If you want to manipulate more than one object on the Stage at a time, you need to create a new layer.
- **ActionScript and sounds should have their own layer.** This lets you easily find and troubleshoot any problems as well as avoid potential conflicts.
- **Special types of layers let you create special effects:**
  - **Mask layers:** Mask layers create a "keyhole" through which you can see layers beneath it.
  - **Guide layers:** Guide layers direct animation along a path.

In addition, you can use layers for your own organizational purposes. For example, you can put text on a separate layer. Then, to focus on just the text, you can hide all the other layers. In this chapter, we explain how to create and manage layers.

Layers add a third dimension to the organization of your Flash document. The Stage lays out your graphics in the horizontal (X-axis) and vertical (Y-axis) dimensions. Using layers is like adding a Z-axis, letting you place graphics on top of each other as if they were on successive transparent sheets.

The Timeline, of course, adds the fourth dimension — time. Layers are intimately connected to the Timeline. For each layer, Flash adds a row of frames in the Timeline.

Working with the Layer List

You work with layers on the Layer list, which you can find to the left of the Timeline, as shown in Figure 4-1. The Layer list contains the following features:

- **Default layer:** You start a new movie with the default layer, Layer 1.
- **Active layer:** The active layer is highlighted in gray. When you create objects, they go on the active layer.
- **Show/Hide Layers:** You can show or hide objects on any layer by clicking the Show/Hide icon for that layer.
- **Lock/Unlock Layers:** You can lock any layer so that you can't select or edit objects. Click the Lock icon for that layer. To unlock a layer, click the Lock icon again.
- **Display Outlines:** You can display objects on a layer as outlines. Each layer uses a different outline color. Outlines may help you see objects on all layers more clearly. Click the Outlines icon for any layer.
- **Insert Layer:** To insert a layer, click the Insert Layer button below the Layer list.
- **Add Motion Guide:** To add a motion guide layer, click the Add Motion Guide button below the Layer list. See the section "An introduction to guide layers," later in this chapter, for more information on guide layers.
- **Insert Layer Folder:** You can organize layers into folders. Click the Insert Layer Folder button below the Layer list.
- **Delete Layer:** To delete a layer, select it and click the Delete Layer button, or drag the layer to the Delete Layer button.

Figure 4-1: Use the Layer list to manage your layers.

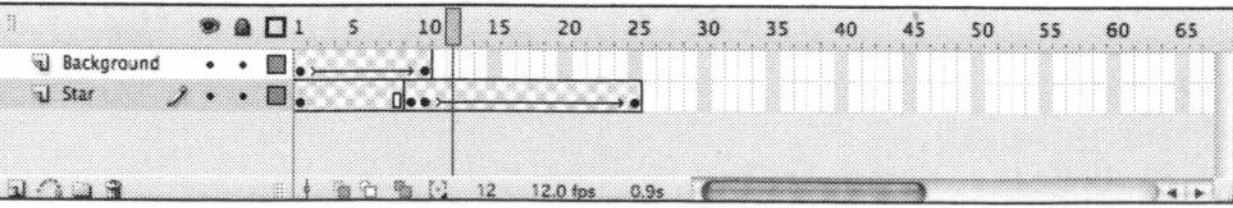

Working with Layers

When you open a new movie, it has one layer, called Layer 1. As you work, you create, delete, move, and copy layers. You also name your layers. Choose a naming system that makes sense to you. ***Note:*** If you make the names too long, you can't see the whole name in the Layer list, so don't get too extravagant. You can drag the right border of the Layer list to the right to see more of the layer names.

Creating layers

When you need to create a new layer, click the Insert Layer button at the bottom of the Layer list (refer to Figure 4-1) or choose Insert⇨Timeline⇨ Layer. The new layer appears above the active layer and becomes the active layer.

You can also create a new layer by right-clicking (or Ctrl+clicking on a Mac) a layer in the Layer list and selecting Insert Layer from the contextual menu that appears.

Rename the new layer from its default name (Layer 1, Layer 2, and so on) immediately after you create it to avoid any confusion about what you're putting on that layer. Double-click the layer name, type a new name, and press Enter.

Using layers

When you draw an object, it appears on the active layer, which is the layer that is highlighted and has a pencil icon next to its name in the Layer list. To draw on a different layer, click the name of the layer that you want to use. When you click a new layer, Flash selects all the objects on that layer. To deselect the objects, click any empty area (on the Stage or in the gray space around the Stage).

Editing layers

You often need to make changes to layers or move objects from one layer to another. You need to keep your layers organized to keep your entire movie under control.

Selecting layers

When editing layers, you may want to select more than one layer at a time, such as when you need to move more than one layer. To select a group of layers that are contiguous (meaning grouped together in a stack), click the first layer name on the Layer list, press and hold down Shift, and click the last layer of the group. To select layers that aren't contiguous, click the first layer, press and hold down Ctrl, and click any additional layers that you want to select.

Moving objects from one layer to another

You often draw objects before you realize that you need them on a separate or different layer. For example, you can only have one object on a layer that you're animating. If you draw additional objects on that layer, you should move them to another layer. First create a new layer, if you don't have one available. (See the section "Creating layers," earlier in this chapter.) To move objects from one layer to another, follow these steps:

1. **Select the frames that represent the objects that you want to move by using the Selection tool.**

   The layer that contains the objects is active and highlighted gray. To select more than one frame in a sequence, select the first frame, press and hold down Shift, and then select the last frame.

2. **Choose Edit⇨Cut.**
3. **In the Layer list, click the layer to which you want to move the objects.**
4. **Choose Edit⇨Paste in Place.**

   The objects appear to be in the same location, but they're now on a new layer.

Distributing to layers

In one of Flash CS3's great features, you can distribute all objects on a layer to separate layers. For example, to animate each letter of a word, you can put each letter on a separate layer. You may want to animate the letters of the word *now* so that each letter flies onto the Stage separately. Follow these steps to distribute objects to separate layers:

1. **Select the text or objects by using the Selection tool.**

   For the purposes of this example, select the Text tool from the Tools section of the Tools panel, type **now** in a single frame, and then select the text.

2. **If you're working with text, choose Modify⇨Break Apart. Otherwise, skip to Step 3.**

   You see a separate box around each letter. Each letter is now a separate object.

3. **Choose Modify⇨Timeline⇨Distribute to Layers.**

   Each object or letter is now on a separate layer. Flash automatically creates the layers for you. In the "now" example, Flash creates three layers, named n, o, and w, for each of the three letters

   The objects also remain on their original layer. Because you won't be needing the entire object any longer, you generally want to delete the original layer and keep only the copies on the individual layers.

Renaming layers

If the content of a layer changes, you probably want to rename the layer to something appropriate to its new content. To rename a layer, double-click the layer name in the Layer list, type the new name, and press Enter.

Deleting layers

To delete a layer, select the layer in the Layer list and click the Delete button (it looks like a trash can) at the bottom of the list. (Refer to Figure 4-1.)

Deleting a layer deletes *everything* on that layer. You may not be able to see everything on the layer because you see only what is on the Stage in the current frame. To see everything on a layer throughout the Timeline, follow these steps:

1. **Right-click the layer name in the Layer list and choose Hide Others from the contextual menu that appears.**
2. **Click the first frame on the Timeline.**
3. **Press Enter to run the animation.**

Copying layers

You can copy an entire layer, and if you do, all the objects on that layer are copied as well. Follow these steps to copy a layer:

1. **Select the layer by clicking the layer's name in the Layer list.**

   Selecting the layer selects all the objects on the layer.

2. **Choose Edit⇨Copy.**
3. **Choose Insert⇨Timeline⇨Layer to create a new layer.**
4. **Choose Edit⇨Paste in Center.**

Reordering layers

Flash displays objects in the order of their layers, from the top down. In other words, objects on the top layer appear in front of objects on the next layer. You can reorder the Layer list to change which objects appear in front on the Stage. See Figure 4-2 for an example.

To move a layer to a different spot in the Layer list, click and drag the layer's name to the location that you want the layer to appear and then release the mouse button.

An introduction to guide layers

A guide layer is a special type of layer that's invisible when you publish your Flash document and play it as a movie. Guide layers have the following main purposes:

- **Drawing guide:** You can place gridlines on the Stage to help you lay out the objects on the Stage, or you can import a bitmap and use it as a guide to help you draw using the graphics tools. The content on the guide layer is invisible when you publish the movie, but having the extra layer helps you draw.
- **Motion guide:** You can place a path on a guide layer that controls the animation of an object. You can read more about this process in Book V, Chapter 5.

To create a drawing guide layer, follow these steps:

1. **Click the Insert Layer button on the Layer list.**
2. **Right-click the layer and choose Guide from the contextual menu that appears.**

   The layer icon changes to the guide icon that looks like a hammer.

Using mask layers

A *mask layer* sits on top of other layers, and acts, you guessed it, like a mask! A mask layer hides everything on its connected masked layers, except what's inside the objects that are on the top mask layer. It, in effect, masks the content on the lower layers. You can use masks to create a spotlight effect, where you only see what's in the spotlight and everything else is hidden. You can see this effect in Figure 4-3, where the circular mask hides everything inside of the circle. The circle is on a *mask layer,* and what you see inside the circle is on a *masked layer.*

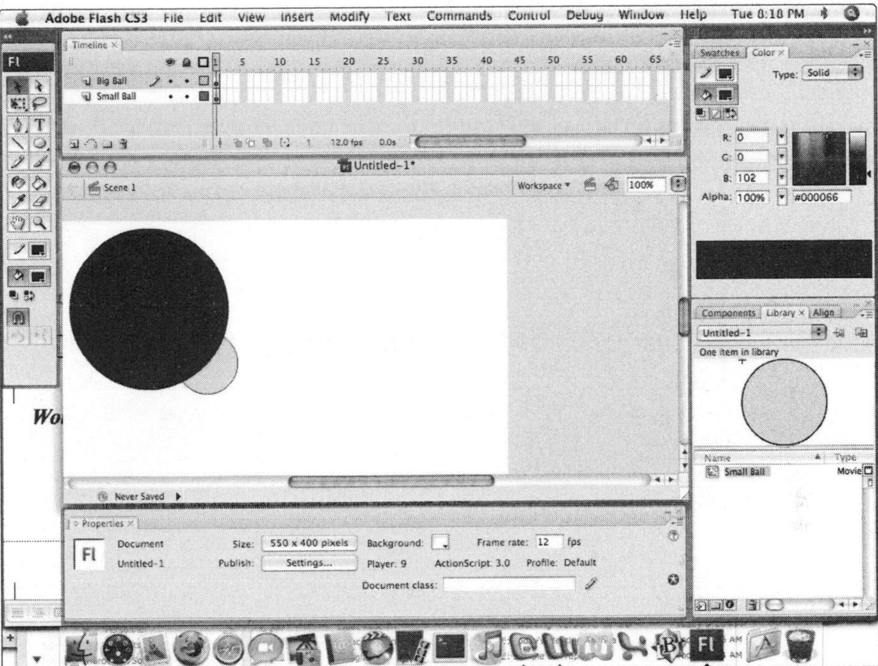

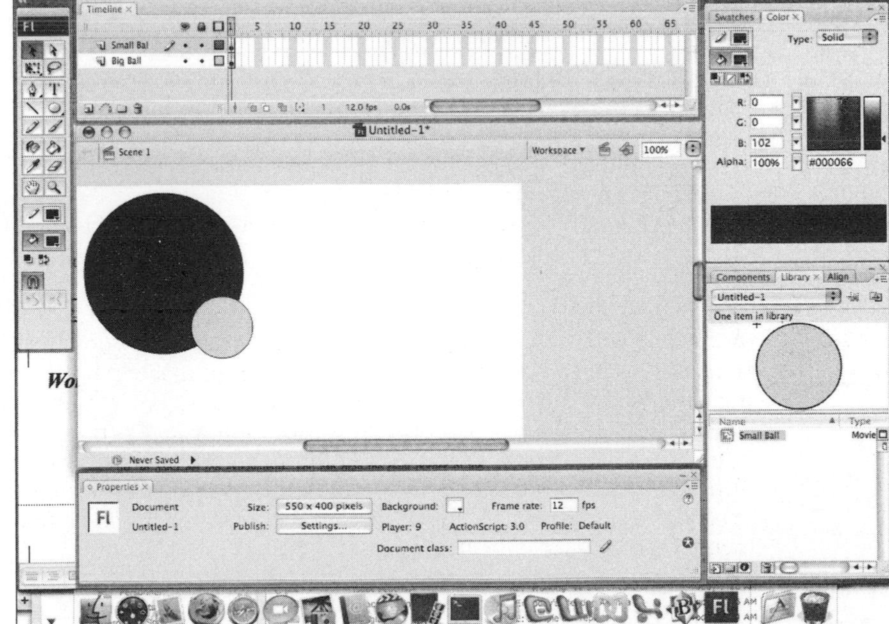

Figure 4-2: By changing the layer order, you change which objects appear in front on the Stage.

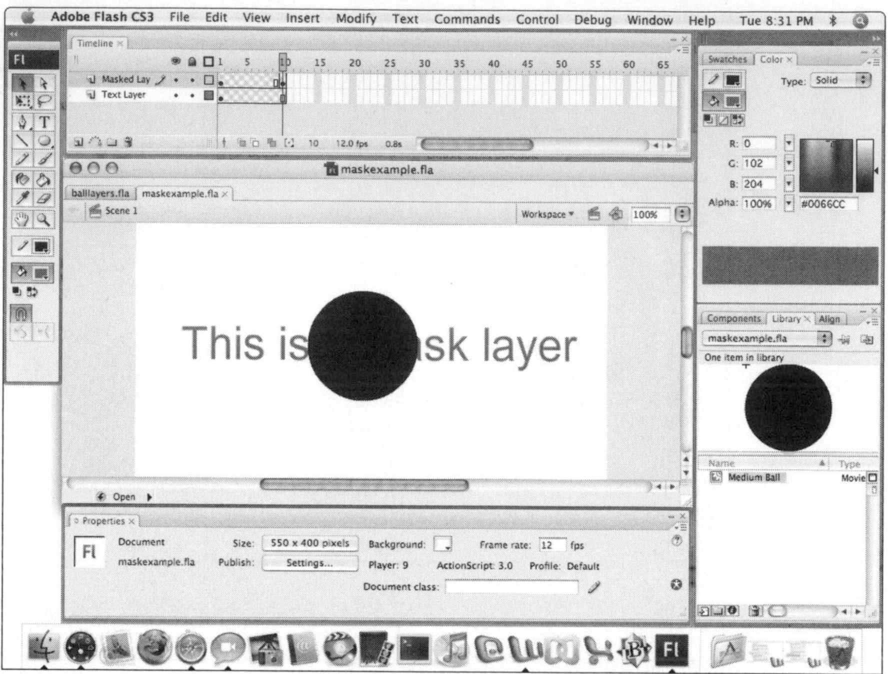

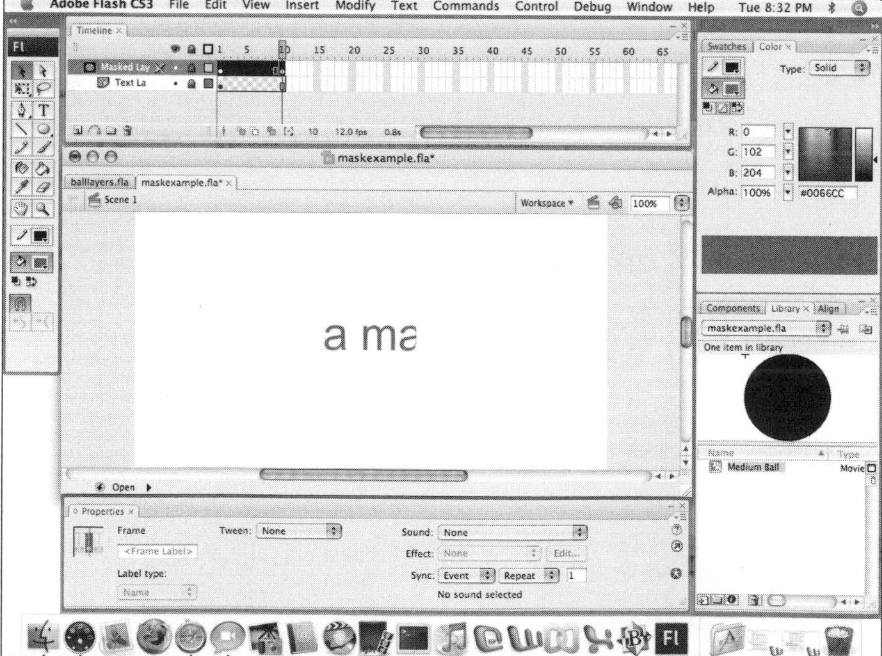

Figure 4-3: The circular mask hides everything except what is inside the circle.

To create a mask layer, follow these steps:

1. **On the top layer of the Layer list, create the objects that you want to be visible through the mask.**
2. **With the top layer selected, click the Add Layer button at the bottom of the Layer list.**
3. **Draw a shape, such as a circle, on this new layer.**
4. **Right-click the new layer and choose Mask from the contextual menu that appears.**

   In the Layer list, the mask layer is locked (meaning it can't be edited) by default, and the masked layer is both locked and indented, showing that it's connected to the mask layer above it. (Refer to Figure 4-3.)

To edit a mask or masked layer, click the lock next to the layer name in the Layer list. Unlocking these layers removes the mask effect. After you finish editing, click the lock column next to the layers' names again to redisplay the mask effect.

To link a layer to a mask layer, drag the layer directly underneath a mask layer. The layer is indented. To display the mask effect, make sure that the layer is locked by clicking it under the Lock column in the Layer list.

Changing Layer Options

You can control the visibility, editability, and display of objects on layers. These tools can really help you when you're trying to isolate certain objects for editing or animation.

Altering the visibility of objects

You can hide all the objects on a layer. If you have a lot of objects on the Stage and want to edit objects on one layer, you can hide other layers that you don't need to see at the moment.

Don't forget about objects on hidden layers. These objects still appear in your published movie.

To hide a layer, click beneath the Eye icon on the layer's row. An X appears in the Eye column to show you that the layer is hidden. Click the X to unhide the layer.

To hide all layers except one, right-click the layer that you want to see and choose Hide Others from the contextual menu that appears.

Locking and unlocking layers

You can lock the objects on a layer so that you can't edit them. You may find yourself accidentally selecting objects that you want to leave alone. This can get annoying, but you can easily avoid the situation by locking that layer.

To lock a layer, click beneath the Lock icon on the layer's row. A lock appears in the Lock column. Click the lock to unlock the layer.

To lock all layers except one, right-click the layer and choose Lock Others from the contextual menu that appears.

Setting layer properties

Many of the layer controls described in this chapter all appear in the Layer Properties dialog box, as shown in Figure 4-4. Most of the time, you just use the controls on the Layer list or the contextual menu that you see when you right-click a layer. However, the Layer Properties dialog box does have some unique features.

To open the Layer Properties dialog box, select the layer that you want to modify and choose Modify⇨Timeline⇨Layer Properties. You can use this dialog box to do the following things:

- **Rename the layer:** Type a new name in the Name text field.
- **Show/Hide the layer:** Select or deselect the Show check box.
- **Lock/Unlock the layer:** Select or deselect the Lock check box.
- **Change the type of layer:** You can turn a layer into a guide, guided, mask, masked, or folder layer.
- **Change the outline color:** Click the Outline Color swatch to choose a new color.
- **Turn outlines on/off:** Select or deselect the View Layer as Outlines check box.
- **Change layer height:** Select a percentage from the Layer Height drop-down list. This percentage can increase the physical size of the layer to make it more viewable.

When you finish making changes, click OK to close the Layer Properties dialog box.

Using Folders to Manage Layers

If you have many layers, you can organize them into folders. For example, you may want to put all your layers containing text in one folder.

To create a folder, click the Insert Layer Folder icon at the bottom of the Layer list. A new folder appears above the current layer. Double-click the folder name and enter a name that describes the folder's contents.

Use the following tips to manage folders:

- **Put layers in a folder:** Drag layers onto the folder's row.
- **Collapse and expand individual folders:** Click the arrow at the left of the folder's icon.
- **Expand and collapse all folders:** Right-click the Layer list, and choose Expand All Folders or Collapse All Folders from the contextual menu that appears.
- **Remove a layer from a folder:** Expand the folder, if it isn't already expanded, and drag the layer above the folder name or to another location where it doesn't darken a folder.
- **Hide or lock an entire folder and its layers:** Click beneath the Eye or Lock icon on the folder's row.
- **Reorder folders:** You can change the order of folders, which also changes the order of the layers contained in the folder relative to other folders. Just drag any folder up or down.
- **Delete folders:** Select the folder and click the Delete (trash can) icon.

WARNING!

Deleting a folder deletes all the layers in the folder and everything on those layers. Flash warns you of this fact if you try to delete a folder.

Chapter 5: Creating Animation

In This Chapter

- Touring the Timeline
- Using frames and keyframes
- Approaching animation frame by frame
- Creating tweened animation
- Making interactive animation
- Working with scenes

Adobe Flash CS3 is basically an animation program, so this chapter focuses on animation, the central purpose of Adobe Flash CS3. In this chapter, we provide the information that you need to create motion and shape animation.

Getting Familiar with the Timeline

The Timeline lays out your animation in time. In order to animate, you need to be thoroughly familiar with the Timeline (shown in Figure 5-1) and its special coding.

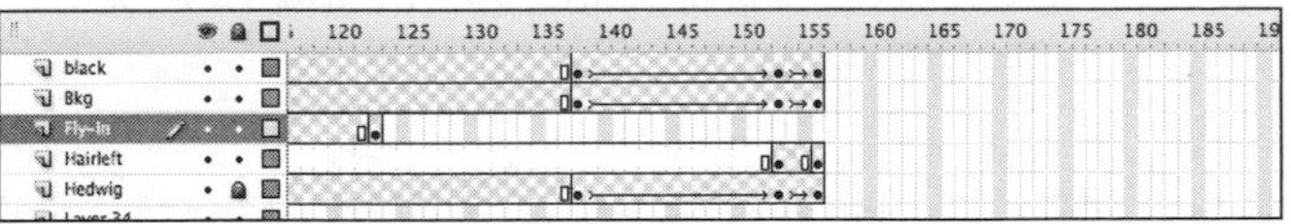

Figure 5-1: The Timeline provides a great deal of information about your animation.

As you can see in Figure 5-1, every fifth frame on the Timeline is numbered and each layer has its own row in the Timeline. (For more information on layers, see Book V, Chapter 4.)

If the Timeline isn't visible, choose Window⇨Timeline (Ctrl+Alt+T). You can collapse the Timeline by clicking its Collapse/Expand arrow at the left side of its title bar.

Understanding the frame rate

The frame rate is the speed at which Flash plays the animation. The default frame rate is 12 frames per second (fps). You can have only one frame rate per document. To change the frame rate, follow these steps:

1. **Double-click the Frame Rate box at the bottom middle of the Timeline.**

   The Document Properties dialog box appears.

2. **In the Frame Rate text field, enter a new number in frames per second.**
3. **Click OK.**

When you use a frame rate that's too slow, the animation appears jerky. Increasing the frame rate may make animation appear smoother, but a frame rate that's too fast can appear blurred. The default frame rate of 12 fps is a good place to start.

The Internet connection rate and the size of the file also affect the rate of animation. A large file (often because of large graphics or sounds) and a slow Internet connection can make the animation stutter. Your viewers can get the best results if you reduce the size of the file as much as possible. In Book V, Chapter 7, we explain how to optimize files for the Web.

Working with the Timeline

You can work with the Timeline in the following ways:

- **Go to a frame:** Click the frame on the Timeline to go to a particular frame. If you want to work on a specific layer, click the frame in that layer's row.
- **Change size and appearance of the frames:** To modify the frames as they appear in the Timeline, click the Frame View button in the upper-right corner of the Timeline and choose one of the options from the menu. You can change the width and height of the frames, turn coloring of frames on and off, and choose to display a small thumbnail of the frame's content in each frame.
- **Add a label or comment to a frame:** To add a label or comment to a frame in the Timeline, select a frame and type a label name in the Frame Label text field in the Properties panel.

- **Select frames:** Click a frame and drag across the frames you want to select. (You can also click the first frame, press Shift, and click the last frame you want to select to select all the frames in between.)
- **Copy and paste frames:** Select the frames you want to copy, choose Edit⇨Timeline⇨Copy Frames, click where you want the frames to go, and choose Edit⇨Timeline⇨Paste Frames.
- **Move frames:** Select the frames you want to move and drag them to the desired location.
- **Add a frame:** To add a frame, right-click the frame to the left of where you want to create a frame and choose Insert Frame from the contextual menu that appears (or press F5).
- **Delete frames:** Select the frames you want to delete. Right-click and choose Remove Frames (or press Shift + F5).
- **Add a keyframe:** Right-click the desired frame and choose Insert Keyframe from the contextual menu (or press F6).
- **Change the length of an animation:** Click and drag the first or last keyframe of the animation to the right or left.
- **Scroll along the Timeline:** Use the horizontal scrollbar to scroll along the Timeline. Use the Vertical scrollbar (which appears when you have too many layers to display) to scroll through the layers.

Onion skinning

When you animate an object, you can display some or all of the animated frames at once, using an effect known as onion skinning. *Onion skinning* produces overlapping translucent images like the translucent layers of an onion. See Figure 5-2 for an example of onion skinning.

To work with onion skinning, use the buttons under the Timeline:

- **Onion skin:** Turns on onion skinning and adjusts the Onion markers to customize the number of frames that display the effect.
- **Onion skin outlines:** Displays single-color outlines of your animation.
- **Edit multiple frames:** Enables you to edit any of the frames on the Timeline, regardless of the current frame.
- **Modify onion markers:** Displays a menu that enables you to always show the markers (even when onion skinning is off), anchor the markers so they don't follow the *playhead* (current frame marker), and set the number of frames that the markers cover.

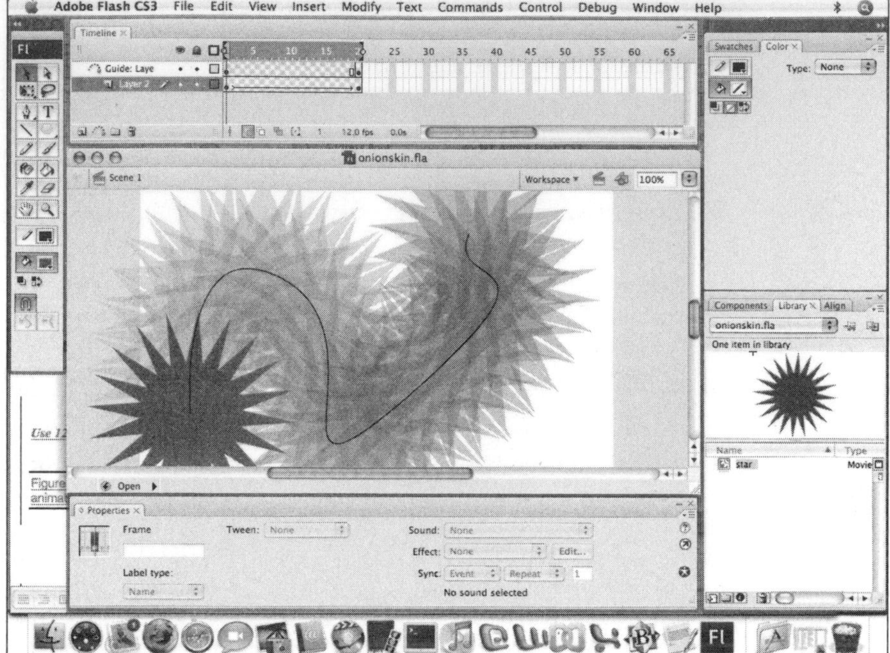

Figure 5-2: Onion skinning shows you the path of your animation.

Using Frames and Keyframes

A frame is actually a unit of time, based on your frame rate. You can place content on any frame, but you can only change content on a keyframe. Use a keyframe whenever you want to start or stop an animation or make any object appear or disappear.

To introduce any new object onto the Stage, you must have a keyframe. Insert a keyframe by right-clicking the frame where you want the keyframe and selecting Insert Keyframe from the contextual menu. Click the keyframe on the layer where you want the object to appear and then do one of the following:

- ✦ Draw something by using the Flash drawing tools. (See Book V, Chapter 2.)
- ✦ Import a graphic. (See Book V, Chapter 3.)
- ✦ Drag an object onto the Stage from the Library. (See Book V, Chapter 1.)

You can create two types of animation in Flash:

- **Frame-by-frame:** In frame-by-frame animation, each frame is a keyframe and contains a slight change in your objects so that when you play the Flash document, you see a smooth animation. This type of animation takes a lot of time and creates bigger files, but you may need to use it to create complex effects. You do cartooning mostly by using frame-by-frame animation.
- **Tweening:** In tweening, the first and last frames of the animation are keyframes, and Flash calculates everything in between. You can tween motion and shapes *(morphing).* You can create tweening much faster than frame-by-frame animation, and tweening creates small file sizes. Tweening does have one down side — you can't do it with any type of object except vector graphics.

Creating Animation Frame by Frame

When your animation doesn't have a simple pattern, such as movement of one object in a direction or the change of one shape to another shape, you need to use frame-by-frame animation. A common example of frame-by-frame animation is cartooning, in which a figure needs to move in complex ways or a mouth moves in time with speech.

To create frame-by-frame animation, follow these steps:

1. **Right-click a frame in the current layer where you want the animation to start and choose Insert Keyframe (or press F6) from the contextual menu.**
2. **Draw or import your image.**

   Book V, Chapter 2 tells you all about creating graphics. To import an image, choose File⇨Import.
3. **Right-click the next frame and choose Insert Keyframe again.**
4. **Change the graphic slightly to create the second frame of the animation.**
5. **Repeat Steps 3 and 4 until you complete your animation.**

   See Figure 5-3 for an example of frame-by-frame animation.

During the process, press Enter to play back your animation and check your work.

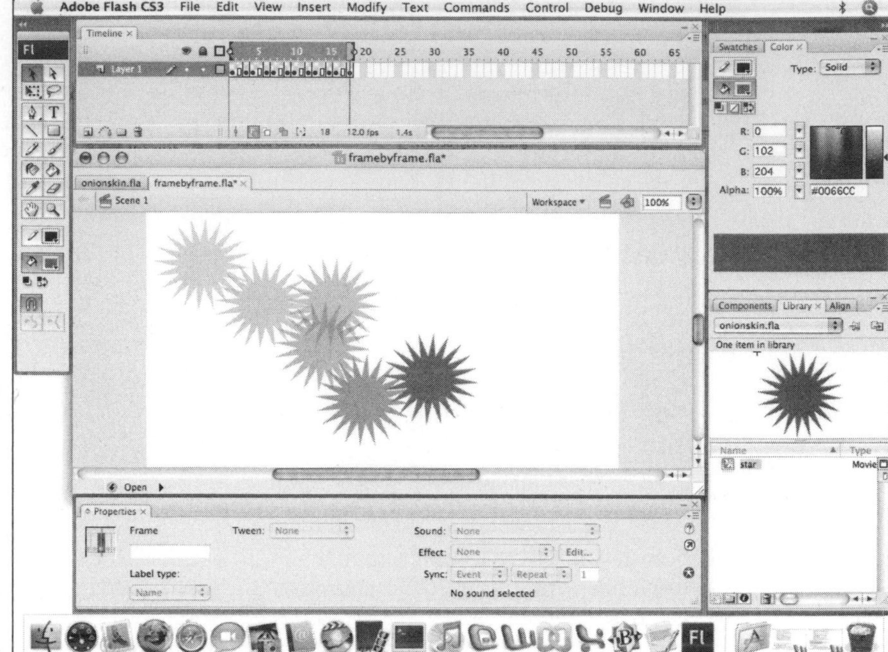

Figure 5-3: This simple frame-by-frame animation is shown using onion skinning.

Creating Tweened Motion Animation

Motion tweening moves a single symbol instance, text object, or grouped set of objects either in a straight line or along a path that you draw (often with the Pencil tool).

Although you can motion tween only one object at a time on any layer, you can tween other objects on other layers to create the overall look of many objects being animated.

You can also change the size, rotation, *skew* (slant), color, and transparency of symbol instances as you motion tween them. To make these changes to text or groups, convert them to symbols. See Book V, Chapter 3 for a discussion of symbols.

Preparing to tween

You can only put one *object* — symbol instance, text, or group — on the layer where you're animating. First, you need to create the object you want to animate and make sure that nothing else is on that layer. Often, you want to create a new layer just for your animation.

Decide how you want your object to move. Do you want its color, size, or rotation to change? After you decide, you're ready to tween.

The Flash Controller is like a control panel for a CD or video player. You may find the Controller helpful when you animate because it offers controls for rewinding and playing your animation. To open the Controller, choose Window➪Toolbars➪Controller.

Creating a simple tween

Before you tween, open the Properties panel by choosing Window➪Properties. To create a simple motion tween that moves the object along a straight line, follow these steps:

1. **On your animation layer, insert a keyframe where you want the animation to start.**

   To add a keyframe, right-click the frame to the left of where you want to create a keyframe and choose Insert Keyframe from the contextual menu.

2. **Click the keyframe and create the object or objects that you want to animate.**

   You can't tween two bitmaps or graphics that are not symbols. If you need to, turn your object or objects into a symbol (see Book V, Chapter 3) or a group (see Book V, Chapter 2). You can tween text without having to change it. You can also import a graphic or drag an instance of a symbol from the Library onto the Stage.

3. **Insert a keyframe where you want the animation to end.**

   The longer the span of frames, the slower the animation. You can always adjust the length of a tween later, as you can read about in the "Working with the Timeline" section, earlier in this chapter.

4. **Click the last keyframe and then move the object to its new location by using the Selection tool.**

   At this point, you can also change the object's color properties and transparency by using the Color box in the Properties panel. In addition, you can use the Free Transform tool or other Flash commands to change the object's size, rotation, and skew, as you can see in Figure 5-4.

5. **Select the range from keyframe to keyframe by clicking the first keyframe and dragging to the last keyframe.**

   If the span of frames is too long to show, click the first keyframe, scroll to the last keyframe, press Shift, and click the last keyframe.

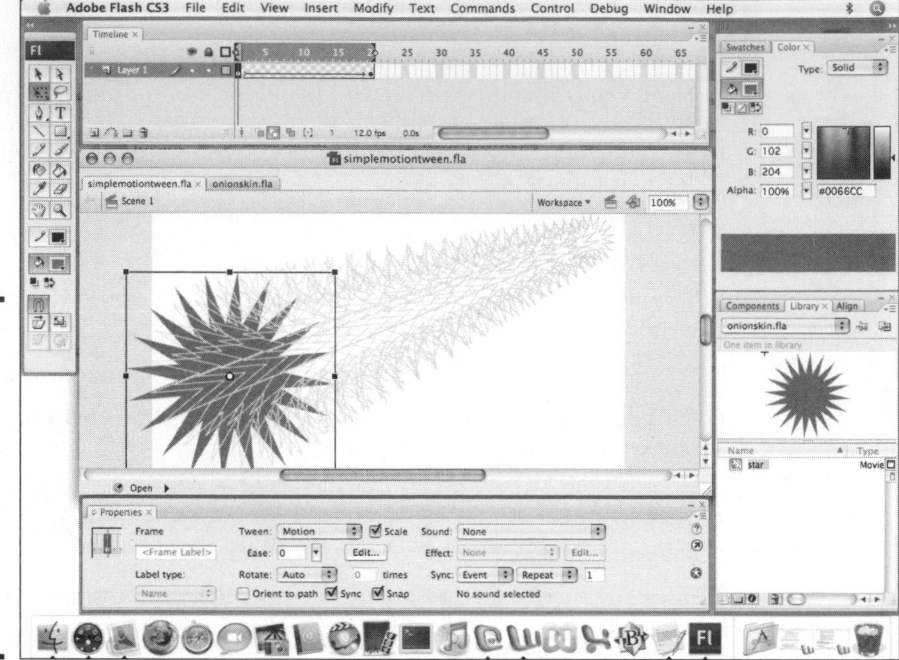

Figure 5-4: A simple motion tween that includes scaling. Onion skinning shows all the frames outlined.

You can click anywhere between the keyframes and get almost the exact same result as you can get with the click-and-drag technique. The last keyframe isn't tweened, but the result looks the same when you play the animation.

6. **From the Tween drop-down list in the Properties panel, select Motion.**

   If you changed the object's size, select the Scale check box in the Properties panel to tween the size.

7. **If you want to rotate the object during the tween (in addition to any rotation you create in Step 4), select CW (clockwise) or CCW (counter-clockwise) from the Rotate drop-down list in the Properties panel and then enter the number of rotations in the Rotation Count text field.**

   To test your animation, click the first keyframe and press Enter or use the Controller to rewind and play your animation.

You can accelerate or decelerate the speed of the tween. To accelerate from beginning to end, enter a value between –1 and –100 in the Ease text field in the Properties panel. To decelerate, use a value between 1 and 100.

See Figure 5-4 for an example of a star that moves along a diagonal line. The star also becomes smaller, so it appears to recede in the distance as it moves.

Motion tweening along a path

To tween along a path that isn't a straight line, you need to draw the path on a guide layer. (See Book V, Chapter 4 for the steps to create a guide layer.) Your animation is on the guided layer (the layer with the animation on it) that is associated with the guide layer (the layer that has the path that the animation follows on it). You can refer back to Figure 5-2 for an example of a motion tween along a path. In that figure, the star moves along a path, which you see with onion skinning on.

To create an animation that moves along a path, follow these steps (which start just like the steps for simple motion tweening):

1. **On your animation layer, insert a keyframe where you want the animation to start.**

   To add a keyframe, right-click the frame to the left of where you want to create a keyframe and choose Insert Keyframe from the contextual menu.

2. **Click the keyframe and create or import the object or objects (symbol instance, group, or text) you want to animate.**
3. **Insert a keyframe where you want the animation to end.**
4. **Select the range from keyframe to keyframe by clicking the first keyframe and dragging to the last keyframe, or click anywhere between the two keyframes.**
5. **From the Tween drop-down list in the Properties panel, select Motion.**
6. **In the Properties panel, select the Snap check box to snap the object to the path.**
7. **If you want the object to rotate in the direction and angle of the path, select the Orient to Path check box.**
8. **Right-click the object's layer and select Add Motion Guide.**

   The new layer is added. The layer is labeled Guide, and the object's layer is indented beneath it.

9. **On the guide layer, draw your path using the Pen tool.**
10. **Click the first keyframe of the object's layer and drag the object by its registration point (a small plus or circle) to the beginning of the path until the registration point snaps to the path.**
11. **Click the last keyframe of the object's layer and drag the object by its registration point to the end of the path until the registration point snaps to the path.**
12. **Press Enter to play the animation.**

If you need to change your path, use the Flash editing tools to edit the path that you created. You can use the Selection or Subselection tools to edit the path. (See Book V, Chapter 2 for details on editing graphics.)

The guide path isn't visible in the published movie. However, you often don't want to see the path even in your document, so you can more easily visualize the animation. Just click the eye column of the guide layer to hide it.

Creating Tweened Shape Animation

If you want your objects to change shape, you need shape tweening, often called *morphing*. In contrast to motion tweening, shape tweening works only with plain vector objects, usually ones that you create with the Flash drawing tools. You can't shape tween a symbol instance, text, or a group unless you break it apart by choosing Modify➪Break Apart.

To turn text into shapes, choose Modify➪Break Apart twice. The first time only breaks apart the text into individual letters. The second time you choose Modify➪Break Apart, you create shapes from the individual letters. However, remember that you can have only one animated object on a layer. You can break apart text once and then choose Modify➪Timeline➪Distribute to Layers to put each letter on a separate layer. If you want to shape tween the letters, break apart each letter a second time.

Creating a simple shape tween

To shape tween a shape, follow these steps:

1. **On a new layer, right-click the frame where you want the animation to start and select Insert Keyframe (or press F6).**
2. **Create the beginning shape.**
3. **Insert a keyframe where you want to end the animation.**
4. **With the second keyframe selected, create the ending shape.**

   You can create the end shape by erasing the first shape and drawing a new one or by modifying the first shape.
5. **If you want to change color, you can simply choose another color for the ending shape from the Color box in the Properties panel.**
6. **If you want to change transparency, open the Color Mixer panel (Window➪Color) and change the Alpha percentage in the Alpha text field.**

   You can also change the color in the Color Mixer.

7. **Click between the keyframes or select the entire span of the tween.**
8. **Select Shape from the Tween drop-down list in the Properties panel.**
9. **From the lower section of the Properties panel, select Angular from the Blend drop-down list if your tween shape has straight lines and sharp corners. Select Distributive for more curvy shapes.**

   You may need to click the Collapse/Expand arrow at the lower-right corner of the Properties panel to display the lower section of the Properties panel.
10. **To play the animation, click the first keyframe and press Enter.**

Using shape hints for more control

When you create your first shape tween, you may find that Flash calculated the transformation differently than you imagined it. You can give Flash cues, called *shape hints,* that tell it which part of the original shape you want to move where, as you can see in Figure 5-5.

Figure 5-5: Shape hints show where you want points on your beginning shape to end up.

To use shape hints, follow these steps:

1. **Create a shape animation, using the steps in the section "Creating a simple shape tween," earlier in this chapter.**
2. **Click the first keyframe of the animation.**
3. **Choose Modify⇨Shape⇨Add Shape Hint or press Ctrl+Shift+H.**

   A small red circle with the letter "a" inside it appears on the Stage.
4. **Drag the shape hint to the area in your shape where you want the shape to transform to your settings.**

5. **Click the ending keyframe of the animation.**

   You again see a small circle with the letter "a" inside it on the Stage.

6. **Drag the shape hint to the area in your shape where you want the beginning hint to move.**

7. **Repeat Steps 3 through 6 to place additional shape hints.**

8. **Press Enter to play the animation and check the results.**

If you want, you can remove or hide existing shape hints:

- **To remove a shape hint:** Drag it off the Stage.
- **To display and hide shape hints:** Select the layer and keyframe with the shape hints and choose View➪Show Shape Hints.

Adding Basic Interactivity to Animation

You often need to control how your animation works. For example, you may want some animation to loop or to stop at a certain point. You may also want to enable viewers to control the animation. Buttons commonly allow users to stop the animation (perhaps some introductory animation for your Web site) or turn off the sound. You introduce interactivity and control by using ActionScript, the Flash programming language.

The following sections offer a few ideas for using ActionScript in animation. We cover interactivity in detail in Book V, Chapter 8.

Go To

You don't need to play your animation from beginning to end. You can add ActionScript (often simply called actions) to control the playing of the frames. The Go To action tells the movie to go to a different frame. At that point, you can tell the animation to stop or to play.

Say that you want your animation to play from Frame 1 to Frame 24, but then you want the last half to loop over and over again. On Frame 24, you can add a Go To action and tell Flash to go to Frame 12 and play. The animation goes to Frame 24 and then loops back to Frame 12 again. In this situation, the first 11 frames play only once, but Frames 12 through 24 play over and over in a loop.

In another situation, you may want animation to play from Frame 1 to Frame 24, and then go to Frame 50 and stop. You may be using Frame 50 to display a menu. In this case, you use the Go To and Stop actions.

Stop

Sometimes, you just want to stop the animation. For example, movie clips automatically loop. If you want them to play just once and then stop, you add a Stop action in the last frame. For any animation, you can add a Stop action at the end to make sure that everything stops at the same time.

Play

After you stop an animation, you may want to play it again. You can use the Play action to play a movie when certain conditions are met (a rollover or a click for example). If the conditions aren't met, the movie doesn't play (because of a Stop action).

On (mouse event)

You use the On action for buttons, which you can read more about in Book V, Chapter 3. To add interactivity, you specify what happens when the button is clicked or released, when a mouse cursor passes over or off the button, or when a mouse cursor is dragged over or off the button. For example, you may want to use the On action to specify that when the button is clicked, you go to a different frame or URL, such as another page on the Web site.

Working with Scenes

A *scene* is a section of an animation. You can divide your animation into scenes, each with its own Timeline. The scenes play back in the order you set. You create a scene to help you organize your animation. By default, you work in Scene 1. The current scene name appears beneath the Layer list. To create a new scene, choose Insert⇨Scene.

To manage your scenes, choose Window⇨Scene. The Scene panel opens, as you can see in Figure 5-6.

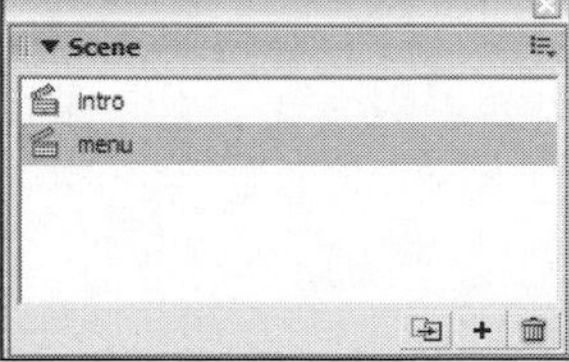

Figure 5-6: The Scene panel helps you manage scenes.

You can use the Scene panel to work with scenes in the following ways:

- **Change scene order:** Drag a scene's name in the Scene panel to a new location to change the order of the scenes.
- **Rename a scene:** Double-click a scene's name, type a new name, and press Enter to rename a scene.
- **Add a scene:** Click the Add Scene button at the bottom of the Scene panel to add a scene.
- **Delete a scene:** Select a scene and click the Delete Scene button at the bottom of the Scene panel to delete a scene.
- **Duplicate a scene:** Select a scene and click the Duplicate Scene button at the bottom of the Scene panel to create a copy of a scene.
- **View a scene:** Select the scene in the Scene panel to view the scene.

Chapter 6: Adding Sound and Video

In This Chapter

- ✓ **Introducing sound and video formats**
- ✓ **Working with sounds**
- ✓ **Working with video clips**

You can make the Web experience richer by adding sound and video to your Web pages. Sounds can range from a simple clicking noise when a user clicks a button to music and narration. You can also include video in your Web site.

Exploring Sound and Video Formats

Both sound and video files come in many formats. Before you can use sound or video, however, you need a file that Adobe Flash CS3 can import.

Sound file formats

Adobe Flash supports several sound formats. These are the most common:

- ✦ **AIFF:** This is the standard sound format for Macintosh computers. These files usually have filenames with the `.aif` or `.ief` extension.
- ✦ **WAV:** This is the standard format for Windows machines. These files usually have filenames with the `.wav` extension.
- ✦ **MP3:** This is a highly compressed format that maintains high-quality sound.

A sound file has several properties that affect its quality and size. You can often adjust these properties to reduce file size without noticeably affecting quality. For sophisticated adjustments, you probably need a sound-editing program, such as SoundForge. Here are the basic properties of a sound file:

- ✦ **Sample rate:** The *sample rate* is the number of times in kilohertz (kHz) that an audio signal is sampled when it's recorded digitally. A higher sample rate results in higher quality sound but also yields a larger file size.

- **Bit rate:** The *bit rate* is the number of bits (pieces of data) used for each audio sample. Sixteen-bit sounds are clearer, but 8-bit sounds are smaller and may be good enough for simple sounds, such as a button click.
- **Channels:** *Channels* are the number of streams of sound in a file and are either mono or stereo. Mono may be just fine and uses half the amount of data as stereo.

You can find a sound's properties when you import the sound into Flash, as explained in the section, "Importing sounds," later in this chapter.

Video file formats

The types of video formats you can use depend on some other software that supports their playback:

- **If you have QuickTime 4 or later installed:** You can import AVI, MPEG (MPG), MOV, and DV formats.
- **If you have DirectX 7 or later installed:** You can import AVI, MPEG (MPG), and WMV/ASF (Windows Media File) formats.

Because video files are usually very large, they are always compressed by using a *codec*. The word *codec* stands for *co*mpression/*dec*ompression. The same codec decompresses the video file when it is used. You need to have the codec that was used for the video file on your computer to be able to import the video file. The same applies to the audio track in a video file.

Working with Sounds

Working with sounds in Flash involves at least two steps: importing the sound and placing it in a movie. You can also do basic sound edits in Flash.

Importing sounds

To import a sound, follow these steps:

1. **Choose File⇨Import⇨Import to Library.**

   The Import dialog box appears.

2. **Select the sound file you want to import and click Open.**

   The sound goes into the Library.

To see a sound's properties, open the Library, right-click the sound, and choose Properties from the contextual menu that appears.

Placing a sound in a movie

After a sound is in the Library, you can place it in your movie. You need to decide when it starts, when it ends, or whether you want to loop the sound.

To place a sound, follow these steps:

1. **Create a new layer for the sound by choosing Insert⇨Timeline⇨Layer.**
2. **Right-click the frame and choose Insert Keyframe from the contextual menu.**

   This selection inserts a keyframe on the sound's layer where you want the sound to start.
3. **Press Ctrl+L to open the Library or choose Window⇨Library.**

   Scroll down to the sound file you're looking for in the Library.
4. **Drag the sound to the Stage.**

   The sound extends to the next keyframe, if one exists.
5. **To specify settings for the sound, open the Properties panel by choosing Window⇨Properties.**
6. **Expand the Properties panel, shown in Figure 6-1, using the Expand/Collapse arrow in the lower-right corner.**

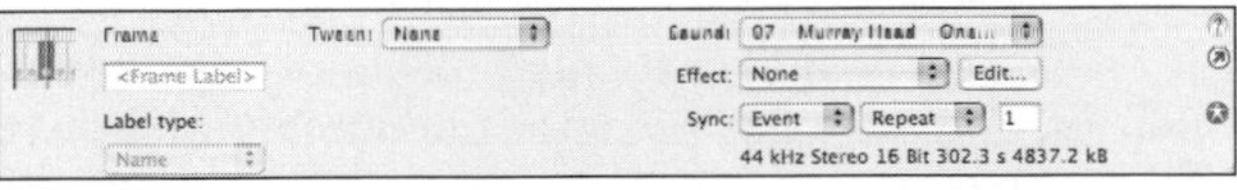

Figure 6-1: Specify sound settings.

7. **From the Sound drop-down list, choose the sound for which you want to specify settings.**

   All the sounds you have imported are listed.
8. **To create a special effect, select an effect from the Effect drop-down list.**

   You have the following choices:

   - **None:** No special effect (the default)
   - **Left channel:** Plays the sound from only the left speaker
   - **Right channel:** Plays the sound from only the right speaker
   - **Fade left to right:** Starts playing from the left speaker and moves to the right speaker

- **Fade right to left:** Starts playing from the right speaker and moves to the left speaker
- **Fade in:** Starts playing softly and increases the volume
- **Fade out:** Starts playing loudly and decreases the volume
- **Custom:** Plays a custom effect if you edit the sound, as explained in the next section

9. **Select a synchronization type from the Sync drop-down list.**

   You can choose from the following options:

   - **Event:** Plays the sound from its first keyframe until it ends (even if the movie stops), replays the sound whenever that keyframe plays, and downloads the entire sound before it plays. This choice is ideal for button sounds that you want to play whenever you click the button. Event is the default synchronization type.
   - **Start:** Plays the sound as the Event option does, but if the keyframe is replayed before the sound is finished, the Start option doesn't replay the sound.
   - **Stop:** Stops playing the sound.
   - **Stream:** Synchronizes the sound with the animation, shortening or lengthening the animation to match the length of the sound. Flash may skip frames if necessary.

10. **If you want to loop or repeat the sound, select either Loop or Repeat from the drop-down list beside it.**

    If you select Loop, the movie simply repeats over and over again. If you select Repeat, you are asked to enter the number of repeats in the field provided.

11. **Press Enter to play the animation and hear the sound.**

    Press Ctrl+Enter to test the movie if you're working on a complex animation.

Editing sounds

Flash contains its own simple sound-editing tool. For example, you can delete some of the beginning or end of the sound if you don't need it. You can also change the volume. To edit a sound, follow these steps:

1. **Click a frame that contains a sound.**
2. **Open the Properties panel by choosing Window⇨Properties.**

   If necessary, click the Collapse/Expand arrow at the lower-right corner to expand the Properties panel fully.

3. **Click the Edit button within the Properties panel.**

   The Edit Envelope dialog box, shown in Figure 6-2, appears. In this context, *envelope* just means the entire snippet of music.

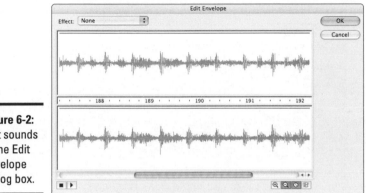

Figure 6-2: Edit sounds in the Edit Envelope dialog box.

You can edit the sound as follows:

- **Change the volume:** Drag an envelope handle up to increase volume or down to decrease volume. Click an envelope line to add a handle so that you can change the volume at that location.
- **Delete the beginning of the sound:** Drag the Time In control to the right.
- **Delete the end of the sound:** Scroll to the end of the sound and drag the Time Out control (the ending control) to the left.

You can use the Zoom In and Zoom Out buttons to change the magnification of the sound wave in the Edit Envelope dialog box. You can also use the Frames and Seconds buttons to change the display between frames and seconds.

Setting sound properties

You can control the properties of a sound to further compress it. If you need to specify different properties for different sounds, set the properties when you place the sound in your movie:

1. **Open the Library by choosing Window⇨Library or by pressing Ctrl+L.**
2. **Double-click the sound icon next to the sound for which you want to see the properties.**

   The Sound Properties dialog box, shown in Figure 6-3, appears.

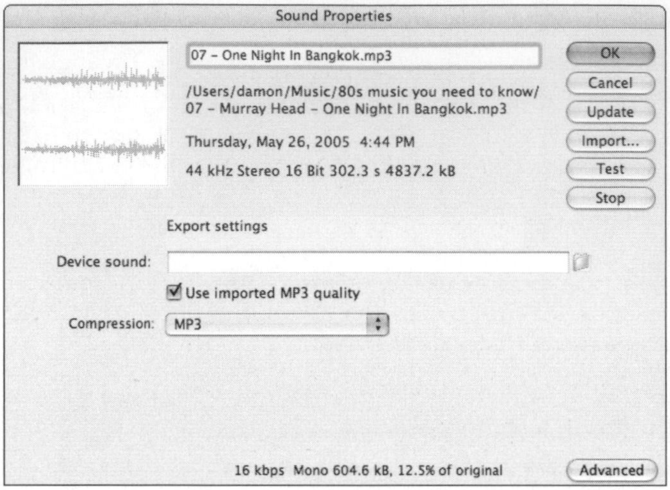

Figure 6-3: Set the properties for individual sounds in the Sound Properties dialog box.

The top part of the dialog box lists the sound's name, original location, and statistics. At the bottom of the dialog box, use the Compression drop-down list to select the file format you want:

- **Default:** Leaves the sound unchanged.
- **ADPCM:** Enables you to convert stereo to mono and to choose a sampling rate and bit rate. This option is used for short sounds.
- **MP3:** Enables you to convert stereo to mono and to choose a bit rate and quality. MP3 is an efficient compression method and is used for longer, more complex sounds, especially music.
- **Raw:** Enables you to convert stereo to mono and to choose the sampling rate. Raw uses no compression.
- **Speech:** Enables you to choose a sampling rate. This option uses compression specially designed for speech.

As you choose an option, you see the resulting statistics at the bottom of the dialog box.

3. **Click the Test button to hear the result of your choice.**

You can also set sound properties for all sounds at once when you publish your movie. (See Book V, Chapter 7.)

Working with Video Clips

In Adobe Flash CS3, you can embed video clips in your Flash movie. A video clip can be live action or animation created with an animation program that outputs a video file format. ***Note:*** Flash may not be able to handle very long video files. You also have no direct control over the video frames.

To use a video, follow these steps:

1. **Select a keyframe already on your Timeline (or create a new keyframe by right-clicking a frame and choosing Insert Keyframe from the contextual menu that appears).**
2. **Choose File⇨Import⇨Import Video.**

   The Import dialog box appears, as shown in Figure 6-4.

Figure 6-4: Use the Import Video window to get video into your Flash movie.

3. **Click the Browse button to select the video you'd like to import.**

   Browse to the movie you'd like to import and then select Open. The location of the movie to import will appear in the File path field.
4. **Click Continue to continue the movie import process.**
5. **Select a compression profile.**

You can select from one of the five compression algorithms that Flash offers by selecting it from the drop-down list, or you can create your own by selecting the Create Your Own Profile option.

6. **To choose the frequency of keyframes in the video clip, drag the Keyframe Interval slider.**

   A *video* keyframe is separate from a *Timeline* keyframe. A *video* keyframe stores the entire image data as compared to the changes from the previous frame that are stored in regular frames.

   A keyframe interval of 0 adds a single keyframe at the beginning of the video stream and no other keyframes.

7. **Select the Synchronize Video to Flash Document Frame Rate option to match the video frame rate to the Flash movie frame rate.**

   If your video display is poor, try deselecting this option.

8. **From the Number of Video Frames to Encode per Number of Flash Frames drop-down list, select a ratio.**

   The default is 1:1, which plays one video frame for each Flash frame. A ratio of 1:2 plays one video frame for every two Flash frames. A 1:2 or higher ratio reduces file size but reduces smoothness of playback as well.

9. **Click Finish.**

   If the video clip is longer than the span of keyframes into which you are placing the video, a message appears, asking whether you want to add enough frames necessary to play the entire clip.

10. **Click Yes to add the frames.**

Chapter 7: Publishing Movies

In This Chapter

- Publishing movies the easy way
- Optimizing movies for speedy download times
- Generating HTML and graphics

After you finish creating your Flash document, you need to publish it in SWF movie format. You then use HTML code to insert the SWF movie in a Web page so that browsers can display the animation. In this chapter, we explain how to place your animation onto your Web site.

Publishing Movies the Simple Way

If you don't need to change any settings, you can immediately publish your file by choosing File⇨Publish. For more control, choose File⇨Publish Settings to open the Publish Settings dialog box, as shown in Figure 7-1.

By default, Adobe Flash CS3 creates two files: the SWF file and an HTML file that contains the HTML code needed for your Web page. You can also export your document to other formats by selecting the format you want on the Formats tab. We discuss the HTML code and other export formats in the "Generating HTML and Graphics" section, later in this chapter.

Flash creates all these files by using the name of your Flash document and tacking on various filename extensions.

To post your movie on your Web site, you use the HTML code either by itself or within another Web page. Then you upload both the Web page and the SWF file as you would any other Web page and image.

Flash has many more options for you to tweak. To set these options, click the other tabs of the Publish Settings dialog box and select the options you want before clicking the Publish button.

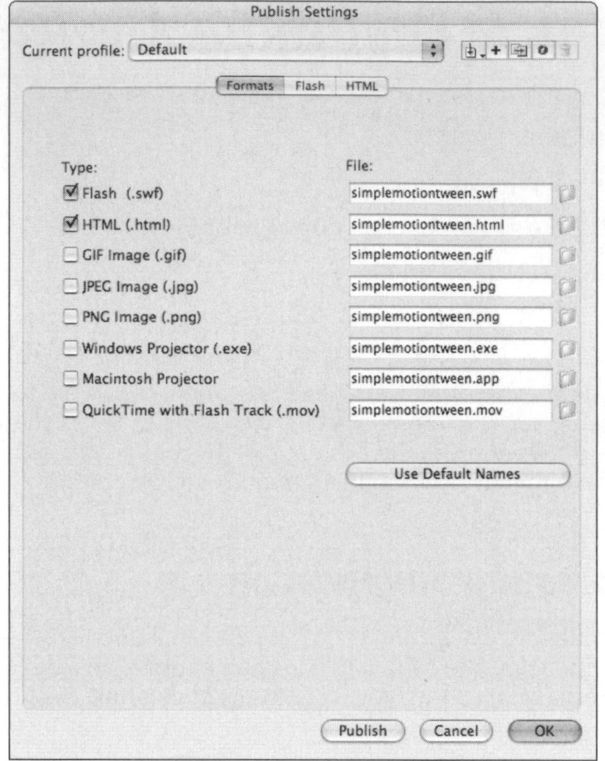

Figure 7-1: Use the Publish Settings dialog box to publish your movies.

Click the Flash tab, shown in Figure 7-2, to see the options for creating the SWF file. You can set the following options:

- **Version:** Saves in previous version formats for backward compatibility.
- **Load Order:** Controls the loading order of layers in your document for the first frame (which usually takes the longest to display).

  Changing the load order can affect how your ActionScript code functions.

- **ActionScript Version:** Enables you to select the version of ActionScript you want to run in your movie. You can click the Settings button to specify the classes to be exported if you select ActionScript 2.0 from the drop-down list.
- **Generate Size Report:** Creates a text file that details the size of the frames of your movie so that you can make adjustments if a movie is loading slowly.

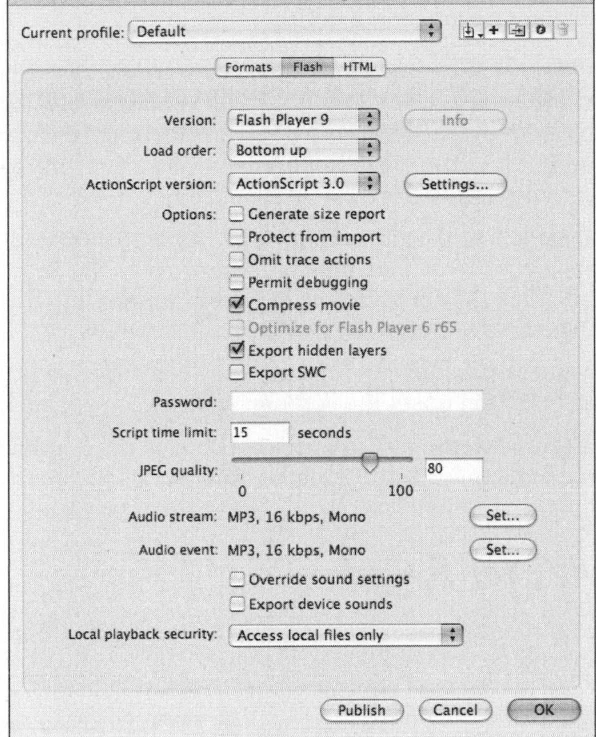

Figure 7-2: Use the Flash tab of the Publish Settings dialog box to set options for the SWF movie file.

- **Protect from Import:** Helps prevent the SWF file from being imported into an FLA file that others can then modify.

  Never trust that your SWF is completely safe. Tools to undo this option are available on the Web.

- **Omit Trace Actions:** Reduces file size by deleting trace actions if you used them in your ActionScript to help you debug your code.

- **Permit Debugging:** Enables you to use the Flash Debugger feature to debug errors in ActionScript.

  The debugger allows you to troubleshoot ActionScript problems from within your browser. You can protect this feature by using a password.

- **Compress Movie:** Compresses your Flash document, especially text and ActionScript. ***Note:*** This feature is compatible only with the Flash Player 6 or later.

- **Optimize for Flash Player 6 r65:** This feature optimizes your movie for playback on the Flash Player 6 or the 6.5 revision.

- **Password:** Enables you to enter a password for debugging so that those without the password cannot debug your movie.
- **Script Time Limits:** Allows you to set a timeout for how long your ActionScripts can run in your application before they give up and decide to display an error message.
- **JPEG Quality:** Sets the quality of bitmaps. Higher quality looks better but means a larger file size.
- **Audio Stream:** Sets the audio compression for all streaming sounds in the movie, if you haven't set individual settings in the Sound Properties dialog box. Click the Set button to set the compression. See Book V, Chapter 6 for more information on streaming sounds.
- **Audio Event:** Sets audio compression for all event sounds in the movie. Click the Set button to set the compression.
- **Override Sound Settings:** Overrides settings in the Sound Properties dialog box and applies settings here to all sounds in your movie.

Optimizing Movies for Speed

As you work, be sure to always design for fast display on a Web site. You can't control the speed of your viewers' Internet connections or how fast their computers' processors are, but you can definitely control the size of your movie file. Before you publish your document, you may want to look it over from within Flash and see how you can make it more efficient. After you publish and test the movie on a Web page, you may find that you need to make some adjustments for faster download. The following four sections offer some tips for optimizing your movies for speedy display.

Simplifying graphics

You can simplify the graphics in your movie and greatly increase its speed. Here are some pointers:

- **Use tweened animation:** Tweened animation is faster than frame-by-frame animation. (See Book V, Chapter 5.)
- **Don't animate bitmaps:** Flash needs to store the location of each pixel in a bitmap, and that storage information greatly increases file size. In fact, avoid bitmaps altogether as much as possible.
- **Turn everything into symbols:** Even backgrounds should be symbols. You can also put symbols inside of symbols. (See Book V, Chapter 3 for details on creating symbols.)
- **Group objects:** Groups also reduce file size.

- **Optimize curves:** Optimizing curves reduces the number of lines in your graphics. (See Book V, Chapter 2.)
- **Use solid lines:** Avoid dashed and dotted lines. Especially avoid custom lines.
- **Use the Pencil tool rather than the Brush tool:** The Brush tool requires your document to store more information.
- **Use the Web-safe color palette:** Avoid custom colors.
- **Use solid fills rather than gradients as much as possible:** Gradients are more complex to calculate.
- **Avoid transparency:** As much as possible, avoid using alpha values of less than 100 percent.

Optimizing text

Text takes up more bytes in your file than vector graphics. Here are some options for reducing the load:

- **Reduce the number of fonts:** Use simpler fonts, fewer font styles (bold, italic), and fewer fonts overall. Use device fonts (Verdana, Arial, Times, and Courier) if possible.

  The device fonts display correctly in any browser and on any computer.
- **Put text into your HTML document:** Not all text needs to be in your Flash document. If you put some of your text in HTML format, you get faster download times.

Minimizing the size of sound files

Sound and music can really hog up the download stream. (See Book V, Chapter 6 for details about working with sounds.) You can use the following techniques to minimize the size of sounds:

- **Compress sounds:** Use the Sound Properties dialog box (right-click the sound in the Library and choose Properties from the contextual menu) to fine-tune settings for individual sounds, or compress sounds by using the sound settings (Audio Stream and Audio Event) on the Flash tab of the Publish Settings dialog box, described earlier in this chapter. Use the MP3 format whenever possible.
- **Remove silent areas:** Edit sounds to remove unnecessary beginnings and endings by adjusting the Time In and Time Out controls.
- **Reuse sounds:** You can reuse a sound with different in and out points or loop different parts of the same sound.
- **Don't loop streaming sound:** Looping is not necessary, and the browser continually downloads streaming sound.

Testing download time

Flash can simulate various Internet connection speeds and give you feedback on which frames may cause a delay in download time. Don't miss out on this excellent tool. If the results indicate delays, go back and adjust your movie until the display is quick. You don't want to lose your Web site visitors because they become impatient while waiting for your Flash movie to download! Follow these steps to test your movie's download time:

1. **Choose Control➪Test Movie.**
2. **From the menu bar of the new window, choose View➪Download Settings and choose a download speed.**
3. **From the menu bar of the new window, choose View➪Bandwidth Profiler.**

   The Bandwidth Profiler is shown in Figure 7-3.

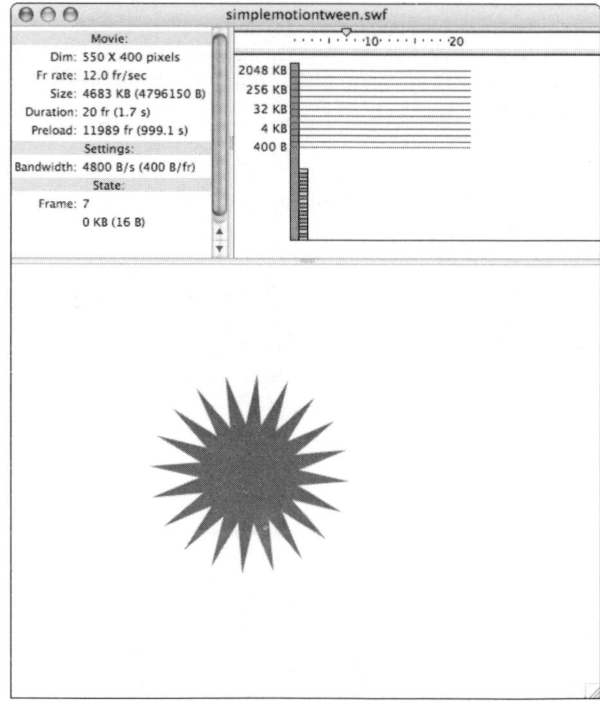

Figure 7-3: Use the Bandwidth Profiler to show the frames that are displayed slowly on a Web site.

4. **Choose View⇨Simulate Download to simulate playing the animation over an Internet connection.**

   Watch for any jerkiness and listen for any breaks in the sound.

5. **Choose View⇨Streaming Graph to see all the frames that may cause delays or View⇨Frame by Frame Graph to see the size of each frame.**

   These are just two ways of viewing the information. You can use either view. Click on any bar (which represents a frame) to see the information for that frame. Frames that extend above the red horizontal line may cause a delay in the display of the movie.

6. **Choose File⇨Close to close the movie-testing tools.**

A short delay in the first frame is often acceptable as Flash downloads all the information. After the first frame, try to avoid any delays because they result in pauses or uneven animation.

Although the best solution is to minimize delays, another possible choice is a preloader, a short animation that plays repeatedly while the main animation is loading. If you want your viewers to get to your movie quickly, work to reduce file size rather than use a preloader. If the artistry and special effects are primary, use a preloader.

Generating HTML and Graphics

When you publish your Flash document, you also generate the HTML code that you need to create a Web page that plays your animation. You can also export your movie in several other graphic and animation formats.

Creating HTML code

You can use the HTML code that Flash generates to create a new Web page that contains nothing but your movie, or you can insert the HTML code into an existing Web page that may contain many other components. On the HTML tab of the Publish Settings dialog box, you can specify the following settings:

- **Template:** Specifies the content of the HTML file. The Flash Only (the default) option includes only `<OBJECT>` and `<EMBED>` tags. Other templates add code to detect earlier Flash Players or offer other features. To see what each template does and which formats you need to choose, select the template and click the Info button.
- **Dimensions:** Controls the size of the movie in the browser. The default option, Match Movie, matches the width and height of your Stage. You can also specify the size in pixels or by percent.

- **Playback: Paused at Start:** Pauses the movie until your viewer clicks a button (that you have coded to start the movie) or right-clicks and chooses Play. By default, this option is off, so the movie plays automatically.
- **Playback: Loop:** Repeats the movie over and over. By default, this option is on.
- **Playback: Display Menu:** Displays a contextual menu if viewers right-click. The menu allows viewers to play, loop, and print the movie. However, not all viewers know that this contextual menu exists. This option is on by default.
- **Playback: Device Font:** Substitutes anti-aliased fonts (that look smoother) for fonts not available on the user's computer. This option is not selected by default.
- **Quality:** Sets the quality of playback. Choose one of the following:
  - **Low:** Uses no anti-aliasing (smoothing)
  - **Auto Low:** Starts at low quality and switches to the highest quality that the user's computer (detected by the Flash Player) can handle
  - **Auto High:** Starts at high quality and switches to a lower quality if the user's computer (detected by the Flash Player) cannot handle high quality
  - **Medium:** Uses some anti-aliasing but doesn't smooth bitmaps
  - **High:** Uses anti-aliasing for everything except tweened bitmaps (the default)
  - **Best:** Uses anti-aliasing for text, unanimated bitmaps, and tweened bitmaps
- **Window Mode:** Specifies how the movie's window relates to the rest of the page on the PC. Choose Window (a separate window), Opaque (an opaque background), or Transparent (a transparent background).
- **HTML Alignment:** Aligns the movie in the browser window. You can choose Default (centered), Left, Right, Top, or Bottom.
- **Scale:** Specifies how the movie is placed in its boundaries when you use the Pixels or Percent option of the Dimensions setting and the width and height are therefore different from the movie's original size. The choices are Default (Show All), No Border, Exact Fit, and No Scale.
- **Flash Alignment:** Specifies how the movie fits in the movie window (not the browser window). The Horizontal setting can be Left, Center, or Right. The Vertical setting can be Top, Center, or Bottom.
- **Show Warning Message:** Displays warning messages if problems occur during publishing.

Creating graphic files

You can create GIF, JPEG, and PNG graphics files from a frame of your Flash movie. Each type of graphics file has its own options. By default, Flash creates the image from your first frame.

To add a label to a frame, click the frame and open the Properties panel (choose Window⇨Properties). Expand the Properties panel by using the Collapse/Expand arrow at the bottom-right corner. Type the label name in the Frame text field. You can name a frame anything you want. Certain names, such as the #Static label, have specific meanings for the way Flash functions.

GIF files

GIF files have limited colors but allow transparency. Select the GIF check box on the Formats tab of the Publish Settings dialog box. When you do that, a GIF tab appears. Then click the GIF tab, where you have the following settings:

- **Dimensions:** Enables you to select the Match Movie option to match the size of the Stage. To use a different size, deselect the Match Movie option and type the new dimensions.
- **Playback:** Enables you to select either the Static (a single image) or Animated (an animated GIF of the entire movie) option. If you select Animated, you can choose to loop continuously or repeat a specified number of times.
- **Options:** Offers several options. Choose from the following:
  - **Optimize Colors:** Removes unused colors
  - **Interlace:** Loads in increments of greater resolution (starting from fuzzy)
  - **Smooth:** Anti-aliases the artwork
  - **Remove Gradients:** Removes gradients from the GIF images
  - **Dither Solids:** Approximates colors not available on the GIF color palette
- **Transparent:** Allows you to set transparency (alpha) of the background.
- **Dither:** Defines the type of *dithering,* which is the approximation of a color from a mixture of other colors when the desired color is not available. You can choose Ordered dithering, which provides good-quality dithering without much increase in file size, or you can choose Diffusion dithering, which provides top-quality dithering for the 216 Web-safe colors but makes for a larger file size.

- **Palette Type:** Defines the GIF color palette. If you choose an adaptive palette, a unique color palette is created for the GIF. You can then choose the maximum number of colors. If you choose a custom palette, click the ellipsis button and choose a palette file. To save a palette of colors that you use in Flash, choose Window➪Color Swatches, click the Options menu icon in the upper-right corner of the Color Swatches panel, and choose Save Colors.

JPEG files

JPEG files allow for many colors but do not allow transparency. They decompress when downloaded, taking up more memory. Select the JPEG check box on the Formats tab of the Publish Settings dialog box. Then click the JPEG tab (it appears after you select the JPEG check box), where you have the following settings:

- **Dimensions:** Enables you to match the size of the Stage or specify another size.
- **Quality:** Enables you to choose the quality. Higher quality means a better picture but a larger file size.
- **Progressive:** Displays the JPEG file in increments of greater resolution (starting from fuzzy) as it downloads in a browser.

PNG files

PNG files offer many colors and transparency, too. Select the PNG check box on the Formats tab of the Publish Settings dialog box. Then click the PNG tab (it appears after you select the PNG check box), where you have the following settings:

- **Dimensions:** Enables you to match the size of the Stage or specify another size.
- **Bit Depth:** Controls the number of colors the image can contain and the availability of transparency (alpha). More colors — and more transparency — increase the file size.
- **Options:** Offers several options. Choose from the following:
  - **Optimize Colors:** Removes unused colors.
  - **Interlace:** Loads the PNG file in increments of greater resolution (starting from fuzzy).
  - **Smooth:** Anti-aliases the artwork.
  - **Remove Gradients:** Removes gradients from the PNG images.

- **Dither Solids:** Approximates colors not available on the GIF color palette. This option is the same as for GIF images (explained previously).

✦ **Dither:** Enables you to use the same Dither settings as for GIF images, if you choose an 8-bit depth. This option is not available for other bit depths.

✦ **Palette Type:** Enables you to use the same Dither settings as for GIF images, if you choose an 8-bit depth.

✦ **Max Colors:** Same as for GIF images.

✦ **Palette:** Same as for GIF images.

✦ **Filter Options:** Determines the method of compression (the method of combining pixels in an image). Choose from the following options:

- **None:** No compression
- **Sub:** Filters adjoining pixel bytes, going horizontally
- **Up:** Filters vertically
- **Average:** Uses both horizontal and vertical
- **Path:** Creates an algorithm using the three nearest pixels to predict the next pixel
- **Adaptive:** Provides the most accurate colors

Creating QuickTime movies

QuickTime is a video format that plays on the QuickTime player. To use QuickTime movies, you need to have QuickTime 4 or higher installed.

Select the QuickTime check box on the Formats tab of the Publish Settings dialog box. Click the QuickTime tab that appears, where you have the following settings:

✦ **Dimensions:** Enables you to match the size of the Stage or specify another size.

✦ **Alpha:** Sets the transparency of the Flash track within the QuickTime movie, if you have combined a QuickTime movie with a Flash movie. A QuickTime movie can contain a separate layer with the Flash movie. The Auto option makes the Flash track transparent only if it is on top of other tracks. The Alpha-transparent option always makes the Flash track transparent. The Copy option makes the Flash track opaque, hiding all content behind it.

- **Layer:** Specifies how the Flash track is layered with the QuickTime content. Choose from Auto (Flash track on top if Flash content appears in front; otherwise on the bottom), Top (Flash track on top), or Bottom (Flash track at the bottom).
- **Streaming Sound:** Enables you to control how streaming sound is used with QuickTime content. Select the Use QuickTime Compression check box to export sound to a QuickTime soundtrack. Click Setting to specify how the sound is compressed.
- **Controller:** Creates a control panel to play the movie. Choose None if you have created your own controller or don't want viewers to have any control. The Standard option displays the QuickTime controller. The QuickTime VR option offers special panoramic and 3D viewing features.
- **Playback:** Enables you to control movie playback. Select the Loop check box to repeat the movie, the Paused At Start check box to let viewers use the Controller to start the movie, or the Play Every Frame check box to disable skipping frames and sound to maintain timing.
- **File:** Enables you to determine how files are referenced. The Flatten (Make Self-Contained) option combines the Flash movie with imported content into a QuickTime movie. If you don't select the Flatten check box, the QuickTime movie references the Flash SWF file.

Creating self-playing movies

Self-playing movies are called *projectors.* A projector doesn't require a separate Flash Player and is ideal when you are putting a Flash movie on a CD-ROM. To create a projector, select the Windows Projector or the Macintosh Projector check box on the Formats tab of the Publish Settings dialog box. Then click the Publish button. The result is a file with an `.exe` extension (for PCs) or an `.hqx` extension (for Macs). The projector file is larger than an SWF file, but users can download it from a Web site and play it without needing the Flash Player.

Exporting movies and images

Export a movie or image, instead of publishing it, when you need to use it in another application. For example, you can export a frame as a GIF file and insert it into a PowerPoint presentation. If you already have the HTML code and just want to update an SWF file, you can export instead of publish. To export a movie, or frame, just follow these steps:

1. **Select the frame you want to export, if you are exporting an image.**
2. **Choose File⇨Export⇨Export Image or File⇨Export⇨Export Movie.**

3. Type a name for the image or movie in the File Name field.

4. From the Save as Type drop-down list, select a file type.

5. Click Save.

A dialog box may appear if the format you choose has settings that you can specify. These settings are the same as you have when you publish a file and are explained in the "Generating HTML and Graphics" section, earlier in this chapter. You can export the following file types:

- ✦ Adobe Illustrator (`.ai`)
- ✦ Encapsulated PostScript (`.eps`)
- ✦ Drawing Exchange Format (`.dxf`)
- ✦ Windows Bitmap (`.bmp`)
- ✦ Metafile (`.emf`/`.wmf`)
- ✦ FutureSplash Player (`.spl`)
- ✦ Graphics Interchange File (`.gif`)
- ✦ Joint Photographic Experts Group (`.jpeg`/`.jpg`)
- ✦ QuickTime (`.mov`)
- ✦ PICT Sequence (`.pct`)
- ✦ Portable Network Graphic (`.png`)
- ✦ Video for Windows (`.avi`)
- ✦ Windows Audio (only) (`.wav`)

Chapter 8: Using Flash's Components

In This Chapter

- ✔ **Understanding components**
- ✔ **Inserting components**

Adobe Flash CS3 is not limited to creating animation. You can use Flash to develop an entire interface, including buttons, menus, forms, scrollbars, and more. Flash includes a set of interface elements called components that you can use to efficiently add interfaces and interactivity to your Web site. In this chapter, we show how you can use components and create forms with Flash.

Flash can create very innovative interfaces. As long as you keep your Flash interfaces user friendly and easy to understand, your viewers will appreciate the new look and feel. Scrollbars created with Flash are a lot cooler than the ones created with conventional HTML editors because you can customize how they look and function. Creating scrollbars and other interface elements for your Web page with Flash may actually be easier than with other, more complex programming environments. Some of these techniques, however, require a bit of ActionScript programming to make them fully functional.

Components are actually movie clip symbols that contain a set of defined parameters and properties. (For an explanation of movie clip symbols, see Book V, Chapter 3.) You can specify the values of these parameters and properties when you create your Flash document. Using these components ensures that your interface items work together and in a similar manner. Because of the programming that has been done in advance to create the parameters and properties, you need to do less programming for each Flash document you create.

You can customize the appearance of components to match the rest of your Web site's style. If you know some ActionScript, you can even create your own components, and you can find components that Flash developers have created on Flash resource Web sites.

Adding Components

A component can be as simple as a check box or as complex as an entire graphical user interface. The following list represents the basic set of components included in Adobe Flash CS3. There are several other components, many of which are native to ActionScript 3.0. For the purposes of this book, however, we focus on the essential ones, most of which are designed for ActionScript 1.0 and 2.0. (You can find them in the User Interface section of the Components panel.)

- **Button:** A simple button within the movie that performs some action.
- **Radio buttons:** Radio buttons are small round buttons. Users can select one choice from several options.
- **Check boxes:** Users can select or deselect each check box.
- **Push buttons:** Clicking a button makes something happen, like a button symbol in Flash. (See Book V, Chapter 3 for more information on working with buttons.)
- **Combo boxes:** Combo boxes provide drop-down lists.
- **List boxes:** List boxes enable you to offer users a scrolling list of choices.
- **Scroll panes:** Scroll panes enable you to create scrollable windows for movie clips.
- **Label:** A label is a simple one-line text descriptor that accompanies a field.
- **ProgressBar:** This handy component shows your viewers a growing percentage bar that represents the progress of a file being loaded.
- **TextArea:** This multiline text area can accept text inputs.
- **TextInput:** Unlike the multiline text area, the TextInput is a single line of text.
- **Numeric Stepper:** This handy component is great for drop-down-like lists. Use it to make lists of numbers that can be incremented or decremented depending on the keystroke.
- **Window:** The Window component creates a window within your Flash movie. This window can have a specific size, as well as header text and even a Close button.

The procedure for working with a component is similar for all the components. However, individual items vary. The general procedure is as follows:

1. **Open the Components panel by choosing Window⇨Components.**

   The Components panel is shown in Figure 8-1.

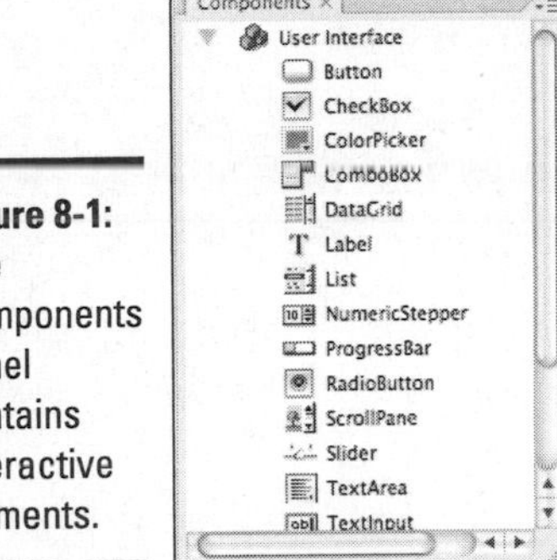

Figure 8-1: The Components panel contains interactive elements.

2. **Drag one of the components onto the Stage.**
3. **With the component still selected, open the Properties panel, if it isn't open already, by choosing Window➪Properties.**

   If the Properties panel is open but collapsed, click the Expand/Collapse arrow on its title bar.
4. **Click the Parameters tab.**

   The Properties panel with the Parameters tab displayed is shown in Figure 8-2.

Figure 8-2: The Properties panel when a radio button component is selected.

5. **In the Instance Name text field of the Parameters panel, type an instance name.**

   Remember that an instance is a single iteration of a symbol. By naming each instance of the component, you can refer to it in your ActionScript.
6. **Set the parameters for the component in the Properties panel by clicking each parameter and entering the value in the field to its right.**

Repeat this procedure with all the components. The individual requirements of the components are listed in the next several sections.

Use the Align panel, which you access by choosing Window⇨Align, to line up and evenly distribute a series of components, such as radio buttons or check boxes.

You can resize components using the Free Transform tool, but they are not all infinitely flexible. For example, you can change the width of a check box, but not its height.

Check boxes

The CheckBox component allows users to select one or more choices from a list. Each item on the list has a small box next to it that has a check inside when the user clicks the box. The CheckBox component has the following parameters:

- **Label:** This parameter determines the text that is attached to the component.
- **LabelPlacement:** This parameter places the text relative to the rest of the component. You can choose Left or Right.
- **Selected:** This parameter, when set to true, shows that your check box is already selected when the page is first viewed.

Radio buttons

Radio buttons are like check boxes, except that users can select only one at a time in any group of radio buttons. When a radio button is selected, it has a dot inside its circle. The RadioButton component has the following parameters:

- **Label:** This parameter determines the text that is attached to the component.
- **Selected:** This initial state parameter determines if a radio button is initially selected.
- **Group Name:** This parameter enables you to create independent groups of radio buttons. Say that you want to poll your users to see whether they like to swim and like to run. You want a Yes or a No for each. To create such groups of radio buttons, enter a Group Name parameter. Users can select one radio button in each group. For example, if you have four radio buttons, you can put two into a group named Swim and two into a group named Run. You can then label buttons Yes and No in

each group and ask users "Do you like to swim?" for the buttons in the Swim group and "Do you like to run?" for the buttons in the Run group. Users can then answer Yes or No to each question.

- **Data:** The Data parameter stores data related to a button. For example, if you want to know whether a user selected the radio button named Yes, you can put Yes in the Data field and use ActionScript to execute an action (perhaps go to a specific Web page) if a user selected the Yes radio button.
- **LabelPlacement:** This parameter places the text relative to the rest of the component.

Push buttons

Push buttons are similar to the buttons you create in Flash. The main reason to use push button components is to create a consistent look with other components. However, the included parameters may make them quicker to use and require less code. They have a Label parameter that places text on the button and a Click Handler that uses a function you write to specify what happens when a user clicks the button.

Combo boxes

A combo box is a menu list of items with a scrollbar to its right. Users can scroll through the list of items and choose one.

As do radio buttons, combo boxes have change handler and data parameters. You add the labels for the list items in the Parameters tab as follows:

1. **With the combo box selected, open the Properties panel, if it isn't open already, by choosing Window⇨Properties. Alternatively, click the Expand/Collapse arrow on the Properties panel's title bar.**
2. **Click the Parameter tab.**
3. **Click the magnifying glass icon next to the dataProvider field, which opens the Values dialog box.**

   The Values dialog box is shown in Figure 8-3.
4. **To add a new list item, click the plus (+) sign and type the label.**

   You can click any label to edit it.
5. **When you're done, click OK.**

The Editable parameter in the Parameter list specifies whether the combo box is editable. If this parameter is set to true, users can enter text to search for a matching item. If it is set to false, users can only select an item.

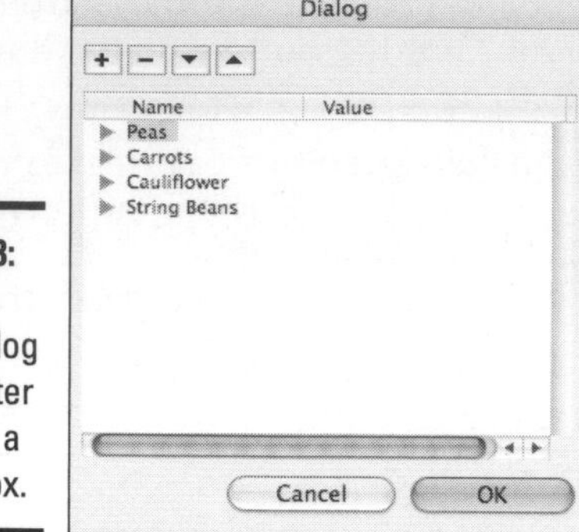

Figure 8-3: Use the Value dialog box to enter labels for a combo box.

The Row Count parameter in the Parameter list determines how many items must be in the combo box before the scrollbar is displayed. The default is eight items.

List boxes

A list box is like a combo box, except that (unlike a combo box) users cannot edit it and they can select multiple items. To allow this capability, set the Select Multiple parameter to true. You add the labels as described in the "Combo boxes" section.

Scroll panes

Scroll panes are rather unusual. They allow you to put movie clips (and only movie clips) inside a scrollable pane. The advantage is to display large movies or images without taking up a lot of space. No programming is necessary. The movie clip must be in the Library, but it doesn't need to be on the Stage.

Label

The Label component is perhaps the simplest of the components in that it is not dynamic in any way. It is simply a label for another form element. That said, some settings can be applied to a label. You can align the text within the label by selecting an autoSize option. You can also specify whether the label will be HTML text by selecting true or false from the HTML option.

Loader

The Loader component allows you to load an SWF movie or a JPEG within a Flash movie, effectively allowing you to play a movie within a movie. You can specify only a few options for this component:

- Set autoload to true to let Flash load the movie for you in the keyframe where the movie begins.
- Provide a path to the SWF or JPEG file to be loaded using the contentPath field.
- Allow the movie to be scaled up or down by setting the scaleContent property to true.

When you render the movie, Flash renders not only your movie but also the one you've pointed to with the Loader component.

TextArea

The TextArea component creates, as you might expect, a text area on the screen. Four simple options apply to this component. To take advantage of this component, simply drag an instance of it from the Components panel onto the Stage. Here's what you can specify using parameters in the Properties panel:

- Make the text box editable (meaning you can type in it on-screen) by selecting true from the Editable property field.
- If you want the box to be in HTML format, select true from the HTML property field. For ease of use, you probably want to keep this property set to false.
- If you want the field to be prefilled with text, input some text in the Text property field.
- Finally, if you want to use word wrap, be sure to select true in the wordWrap property field.

TextInput

Much like the TextArea component, the TextInput component allows viewers to input text on the screen. Again, you add it to your document by dragging an instance of it from the Components panel onto the Stage. In the Properties panel, you can set the following parameters:

- Make the text box editable (meaning you can type in it on-screen) by selecting true from the Editable property field.
- If you want the text field to be a password field, meaning that only **** shows up instead of characters, select true from the Password property field. The default value is true.
- If you want the field to be prefilled with text, input some text in the Text property field.

NumericStepper

The NumericStepper component can be handy when you have lists that have incremental numeric values in them. Essentially, this component creates a list that you can cycle either up or down by using arrows. To use a NumericStepper, simply drag it from the Components panel onto the Stage. There, you can specify the following through the Properties panel:

- ✦ To set the maximum value of the NumericStepper, input an integer in the Maximum property field.
- ✦ To set the minimum value of the NumericStepper, input an integer in the Minimum property field.
- ✦ Input an integer in the StepSize property field. It determines how big the increments are from step to step.
- ✦ In the Value property field, input the initial value of the NumericStepper.

Window

Another interesting tool for adding some cool interactivity to your interface is the Window component. This component adds a window to your Flash movie. This feature can be useful if you're zooming in or loading a picture in your movie. You create a window by dragging it from the Components panel onto the Stage. Then you can specify the following:

- ✦ If you want to be able to close the window, select true from the CloseButton property field.
- ✦ To load a picture into the window, provide a path to the image in the contentPath property field.
- ✦ If you want the window to have a text title, enter it in the Title property field.

Setting component properties

You can set the color and text properties of a component by using ActionScript. You can also globally set properties of all the components in your movie. Finally, you can create *skins,* graphic elements that affect how components look. These methods are beyond the scope of this book. For more information, see Flash Help.

Book VI

Contribute CS3

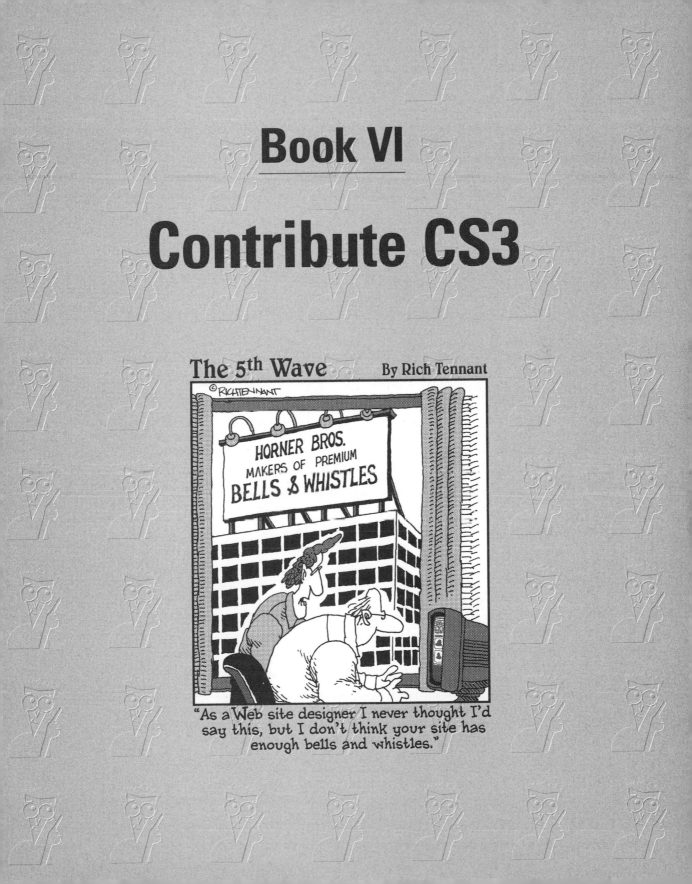

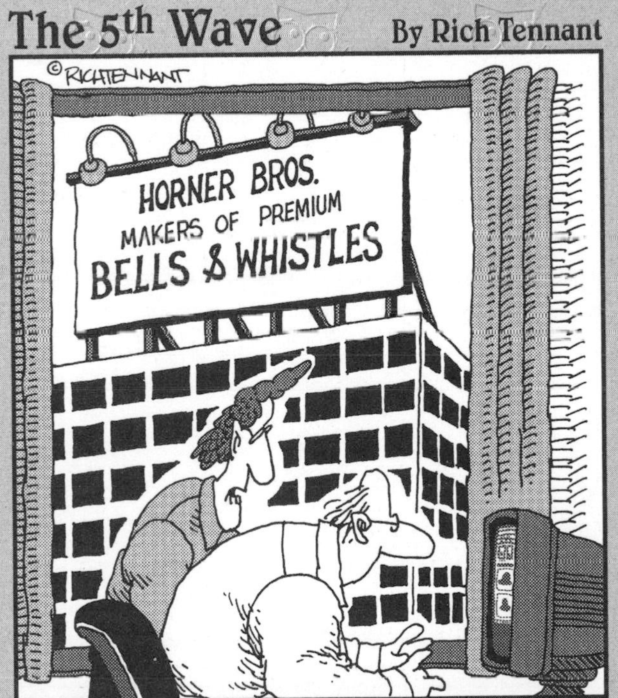

"As a Web site designer I never thought I'd say this, but I don't think your site has enough bells and whistles."

Chapter 1: Introduction to Contribute CS3

In This Chapter

- **Deciding when to use Contribute**
- **Checking out the Contribute interface**
- **Setting your preferences**

For many big Internet and intranet sites these days, Web development experts are the authors (that is, they design and build it from scratch, or at least set up its basic framework). After a site is established, it may then need to grow and change — which in the past meant calling in that handy Web development expert again to update a Web site. Now, however, people more familiar with the content that needs to go on the site than with the vagaries of Web development are being asked to take on the responsibility of updating the original pages or adding new pages based on existing designs.

The original version of Dreamweaver was built to enable people to create and modify Web pages without having to learn the boring ins and outs of HTML. The funny thing is that Dreamweaver CS3 has become so powerful as an authoring tool that for many day-to-day editors and authors of Web sites, Dreamweaver offers far more functionality than is required.

So what's a nonexpert to do? Read on to discover the answer.

Why Contribute?

When Dreamweaver is too much, Contribute is just right. Contribute is designed especially for people who must contribute to an existing site but don't need to know how to develop a site from scratch.

Contribute is streamlined to make Web page production as simple as possible, which means that the application can't do many things, such as edit the HTML making up the page. (However, Contribute CS3 can be set up to allow specified users to launch and edit HTML in Dreamweaver.) For those kinds of tasks, you definitely still need Dreamweaver. Table 1-1 offers a list of some common Web page tasks for which each application can be used.

Table 1-1 Comparing the Capabilities of Dreamweaver and Contribute

Task	*Dreamweaver*	*Contribute*
Creating a new page from scratch	X	x
Creating a new page from a Dreamweaver template	X	x
Creating a Dreamweaver template	X	
Viewing and editing the underlying HTML code directly	X	
Adding, deleting, and modifying text and tables	X	x
Adding and deleting images	X	x
Creating DHTML navigation bars	X	
Adding, modifying, and deleting behaviors (such as JavaScript button rollovers)	X	
Creating and modifying framesets	X	
Modifying content (such as text and images) within frames	X	x
Creating forms	X	
Creating and editing Cascading Style Sheets (CSS)	X	
Applying CSS styles to text	X	x
Working offline	X	x
Uploading and downloading Web Pages to/from a remote server	X	x

As you can see, the capabilities overlap quite a bit, but the more complicated tasks are best accomplished using Dreamweaver.

Exploring the Contribute Interface

The Contribute interface is as streamlined as its functionality, as you can see in Figure 1-1. Two panels are on the left, with a big work area — known as the *Browser* — on the right.

Panel basics

While other applications in Adobe CS3 have many customizable panels, Contribute has just two basic panels: Pages and How Do I, as shown in Figure 1-1. In contrast to the panels in other Adobe CS3 applications, you can't move, group, or delete the panels in Contribute.

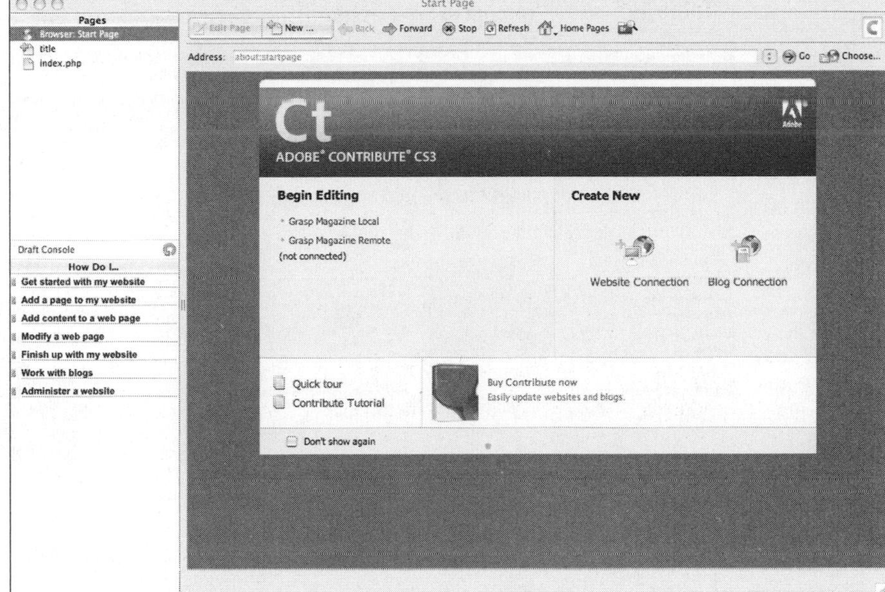

Figure 1-1: Contribute's streamlined interface includes two panels (at left) and the Browser.

You can, however, collapse and expand the panels by double-clicking the panel name. If the panel was expanded before you clicked, it collapses. If it was collapsed originally, it expands.

The Pages panel

The Pages panel displays the name of the most recent page you browsed to, any *unpublished drafts* (that is, any pages you have downloaded and edited but not uploaded back to the server), and the page on which you're currently working. Figure 1-2 shows that we're connected to the Grasp Magazine site, and that we have a draft of the home page that has been edited but not yet uploaded.

To navigate to any page listed in the Pages panel, click the title or the icon to the left of the page you want displayed in the Browser.

If you click the page at the top of the list, the Browser automatically switches to Browse mode. If you're already in Browse mode and you click a draft, the Browser automatically switches to Edit mode and displays your page, ready to edit.

The Browser is always at the top of the list in the Pages panel. See "The Browser/Editor" section, later in this chapter, for more information on the Browser itself.

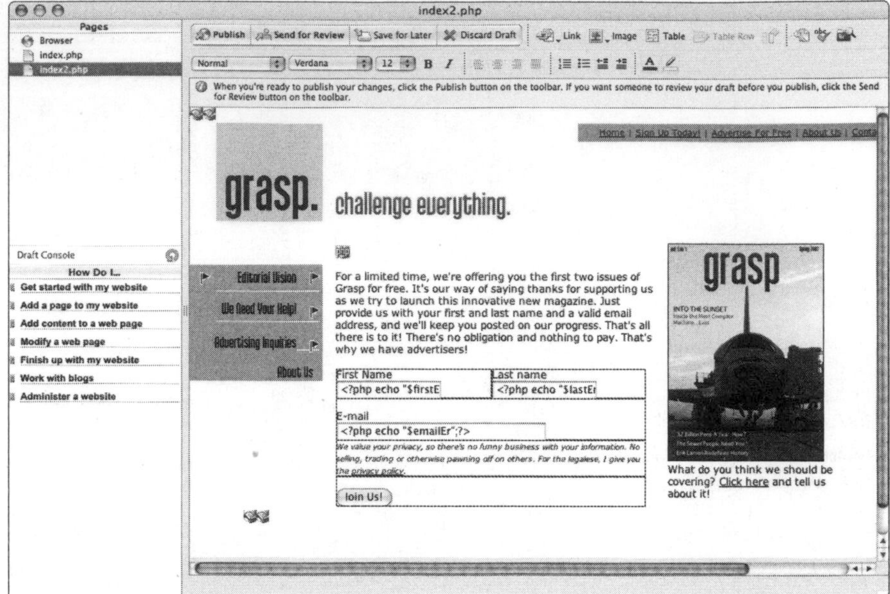

Figure 1-2: The title of the page currently being edited is highlighted in the Pages panel; the page itself is available for editing in the Browser.

The How Do I panel

The How Do I panel shows several options when you open Contribute for the first time

- Get Started with My Website
- Add a Page to My Website
- Add Content to a Web Page
- Modify a Web Page
- Finish Up with My Website
- Work with Blogs
- Administer a Website

It's easy to collapse or expand a section; just click the arrow at the left of the section name, or click the section name itself. If the section is expanded when you click, it collapses. If the section is collapsed when you click, it expands.

Each section has a list of actions you might want to perform. The list is in the form of text links, just as on a Web page. The list of links changes, based on what you're currently working on. We collapsed the sections in Figure 1-2 so that you can see some of the other sections that show up automatically in the How Do I panel when you're editing a page.

When you click a link, the How Do I panel updates, as shown in Figure 1-3. To return to the previous page of information in the panel, click the Back button at the top left of the How Do I panel. To go back to the original list of links, click the Topics icon at the top right of the panel.

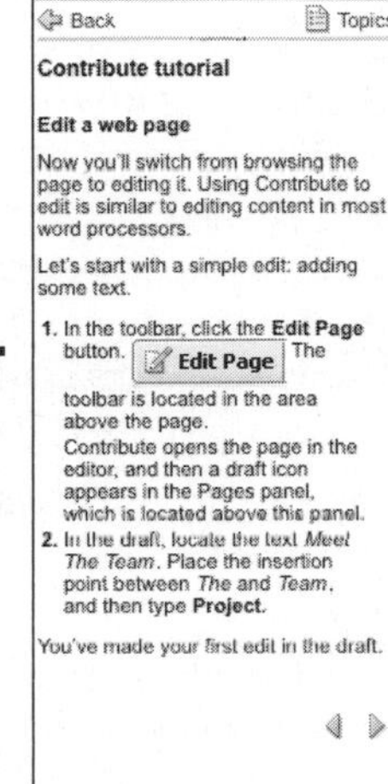

How Do I...
Back
Topics
Contribute tutorial
Edit a web page
Now you'll switch from browsing the page to editing it. Using Contribute to edit is similar to editing content in most word processors.
Let's start with a simple edit: adding some text.
1. In the toolbar, click the Edit Page button. Edit Page The toolbar is located in the area above the page.
Contribute opens the page in the editor, and then a draft icon appears in the Pages panel, which is located above this panel.
2. In the draft, locate the text Meet The Team. Place the insertion point between The and Team, and then type Project.
You've made your first edit in the draft.

Figure 1-3: The How Do I panel fits a lot of information into a very compact space.

The Browser/Editor

The main work area is called the Browser/Editor. (We call it the Browser to save space.) The Browser has two modes, Browse and Edit, and you can only be in one mode at a time. The appearance and functionality of the Browser depend on which mode you're in.

When you're in Browse mode in the Browser, you can navigate anywhere a regular Web browser, such as Internet Explorer, Firefox, or Safari, could take you. When you're in Edit mode, you can make changes to a Web page.

Browse mode

To browse to a page you want to update, you must use the Browser in its Browse mode. You can tell when the Browser is in Browse mode by looking at the buttons at the top. The following buttons (as shown in Figure 1-4) allow you to navigate as you would using any browser, such as IE:

- **Back:** Click this button to view the page you were previously viewing in the Browser. You can step back one page at a time through each of the pages you viewed since you opened the Browser. The Back option in the View menu performs the same function.
- **Forward:** Click Forward to go one page at a time from pages you viewed earlier to pages you viewed most recently.

- **Stop:** Pages with lots of big images or complex Flash movies sometimes take awhile to load in the Browser. Click this button to stop a page from loading further in the Browser.
- **Refresh:** As with your regular Web browser's Refresh button, this button reloads the current Web page in the Contribute Browser. The rest of the buttons are specific to the Contribute Browser.

- **Edit Page:** Click this button to edit the page you have browsed to. When you click Edit, Contribute downloads the page and automatically sets the Browser to Edit mode. This option is not available if you don't have what Contribute calls a *connection* — that is, permission to edit the page.
- **New Page:** Click this button to create a new page on the current Web site. You are prompted to name the page and, if you desire, to choose a page or template to use as a basis for the new page. See Book VI, Chapter 2 for more details.
- **Home Pages:** Use this button to navigate quickly to the home pages of the sites to which you have Contribute connections. Click and hold to see a drop-down list of eligible home pages.
- **Go:** This button works in conjunction with the Address text input field. See the following instructions for browsing to a page on the Internet.
- **Choose:** Click this button to open a dialog box in which you can navigate quickly to any page on the Web site you're currently updating.
- **Go to Bridge:** This is a new feature to Contribute CS3 that allows you to connect to Adobe Bridge to manage all your files across the various CS3 products.

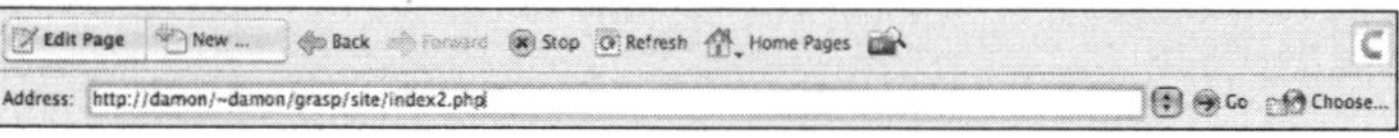

Figure 1-4: The Browser toolbar in Browse mode.

To browse to a page on the Internet, just follow these simple steps:

1. **Type or paste a URL (such as `www.graspmagazine.com`) into the Address field at the top of the Browser.**
2. **Click the Go button at the right of the Address input field or press Enter.**

   The requested Web page opens in the Browser.

When you browse to a site that you have been set up to edit, the top left of the Browser toolbar has two buttons: Edit Page and New Page. When you browse to a page that you are not set up to edit, the buttons are replaced by the Create Connection button. (See the section on connecting to a site in Book VI, Chapter 2 for more information on creating connections.)

Edit mode

The Edit mode is what Contribute is all about: It's the mode that you use to make changes to Web pages. To get into Edit mode after you've browsed to an editable page, do one of the following:

- ✦ Click the Edit Page button at the top left of the Browser.
- ✦ Choose File⇨Edit Page.
- ✦ Press Ctrl+Shift+E (⌘+E on a Mac).

To get into Edit mode if you haven't yet browsed to a page you have permission to edit, click the name of an existing draft in the Pages panel (or click the icon next to the name). The draft opens in the Browser, and the Browser automatically switches to Edit mode.

Most of Book VI, Chapter 2 is about the things you can do in Edit mode, so if you're anxious to get to work on a site, skip ahead to the next chapter.

Menus

The Contribute menu bar sports eight menus, each of which includes several choices. (Many of the choices are also available from buttons at the top of the Browser.) We give you some details about the most important functions in the first three menus, as well as brief descriptions of what the other five offer:

- ✦ **File:** Every computer program has a File menu, with options such as Open, Save, and the like. The Contribute File menu offers the following:
  - **New Page:** Select this option to create a new Web page. You can create a new page from scratch, from an existing page, or from a Dreamweaver CS3 template. See Book VI, Chapter 2 for details.
  - **Actions:** The Actions option groups the most common functions in a submenu. See File⇨Actions, later in this list, for details.
  - **Save:** Select this option to save the work you have done on a draft without publishing the edited page. After saving, you may continue working on the draft.
  - **Save for Later:** Select this option to save the work you have done on a draft without publishing the edited page; the Browser will automatically change from Edit mode to Browse mode and load the last page you were looking at in Browse mode.

- **Publish File from My Computer:** With this option, you can move a file directly from your computer or shared network to a remote server where your Web site is located. This is handy when you need to move files — an Excel file for example — that you don't need to edit in Contribute.
- **Send File from My Computer:** This is similar to the preceding Publish option except that it's used for situations in which a user needs to have a file reviewed before sending, or when the user doesn't have access to a remote server.
- **Preview in Browser:** Select this to see what your draft looks like in your regular browser (IE, Firefox, Opera, Safari, and so on).
- **Export:** Select Export to save a copy of the page you're working on to your local hard drive (or to a removable disk or remote hard drive).
- **Page Setup:** Select this option to open a dialog box that allows you to customize how your printer deals with your page (paper size, orientation, and so on).
- **Print:** As you might expect, you can print your Web page by selecting Print from the File menu.
- **Print Preview:** Select Print Preview to see on your computer screen a representation of how your Web page will appear on paper when you print it.
- **Delete Page:** Select Delete Page to remove a page from your Web site. This option is available only when the Browser is in Browse mode.
- **Work Offline:** Select this option if you don't need to upload or download any unpublished drafts you're editing, or if you're temporarily unable to connect with your network or the Internet.
- **Drafts:** Use this option to open an unpublished draft of a page.
- **Recently Published Pages:** Use this option to view in the Browser a page you recently published.

- **Exit:** Select this option to close Contribute. You can also close Contribute by pressing Ctrl+Q or Alt+F4 on your keyboard.

✦ **File⇨Actions:** This new submenu groups together all the most common publishing actions (as shown in Figure 1-5). Many of these actions are available as buttons in the Browser.

- **Edit Page:** This option is available only when the Browser is in Browse mode and is currently displaying a page you have permission to edit. When you choose File⇨Actions ⇨Edit Page, Contribute downloads the page to your computer and makes it available for modification. Clicking the Edit Page button in the Browser does the same thing.

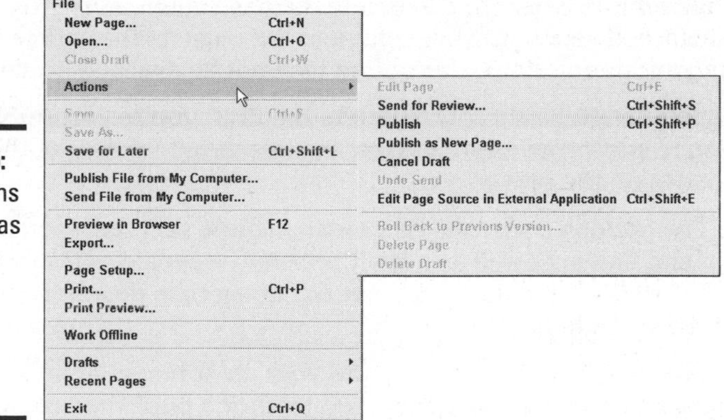

Figure 1-5: The Actions submenu as it appears when a page is being edited.

* **Send for Review:** Select this to upload a temporary version of your page to the server and send an e-mail to a co-worker with a link to the temporary page. If you need someone's approval before you *publish* a page (that is, before you make it live on the site so users can see it), E-mail Review is a handy automated way to show your work to the person who can approve it.
* **Publish:** Select this option to upload an edited page to the server.
* **Publish as New Page:** Select this option to upload a page to the server with a new filename (such as aboutus.htm). You're prompted to type or paste in the new filename. See Book VI, Chapter 2 for details.
* **Cancel Draft:** Select this to delete the draft you're currently working on from your computer. ***Note:*** Selecting Cancel Draft does not delete the page from your Web site.
* **Undo Send:** Select this to remove a draft from a reviewer's Pages panel and put it back in yours. If the reviewer has sent the draft to another reviewer, you can't undo the send.
* **Edit Page Source in External Application:** Select this to launch Dreamweaver (or another text editor) to edit the underlying HTML source code of the page. Your site administrator must enable this option in order for you to use it.
* **Roll Back to Previous Version:** If you find that you've published a page that has a mistake on it, select Roll Back to Previous Version to restore the previously published version of the page. See Book VI, Chapter 3 for more information on this feature, which must be set up by an administrator.

- **Delete Page:** Select this to delete the page you're currently editing. This will delete both your draft and the page on the server. Depending on your permissions, this option may not be available to you.
- **Delete Draft:** Select this to delete the draft you're currently editing. If you're editing an existing page, the last saved version of the page will remain on the server.

✦ **Edit:** The options under the Edit menu include such perennial favorites as Cut and Paste, as well as a few Contribute-specific options. Which options are *live* (not grayed out) at any given time depends on your most recent action.

- **Undo:** Select this option to undo your most recent actions in a draft, one at a time. You can't use Undo to alter a published page; for that, you need to choose File⇨Actions⇨Roll Back. The keyboard shortcut for Undo is Ctrl+Z.
- **Redo:** Redo is sort of an undo of an undo. Select this option to redo the last actions you undid in your draft, one at a time, or press Ctrl+Y.
- **Cut:** Select this option to remove highlighted text or objects from your draft. You can then paste the text or objects into the same page, a different page, or even a different kind of document (for example, a Word document). The keyboard shortcut to cut highlighted objects is Ctrl+X.
- **Paste:** After you've selected some text or objects (images, for example), select this option to paste the text or objects into your draft, or press Ctrl+V.
- **Paste Text Only:** After selecting a block of text that also includes images or other objects, you can use this option to paste only the text from your selection. You can also press Ctrl+Shift+V.
- **Clear:** Use this option to remove selected text or objects from your Web page. In contrast to Cut, this option does not allow you to paste the removed text or objects elsewhere.
- **Find:** Use this option to find any string of characters (a word or phrase, for example) on a page you're currently editing. You can also automatically replace that string with another string (such as changing, say, "Go back to top" to "Go to top"). If the string appears multiple times on the page, you can change each instance one at a time or click Replace All and change every instance at once.
- **Select All:** Use this option to select everything in a draft. You can then cut, paste, or clear everything at once. The keyboard shortcut for selecting all is Ctrl+A.
- **Preferences:** Select this option to open a dialog box that allows you to customize the way Contribute works. See the "Setting Preferences" section, later in this chapter, for details.

- **My Connections:** Use this option to view, edit, and delete the connections you have to the sites you maintain.
- **Administer Websites:** If you have Administrator privileges on a site to which you have a connection, use this option to open the Administration dialog box and change any settings for the selected site. See Book VI, Chapter 3 for information on sitewide settings, permission groups, and setting up users.

If you're using the Mac version of Adobe Contribute CS3, you'll find the final three items on the preceding list under the Contribute menu just to the right of the Apple menu.

✦ **View:** The View menu offers options related to what you see on-screen in Contribute.

- **Sidebar:** Select this option to show or hide the sidebar, which contains the Pages and How Do I panels.
- **Home Pages:** Select this option to open the home page for any site you can connect to in Contribute.
- **Draft Console:** Select this option to view the Draft Console, which shows you any drafts you have edited but not published, as well as any drafts you have been asked to review or have sent to someone else to view.
- **Refresh Drafts:** Select this option to update the Draft Console.
- **Draft History:** If you have received a draft for review, you can select this option to open a window in which you can read a history of the changes made to the draft.
- **Browser:** Select this option to switch to Browse mode. The last page you looked at in that mode appears in the Browser. You can press Ctrl+Shift+B or click the top line in the Pages panel to do the same thing.
- **Go to Web Address:** If you select this option, a dialog box opens in which you can type or paste a URL to open a particular Web page in the Browser. When you click OK, the Browser switches to Browse mode — if it wasn't already — and loads the page you requested. You can also press Ctrl+O (⌘+D on a Mac) to open the Go to Web Address dialog box.
- **Choose File on Website:** This option allows you to navigate directly to an editable page from a window that displays all the sites to which you have a Contribute connection.

  The Back, Forward, Stop, Refresh, and Home Pages options function just the same as their corresponding buttons in the Browser. See the "Browse mode" section, earlier in this chapter, for the skinny on them.

- **Bookmarks:** A *bookmark* is a link to a Web page. Options here allow you to add and delete bookmarks to Web pages that you visit often. If your main Web browser is IE, you see all your IE bookmarks listed under the Other Bookmarks option.
- **Insert:** Select an option in this menu to insert an item into a draft. The Insert menu allows you to insert the following items into a draft:
  - Table
  - Link
  - Shared asset
  - Image
  - Flash
  - Video
  - PDF document
  - Enclosure
  - Date
  - Section anchor
  - Horizontal rule
  - Line break
  - Special characters
  - PayPal tool
  - Google search field
  - HMTL snippets
- **Format:** You can use the options in this menu to format selected text in a draft. You can apply CSS styles, as well as more traditional HTML text treatments such as bold and italic. See Book VI, Chapter 2 for details on text formatting in Contribute. The Format menu also gives you access to the Contribute spell checker (keyboard shortcut: F7) and allows you to edit page properties, such as title and background color (keyboard shortcut: Ctrl+J).
- **Table:** This menu offers commands that allow you to insert and edit tables in your draft.
- **Help:** The Help menu gives you a choice of several kinds of help:
  - **Adobe Contribute Help:** Select this option to view standard help files, with step-by-step instructions.
  - **Quick Start Guide:** Select this option to see instructions on Contribute to help get you up and running quickly.
  - **Contribute Support Center:** When you select this option, your regular Web browser opens to the Contribute Support home page on Adobe's Web site.
  - **Contribute Tutorial:** Select this option to access a set of guided lessons on basic tasks you can perform with Contribute.

  The Help menu also allows you to open the Contribute Welcome page in the Browser, print your Contribute registration form, submit your registration online, and see the About Contribute window, which shows information about the version you're running.

Setting Preferences

For most users, the default Preferences should suffice, but you may wish (or need) to make a few changes in order to use Contribute most efficiently. To open the Preferences dialog box, choose Edit➪ Preferences on a PC, or Contribute➪Preferences on a Mac.

The Preferences dialog box includes nine "screens"; you access the different screens by selecting one of the items in the list on the left side of the dialog box; see Figure 1-6. A brief overview of each page follows.

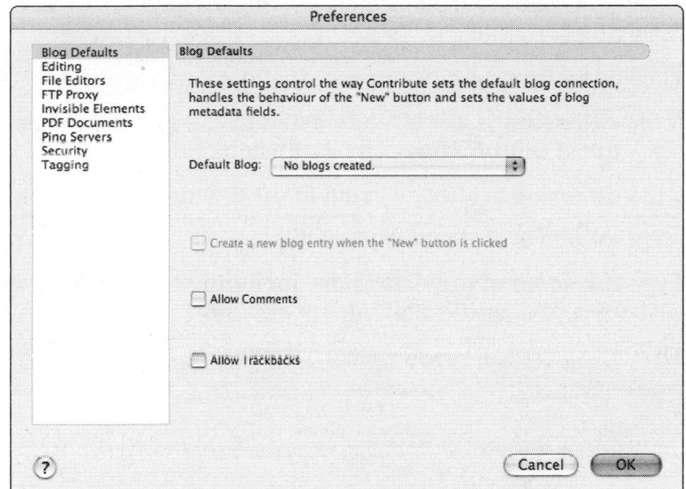

Figure 1-6: The Preferences dialog box.

Setting Blog Defaults preferences

By default, the Preferences dialog box opens to the Blog Defaults screen. Here, if you're using Contribute to manage your personal or corporate blog, you can set the following items:

- ✦ Select which blog should be the default blog for your Web site.
- ✦ Change the default behavior of the New button in Contribute so that it maps to creating a blog entry as opposed to creating a new Web page.
- ✦ Set up your blog to allow outside users to add their comments.
- ✦ Enable the trackback URL feature so that other blog authors can link from their Web site to your blog entries.

Setting Editing preferences

From this screen, you can choose a dictionary language from the drop-down list. Contribute uses the dictionary to spell-check Web page drafts.

Setting File Editors preferences

You can tell Contribute what application you want it to use to open various types of files when you double-click the files in the Browser in Edit mode. To set Contribute to open a particular type of file with a particular application, just follow these steps:

1. **Select File Editors from the list on the left side of the Preferences dialog box.**

   The File Editors options appear, as shown in Figure 1-7.

2. **If the extension is not already listed in the Extensions list box, click the + (plus) button above the Extensions box.**

   If the extension is already listed in the Extensions box, skip to Step 4.

   A cursor blinks at the bottom of the list.

3. **Type the name of the extension, including the dot (for example, type** .wav **for a WAV audio file), and press Enter.**

   The extension you typed remains highlighted.

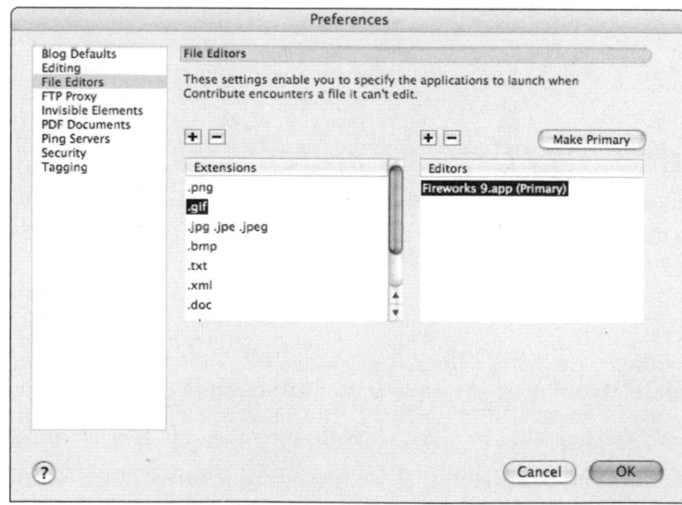

Figure 1-7: Setting the File Editors preferences for GIFs.

4. **If the application is not already listed, click the + button above the Editors box.**

   If the application is listed, click its name to select it and skip to Step 6.

   The Select External Editor dialog box pops up.

5. **Navigate to the application and double-click its icon, or type the pathname (including the application name) into the File Name text field.**

   The application name appears in the Editors box.

6. **Set any other file editor preferences and click OK when you're finished.**

Contribute comes with quite a few defaults (naturally, Adobe Studio CS3 applications feature prominently), so you may never need to touch the File Editors preferences. You can assign more than one application to edit a particular file type. If you do that, you need to designate one of the programs as the primary application by selecting it in the File Editors screen of the Preferences dialog box and clicking the Make Primary button.

Setting FTP Proxy preferences

If your computer is separated by a firewall from the server that houses your site (or sites), use the FTP Proxy screen of the Preferences dialog box to input the host name and port number that allow you to tunnel through the firewall. If you're not sure what all that means, ask someone in your IT department.

Setting Invisible Elements preferences

When you link some text or an image to a particular line on a Web page, you need to place an invisible target (an *anchor*) at that line. Select Invisible Elements in the list box on the left of the Preferences dialog box to see the Invisible Elements options. Leave the Show Section Anchors When Editing a Page check box selected if you want to be able to see icons that identify where invisible anchor links are in your draft.

Setting PDF Documents preferences

In previous versions of Contribute, a preferences area was dedicated to Microsoft integration. With the Adobe purchase of Macromedia and subsequent integration, that preference area is history. In its place, you now find an Adobe PDF Preferences pane. Ironically, though, the contents of the Preferences pane are nearly identical to the other Microsoft one.

When inserting a PDF document into Contribute, you can choose to have it be a link, have it directly embedded in the document, or have Contribute prompt you to choose one of those options when inserting.

Setting Ping Servers preferences

The Ping Servers preferences panel is another nod toward the fact that Contribute is a blog-oriented product. In many cases, you want to notify other sources when you make a blog post. This notification, often called a "ping," can be automated with Contribute. The Ping Servers panel is where you can set up these pings. Using the plus (+) or minus (–) buttons, you can add a server to notify you when a blog entry is posted. In addition, you can specify the number of blog entries.

Setting Security preferences

If you share a computer with other people and don't want them to have access to Contribute (and therefore to the sites you maintain), open up the Security options in the Preferences dialog box and select the Encrypt Connection Information For All Websites check box. Then follow these steps:

1. **Click in the Password text field, type a password, and press the Tab key.**

   The cursor moves to the Confirm Password text field.

2. **Retype your password in the Confirm Password text field exactly as you typed it in the Password text field. Go on to Step 3, or press Enter or click OK.**

   Contribute asks for a password when you launch the application.

3. **Select the Require Password at Startup option if you want users to enter a password in order to launch the application.**
4. **Press Enter or click OK.**

You can change your preferences at any time by choosing Edit⇨Preferences (Contribute⇨Preferences on a Mac).

Setting Tagging preferences

Tags are a way to both gain exposure for your blog and help it get organized. A tag is simply a way to identify the content of a blog posting by using a handful of words. So, if you have an entry about remodeling your kitchen, you might use the tags "appliances," "counter," and "cabinets." You can create your own tag repository or use others that are out there on the Internet. Using the Contribute tagging preferences, you can select the location within your posting of where the tags will show up, in addition to adding tag repositories and prefixes for your tags.

Chapter 2: Basics for Contributors

In This Chapter

- Getting a site connection
- Opening an existing page for editing
- Creating a new page
- Working with text and tables
- Inserting images and links
- Taking a look at your work
- Putting a page on the Web
- Working with others

Contribute CS3 is a remarkably easy-to-use tool for editing existing pages on — or adding new pages to — a Web site. As with the original Contribute version, many of the things you need to do to add or replace content (or build a page based on an existing design) take little more than a click — and you don't have to know a thing about HTML.

With Contribute CS3, Adobe has added many features to the last version of the application while keeping it simple enough for nontechnical users — no small task. This chapter is all about how using the Contribute CS3 tools can make modifying or creating a basic Web page easier. If you need to know about things such as setting yourself up as a site administrator or sending a connection key to a fellow site contributor, see Book VI, Chapter 3.

Connecting to a Site

To put Contribute CS3 to use when working on a Web site, you must be connected to that site. Being *connected* means establishing an *FTP (File Transfer Protocol)* connection between your computer and the remote server that your site lives on. If that sounds complicated, don't worry. It's actually pretty simple.

You can connect in two ways:

- By using a connection key that the site administrator has e-mailed to you
- By entering information in the Connection Wizard

Both ways are pretty simple, but you'll need some information about your Web server to employ the latter method. If you've been sent a connection key, read the next section to find out how to use it. If you need to connect to a site but don't have a key, skip ahead to the "Connecting to a site with the Connection Wizard" section.

Connecting to a site with the connection key

A connection key is an encrypted file that contains nearly all the information Contribute needs to connect your program copy to the Web site you're updating. (You also need to get a password from your administrator.) You might receive a connection key

- Via e-mail from the site administrator
- By downloading it from your local network

Most likely, you'll get your connection key via e-mail, but it works the same either way (just skip Step 2). To open a connection to the Web site you'll be working on, just follow these simple steps:

1. **Open the e-mail from your site administrator that contains the connection key.**

   The connection key shows up as an attachment; see Figure 2-1. The e-mail body contains instructions on using the key. The connection key name is based on the name the site administrator gives the site connection in Contribute.

2. **Double-click the connection key.**

   Contribute starts up (if it's not already open), and the Import Connection Key dialog box opens.

3. **If your name is not already there, click in the What Is Your Name? text field and type your name.**
4. **Press Tab or click in the E-mail text field.**
5. **If your e-mail address is not already there, type your e-mail address in the next field.**
6. **Press Tab or click in the next text field.**

   If you already have a connection to another Web site, your e-mail address may already be entered in the field.

7. **In the What Is the Connection Key Password? text field, type the password given to you by the site administrator.**

   The password may have been sent in a separate e-mail or told to you on the phone. If you don't yet know the password, check with the site administrator.

8. **Click OK.**

   The Contribute Browser loads the site's home page.

The connection key should have all the FTP information that allows you to connect to your Web server. In some cases, you may have to input the FTP information manually. The next section tells you how.

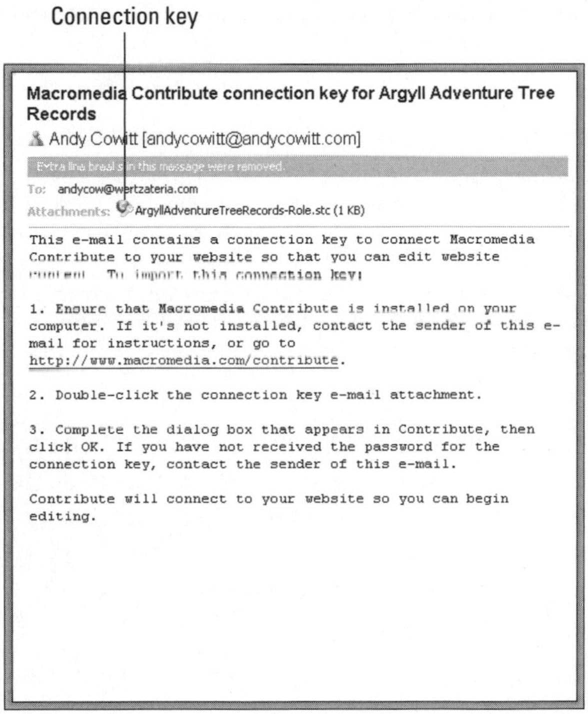

Connection key

Macromedia Contribute connection key for Argyll Adventure Tree Records

Andy Cowitt [andycowitt@andycowitt.com]

Extra line breaks in this message were removed.

To: andycow@wertzateria.com

Attachments: ArgyllAdventureTreeRecords-Role.stc (1 KB)

This e-mail contains a connection key to connect Macromedia Contribute to your website so that you can edit website content. To import this connection key:

1. Ensure that Macromedia Contribute is installed on your computer. If it's not installed, contact the sender of this e-mail for instructions, or go to http://www.macromedia.com/contribute.

2. Double-click the connection key e-mail attachment.

3. Complete the dialog box that appears in Contribute, then click OK. If you have not received the password for the connection key, contact the sender of this e-mail.

Contribute will connect to your website so you can begin editing.

Figure 2-1: The connection key is marked as an attachment to this e-mail.

Connecting to a site with the Connection Wizard

Contribute saves you the trouble of having to use an FTP client to move Web pages back and forth between your computer and the server that hosts your Web site. When you click the Edit button in the Browser, Contribute automatically gets *(downloads)* the page for editing. When you click the Publish button, Contribute puts *(uploads)* the page on the Web server. After you've set up a connection, Contribute transparently handles all the downloading and uploading.

The Connection Wizard makes connecting to a remote Web server a snap, if you have the login information at hand. Just follow these steps to set up a connection, after you've opened Contribute:

1. **Type or paste the URL for your site (for example,** `www.MySite.com`**) into the Address field of the Contribute Browser.**
2. **Either press Enter or click the Go button.**

   The Contribute Browser takes you right to your site.

   You can use the Contribute Browser to view any site on the Web, but you can only set up a connection to a site if you have FTP information for that site.
3. **Click the Create Connection button at the top left of the Browser.**

   The Connection Wizard opens to its Welcome screen.
4. **We're assuming that you don't have a connection key, so click the Continue button at the bottom of the wizard.**

   The Website Home Page screen appears.
5. **Enter the URL (**`www.MySite.com`**, for example) for the Web site you'll be editing into the text field and then click Continue.**

   You can also click the Browse button, which opens a browser window for navigating to the site.

   When you click Continue, the Connection Information screen appears in the wizard.
6. **Select a connection method from the drop-down list.**

   You have the following options: FTP, Secure FTP (SFTP), Local/Network, and WebDAV. If you're not sure what to select, check with your IT person or site administrator. Depending on what you choose, different text fields appear below the drop-down list. As you can see in Figure 2-2, we've entered FTP.

7a. **If in Step 6 you selected FTP or SFTP, enter the FTP server name (for example, ftp.EarlsBowlateria.com), the FTP login, and the FTP password in the respective text fields. Click Continue.**

   The FTP login is sometimes called the *username.*

   The Testing Connection window appears. When the connection is confirmed, the User Information screen appears.

7b. **If in Step 6 you selected Local/Network, enter the network path (for example, \\mynetwork\mydepartment\site) by typing, by pasting, or by clicking the Choose Folder button and browsing in your network to the folder containing your site. Click Continue.**

    The User Information screen appears.

8. **Enter your name in the What Is Your Full Name? text field.**

    Your name may already appear. The name in this field identifies you to other contributors to your site, if there are any.

9. **If it's not already there, enter your e-mail address in the What Is Your E-mail Address? text field and then click Continue.**

    If your site already has an administrator, the Role Information screen appears. Go to Step 10. If the site doesn't have an administrator, the Summary screen appears. Go to Step 11.

10. **Click the role you're assigned to and click Continue.**

    If you click Administrator, a pop-up window may appear. Enter the Administrator password and click OK. Congratulations! You've made it to the Summary screen.

11. **Make sure that the Summary screen information is correct.**

    If it isn't, use the Back button to go to the screen with incorrect info and fix the mistake; then use the Continue button to return to the Summary screen.

12. **Click Done.**

Unless any of the information you put in the Connection Wizard changes, you never have to think about it again — from here on, you can just get straight to work making changes to your site.

If you want to make yourself the site administrator, see Book VI, Chapter 3.

Figure 2-2: Setting up your site connection.

Opening an Existing Page for Editing

After you've established a connection to your site, you're ready to start making changes to existing pages and even creating new ones. Downloading a page to edit is extremely easy — just follow these steps:

1. **Type or paste the URL of the page you want to edit (for example, `www.MySite.com`) into the Address field of the Contribute Browser.**
2. **Either press Enter or click the Go button.**

   The Browser loads your page, and the Edit Page and New Page buttons appear at the top left of the Browser. If the page is not available for editing, the warning `You are viewing a page on a Web site that you haven't created a connection to` appears under the Address field in the Browser.
3. **Click the Edit Page button.**

   The Browser switches to Edit mode, and the page appears as a draft in the Browser. The Browser's toolbar at the top changes to show buttons for inserting links, images, tables, and text, as shown in Figure 2-3.

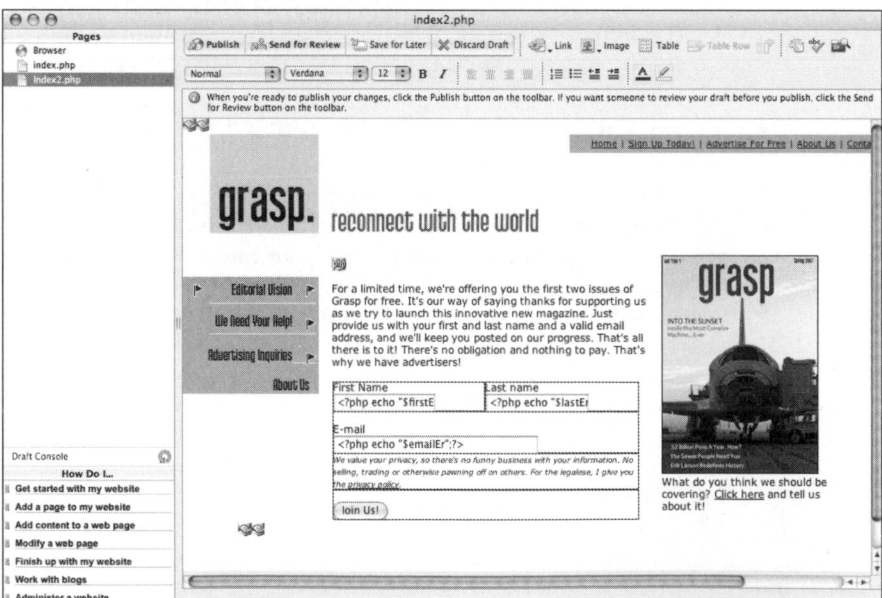

Figure 2-3: A Web page ready for editing.

Creating a New Page

If opening a page for editing is a snap, creating a new page is maybe three snaps. To create a new page for your site, follow these simple steps:

1. **If you have connections to more than one Web site, use the Contribute Browser to go to the site to which you want to add a page. Otherwise, skip to Step 2.**

   The Browser loads your page, and the Edit Page and New Page buttons appear at the top left of the Browser. If the site is not available for editing, the warning `You are viewing a page on a Web site that you haven't created a connection to` appears under the Address field in the Browser.

2. **Click the New Page button or choose File⇨New Page.**

   The New Page dialog box appears.

3a. **If you want the new page to have the same basic appearance and structure (for example, to have the same navigation items and basic layout) as the page currently showing in your browser, click the Copy of Current Page in the New Page dialog box.**

3b. **If you want to create a page from a Dreamweaver CS3 template, click the template name in the Create New Page From pane.**

   If the templates are in a folder and you don't see them, click the arrow next to the folder that holds the templates; the contents of the folder appear. A template preview appears in the Preview pane, as shown in Figure 2-4.

3c. **If you want to start the page from scratch, skip to Step 4.**

   The Blank Web Page option may not be available to you, depending on how the administrator has set up your connection.

4. **Type or paste a page title in the Page Title text field. Click OK.**

   Your new page opens in the Browser, as a draft ready for editing. The page title appears at the top of the Web browser's window when people view your Web site.

TIP

You can also create a new page by using the keyboard shortcut Ctrl+N.

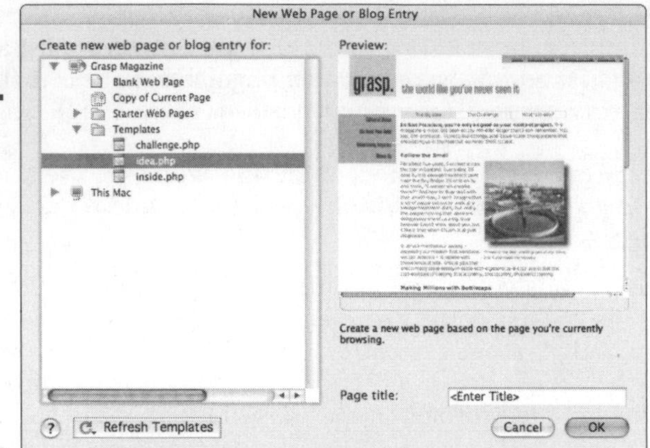

Figure 2-4: The New Page dialog box allows you to select a template on which to base your new page.

Working with Text

Text is often the most abundant element on a Web site. Contribute makes adding, formatting, and deleting text a piece of cake.

Adding text

To add text to a *draft* (that is, to a page that's ready for editing; see the previous sections, "Opening an Existing Page for Editing" or "Creating a New Page"), just follow these easy steps:

1. **Click the place in the draft where you want to insert text.**

   A cursor blinks in the spot you selected.

2. **Type or paste the text.**

   You may need to format the text. See the next section for the lowdown.

Formatting text

Text *formatting* entails everything from setting a font face and font size, to emphasizing words or phrases by making them bold or italic, to creating numbered or bulleted lists. It's all as easy as clicking a button in Contribute.

You can format text either before or after you insert it on a page. If you're working from a template, text areas may be preformatted for things like font size, color, and face. If not, the text you insert conforms to the settings in the text toolbar (the second row of the Browser).

Setting a text style

To set the font style, choose a style from the Style drop-down list at the top left. If you have CSS styles attached to your page, they appear in the menu; otherwise, your choices are Normal and Heading 1 (largest) through Heading 6 (smallest).

Setting a text face

To set a face for your font (for example, Arial, Verdana, and so on), choose one from the Font drop-down list (to the right of the Style list). If you leave the setting at Default, the text's appearance is determined by a site visitor's browser settings.

Setting a text size

Choose a text size from the Size drop-down list. The smallest is 11, and the largest is 96 (too big for most uses). If you select Default, the text's size is determined by a site visitor's browser settings. Figure 2-5 shows just some of the ways you can format text.

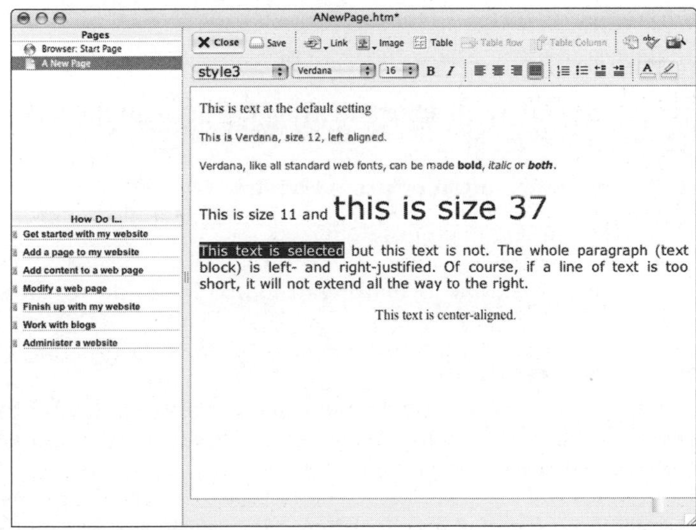

Figure 2-5: You can format text in many different ways.

Selecting text

To select text, click and drag over the text you want. The selected text is highlighted. If you change the style, font face, size, color, or background color settings while text in your draft is selected, the selected text (and only it) changes to reflect the new settings.

Aligning text

Contribute allows you to align text to the left, center, or right, or to justify the text at the left and right (though the latter is extremely rare on the Web). To align text, place the cursor anywhere in the block of text you want to align (or select a block of text by clicking and dragging) and click an Align button (from left to right, the Align buttons are Align Left, Align Center, Align Right, and Justify).

Adding boldface to your text

To make some text bold, follow these steps:

1. **Select the text by clicking and dragging until all the text you want bold is highlighted.**
2. **Click the Bold button or press Ctrl+B.**

   The selected text becomes bold.

You can remove the bold formatting from text by following the same steps.

Italicizing your text

To italicize some text, follow these steps:

1. **Select the text by clicking and dragging until all the text you want changed is highlighted.**
2. **Click the Italic button or press Ctrl+I.**

   The selected text becomes italicized.

You can remove the italic formatting from text by following the same steps.

Changing the text color

Web text is typically black by default but can be set to default to other colors. If you're working with CSS styles or Dreamweaver templates, default text colors may be set for you already.

To change the color of a specific block of text, follow these steps:

1. **Select the text by clicking and dragging until all the text you want changed is highlighted.**
2. **Click the Text Color button in the Browser's Text toolbar.**

   The Text Color button is the one on the second row, toward the right, with a capital A on it. When you click it, the color picker pops up.

3. **Click a cube of color with the eyedropper to make the selected text that color.**

Changing the text background color

When you change the text background color, you're changing just that: the background of each chunk of text, be it letters or numbers.

To change the text background color of some text, follow these simple steps:

1. **Select the text by clicking and dragging until all the text you want changed is highlighted.**
2. **Click the Highlight Color button in the Browser's Text toolbar, as shown in Figure 2-6.**

   The Highlight Color button is the one with the highlighter marker; it's just to the right of the Text Color button. When you click the Highlight Color button, the color picker pops up.
3. **Click a cube of color with the eyedropper to make the background of the selected text that color.**

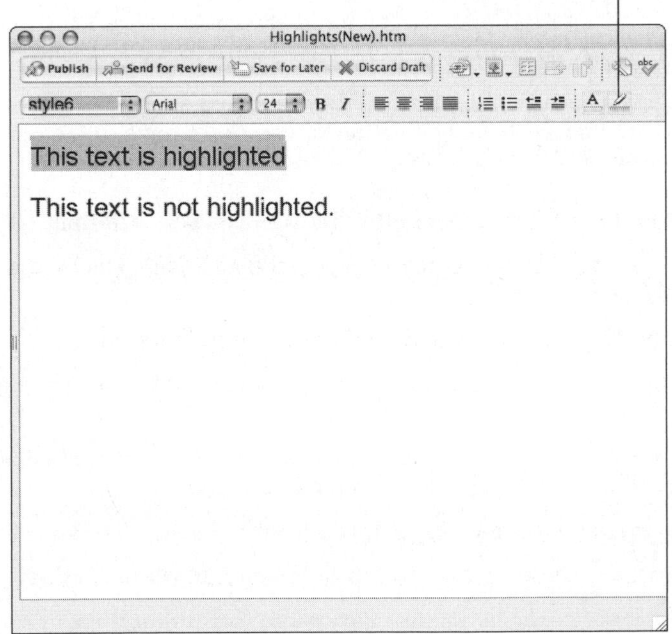

Figure 2-6: The text background color acts like a highlighter marker.

Creating a numbered list

You can create a numbered list the fancy way, with complicated tables and such, or you can do it the easy way, using the numbered list convention built into HTML. Contribute makes the easy way even easier. To create a numbered list, just follow these steps:

1. **Click the Numbered List button in the Browser's toolbar, as shown in Figure 2-7.**

   The indented number 1 appears, followed by a period, a space, and a blinking cursor.

2. **Type the first item in your numbered list. Press Enter when you're finished.**

   The number 2 automatically appears on the next line, followed by a period, a space, and a blinking cursor.

3. **Type the second item in your numbered list, press Enter, and continue to enter items until you have completed your list.**

   Leave the extra number for which you don't have an item.

4. **Click the Numbered List button to deactivate the numbering.**

   The last (extra) number disappears and the cursor goes to its non-indented position below the list.

Creating a bulleted list

HTML has a specification for bulleted lists, just as it does for numbered lists. Contribute knows the specification so you don't have to. To create a bulleted list, simply follow these steps:

1. **Click the Bulleted List button in the Browser's toolbar.**

   An indented bullet appears, followed by a little space and a blinking cursor.

2. **Type the first bullet item and press the Enter key.**

   A bullet appears on the next line, followed by a little space and a blinking cursor.

3. **Type the second bullet item, press the Enter key, and repeat the process until you have completed your list.**

   An extra bullet remains temporarily at the bottom of your list.

4. **Click the Bulleted List button to deactivate the bulleting.**

   The last (extra) bullet disappears and the cursor goes to its non-indented position below the list.

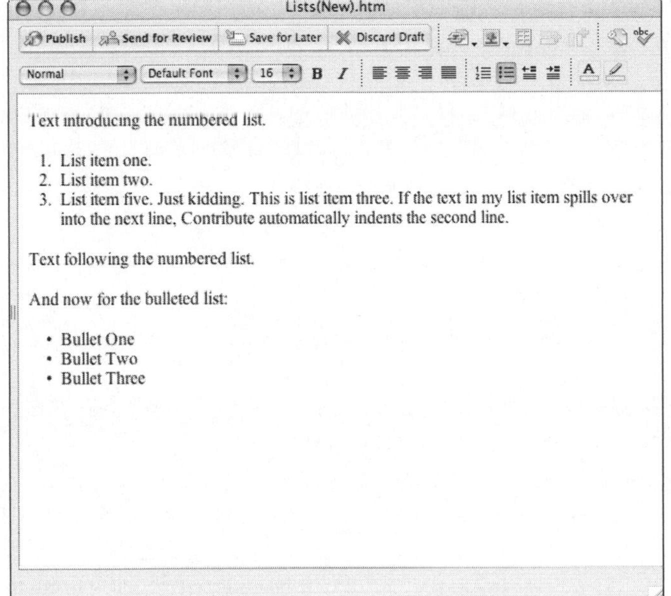

Lists(New).htm
Publish
Send for Review
Save for Later
Discard Draft
Normal
Default Font
16
Text introducing the numbered list.
1. List item one.
2. List item two.
3. List item five. Just kidding. This is list item three. If the text in my list item spills over into the next line, Contribute automatically indents the second line.
Text following the numbered list.
And now for the bulleted list:
• Bullet One
• Bullet Two
• Bullet Three

Figure 2-7: Contribute allows you to create numbered and bulleted lists easily.

Working with Tables

You might use tables on a Web page in two basic ways:

- ✦ To display tabular information, such as a spreadsheet
- ✦ To control page layout

No matter which function you want the table to have, you can add, modify, and delete the table using the same simple methods. Tables are made up of *cells,* arranged in rows and columns. Picture a basic tic-tac-toe game. It's played on a kind of table, with nine cells arranged in three rows and three columns. If you can draw a tic-tac-toe game, you can make a table on a Web page.

Inserting a table

To insert a table into your page, just follow these steps:

1. **Click the spot in your draft where you want the top-left corner of the table to go.**

   A blinking cursor marks the spot.

2. **Click the Insert Table button in the top row of the Browser toolbar.**

   The Insert Table dialog box appears, as shown in Figure 2-8.

Figure 2-8: The Insert Table dialog box asks for enough information to create a basic HTML table.

3. **Enter the number of rows you want the table to have in the Number of Rows field.**

   You can always add or delete extra rows later, if you need to.

4. **In the Number of Columns field, enter the number of columns you want the table to have.**

   You can always add or delete extra columns later.

5a. **If it doesn't matter how wide the table is, leave the Default Width setting as is and skip to Step 6.**

5b. **If you want a particular width, select the Specific Width radio button, enter a number for the width, and then choose either Pixels or Percent from the drop-down list to the right.**

   If you choose Pixels, the table will be the number of pixels wide that you specified. If you choose Percent, you must choose a numeral between 1 and 100; the table's width will vary according to the overall page layout, and it may vary according to the width of a site visitor's browser window.

6. **In the Border Thickness field, enter a number for how many pixels thick you want the border of your table to be.**

   If you don't want the table border to show (which you probably don't if you're using the table for page layout purposes), enter 0 (zero).

7. **In the Cell Padding field, enter a number for the amount of pixels you want between the border of the cell and the text or object inside the cell.**

   The cell padding applies to the top, bottom, left, and right of the inside of each and every cell.

8. **In the Cell Spacing field, enter a number for the amount of pixels you want between the cells.**

   The cell spacing applies to the whole table; you can't have different cell spacing for individual rows or columns.

9. **If your table has a header row or header column (or both), click the icon that represents the header structure.**

   Figure 2-9 shows a table with a single header row. The text in that row is automatically bold and center-aligned in the cells.

10. **Click OK.**

    The Insert Table dialog box closes, and an empty table appears in your draft, built to your specifications and ready to be filled with content.

Adding information to a table

Adding text and images to a table is pretty much the same as adding them anywhere else on a draft. To add text to a table, follow these steps:

1. **Click in the cell where you want to put the text.**

   A cursor blinks in the cell.

2. **Type or paste in the text.**

   The cell expands downwards. In some cases, the cell also expands to the right, depending on its width and the nature of the text. For example, a long e-mail address, which is made of many characters strung together without a space, can stretch a cell. (Refer to Figure 2-9.) The other cells may become narrower to compensate.

3. **Click in another cell or outside the table if you want to add more information to the table or elsewhere on the draft.**

To add an image or other object to a cell, click in the cell and then follow the directions in the "Adding Images, Links, and More" section, later in this chapter.

Modifying a table

You can modify many properties of an existing table quickly and easily. In some cases, you can make the changes by clicking and dragging table or cell borders; in other cases, you can enter new settings in the Table Properties dialog box.

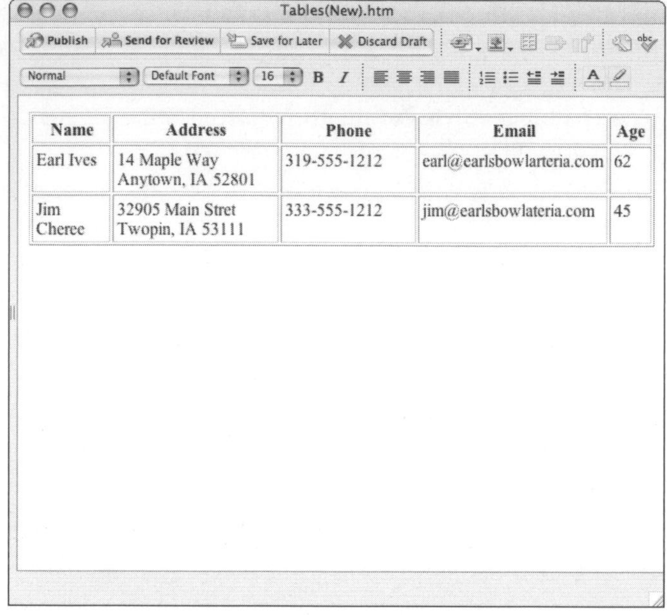

Name	Address	Phone	Email	Age
Earl Ives	14 Maple Way Anytown, IA 52801	319-555-1212	earl@earlsbowlarteria.com	62
Jim Cheree	32905 Main Stret Twopin, IA 53111	333-555-1212	jim@earlsbowlateria.com	45

Figure 2-9: A small table, built according to the specifications shown in Figure 2-8.

Changing the whole table using the Table Properties dialog box

To make changes to the entire table at once, follow these steps:

1. **Select the table by placing your cursor over the top-left or bottom-left corner of the table until the cursor changes into a four-pointed arrow; then, click.**

   The border of the table highlights.

2. **Click the Table button on the Browser toolbar.**

   Yes, it's the same button you click to insert a table, but when you've selected a table that's already there, the button opens the Table Properties dialog box. The dialog box has two tabs: Table and Row and Column. (The default view opens to the Table tab, as shown in Figure 2-10.)

3. **Select an alignment from the Table Alignment drop-down list.**

   A table can be justified left, center, or right.

4. **Change the table width, border thickness, cell padding, and cell spacing as needed.**

   For more information on those table properties, see the "Inserting a table" section, earlier in this chapter.

5. **To change the border color, click the Border Color icon and use the color picker to choose a color.**

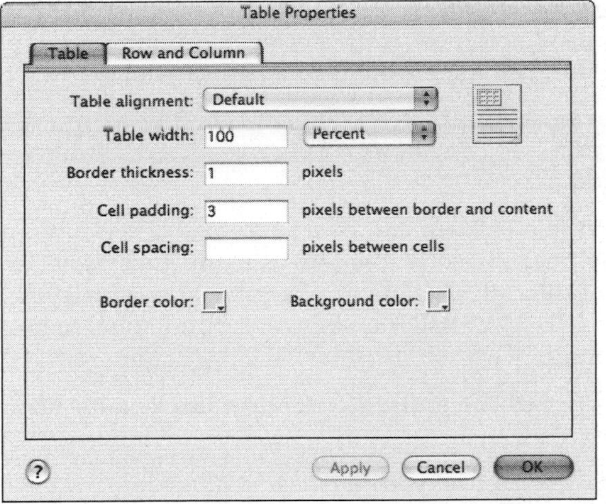

Figure 2-10: Change the table's alignment, width, and other properties in the Table Properties dialog box.

6. **To change the color of the table's background, click the Background Color icon and use the color picker to choose a color.**

7. **To change other properties, click the Row and Column tab at the top of the dialog box.**

   The Row and Column options appear. If you have selected only a row and not the whole table, the tab says Row. Likewise, if you have selected only a column and not the whole table, the tab reads Column.

8. **To change the horizontal alignment of elements in each cell, select an option from the Horizontal Alignment drop-down list.**

   Your options are Default, Left, Center, and Right. Choosing Default allows the visitor's browser to set the cells' alignment.

9. **To change the vertical alignment of elements in each cell, select an option from the Vertical Alignment drop-down list.**

   Your options are Default, Top, Middle, and Bottom. Choosing Default allows the visitor's browser to set the cells' alignment.

10. **To change the background color for the cells in the table, click the Background Color icon and use the color picker to choose a color.**

11. **Decide how you want to determine column width:**

    - If you want the table's column width to be allotted automatically, select the Fit to Contents radio button.
    - If you want to set the column widths to a specific number of pixels or percentage of the overall width, select the radio button underneath the Fit to Contents radio button, enter a number in the text field, and select either Pixels or Percent from the drop-down list.

If you insert something in a cell that is wider than you have set the column to handle, the cell overrides your column width setting to accommodate the element, be it an image or a long string of text.

12. **If you want to keep all the text on a single line within the cells, deselect the Wrap Text check box. Otherwise, leave the Wrap Text check box selected.**

    If all the text in a cell won't fit on a single line and the Wrap Text check box is selected, the text is split into as many lines as necessary, given the width of the cell. The line breaks come at spaces, dashes, and carriage returns. Deselecting the Wrap Text option may increase the width of your table.

13. **If you've selected the entire table, leave the Header Row check box alone.**

    If you've selected a row, you can make it a header row by selecting the Header Row check box, or you can remove its header row formatting by deselecting the Header Row check box.

14. **Decide how you want to determine row heights:**

    - If you want them determined by the content in the rows (each row is only as large as the biggest cell in that row), select the Fit to Contents radio button next to the Row Height section.
    - If you want them set in pixels, select the radio button below the Fit to Contents radio button and enter a number for the height you want the row to be in pixels.

15. **When you've made all the changes you want, click OK.**

    At any time while you are changing settings, you can click the Apply button to see the effect before moving on to the next property.

Changing rows, columns, or individual cells using the Tabl Properties dialog box

There may be times when you want to change the text alignment in some cells but not others, or you want to perform some other task that applies only to a particular row or column. In those circumstances, you need to select only the cells you want to affect; then you can make the changes using the Table Properties dialog box.

Selecting a row

To select a row, place your cursor on the table border at the left of the row you want to select and click when the cursor becomes a bold right-pointing arrow, as shown on the top in Figure 2-11. The row will highlight.

Selecting a column

To select a column, place your cursor on the table border at the top of the column you want to select and click when the cursor becomes a bold down-pointing arrow, a shown in the middle in Figure 2-11. The column will highlight.

Selecting an individual cell or group of cells

To select an individual cell, triple-click the cell. The cell is highlighted. To select multiple cells, click in one cell, hold the Shift key, and triple-click in another cell. The two cells you clicked in and every cell between them are highlighted.

After you've made your selection, click the Table button to open the Table Properties dialog box and make the changes just as outlined in the "Changing the whole table using the Table Properties dialog box" section, earlier in this chapter. If you have selected a row, the Rows and Columns tab says only Row, and if you have selected a column, the Rows and Columns tab reflects that by saying only Column.

Name	Address	Phone	Email	Age
Earl Ives	14 Maple Way Anytown, IA 52801	319-555-1212	earl@earlsbowlateria.com	62
Jim Cheree	32905 Main St. Twopin, IA 53111	333-555-1212	jim@earlsbowlateria.com	45

Name	Address	Phone	Email	Age
Earl Ives	14 Maple Way Anytown, IA 52801	319-555-1212	earl@earlsbowlateria.com	62
Jim Cheree	32905 Main St. Twopin, IA 53111	333-555-1212	jim@earlsbowlateria.com	45

Name	Address	Phone	Email	Age
Earl Ives	14 Maple Way Anytown, IA 52801	319-555-1212	earl@earlsbowlateria.com	62
Jim Cheree	32905 Main St. Twopin, IA 53111	333-555-1212	jim@earlsbowlateria.com	45

Figure 2-11: Selecting a row (top), a column (middle), and a group of adjacent cells (bottom).

Adding Images, Links, and More

Adding images to a page is a snap with Contribute. In a way, it's easier than adding a table, because images have fewer properties to set. Same goes for adding Flash movies to a page.

Inserting an image

If the image you want to insert in your page is on your computer's hard drive, just follow these steps to insert it:

1. **Place your cursor in the draft and click where you want to add the image.**

   The cursor blinks where the top-left corner of your image will appear on the page. You can insert an image in a table cell or anywhere else on the page.

2. **Choose Insert⇨Image⇨From My Computer or press Ctrl+Alt+I.**

   The Select Image dialog box appears.

3. **Navigate to the folder the image is in and then either double-click the image's filename or click the filename and click Select.**

   The image is placed in your draft. When you publish the page, Contribute automatically uploads the image. Your site administrator can set a maximum file size for any image uploaded to your site. If you get an error message saying your image is too big, see your site administrator or re-export the image from Fireworks at a smaller file size.

Inserting a Flash movie

Adding a Flash movie to your page from your computer's hard drive is easy. Just follow these steps:

1. **Place your cursor in the draft and click where you want to add the Flash movie.**

   The cursor blinks where the top left of your movie will appear on the page. You can insert a movie in a table cell or anywhere else on the page.

2. **Choose Insert⇨Flash⇨From My Computer.**

   The Open dialog box appears.

3. **Navigate to the folder the movie is in and then either double-click the Flash movie's filename or click the filename and click Open.**

   The Flash movie is placed in your draft. When you publish the page, Contribute automatically uploads the `.swf` file.

Flash movies have *parameters* that can be set on a Web page — they affect how the movies appear and function — but Contribute only gives you access to a couple of them. To make these (limited) changes, select the movie by clicking it and then choosing Format⇨Flash Movie Properties to open the Flash Movie Properties dialog box and set the Play on Page Load and Loop properties.

Inserting a link

Links (short for *hyperlinks*) are what the Web is all about, so naturally Contribute allows you to add links to your pages. You can link *from* both text and images, and you can link *to* other pages on your site, other pages on the Web, e-mail addresses, and things like PDF files.

Linking to a Web page

To add a link from text or an image to a page on your Web site or any other Web site, just follow these steps:

1. **Click an image or click and drag to select some text that you want to link to another page on the Web.**

   The image or text highlights.

2. **Choose Insert⇨Link⇨Browse to Web Page.**

   The Insert Link dialog box opens, with Browse selected at the top, as shown in Figure 2-12. Alternatively, you can choose to link to a draft or recently edited page.

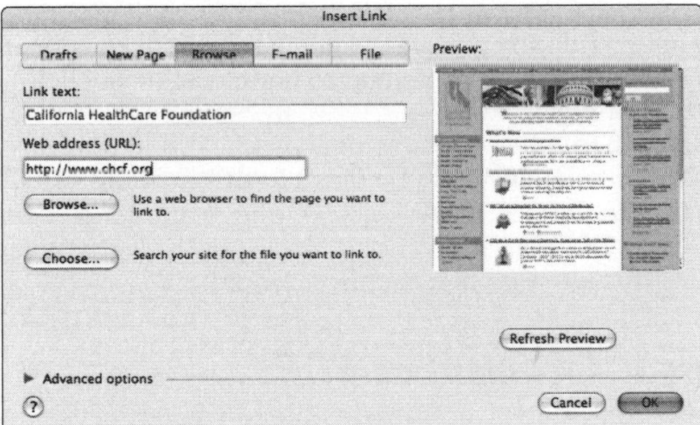

Figure 2-12: The Insert Link dialog box varies slightly in appearance, depending on what type of link you're creating.

3. **Enter a URL (for example,** `www.MySite.com/contactus.htm`**) in the Web Address text field, or click the Browse button to go to the page you want to link to.**

   Browsing to the page is often the best way to ensure that you link to the correct page. The page you browsed to appears in the Preview area on the right.

4. **Click OK.**

   You've just created a hyperlink.

Linking to an e-mail address

When you link to an e-mail address, the link on your Web page opens a new e-mail message in your visitor's e-mail program. The e-mail is automatically addressed to the e-mail address you specify in the link.

To add an e-mail link to some text or to an image:

1. **Click and drag to select text or click an image that you want to link to an e-mail address.**

   The image or text highlights.

2. **Choose Insert⇨Link⇨E-mail Address.**

   The Insert Link dialog box opens, with E-mail selected at the top.

3. **Enter the text that will link to the e-mail address in the Link Text text field.**
4. **Enter the e-mail address in the E-mail Address text field.**
5. **Click OK.**

   The selected text or image links to the e-mail address.

Linking to an e-mail address opens the visitor's e-mail program only if his or her program is set up to open when such a link is clicked. Most current e-mail programs are set up by default to handle an e-mail link.

You can also link to other drafts, to new pages, and to files on your computer (such as Word documents and PDF files). See Contribute's Help files for details on how to perform those tasks, or check out *Adobe Contribute For Dummies,* by Janine Warner and Frank Vera (published by Wiley), which has many details that we can't fit into this minibook.

Inserting a document as PDF

Starting with Contribute 2, users were able to convert Office documents into compact Flash movies that could be displayed in a Web page and viewed by anyone with the Flash plug-in in his or her browser. Called FlashPaper, this functionality basically competed with Adobe's PDF format. With the merger between Adobe and Macromedia, FlashPaper has been put out to pasture and replaced throughout the entire old Macromedia product line with Adobe's PDF. Nowhere is this more noticeable than in Contribute.

To insert a PDF document into your page, just follow these steps:

1. **Place your cursor in the draft and click where you want to add the document.**

   The cursor blinks where the top left of your image will appear on the page. You can insert an image in a table cell or anywhere else on the page.

2. **Choose Insert⇨PDF Document⇨From My Computer.**

   The Open dialog box appears.

3. **Navigate to the document's folder and then either double-click the document's filename or click the filename once and click Open.**

   The Insert PDF Document dialog box appears, as shown in Figure 2-13.

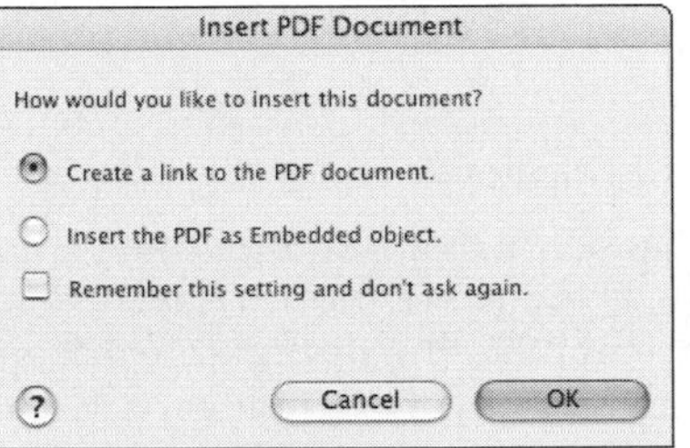
Insert PDF Document
How would you like to insert this document?
Create a link to the PDF document.
Insert the PDF as Embedded object.
Remember this setting and don't ask again.
?
Cancel
OK

Figure 2-13: You can either link to a PDF document or embed it in your Web page.

4. **Select either to link to the PDF document or embed the document in your draft page.**

   You can also select the Remember This Setting and Don't Ask Again check box to avoid seeing the dialog box on subsequent inserts.

5. **Click OK to insert the document or link.**

Previewing Your Work

If you make minor text changes to a page, you may not need to see the pagein a browser such as Internet Explorer or Opera before you put it on your Web site for the whole world to see. But if you make extensive changes, or if you've created a new page, you may want to check out how it looks in your regular Web browser before you publish it to your site.

To preview a draft in your regular Web browser, choose File⇨Preview or press F12. Your regular Web browser (such as Internet Explorer) opens and displays the page you're editing.

Uploading (Publishing) a Page

When you've finished editing a page or creating a new one, you'll want to put it on your Web site where people can browse to it — that is, if you don't want to preview the page (see the preceding section, "Previewing Your Work") and you don't need approval to post the page (see "Collaborating," later in this chapter). In Contribute, uploading the page to your Web server, where it can be seen by any visitor who goes to the right URL, is known as *publishing a draft.*

Publishing a draft is incredibly simple: Just click the Publish button at the top left of Contribute's Browser. The page and any images or Flash movies you've added to it are uploaded to the server, and Contribute's Browser automatically switches to Browse mode to display the uploaded page as it will appear to visitors to your site.

Working Offline

Unless you tell it otherwise, Contribute maintains an open connection to the server that hosts your Web site. If you prefer not to have a connection open the whole time you're working, you have the option to work offline. Simply choose File➪Work Offline (Contribute➪Work Offline on a Mac). The Contribute Browser shows that you are working offline.

When you create a new page offline, the Work Online button instead of the Publish button appears, as shown in Figure 2-14. To reconnect to your site, simply click the Work Online button.

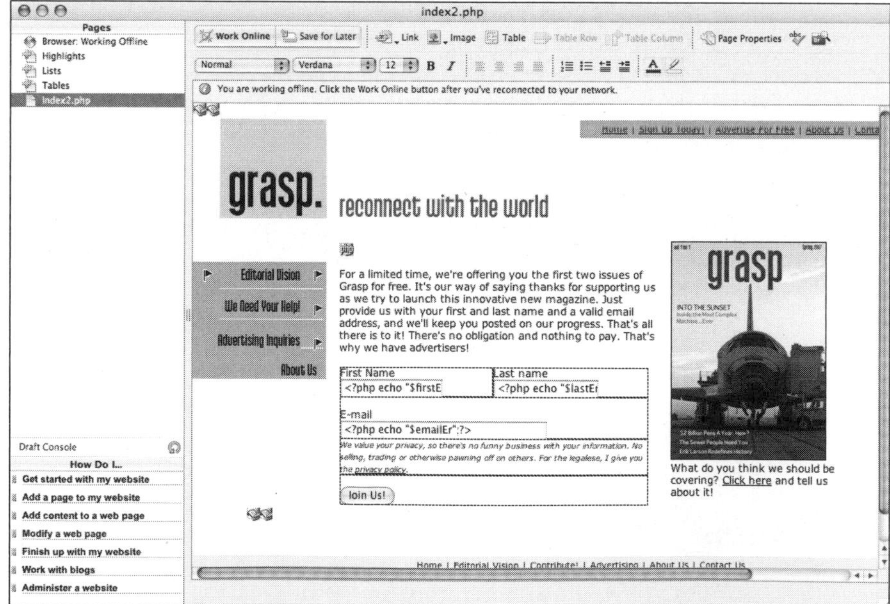

Figure 2-14: Working offline is a great way to keep working when you're traveling.

Collaborating

Contribute has several features that make collaborating on a site easy. For example, when you edit a page, Contribute prevents anyone else from editing the page at the same time. That way, you never accidentally overwrite someone else's changes — and nobody overwrites yours!

If you need approval before you publish a draft, you have two methods for submitting the draft to a colleague:

- **Email Review:** Contribute uploads a copy of your draft to a hidden part of your Web site, and you send an e-mail to your colleague with a link to the hidden page. When you get approval, you publish the page.
- **Send Draft for Review:** Contribute makes the hidden page available to your colleagues so that they can review and publish it.

To make a preview of your draft and send an e-mail to a colleague with a link to the preview, just follow these steps:

1. **While you're in Edit mode on the page you want to show to your colleague, click the Send for Review button in the Browser.**

   The Send for Review window appears.
2. **Select Send E-mail with a Link to a Preview of the Draft.**
3. **Click the Send button.**

   An e-mail appears with a message to the person you're asking to review your work.
4. **Edit the e-mail if necessary and then send it.**
5. **If you think you may have to wait awhile for approval, save the draft by clicking the Save for Later button at the top of the Browser.**

   The draft appears in the Pages panel.
6. **When you have approval, click the draft's name in the Pages panel.**

   The Browser switches to Edit mode and loads the draft in the Browser.
7. **Click Publish.**

   The Browser switches to Browse mode and displays the published page as it appears on your Web site.

To send a draft of the page to a colleague for review and publishing, just follow these steps:

1. **While you're in Edit mode on the page you want to show your colleague, click the Send for Review button in the Browser.**

   The Send for Review window appears.

2. **Select Send the Draft to Another Contribute User.**

   A list of users and groups becomes available.

3. **Click to select a recipient or multiple recipients.**

   Press the Shift key to make multiple, contiguous selections from the list; press the Ctrl key and click to make multiple, noncontiguous selections.

4. **If the page is a new draft of an existing page, you can enter a description of the changes you've made.**

   This step is optional.

5. **If you want to send an e-mail notifying your colleagues of your request, leave the Notify Recipients Through E-mail option selected and proceed to Step 6.**

   Otherwise, deselect the box and click Send. Depending on your setup, the Send New Page or Send Linked New Files dialog box may appear. You can rename your draft and navigate to a directory to copy the draft into. A window appears to confirm that your draft has been sent for review (unless you have previously selected the Don't Show Me This Message Again check box).

6. **Edit the e-mail if necessary and send it.**

   The e-mail opens in your default e-mail program. After you send it, Contribute updates to show the latest draft in the Draft Console. If you want to cancel the review request, click the Undo Send button.

Chapter 3: Contribute CS3 Administration

In This Chapter

- Making yourself a site administrator
- Making general settings, including rollbacks
- Working with users and roles
- Revising role settings
- Utilizing shared assets
- Creating connection keys

If you're set up in the role of Contribute CS3 site *administrator,* you can do everything a regular user can do — edit existing pages and make new ones — but you also control who the regular users are, what access they have to a site, and more.

A site may have multiple administrators as well as multiple users. All administrators have the same privileges, including the privilege to set up groups of users in roles with distinct privileges. If reading that last sentence makes you feel as though you've just stumbled into a hall of mirrors, don't worry. Read on, and you'll be a site administrator in no time.

Setting Yourself Up as Site Administrator

You can set yourself up as an administrator, or you can set someone else up as an administrator. But first things first: If you want to make site administrators of your colleagues, you have to make yourself a site administrator beforehand. By the way, if you want to be an administrator on a site that already has one, you need that site's administrator to set you up in a role with administrator privileges.

Though you may be able to set yourself up as a site administrator at any time by editing your settings, we assume for the purposes of this book that you are setting yourself up as an administrator at the same time you are making your first connection to the site in Contribute, and that nobody else has yet done so. To set yourself up as an administrator, just follow these steps:

1. **Browse to the site via Contribute's Browser by typing or pasting a URL (for example, `www.MySite.com`) into the Address text field.**
2. **Press Enter or click the Go button.**

   The Contribute Browser takes you right to your site.

   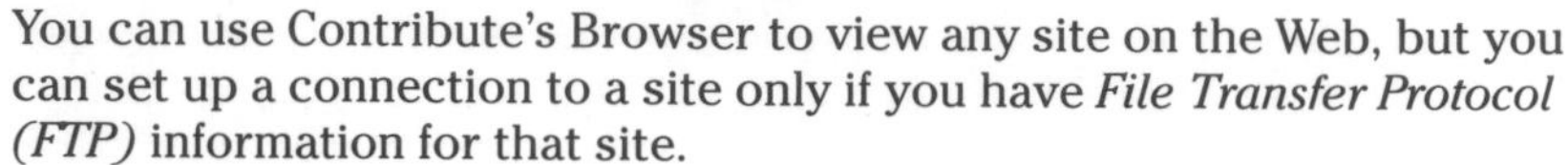

   You can use Contribute's Browser to view any site on the Web, but you can set up a connection to a site only if you have *File Transfer Protocol (FTP)* information for that site.
3. **Click the Create Connection button at the top left of the Browser, as shown in Figure 3-1.**

   The Connection Wizard opens to its Welcome screen.
4. **We're assuming you don't have a connection key, so click the Continue button at the bottom of the wizard.**

   The Website Home Page screen appears. For more information about connection keys, see the "Creating Connection Keys to Provide Access to Contributors" section, later in this chapter.
5. **If necessary, enter the URL (`www.MySite.com`, for example) for the Web site you'll be editing by typing or pasting it into the text field. Click Continue.**

   The URL should be there already because you browsed to the site to start the connection process. When you click Continue, the Connection Information screen appears in the wizard.

Figure 3-1: Getting ready to connect to a Web site.

6. **Select a connection method from the drop-down list.**

   You have the following options: FTP, Secure FTP (SFTP), and Local/Network. Depending on what you choose, different text fields appear below the drop-down list. As you can see in Figure 3-2, we entered FTP.

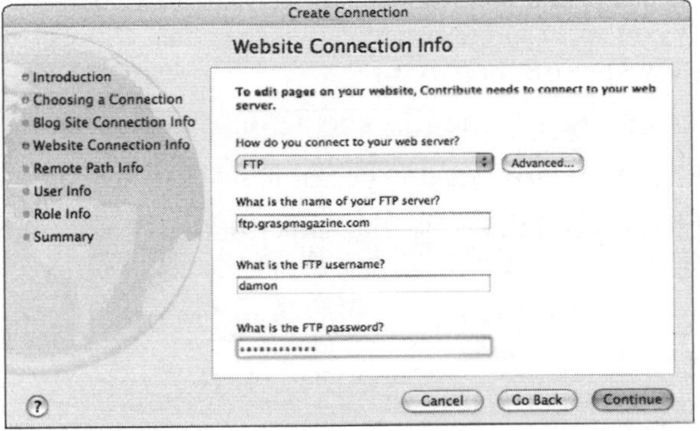

Figure 3-2: FTP information is entered in the Connection Information screen.

7a. **If you selected FTP or SFTP, enter the FTP server name (such as `ftp.graspmagazine.com`), login, and password in the respective text fields. Click Continue.**

   The login is sometimes called the *username*. When you click Continue, Contribute tests the connection and then the User Information screen appears.

7b. **If you selected Local/Network, enter the network path (for example, `\\mynetwork\mydepartment\site`) by typing it, pasting it, or clicking the Choose Folder button and going to the folder that contains your site. Click Continue.**

   When you click Continue, Contribute tests the connection and then the User Information screen appears.

7c. **If you selected WebDAV, enter the URL, username, and password that you use to connect to the site under WebDAV.**

   When you click Continue, Contribute tests the connection and then the User Information screen appears.

8. **Enter your name in the What Is Your Full Name? text field.**

   Your name may already appear. The name in this field identifies you to other contributors to your site, if there are any.

9. **If it's not already there, enter your e-mail address in the What Is Your E-mail Address? text field and click Continue.**

   The Summary screen appears.

10. **Click Done.**

    The Connection Wizard closes.

11. **Choose Edit⇨Administer Website⇨*Name of Site,* where *Name of Site* is the site you want to administer. (On the Mac, this option can be found in the Contribute menu.)**

    Contribute connects to the site, and a Contribute window opens.

12. **Select either Standard Word Processing or Dreamweaver-style editing.**

    These options affect the code that Contribute writes, but they do not affect the Contribute user's editing experience.

13. **Click the Yes button, indicating you would like to become the site's Contribute administrator.**

    The Administer Website window opens to the Users and Roles screen, with Administrator selected by default; see Figure 3-3. Your name may appear under Administrator.

14. **Click Administration in the list on the left.**

    The Administration screen appears on the right.

15. **Enter a contact e-mail address as needed.**

    The contact e-mail address appears when Contribute throws a Contact Your Administrator error message to a user.

16. **Click the Set Administrator Password button.**

    The Change Administrator Password window appears.

17. **Enter a password in the top text field of the Change Administrator Password window.**

18. **Re-enter the password in the text field below, exactly as you typed it in Step 17. Click OK.**

    You can use any combination of numbers and letters for your password. The password is *case sensitive* (so as far as the password is concerned, a big *S* and a small *s* are different characters). Only contributors who know that password can perform administrator functions on the site. When you click OK, the window closes.

You are now the site administrator. You can click the Close button or set options for users on the other screens of the Administer Website window. To find out about those other screens, read on.

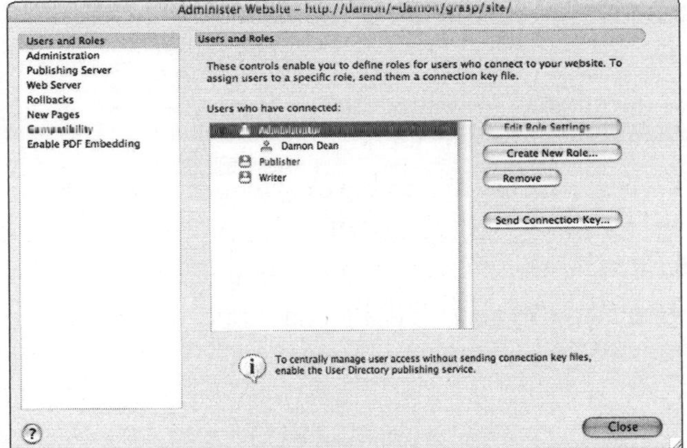

Figure 3-3: The Administer Website window centralizes all your site administration options.

Creating General Settings

General settings apply to all site contributors, regardless of any role settings you make. (We deal with role settings later in this chapter.) Using the Administer Website dialog box, shown previously in Figure 3-4, you can

- Change the administrator's e-mail address and password
- Enable Contribute Publishing Services
- Set up index and URL mapping
- Enable rollbacks and customize rollback settings
- Establish default encoding and file extension settings for new pages added by users
- Delete all permissions and settings simultaneously

We discuss each of those settings in the following subsections.

Changing the administrator's e-mail address

To change the administrator's e-mail address, just follow these steps:

1. **Choose Edit⇨Administer Website⇨*Name of Site*, where *Name of Site* is the site you want to administer.**

   If the Administrator Password dialog box appears, go to Step 2. Otherwise, when the Administer Website dialog box appears, it opens to the Users and Roles screen. Skip to Step 3.

2. **Enter your password and click OK or press Enter.**

   The Administer Website dialog box appears.

3. **Click Administration in the list on the left.**

   The Administration screen appears on the right, as shown in Figure 3-4.

4. **Select the existing administrator e-mail address by clicking and dragging until the address is highlighted.**

5. **Enter a new address by pasting or typing it into the administrator Contact E-mail Address text field.**

6. **Click Close.**

   The Administer Website dialog box disappears and the new e-mail address is set.

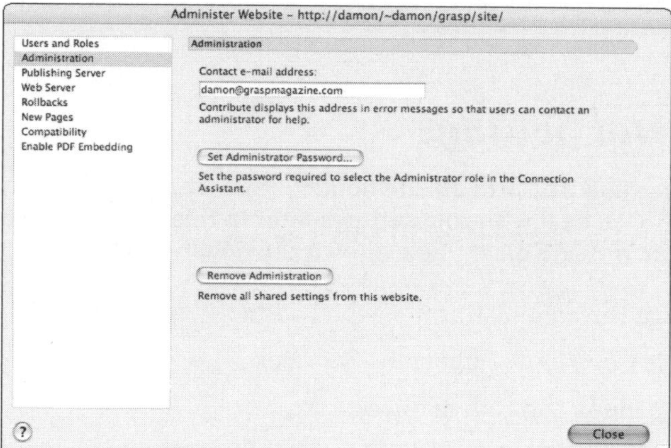

Figure 3-4: The Administration tab.

Changing the Administrator password

To change the Administrator password, follow Steps 1 through 3 in the previous section and then do the following:

1. **Click the Set Administrator Password button.**

   The Change Administrator Password dialog box appears.

2. **In the top field, enter your current Administrator password.**

3. **Press the Tab key or click in the second field and enter the new password that you want to use.**

4. **Press the Tab key or click in the third field and re-enter the new password exactly as you entered it in the second field.**

5. **Click OK.**

   The Change Administrator Password dialog box closes. If you want to make changes to other settings, do so. Otherwise, click Close to close the Administer Website dialog box and save your changes.

Setting up Contribute Publishing Services (CPS)

Contribute Publishing Services (CPS) is a scalable, extensible server application that can add administrative capabilities to Contribute while integrating with your existing Active Directory or LDAP setup. CPS logs all publishing activities on Web sites and offers administrators centralized control over user access. If you're having trouble understanding the terminology in this paragraph, ask for help from your IT director.

You must install and configure CPS before you can enable it from the Administer Website dialog box. For information on installing and configuring CPS, see your documentation.

To enable CPS, follow these steps:

1. **Choose Edit⇨Administer Websites⇨*Name of Site*, where *Name of Site* is the name of the site you want to administer.**
2. **Enter your password and click OK or press Enter if prompted.**

   The Administer Website dialog box appears.
3. **Click Publishing Server in the list on the left.**

   The Publishing Services screen appears on the right.
4. **Click the Enable Publishing Services button.**

   The Enable Publishing Services dialog box appears.
5. **Enter the URL for Publishing Services.**
6. **Leave Enable User Directory selected if you want to use Contribute's ability to authenticate users and manage the Web site connection.**
7. **Click OK.**

   The Enable Publishing Services window closes.
8. **Perform further administrator tasks or click Close to save your settings and close the Administer Website dialog box.**

Establishing Web server settings

In some cases, the way your Web server is configured to retrieve index pages may require you to adjust some settings in Contribute to get your connections between Contribute and the server working properly. The Web Server pages in the Administer Website dialog box offer you the ability to customize index pages and URL mapping, and to change from the default *guard page* (a hidden file that Contribute uses to control access to drafts and administrative files).

Mapping to alternate Web site addresses

If you have multiple *domain name system (DNS)* entries pointing toward a single *Internet protocol (IP)* address — that is, if `www.graspmagazine.com` and `grasp-magazine.com` both point to the same Web server — or if your contributors access your Web server using different addresses — from the Web and from your internal network, for example — you need to set up Contribute to recognize the additional addresses. Luckily, doing so is simple. To map Contribute to an alternate Web site address, just follow these steps:

1. **Choose Edit⇨Administer Website⇨*Name of Site*, where *Name of Site* is the site you want to administer.**
2. **Enter your password and click OK or press Enter if prompted.**

   The Administer Website dialog box appears.
3. **Click Web Server in the list on the left.**

   The Web Server screen appears on the right, open to the Web Addresses tab.
4. **Click the Add button.**

   The Add or Edit Alternate Address dialog box appears.
5. **Enter the URL(s) in the Alternate Addresses text field.**
6. **Click OK.**

   The Add or Edit Alternate Address dialog box disappears and the additional address appears highlighted at the bottom of the list.
7. **Make any other changes to the Web server settings, if necessary, and click Close.**

   This step saves your settings and closes the Administer Website dialog box.

To edit or delete an alternate Web site address, do the following:

1. **Follow Steps 1 through 3 in the previous list to open to the Web Addresses tab of the Web Server screen of the Administer Website dialog box.**
2. **Click the address you want to edit or delete.**

   The address is highlighted. Now you can perform one of the following actions:

   - **To edit the address, click the Edit button.** The Add or Edit Alternate Address dialog box appears, with the address highlighted. Edit the URL in the Alternate Website Address text field and click OK to close the Add or Edit Alternate Address dialog box.
   - **To delete the address, click the Remove button.** The address disappears from the dialog box.

3. **Make any other changes to the Web server settings, if necessary, and click Close.**

   This step saves your settings and closes the Administer Website dialog box.

Mapping to index files

Assume that your server is configured to default to home pages in a nonstandard way. For example, the server first checks a directory for `start.php` and then looks for `index.htm` if it doesn't find `start.php`. You can set up Contribute to mirror that configuration.

Contribute has 30 possible index page filenames listed (index and default, for each of 15 extensions). If your server is configured to look for a page with a different filename (such as `start.php` or `main.html`), you need to add that filename to the list.

To add a filename to the list, just follow these steps:

1. **Choose Edit⇨Administer Website⇨*Name of Site,* where *Name of Site* is the site you want to administer.**
2. **Enter your password and click OK or press Enter if prompted.**

   The Administer Website dialog box appears.
3. **Click Web Server in the list on the left.**

   The Web Server screen appears on the right, open to the Web Addresses tab.
4. **Click the Index Files tab.**

   The Index Files page appears.
5. **Click the Add button.**

   The Add or Edit Index Filename dialog box appears.
6. **Enter the filename in the Index Filename text field.**
7. **Click OK.**

   The Add or Edit Index Filename dialog box disappears and the new filename appears at the bottom of the list in the Index and URL Mapping dialog box.
8. **Use the arrow buttons on the right to move the new filename to the spot in the list that reflects the order the server uses.**

   For example, if the server checks `index.htm` first, that filename should be at the top of the list (as it appears in Figure 3-5). Each time you click the up-arrow button, the selected name moves up one spot in the list.

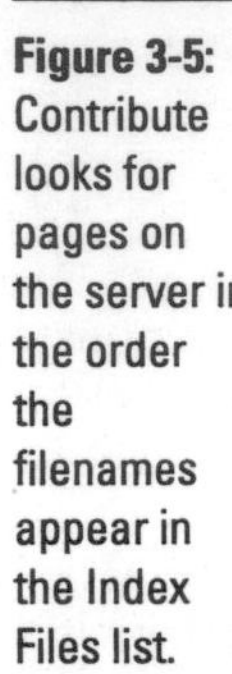

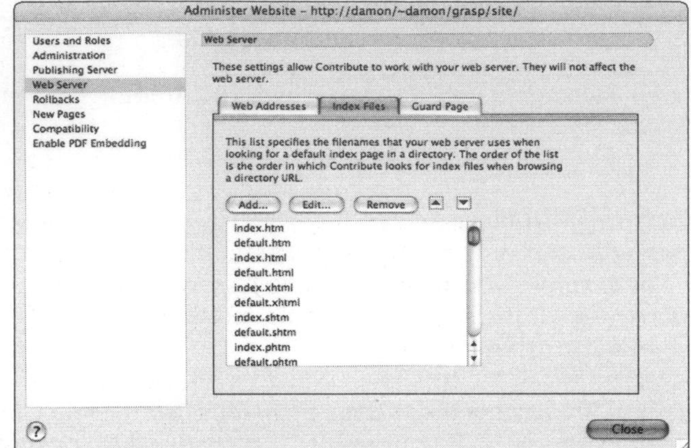

Figure 3-5: Contribute looks for pages on the server in the order the filenames appear in the Index Files list.

9. **Make any other changes to the Web server settings, if necessary, and click Close.**

   This step saves your settings and closes the Administer Website dialog box.

To edit or remove a filename from the list, just follow these steps:

1. **Follow Steps 1 through 4 in the previous list to open the Index Files tab of the Web Server pages of the Administer Website dialog box.**
2. **Click the filename you want to edit or remove.**

   The filename is highlighted.

   - **To edit the filename, click the Edit button.** The Add or Edit Index Filename dialog box appears, with the current filename highlighted. Type a new filename and click OK. The Add or Edit Index Filename dialog box closes and the edited filename appears in the list.
   - **To remove the filename from the list, click the Remove button.** The filename disappears from the list.
3. **Make any other changes to the Web server settings, if necessary, and click Close.**

   This step saves your settings and closes the Administer Website dialog box.

Using the Rollback feature to save file backups

Contribute's Rollback feature allows contributors to *roll back* to a previously published version of a page. You'll find this useful because reverting to a prior state of things is sometimes the best way out of a jam. To make it possible to roll back, Contribute keeps backup copies of edited pages on the Web server. Administrators can specify how many versions Contribute backs up. Administrators can also disable the Rollback feature.

The main advantage to the Rollback feature is pretty obvious: Backups can help you recover quickly if a newly published version of a page has multiple errors. Rather than having to scramble to fix the errors while the world sees your faulty page, you can just roll back almost instantaneously to the previously published version of the page. It's less likely you'll end up in a Rollback scenario if your draft has gone through the review process.

The major disadvantage of the Rollback feature, particularly for large sites, is that backups take up space on the Web server. If you have Contribute set to save three versions of each page, for example, by the time your colleagues have published changes to 100 pages, 300 backup pages have been created and stored in the `_baks` directory that Contribute has placed on the Web server that contains your site.

To activate and customize the Rollback feature, just follow these steps:

1. **Choose Edit⇨Administer Website⇨*Name of Site,* where *Name of Site* is the site you want to administer.**
2. **Enter your password and click OK or press Enter if prompted.**

   The Administer Website dialog box appears.
3. **Click Rollbacks in the list on the left.**

   The Rollbacks screen appears on the right.
4. **Select the Enable Rollbacks check box.**

   A check appears in the check box and the text field below is no longer grayed out.
5. **Use the toggle buttons at the right of the text field to increase the number of backups from 0, or double-click the 0 and enter a whole number between 1 and 99.**

   Though you may elect to keep up to 99 versions of each page, you're probably better off limiting the number to 2 or 3 to conserve space on your Web server.
6. **Make any other changes and click Close.**

   This step saves your changes and closes the Administer Website dialog box.

To disable rollbacks, follow Steps 1 through 3, deselect the Enable Rollbacks check box, and click Close. Disabling rollbacks does not remove existing backups. To remove existing backups, disable rollbacks and then use Dreamweaver or your favorite FTP client to delete the files. Do not delete the `_baks` folder because doing so can affect the way the program works.

Setting New Pages defaults

You can use the New Pages screen of the Administer Website dialog box to set the default encoding and file extension for any new page generated by a user. To set New Pages defaults, just follow these steps:

1. **Choose Edit⇨Administer Website⇨*Name of Site*, where *Name of Site* is the site you want to administer.**
2. **Enter your password and click OK or press Enter if prompted.**

   The Administer Website dialog box appears.
3. **Click New Pages in the list on the left.**

   The New Pages options appear on the right.
4. **Select a Default encoding from the drop-down list.**
5. **Enter a file extension in the Default File Extension text field.**
6. **Make any other changes and click Close.**

   This step saves your changes and closes the Administer Website dialog box.

Deleting all permissions and settings at one time

The Administration page of the Administer Website dialog box includes a button that allows you to delete all your custom sitewide settings and roles with a single click. You might find it efficient to delete all the settings at one time if your company or your Web site has just gone through a massive reorganization.

If you click this button, you nullify all restrictions you may have placed on any of your contributors. This means that all contributors have standard user access to all files on your site. It also means that if you have an elaborate array of restrictions and roles and you change your mind the next day, you have to re-create all those settings from scratch.

To delete all your sitewide settings and roles, simply click the Remove Administration button in the Administration page of the Administer Website dialog box. A Warning dialog box appears to give you a chance to back out. If you're sure that you want to delete the settings, click Yes. Then click Close in the Administer Website dialog box.

Setting Up Users and Roles

After you have designated yourself as an administrator, you have access to the Administer Website dialog box, in which you can do things such as configure general settings, send connection keys, and more.

When you set up a connection, Contribute automatically creates three default roles for contributors: Administrators, Publishers, and Writers. By default, users in all three roles may edit and create new pages, but only administrators and publishers can publish pages. You can set up as many additional roles as you like; each role might have different new page-creation permissions or access to different directories on the site, or other settings and permissions.

Opening the Administer Website dialog box

To open the Administer Website dialog box for a site to which you have administrator access, simply do the following:

1. **Choose Edit⇨Administer Website⇨*Name of Site*, where *Name of Site* is the site you want to administer.**
2. **Enter your password and click OK or press Enter if prompted.**

   The Administer Website dialog box appears, open conveniently to the Users and Roles screen.

Setting up a new role

If you don't need more than one set of users and one set of administrators, you can skip this section.

If you're creating a new role whose settings largely overlap with those of an existing role's, you can duplicate the existing role and then edit the duplicated role's settings as necessary. In fact, in Contribute CS3, all new roles must be created this way. To create a new role by duplicating an existing role, just follow these steps:

1. **Open the Administer Website dialog box by following the steps described in the earlier section, "Opening the Administer Website dialog box."**
2. **Click the Create New Role button in the Users and Roles page of the Administer Website dialog box.**

   The Create New Role dialog box appears.
3. **Select an existing role from the list at the top.**

4. **Enter a name for the new role in the Name of New Role field and click OK or press Enter.**

   The Create New Role dialog box closes. The new role's name is highlighted in the Administer Website dialog box, as shown in Figure 3-6, where we added a role called "Editor." If you want to edit that role's settings, just click the Edit Role Settings button. The "Editing Role Settings" section, later in this chapter, details the settings you can make.

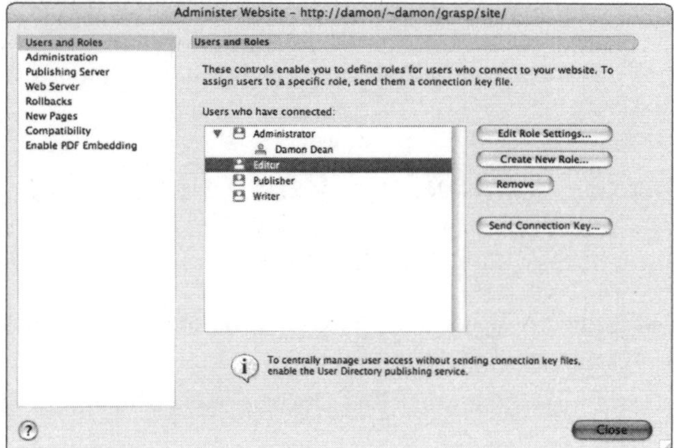

Figure 3-6: The new role "Editor" is highlighted in the Administer Website dialog box.

Deleting roles

Deleting a role is easy. Simply follow these steps:

1. **Open the Administer Website dialog box by following the steps described in the earlier section, "Opening the Administer Website dialog box."**
2. **In the Users and Roles page of the Administer Website dialog box, click the name of the role you want to delete.**

   The role name is highlighted.
3. **Click the Remove button.**

   A dialog box pops up, warning you that you are about to remove a role.
4. **Click Yes to remove the role.**

   The Warning dialog box closes and the role's name disappears from the Administer Website dialog box.

Editing Role Settings

After you've created a role (or decided to go with the default Administrators, Publishers, and Writers), you can adjust the permissions granted to the users who perform that role. Permissions may be *wholesale* (contributors in the Writers role may upload any images) or *conditional* (Writers may upload images, but only if the images' file sizes are smaller than 32 kilobytes, for example).

In contrast to general settings, role settings apply only to individual roles, not to all roles. Each role may have its own permissions or settings in the following areas:

- ✦ General
- ✦ Folder/File Access
- ✦ Editing
- ✦ Styles and Fonts
- ✦ New Pages
- ✦ File Placement
- ✦ Shared Assets
- ✦ New Images

We discuss each of the areas in detail in the following subsections.

Making general settings

When you open the Role Settings dialog box, you see the General screen by default. The General options allow you to make three types of settings for a role:

- ✦ **Publish Permission:** Give or deny users in the role permission to publish pages to the Web site.
- ✦ **Role Description:** A sentence or two that describes the role. The Role Description is what people see when they click the role name in the Connection Wizard.
- ✦ **Role Home Page:** The page that loads when users assigned to the role connect to the Web site in Contribute.

To create general settings for a role, follow these simple steps:

1. **Click to select the role for which you want to edit settings.**

   The role is highlighted.

2. **Click the Edit Role Settings button.**

   The Edit Role Settings dialog box appears, with the name of the role and Web site in the title bar.

3. **Select the Allow Users to Publish Files check box if you wish people in the selected role to be able to publish files to the Web site.**

   If no mark is in the check box, users in the selected role will have to send drafts to someone with publishing permission.

4. **Enter a role description by typing or pasting it into the Role Description text field.**

   Note that if you have selected the Allow Users to Publish Files check box, you'll probably want to change the default role description.

5. **Click and drag to select the current role home page and enter a new URL by typing or pasting it into the Home Page for Users in This Role text field.**

   Alternatively, you can click the Choose button at the right and navigate to the page in the Choose File on Website dialog box.

   One advantage of navigating via the Choose File on Website dialog box is that you avoid the possibility of misspelling the URL.

6. **Make other changes to the role's permissions as needed and click OK.**

If your Web site has several directories, each of which is maintained by a different department, you can make a role for each department and set a default home page for each role. For example, senior members of the Editorial Department, who are responsible only for all Web site content, might have `www.graspmagazine.com /edit/index.php` as their home page. Figure 3-7 shows the local network version of that same page.

Granting access to folders and files

You may wish to restrict certain groups of contributors from editing particular files on your site. For example, you may want the members of your Marketing Department to be able to update the News section of your site but not have access to the Products section. Contribute allows you to specify which folders (directories) a user in a particular role may access to edit the files within. (See Figure 3-8.)

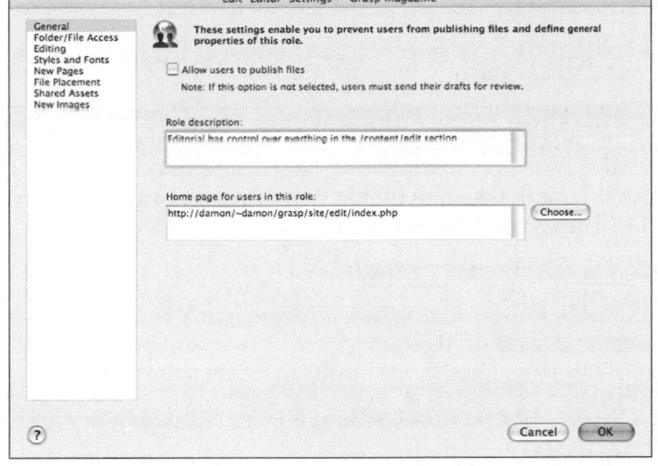

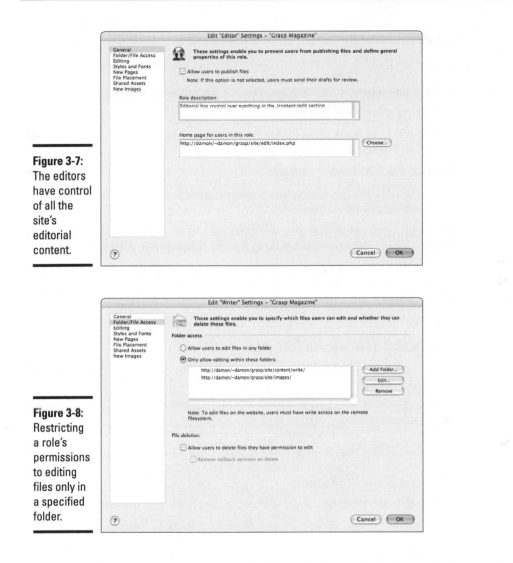

Figure 3-7: The editors have control of all the site's editorial content.

Figure 3-8: Restricting a role's permissions to editing files only in a specified folder.

To grant a role access to the files in a particular folder that already exists on your site, just follow these steps:

1. **From the Administer Website dialog box, select Users and Roles.**
2. **Click to select the role for which you want to edit settings.**

   The role is highlighted.
3. **Click the Edit Role Settings button.**

   The Edit Role Settings dialog box appears, with the name of the role and Web site in the title bar.

4. **Click Folder/File Access in the list on the left.**

   The Folder/File Access screen, as shown in Figure 3-8, appears, replacing the General screen.

5. **Select the Only Allow Editing Within These Folders option.**

   If a dialog box asks if you'd like Contribute to add a folder automatically to the list, click OK. The dialog box disappears and the Allow Editing Within These Folders text field becomes editable.

6. **Click the Add Folder button.**

   The Choose Folder dialog box appears, with your site's directory structure represented on the left.

7. **Double-click the folder you want the role to be able to edit, and then click Select *Folder Name,* where *Folder Name* is the name of the folder.**

   The Choose Folder dialog box disappears and the URL for the folder you selected appears in the Folder Access text field (refer to Figure 3-8).

8. **Make other changes to the role's permissions as needed; then, click OK.**

Extending file deletion privileges

The Folder/File Access screen in the Role Settings dialog box also allows you to choose whether a role is permitted to delete files from the site. Users in a given role can delete only files that they have permission to edit.

To allow users to delete files from a site, follow these simple steps:

1. **In the Folder/File Access screen, select the Allow Users to Delete Files They Have Permission to Edit check box at the top of the File Deletion section of the dialog box.**

   The Remove Rollback Versions on Delete check box becomes available.

2. **(Optional) If you want rollback files for a page to be deleted when that page is deleted, select the Remove Rollback Versions on Delete check box.**

3. **Make other changes to the role's permissions as needed; then, click OK.**

Customizing editing settings

The Editing options (shown in Figure 3-9) in the Edit Role Settings dialog box allow you to set what aspects of a page's underlying HTML code a role can edit. The Edit Role Settings dialog box also allows you to specify how Contribute writes some basic HTML formatting code.

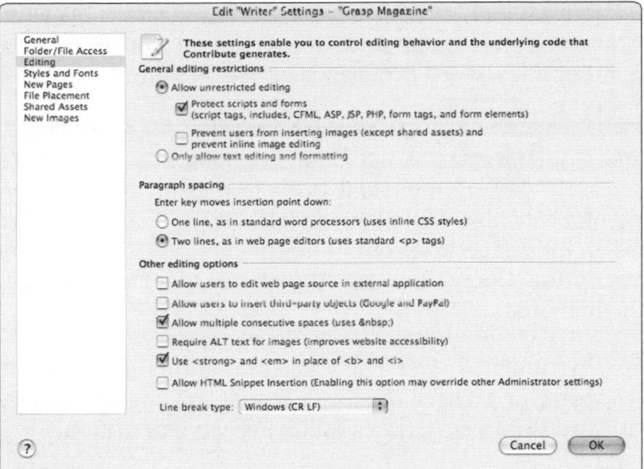

Figure 3-9: Editing options allow an administrator to restrict the number of functions a user can perform while editing a page.

Setting general editing restrictions

Dreamweaver templates "lock" certain chunks of code so that people editing pages based on those templates cannot change certain aspects of the way the page is built. This preserves the structure and look of the page. (For details on creating Dreamweaver templates, see Book II, Chapter 6.)

If you're not using Dreamweaver templates but you still want to protect any specialized code (ColdFusion markup, for example) from being edited, make sure that the Protect Scripts and Forms check box in the General Editing Restrictions section is selected. (The Allow Unrestricted Editing option is selected by default; if you want to allow everything on the page to be edited except scripts and forms, the Allow Unrestricted Editing option must be selected before the Protect Scripts and Forms check box can be selected.)

If you want users in the selected role to be unable to insert images or edit them using Contribute's new inline image-editing capabilities, select the Prevent Users from Inserting Images check box.

If you want users in a role to be able to edit and format text only, select the Only Allow Text Editing and Formatting option.

Setting the Paragraph Spacing option

When you're writing text in a regular word-processing program (such as Microsoft Word) and you press the Enter key on your keyboard, your cursor goes to the next line, just as a carriage return works on a typewriter. When you press Enter to go to a new line in a *WYSIWYG (What You See Is What You*

Get) HTML editor such as Dreamweaver, a blank line is inserted between the previous line you were on and the new line. You can set up Contribute to function either like a word processor or like Dreamweaver when a contributor presses the Enter key.

It's not just Contribute's behavior that changes when you change this setting, it's also the underlying HTML code that Contribute generates. When you select the One Line option in the Paragraph Spacing section, Contribute generates an inline CSS style to create the line break. When you select the Two Lines option, Contribute uses the standard HTML paragraph tag `<P>` to create the line break.

To set up Contribute to start a new line of text directly under the old one when a contributor presses the Enter key, select the One Line, As in Standard Word Processors (Uses Inline CSS Styles) option.

To set Contribute to start a new line of text two lines down from the old line, leaving a space in between, select the Two Lines, As in Web Page Editors (Uses Standard <P> Tags) option.

Setting other editing options

In the Other Editing Options section of the Editing screen, the Use `<STRONG>` and `<EM>` in Place of `<B>` and `<I>` option is selected by default. Leave it as is if you want Contribute to use the latest HTML tags for bold and italicized text.

Select the Allow Users to Insert Third-party Objects option if you want users in the selected role to be able to insert Google and PayPal extensions into pages.

Select the Allow Multiple Consecutive Spaces (Uses) option to enable contributors to create horizontal space in a page by inserting multiple spaces.

Select the Require ALT Text for Images option if you want Contribute to prompt contributors to include information that makes the page more accessible to visitors who are visually impaired.

To choose a line break type for the underlying code (not the text as it appears in a browser), select from the Line Break Type drop-down list. In most cases, you may leave this at its default setting; if the people working directly on the HTML use a particular type of computer, you may wish to select the line break type accordingly. *CR* stands for Carriage Return, and *LF* is short for Line Feed. Contribute offers the following line break types:

- Windows (CR LF)
- Macintosh (CR)
- UNIX (LF)

Granting styles and fonts permissions

To change the permissions for a role's ability to format text on Web pages, click Styles and Fonts in the list on the left side of the Role Settings dialog box; see Figure 3-10. Formatting text is usually one of the main responsibilities of anybody maintaining a Web site. Contribute makes formatting text easy as it is; setting styles and fonts permissions can make formatting text even easier for contributors by taking away options that might lead to incorrect formatting.

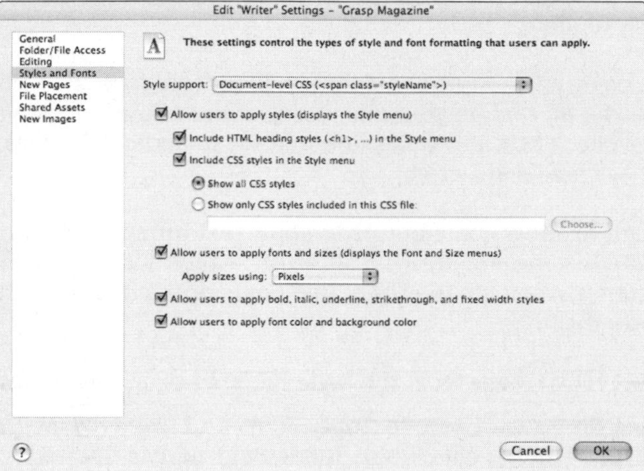

Figure 3-10: The Styles and Fonts screen of the Edit Role Settings dialog box allows you to limit text-formatting options by removing menus from Contribute's Browser.

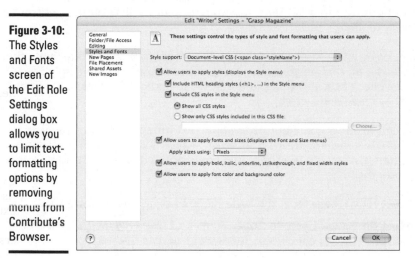

Setting styles options

By default, contributors are permitted to apply CSS styles and HTML paragraph and heading styles to text on pages they have permission to edit. The Style Support drop-down menu allows you to prevent users from applying any styles to the text by selecting the Don't Allow Users to Create Styles option. If you select that option, the rest of the Styles and Fonts options disappear.

If you don't want contributors to be able to apply CSS styles but you *do* want them to be able to apply styles to `<P>` tags and to insert header tags (`<H1>`, `<H2>`, and so on), deselect the Include CSS Styles in the Style Menu check box, but leave the other two check boxes selected.

If, on the other hand, you have set up a thorough CSS style sheet and don't want contributors using generic HTML paragraph and heading styles to format text, deselect the Include HTML Heading Styles (`<H1>`, . . .) in the Style Menu check box, but leave the other two check boxes selected.

Note that with Contribute CS3, you can limit the styles that appear in the Contribute Browser's toolbar to those that appear on a specific stylesheet. Simply select the Show Only CSS Styles Included in This CSS File option and input the pathname or URL of the style sheet, or click the Choose button and browse to the style sheet.

Setting fonts options

When the Allow Users to Apply Fonts and Sizes (Displays the Font and Size Menus) check box is selected, as it is by default, contributors can format text by choosing a font face and size from drop-down lists on the Contribute Browser's toolbar.

If you're using a CSS style sheet that includes font face, size, color, and other attributes for all text on your site, deselect the Allow Users to Apply Fonts and Sizes check box and make sure that the Include CSS Styles in the Style Menu check box is selected.

If you want to allow contributors to apply text formatting, and you want Contribute to generate basic HTML `<FONT>` tags, just follow these steps. This assumes you have the Styles and Fonts options of the Edit Role Settings dialog box showing.

1. **Select HTML Tags from the Style Support drop-down menu.**
2. **Select the Allow Users to Apply Fonts and Sizes (Displays the Fonts and Size Menus) check box, if it isn't already selected.**

   This box is selected by default.
3. **Select the Include HTML Heading Styles option.**
4. **Edit the settings as necessary.**

   By default, users are permitted to apply fonts and sizes, bold, italics, underline, strikethrough, and fixed-width styles, and to edit font and background colors.
5. **Make other changes to the role's permissions as needed, then click OK.**

If you want to allow contributors to apply text formatting, but you want Contribute to generate CSS-style code instead of HTML `<FONT>` tags, just follow these steps. We assume that you have the Styles and Fonts options of the Edit Role Settings dialog box showing.

1. **Select Document-Level CSS from the Style Support drop-down menu.**
2. **Select the Allow Users to Apply Fonts and Sizes check box, if it isn't already selected.**

   This box is selected by default.

3. **Select the Include CSS Styles in the Style Menu option.**

   For more details on this option, see "Setting styles options," earlier in this chapter.

4. **Select the Allow Users to Apply Fonts and Sizes check box.**

   If you want users to be restricted to font faces and sizes as defined in your style sheets, deselect this check box and skip to Step 6.

5. **Select a unit of font measurement from the Apply Sizes Using drop-down list.**

   The choices are Pixels, Points, or Ems. Whichever you choose is available from a drop-down list in the Contribute Browser.

   For information about the relative advantages and disadvantages of using each of the units of font measurement, browse to Mulder's style sheet tutorial at the Webmonkey Web site (`WebMonkey.wired.com/webmonkey/98/35/index2a.html?tw=authoring`).

6. **Edit other settings as necessary.**

   You can allow users to apply custom text formatting, font color, and background color to pages, or restrict users to options in your style sheet.

7. **Make other changes to the role's permissions as needed and then click OK.**

Granting permission to create new pages

Chances are, your contributors are going to need to create new pages for your Web site. If your company paid good money to have the site professionally designed, however, you probably don't want the people maintaining your site to fashion pages that diverge from the approved design.

Contribute gives administrators a way to force contributors to use Dreamweaver templates (the safest bet) or to use existing pages to create new ones. That helps keep the site design uniform and saves time for the people maintaining the site, as well.

To control the types of Web pages contributors can create, just follow these steps:

1. **If you have the Edit Role Settings dialog box open already, skip to Step 5. Otherwise, continue with Step 2.**

2. **Choose Edit⇨Administer Website⇨*Name of Site,* where *Name of Site* is the site you want to administer.**

   The Administer Website dialog box appears, open conveniently to the Users and Roles screen.

3. **Click to select the role for which you want to edit settings.**

   The role is highlighted.

4. **Click the Edit Role Settings button.**

   The Edit Role Settings dialog box appears, with the name of the role and Web site in the title bar.

5. **Click New Pages in the list on the left.**

   The New Pages screen replaces the General screen, as shown in Figure 3-11.

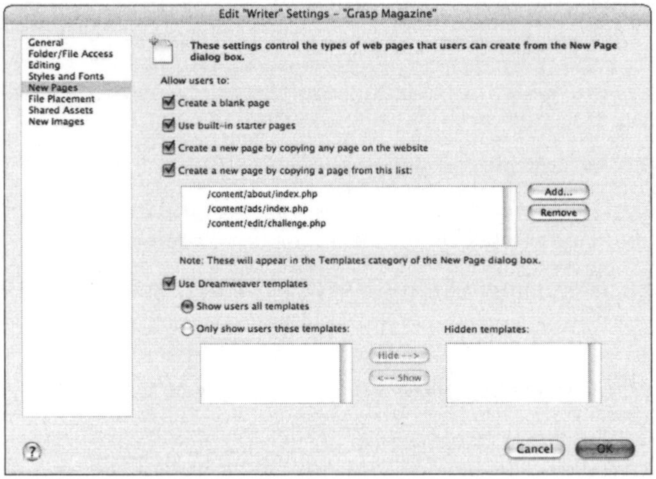

Figure 3-11: Granting permission to create new pages.

6. **If you want roles to have the option of creating a page from scratch, select the Create a Blank Page check box.**

   If you don't want users to be able to create a page from scratch, deselect the check box. This check box is selected by default.

7. **If you want roles to be able to create new pages based on Contribute's sample pages, select the Use Built-In Starter Pages check box.**

   If you don't want roles to be able to create a page from one of Contribute's sample pages, deselect the check box. This check box is selected by default.

8. **Decide which option you want:**

   - If you want roles to be able to use any page on your Web site as a basis for a new page, select the Create a New Page by Copying Any Page on the Website check box and then skip to Step 10a.

- If you want contributors to be able to use only specific existing pages on the site to create new ones, make sure that the Create a New Page by Copying Any Page on the Website check box is deselected and then proceed to Step 9a.

9a. Decide which option you want:

- If you want roles to be able to create a new page based on a specific page (or set of pages) on your site, select the Create a New Page by Copying a Page from This List check box.
- If you do not want roles to be able to create a new page based on a specific page, skip to Step 10a.

The Add and Remove buttons become active.

9b. Click the Add button.

The Choose File dialog box appears, with the directory structure of your site on the left.

9c. Click the page on which you want contributors to be able to model a new page.

If the page is in a folder, double-click the folder to open it in the dialog box, and then click the page. The preview section on the right displays the page you selected.

9d. Click OK.

The Choose File dialog box disappears, and the selected page appears in the list. Repeat Steps 9a through 9d if you want to add more pages. These pages appear as choices when the user in the role tries to create a new page.

10a. If you want roles to work from a Dreamweaver template when creating a new page, select the Use Dreamweaver Templates check box and continue with Step 10b. Otherwise, skip to Step 11.

When the Use Dreamweaver Templates check box is selected, the Use Dreamweaver Templates section of the dialog box becomes active.

10b. Decide which option you want:

- If you want roles to be able to base a new page on any Dreamweaver template on your site, select the Show Users All Templates option and proceed to Step 11.
- If you want roles to be able to base a new page only on a specific template (or set of templates), select the Only Show Users These Templates option and proceed to Step 10c.

10c. Double-click the template name (or names) in the Hidden Templates field, or click the template name and then click the Show button.

11. **Make other changes to the role's permissions as needed, then click OK.**
12. **Click OK in the Administer Website dialog box to save the changes.**

Setting file placement rules

Administrator lets you configure settings for placing various types of files when users upload them. Contribute offers default rules for style sheets, images, Microsoft Office files (such as Word docs and Excel spreadsheets), PDFs, and any other file types that have no specific file placement rule.

To add a file placement rule, follow these steps:

1. **If you have the Edit Role Settings dialog box open already, skip to Step 5. Otherwise, continue with Step 2.**
2. **Choose Edit⇨Administer Website⇨*Name of Site,* where *Name of Site* is the site you want to administer.**

   If the Administrator Password dialog box appears, go to Step 3. Otherwise, when the Administer Website dialog box appears, open to the Users and Roles screen, skip to Step 4.
3. **Enter your password and click OK or press Enter.**

   The Administer Website dialog box appears, open conveniently to the Users and Roles screen.
4. **Click to select the role for which you want to edit settings.**

   The role is highlighted.
5. **Click the Edit Role Settings button.**

   The Edit Role Settings dialog box appears, with the name of the role and Web site in the title bar.
6. **Click File Placement in the list on the left.**

   The File Placement options appear on the right.
7. **Click the Add button.**

   The File Placement Rule dialog box appears.
8. **Type or paste an extension (`.mov` or `.swf`, for example) in the File Type Extensions text field.**

9a. **If you want the uploaded file to reside in the same folder as the Web page that links to it, select the first Location option and go to Step 12.**

9b. **If you want the file to be placed in a folder that resides at the same level as the Web page, select the second option, enter a folder name in the text field, and go to Step 12.**

   Contribute creates the folder.

9c. **If you want the uploaded file to be put in an existing folder on your site, select the Specific Folder on Your Website option.**

Two further options become available.

10. **Click Choose and navigate to the folder where you want to put the uploaded file.**

11. **If you want Contribute to write links to uploaded files relative to the root of the Web site, select the check box.**

If, on the other hand, you want Contribute to write links relative to the page, don't mark the check box.

12. **Click OK.**

The File Placement Rule dialog box disappears and the File Size section appears in the Edit Role Settings dialog box.

13. **If you want to specify a maximum size for uploaded files, select Reject Linked Files (Except Images) That Exceed Max File Size. Otherwise, skip to Step 15.**

The Max File Size text field becomes active.

14. **Double-click or click and drag to highlight the default value and enter a new number in the Max File Size text field, as shown in Figure 3-12, to set a maximum file size.**

If you don't want users to be able to upload files, set Max File Size to 0.

The field uses kilobytes as its unit of measurement. If your maximum file size is greater than 1 megabyte (MB), calculate 1,024 kilobytes per MB. For example, a 5MB file is 5,120 kilobytes. Note that the text field will not accept a value greater than 9,999 kilobytes.

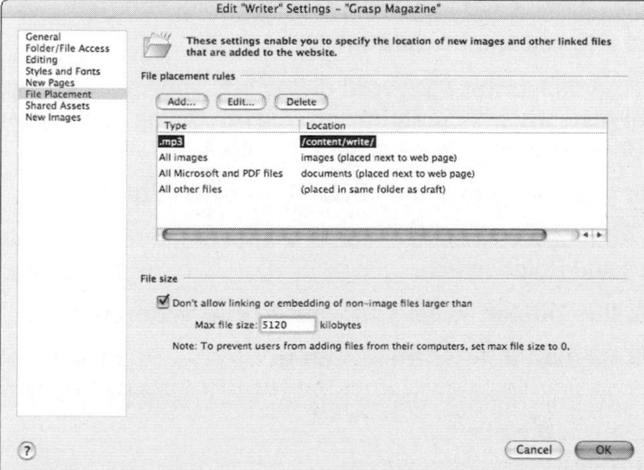

Figure 3-12: Limiting the size of mp3 files a user may upload to 5MB.

If you create file placement rules, be sure that your users have access to the folders in which you're doing the restricting! For example, if you have designers updating style sheets, make sure that they have access to that directory. See the previous section for details on enabling users to create pages in specific directories.

15. **Make other changes to the role's permissions as needed and then click OK.**
16. **Click OK in the Administer Website dialog box to save the changes.**

To edit a File Placement rule, follow Steps 1 through 6, click a rule to select it, and click the Edit button. Change any rule options as outlined in Steps 8 through 15.

To delete a rule, simply follow Steps 1 through 6, click a rule to select it, and click the Delete button. A warning may appear, asking if you really want to remove the rule. Click Yes to remove the rule and close the warning dialog box. Note that you may not delete any of Contribute's default rules, though you can edit them.

Working with shared assets

Shared assets are things such as Dreamweaver library items, Flash movies, and images that you want available for users to place easily in Web pages.

Adding a shared asset

To add a shared asset, follow these steps:

1. **If you have the Edit Role Settings dialog box open already, skip to Step 5. Otherwise, continue with Step 2.**
2. **Choose Edit⇨Administer Website⇨*Name of Site*, where *Name of Site* is the site you want to administer.**

   If the Administrator Password dialog box appears, go to Step 3. Otherwise, when the Administer Website dialog box appears, open to the Users and Roles screen, skip to Step 4.
3. **Enter your password and click OK or press Enter.**

   The Administer Website dialog box appears, open conveniently to the Users and Roles screen.
4. **Click the role for which you want to edit settings.**
5. **Click the Edit Role Settings button.**

   The Edit Role Settings dialog box appears, with the name of the role and Web site in the title bar.

6. **Select Shared Assets in the list on the left.**

   The Shared Assets options appear on the right, as shown in Figure 3-13.

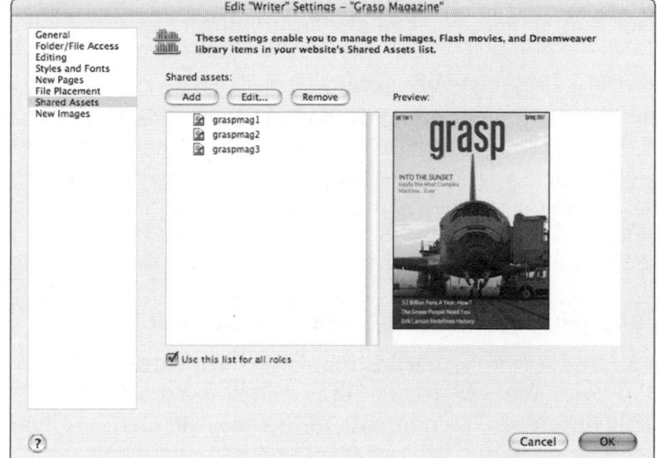

Figure 3-13: We've limited the writers to having access only to covers.

7. **Click Add and select an asset type from the pop-up menu.**

   The choices are Image, Library Item, and Flash. The Choose window appears.

8. **Navigate to the asset you want to share.**

   Shift+click to select multiple contiguous items; Ctrl+Click to select multiple noncontiguous items. You can also click the Select All Files in Folder button if you want to share all the items. If the Shared Asset Properties dialog box appears, see the instructions in the upcoming "Editing a shared asset" section for details on options.

9. **Click OK.**

   The Choose window disappears and a dialog box informs you that you have the option to prevent users from editing the asset.

10. **Click OK to close the dialog box.**
11. **Make other changes to the role's permissions as needed; then, click OK.**
12. **Click OK in the Administer Website dialog box to save the changes.**

Editing a shared asset

You can edit the name of any shared asset, regardless of type. The asset name is what shows up for the user when he chooses Insert⇨Shared Asset. By default, the asset name is the filename, minus the extension. For example, if the filename is di_113_small_2006.gif, it appears to the user as di_113_small_2006. An asset name like that might not be helpful to the user, so Contribute gives you the power to name the asset something more user friendly, such as Logo - Small.

If the asset is an image, you can also input an Alt tag.

If the asset is a Dreamweaver library item, you can change the asset name that appears to users and prevent users from editing the item. (By default, the Lock Item on Page check box is unselected, so users can edit the library item.)

To edit a shared asset, follow Steps 1 through 6 in the "Adding a shared asset" section, earlier in this chapter, and then do the following:

1. **Click to select an asset and then click the Edit button.**

   The Shared Asset Properties dialog box appears, as shown in Figure 3-14. If you have selected multiple items, the dialog box will appear slightly different. The contents of the box will also be slightly different depending on which type of asset you have selected.

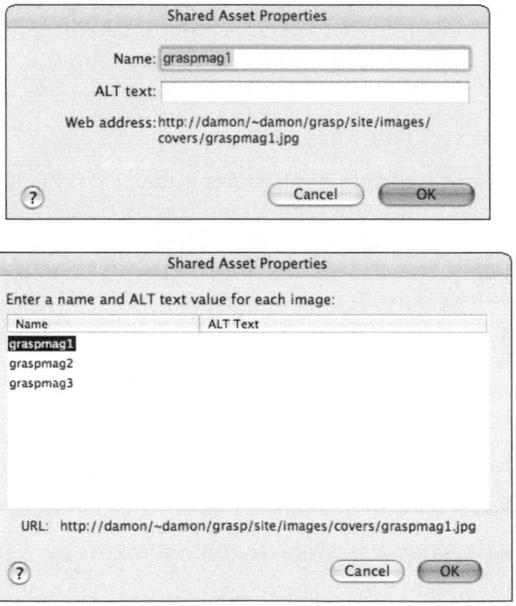

Figure 3-14: The Shared Asset Properties dialog box offers different options depending on which type of asset you choose and how many assets you choose.

2a. **If the asset is an image, change the asset name and Alt tag as needed.**

2b. **If the asset is a Dreamweaver library item, change the asset name and select or deselect the Lock Item on Page check box as needed.**

2c. **If the asset is a Flash SWF, change the asset name as needed. Click OK to close the dialog box.**

3. **Make other changes to the role's permissions as needed and then click OK.**

4. **Click OK in the Administer Website dialog box to save the changes.**

Deleting a shared asset

To delete a shared asset, follow Steps 1 through 6 in the "Adding a shared asset" section, earlier in the chapter, and then click an asset or assets and click the Remove button. A warning dialog box appears, asking whether you're sure that you want to remove the asset. Click Yes. The dialog box closes. Then you can make other changes in the Administer Website dialog box, or click OK to save your changes and close the Administer Website dialog box.

Customizing options for adding new images

As an administrator, you can set a file size limit for images; Contribute won't allow a role to add an image with a file size greater than the maximum you set. By default, there's no limit. You can also set maximum image dimensions. Note that these settings apply only to new images, not to shared assets or images inserted from the Web site.

If you want to allow users to edit new images using the built-in Contribute CS3 image-editing tools and to constrain the user's image-editing options, just follow these steps:

1. **If you have the Edit Role Settings dialog box open already, skip to Step 5. Otherwise, continue with Step 2.**

2. **Choose Edit⇨Administer Website⇨*Name of Site*, where *Name of Site* is the site you want to administer.**

   If the Administrator Password dialog box appears, go to Step 3. Otherwise, when the Administer Website dialog box appears, open to the Users and Roles screen, skip to Step 4.

3. **Enter your password and click OK or press Enter.**

   The Administer Website dialog box appears, open conveniently to the Users and Roles screen.

4. **Click to select the role for which you want to edit settings.**

   The role is highlighted.

5. **Click the Edit Role Settings button.**

   The Edit Role Settings dialog box appears, with the name of the role and Web site in the title bar.

6. Click New Images in the list on the left.

   The New Images options appear in the Edit Role Settings dialog box, as shown in Figure 3-15, replacing the General options.

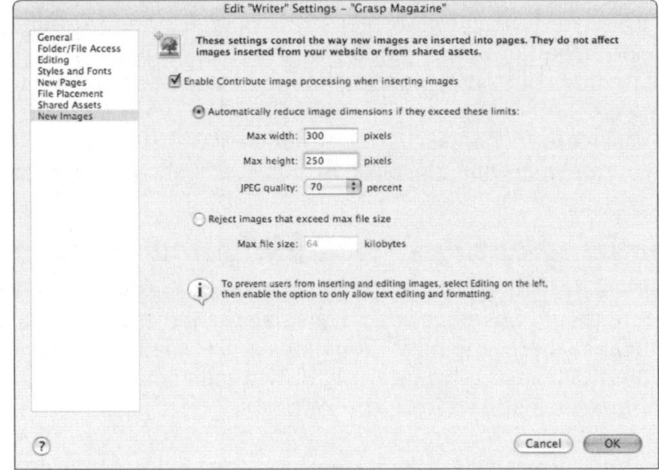

Figure 3-15: The New Images screen offers two ways to constrain altered, new images.

7. **Select the Enable Contribute Image Processing When Inserting Images check box if you want users to be able to use Contribute's built-in image-editing capabilities.**

   This option is selected by default. If you deselect this option, all the other options on the page lose their editability.

8. **Choose either the Automatically Reduce Image Dimensions if They Exceed These Limits option or the Reject Images That Exceed Max File Size option.**

   If you choose the former, go to Step 9. If you choose the latter, skip to Step 12.

9. **Double-click or click and drag to highlight the default Max Width value and enter a new number in pixels.**
10. **Double-click or click and drag to highlight the default Max Height, and set it in pixels.**
11. **Select a JPEG quality from the drop-down menu.**

    After making your selections, skip to Step 13.
12. **Double-click or click and drag to highlight the default value and enter a new number in the Max File Size field.**

    If you want the maximum file size to be 64 kilobytes, you can skip this step, of course.
13. **Make other changes to the role's settings as needed and then click OK.**

Creating Connection Keys to Provide Access to Contributors

Connection keys are password-protected, encrypted text files that contain the data Contribute needs to establish a connection with a Web site. When you send a connection key to a user in a role, all the user must do to establish a connection is double-click the key and enter a password. That can be pretty handy if you have several people in a group, since you can e-mail the same key to all of them, or post the key on your internal network.

You don't have to go to each member's machine to set up the connection, nor do you have to worry about providing tech support if you've decided to let people establish their own connections. Best of all, connection keys are specific to roles, so you don't have to worry that a contributor will choose to be in the wrong role.

To create a connection key, follow these steps:

1. **Choose Edit⇨Administer Website⇨*Name of Site,* where *Name of Site* is the site you want to administer.**

    If the Administrator Password dialog box appears, go to Step 2. Otherwise, when the Administer Website dialog box appears, open to the Users and Roles screen, skip to Step 3.
2. **Enter your password and click OK or press Enter.**

    The Administer Website dialog box appears, open conveniently to the Users and Roles screen.

3. **Click the Send Connection Key button.**

   The Export Wizard's welcome screen appears, as shown in Figure 3-16.

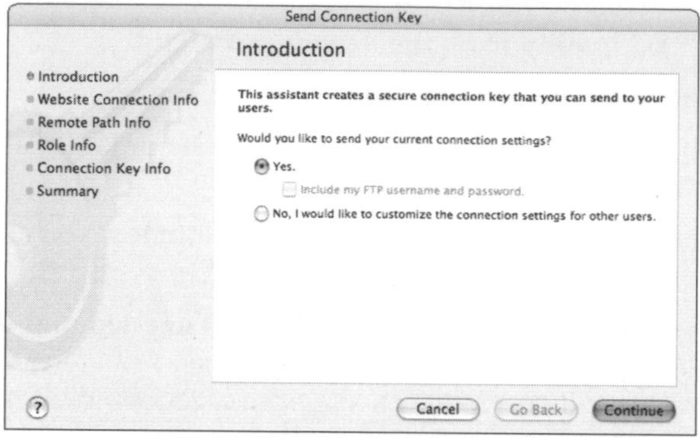

Figure 3-16: The Export Wizard's welcome screen starts you off with a basic Yes or No question.

4a. **If the role will connect to your Web server in the same way as you do, leave the Yes option selected under the question Would You Like to Send Your Current Connection Settings? and proceed to Step 4b. If not, skip to Step 4c.**

4b. **If you want to include FTP or SFTP login information in the connection key, select the Include My FTP Username and Password check box. Click Continue and skip to Step 6.**

   If your connection to the site is Local/Network, the box will be grayed out. When you click Continue, the Role Information screen appears.

4c. **If users in the role will be connecting to the site in a different way than you do, select the No, I Would Like to Customize the Connection Settings for Other Users option. Then click Continue and go to Step 5.**

   If users in the role will be connecting via the Web while you connect via your network, customize the connection settings for the role. When you click Continue, the Connection Information screen appears.

5. **Enter the information and click Continue.**

   For information about the Connection Information screen, see the section on connecting to a site with the Connection Wizard in Book VI, Chapter 2. When you click Continue, the Role Information screen appears.

6. **In the Select a Role area, click the name of the role that will use the connection key you're creating. Click Continue.**

   When you click the role, its description appears at the right, as shown in Figure 3-17. When you click Continue, the Connection Key Role Information screen appears.

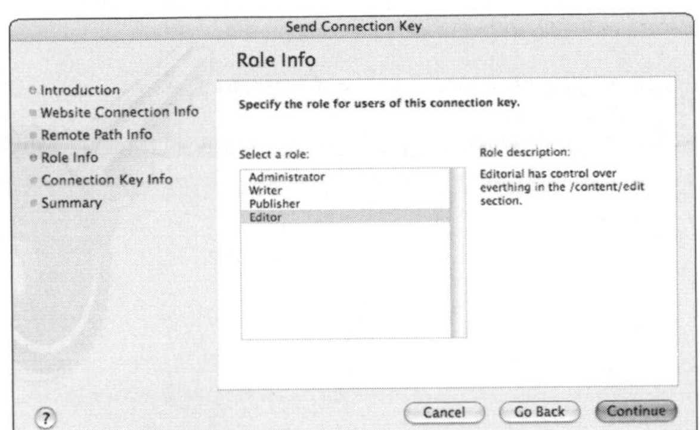

Figure 3-17: When you select a role, its description appears at the right.

7. **Answer the question How Would You Like to Export the Connection Key File? by selecting either the Send in E-mail or the Save to Local Machine option.**

   Adobe recommends that you not send the key via Web-based e-mail (such as Hotmail or Yahoo!) because even though the key is encrypted, it contains sensitive information that should never be sent via inherently less-secure, Web-based e-mail.

8. **In the top text field, enter a password that enables users in the role to use the key. Press the Tab key or click in the bottom text field.**

   A contributor must have the password to use the key. The password may contain spaces, numbers, and letters and be up to 30 characters long; the password is case sensitive. If you send the key in an e-mail, it's safest not to include the password in the same e-mail. Instead, send the password in a separate e-mail or, better yet, reveal the password verbally to users in the role.

9. **Re-enter the password exactly as you entered it in the text field in the previous step and click Continue.**

10. **Carefully check the information on the Summary screen to make sure that it's correct.**

    - If it isn't, use the Back button to go back and correct any information on previous screens; then, click Continue to return to the Summary screen.
    - If the information is correct, click Done.

If you selected the Send in E-mail option, a new e-mail with the connection key attached opens automatically in your e-mail program. Customize the e-mail as necessary, add a recipient or recipients, and send the message. If you selected the Save to Local Machine option, the Export Connection Key dialog box opens. Navigate to the folder on the local machine or on your network where you want to place the key and click Save.

Book VII

Acrobat 8

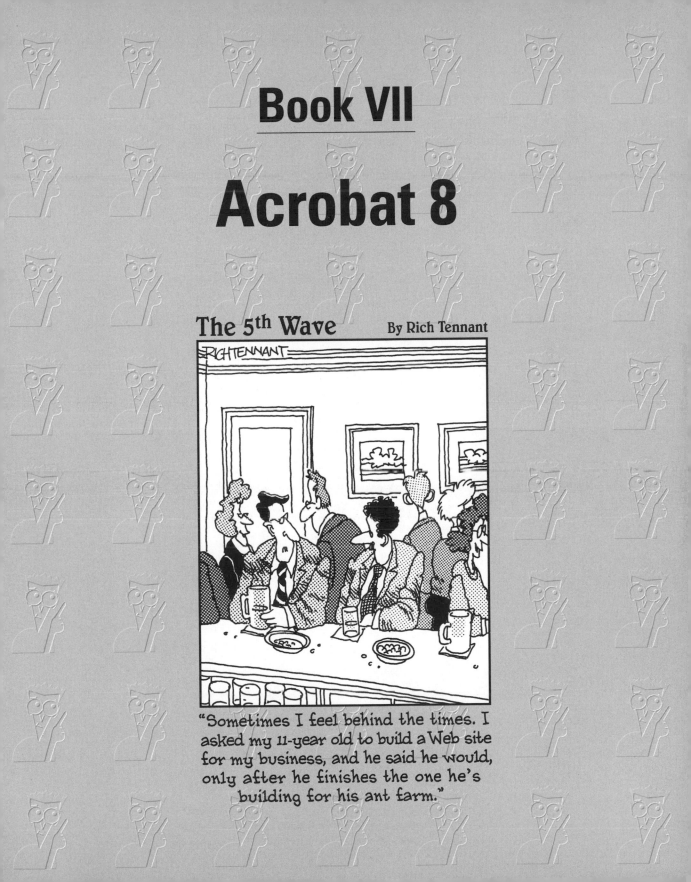

The 5th Wave By Rich Tennant

"Sometimes I feel behind the times. I asked my 11-year old to build a Web site for my business, and he said he would, only after he finishes the one he's building for his ant farm."

Chapter 1: Discovering Essential Acrobat Information

In This Chapter

- **Discovering Acrobat and PDF files**
- **Knowing when to use PDF files**
- **Becoming familiar with the Acrobat workspace and tools**

Adobe Acrobat 8 provides a variety of tools for sharing and reviewing documents. Although the Adobe Creative Suite applications can create Portable Document Format (PDF) files without Acrobat, you can use Acrobat to create PDF files from programs that aren't part of the Creative Suite. You can also use Adobe Acrobat to enhance PDF files, regardless of how they were created. You can add security to restrict features such as printing or editing, change the page order, merge documents together, add comments and annotations, and even create PDF forms.

In this chapter, you find out why you may want to create PDF files and acquaint yourself with the Adobe Acrobat tools and workspace. You'll see how easy it is to navigate through PDF files using the navigational tools, tabs, and viewing options in Acrobat. In the following chapters of this minibook, you explore how to use Acrobat to create Adobe PDF files from documents produced in a variety of programs and discover ways to enhance your Adobe PDF files.

Working with PDF Files

Adobe Acrobat is used to create Adobe PDF files, review existing PDF files, and modify existing PDF files. When you work with programs in the Adobe Creative Suite, such as Adobe InDesign, and you want to share your work with colleagues or clients, you need to find a way to deliver the documents to them. Of course, you can always print your documents and send them via courier, the mail, or even fax. But all these methods take time and don't provide for easy collaboration. This area is where PDF files are helpful.

Many people prefer to receive documents electronically, but there's a small problem: All the people with whom you need to share files probably don't have the same software you use. They may not all have InDesign — or whatever part of the Adobe Creative Suite you're using. PDF provides a common file format that everyone can open to review your documents. PDF provides an application independent method for viewing your files, regardless of what computer program was used to create them. The PDF file format also lets Mac users share their files with Windows users, and vice versa. Additionally, Acrobat provides extensive tools for review, commenting, and marking up so that you can easily collaborate on a project without modifying the original document.

You can view PDF files on many different computer types, including Macintosh computers, Windows computers, Unix computers, and even some cell phones and handheld PDAs. Because the software to view Adobe PDF files is free, you can be assured that those receiving your files don't need to purchase any special software. In fact, the odds are quite good that most users already have this free software, called Adobe Reader, as more than 500 million copies have been distributed. Adobe has actually released the underpinnings of PDF to all computer software makers, allowing them to freely create different programs to read and create PDF files.

What makes PDF so useful is that it provides a true reproduction of original documents. The fidelity of PDF files is so good that the Internal Revenue Service uses this format to distribute tax forms online. Likewise, many banks, insurance agencies, and financial services firms use PDF as a method for distributing documents. We even use PDF files to send books like the one you're reading now to the printing plant.

Although PDF files provide a high-quality representation of an original file, they're more than just a picture of the document from which they were created. PDF files retain the high-quality appearance of text so that they print clearly and are searchable. Logos and illustrations created using Adobe Illustrator retain the same high-quality appearance within a PDF file. PDF files also may contain the intricate details that are captured in bitmap images, such as those edited using Adobe Photoshop — but PDF files are able to keep both bitmap and vector information together in the same file, making them a great choice for distributing documents electronically. You don't have to sacrifice quality to distribute a file electronically. You do need to know a few things about Acrobat to create the right type of PDF files for your needs, though. The PDF file you'd send to a printer may be too big for anyone to post on a Web site or send as an e-mail attachment, for example.

One new feature in Acrobat 8 lets you create PDF packages. A PDF package contains multiple PDF files and can also contain other file types that aren't PDF files. A PDF package may contain a few pages from a PowerPoint presentation, part of a spreadsheet, a CAD drawing, some text documents, perhaps an e-mail or two, and so on. This great flexibility is a powerful enhancement to Adobe Acrobat.

Adobe Acrobat is a tool for distributing documents; it's *not* a design tool. You generally don't use Acrobat to build new documents, although Acrobat 8 does let you create a blank page and put text and objects on that page.

However, Acrobat is meant to be a medium for sharing files, not for creating them. Simply put, you don't use Acrobat to create new documents. But Acrobat is still incredibly useful. Using Acrobat, you can

- Share documents with users who don't have the same software or fonts that you use.
- Review and mark up PDF files that others send you. You can also enable a PDF file to be reviewed by users with the free Adobe Reader software.
- Combine documents created in other programs. You can use Acrobat to merge PDF files that may have been originally created in different programs.
- Create a PDF Package. You can combine various file formats into a single PDF Package and yet retain the files in their original file formats.
- Edit Adobe PDF files.
- Apply security to PDF files when you don't want them changed.
- Add interactivity to PDF files by infusing them with sounds, movies, and buttons.
- Create interactive forms, where you can collect information without requiring a user to print, write, and then fax or mail information back to you.

We cover these capabilities throughout the rest of this minibook.

Knowing When to Use Adobe PDF Files

So when does it make sense to use Adobe PDF files? Here are some examples:

- **When you've created a spreadsheet that includes numbers, formulas, and tables that you don't want others to edit:** Your recipients may have the same software you used to build the document, but you can keep them from editing the original spreadsheet file by distributing it as a PDF file.
- **When you've created a presentation that you want others to deliver, but you work on a PC and some of them use Macintosh systems:** By converting the document to PDF, you don't have to worry about issues that can arise when sharing files between different computer types. For example, fonts are typically included within PDF documents and can be used on any computer systems with the free Adobe Reader or the complete Adobe Acrobat software.

  In addition, by sending the presentation in PDF format rather than in the original presentation file format, you don't have to be concerned that the recipients may edit the file.

- **When you have a sensitive document that will be shared only with certain authorized colleagues:** If you have a document containing information that you don't want unauthorized persons viewing, you can add security to a PDF file by using Adobe Acrobat's security tools. Using these options, you can require users to enter a password to view the file, and you can limit other features, such as the ability to print or edit the document.
- **When you want to review a document quickly and efficiently:** When documents need to be reviewed or approved, Acrobat really shines. You can use commenting, markup, and annotation tools to add suggestions and edits to a file, regardless of where it was created. You can even combine comments from multiple reviewers into a single document.

Introducing the Adobe Acrobat Workspace and Tools

To take advantage of all that Adobe Acrobat has to offer, you'll want to discover the workspace and tools Acrobat uses. Adobe has significantly revised the Acrobat 8 interface. Unlike previous versions of Acrobat, which opened with a blank workspace, Acrobat 8 opens with a Getting Started screen. It provides eight possible tasks: Create PDF, Combine Files, Export, Start Meeting, Secure, Sign, Forms, and Review & Comment. These tasks are also incorporated in Acrobat's toolbar once you begin working with your document. You can click a task in the Getting Started window, or if you just want to review a file, you can close the Start Up window like you would any other document window by clicking the Close Window button in the corner.

The Getting Started window appears each time you open Acrobat unless you click the Do Not Show At Startup check box.

Once you open a document, you see the Acrobat workspace, which is divided into three areas: the document window, the toolbar well, and the navigation panes. When you open a PDF document using Acrobat, you can use the toolbars, buttons, and navigation panes to work with and manipulate the PDF file. For example, a PDF file may contain multiple pages. You can use the navigational buttons or the Pages navigation panel to move between pages and then use commenting tools to mark up the file.

The toolbar provides useful information for navigating through your document, including:

- **Current page and total pages:** Click in the area showing the current page, type a different page number, and press Enter (Return on a Mac) to view a specific page.
- **Previous Page/Next Page:** Use these navigational buttons to skip forward or backward by one page.

The Zoom tools

If things are a bit too small for you to see clearly, increase the magnification used for viewing pages with the Zoom drop-down menu in the toolbar. Using the toolbar, select from a preset magnification by choosing the drop-down list showing magnification percentages. The preset magnification choices are available to the right of the current magnification level, which is displayed in the menu bar. You can use the minus (–) and plus (+) symbols to the left of the current magnification level to zoom out or in from the current magnification.

The Marquee Zoom tool is the magnifying glass icon, and you can use it to identify specific portions of a page that you want to magnify. Select this tool and then click and drag around a portion of the page to increase the magnification. You can also click multiple times on an area to increase its magnification, but clicking and dragging a box with the Zoom In tool is generally a much faster way to focus on a portion of a page you want to view. You can change the Zoom In tool to the Zoom Out tool (magnifying glass with a minus sign) by selecting the Marquee Zoom tool and Alt+clicking (Option+clicking on a Mac) in the document window. The magnifier's plus (+) sign changes to a minus (-) to indicate that you're decreasing the document's magnification. But it's usually faster to choose a preset zoom percentage.

To the right of the magnification percentage box are page icons that you can use to change the page magnification:

- **Scrolling Pages:** Use this button to avoid scrolling from left to right when reading a document. The view is changed to fit the document's width in the available space on your display, making it necessary to only scroll up and down on a page. This also sets the page view to display the top or bottom of adjacent pages. When you scroll and reach the bottom of one page, the top of the next page becomes visible.
- **One Full Page:** Use this button to fit the current page within the available screen space on your monitor. For smaller documents, such as a business card, the magnification is increased. For larger documents, the magnification is generally decreased unless you have a large monitor. When viewing pages in the Fit Page mode, only one page is displayed at a time. This mode is good for viewing the entire display of a page layout.

Toolbars

The toolbars in Acrobat 8 are now customizable, so you can combine functions from different toolbars to meet your needs.

For example, Acrobat also includes several additional tools for navigation, which are accessible by choosing View➪Toolbars➪More Tools. In the More Tools window that appears, select the navigation tools you'd like to have displayed in the toolbar. The Selecting and Zoom Toolbar section displays the navigation tool choices that can be displayed.

Less than half of the toolbars are visible in the default Acrobat display. You can add to the tools that are displayed or limit them by clicking the check box next to those you want to display or hide in the More Tools window. Toolbars that have a check mark next to their names are visible, while those without a check mark aren't visible.

Customizing the location of toolbars on your screen can make it easier for you to work with PDF files using Acrobat. For example, you may want all the tools for navigating through your documents in one section of the toolbar well. To achieve this, you can rearrange the location of specific toolbars.

Along the left edge of every group of tools is a dotted double line. By clicking and holding onto this edge with your mouse, you can drag any toolbar to a new location on your screen. This new location can be within the same area holding the other toolbars, or anywhere in the Acrobat work area. If you pull a toolbar out of the docking area, it becomes an independent, floating toolbar. You can reposition or drag floating toolbars back into the docking area when you're finished working with them. You can also close a floating toolbar by clicking its Close Window button. You can place toolbars along the left or right of the Acrobat work area — turning either side of the Acrobat workspace into a docking area for toolbars.

Although the flexibility of placing toolbars anywhere you like is useful, it may lead to a chaotic work environment. Instead of leaving toolbars all over your screen, you can have Acrobat clean up the workspace by choosing View⇨Toolbars⇨Reset Toolbars.

Toolbars contain both tools and buttons. For example, you choose the Marquee Zoom tool to change the magnification by clicking or selecting an area of the page. Buttons perform an immediate task, such as printing, saving, or applying security to a PDF document. In general, most of the task buttons are on the top row of the docking area, immediately below the menu bar, and most of the tools are on the bottom row — but you can move these toolbars.

Some tools and task buttons also include additional options that you can access through drop-down lists within the toolbars. Tools and buttons that contain additional choices are noted by the small triangle immediately to the right of the icon. Click this small triangle, and you see a menu listing the additional choices for that tool or button.

Viewing modes

Acrobat provides several viewing modes that control how the entire document is displayed. You can choose which viewing mode is used by choosing View⇨Page Display and selecting the viewing option you want.

The viewing modes are

- **Single Page:** This mode displays only the current document page on-screen and does not show any adjoining pages. When you scroll to the top or bottom of the current page, other pages aren't visible at the same time as the current page.
- **Single Page Continuous:** With this mode, you can see the current document page, and if you scroll to the top (or bottom) of the current page, the adjoining page is also visible. If you reduce your page viewing magnification, many document pages are visible.
- **Two-Up (previously known as Facing):** Use this mode to see pages as a *spread,* where you can view both the left and right side of adjoining pages at the same time. When you have documents with pictures or text that spans a pair of pages, use this option to see the pages presented side-by-side in Acrobat. As with the Single Page mode, other pages that go before or fall after the spread aren't visible — only the one pair of pages is visible on-screen, regardless of the magnification or scrolling.
- **Two-Up Continuous (previously known as Continuous-Facing):** If you have a document with many pages containing text or pictures on their adjoining pages, you can use this mode to scroll from one pair of visible pages to the next. When the Continuous-Facing view is selected, you can see adjoining page spreads. This option is identical to the Facing option, but it also shows pages above or below the spread you are presently viewing.

If you have pages where images or text go across pages, the Two-Up choice is useful. By default, the pages generally display incorrectly. For example, a magazine will display the cover (page 1) and page 2 together, instead of pages 2 and 3. To correct this, you need to choose View⇨Page Display⇨Show Cover Page During Two-Up.

TIP

You can add viewing modes as menu buttons using the More Tools window, described earlier in the Tools section.

Additional viewing options

Acrobat has two options for changing your document display.

- **Full Screen Mode (View⇨Full Screen Mode):** You can use the Full Screen View option to hide all menus, toolbars, and other parts of the Acrobat interface. This option is useful if you want to focus on the document being displayed, not the program being used to view it. Use this mode, for example, when you've a converted PowerPoint file to a PDF document and want to deliver the presentation using Acrobat. If you're viewing a document in the Full Screen Mode, press the Esc key to return to the regular viewing mode.

You can set a document to automatically open in Full Screen Mode by choosing File➪Properties and choosing this option from the Initial View panel of the Document Properties window. Additionally, you can choose Edit➪Preferences and select the Full Screen option along the top left side of the Preferences window to control various aspects of the Full Screen Mode. Some choices include the transition between pages and whether pages advance automatically, allowing you to create a self-running PDF presentation.

✦ **Reading Mode (View➪Reading Mode):** With so many toolbars, they sometimes get in the way. Reading Mode temporarily hides all your toolbars.

Navigation panels

Acrobat offers a variety of panels that are helpful when navigating through PDF documents. The term *panel* may be a bit misleading because similar options are called *palettes* or *panes* in the other Adobe Creative Suite programs. Regardless of the name, however, you use them to get around PDF files more easily.

The navigation panels are visible along the left side of your document window as small icons (refer to Figure 1-2). Click an icon to make its panel visible. For example, click the Pages icon to display thumbnail-size representations of each page, as shown in Figure 1-5. You can click a thumbnail page to have that page displayed in the document window. You can also choose View➪Navigation Panels to access the panels. There are 14 panels: Articles, Attachments, Bookmarks, Comments, Content, Destination, How To, Info, Layers, Model Tree, Order, Pages, Signatures, and Tags.

Many panels have more advanced uses that are covered in later chapters of this minibook. In this chapter, we provide you with a brief understanding of how you can use the Pages tab to more easily navigate through a PDF document. Just do this:

1. **Make sure that the Pages panel is visible by clicking its panel icon.**
2. **In the Pages panel, click any page thumbnail to navigate directly to that page.**

   A dark border appears around the selected page. In the lower-right corner of the page is a very small red box.
3. **Drag the small red box up and toward the left, in a diagonal movement, to focus the magnification on a smaller portion of the page.**

Chapter 2: Creating PDF Files

In This Chapter

- Creating PDF files from Microsoft Word, Excel, and PowerPoint documents
- Creating PDF files from Adobe Creative Suite applications
- Creating PDF files from all other electronic formats
- Creating PDF files from paper documents and the Web

You don't need Adobe Acrobat to create Portable Document Format (PDF) files from Adobe Creative Suite documents — this capability is built right into the Creative Suite application — but you do need Acrobat for creating PDF files from many other programs. Converting documents to the PDF format is a great way to share information. In this chapter, you find out how to create Adobe PDF files from a variety of programs.

Creating PDF Files from Microsoft Office

Adobe Acrobat includes tools that make it easy to convert Microsoft Word, Excel, and PowerPoint files to PDF. These capabilities are much more robust for the Windows versions of these programs, so Macintosh users may find that not all these options are available.

When you install Acrobat on your computer, it looks for Microsoft Office programs. If it locates Word, Excel, PowerPoint, or Outlook, it installs a utility called PDF Maker 8 that helps convert Microsoft Office documents to PDF. This utility installs a PDF Maker 8 toolbar that appears in these programs, allowing for one-click PDF creation.

You can tell whether Adobe Acrobat PDF Maker 8 has been installed for these Microsoft Office programs by looking for the Adobe PDF menu to the right of the Help menu, and the PDF Maker 8 toolbar. If the Adobe PDF menu is not there, check View⇨Toolbars to see whether Adobe Acrobat PDF Maker 8 is available to select in the Toolbars submenu. If it still isn't available, it's possible that Acrobat did not install Adobe PDF Maker 8. To gain access to the Adobe PDF Maker 8 utility, you can reinstall Adobe Acrobat.

When you convert documents to Adobe PDF, the original file remains unchanged, so you'll have both the original file and a separate PDF document. The original document and the PDF aren't linked, so changes to the original source file aren't reflected in the PDF file.

PDF conversion options

Adobe PDF Maker 8 provides a variety of controls over how PDF files are created. For example, you can have Acrobat create the file without asking you to confirm the location and name of the file each time you click the Convert To Adobe PDF button, and it will simply save the file in the same location as the original document. Similarly, you can choose to create PDF files that balance your need for quality and file size.

PDF Maker 8 provides controls over the type of PDF file you create. This is because some PDF files may need to be of a higher quality for printing, and others may need to be smaller to allow for fast electronic distribution. For example, you may want to post a PDF document to a Web site, where you want to make the file small so that it can be quickly downloaded.

When working in Microsoft Word, Excel, or PowerPoint, you can access the PDF Maker 8 controls by choosing Adobe PDF➪Change Conversion Settings. In the Acrobat PDF Maker 8 dialog box that appears, you can then choose from a variety of settings that control how the PDF file is created. In this section, we focus on the most useful options for Microsoft Office users.

From the Conversion Settings drop-down list in the Acrobat PDF Maker 8 dialog box, you can find these useful options that control how the PDF file is generated:

- **Standard:** Choose this option to create PDF files that will be printed on an office laser printer or distributed via e-mail. This setting meets the needs of most users — it provides some compression of graphics, but they remain clear on-screen and look reasonably good when printed. In addition, this setting builds the fonts into the PDF file to maintain an exact representation of the document, regardless of where the file is viewed.
- **Smallest File Size:** With this setting, you can control the file size of the PDF documents you create. This setting provides significant compression of images and also reduces resolution, which causes graphics within the files to lose some clarity and perhaps appear jagged.

  In addition, fonts aren't embedded in PDF files created with this setting. If the fonts used in the document aren't available on a computer where a PDF created with the Smallest File Size setting is viewed, Acrobat uses a font substitution technology to replicate the size and shape of the fonts used in the document. This feature typically provides a similar appearance to the original document, but it's not always an exact match of the original file.

  Because this setting is so lossy you would only want to use it if you needed to compress a large file to a small enough size to send as an email attachment. Make certain the recipient has the fonts used in the document installed on their computer. Otherwise, Adobe uses font substitution.

✦ **Press Quality:** If you need to provide PDF files to your commercial printer or copy shop, use this setting to create a PDF file that is designed for high-quality print reproduction. Along with including fonts in the PDF file, the graphics aren't significantly compressed, and they maintain a much higher resolution. Overall, these files tend to be larger than similar PDF files created using different settings, but the quality of the PDF file is more important than the file size when you're having the PDF professionally printed.

PDF conversion options from Microsoft Word and Excel

Although Microsoft Word and Excel are widespread standards on many corporate computers, they aren't always the best choice for distributing documents. Formatting of Microsoft Word documents and Excel spreadsheets changes depending on the fonts available on users' computers or even the printer they choose to print with. In addition, Microsoft Word and Excel files can be easily edited, and users can also copy and extract information from these files with very few limitations.

Converting a Word or Excel file to PDF overcomes these limitations and is quite straightforward. Choose from two methods:

✦ From inside Microsoft Word or Excel (make sure that the document you want to convert to an Adobe PDF file is open), simply click the Convert To PDF button in the main toolbar to convert the document.

✦ Alternatively, choose Adobe PDF⇨Convert To Adobe PDF.

No matter which method you choose, you must specify the location of the PDF file that is created and name the file.

Choose Adobe PDF⇨Change Conversion Settings and deselect the Prompt For PDF Filename option so that PDF files are generated in one step, without having to input the name of the PDF file.

Not only can you create PDF files from Microsoft Office applications, but you can add other functionality into PDF documents. Choose Adobe PDF⇨Change Conversion Settings and in the dialog box that appears, use the following settings:

✦ **Add Links:** Automatically converts Word links, such as Web addresses, into PDF links that you can use when viewing the file in Acrobat or the Adobe Reader. Click the Word tab to access additional link options that can be built into PDF files created from Word.

✦ **Add Bookmarks:** Adds interactive bookmarks that make navigating the PDF file easy. Bookmarks are added based on Microsoft Word styles, such as text that is styled as Heading 1. The bookmarks appear in the Bookmarks palette when viewing the PDF.

Converting PowerPoint files to PDF

You can convert your PowerPoint presentations to Adobe PDF documents using PDF Maker 8. PDFs make it easy to distribute electronic versions of presentations, without worrying that the file may be edited, or that the recipient may not have the same fonts that you used.

From PowerPoint, click the Convert To Adobe PDF button to save the file as an Adobe PDF file. (Make sure that the presentation you're converting is open before you click the button!).You can also choose Adobe PDF⇨Convert To Adobe PDF from PowerPoint's main menu. If you're working with a new file, you must save it before Adobe PDF Maker 8 will convert it.

As with Word and Excel, you can choose Adobe PDF⇨Change Conversion Settings within PowerPoint to select options relating to the conversion. Along with the conversion settings that impact the quality of the resulting PDF file, you should select two additional options:

✦ **Save Slide Transitions In Adobe PDF:** With this option, you can have the slide transitions that were created in PowerPoint converted into PDF transitions that will be used when the presentation is delivered using Adobe Acrobat's Full Screen View option.

✦ **Convert Multimedia To PDF Multimedia:** Because Adobe PDF files are able to contain integrated sound and movie files, you can choose this option to have sounds and movies used in a PowerPoint file converted into the PDF document.

You can even use PDF as the method for delivering presentations that have been created using PowerPoint by choosing Window⇨Full Screen View after you've converted the file to PDF. You can also click the Full Screen option in the lower left corner of the document window. Press the Esc key to stop viewing the document in the Full Screen mode.

Creating PDF Files from Adobe Creative Suite Applications

Throughout this book, we discuss how to integrate the applications within the Adobe Creative Suite. You won't be surprised to know that you can easily convert a Photoshop file, an Illustrator file, or an InDesign document to the PDF format. In this section, we show you how.

Converting Photoshop and Illustrator files to PDF

Both Adobe Photoshop CS3 and Adobe Illustrator CS3 can save documents directly in the Adobe PDF file format. To do so, simply choose File⇨Save or File⇨Save As. Then, from the File Type drop-down list, choose Adobe PDF (Illustrator) or Photoshop PDF (Photoshop). In these programs, you can create PDF files without Adobe Acrobat or Acrobat Distiller.

You can view PDF files created from Photoshop or Illustrator using Adobe Acrobat or Adobe Reader. But you can also open and edit these PDF files using the same program in which they were created. For example, you can open and modify a logo created using Adobe Illustrator and saved as a PDF file from Illustrator at a later time with Illustrator. You can also view the same file using either Adobe Reader or Adobe Acrobat software.

Converting InDesign documents to PDF

As with Photoshop and Illustrator, the ability to convert InDesign documents to PDF is integrated into the application. Using Adobe InDesign CS3, you can choose File⇨Export and select Adobe PDF from the File Type drop-down list. InDesign provides a significant number of options for controlling the size and quality of the resulting PDF file. Many of these options are similar to those available for PDF Maker 8 for Microsoft Office.

In the Adobe InDesign Export PDF dialog box, you can choose from the Preset drop-down list at the top of the dialog box. The choices are many, but we list and describe here the most commonly used settings:

- ✦ **Smallest File Size:** Creates compact Adobe PDF files that are intended for display on the Internet or to be distributed via e-mail. Use this setting to create PDF files that will be viewed primarily on-screen.
- ✦ **High Quality Print:** Creates Adobe PDF files that are intended for desktop printers and digital copiers.
- ✦ **Press Quality:** Use this setting to create PDF files that will be delivered to a commercial printer, for high-quality, offset print reproduction.

TIP

When creating PDF files to be used for high-resolution printing, be certain to select Marks And Bleeds in the list on the left in the Export PDF dialog box, as shown in Figure 2-1, and specify the amount of space items need to extend off the page (*bleed*). If you're delivering the file to a printing firm, they can provide you with guidance as to the value you should use for bleed and marks offset. A good rule to follow is to use at least .125 inches if you have items extending all the way to the edge of your document pages. Specify the value you want by entering the value in the Bleed And Slug section of the Marks And Bleeds tab. If the amount of bleed is to be the same on all four sides, type the value in the Top text field and then click the link icon to the right of the Top and Bottom Bleed text fields.

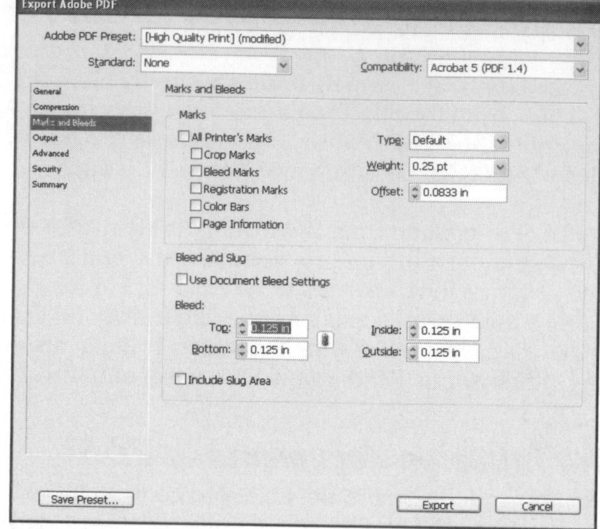

Figure 2-1: Setting the bleed values in the InDesign Export Adobe PDF dialog box.

Converting Other Electronic Documents to PDF

Adobe has made it quite easy to create PDF files from other Adobe Creative Suite applications and Microsoft Office programs, but you can also create PDF files from many other programs. When you installed the Adobe Creative Suite on your computer, you also installed a new printer, called the Adobe PDF 8 printer, which is used to convert documents to Adobe PDF files. This printer captures all the same information that is normally sent to your printer, and, instead of creating a piece of paper, the information is converted into an Adobe PDF file.

To create a PDF file from any program, choose File➪Print. In the Print dialog box, select Adobe PDF 8 as the printer and click OK (click Print on a Mac).

To change the type of PDF file that is created, such as a smaller file for Internet Web posting, or a higher quality file for delivery to a commercial printer, do this:

✦ **Windows:** Click the Properties button in the Print dialog box to open the Adobe PDF Document Properties dialog box, shown in Figure 2-2. Here, you can choose the PDF settings you want to use to control the quality and size of the resulting PDF file.

✦ **Mac OS:** Choose PDF Options from the Copies And Pages menu and then choose the PDF settings.

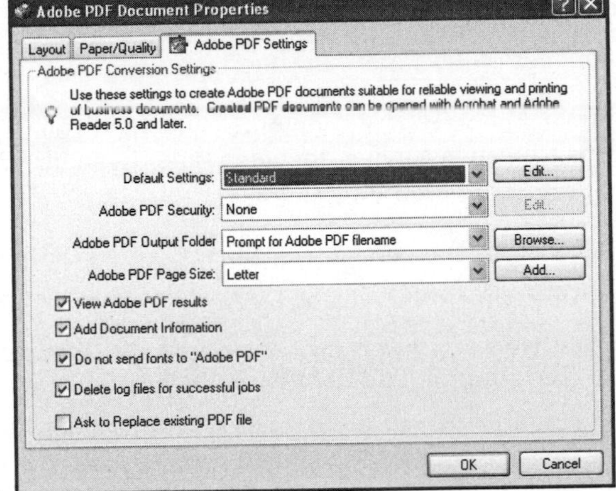

Figure 2-2: You can change conversion settings when printing to the Adobe PDF printer.

We discuss the settings earlier in this chapter, in the "PDF conversion options" section.

This process of navigating through the Print menu may appear strange, but it is probably the easiest way for Adobe to capture all the same information that you'd expect to see when you print your files. This provides an easy and standard method for generating PDF files from any program. In fact, you can even use this method for creating PDF files from Microsoft Office programs or other programs in the Adobe Creative Suite if you want.

Bookmarks and links aren't exported if a PDF is generated using the Print menu option.

Creating PDF Files from Paper Documents and the Web

PDF files don't need to start as electronic publishing files. Adobe Acrobat provides options for converting both paper documents and Internet Web pages into PDF format.

Converting paper documents to PDF

To convert paper documents into PDF, you need a scanner to digitize the information. If you expect to scan a large number of pages into PDF, consider purchasing a scanner with an automatic document feeder. Some scanners can scan both the front and backside of a document at the same time.

Unfortunately, we can't fully describe all the ins and outs of choosing a scanner to fit your needs, but Mark L. Chambers does a swell job of it in his book, *Scanners For Dummies* (Wiley Publishing, Inc.).

If a scanner is already hooked to the computer on which you use Acrobat, follow these steps to scan in a paper document and then convert it to PDF format:

1. **From the Acrobat main menu, choose File⇨Create PDF⇨From Scanner.**

   The Create PDF From Scanner dialog box appears.

2. **Make sure that your scanner is turned on, put the document to be scanned into the scanner, and then click the Scan button.**

   If necessary, continue to scan multiple pages into a single document. When you're done scanning, the scanned page appears in Acrobat.

3. **Choose File⇨Save to save the PDF.**

   If you have a PDF open and choose Create PDF From Scanner, a window appears, giving you the opportunity to *append* the file (add to the existing file) or create a new PDF file.

   The document opens in Acrobat.

If the pages need to be rotated, you can choose Document⇨Rotate Pages. Some scanners now automatically convert scanned documents to Adobe PDF files and automatically rotate them.

Use the Zoom In tool to increase the magnification of what you've just scanned. You can see that the text is jagged because it's a picture of the text. If you need the text to be searchable, use Document⇨OCR Text Recognition⇨Recognize Text Using OCR. This command makes the text you have just scanned searchable. Otherwise, you have only a picture of the text.

Scanned text is unlike text from electronic documents that you create using either PDF Maker 8 or the Adobe PDF Printer. Both of these options create text that looks very clear, even when enlarged.

Converting Web pages to PDFs

By converting online content to Adobe PDF, you can capture contents from an Internet Web site. Because Web content can change rapidly, you can capture something that may not remain online for a long period of time. You can convert things such as news stories or competitive information ca from a Web site into PDF in a single click. And because PDF files can easily be combined with other PDF documents, you can merge information from a variety of sources, such as spreadsheets, word-processing documents, and brochures.

If you want to convert only a single page and are using Internet Explorer, click the Convert Web Page To PDF button. This step converts the current web page to a PDF. If you want to convert more than a single page, follow these steps from within Acrobat (not your Web browser):

1. **From the Acrobat main menu, choose File⇨Create PDF⇨From Web Page.**

   The Create PDF From Web Page dialog box opens.

2. **In the URL text field, enter the URL for the Web site you're converting to PDF.**
3. **To capture additional pages that are linked from the main page you're capturing, select the Get Only radio button (selected by default), enter the number of levels to be captured in the Levels text field, and then select one of the following:**
   - Select the Stay On Same Path check box if you want only URLs (pages) subordinate from the entered URL converted to PDF.
   - Select the Stay On Same Server check box to download only pages that are on the same server as the entered URL.

   Be cautious about selecting the Get Entire Site radio button instead of the Get Only radio button. The Get Entire Site option may take an enormous amount of time and not have any relevance to what you need.

4. **Click the Settings button to open the Web Page Conversion Settings dialog box and see accepted File types and change PDF settings (on the General tab), as shown in Figure 2-3.**

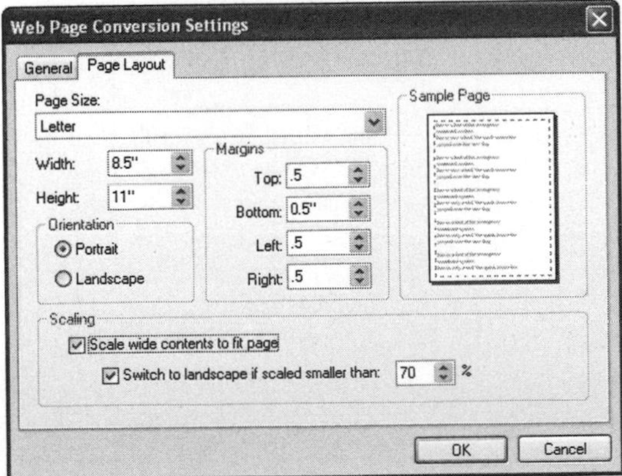

Figure 2-3: Changing file type and PDF settings.

5. **On the Page layout tab of the Web Page Conversion Settings dialog box, make changes to page size, orientation, and margins.**
6. **When you're done making changes in the Web Page Conversion Settings dialog box, click OK.**
7. **Back in the Create PDF From Web Page dialog box, click the Create button.**

   The Downloading Status window opens, showing the rate of download.

When the download is complete, the Web page (for the entered URL) selected appears as a PDF with existing hyperlinks (links to other pages within the site) left intact. When links on the converted Web page are selected, the viewer can open the page either in Acrobat or the Web browser.

Chapter 3: Adding Interactivity to PDF Files

In This Chapter

- Adding interactive bookmarks
- Creating and editing links
- Using buttons for easy navigation

Because many Adobe PDF documents are viewed online, you need to make the documents easy for readers to navigate. Using Acrobat, you can design documents that are easier to navigate than their printed counterparts and that include rich interactive features that simply aren't available with paper documents.

Rather than making readers scroll through a document to find what they want, you can add links within an index or table of contents, or you can add links to Web sites and e-mail addresses. Acrobat also includes features (known as *bookmarks*) to build your own online table of contents, and you can add buttons that link to specific pages within a PDF document or that cause an action to occur when clicked, such as closing the document. We discuss all these features in this chapter.

Adding Bookmarks to Ease PDF Navigation

One reason for distributing PDF documents is that it's convenient and cost-effective. But if users can't easily find the information they need, or they're unable to effectively understand how the contents of a file are structured, they may become frustrated, or they may need to print the document, which defeats the purpose of electronic distribution.

A table of contents in a traditional, printed book doesn't work well with electronic PDF files. It requires you to constantly return to the page containing the contents and then navigate to the page containing the data you need. But you can make your documents more user-friendly by adding bookmarks, which are the equivalent of a table of contents that is always available, no matter what page is being viewed in the document window.

Bookmarks provide a listing of contents that reside within a PDF file, or links to relevant external content. Bookmarks sit within a panel, and when you click one, you're taken to a specific destination in the PDF document (or possibly to an external file), much like a hyperlink. Acrobat technically calls the panel a panel, but all other Adobe Creative Suite programs call them panels — so that's what we call them here. You can create bookmarks from existing text, or you can use your own text to describe the content, such as a chart or graphic.

By default, the Bookmarks icon resides along the left side of the Acrobat document window in what is called the *navigation pane.* Click the Bookmarks icon to make the panel appear; click the Bookmarks icon a second time to hide it. If the icon isn't visible, choose View⇨Navigation Panels⇨Bookmarks to make it appear.

Creating bookmarks that link to a page

By navigating to a page, and to a specific view on a page, you can establish the destination of a bookmark link. With a PDF document open, follow these steps:

1. **If the Bookmark icon isn't visible, choose View⇨Navigation Panels⇨Bookmarks.**

   The Bookmarks panel appears on the left of the document window.

2. **In the document window, navigate to the page that you want as the bookmark's destination.**

3. **Set the magnification of the view that you want by using the Marquee Zoom tool to either zoom in or zoom out.**

   The zoom level that you are at when you create the bookmark is the view that viewers see when they click the bookmark.

4. **In the Bookmarks panel, choose Options⇨New Bookmark.**

   The new bookmark appears in the Bookmarks panel as Untitled.

5. **Change the name by typing something more descriptive.**

   If you leave the bookmark as Untitled but want to rename it later, you must click the bookmark and then choose Options⇨Rename Bookmark from the menu in the Bookmark panel.

6. **Test your bookmark by scrolling to another page and view in the document window; then click your saved bookmark in the Bookmark panel.**

   The document window shows the exact location and zoom that you selected when you created the bookmark.

If you use the Selection tool to highlight text, such as a headline or a caption, that is a part of the bookmark destination and then choose Options⇨New Bookmark, the selected text becomes the title of the new bookmark. You can use this shortcut to avoid entering a new name for new bookmark titles. You can also press Ctrl+B (⌘+B on a Mac) to quickly create a bookmark.

Creating bookmarks that link to external files

Although bookmarks are most commonly used to link to content within a PDF file, you can also use bookmarks to create links to other documents. To create a link to an external file, follow these steps:

1. **Choose Options➪New Bookmark in the Bookmarks panel.**
2. **Replace the Untitled bookmark entry that appears in the Bookmarks panel with an appropriate title for the bookmark.**
3. **Choose Options➪Properties from the Bookmarks panel.**

   The Bookmark Properties dialog box appears. Using this dialog box, you can change a bookmark so that it links to any type of file. In this example, we use a PDF document, but the bookmark could be a link to another PDF file, a Photoshop file, or even a Microsoft Excel file. Just remember that this bookmark creates a relative link. The linked file must travel with the PDF document in order for the link to work.
4. **In the Bookmark Properties dialog box, click the Actions tab and choose Open A File from the Select Action drop-down list and then click the Add button.**

   The Select File To Open dialog box appears.
5. **Click the Browse button, choose a file to which the bookmark will navigate, and then click the Select button.**
6. **In the Specify Open Preference window, choose whether you want the linked file to open in a new document, new window, or existing window and then click OK.**

Note that the other file isn't attached to the current document. If you distribute a PDF file containing the bookmarks to external files, you must distribute any external files that are referenced along with the source file; otherwise, the links will not work. In addition, the linked files need to be in the same relative location as the original documents — so don't change the name of the linked file or the folder in which it is located.

You can create links to non-PDF files. Instead of choosing Go To A Page In Another Document, choose Open A File to open a non-PDF file or choose Open A Web Link to access an Internet Web address.

Using bookmarks

Bookmarks are intuitive to use, which makes them an attractive option to add to PDF files. After you click a bookmark, the action associated with it is performed, which typically navigates you to a certain page within the PDF file.

Unfortunately, the Bookmarks panel doesn't open automatically with a document, even when bookmarks are present within a file. To display the Bookmarks panel when a file is opened, follow these steps:

1. **Choose File➪Properties.**
2. **In the Document Properties dialog box that opens, select the Initial View tab, as shown in Figure 3-1.**
3. **From the Navigation drop-down list, choose Bookmarks Panel And Page and then click OK.**

   After the file is saved and then reopened, the Bookmarks panel is displayed whenever the document is opened.

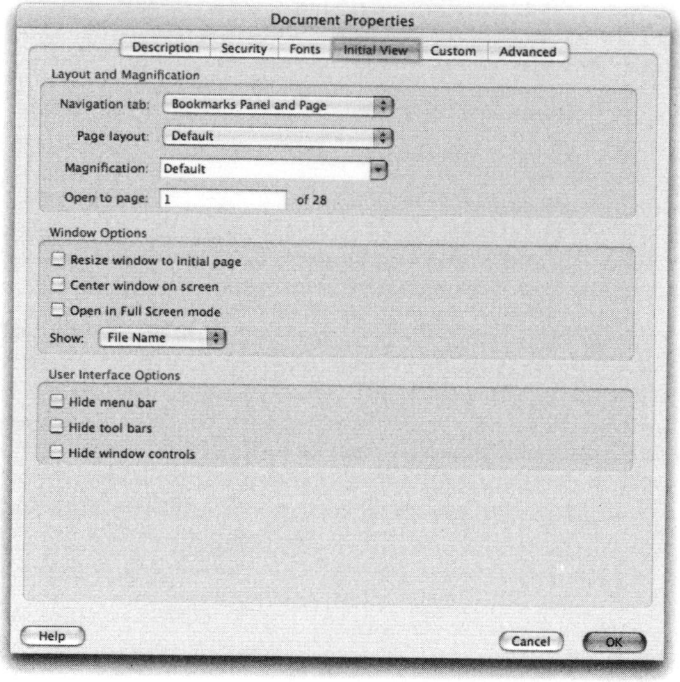

Figure 3-1: The Documents Properties window in Adobe Acrobat.

Editing bookmarks

You can change the attributes of bookmarks so that they link to other locations by clicking to select a bookmark and then choosing Options➪Properties in the Bookmarks panel. In the Bookmark Properties dialog box, choose the color and font type of the bookmark on the Appearance tab: To change the bookmark's font style, choose a style from the Style drop-down list; to change the bookmark's color, click the Color box and choose a color from the color picker.

On the Actions tab of the Bookmark Properties dialog box, you can delete existing actions (in the Actions section of the Actions tab) by clicking to select an action and then clicking the Delete button. Also, you can add actions by choosing another action from the Add Action section and then clicking the Add button. You can add more than one action to a bookmark.

Adding Interactive Links

When viewing a PDF file electronically, you can add links for e-mail addresses, Web addresses, and references to other pages. Links are attached to a region of a page, which you identify with the Link tool.

To add an interactive link to your PDF document, follow these steps:

1. **Choose Options⇨New Bookmark in the Bookmarks panel.**
2. **After locating an area of a page where you want to add a link, Choose View⇨Toolbars⇨Advanced Editing to display the Advanced Editing toolbar.**

3. **Select the Link tool and then click and drag to select the region that you want to link to.**

   The Create Link dialog box appears.
4. **Choose a Link Action:**
   - **Go To A Page View:** This option is the default, where you can scroll to the page that is the destination of the link.
   - **Open A File:** Alternatively, you can choose to link to another file; click the Browse button to locate the file.
   - **Open A Web Page:** If you choose this option, you're choosing to link to a Web address. In the Address text field, enter the complete address of the Web site to which the link should direct viewers. To create a link to an e-mail address, type **mailto:** followed by an e-mail address. Note that mailto: is all one word with no spaces.
   - **Custom Link:** Use this option to choose from other types of links in the Link Properties dialog box.
5. **Click Next, and follow the instructions in the next dialog box before clicking OK.**

The Link tool is relatively simple to use, but you may prefer to create links from text in another way: Using the Selection tool, select the text, right-click (Ctrl+click on a Mac) the selected text, and then choose Create Link from the contextual menu that appears.

Remember that you can also have links automatically transferred from your original Microsoft Office documents when using PDF Maker.

You can edit links by choosing the Link tool and double-clicking the link to open the Link Properties dialog box. While editing a link, you can change how it's presented in the Appearance tab. Make a link invisible or add a border to the link, such as a blue border that commonly is used to define hyperlinks. On the Actions tab of the Link Properties dialog box, you can add, edit, or delete actions, just as you can with bookmarks (see the preceding section).

Adding Buttons to Simplify Your PDF Files

Along with links and bookmarks, buttons provide another way to make your files more useful when they're viewed online. You can create interactive buttons entirely within Acrobat — designing their appearance and adding text to them. Or you can import buttons created in other Adobe Creative Suite applications, such as Photoshop and Illustrator. For example, you can create buttons that advance the viewer to the next page in a document.

Buttons are added by using the Button tool located on the Forms toolbar. Choose View⇨Toolbars⇨Forms to open the Forms menu.

To add a button to your PDF document, follow these steps:

1. **Click the OK Button tool and click and drag to create the region where the button will appear.**

   The Button Properties dialog box appears.

2. **In the General tab, you can enter a name for the button in the Name text field and provide a Tooltip in the Tooltip text field.**

   A *ToolTip* is the text that appears whenever the mouse cursor is positioned over the button.

3. **In the Appearance tab, establish how your button will look:**

   - **Border Color/Fill Color:** Click the square to the right of the appropriate attribute in the Borders And Colors section of the Appearance tab and then choose a color from the color picker.
   - **Line Thickness and Style:** These options don't appear unless you change the border color from none (red diagonal line) to another selection.

- **Font Size/Font:** Change the size and font of the button text by making a selection from the Font Size and the Font drop-down lists.
- **Text Color:** Change the color of the text by clicking the color square and choosing a color from the color picker.

4. **In the Options tab, make these selections:**
   - **Layout:** Use the Layout drop-down list to specify whether you want to use a *label* (text that you enter in Acrobat that appears on the face of the button) or whether you want an *icon* (an imported button graphic that you may have designed using Photoshop or Illustrator).
   - **Behavior:** Choose Push from the Behavior drop-down list to create different appearances for a button so that it changes based upon whether the mouse cursor is positioned over the button. The button appearance can also change when clicked.
   - **State:** To specify the different appearances (see Behavior, discussed in the preceding paragraph), click the State on the left side of the Options tab and then choose the Label or Icon status for each state.
   - **Label:** If you choose to use a label, enter the text for it in the Label text field.
   - **Icon:** If you choose to use an icon, specify the location of the graphic file by clicking the Choose Icon button. You can create button icons in either Photoshop or Illustrator.

5. **In the Actions tab, you can choose an action from the Select Action drop-down list and then click the Add button.**

   Actions are applied to buttons similar to the way in which they're applied to links and bookmarks.
   - To choose actions that are a part of the menu commands, such as printing a document, closing a file, or navigating to the next or preceding page, choose the Execute Menu Item action and then specify the command to be accessed.
   - You can also choose the activity that causes the action to occur, known as the *trigger*. The default trigger is Mouse Up, which causes the action to occur when the mouse button is depressed and then released. You can choose other actions, such as the mouse cursor merely rolling over the button without the need to click it.

6. **After you make all your changes in the Button Properties dialog box, click Close and you're done.**

Chapter 4: Editing and Extracting Text and Graphics

In This Chapter

- **Manipulating text with the TouchUp tools**
- **Modifying graphics with the TouchUp tools**
- **Pulling text and graphics out of PDFs for use in other documents**

You may assume that PDF files are mere pictures of your documents and can't be edited, but nothing is further from the truth. Adobe Acrobat includes a variety of tools for editing both text and graphics. You can use these tools as long as the file has not been secured to prohibit editing. We introduce you to these great tools in this chapter. (We discuss security, which allows you to limit access to these tools, in Chapter 6 of this minibook.)

Editing Text

The tools for editing text and graphics are located on the Advanced Editing toolbar (see Figure 4-1). You can add several TouchUp tools to the Advanced Editing tool bar by choosing View⇨Toolbars⇨More tools and checking the tools you want to add. You have three choices:

- **TouchUp Text Tool:** Used to manipulate text.
- **TouchUp Object Tool:** Used to manipulate objects.
- **TouchUp Reading Order Tool:** Used to correct the reading order or structure of the document.

The TouchUp Reading Order tool isn't used for changing the appearance of the document, so we don't discuss it in this chapter.

Figure 4-1: The Advanced Editing toolbar.

Using the TouchUp Text tool to manipulate text

The TouchUp Text tool is used for *touching up,* or manipulating, text. This touchup can include changing actual text characters or the appearance of text. You can change the word "cat" to read "dog," or you can change black text to make it blue, or you can even change the Helvetica font to the Times font.

When you change a PDF file, the original source document isn't modified.

You have a few ways to accomplish text edits:

- ✦ Choose the TouchUp Text tool, click within the text that you want to change to obtain an insertion point, and then start typing the new text.
- ✦ Insert the TouchUp tool into your text and press the Backspace or Delete key to delete text.
- ✦ Drag, using the TouchUp tool, to highlight text and enter new text to replace the highlighted text.

When changing text — whether you're adding or deleting — Acrobat tries to use the font that was specified in the original document. Sometimes, this font is built into the PDF file, which means that it's *embedded* in the file. Other times, the font may not be available either because it hasn't been embedded or it's been embedded as a *subset* where only some of the characters from the font are included in the PDF file. In these cases, Acrobat may provide the following warning message:

```
All or part of the selection has no available system font. You cannot add or
    delete text using the currently selected font.
```

Fortunately, you can change the font if you need to edit the text. However, when you change the font, the text may not retain the same appearance as the original document. In some instances, you may not have the exact same font on your computer as the font used in the PDF document, but you may have a similar font you can use without causing a noticeable change — most people won't notice the difference between Helvetica and Arial or between Times and Times New Roman. Fonts with the same name but from different font designers often look very similar. For example, Adobe Garamond looks similar to ITC Garamond, even though they're two different fonts.

To change the font that is used for a word or range of words, follow these steps:

1. **Select the text with the TouchUp Text tool by dragging across it.**

   You will probably get a message that reads `Loading System Fonts` followed by another message that reads `Loading Document Fonts.` Depending on the number of fonts installed on your system, it may take a while for this message to appear.

2. **Right-click (Ctrl+click on a Mac) the highlighted text and then choose Properties from the contextual menu.**

   The TouchUp Properties dialog box appears, as shown in Figure 4-2.

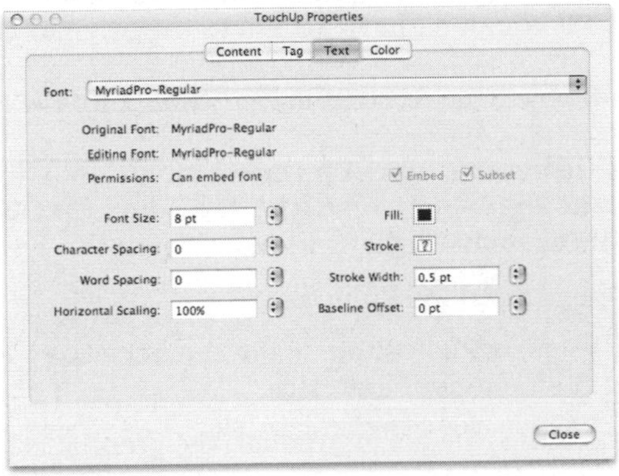

Figure 4-2: The TouchUp Properties dialog box.

3. **In the Text tab, choose the typeface you want to use from the Font drop-down list and make any other changes you want.**

   In this dialog box, you can also change the size by selecting or typing a number into the Font Size drop-down list. In addition, you can modify the color by clicking the Fill color swatch.

4. **When you're satisfied with your changes, click the Close button to apply your changes to the selected text.**

Typewriter tool

You can use the Typewriter tool to type anywhere on the document. This tool resembles the Text Box tool, though its default properties are different. Access the Typewriter tool by choosing Tools➪Typewriter➪Show Typewriter Toolbar. Then, select the Typewriter icon, position your cursor where you want to begin typing and type, pressing the Enter key whenever you want to add a line. The Increase and Decrease size buttons will enlarge or diminish your type size.

Likewise, to change the leading, you select the text and choose the Increase or Decrease Line Spacing buttons. You can move or resize the Typewriter block by selecting it with the Select tool and either moving or resizing the text box. Your text remains editable. So, if you've made a mistake and want to correct it, or want to add or delete text, you select the Typewriter tool again and double-click in the type box.

Using the TouchUp Object tool to edit graphics

You can use the TouchUp Object tool to access editing software for modifying graphics. For example, you can use the TouchUp Object tool to select a graphic, bring the graphic into Photoshop, and then save the modified version back into the PDF file. In other words, you can edit the graphics used in PDF documents, even if you don't have access to the original graphic files.

To edit a photographic file from Acrobat in Photoshop, follow these steps:

1. **Select the image using the TouchUp Object tool, right-click (Ctrl+click on a Mac) on a photographic image with the TouchUp Object tool, and then choose Edit Image from the contextual menu.**

   The image file opens in Adobe Photoshop.

2. **Using the many tools of Photoshop, make the necessary changes to the graphic and then choose File⇨Save.**

   When you return to the PDF file in Acrobat, the graphic is automatically updated in the PDF document.

If you have the original graphic file, it remains untouched — only the version used within the PDF file is modified. It isn't necessary to have the original graphic file to perform these steps.

You can also use Acrobat to edit vector objects from within PDF files, such as those created using Adobe Illustrator. Just follow these steps:

1. **Select a piece of vector artwork using the TouchUp Object tool, right-click (Ctrl+click on a Mac) on the vector artwork, and then choose Edit Object from the contextual menu.**

   Note that Acrobat displays Edit Object in the contextual menu if it detects a vector object, and it displays Edit Image if it detects a bitmap image. Acrobat also displays Edit Objects (note the plural) if you have more than one object selected.

   If you're editing a complex illustration, be sure to select all its components by holding down the Ctrl key (⌘ on a Mac) while clicking them with the TouchUp Object tool.

   After you choose Edit Object, the object opens for editing in Adobe Illustrator.

2. **Make the necessary changes in Illustrator, choose File⇨Save.**

   The graphic is updated in the PDF document.

If Acrobat doesn't start Photoshop or Illustrator after choosing the Edit Image or Edit Object command, you may need to access preferences by choosing Edit⇨Preferences⇨Touch Up and then specify which programs should be used for editing images or objects.

You can also use the TouchUp Object tool to edit the position of text or graphic objects on a page, which includes the ability to relocate individual lines of text or to change the position of a graphic on a page. After you've selected an object with the TouchUp Object tool, you can simply drag it to a new location on the page.

Exporting Text and Graphics

Although editing text and graphics is helpful, you may need to take text or images from a PDF document and use them in another file. Fortunately, Acrobat also includes tools to make this a breeze. Of course, you should always make certain that you have the permission of the owner of a document before reusing content that is not your original work.

You need the Select & Zoom toolbar for extracting text and graphics, so make sure that it's visible. If it isn't, choose View⇨Toolbars⇨Select & Zoom.

You can export text, images, or charts from Acrobat in three ways:

- ✦ Select/Copy/Paste.
- ✦ Save As To Word Document, JPEG, TIFF, HTML Web Page, XML 1.0, Encapsulated PostScript, HTML 3.2, JPEG 2000, PNG, PostScript, Rich Text Format, Text Accessible, Text (Plain).
- ✦ Use the Snapshot tool to send selected areas to the Clipboard where they will be available to use in other applications or save the selected area as a TIFF file.

Exporting text using Select, Copy, and Paste

Make sure that the Select & Zoom toolbar is visible and then follow these steps to select, copy, and paste text from a PDF file:

1. **Using the Select tool, highlight the text you want to export.**

   The Select tool is the I-Bar/Black Arrow in the toolbar. When you hold the arrow over a section of your document, it will turn into an I-Bar cursor, which you can drag to select the text you want to copy.

If the Cut, Copy, and Paste commands are unavailable after you've selected some text, the author of the document may have set the security settings to disallow copying. If you can't select the text, you may be trying to copy text that is part of an image.

2. **Right-click (Ctrl+click on a Mac) the selected text and choose Copy from the contextual menu.**

   Being able to extract the text out of a PDF document by selecting and copying it is useful if you don't have access to the original source document, but you need to use the text from a PDF file.

3. **Open another text-editing program, such as Adobe InDesign or Microsoft Word.**

   You can paste the copied text into a new document or a preexisting file.

4. **Insert your cursor in the document at the appropriate spot and choose File⇨Paste.**

   The text is pasted into the document, ready for you to use.

Exporting text using Save As

The File⇨Save As command exports all the text in your PDF file. A drop-down menu gives you various format options. After choosing an option and any settings, click the OK button to select the settings and the Save button to save the text. The File⇨Export command gives you the same options.

Here are the formats you can use to export text:

- **Microsoft Word Document:** Use the Settings button to choose whether or not to save the comments or images with your document. If you choose to save the comments or images, you can select additional formatting options.
- **Rich Text Format:** Use the Settings button to choose whether or not to save the comments or images with your document. If you choose to save the comments or images, you can select additional formatting options.
- **Text (Accessible):** Use this format to create a file that can be printed to a Braille printer.
- **Text (Plain) (secondary Settings):** This format creates a plain vanilla file with no formatting. You can save some secondary options in various file encodings. Also, you can select to save the images in your PDF in a separate images folder.
- **Adobe PDF, Encapsulated PostScript, PostScript.**
- **Various Adobe PDF Options.**

✦ **Various graphics formats (JPEG, JPEG2000, PNG, TIFF), but your text will no longer be editable.**

Text that is copied from a PDF file is no longer linked to the original document. Edits made to the extracted text aren't reflected within the PDF file, and it is extremely difficult to have the extracted text reinserted into the PDF document. Think of the extraction process as a one-way trip for the text, which can be extracted but not reinserted.

You can also copy text within a table to the Clipboard or open it directly in a spreadsheet program, such as Microsoft Excel. And you maintain the table's formatting after it is extracted. Just follow these steps:

1. **Click the Select tool and click and drag to select the text in the table.**

   You can also position your cursor just outside the edge of the table and then draw a box around a table.

   A border appears around the selected table.

2. **Right-click (Ctrl+click on a Mac) and choose Open Table In Spreadsheet from the contextual menu or save the table directly to a file or save a copy to the Clipboard to be later pasted.**

   The table opens in Excel or whatever spreadsheet program you have installed on your computer.

   To save the table directly to a file, choose Save Table As from the contextual menu.

   To copy the table to the Clipboard so that you can paste it into other documents, choose Copy As Table from the contextual menu.

   And that's it. You can now use that table in another program.

Extracting graphics

You can also extract graphics from DF files, but extracting graphics is very different from editing them. We discuss editing graphics and vector objects earlier in this chapter. When editing graphics, you open the original graphic file at its highest possible quality. Extracting graphics is different because they're removed at the quality of the screen display resolution, which may be of much lower quality than the original, embedded graphics.

With the Select tool, right-click (Ctrl+click on a Mac) an image, or drag with the Select tool to select a part of the image. Then you can either drag and drop the selection into an open document or choose Copy Image from the contextual menu. The image is now available to be pasted into other applications. The other option in the contextual menu is to Save Image As and save the selected area as a TIFF file.

Snapshot tool

You can use the Snapshot tool to select both text and images and create a picture of a certain area within a PDF file. The result is commonly referred to as a *screen grab* of a section within a PDF file. The result is an image, and your text is no longer editable.

To use the Snapshot tool, choose Tools➪Select & Zoom➪Snapshot Tool. You then have two options.

✦ After you select the Snapshot tool, click anywhere in the page. The snapshot tool automatically captures everything displayed on the screen.

✦ After you select the Snapshot tool, click and drag a rectangle around an area of the page.

You can include text and images. The area you've selected will be saved to the Clipboard so that you can paste it into another document. The Snapshot tool remains active so that you can keep selecting areas and saving them to the Clipboard. However, the previous selection in your Clipboard is deleted when you make a new selection. So, make certain you've pasted a selection into your other document before you make a new selection.

You have to select another tool to deactivate the Snapshot tool.

Chapter 5: Using Commenting and Annotation Tools

In This Chapter

- Adding comments to PDF files
- Working with comments

One of the fantastic features of Acrobat is the capability to mark up documents electronically using virtual sticky notes called *comments.* You can mark up text to indicate changes and add annotations and drawing comments to a PDF file. The Acrobat commenting tools do not change the original file, and you can remove the comments at any time, which means you can disable comments for printing or viewing at any time. In this chapter, we describe these great features and show you how to put them to work for you.

Creating Comments

You can easily add annotations to PDF files, including stamps, text highlights, callouts, and electronic sticky notes, by using the Comment & Markup Toolbar, which you can access by clicking the Review & Comment option in the Tasks toolbar. You can then choose to display the Comment & Markup Tools.

You can also access the Comment & Markup toolbar by choosing View⇨Toolbars⇨Comment & Markup.

The Comment & Markup toolbar

The Comment & Markup toolbar, shown in Figure 5-1, provides several tools for adding comments to PDF documents. It also includes a Show menu to help manage comments and the process of adding comments. We discuss these tools in the following sections.

The Sticky Note tool

Use the Sticky Note tool to add electronic sticky notes to your files. You can click the location where you want the note to appear within a PDF document. An icon, representing the note, appears, along with a window where you can enter text. After entering text in the sticky note, close the window so that the document isn't hidden beneath it. You can change the icon and color used to represent the note by right-clicking (Ctrl+clicking on a Mac) the note and choosing Properties from the contextual menu. In the Properties dialog box that appears, make the changes to the note icon or color and then click Close.

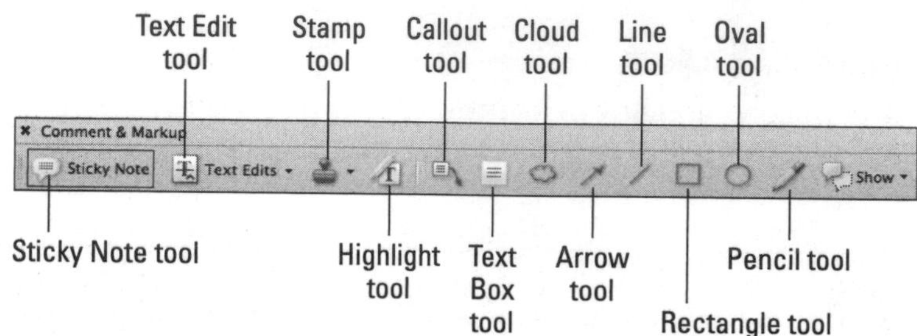

Figure 5-1: Use the Comment & Markup toolbar to add comments to your document.

The Text Edits tool

The Text Edits tool is actually six separate text commenting tools. Use these tools to replace selected text, highlight selected text, add a note to selected text, insert text at cursor, underline selected text, and cross out text for deletion.

To use the Text Edits tool, follow these steps:

1. **Choose the Text Edits tool and drag to select text that requires a change or comment.**
2. **Click the arrow to the right of the Text Edits tool to access the drop-down list containing your six choices.**
3. **Choose an option from the list of available editing choices:**
   - **Replace Selected Text:** Replaces the selected text.
   - **Highlight Selected Text:** Highlights the selected text.
   - **Add A Note To Selected Text:** Allows you to add a note to the selected text.
   - **Insert Text At Cursor:** Places a cursor at the end of the selected text.
   - **Underline Selected Text:** Underlines the selected text.
   - **Cross Out Text For Deletion:** Crosses out the selected text.

   Your selected text changes, depending on what you choose from the list.

After selecting the text that requires a comment, you can press the Delete or Backspace key to indicate a text edit to remove the text. Similarly, you can start to type, and Acrobat will create an insertion point. Also, if you right-click (Ctrl-click on a Mac) after selecting the text, you can select the type of edit or comment you want to insert from the contextual menu.

The Stamp tool

You can use stamps to identify documents or to highlight a certain part of a document. Common stamps include Confidential, Draft, Sign Here, and Approved.

The stamps are grouped into sections. Some stamps automatically add your default user name along with the date and time you applied them to the document; these stamps are available under the Dynamic category in the Stamps menu. The more traditional business stamps, such as Confidential, appear under the Standard Business category. You can access each of the different categories by clicking the arrow to the right of the Stamp tool in the Comment & Markup toolbar, as shown in Figure 5-2.

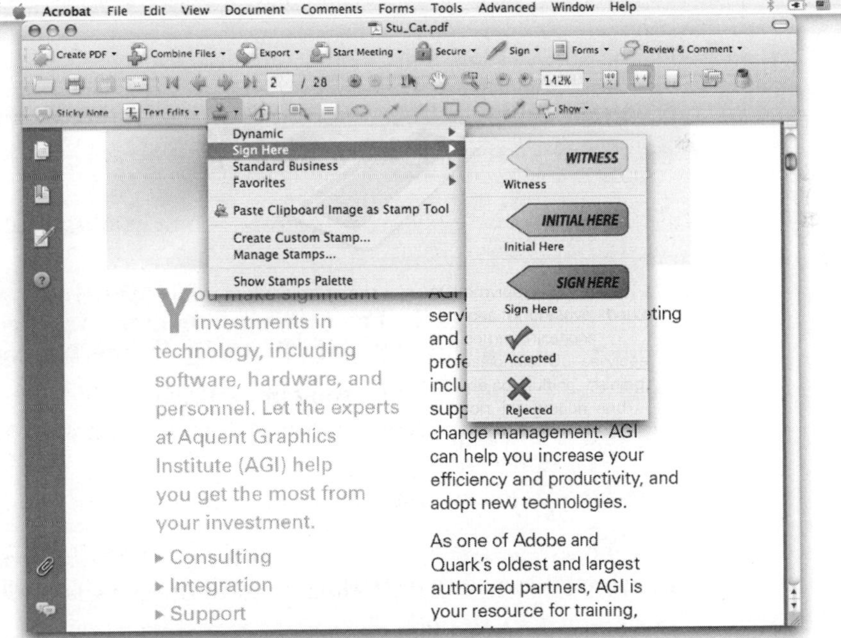

Figure 5-2: Access the different types of stamp groups by clicking the arrow to the right of the Stamp tool.

To apply a stamp to your document, follow these steps:

1. **Select the Stamp tool from the Comment & Markup toolbar.**
2. **Click the arrow to the right of the stamp tool and, from the menu, choose the stamp you want to apply to the document.**
3. **Drag within your document at the location where you want the stamp to appear.**

The Highlight, Underline Text, and Cross-Out, Callout, and Text box tools

The Highlight, Cross-Out, and Underline text tools provide the same functionality and options that are available with the Text Edits tool, but with easier access. If you want to delete the highlighted, crossed-out, or underlined formatting to your text, just click the formatted area and hit the Delete key. Your text will remain, but the formatting will disappear.

You can also call attention to areas in your document by using the Callout and Textbox tools. If you want to delete a Callout or Text box after you've added them, just highlight them and hit the Delete key.

To highlight text, follow these steps:

1. **Select the Highlight Text tool from the Comment & Markup toolbar.**
2. **Drag over the text that you want highlighted.**

   The text is now highlighted.

To underline text, follow these steps:

1. **Select the Underline Text tool by selecting in the Task tools Review & Comment⇨Comment & Markup Tools⇨Underline Text tool.**
2. **Drag over the text that you want underlined.**

   The text is now underlined.

To cross-out text, follow these steps:

1. **Select the Cross-out Text tool by selecting in the Task tools Review & Comment⇨Comment & Markup Tools⇨Cross Out Text Tool.**
2. **Drag over the text that you want crossed out.**

   The text is now crossed out.

The Attach File tools

Using the Attach File tools, you can attach an existing text file, sound file, or any file copied to the Clipboard from your computer (or computer network) and attach it to the PDF.

Follow these steps for file and sound attachments:

1. **In the Task tools, choose Review & Comment⇨Comment & Markup Tools⇨Attach A File As A Comment.**

   A pushpin icon appears.

2. **Click where you want the attachment noted.**

   The Add Attachment dialog box appears.

3. **In the Add Attachment dialog box, browse to the file that you want to attach and click the Select button.**

   You can attach text, graphic, or sound files.

4. **Select the type of icon to represent the attached file and then click OK.**

   There are several types of icons to represent the attached file. You can select a paperclip, graph, pushpin, or tag. Whatever icon you select appears on your document to denote that another file is attached. When you roll over the icon, a little annotation appears telling you the filename.

   With the Record Audio Comment tool, you can share a verbal comment by using a microphone and recording a message directly into the PDF. The sound is added as a comment.

The file(s) that you attach with the Attach File tools becomes embedded within the PDF file. The attached file remains in its original file format, even if the attached file is not a PDF file. For example, you can attach an Excel spreadsheet to a PDF document.

The Drawing tools

There are three shape tools, two line tools, and a pencil in the Comment & Markup toolbar. Use the drawing tools to add lines, ovals, rectangles, and other shapes to your PDF file. These shapes can call attention to specific portions of a document.

To use the Cloud Shape tool:

1. **Select the Cloud Shape from the Comment & Markup toolbar.**
2. **Click in your document to begin the shape.**

3. **Click again in another position to set the length of the first part of the cloud and then click again to begin shaping your cloud.**

   Click as often as you like to create your shape.
4. **When you're finished with your shape, double-click to close the Cloud Shape.**
5. **While the Drawing tool is selected, click the shape you created and drag the corner points to resize, if necessary.**
6. **After creating the cloud shape, right-click (Ctrl+click on a Mac) the shape and choose Properties from the contextual menu to change the color and thickness of the line values; when you're finished, click OK.**

   You can also use the Properties toolbar to change the appearance of a selected comment. Instead of the cloud edges, you can change them to dotted lines, dashed lines, and so on.

To use the Rectangle and Oval Shapes:

1. **Select either the Rectangle or Oval Shape from the Comment & Markup toolbar.**
2. **Click and drag in your document to draw the shape.**
3. **While the Drawing tool is selected, click the shape you created and drag the corner points to resize, if necessary.**
4. **After creating the shape, right-click (Ctrl+click on a Mac) the shape and choose Properties from the contextual menu to change the color and thickness of the line values; when you're finished, click OK.**

   You can also use the Properties toolbar to change the appearance of the shape.

The Text Box tool

When creating notes that you want to prominently display on a document, you can use the Text Box tool.

Follow these steps to add a text box to hold your comments:

1. **Select the Text Box tool from the Comment & Markup toolbar.**

   A text field is placed directly on the document.
2. **Drag to add the comment.**
3. **Right-click (Ctrl+click on a Mac) and choose Properties from the contextual menu to set the color of the text box that contains the note.**

   You can also use the Properties toolbar to modify the selected text box.
4. **Make your choices to modify the appearance of the text box and then click OK.**

You can select the text box and move it to another position any time you want. You can resize the text box by dragging an anchor point.

The Callout Box tool

The Callout Tool creates a callout text box that points to a section of your document with an arrow. The Callout text box is made up of three parts: the text box, the knee line, and the end point line. You can resize each part individually to customize the callout area of your document. To use the Callout tool, follow these steps:

1. **Select the Callout Tool from the Comment & Markup toolbar.**
2. **Click where you want the arrowhead point to be.**
3. **Drag down or to the side to position the text box and begin typing.**

   You can click anchor points on the knee line, end point line, or text box to resize them. You can change the size, color, and font characteristics of the text in the Callout text box.
4. **Right-click (Ctrl+click on a Mac) and choose Properties from the contextual menu to set the color of the Callout text box.**
5. **Make your choices to modify the appearance of the Callout text box and then click OK.**

You can select the Callout text box and move it to another position any time you want. You can resize the text box by dragging an anchor point.

The Pencil tool

With the Pencil tool, you can create freeform lines on your documents. These lines can be useful when you're trying to attract attention to a specific portion of a page. Just follow these steps:

1. **Select the Pencil tool from the Comment & Markup toolbar.**
2. **Click and drag to draw on your document.**
3. **Edit the color and thickness of lines created with the Pencil by right-clicking (Ctrl+clicking on a Mac) on the line and choosing Properties from the contextual menu or press Ctrl+E (⌘+E on a Mac) to access the Properties toolbar.**
4. **Make your choices and click OK.**

By right-clicking (Ctrl+clicking on a Mac) on the Pencil tool, you can choose the Pencil Eraser tool. Use the Pencil Eraser tool to remove portions of lines that had previously been created with the Pencil tool.

Managing Comments

One of the most powerful features of PDF commenting is the ability to easily manage and share comments and annotations among reviewers. For example, you can determine which comments are displayed at any time, and you can filter the comments by author or by the type of commenting tool used to create the comment. In addition, you can indicate a response to a comment and track the changes that may have been made to a document based upon a comment. Also, you can consolidate comments from multiple reviewers into a single document.

Viewing comments

You can use any of several methods to see a document's list of comments:

- Click the Comments tab along the left side of the document window in the Navigation pane.
- Choose Review & Comment⇨Show Comments List.
- Choose View⇨Navigation Panels⇨Comments.

No matter which method you use, the Comments List window that shows all the comments in the document appears along the bottom of the document window. You can see the author of each comment and any notes entered by reviewers. By clicking the plus sign to the left of a comment, you can view more information about it, such as what type of comment it is and the date and time it was created.

If you've clicked the plus sign to the left of the comment to expand the view, it changes to a minus sign, which you can then click to return to the consolidated view showing only the author and the initial portions of any text from the note.

To the right of the plus sign is a check box that you can use to indicate that the comment has been reviewed or to indicate that a certain comment needs further attention. Use these check boxes for your own purposes; their status doesn't export with the document if you send the file to others, so they're for your own personal use only.

Changing a comment's review status

Acrobat makes it easy to indicate whether a comment has been reviewed, accepted, or has additional comments attached to it. To change the status of a comment, follow these steps:

1. **Choose Comments⇨Show Comments List to see the entire list of comments and the status of each one.**

   You can also click the Comments tab located on the bottom left side of the screen to display the comments.

2. **In the Comments List, right-click (Ctrl+click on a Mac) on a comment and choose Set Status⇨Review from the contextual menu.**

3. **Select Accepted, Rejected, Cancelled, or Completed, depending on what's appropriate to your situation.**

   The comment you modified appears in the list, showing the new status you assigned to it.

Replying to a comment

You can right-click (Ctrl+click on a Mac) on a comment in the Comments List and choose Reply from the contextual menu to add a follow-up note to the comment. This way, new comments can be tied to existing comments. If your documents go through multiple rounds of review, adding a reply allows a secondary or final reviewer to expand on the comments from an initial reviewer. This also allows an author or designer to clearly respond to the suggestions from an editor.

Collapsing or hiding comments

Because the Comments List can become rather large, you can choose to collapse all comments so that only the page number on which comments appear is displayed in the list. To do so, click the Collapse All button in the upper-left of the Comments List window; it has a minus sign next to it. To view all comments, click the Expand All button in the same location; this button has a plus sign next to it.

To hide all the comments within a document, click and hold the Show button on the Commenting toolbar and choose Hide All Comments. You can then click the Show button in the Comments toolbar and choose to show comments based upon:

- ✦ Type of comment, such as note, line, or cross out
- ✦ Reviewer, such as Bob or Jane
- ✦ Status, such as accepted or rejected
- ✦ Checked State, which can be checked or unchecked

Use these filtering options to view only those comments that are relevant to you.

Sharing comments

You can share your comments with other reviewers who have access to the same PDF document by following these steps:

1. **Make sure that the Comments List is visible by clicking the Comments tab on the left side of the document window.**
2. **Select the comment that you want to export by clicking it (Shift+click for multiple selections).**
3. **Choose Options⇨Export Selected Comments from the Comments List window.**

   The Export Comments dialog box appears.
4. **Browse to the location where you want the comments to be saved and give the saved file a new name.**

   You now have a file that includes only the comments' information, and not the entire PDF file.

You can share your file with reviewers who have the same PDF file, and they can choose Options⇨Import Comments in the Comments List window to add the comments into their document. You can use this method to avoid sending entire PDF files to those who already have the document.

Summarizing comments

You can compile a list of all the comments from a PDF file into a new, separate document. To summarize comments, follow these steps:

1. **Choose Options⇨Summarize Comments in the Comments List window.**

   The Summarize Options dialog box appears.
2. **Create a listing of the comments with lines connecting them to their locations on the page by selecting the second radio button from the top of the list.**

   In the Include section, you can choose which comments should be summarized.
3. **Click Create PDF Comment Summary.**

   This step creates a new PDF document that simply lists all the comments, as shown in Figure 5-3.

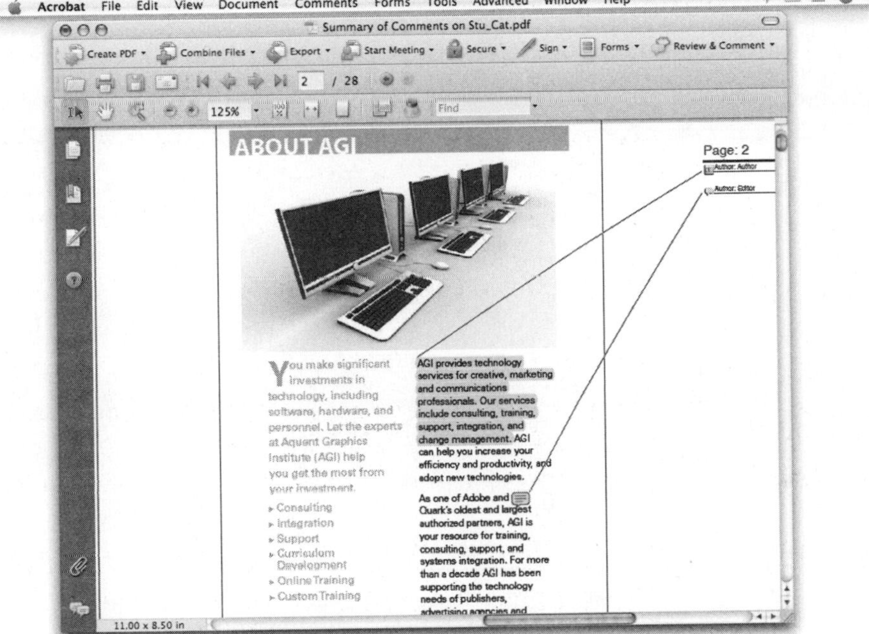

Figure 5-3: A new PDF document is created, listing all of the comments.

Enabling commenting in Adobe Reader

Acrobat 8.0 Professional makes it easy to include users of the free Adobe Reader in a review process. To include Adobe Reader users in a review, choose Comments⇨Enable For Commenting in Adobe Reader. After saving the file, you can share it with users of Adobe Reader, who can then use commenting and markup tools and save their comments into the file. A user of Adobe Acrobat 8.0 Professional must enable commenting in a PDF file before users of Adobe Reader can add comments to a file.

Chapter 6: Securing Your PDF Files

In This Chapter

- Finding out about security in Acrobat
- Using passwords
- Setting limits for editing and printing

You may think that because you've converted your documents to PDF that they're secure. This is not quite true, because Adobe Acrobat includes tools for changing text and images, as well as extracting them. For example, you can use the Select tool (see Chapter 4 of this minibook) to select and copy a passage of text or graphics.

Applying security provides you with control over who is able to view, edit, or print the PDF documents you distribute. You can restrict access to certain features, which deters most users from manipulating your files. All Adobe applications recognize and honor security settings applied in Acrobat, but some software ignores Adobe's security settings or can bypass them all together. For this reason, we recommend that you share your most sensitive documents only when you've applied password security protection. This way the only users who can open a file are those who know the password.

In this chapter, we discuss using password protection to limit access to PDF files and show you how to limit what users can do within your PDF documents.

Understanding Password Security

By requiring users to enter a password to open and view your PDF files, you limit access to those files so that only certain users can view them. You can also apply security to limit access to certain Acrobat and Adobe Reader features, such as copying text or graphics, editing the file, and printing. Adobe calls this type of security *password security* because it requires a password to either open the document or to change the security that has been applied to the document.

Apply security options that limit the opening and editing of your PDF document to those who supply the proper password by using the Secure button on the Tasks toolbar. If the Secure button isn't visible, choose View⇨Toolbars⇨Tasks.

Click and hold down the Secure button in the Tasks toolbar and choose 2 Password Encrypt to bring up the Password Security – Settings dialog box.

In the Password Security – Settings dialog box, you choose an Acrobat version from the Compatibility drop-down list. The higher the version of Acrobat, the greater the level of security.

Your choice here is based on your needs for security and also the version of Acrobat or Adobe Reader that your audience will be using. In the following list, we explain the compatibility choices before showing you how to enable security in the following sections:

- **Acrobat 3 And Later:** If the users who receive your PDF files may have older versions of the software, you can choose Acrobat 3 And Later from the Compatibility drop-down list to ensure that they can work with the files you provide. This option provides compatibility for users who may not have updated their software in many years, but the level of security is limited to 40-bit encryption. While this amount will keep the average user from gaining access to your files, it won't deter a determined hacker from accessing them.
- **Acrobat 5 And Later:** When sharing files with users who have access to Adobe Reader or Adobe Acrobat Version 5 or 6, this option provides expanded security, increasing the security level to 128-bit, which makes the resulting PDF files more difficult to access. Along with the enhanced security, you can also secure the files while still allowing access to the file for visually impaired users. Earlier versions of security don't provide this option, but it's included when you choose either Acrobat 5- or 6-compatible security.
- **Acrobat 6 And Later:** Along with the enhanced security offered with Acrobat 5 compatibility, this setting adds the ability to maintain plain text metadata. In short, this option allows for information about the file, such as its author, title, or creation date, to remain visible while the remainder of the file remains secure.
- **Acrobat 7 And Later:** This choice includes all security options of Acrobat 6 compatibility and also allows you to encrypt file attachments that are a part of a PDF file. It uses the Advanced Encryption Standard, which is a very high level of encryption, making it unlikely that an unauthorized user can decrypt the file without the password.

Applying password security to your PDF documents

Selecting the Require A Password To Open The Document check box in the Password Security – Settings dialog box limits access to the PDF file to only those who know the password. The only practical way to open password-protected files, especially those secured with the most recent versions of Acrobat, is by entering the password. This safeguard provides a good incentive to use passwords that you can easily remember but are difficult for others to guess.

To apply password security to a file, follow these steps:

1. **With a PDF file open, click and hold the Secure button on the Security taskbar and choose Manage Security Policies.**

   The Managing Security Policies window appears, as shown in Figure 6-1.

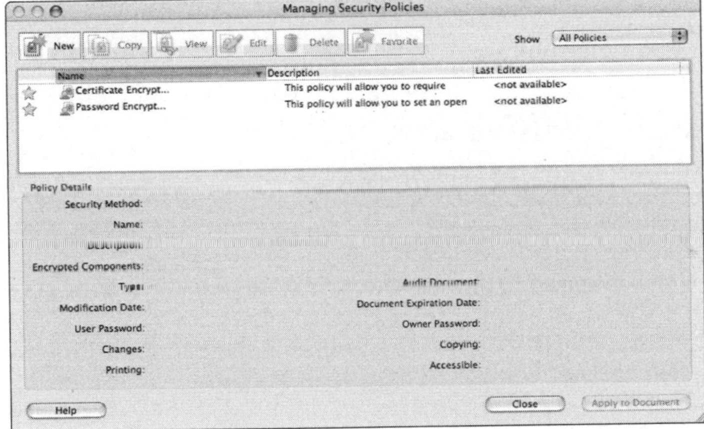

Figure 6-1: The Managing Security Policies window.

   If there is no Password Encrypt policy showing in the Name/Description/Last Edited section, then you have to create one following the directions in Step 2. If there is a Password Encrypt policy, you can skip Step 2 and go to Step 3.

2. **Close the Managing Security Policies window; hold the Secure button on the Security taskbar and select 2 Password Encryption and create your encryption policy.**

   After you have created your Password Encrypt policy, click and hold the Secure Button on the Security taskbar and choose Manage Security Policies. The Password Security – Settings window opens.

3. **Click the Require A Password to open the document check box.**

   Enter a logical password that will be required to open the file in the Document Open Password text field.

   You can also add additional security settings, which we outline in the next section. Or you can use this setting as the only security to be applied to the document.

   If password protection is the only security measure you apply to the document, authorized users are able to access the document by entering a password. Users with the password are also able to edit or print the document.

4. **Click the OK button.**
5. **Confirm the password, click OK again, and the dialog box closes.**
6. **Save, close, and then reopen the PDF file.**

   A password dialog box appears asking for the proper password to be entered for access to this file. Now, every time a user accesses the file, this dialog box appears.

Limiting editing and printing

In addition to restricting viewing of a PDF file, you can also apply restrictions to editing and printing PDF files. In doing so, you restrict users from making changes to your document. Users are only able to view the file.

To limit editing and printing of your PDF document, follow these steps:

1. **With a PDF file open, click and hold the Secure button on the Security taskbar and choose 2 Password Encrypt.**

   The Password Security — Settings window opens.

2. **In the Permissions area, select the check box labeled Restrict Editing And Printing Of The Document.**

   Whew! This check box may win the prize for the longest name ever placed in a software program, but it allows you to require a password to edit the file or change the security settings.

   With this option selected, you can apply a password for access to features such as printing or editing. This password can be different than the password used to open the document — in fact, you don't even need to use a document open password if you don't want to, but it is a good idea to use both of these passwords for sensitive data.

3. **In the Change Permissions Password text field, enter a password.**

4. **Choose whether users are able to print the document by selecting from the Printing Allowed drop-down list.**

   The choices include low resolution or high resolution.

5. **To restrict editing, choose from the Changes Allowed drop-down list (see Figure 6-2).**

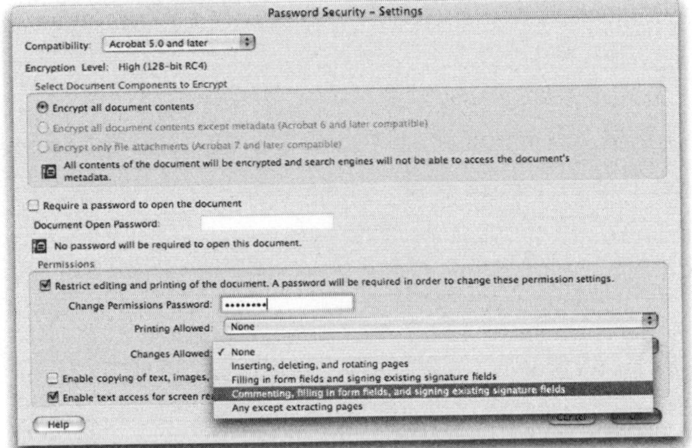

Figure 6-2: The Password Security – Settings window.

6. **If you want, enable the last two check boxes:**

   - **Enable Copying Of Text, Images, and Other Content:** Restrict the ability to copy and paste text and graphics into other documents by deselecting this check box.
   - **Enable Text Access For Screen Reader Devices For The Visually Impaired:** When you choose Acrobat 5 or later compatibility, you can also select this check box to allow visually impaired users to have the PDF file read aloud to them.

7. **After you're satisfied with the settings, click OK.**

By choosing Acrobat 6 and later or Acrobat 7 and later from the Compatibility drop-down list, you can choose to Encrypt All Document Contents Except Metadata. If you choose Acrobat 7 and later from the Compatibility drop-down list the additional option to Encrypt Only File Attachments (Acrobat 7 and later compatible).

Index

Numerics

A

B

C

D

E

F

G

J

K

L

M

N

O

P

S

U

V

X

Z

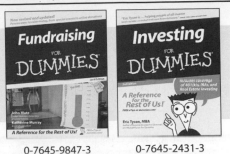

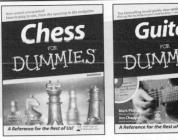

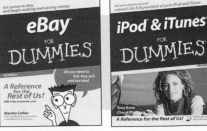

SPORTS, FITNESS, PARENTING, RELIGION & SPIRITUALITY

0-471-76871-5

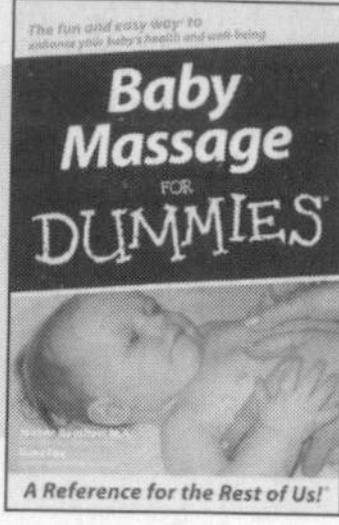

0-7645-7841-3

Also available:

- Catholicism For Dummies 0-7645-5391-7
- Exercise Balls For Dummies 0-7645-5623-1
- Fitness For Dummies 0-7645-7851-0
- Football For Dummies 0-7645-3936-1
- Judaism For Dummies 0-7645-5299-6
- Potty Training For Dummies 0-7645-5417-4
- Buddhism For Dummies 0-7645-5359-3
- Pregnancy For Dummies 0-7645-4483-7 †
- Ten Minute Tone-Ups For Dummies 0-7645-7207-5
- NASCAR For Dummies 0-7645-7681-X
- Religion For Dummies 0-7645-5264-3
- Soccer For Dummies 0-7645-5229-5
- Women in the Bible For Dummies 0-7645-8475-8

TRAVEL

0-7645-7749-2

0-7645-6945-7

Also available:

- Alaska For Dummies 0-7645-7746-8
- Cruise Vacations For Dummies 0-7645-6941-4
- England For Dummies 0-7645-4276-1
- Europe For Dummies 0-7645-7529-5
- Germany For Dummies 0-7645-7823-5
- Hawaii For Dummies 0-7645-7402-7
- Italy For Dummies 0-7645-7386-1
- Las Vegas For Dummies 0-7645-7382-9
- London For Dummies 0-7645-4277-X
- Paris For Dummies 0-7645-7630-5
- RV Vacations For Dummies 0-7645-4442-X
- Walt Disney World & Orlando For Dummies 0-7645-9660-8

GRAPHICS, DESIGN & WEB DEVELOPMENT

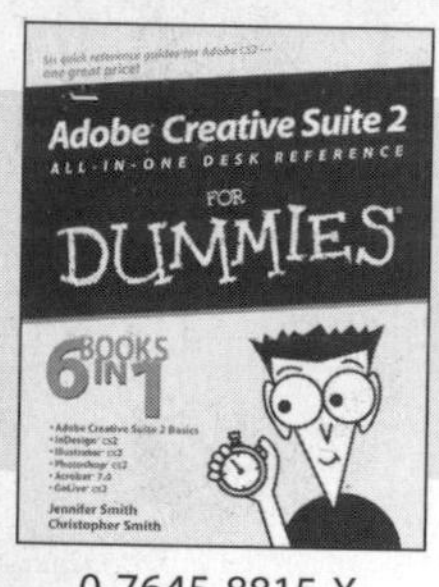

0-7645-8815-X

0-7645-9571-7

Also available:

- 3D Game Animation For Dummies 0-7645-8789-7
- AutoCAD 2006 For Dummies 0-7645-8925-3
- Building a Web Site For Dummies 0-7645-7144-3
- Creating Web Pages For Dummies 0-470-08030-2
- Creating Web Pages All-in-One Desk Reference For Dummies 0-7645-4345-8
- Dreamweaver 8 For Dummies 0-7645-9649-7
- InDesign CS2 For Dummies 0-7645-9572-5
- Macromedia Flash 8 For Dummies 0-7645-9691-8
- Photoshop CS2 and Digital Photography For Dummies 0-7645-9580-6
- Photoshop Elements 4 For Dummies 0-471-77483-9
- Syndicating Web Sites with RSS Feeds For Dummies 0-7645-8848-6
- Yahoo! SiteBuilder For Dummies 0-7645-9800-7

NETWORKING, SECURITY, PROGRAMMING & DATABASES

0-7645-7728-X

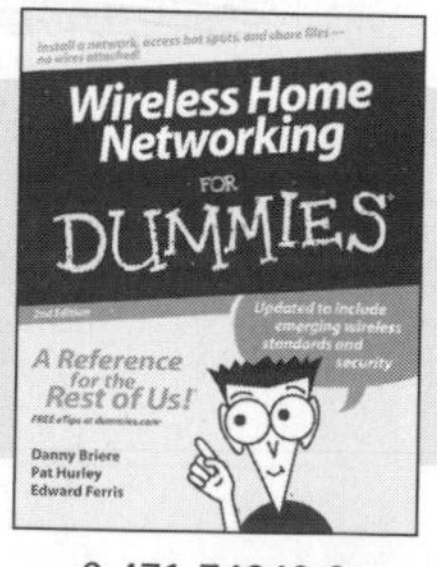

0-471-74940-0

Also available:

- Access 2007 For Dummies 0-470-04612-0
- ASP.NET 2 For Dummies 0-7645-7907-X
- C# 2005 For Dummies 0-7645-9704-3
- Hacking For Dummies 0-470-05235-X
- Hacking Wireless Networks For Dummies 0-7645-9730-2
- Java For Dummies 0-470-08716-1
- Microsoft SQL Server 2005 For Dummies 0-7645-7755-7
- Networking All-in-One Desk Reference For Dummies 0-7645-9939-9
- Preventing Identity Theft For Dummies 0-7645-7336-5
- Telecom For Dummies 0-471-77085-X
- Visual Studio 2005 All-in-One Desk Reference For Dummies 0-7645-9775-2
- XML For Dummies 0-7645-8845-1